The NEW
COMPETITIVE
RUNNER'S
Handbook

Bob Glover and Pete Schuder

D0067539

PENGUIN BOOKS

PENGUIN BOOKS
Published by the Penguin Group
Viking Penguin Inc., 40 West 23rd Street,
New York, New York 10010, U.S.A.
Penguin Books Ltd, 27 Wrights Lane,
London W8 5TZ, England
Penguin Books Australia Ltd, Ringwood,
Victoria, Australia
Penguin Books Canada Ltd, 2801 John Street,
Markham, Ontario, Canada L3R 1B4
Penguin Books (N.Z.) Ltd, 182–190 Wairau Road,
Auckland 10, New Zealand

Penguin Books Ltd, Registered Offices:
Harmondsworth, Middlesex, England

First published under the title *The Competitive Runner's Handbook*
in Penguin Books 1983
This revised edition published 1988
Published simultaneously in Canada

LIBRARY OF CONGRESS CATALOGING IN PUBLICATION DATA
Glover, Bob.
  The new competitive runner's handbook.

  Revise. Originally The competitive runner's handbook: New York: Viking Press, 1983.
  Includes index.
  1. Running—Training.   2. Running—Psychological aspects.   3. Running races.
  I. Schuder, Pete.   II. Title.
[GV1061.5.G54   1988]   796.4'26   87-7379
ISBN 0 14 04.6837 4

Printed in the United States of America by
R. R. Donnelley & Sons Company, Harrisonburg, Virginia
Set in Baskerville

PENGUIN HANDBOOKS
THE NEW COMPETITIVE RUNNER'S HANDBOOK

BOB GLOVER is founder and president of Robert H. Glover and Associates, Inc., a fitness consulting firm that specializes in program development and marketing for corporations and athletic clubs; running; and youth fitness. He writes a column for *Runner's World* magazine and has authored articles for several leading magazines including *GQ, New York* magazine, *Private Clubs,* and *Working Mother.* Glover serves as the director of educational programs for the 25,000-member New York Road Runners Club and coaches 2,000 members per year in classes for beginning and competitive runners. He also co-founded the Achilles Track Club, for disabled athletes, and founded and coaches the elite women's racing team Atalanta, which has won many national honors in both the open and masters categories. Glover serves as a member of the Board of Advisors for the American Running and Fitness Association, is chairman of the Board of Advisors for New York City's prestigious fitness center, the Atrium Club, and consults with the Club Corporation of America on athletic club projects around the country. A high school county champion at 2 miles and a three-time gold medalist at the Hue Sports Festival during the Vietnam War, he has competed for 25 years at distances ranging from the quarter mile to 50 miles. He has 20 years' experience coaching all levels of runners, but achieves his greatest satisfaction from helping the back-of-the-pack runners increase their enjoyment of the sport. Over 50,000 of these "athletes" have participated in his classes, and several thousand more have followed the training programs in his books since *The Runner's Handbook* was released and became an immediate best-seller in 1978. He is currently developing a nationwide family fitness program.

PETE SCHUDER was the 1968 "Athlete of the Year" at Rutgers University, where he was the school record holder in six events and an NCAA finalist in the quarter-mile event. He was a three-time All-American in AAU indoor competition at 600 yards and the mile relay. He also competed for the powerful Sports International running club coached by Brooks Johnson, the 1984 USA women's Olympic track coach. Schuder has been a professional coach for 20 years at the high school, college, and club level. He coached track and cross-country at Columbia University, and in 1979 his cross-country team won the Ivy League Championship and the Heptagonal Games for the first time in over 40 years. He has been head track coach at Boston University since 1985, where his 1986 cross-country team and indoor track team both placed third in the NCAA championships.

Also by Bob Glover

The Runner's Handbook: The Classic Fitness Guide for Beginning and Intermediate Runners
by Bob Glover and Jack Shepherd

The Runner's Handbook Training Diary
by Bob Glover and Jack Shepherd

The Injured Runner's Training Handbook
by Bob Glover and Dr. Murray Weisenfeld

The Family Fitness Handbook (1989)
by Bob Glover and Jack Shepherd

IN MEMORY

On April 12, 1983, Bill "Coach" Coughlin went out for his daily training run in Jackson, Michigan. He was run down by a car and tragically taken away from all his friends. For several decades he was a highly respected high school track coach and athletic director in Rome, New York. Only a few weeks before his death he retired, married, and started a new life with his wife, Dee. He planned to use this book as an aid to a marathon class that they would teach together. Coach was my professional adviser, my training partner, my friend. He was the perfect role model for athletes who sought discipline and dedication. He was a coach's coach. His inspiration will live on in the hearts of thousands of runners and friends.

—Bob Glover

CONTENTS

ACKNOWLEDGMENTS

Both of us have been involved with competitive running since the early sixties. Over the years, many individuals have helped us in our careers as competitive runners and as coaches, and thus have contributed to this book.

Bob Glover especially wishes to thank the athletes he has coached who for many years have served as guinea pigs for his training methods. Their experiences contributed greatly to this book. Members of the elite women's racing team Atalanta have won many individual and team honors in both the open and masters categories. Knowledge gained since 1975 coaching highly competitive female athletes is shared in the following pages. The major source of information within these pages, however, comes from the thousands of beginner runners, novice racers, and back-of-the-pack and middle-of-the-pack runners who have participated in Bob's running classes with the New York Road Runners Club since 1978. A special thanks to all 10,000 of you for your contributions. Over fifty coaches have assisted with the classes, and their service and ideas have also been very valuable.

Several key people from the running community helped Glover in his career. Those from upstate New York need a special thanks for their help in the early seventies: Roman Runners (Rome, New York) Al Stringham, the late Bill Coughlin, Carl Eilenberg, and Dr. Fred Grabo; Utica Pacemakers Joe Ficcaro, Sam Gratch, Tom Hovey, and Syl Pascale; Syracuse Chargers Arnie Briggs, Kathy Switzer, Al Bonney, and Chuck Wiltse.

When Al Melleby recruited Glover in 1975 to become his fitness director at New York City's West Side YMCA, he had the vision—prior to the running boom—to encourage him to promote running as a key part of the Y program. Melleby allowed Glover to turn over part of his dingy office to the then struggling 200-member New York Road Runners Club (NYRRC), and encouraged him to help them grow. Knowledge gained in the mid-seventies from veteran NYRRC officials Joe Kleinerman, Harry Murphy, Kurt Steiner, Ted Corbitt, Dr. Norb Sander, and Gary Muhrcke is utilized in this work. Special mention must go to two key members of the NYRRC. Nina Kuscsik, Bob Glover's heroine, has been a pioneer athlete and women's running promoter. President Fred Lebow engineered the NYRRC's growth from 200 to 25,000 members. He encouraged Bob to develop his running classes, clinics, and teams through the NYRRC, and turned him loose as a writer for the club's newsletter.

From these writings came collaboration with Jack Shepherd, author of nine books (three national best-sellers) and coauthor, with his coach as a beginner runner, of *The Runner's Handbook*. His fine writing skills helped that book sell over a quarter-million copies and make everyone's best-seller list, and he contributed substantially to this work also.

Special thanks also go to Dr. George Sheehan and Dr. Richard Schuster, who freely offered medical advice early in Glover's career that helped keep him and his athletes on the road to better racing. Dr. Murray Weisenfeld, coauthor with Bob of *The Injured Runner's Training Handbook,* contributed significantly to the injury section of this book, as did Dr. Edward Colt and Dr. Hans Kraus. New York City physical therapist Robert Kropf offered his expertise in the area of the mental aspects of running. Inspiration for the original version of this book was contributed by Richard Traum, the one-legged marathoner coached by Glover, who with him founded the Achilles Track Club for disabled athletes; and Jim Ferris, who pushed Bob into a "new dimension" during workouts and challenged him to be daring during his breakthrough races in the late seventies.

A final thanks to the runners who ran countless intervals while photographing the cover of this book: Mike Alber, Colleen Gardner, Renee Landegger, and Stephen Redmon.

Pete Schuder wishes to thank Les Wallack and Art Gulden, his first coaches on the college level, who taught him the basics and inspired him to become a national class runner and a professional coach. John Novak deserves special mention as Pete's roommate, teammate, and partner during Schuder's high school coaching career at Metuchen High School in New Jersey. Their endless discussions on coaching principles and philosophies pushed Pete to search for answers to the many questions of training and racing, and helped shape this work.

Brooks Johnson taught Pete to analyze and evaluate the technical aspects of running. He also made him believe in his talents as a track coach. All of these friends and mentors contributed to Pete's knowledge of running.

Desi Foynes, Paul Heck, and Charles Allen were Pete Schuder's first All-America track and field athletes at Columbia University. They gave him the confidence to continue growing and experimenting as a coach. Members of Columbia's league championship cross-country team of 1979 also must be thanked, particularly Charlie Miers, Paul Loomie, Wally Collins, Paul Hofmann, Jim Hannon, and Rich McNally.

Outside of college track, there were others who contributed to Pete's knowledge and therefore to this book. Cheryl Norton taught Pete how to train women runners. The New York Road Runners Club classes gave him experience with the average adult runner. Thanks also go to the many club runners Pete coached, especially Laurie Schuder—she married the coach—and national class masters runners Anne Bing and Helene Bedrock, who expressed their appreciation in so many ways for his coaching.

INTRODUCTION: CHANGING TRENDS IN RUNNING

Since 1975, when I started working on the first edition of *The Runner's Handbook,* and since 1978, when the book made everybody's national best-seller list, and since 1983, when *The Competitive Runner's Handbook* was a successful release, running and runners have changed a lot. In fact, they changed so much that *The Runner's Handbook* was revised in 1985, and now *The Competitive Runner's Handbook* has been revised. *The Runner's Handbook* revision focused on the beginner and intermediate runner; this book is being revised to better focus on the average runner-competitor who seeks improvement, but must also balance career and family responsibilities.

Back in 1975, I certainly wouldn't have predicted the running boom that was soon to come. For example: the New York Road Runners Club membership exploded from 200 members to 25,000 over a period of 10 years; major marathons attracting thousands of runners took over the streets in cities across the country, including New York, Chicago, Pittsburgh, Columbus, Los Angeles, Houston, Minneapolis-St. Paul, Phoenix, and San Francisco. Also, my modest goal of 5,000 sales of my first book was multiplied by 100, as over a half-million copies of *The Runner's Handbook* series have been sold thus far. The running boom has changed the sport forever. No longer will it be a close-knit fraternity of serious athletes. In fact, the personality of running has changed so much that the serious athlete is no longer the core group, but rather the small minority at the peak of a huge pyramid of thousands of semi-serious and not-so-serious runners. The big mega-races, running shoe companies, magazines, and, yes, running book authors can't survive by only catering to the needs of the elite. You middle-of-the-pack and back-of-the-pack runners are making your needs known, and it is the goal of this book to satisfy you.

The Competitive Runner's Handbook has been revised for two major reasons. The revision allows me the opportunity to update information that has changed because of scientific and technological advances. More important, it allows me the opportunity to simplify and streamline training information and better communicate it to you, the average runner. Many books are written by elite runners or coaches of elite runners. Most often the information contained is over the heads of the majority of the running population. This book is a product not of elite training and trainers, but of the masses. Since the release of *The Competitive Runner's Handbook,* thousands of runners have participated in my running classes and thousands more have been exposed to the training principles in the book and my column in *Runner's World* magazine. Feedback from these sources has been a valued learning experience. A coach is only wise if he learns from his students and thus improves his services. The following pages do not represent new and modern training techniques. Rather, they offer practical training advice that can be easily understood and used by runners of all ability levels.

As the running boom of the late seventies matures in the late eighties and the nineties, here are the trends that are emerging.

HOW MANY EXERCISE? RUN? RACE?

According to a Gallup poll reported in *American Health* magazine, from November 1984 to November 1986 approximately 25 million Americans started exercising for the first time. During that time period, the percentage of Americans who exercise (but not necessarily exercise enough) increased from 54 to 69 percent—more than two-thirds of adults! According to this survey, not only are more people exercising, they are also exercising more: 25 percent exercise 2–4 ½ hours per week, and 27 percent exercise 5 or more hours per week. These trends are expected to continue into the nineties. Many of these exercisers turn to running and eventually to racing.

The running movement died a bit as the fad exercisers moved on to aerobics classes, walking, etc. A Gallup poll conducted in 1986 for *Runner's World,* in fact, demonstrated that from 1984 to 1986 the number of "occasional runners" dropped from 30.2 million to 25.5 million. However, a hard-core group of more than 7 million "life-style" runners, who run at least 120 days a year, has emerged, and this group is sophisticated about its training. Basically, the fringe runners have moved on to other activities, and those who are committed to running as a lifelong activity have emerged stronger than ever. In fact, a *Runner's World* survey of its readers revealed that 97 percent of them intended to continue at their present level of running for at least another 20 years.

According to a 1986 report from the National Running Data Center, between 600,000 and 800,000 compete in races annually—a figure that is expected to remain steady or increase slightly after years of spectacular growth. The running boom has leveled off, leaving us with a smaller but steady influx of new runners and new racers each year. It is expected that the sport will remain strong and steady for years to come, with a 5–10 percent annual growth rate.

RACING

Marathon mania was king a decade ago. If you hadn't yet completed one, you were considered a virgin runner. Those who did compete regularly, myself included, often raced three or more marathons a year. At last, runners are learning to listen to reason rather than ego, and are holding off longer before running that first (if ever) marathon. Veteran marathoners will only put their bodies through the grind of a long, hard race once or twice a year, or even once every 2 or 3 years. Organized road races increased in the USA from 4,058 in 1979 to over 15,000 in the late eighties—mostly 5K–10K events that require less training and have a quicker recovery period. In the mid-eighties, marathon participation was down approximately 20 percent in 1985 but up 10 percent in 1986. Participation in the 10K was up approximately 20 percent, and the 5K—which is very attractive to the low-mileage, semiserious runner and fun racer—was up over 100 percent. These trends are expected to continue into the nineties:

1. Fewer marathons will be run, but the big-city events which are very attractive and exciting will continue to grow. We will not have fewer marathoners, but marathoners will race fewer times and will be more concerned about training properly in order to do as well as possible. A high percentage of big-city marathons will be first-timers attracted by the hoopla and the challenge. These runners will be better prepared for their first marathon than those in the past, and after completing their marathon they will go back to enjoying shorter races, perhaps returning later to improve their marathon time.

2. Runners will race less often, and enjoy it more. Most will race once a month or less—and by not overracing, minimize injury and burnout.

3. Participation in fun events—such as the Bay to Breakers race (this zany event in San Francisco attracts over 100,000 runners), Corporate Challenge races, and couples events such as the Trevira Twosome—will grow. So too will races of 5K and fun runs of 2–4 miles accompanying more serious races of 10K and longer. A good example: the highly competitive Gasparilla Classic 15K in Tampa added a 5K event, and in 1987 the 5K outdrew the 15K 7,000 runners to 5,500.

MILEAGE

The days of the mega-mileage are over. Runners are less compulsive and more intelligent in their mileage distribution. I once ran 100 miles a week for 12 straight weeks. Now I'd advise that a runner that serious should run 70–80 miles a week and add to it some aerobic alternative training. More runners are balancing running mileage with aerobic alternatives such as swimming, biking, and cross-country skiing. These activities when added to a modest mileage base will increase aerobic fitness while minimizing pounding that comes with high mileage on the roads. They also provide variety. A survey of readers of *Runner's World* in the mid-eighties portrayed the average semi-serious runner as one who runs 20–25 miles per week at a 7–9-minute pace. The average marathoner will move up to 40–50 miles a week for several weeks prior to the big race and then move back down. The average runner in the top 25 percent of the field will run 40–70 miles per week year-round.

WOMEN

In the early seventies, 99 percent of subscribers of *Runner's World* were men. By the mid-eighties, 25 percent were women, and that percentage increases yearly. In the early seventies, approximately twenty men participated in the average running event per single female entry. By the mid-eighties, in events of 10K and less the ratio was better than three to one. As we enter the nineties, female participation in races will continue to grow compared with male participation. A mid-1980s study by American Sports Data indicated that 47 percent of runners were women and that 57 percent of first-year runners were women. Since women make up approximately 50 percent of our population, it is only a matter of time before they equal men in participation in running and racing. In fact, the 1985 Bloomsday 12K in Spokane drew 19,000 women—50 percent of the field, which was a first for a major road race. A May 1986 Fun Run in New York City's Central Park drew 465 women and 461 men—the first time in the 30-year history of the New York Road Runners Club that women had outnumbered men in a running event. Because of physiological differences, women won't outrun the faster men; however, they will continue to improve as runners faster than men will, since they have had less experience in competitive athletics. More and more research will be done concerning women and athletics. Although most races for the masses will continue to have coed starts, many races will offer a separate start for women, enabling them to better get the feel of running head-to-head without interference from male runners. Women-only events will continue to grow in size, since women new to racing are less intimidated by women-only events such as the 8,000-woman L'Eggs Mini Marathon in New York City.

AGE

On July 1, 1983, for the first time in this country, our population included more people over the age of 65 than under the age of 25. In 1880 the average life expectancy was 45; now it is over 75. The average age of *Runner's World* readers will pass age 40 for the first time by the end of this decade. More emphasis will be placed on "masters" (age 40+) competition, and more races will include 5-year breakdowns for older age brackets. Those of us, including myself, who were the bulk of the runners making up the running boom in the late seventies are now over 40 and still going strong. More and more runners are competing into their 50s, 60s, 70s, and even 80 and beyond. In fact, for the 1986 racing season the New York Road Runners Club nominated five strong candidates for age 70+ Runner of the Year—an award that in previous years automatically went to anyone still alive and moving at that age. Masters runners will organize more events and more clubs that cater to their needs. As I've learned, it's great to get older if you are a runner. Every 5 years you get to move into another age group as a "kid" and can start all over again recording personal records. We can't continue to keep running faster as we age, but we can sure enjoy the benefits of keeping fit and seek to be competitive with our peers.

WELLNESS

More and more runners are realizing that running alone isn't enough to guarantee a longer, healthier life. The term "wellness" can be defined as the marriage of good fitness practices and good health practices. The runner's fitness level is determined not only by his or her reaching the minimum standard of 30 minutes of aerobic training three to five times per week, but also by his or her flexibility and postural muscular strength.

Being able to control your body weight and the stress in your life and maintaining a proper diet are critical to your overall health. Best-selling running book author Jim Fixx died of a heart attack while on the run. His 10-miles-per-day routine didn't make up for his strong family history of heart disease, high cholesterol, and previous life-style of being overweight and a heavy smoker. The healthy trend is to make wellness a part of your daily life. Eat properly, get adequate sleep, exercise prudently.

REALISTIC VS. IDEAL

Each runner has two levels of running potential—ideal and realistic. Ideally, you should maximize your abilities by spending enough time and effort on all aspects of training. Realistically, you do your best and recognize that you are not a full-time runner. Being totally committed to running takes time. Bill Rodgers once remarked: "No one who works a forty-hour week will ever beat me." He's got a good point—and we working stiffs should accept that.

This book explains the key aspects of successful running. Don't let them overwhelm you. Budget your time and energy to become a better runner within the limits of your career and family responsibilities. Don't let anyone push you beyond these goals. Good luck!

—Bob Glover

Part I
TRAINING

1. CATEGORIES OF RUNNERS

Male or female, young or old, all runners who race have the same goal: personal improvement. In this chapter, we discuss why female runners can't run as fast as comparable male runners, but should train the same; why older runners slow down over the years, but can minimize the slowdown with quality training; and why youth should concentrate on shorter distances.

In this chapter, runners are divided into four categories: novice, basic, advanced, and champion competitors. By identifying your level, you can use this book to structure your own training program and fit it to your needs. You can set approximate goals for your weekly mileage, long runs, speed workouts, training schedule, and races.

Obviously, these categories are only approximate guides to help you determine what program is best for you. In many cases, a runner may be putting in less or more mileage than that indicated for his or her racing time. Young, fast runners will get away with less mileage. Older runners, who need more rest time between runs, often run somewhat less mileage than indicated for their category; this is especially true for those runners age 50 or older. Generally, most runners fit into one of these categories and are training to move into the next level. We have adjusted the categories for age and sex. The racing time range for your age group can be used to help you set racing goals and to predict your race times for all racing distances.

WOMEN RUNNERS

Physical characteristics make women runners different from men. Women have only 85 to 90 percent of the heart size of men, have smaller lungs, and have lower hemoglobin readings (a measure of the oxygen-carrying capacity of the blood). They have more body fat, but smaller bones and less muscle. Forty percent of a man's body weight is muscle; in a woman, muscle amounts to only 23 percent. This sex-specific fat cannot be eliminated by diet or training, and excessive attempts to lower weight and body fat percentage often leads to anorexia and other health problems.

Women differ dramatically from men in maximal oxygen uptake (the ability to consume, transport, and utilize oxygen). Exercise physiologists in 1975 conducted extensive tests on many of the nation's elite male runners at Dr. Ken Cooper's Aerobics Center in Dallas. Their results: the elite averaged a score of 76.9 ml/kg/min for their maximal oxygen uptake. Similar tests were conducted on elite women runners in 1982 and 1983 at the Nike research labs in Oregon and New Hampshire, and in 1985 at the Georgia Institute of Technology in Atlanta. Their results: the elite women on the average scored 10 ml/kg/min lower than the elite men. The best men and women differ by about 11 percent in terms of maximal oxygen uptake—very close to the difference between the men's and women's world records in the distance events.

According to exercise physiologist Dr. Jack Daniels, who conducted the Nike research, "The basic physiological systems function the same way in men and women; likewise, training principles should be the same for both genders; and men and women can train and race at the same relative intensity." Dr. William Morgan, a sports psychologist who participated in both the men's study in Dallas and the women's study in Atlanta, conducted psychological tests on both elite men and women athletes and concluded that "biologically you see differences . . . but you don't see a difference from a psychological perspective." He agrees with Daniels: male and female athletes do not require different coaching or training methods.

We do find, however, that often women in our classes can't keep up with the men in their group who run similar 10K times when doing short, fast workouts. They keep up better on longer intervals and often beat the same men in the marathon event. At shorter distances, men have more power for speed and run away from most women. So ladies, don't get frustrated if you struggle to keep up with the guys in the speed workouts; you'll give them a good run on race day.

In this book, and in our classes and teams, we coach women in the same way as men. We have adjusted our race time categories to compensate for the physiological differences between men and women. For more information particular to women, such as menstruation, pregnancy, and menopause, consult *The Runner's Handbook.*

A Note on Pacing: In the back of the pack, women and men can intermingle comfortably and even pace each other to improved performances. Men often run with slower women to help them do better. But if you are a woman, when you get fast enough to compete for awards, this practice should be eliminated. A male pacer can hand you water, read your splits, set your pace, let you know where your competitors are, and encourage you to keep going despite fatigue, hot weather, or loss of confidence. It is unfair to the other women you are competing with to have a faster man help you beat them. Once you are no longer a fun racer in the pack, you should strive to beat all of your competitors—male and female—without benefit of unequal assistance.

SENIOR RUNNERS

One of the growing trends in running is the growth of the age 40+ masters runners, including the co-authors of this book. Even the elite are joining us: marathon superstars Frank Shorter, Bill Rodgers, and Carlos Lopes all turned 40 in 1987.

Not only are more of us running at an older age, more of us will live longer because of our running. In a paper published in 1986 in the *New England Journal of Medicine,* Dr. Ralph Paffenbarger and other researchers reported results of a 16-year—and ongoing—study of 16,936 Harvard University male alumni who graduated between 1916 and 1950. They reported "a considerable gain in man-years of life for the habitually energetic." According to the study, men who exercise regularly (approximately 20–35 miles a week for runners) will increase their life span, on the average, by 1 to more than 2 years when compared with their sedentary counterparts. Since this is an average figure, some of us can extend our lives by even more than this figure as a result of our exercise routine. But don't go out and start running a marathon a day in an effort to live forever. There are minimal additional longevity returns after about 35 miles a week.

Most of us are more concerned with quality of life rather than adding a few years to our lives. Many of us are concerned with the quality of our racing performance. As we age, our bodies betray us. Scientific studies, and most stopwatches, show that we peak as athletes between ages 25 and 30 and go downhill steadily from there. As we age, we lose lung function, muscle strength, joint mobility, and elasticity, and our cardiac output decreases about 1 percent per year. But do we have to slow down dramatically?

A long-term study being conducted at Washington University in St. Louis involving competitive runners age 50 and older reports encouraging news: people don't slow down with age as fast as many have believed. That research shows only a 5 percent per decade decrease in performance after the age of 30 if training is steady.

Another long-term study of competitive runners under the direction of exercise physiologist Michael Pollock since 1971 continues to offer further information about aging and performance. A 10-year follow-up test showed that runners who eased up on their training lost 9 percent of their aerobic capacity in a decade—similar to what most studies show for sedentary people. However, since they started with an aerobic capacity far superior to that of the sedentary population, they still were in pretty good shape. Those athletes who continued to train hard showed *no* statistical loss of aerobic capacity despite aging 10 years. Those athletes will slow very slightly over time. Pollock suggests that if we want to hold on to our performance longer as we age, we need to maintain hard work, not just run easy mileage. But we must be careful. As we age, it takes longer to properly recover from hard workouts, long runs, and races, and we are much more prone to injury. It is much harder to recapture fitness after a layoff resulting from injury as we age.

Some of us will actually improve with age. I've seen 65-year-olds run faster than they did when they were 60. This is due to the fact that they didn't have the training background and experience to run faster when they were younger. Most of us have to accept the fact that we will gradually run a bit more slowly and readjust our goals. According to Dr. George Sheehan, columnist for *Runner's World* and himself a septuagenarian competitor, "We are continually capable of doing everything we did in our prime—a little slower, perhaps, somewhat weaker, surely, but if they wait around long enough we'll finish."

Running is one of the few sports that rewards you for getting older. Most races score according to 5- or 10-year age groups after age 40. We've coached many women who have celebrated 40th, 45th, 50th, and even 60th birthdays with a big party because they get to be a "kid" in a new age group. We never imagined ever seeing women brag about getting older! After age 35, try recording your personal records all over again at each 5-year mark you pass. That will keep you motivated and give you attainable goals. Be proud that you look and feel so good at your age. Join together with other older runners to provide one another support and motivation. Form your own masters running club. I challenge you to come up with a better name and more enthusiasm than my friends in the Scarsdale (New York) Antiques!

We have included age breakdowns in the following category charts to help you better adjust your training. But in general, our guidelines in this book are based on time goals. Enjoy yourself as a masters runner—we are quickly becoming the majority rather than the minority!

YOUNG RUNNERS

Several recent studies have proven that the fitness level of our children—from preschoolers to teenagers—is poor and getting worse. *The Runner's Handbook* includes detailed guidelines for young runners of all ages, and even baby carriage running tips for parents. We do not encourage children age 12 and under to compete in long distance racing. Rather, we prefer to have them experience the joys of running for fitness and for fun, as well as participating in a variety of sports. Young children should be encouraged to let their bodies fly, their legs run. But they must be harnessed so that growing bones and growing minds are not damaged. Parents are cautioned: don't push them too soon; let your children *choose* to run—for themselves, not for you.

Preschool: Christopher Glover took off running at 10 months before he walked his first step. He hasn't stopped running since, but even as a first grader in 1988 he still doesn't train. But he runs while playing baseball, basketball, and several other sports. He skates, swims, bikes, hikes, climbs, and more with enthusiasm. He picks his activities; his daddy supports him and tries to keep up. Even though his daddy founded the Pee Wee Races for age 6 and under with the New York Road Runners Club, Christopher didn't want to participate. So his daddy was disappointed, but patient. All of a sudden at age 5, he wanted to know why he never got to run in races like Mommy and Daddy. He ran all six races in the series that year and has been participating in them ever since. But it isn't racing. The distance is kept short: anywhere from 100 yards to a quarter mile. There are no winners; every participant gets a ribbon at the finish. Christopher is sometimes one of the top finishers, sometimes back in the pack—depending on his mood that day. But he enjoys each "race" because he loves to run fast and, most of all, he loves to get another ribbon to put on his bulletin board. His biggest thrill thus far was receiving one of his daddy's old trophies after finishing his first race. Preschoolers should be encouraged to "sprint" short distances, not run long. Let them think they are doing really well, no matter how fast or slow they run. At this age the most important goal should be to establish in their minds that running and exercise are not only good for them, but fun. Winning and losing, the thrills and agonies of competition, should be learned later in life.

Age 6–12: Low-key competition can be introduced at this age if the child is interested. The guidelines above will still apply to many 6- and 7-year-olds. Racing distance should be limited to 1 mile or less. Often children at this age volunteer to jog a little with their parents. Go at their pace for whatever distance they can maintain interest—it might be around the block or a 3-mile loop of the park. You might want to ease them into fitness racing by running with them for a local 2-mile fun run. Encourage them to participate in activities in which they do a lot of running without realizing it—such as soccer and tennis. Biking, skating, and swimming are activities you can do together at this age, when they are building up a good aerobic base of fitness. Many kids this age enjoy riding their bikes to accompany parents on the run. This can be a great way to get in your run while chatting with your child. He or she can learn from your attitude that running and fitness are important and fun. Establish a good motivational base for a lifelong interest in aerobic exercise, not just running.

Teens: The guidelines for enjoying running and exercise with your preteen child still apply to teenagers. At this age some of them may wish to become more serious about running and sign up for a school or club track or cross-country team. Teenage runners should learn how to run fast over short distances and have fun. They should concentrate on the distances run in their schools—up to 5K, and if they wish, during the off-season on road races, up to 10K. Marathons are not advised until their bodies and minds mature. We can only be young once, so let them enjoy their school races while they can. They can run marathons when they are 60 years old, so why be in a rush? Most 13–15-year-old runners should limit mileage to less than 30 miles per week. High school runners shouldn't go above 40–50 miles per week; most should run 20–40 miles a week depending upon their event, experience, and enthusiasm for the sport. Track runners should concentrate on races from 440 yards to 2 miles. Teenagers age 17–19 may move up to 5K on the track; all teens may wish to run some 5K–10K road races during the off-season for fun. If you are a teenager, don't train for them seriously, save your speed training to peak for school races. See chapter 17 for guidelines for training for the track mile. Chapter 18 contains guidelines for cross-country. This sport is very popular with junior high and senior high boys and girls across the country. You don't have to be real good to be on the team. All you need is the desire to get out and run over challenging courses and, perhaps as important, an interest in improving your fitness level and in taking advantage of the social benefits of being on a team with friends.

The Physically Disabled

More and more men, women, and children with a wide variety of physical disabilities are finding that they can enjoy running too. Some of them "run" in wheelchairs or use devices such as an artificial leg or crutches. Bob Glover co-founded the New York City–based Achilles Track Club with one-legged marathoner Dick Traum. Under Traum's leadership, the club has added chapters across the country that have guided hundreds of physically "challenged" individuals into races, including over a hundred each year in the New York Marathon. Contact Traum (Personnelmetrics, 356 West 34th Street, New York, NY 10001; 212–967–9300) for information on running for the physically disabled or about starting an Achilles Track Club chapter in your area. A complete chapter in *The Runner's Handbook* is devoted to guidelines for running for the physically handicapped.

NOVICE COMPETITOR

This runner has raced little or lacks the time or ability to improve and move into the next level.

Experience: Has been running at least 6 months and has just started racing, or has been racing only a few months, or may be an experienced runner who hasn't trained seriously.

Mileage: 15 to 30 miles per week, and moves to 40 for a marathon.

Frequency: 4 to 6 days per week.

CHART A NOVICE COMPETITOR—
RACE-TIME RANGES FOR MEN

DISTANCE	(OPEN)	(40–49)	(50–59)	(60–69)
5K	23:30+	25:30+	27:30+	29:30+
10K	48:00+	52:00+	56:00+	60:00+
15K	75:00+	81:00+	87:00+	93:00+
10 miles	80:00+	86:40+	93:20+	1:40+
20K	1:42+	1:51+	1:59+	2:07+
Half marathon	1:50+	2:00+	2:10+	2:20+
25K	2:10+	2:20:30+	2:31:30+	2:42:30+
30K	2:38+	2:51:30+	3:04:30+	3:17:30+
Marathon	3:50+	4:10+	4:30+	4:50+

Note: Times for the novice competitor reflect a wide range of performance, from being able to just finish the distance to running near the basic competitor times. For example, 48:00+ for an open man for 10K means his time would be more than 48 minutes, and thus this runner is a novice competitor. For example, his time could be 50 or 60 minutes. His goal would be to move up to the basic competitor category by improving his time in order to break 48 minutes.

CHART A NOVICE COMPETITOR—
RACE-TIME RANGES FOR WOMEN

DISTANCE	(OPEN)	(40–49)	(50–59)	(60–69)
5K	25:30+	27:30+	29:30+	31:30+
10K	52:00+	56:00+	60:00+	64:00+
15K	81:00+	87:00+	93:00+	99:00+
10 miles	86:40+	93:20+	1:40+	1:46:40+
20K	1:51+	1:59+	2:07+	2:15+
Half marathon	2:00+	2:10+	2:20+	2:30+
25K	2:20:30+	2:31:30+	2:42:30+	2:53:30+
30K	2:51:30+	3:04:30+	3:17:30+	3:30:30+
Marathon	4:10+	4:30+	4:50+	5:10+

Note: Times for the novice competitor reflect a wide range of performance, from being able to just finish the distance to running near the basic competitor times. For example, 52:00+ for an open woman for 10K means her time would be more than 52 minutes, and thus this runner is a novice competitor. For example, her time could be 55 or 60 minutes. Her goal would be to move up to the basic competitor category by improving her time in order to break 52 minutes.

Long runs: 4 to 12 miles every 2 to 3 weeks, and moves into the 15- to 20-mile range for marathon training.

Speed work: 1 day a week or less, *after* experiencing a few races.

Races: 1 to 10 times per year, usually 10K or less.

Race times: See Chart A on the previous page.

BASIC COMPETITOR

This is the majority of the runners in the middle of the pack and back. They run half marathons and shorter races well. They can finish a marathon with their heads up in a respectable time. These runners do some speed work to improve their times. They may be first-time marathon runners, and train more than the novice competitor to run that race in reasonable time.

Experience: Has been running at least 2 years, racing at least 1 to 2 years.

Mileage: 25 to 60 miles a week.

Frequency: 5 to 7 days per week.

Long runs: 10 to 20 miles, once every other week.

Speed works: 1 day a week when preparing for races, 2 if experienced.

CHART B   BASIC COMPETITOR—RACE-TIME RANGES FOR MEN

DISTANCE	(OPEN)	(40–49)	(50–59)	(60–69)
5K	19:30–23:30	20:30–25:30	21:30–27:30	22:30–29:30
10K	40:00–48:00	42:00–52:00	44:00–56:00	46:00–60:00
15K	63:00–75:00	66:00–81:00	69:00–87:00	72:00–93:00
10 miles	66:40–80:00	70:00–86:40	73:20–93:20	76:40–1:40
20K	1:25–1:42	1:29–1:51	1:34–1:59	1:38–2:07
Half marathon	1:30–1:50	1:35–2:00	1:40–2:10	1:45–2:20
25K	1:46–2:10	1:53–2:20:30	1:59–2:31:30	2:05–2:42:30
30K	2:12–2:38	2:18–2:51:30	2:25–3:04:30	2:32–3:17:30
Marathon	3:10–3:50	3:20–4:10	3:30–4:30	3:40–4:50

Note: A runner may qualify as a basic competitor in one distance, such as the 5K, but because of a lack of mileage or experience be classified as a novice competitor in another distance, such as the marathon.

CHART B   BASIC COMPETITOR—RACE-TIME RANGES
FOR WOMEN

DISTANCE	(OPEN)	(40–49)	(50–59)	(60–69)
5K	21:30–25:30	22:30–27:30	24:30–29:30	26:30–31:30
10K	44:00–52:00	46:00–56:00	50:00–60:00	54:00–64:00
15K	69:00–81:00	72:00–87:00	78:00–93:00	84:00–99:00
10 miles	73:20–86:40	76:40–93:20	83:20–1:40	90:00–1:46:40
20K	1:34–1:51	1:38–1:59	1:46–2:07	1:54–2:15
Half marathon	1:40–2:00	1:45–2:10	1:55–2:20	2:05–2:30
25K	1:59–2:20:30	2:05–2:31:30	2:15–2:42:30	2:26–2:53:30
30K	2:25–2:51:30	2:32–3:04:30	2:45–3:17:30	2:58–3:30:30
Marathon	3:30–4:10	3:40–4:30	4:00–4:50	4:20–5:10

Note: A runner may qualify as a basic competitor in one distance, such as the 5K, but because of lack of mileage or experience be classified as a novice competitor in another distance, such as the marathon.

Races: 5 to 12 a year, usually from 5K to a half marathon; typically, no more than one marathon a year.

Race times: See Chart B above and on previous page.

ADVANCED COMPETITOR

This is the highest level of competition most runners can achieve, because of limited natural ability, lack of time, or family responsibilities. This runner is serious about the sport, and races well at the marathon distance and under, usually placing in the top 10 to 25 percent of the field and winning awards in local races.

Experience: Has been running at least 4 years and racing for at least 2 years.

Mileage: 40 to 60 miles per week.

Frequency: 6 to 7 days a week; perhaps a few two-a-days.

Long runs: 10 to 20 miles, once every 2 weeks, or 2 out of every 3 weeks.

Speed work: 1 or 2 days per week while preparing for races.

Races: 10 to 20 times a year at a variety of distances. Runs no more than 1 or 2 marathons per year.

Race times: See Chart C on the following page.

CHART C ADVANCED COMPETITOR—RACE-TIME RANGES FOR MEN

DISTANCE	(OPEN)	(40–49)	(50–59)	(60–69)
5K	16:30–19:30	17:30–20:30	18:30–21:30	20:30–22:30
10K	34:00–40:00	36:00–42:00	38:00–44:00	42:00–46:00
15K	53:00–63:00	56:00–66:00	59:00–69:00	66:00–72:00
10 miles	56:40–66:40	60:00–70:00	63:20–73:20	70:00–76:40
20K	1:12–1:25	1:16–1:29	1:21–1:34	1:29–1:38
Half marathon	1:15–1:30	1:20–1:35	1:25–1:40	1:35–1:45
25K	1:31–1:46	1:37–1:53	1:42–1:59	1:53–2:05
30K	1:51–2:12	1:58–2:18	2:04–2:25	2:18–2:32
Marathon	2:40–3:10	2:50–3:20	3:00–3:30	3:20–3:40

CHART C ADVANCED COMPETITOR—RACE-TIME RANGES FOR WOMEN

DISTANCE	(OPEN)	(40–49)	(50–59)	(60–69)
5K	18:30–21:30	20:30–22:30	22:30–24:30	24:30–26:30
10K	38:00–44:00	42:00–46:00	46:00–50:00	50:00–54:00
15K	59:00–69:00	66:00–72:00	72:00–78:00	78:00–84:00
10 miles	63:20–73:20	70:00–76:40	76:40–83:20	83:20–90:00
20K	1:21–1:34	1:29–1:38	1:38–1:46	1:47–1:54
Half marathon	1:25–1:40	1:35–1:45	1:45–1:55	1:55–2:05
25K	1:42–1:59	1:53–2:05	2:05–2:15	2:15–2:26
30K	2:04–2:25	2:18–2:32	2:32–2:45	2:45–2:58
Marathon	3:00–3:30	3:20–3:40	3:40–4:00	4:00–4:20

CHAMPION COMPETITOR

This level is achieved by those with the time, talent, and energy to reach at least the top local class. This runner often competes at the edge of national class. This is a serious level of competitive training. The champion usually places in the top 10 to 20 runners overall in local races, or in the top 5 in the masters age groups. These runners are also very often race winners.

Experience: Has been running at least 5 years, and racing at least 4 years.

Mileage: 60 to 80 miles per week.

Frequency: 7 days a week, with several two-a-days.

Long runs: 12 to 20 miles, 2 out of 3 weeks or 3 out of 4 weeks.

Speed work: 1 to 2 days per week when preparing for a key race.

Races: 10 to 20 times a year at a variety of distances. Runs no more than two marathons a year.

Race times: See Chart D, below.

CHART D CHAMPION COMPETITOR—RACE-TIME RANGES FOR MEN

DISTANCE	(OPEN)	(40–49)	(50–59)	(60–69)
5K	14:30–16:30	15:30–17:30	17:00–18:30	19:00–20:30
10K	30:00–34:00	32:00–36:00	35:00–38:00	39:00–42:00
15K	46:00–53:00	49:00–56:00	55:00–59:00	61:00–66:00
10 miles	50:00–56:40	53:20–60:00	58:20–63:20	65:00–70:00
20K	1:03–1:12	1:07–1:16	1:14–1:21	1:23–1:29
Half marathon	1:06–1:15	1:10–1:20	1:17:30–1:25	1:27:30–1:35
25K	1:20–1:31	1:25–1:37	1:34–1:42	1:45–1:53
30K	1:37–1:51	1:44–1:58	1:54–2:04	2:08–2:18
Marathon	2:20–2:40	2:30–2:50	2:45–3:00	3:05–3:20

CHART D CHAMPION COMPETITOR—RACE-TIME RANGES FOR WOMEN

DISTANCE	(OPEN)	(40–49)	(50–59)	(60–69)
5K	17:00–18:30	19:00–20:30	20:30–22:30	23:00–24:30
10K	35:00–38:00	39:00–42:00	42:00–46:00	47:00–50:00
15K	55:00–59:00	61:00–66:00	66:00–72:00	73:00–78:00
10 miles	58:20–63:20	65:00–70:00	70:00–76:40	78:20–83:20
20K	1:14–1:21	1:23–1:29	1:29–1:38	1:40–1:47
Half marathon	1:17:30–1:25	1:27:30–1:35	1:35–1:45	1:47:30–1:55
25K	1:34–1:42	1:45–1:53	1:53–2:05	2:07–2:15
30K	1:54–2:04	2:08–2:18	2:18–2:32	2:35–2:45
Marathon	2:45–3:00	3:05–3:20	3:20–3:40	3:45–4:00

NATIONAL CLASS AND ELITE RUNNERS

Beyond these four categories are the national class and elite runners. Since some of the champion runners may aspire to the national class level, we have included racing times (Chart E, below) for this category. In fact, several of the runners we coach ranging in age from 20 to 65 have entered this level.

We do not set specific training guidelines for national class runners, who include, for example, a sub-2:20 male marathoner and a sub-2:40 female masters marathoner. Runners at this level would follow the same general guidelines as the champion competitor.

The elite runner was made in heaven and seldom runs in hell. They are the big guns: Rodgers, Shorter, De Castella, Benoit-Samuelson, Kristiansen, Waitz. There is little anyone can teach them except, perhaps, to remind them that they wouldn't be at the top if the rest of us weren't behind them.

CHART E   NATIONAL CLASS COMPETITOR—RACE-TIME RANGES FOR MEN

DISTANCE	(OPEN)	(40–49)	(50–59)	(60–69)
5K	14:30	15:30	17:00	19:00
10K	30:00	32:00	35:00	39:00
15K	46:00	49:00	55:00	61:00
10 miles	50:00	53:20	58:20	65:00
20K	**1:03**	**1:07**	**1:14**	**1:23**
Half marathon	**1:06**	**1:10**	**1:17:30**	**1:27:30**
25K	**1:20**	**1:25**	**1:34**	**1:45**
30K	**1:37**	**1:44**	**1:54**	**2:08**
Marathon	**2:20**	**2:30**	**2:45**	**3:05**

CHART E   NATIONAL CLASS COMPETITOR—RACE-TIME RANGES FOR WOMEN

DISTANCE	(OPEN)	(40–49)	(50–59)	(60–69)
5K	17:00	19:00	20:30	23:00
10K	35:00	39:00	42:00	47:00
15K	55:00	61:00	66:00	73:00
10 miles	58:20	65:00	70:00	78:20
20K	**1:14**	**1:23**	**1:29**	**1:40**
Half marathon	**1:17:30**	**1:27:30**	**1:35**	**1:47:30**
25K	**1:34**	**1:45**	**1:53**	**2:07**
30K	**1:54**	**2:08**	**2:18**	**2:35**
Marathon	**2:45**	**3:05**	**3:20**	**3:45**

2. THREE BASIC QUESTIONS: HOW FAR? HOW FAST? HOW OFTEN?

The most common questions runners of all levels ask are: How far should I run? How fast should I run? How often should I run? Mileage, pace, and frequency of runs comprise the ingredients of a successful running program. Most exercise physiologists agree that the answer to these basic questions for those interested in meeting minimal fitness standards is to run 30 consecutive minutes, three to five times per week, at a brisk, but comfortable pace. Any training done beyond this level is for reasons other than fitness, since you receive minimal health benefits and increase your chance of injury.

But many runners strive to challenge themselves in races, whether they are 5-minute-per-mile athletes or 12-minute-per-mile athletes. If you wish to challenge yourself, then you are an *athlete*. And an athlete is concerned with more than fitness; he or she is interested in performance. To perform well you need more mileage than the fitness runner. You'll run at a faster pace and run more often. But you may not be able to attain certain running goals because your body or your environment, including work and family responsibilities, won't allow you to put in the needed work. Most often runners fail because they want too much too soon and do not respond to warning signals of injury and overtraining. The following guidelines will help you safely improve your realistic race times.

HOW FAR SHOULD I RUN?

When you first start running your goal is to run 20 and then 30 minutes nonstop. The goal is to train the heart and lungs to work hard for a half hour, thus strengthening them and improving your level of fitness. For minimal fitness, mileage means nothing—you must train the cardiovascular system for the recommended time period. Once runners are averaging 30 minutes of nonstop running and are starting to ease into longer runs, they often wish to start counting daily and weekly mileage instead of minutes run. Although it often makes more sense to record minutes run rather than mileage, most runners eventually switch to counting mileage, since all their friends do and all races and training for races are measured in miles run. Besides, how can you answer the inevitable question at runners' parties, "How many miles a week do you run?" if you don't faithfully record mileage in your log? Thus, in this book we give you guidelines for daily and weekly mileage. How much mileage you should run depends on your goals, what distances you intend to race, what you can tolerate, and your running experience. Chapter 6 provides detailed information about your running mileage. Your training mileage is such an essential ingredient in your training program that we have devoted a separate chapter to this topic.

HOW FAST SHOULD I RUN?

Just as you can measure how far you can run two ways, by time or by mileage, you can measure how fast you run in two ways: by your pulse and by your pace per mile. The quality of your runs is determined by your goals. We run for two reasons: fitness and racing. Running for fitness means running aerobically within your training heart-rate range and at a comfortable pace. You run at a pace at which you can converse with others. By running at an even pace during which your heart rate levels off at a "steady state" well within your training heart-rate range, you safely increase your aerobic endurance. You strengthen the engine that powers the racing machine.

If you run too fast, you become breathless and your muscles may tighten, perhaps causing injury. Mostly, you are forced to slow down because you feel uncomfortable. This happens when you run at a pace above your training heart-rate range (see chart on page 30). Only experienced runners train and race above their training heart-rate range and at a pace where they can't talk comfortably. This is called running "anaerobically" or "going into oxygen debt": at this pace, these runners cannot meet their bodies' demand for oxygen, and they have to borrow chemically from their bodies, causing a buildup of lactic acid in their muscles. You have to practice running anaerobically, with speed training and racing, in order to improve as a racer. You also have to learn to pace yourself properly in races, since starting too fast or too slowly may ruin your race.

Almost all of your running should be done aerobically, and to make sure you don't run too fast, you should listen to the best pacer you have—your heart. Many veteran runners can easily tell, by how they feel, when their heart rate is within their training range. This is perceived exertion, and you may develop it as you train. Check your pulse (heart rate) periodically to monitor the intensity of your workouts. This keeps you from running too fast.

Pulse

Your pulse, or heart rate, is the number of times your heart beats per minute. The faster it beats, the harder you are working. The slower it beats when you are under stress, the better shape you are in. For example, before training, your heart rate may go to 140 beats per minute when you run at a pace of 10 minutes per mile. After perhaps 2 months of training, it may rise to only 120 beats per minute at the same speed. This is one indication of improvement in your cardiovascular system from a consistent running program.

You can count your heartbeat at several places on your body: over the left side of the chest, at about the middle of your upturned wrist, at the carotid artery just in front of the large vertical muscle along the sides of your neck, or at any convenient place where you feel a pulse. The most common method is to gently press your wrist or neck with the tips of your first two fingers. Don't use your thumb and don't press too hard. Excessive pressure at the carotid artery can be dangerous and may slow the heart rate by 3 or 4 beats per minute.

When you feel a pulse, count the number for 10 seconds, then multiply it by 6. That will give you your heart rate per minute. (For example, if you count 12 beats in 10 seconds and multiply by 6, that will give you a heart rate of 72 beats per minute.) This enables you to determine your resting heart rate easily.

Obtaining your exercise heart rate can be more difficult. Take your pulse immediately after stopping. (This may be for a pulse check break during your run or at the conclusion of your run.) If you don't, your heart rate drops too quickly to give you an accurate estimate. If you take the pulse immediately—you don't have to jog in place to keep your heart rate up—you should get a close reading of your exercise heart rate. Note that counting your heart beats for 15 seconds (and multiplying by 4) sometimes gives a lower rate.

Four types of heart rates are important in developing a safe exercise training program.

1. Resting Heart Rate (Base Pulse) This is your heart rate when you first wake up in the morning, or when you are very relaxed during the day. The average resting heart rate for men is 60 to 80 beats per minute; for women, the average is 70 to 90 beats per minute. A well-conditioned person's heart rate may be around 60 or below; the serious runner often has a resting heart rate in the 40-to-50-beats-per-minute range.

This base pulse is helpful in several ways. First, most people chart their resting heart rates over the course of months or years as a measure of how they are progressing. Generally, as you get in better shape, your resting heart rate lowers. Second, the pulse rate may serve as a warning signal of overtraining. A higher than usual morning resting heart rate may indicate that you are training too hard, not sleeping well or long enough, or are overstressed. You should take a day off from running, or exercise less until the rate returns to normal.

2. Maximum Heart Rate This rate is at or near the level of exhaustion, where the heart "peaks out" and cannot satisfy your body's demand for oxygen or beat much faster. You should *estimate* your maximum heart rate by subtracting your age from 220. *This is not a goal.* It is merely a figure from which you can obtain your training heart-rate range. (Your exact maximum heart rate can only be obtained by taking a stress test, supervised by a physician.)

3. Training (Exercise) Heart Rate Each of us has a specific range—between two heart rates—in which we should achieve sufficient and safe cardiovascular training. This "target zone" or training range falls between two numbers: the minimal target of 70 percent of your maximum heart rate and the cutoff figure of 85 percent of your maximum heart rate. (The 85 percent figure is the approximate border between aerobic and anaerobic conditions.)

Exercising at a heart rate below the lower of the two numbers will not provide much conditioning for your cardiovascular system. Exercising at a heart rate above the higher number will cause a great deal of extra effort (and agony) and potential musculoskeletal injury. It will not improve your cardiovascular conditioning because you will not be able to sustain it long enough for the conditioning to take place.

To find your approximate training heart-rate range, subtract your age from 220. Your minimum training heart rate is 70 percent of this number, and your maximum (slowdown) rate is 85 percent. For you runners counting on your fingers and toes, we have included a chart on page 30.

The pulse rates are based on a predicted maximum, and thus some error is possible. One runner may be able to exceed his or her cutoff rate without "breathing hard," or he or she may feel tired at a lower level of exertion. The "talk test" is a good monitoring device. If you are running so fast that you cannot converse with someone, slow down! Exercise should be fun and beneficial, not exhausting.

The key is to keep your heart rate between 70 and 85 percent of your maximum heart rate. Your goal is to hold your heart rate in a "steady state" near the 70 percent figure where your

HEART-RATE CHART

The following chart designates heart-rate targets for various age groups:

Age	Target HR (70%)	Cutoff HR (85%)
20–25	140	167
26–30	134	163
31–35	131	159
36–40	127	155
41–45	124	150
46–50	120	146
51–55	117	142
56–60	113	138
61–65	110	133
66–70	106	129

Training range

body handles the workout easily yet gets aerobic conditioning. Your heart rate will increase as you run uphill, increase your speed, run in heat and humidity, or grow tired. At this point you should slow down or walk briskly to keep your heart rate in that 70–85 percent range.

Your training pulse and pace are particular to you. A comfortable 7-minute pace for an advanced runner may only be 70 percent of his or her maximum, whereas another runner may be out of breath trying to keep up. Conversely, at an 8-minute pace, which may be the slower runner's 70 percent level, the advanced runner would be below his or her training range. Be careful when running with others that you don't run too fast or too slowly; set your own pace for maximum benefit.

Stop and take your pulse periodically during your run or at the end of an evenly paced run. With practice you will be able to guess it, just as you can guess your per-mile pace pretty accurately. Judge by perceived exertion and forget the numbers. If you can talk comfortably and are running fast enough to perspire, you are training aerobically (70–85 percent). If you talk, but not easily, you are at the aerobic-anaerobic borderline (85 percent). If you are out of breath, straining, and unable to talk, you are in oxygen debt (over 85 percent).

Recovery Heart Rate Your recovery heart rate is your post cool-down pulse. After training runs, following 15 to 20 minutes of walking and stretching, your pulse rate should be below 100 beats per minute. If it isn't, either you didn't cool down properly, or you ran too hard.

Training Pace

In deciding how fast to run, most runners think in terms of pace per mile, not pulse rate. But your pulse rate will reflect factors such as heat, fatigue, hills, and head winds, which would be neglected if you measure only your exertion at pace per mile. The safest bet is to learn what your pulse feels like at various paces: for example, a 9:00–9:15–minute-mile pace may keep you within your training range at a steady 140–145 pulse per minute. Be flexible enough to adjust to environmental conditions and other stresses. The bottom line should not be to stubbornly stick to a prearranged training pace per minute, but rather to keep your perceived exertion constant and your pulse within your training range. Some days factors such as uphills and head winds will temporarily cause you to slow the pace, just as downhills and tail winds may cause you to temporarily pick up the pace. Heat, fatigue, slippery footing, and other factors may cause you to run at a slower pace for your entire workout.

Since we most often refer to our training runs in terms of pace per mile and since your daily training pace is such an unglamorous but essential ingredient in your training program, we have devoted chapter 5 to this topic.

HOW OFTEN SHOULD I RUN?

You must peform some form of aerobic exercise at least 3 times a week to maintain a minimal level of fitness, but don't run 3 or 4 days in a row and then take the rest of the week off. Spread the exercise out over the entire week. Most runners easily find the time to exercise on the weekend, but have trouble getting out during the week. As a minimum goal for these runners we suggest the following: run Saturday and Sunday, taking Monday and Friday off; make every effort to run on Tuesday, Wednesday, and Thursday. You'll have trouble keeping fit enough for racing on less than 5 days of running per week. Most basic competitive runners should run 5–6 days per week, and most advanced runners should run 6 days per week.

Should I Run Every Other Day?

Some coaches and runners advocate running every other day: running the same or slightly less mileage per week as if you ran every day, but running longer each day followed by a day of rest. The theory behind this strategy is that it takes approximately 48 hours for the body to recover properly from a run. Running fewer days per week certainly saves time warming up, cooling down, dressing, undressing, and showering. More recovery between runs minimizes the chance of injury and allows you to feel fresher and run with better form on your runs. Because of time constraints or susceptibility to injury, you might find this system helpful to you. You may fill in the off days with running equivalent mileage (see chapter 7) to help keep your aerobic endurance up.

Many of us enjoy running every day. We run as much for pleasure or stress management as we do for performance. Runners often feel very antsy if they don't get in their daily run. As long as you take a few days easy, there is really no reason why you can't run every day if you really enjoy it. But you don't have to run every day. We recommend a minimum of one day off per week for all but the very serious competitors. Give the body a day of rest and it will respond better for the remainder of the week. Take your day off on a regularly scheduled day (Monday following a couple of good weekend runs is a typical off day), or save it for a busy workday or a day when you feel a little tired.

Beware: Taking days off can get too easy. If you don't keep a consistent running schedule going, you will not achieve your desired level of fitness. Keeping a weekly training log helps here: too many big zeros entered will make you feel guilty. We suggest that most runners take a day off following their long runs while marathon training. No sense pounding the pavement with tired legs. If you really need to train every day, try substituting biking, swimming, rowing, or cross-country skiing once or twice a week as detailed in chapter 7. Alternative aerobic training allows for "active rest"—you still gain aerobic benefit, but eliminate the impact stress that comes with daily running.

A 1986 study of British women marathoners reported in the *Journal of Sports Science* indicated that the frequency of runs (more workouts were better) better predicted superior racing times than any other variable, including weekly mileage and years of running experience. Consistently getting out the door and running pays off if you listen to your body and don't do too much. Our suggestion is to run 5–7 days per week and to supplement running days with alternative aerobic training.

Should I Run Twice a Day?

No! Unless you are

1. Running through an injury, or recovering from an injury when two 4-mile runs (for example) may be less stressful than one 8-miler.

2. Running in difficult footing—on an indoor track or in the snow—that will tire out your muscles. You are more prone to injury the longer you run under such conditions. You might run two 5-mile runs, or run one indoors and one outdoors instead of a single longer run. Remember this rule of thumb: to avoid muscle strain or injury, don't run more than 45 minutes in difficult footing.

3. Running in rain, extreme cold, or heat. Two short runs are better than risking your health for a longer time. No matter how hot or cold it is, you won't get too uncomfortable for the first 30 to 45 minutes.

4. Running with a busy schedule. You may have to break up your runs into two-a-days occasionally to have time to meet the demands of family and job. Some runners choose to save time and money by running to and from work.

5. Running for recovery. In the day or days following a hard race, you may find it beneficial to run two short workouts; 2 light miles with a morning swim and an evening 3-miler may speed recovery.

6. Running before a speed workout. If your workout is in the evening, a short run in the morning or at noon will loosen you up.

7. Running with high mileage. The high-mileage runner can increase his or her mileage by adding a few extra morning or evening runs a week of about 5 miles each. One of the problems of high mileage is that you run more slowly because of fatigue. Also you may pick up bad habits, such as altered form. You may not even run fast enough to improve your fitness level. For this runner, two-a-days are essential.

Most runners need not run twice a day. Medical researchers haven't decided which is more beneficial—a single 10-miler or two 5-milers. Certainly you shouldn't eliminate the single long run. Unless you are a top runner wanting to move up to a more competitive level, you should run only once a day. The runner averaging more than 10 miles a day almost has to use two-a-days. If you decide to use this method, experiment with it to see if it agrees with your body and mind.

Start with a few 2-milers in the morning in addition to your evening run. Make the morning runs slow and easy. Later, move up to 4- or 5-milers. When doing two-a-days, any run below 4 miles won't improve your aerobic fitness.

Two-a-days also take time. You may feel as if you do nothing all day but stretch, run, shower, eat, and sleep. Running once a day gives you the most miles per hour of time invested. Since you must warm up and cool down twice for two-a-days, beware of shortchanging yourself in that important area. Forcing two-a-days will increase your risk of injury.

What Time of Day Should I Run?

Morning, noon, or night? Most runners do the bulk of their training on weekdays after work and on weekend mornings. But there are plenty of runners who prefer early morning runs and several who like to break up the day with an afternoon run. In terms of training for performance, the time of day that you run doesn't matter much. In fact, elite runners can be found working out at all times of the day. When you run should depend mostly on how easily you can fit running into your schedule and the time of day you enjoy it best.

Morning runs may start your day on a pleasant note or leave you the rest of the day free. Those who develop the first-thing-in-the-morning routine tend to be more consistent in their training: by getting in the run before work, last-minute business or personal problems don't cause you to miss your run or force you to do it in a rush. Morning runs in the summer avoid the heat of the day.

For people like Bob Glover, morning runs are at noon. It is hard to get up and get moving for some of us. But morning run enthusiasts swear that their run gets them off to a running start on a great day. Winter brings cold, dark mornings that are easy to skip unless you are very dedicated. Make sure you get to sleep early if you intend to run early in the morning. Some of the most restful sleep is during the last 2 hours, and to wake up before your body is ready to go for a run may leave you fatigued rather than refreshed. When you wake up in the morning your muscles are stiff. According to circadian (daily) rhythms, body temperature is lowest between 4:00 A.M. and 6:00 A.M. Since your body is both stiff and cold, it is much more prone to injuries. In fact, a study by podiatrist Dr. John Pagliano indicated that morning runners get injured more often than noontime or evening runners.

You can counteract the danger of early morning running by warming up properly. Don't attempt vigorous stretching exercises—your muscles are too cold to stretch properly. Do some easy limbering exercises and go for a brisk walk for 5 minutes and then ease into a slow run for a mile or two before you settle into your normal pace. You can stretch in more detail after the run. A better idea: ride an indoor bike for 15 minutes to warm up the body and then stretch gently before going out to run. Too many early morning runners are in a hurry and skip the warm-ups, thus making themselves more prone to injury. Better to skip a mile or two of running than to risk injury. Says podiatrist Dr. Steve Subotnik: "You need a good half-hour to warm up and get the metabolism going. You've been in bed all night and when you're resting, the soft tissues contract a little." When Bob Glover is traveling on business and wakes up stiff all over in an uncomfortable hotel bed, he sits in a warm tub for 10 minutes to warm up and then walks 10 minutes slowly before starting a run: by the time his run is over he feels loose and awake. Avoid hard running or speed training until you have been awake and about for at least 2 hours.

Morning runs can be enjoyable to many; just be certain to take it easy. Since most races are on weekend mornings, you should do at least some of your runs at that time of day on the weekends. You don't need to eat before early morning runs; if you do, you might cause cramps. If you feel weak in the stomach and desire something before you run, try something simple like a glass of orange juice and a piece of toast to settle your stomach.

Midday runs are great for those who have flexible work hours. You don't have to worry about darkness, and it isn't as cold in the winter. You also aren't as stiff. A run will stifle your appetite, so a light lunch afterward will help you manage your weight. Taking a time-out during the day to enjoy a run provides the mind with a break. Bob Glover prefers these kinds of runs, which allow him to better break up his day. It also eliminates hassles at home when your spouse or kids want your attention after work. More and more workers negotiate for company showers or join a nearby fitness club in order to escape from work for a midday run. With proper planning and the flexibility to work a little later perhaps to make up for a longer lunch break, the midday run can be the working runner's dream. Of course, you may need to pass on midday runs during the heat of the summer unless you wish to substitute a swim, bike ride, or treadmill run at your club.

Evening is when most runners are on the road. The pressures of the day are left behind, and you come home refreshed and ready for the evening. It is the easiest time to find running partners. These runs, however, are most likely to interfere with the rest of your social life, and dinners and evenings out often have to be rescheduled to accommodate the evening runner. A solution: run with your date and then go out for dinner. Evening runs, as Bob Glover found out, are not popular with the kids at home. They want Daddy and Mommy when they want them, not after a run when it is their bedtime. But for the singles crowd, hanging out in the park after a run is healthier than the singles bar scene. Running too hard late in the day may make it hard for you to relax and get to sleep. Try some relaxation exercises and a warm bath. As with morning runs, during the winter you need to cope with the cold and the dark. Be sure to run wearing reflectorized materials, run where it is well lit, keep as far away from cars as possible, and run in groups if possible. Another plus for evening runners: according to a study at the Cooper Clinic Research Institute, exercising in the evening is most effective in controlling weight.

3. BASIC TRAINING PRINCIPLES

This book is for men and women who wish to improve as runners. You wish to learn more about the sport, race longer distances, faster times. You may be a 12-minute-per-mile or a 6-minute-per-mile runner, but you seriously want to get better by following a well-organized training program. You hold that program in your hands.

A competitive runner plans his or her runs and develops a training schedule directed toward a key race or races several weeks ahead. Running is still enjoyable, but involves more dedication, structure, regularity, and work. Some of these runs, particularly long runs and speed sessions, carry a different kind of reward. You learn the satisfaction of completing hard workouts that help you accomplish training and racing goals. You learn what it means to "pay your dues," and see a new personal record (PR) on the clock at the finish line. Training teaches both the body and the mind to meet racing's many challenges.

Training methods are based on established principles. Each coach or athlete "steals" hints from this person or that person, and processes them through the trial and error of personal experience. The result is different applications of the same basic knowledge. We do not pretend to have invented competitive training. We are greatly indebted to those pioneer coaches, runners, and scientists who have contributed to the resource bank we draw on. Other coaches may tell you to train differently; they are neither right nor wrong. They have interpreted the basic training principles in a different way.

> Before you proceed with this chapter, review the list of physiology terms in the Appendices. A basic understanding of key terms is essential to proper training.

The following ten principles form the backbone of your training program as a competitive runner.

I. THE PRINCIPLE OF FOUNDATION TRAINING AND SHARPENING

When you construct a house, you start with the foundation and build on that. The same is true of competitive running.

You must build a *foundation* of aerobic endurance. You do this by progressively increasing your work load, and then, as you approach your race target, you *sharpen* your training with specific speed workouts designed so that you peak for your race or series of races. Then you recover and rebuild with foundation endurance running.

This basic principle is used by two types of runners:

1. The runner "on the way up"—the beginner racer or marathoner—slowly develops a foundation of endurance before adding miles to his or her schedule. For the true beginner, this means building to a base of 30 minutes of running 5 times a week before building toward the first race. The novice marathoner builds to a foundation of 30 to 40 miles a week and then adds to this base.

The mileage foundation for this type of runner is essential. Sharpening means increasing the number of miles with more foundation endurance work in order to have the stamina to complete the aimed-for event. After the goal (race) is reached, the runner cuts back on mileage, recovers, and then rebuilds a foundation at a higher level of mileage for the next challenge, and either improves the time or increases the distance raced. For the first 1 to 2 years of running and racing, the novice puts in almost exclusively foundation aerobic runs at a conversation pace.

2. The experienced competitor wants to improve his or her time. To do this, he or she expands from a foundation of endurance and sharpens for the race with speed workouts. Having peaked for a race, the competitive runner needs a period of decreased activity to rebuild the foundation and sharpen again to reach an even higher level of performance.

In other sports this principle is applied as a seasonal approach. Professional teams have spring training or summer camps and preseason workouts and games. High school and college track teams have well-defined seasons: cross-country in the fall, indoor track in the winter, and outdoor track in the spring. The average competitive road racer has neither well-defined seasons, nor a coach to develop him or her, following the principle of foundation training and sharpening.

A training program for competitive runners consists of three parts: the off-season (rebuilding—light running), the preseason (progressive foundation endurance running), and the competitive season (specific training to sharpen and build to peak performance). Some competitive road racers only "peak" once a year. For the average competitive runner, this may mean an increase in mileage and workouts leading to a popular mass marathon. For others, it may mean building up for key races two or three times a year. Some elite runners spend 6 months to a year building toward one key race, perhaps to run a fast time or qualify for the Olympic team. Most runners, however, have varying peaks and valleys in their running year.

The average competitor follows a two-season approach. He or she may back off during the cold weather and then build for a spring race—perhaps the Boston Marathon. Then he or she may back off during the hot summer to build for the fall races—maybe the New York Marathon. Most popular races are held in the spring and fall, when the weather is cooler.

Foundation training is done year-round. During the off-season, it is used for recovery and maintenance running. During the buildup period, it increases progressively to improve aerobic and muscular endurance. During the sharpening periods of the competitive season, foundation endurance runs form the backbone of a weekly schedule. Remember, the better the base developed through foundation training, the more hard work your body will be able to do as you prepare for your big race, and the more likely you are to become a successful competitive runner.

II. THE PRINCIPLE OF CONSISTENCY

Foundation training is based on steady, *consistent* work. Constant training—52 weeks a year—is necessary for the competitive runner. You run when it's hot or cold, when you are high or low, alone or with friends, when aiming toward a big race or when your goal has been achieved.

You must train all week—not just on Saturday and Sunday. Even small amounts of running on a regular basis are better for you than sporadic hard days followed by days of inactivity.

If you decide to cut back for a change of pace, replace the aerobic exercise with another. Develop a minimal fitness base of running—anywhere between 50 and 75 percent of your peak mileage—and don't fall below it except in case of injury or illness. For example, if you normally build to 50 miles a week for a marathon, don't fall below a base of 25–35 miles a week during your lull in training. If you do, it will be too hard to build back up. Train consistently all year in order to grow stronger year after year. "Put miles in the bank."

Consistency requires discipline. Force yourself out the door. An advanced competitor puts in some mileage every day; less serious competitors run 4–6 days a week. Log your runs in your diary. It is easy to fall into the habit of taking a day off when things get a little tough. Instead of not running at all, cut back your mileage on days when you are faced with obstacles; force yourself to do a minimal amount to keep the habit of consistency alive. To succeed as a runner, you must be a little crazy about getting in your daily run. If possible, schedule your run for the same time every day; make it an important appointment with yourself.

When you build to your intended mileage level for base

training for a big race, try to stay consistent. In 1978, Bob Glover ran exactly 100 miles each week for 12 consecutive weeks of foundation work. This consistency seemed fanatical even to other runners. After lowering his mileage to 80–90 miles a week and doing some quick speed work with Pete Schuder yelling at him, Glover enjoyed two months of racing times he had never before dreamed he could accomplish, peaking with a 1:43 30K race.

On the other hand, consistent training needs to be practical. If your body asks for a day off—take it. But only sound reasons like physical fatigue, injury, or major travel conflicts should excuse you. The training diary helps here. By logging miles in it and keeping a record of daily, weekly, and monthly totals, you are forced to be consistent and disciplined. Count your weekly mileage from Monday through Sunday, so that you have the full weekend at the end of your training week and can make up a few miles on those days. Also, since many races fall on Sundays, you can plan your weekly training going into a race.

Consistency in mileage is best measured by counting your monthly mileage. For example, if your goal is 5 miles a day, that would be about 150 miles a month. You may log 35, 30, 40, 35 miles during the 4 weeks and still be very consistent. This allows you flexibility as you taper for races or take days off. When training seriously, set a range limit on your weekly and monthly goals and record it. For example, you should run not less than 30 miles in a single week, but not more than 40 miles; that would mean 35 miles on the average as a consistent foundation.

If you miss a day or two, don't try to make it up all at once. Add a mile or two a day, or forget the missed mileage. Consistency means training daily in manageable amounts. Running twice as far one day to make up for a lost day is not consistent training; it's overtraining. Forget the lost day and continue the next day at the *rate of training* you would normally have followed for the week. Also, the day off may have been necessary to prevent injury from stress.

Unfortunately, your body builds fitness slowly and loses it quickly. It takes only a few weeks to lose most of the adaptation to training that you have worked so hard to achieve. It takes less time to get out of shape than to get into shape—unfair, but true. You can maintain fitness with consistency on a year-round basis, avoiding injury by avoiding the causes and listening to the warning signals.

III. THE PRINCIPLE OF ADAPTATION TO PROGRESSIVE STRESS

The body—and mind—gradually adapts to increasing levels of stress. The body is a remarkable organism, and will surprise you in its ability to get stronger in order to adapt to stress. But it can also surprise you by breaking down if you overstress it. The stress shouldn't be either too little or too much. It must be intense enough and regular enough to promote adaptation to a higher level of racing fitness—the "training effect." On the other hand, if the stress is too much (overtraining), you overtax the adaptation system, causing fatigue, injury, or poor performance. "Train, don't strain" is the rule to follow. You train hard enough to improve, but don't strain so much that you defeat the improvement. More—faster and longer—isn't always better.

Thus, you apply a training stress in the form of your *hard* workouts (or gradually increased mileage) and balance it with easy days to allow for *recovery* between, and you do this for a training season followed by a rest season. If the stress is applied regularly and is nearly equal to your body's capacity to handle the work (harder than your normal easy run, but not all out), your body will adapt by increasing its capacity. As the body becomes accustomed to handling a specific amount of work, the work load should be increased slightly until the body can adapt to running with the same effort as before. As your fitness improves, you should be able to handle a greater training load with the same effort. The progress continues until you reach your ultimate capability, the limit of your body's ability to adapt without breaking down.

For the beginning runner and racer, progress comes fairly rapidly with visible results: improved finishing times for races. Students in our classes often see their times improve by several minutes. But as you approach your maximum potential, progress becomes less dramatic. The more you improve, the harder it is to continue improving. Some runners make a major jump in progress and then level out for a long time. Plateaus are a natural part of progress. Expect them. You can't keep on improving your time at the same rate; rather, you'll improve and then level off, and then improve again. Little by little your performance base will increase. These improvements, especially at the longer distances, will be greatest for the least experienced runners; elite runners measure improvements in seconds.

Athletes at all levels are finding that by pushing themselves progressively farther and faster, they are reaching performances they never dreamed possible. The danger here is overloading your body. You can avoid that by following the 10 percent rule: never increase your mileage or speed by more than 10 percent from one week to the next, or one month to the next. Also, do no more than 10 percent of your running as racing.

IV. THE PRINCIPLE OF RECOVERY

It is essential to alternate stress and recovery periods. Here are some basic rules:

1. In your day-to-day schedule, you should precede and follow each hard day (speed workout, race, or long run) with one or more easy days (of short or medium runs, or time off). It usually takes 48 hours to recover from hard runs, and 72 hours or more to recover from races. Light running the day after a hard session helps prevent injury and circulates blood to fatigued muscles, helping remove accumulated waste products and getting them ready to work again. Consider active rest after hard runs or on the day following; this includes stretching, biking, swimming, walking, massage, warm baths, etc.

2. During your speed workout, you should rest following each repetition or hard run.

3. Rest (taper) before a race, and slowly rebuild following the race. A common mistake is to rush back into training.

4. For your yearly schedule, you should build your foun-

dation and then sharpen for a few races, and follow this with several weeks of recovery running. You can't train hard year-round.

When scheduling your daily, weekly, or seasonal routine, you should alternate stress with recovery. Your body responds best to stressful hard work if it's also given the chance to recover and repair itself. Stress applied on top of stress equals breakdown; stress followed by recovery equals progress. If sufficient recovery does not occur, then the body's resources are depleted. The concept of alternating work and rest is popularly called the "hard-easy method."

What is easy for one runner, however, may be difficult for another. Also, it may take some runners longer to recover after certain runs. Perhaps you ran your workout too hard, your course was unusually hilly, it was a very hot day, or you were short on sleep and long on stress. Listen to your body and learn to recognize its warning signs—sore muscles, fatigue. Sometimes your body tricks you. After a hard workout or race you may feel very strong the next day and be tempted to run hard. Don't! Often "the 2-day lag" occurs—you feel fine the day after your hard day, but are wiped out the following day. If you ignore this principle of recovery, you can dig yourself into a very deep hole.

Some runners alternate weeks of hard-easy training. After every 3 weeks of normal training, take a week of rest—no speed work, no long runs, and only 50 percent of your normal mileage. This system is especially good for the runner who has a tendency to overtrain, since it has its own built-in physical and mental relief.

The hard-easy concept is perhaps the most difficult principle to teach in our running classes. Runners want to run a hard or long race on Sunday and go for a 10-miler on Monday, and then on Tuesday they wonder why they are outsprinted by the grandmothers in our class. *You must rest before and after all long runs, speed workouts, and races.* The average working man or woman must be careful not to try to squeeze in hard days on both Saturday and Sunday—the result can be total fatigue by Monday or Tuesday, or worse, an injury.

Do not train the same number of miles every day. Run slowly

some days, and vary your mileage. Some runners actually need to be taught how to run slowly. Coaches should be as concerned about holding back their athletes as they are about pushing them.

Hard-easy training involves mixing the distance and speed of your runs in such a way as to induce the right amount of stress, and the needed types of both stress and recovery, that will help you in your running. We will teach you how to plan your training schedule safely and wisely by balancing speed, distance, and rest. The formula is easy: hard work + rest = faster times.

V. THE PRINCIPLE OF SPECIFICITY OF TRAINING

You will train differently for a 5K race and a marathon, to run on a fast, flat course or a rugged, hilly one, to race in cool weather or in the heat. After building your foundation of endurance, and as you sharpen for your race, you need to train your body and mind for the specific demands of the race or series of races you plan to enter.

When you run different types of races over varying terrains in varied weather conditions, you ask your body to work differently from your normal training runs. You should alter your training so that the speed, distance, resistance, form, and temperature conditions will be as nearly as possible the same as for your race. Specific training will allow your body to adapt to the specific stresses it will encounter on race day.

The best way to train your body for running is by running. No matter how many hours you spend swimming or biking, you still won't be using the same muscles the same way as you do in running. Running consists of several types of runs. With running itself, you must choose the specific types of endurance and speed runs and apply them in your training to help you prepare for particular races. You need to practice certain skills of running so that you become good at them, feel comfortable with them, and your body adapts physiologically to them. A sprinter's success depends largely on his or her ability to contract muscles powerfully and run in oxygen debt. The marathon runner needs a well-developed cardiorespiratory system and muscular endurance—strength over distance. The 5K–10K runner is somewhere in between, and needs the capacities of both the marathoner and the sprinter. If you are increasing your distance, you need to do more specific training for endurance. If you are decreasing your distance, you need to develop more specific training for speed.

Do not, however, become obsessed with this training. You shouldn't run long every day in preparation for a marathon, nor run only uphill for a hilly event. Most of your training sessions should be the same, except that for 1 to 3 days a week (from a few weeks for shorter races to a few months for longer ones), as you sharpen you should also alter your training.

Specific training should be used in five basic areas:

Distance

You need to train your muscles, mind, and cardiorespiratory systems to handle the stress of fatigue associated with running long distances. The longer the race, the more important it is to train with higher mileage and longer single runs. Any increase in the distance of your usual race (such as from 1 mile to 10K) and any training for the marathon distance or beyond require two specific changes in your training: increases in total mileage and increases in long runs.

Speed

You need to train yourself to be comfortable at your race pace. Do some training at race pace or faster. The miler would do specific training much faster than the 10K runner, since, obviously, the required pace is much quicker. The marathoner would run many workouts more slowly and over longer distances than the 10K runner.

It makes sense that if you do most of your daily running at 8:30 per mile and the fastest you have ever run a single mile is 6:50, you are going to be uncomfortable if you start a race at a 7-minute-mile pace. Thus, you need to improve your speed so that you can be comfortable at the early brisk pace and can generate speed for tactical bursts during the race and at the finish.

Racing Form

You should practice the biomechanics of racing form at race pace or slightly faster so that your body feels comfortable at this pace. This includes uphill and downhill form.

Terrain

If you are planning to run a flat, fast course on a track or road, you should prepare yourself by doing some quick track or roadwork at race pace or faster. The race pace will be quicker than what you are used to. A hilly course requires some hill running in your normal training, and some hill speed sessions. In brief, train for the course you will run.

Heat

Avoid training in the heat, but if you usually run in the early morning or late evening and your race starts at noon, you must also do some running at that time of day. Be sure to slow the training pace and drink plenty of fluids, even when you're not thirsty. If you plan to race in hot weather but must train in cool weather, you have three options: move into the climate zone of the race for 1 to 2 weeks to allow yourself to acclimatize; artificially simulate heat conditions by running with extra clothing for a few days a week; get into the best shape you can, and pray for clouds and rain.

VI. THE PRINCIPLE OF INDIVIDUALITY AND FLEXIBILITY

All training must be flexible, adapting to the needs of the individual runner. A coach shouldn't establish a single training schedule for all athletes; each runner has personal likes and dislikes, strengths and weaknesses. Your ability level and training goal are unique to you. Use the guidelines in this book to write your own training program—a program that will change as your individual needs change.

Find out what training works best for you. Some runners will thrive on a steady diet of high mileage and weekly 20-milers, while others would break down physically or mentally following this program. Some benefit most from 1-mile speed workouts, while others feel they race better at all distances by doing shorter, faster 440s. Some need more rest than others after races and between hard workouts.

Learn to "go with your strengths." If you can pound out high mileage and have lots of endurance for long races, you are a natural endurance runner. You may find that no matter how much you train to improve your speed, you make only minimal gains at best. We can't make a sprinter out of a turtle. But by going with your strengths you can train with high mileage and concentrate on longer speed workouts—such as 1- or 2-mile interval workouts or quick tempo runs of 5 to 10 kilometers. You work on improving your speed over longer distance, rather than for a shorter sprint. Try to improve in the areas you have less talent in, but don't waste a lot of time on them if you will get better results by maximizing your natural ability in other areas.

Your training program must be flexible. You should be prepared to adapt to weather conditions, available facilities, your health, and family obligations. Alter your training to fit your needs—be practical, not stubborn. On the other hand, don't be so flexible that you lose consistency and discipline. Include variety in your training program. Don't run the same distance every day over the same course at the same time of day with the same people at the same pace. Vary your training and speed workouts. For the most part, the competitive athlete in training should pick a few basic courses of varying lengths and stick to them. Putting in high mileage is often an unglamorous, robotlike task, and being familiar with the terrain is quite helpful when you are tired and just want to push automatic and cruise without thinking. Save the joys of exploring for when you are especially bored or when traveling. Having a trusty course is a kind of security blanket—you feel comfortable with it. And it is safer—you make friends along the route who will help take care of you and offer you encouragement. If a group of runners meet to run, chances are that the pace they will run will be too fast for some and too slow for others—just as in a race. You must be willing to compromise a little, but in general find training partners who will help you—neither push you too hard nor hold you back too much.

To vary your racing distances, try cross-country in the fall and shorter races, maybe even track, in the summer. Take time off between racing seasons; perhaps try an alternative like cross-country skiing. Don't train only for marathon races all year long.

VII. THE PRINCIPLE OF CONFIDENCE BUILDING

Confidence comes with experience and the triumph of progressive training work loads and improved race performances. If you believe in yourself and know you have a strong foundation of training, success is only a few miles down the road.

As you approach big races, use key workouts and smaller races to increase your confidence and mental toughness. Surviving long runs and speed workouts and pushing yourself in training toughens you and builds confidence that you can meet a challenge and not quit.

Some highly trained runners will toughen themselves by "pulling a max." This means that about 2 or 3 weeks before a big race they will run a much harder workout than usual. Bob Glover's all-time "max workout" was twenty 440s at hard pace with little recovery on a hot day. To make it worse, Pete Schuder yelled at him the whole time and clocked the recovery to the second so that Glover couldn't cheat. He rested for several days, and then 2 weeks later went out confident on a hot day and ran one of his best races. Other coaches use such a method, commonly known as "callousing." They want their runners to experience stress in workouts so they will be tougher on race day. Obviously, this practice should be limited to those more experienced runners who are very fit.

Every runner can increase his or her toughness and confidence by applying a little more stress in order to "enter a new dimension" on race day. We all have more physical potential than our minds allow us to use. The trick is to reach down deep, run through those psychological barriers, and maximize our potential as athletes.

VIII. THE PRINCIPLE OF PATIENCE AND EXPERIENCE

Successful racing doesn't happen overnight. For the competitive runner, success is measured in years, not weeks. Each day you put more miles in the bank and build for the future. With increased experience as a competitor, you become a wiser and more efficient racer. You *experience* your first marathon, for example, then *race* the next. Important lessons have to be learned: dressing for races, drinking on the run, handling heat and cold, pacing and race strategy. No matter how many times you have read what to do, until you have experienced it and learned by doing—possibly learned through error—you won't be a skilled competitor. You will learn more from every race you run— even after years of competition. Take your time and be patient as you progress slowly but steadily. Learn from your racing experience over the years so that you will be able to get more out of your body with every race and every year of racing. The more years you log in your diary, the better competitor you will be.

IX. THE PRINCIPLE OF EXTENDED GOALS

Competitive running offers the average athlete a never-ending finish line. There seem always to be new challenges—longer distances to conquer or more minutes and seconds to knock off the clock. Even as we slow down with age, we are presented with new opportunities as we move into new age classifications, with new standards of excellence. You may remember when your goal was only to run a mile or complete a local 10K race or a marathon. After you conquer the distance goals, you can establish time goals for each distance—breaking 4 hours for the marathon, then 3:30, and so on.

Our sport gives us a tremendous incentive to keep improving—the extended goal. No matter how fast you run a race, once it is over you can plan to improve on that effort. But progress comes slowly. You should always set your goals—reasonable ones—for a full year ahead. This way you won't be in a rush and overdo it.

X. THE PRINCIPLE OF MODERATION AND BALANCE

Too much of anything—food, drink, parties, training miles, speed work, races, even sex—isn't good. You need to take a moderate approach to your life. Balancing the major stresses of your life—career, family, and running—is as important as balancing the individual parts of your training program.

4. KEY INGREDIENTS FOR SUCCESSFUL RACING

The preceding chapters gave you an introduction to how far, how fast, and how often you should run and an overview of the basic training principles that are essential to your running program. The following chapters will be more specific.

The competitive runner wants more than fitness; he or she wants improved performance. There are several key ingredients to successful racing. You will most likely never master all of them, but you should be aware of the factors that can limit, or enhance, your performance. Follow the guidelines in this book to improve on your areas of weakness and take advantage of your areas of strength.

LIMITING FACTORS IN RACE PERFORMANCE

Heredity

To a large degree, you are limited as an athlete by the selection of your parents. That doesn't necessarily mean that if both your parents were either great or poor athletes you will follow suit. If one or both of your parents were athletically gifted, your chances of being athletic are increased. But the nonathletic parent(s) may have had the genetic ability to be a good athlete and never took advantage of it. To be a great runner, you also need to inherit the right genes for your sport. Kareem Abdul-Jabbar, a great 7-foot+ basketball star, wouldn't be a great runner—because of his height and weight he just isn't well-suited for the sport. On the other hand, skinny, small-boned runners like Bill Rodgers and Frank Shorter weren't born to play professional basketball.

Some of you were born tall and big-boned, or with a "well-cushioned" body type: you weigh too much to excel at running. You can run well for your weight, and use running to control your weight—but your ability is hindered by genetics.

You are born with a certain muscular type. Some of us are naturally strong, some much weaker. Weight training and running hills can help all runners get much stronger, and thus race better. You are born with a certain ratio of fast twitch to slow twitch muscle fibers. Those greatly lacking in fast twitch fibers won't have natural leg speed. Those lacking in slow twitch fibers won't have a natural ability to run long distances. We can improve our speed and our endurance by speed training and by aerobic training, but how good we can get is limited by genetics.

Your heart-lung machine—the cardiorespiratory system— is also inherited. Your ability to exercise aerobically and anaerobically is greatly affected by genetics. Fortunately, all of us can greatly improve in this area with proper training.

You are born with certain biomechanical features and weaknesses that help or limit your performance. A leg that is longer than the other, weak arches and the tendency to pronate, are examples of inherited biomechanical weaknesses that can limit your ability as a runner.

It is important to pick the right parents. But few of us are born to be a natural elite runner. You can achieve performances—despite genetic imperfections—that will satisfy you and amaze your friends who didn't make the most of what they were given. Regardless of your genetic limitations, you can become a better runner than you are now! Let the genetically gifted, well-trained athlete have the glory up front; you will still be very satisfied with your improvement as a runner.

Age

As noted in chapter 1, we slow down as we get older and we must accept this fact. However, we can greatly minimize this slowing process with proper training.

Aerobic Capacity

The ability to consume, transport, and utilize large volumes of oxygen is a key factor in running performance. We breathe in air containing oxygen which is then absorbed by blood as it passes through the lungs. The heart then pumps this oxygen-enriched blood to the muscles, which utilize it to produce the needed energy to carry out work. Exercise physiologists believe that the best single indicator of a runner's endurance potential is his or her aerobic capacity—also known as maximal oxygen uptake (max VO_2). This can be measured in a laboratory while running on a treadmill.

Your aerobic capacity can be improved by consistent, progressive aerobic endurance running as well as the use of aerobic alternative activities. (See chapters 5–7 for guidelines for aerobic endurance training.) Research also indicates that you can improve your aerobic capacity by running controlled speed workouts, especially interval runs at 10–20 seconds faster per minute than your 10K race pace (see chapters 8–11).

Your aerobic capacity is expressed as milliliters of oxygen per kilogram of body weight per minute (ml/kg/min). Studies of elite runners found an average value of 76.9 for men and 67.0 for women. Joan Benoit-Samuelson, winner of the first Olympic Marathon for women in 1984, was tested at 78.6!

You can estimate your aerobic capacity from your 10K race time. Exercise physiologist Dr. David Costill gives these estimated values in his book *Inside Running: Basics of Sports Physiology:*

AEROBIC CAPACITY (ML/KG/MIN)	10K TIME
above 70	33:00 and faster
65 to 69	36:15 to 33:40
60 to 64	39:30 to 36:50

55 to 59	42:45 to 40:10
50 to 54	46:00 to 43:35
45 to 49	49:15 to 46:40
40 to 44	52:30 to 49:50
below 39	53:10 or slower

Generally, the higher the aerobic capacity the better the runner. However, some runners are mentally tougher than others, and some are able to perform at a higher percent of their aerobic capacity than others. Most distance runners, according to Costill, perform at 75 to 80 percent of their aerobic capacity during a marathon.

Anaerobic Threshold

Some runners, like Frank Shorter, Bill Rodgers, and Grete Waitz, are able to compete for the marathon distance at 85 to 90 percent of their aerobic capacity because they have a higher anaerobic threshold: they can run in reasonable comfort at a higher percentage of their aerobic capacity. You can improve your anaerobic threshold—the borderline between aerobic and anaerobic running at which running becomes uncomfortable— with speed training, especially training runs of 3–4 miles at your estimated anaerobic threshold: 30 seconds slower than your 10K pace. See page 135 for more guidelines for anaerobic threshold training runs. With an improved anaerobic threshold, you can run farther and faster before your muscles give in to oxygen debt. Any combination of improving your aerobic capacity and your anaerobic threshold will result in improved race performances.

Anaerobic Capacity

This is the ability to withstand oxygen debt: the buildup of lactic acid that occurs because you are running so fast that you can't supply enough oxygen by normal aerobic means to fuel the working muscles. When lactic acid accumulates in the muscles, you are forced to slow down dramatically. The body is very limited in its ability to perform without sufficient oxygen. But your anaerobic capacity can be improved some with short, fast speed workouts in which you practice going into oxygen debt. Anaerobic capacity is of increased importance in races of 5K and less.

Speed

In a short sprint, or finishing kick, neither aerobic capacity nor anaerobic capacity is the limiting factor. Rather, you are limited by your ability to generate leg speed quickly over 220 yards or less. You are mostly limited here by your percentage of fast twitch muscle fibers, although you can improve your speed some by improving your running form (see chapter 29), practicing your finishing kick (see page 404), and doing short, fast speed training.

Strength

Runners need two types of strength. General strength of key postural muscles can be improved by weight training (see chapter 35). Leg strength can be improved to allow you to run more comfortably over long distances and to minimize leg fatigue late in a race. Running strength is best improved by running hill workouts and strength training runs (see chapter 10).

Aerobic Endurance

The ability to run long distances within your training heart-rate range allows you to build muscular and aerobic endurance, increases your aerobic capacity, controls your body weight, and builds confidence. Aerobic endurance training supplies the base for competitive training. There are four key factors in building aerobic endurance:

    A. weekly mileage (see chapter 6)
    B. pace of the aerobic runs (see chapter 5)
    C. the need for long runs (see chapters 6 and 22)
    D. the use of alternative aerobic activity to improve endurance (see chapter 7)

The Goal-Directed Training Schedule

You can't just go out the door each day and go for a run if you wish to reach your potential. Set challenging, realistic goals (chapter 26), and then develop a training schedule that allows you to develop a base, sharpen, and reach a peak performance (see chapters 12 and 13). The training should be specific to your racing distance (see the specific racing chapters in this book for guidelines for 5K, 10K, marathon, and more).

Consistency of Training

In terms of long-range development, three key factors are the difference between reaching your ultimate goals and only achieving modest success:

1. Consistent mileage at a reasonable level week after week, month after month, year after year: "packing miles into the bank."

2. Consistent long runs over several weeks as you are building endurance and strength for key races.

3. Consistent speed workouts of good (not necessarily fantastic) quality as you are sharpening and peaking for key races.

Rest

You need plenty of sleep—7–8 or more hours per night on a consistent basis—for your body to be able to withstand the stresses of competitive training. Follow the hard-easy system of training: always follow hard running days with one or more easy running days in order to allow the body to properly recover and strengthen itself. Follow each racing peak season with a rebuilding phase (see page 164) to allow the body to regenerate.

Mental Preparation

You can train the body to run well, but if the mind isn't prepared for a peak performance also, your physical preparation will be wasted. Chapter 27 details the many factors involved with mental preparation for racing.

Strategy

You must run your races at a challenging yet sensible pace. You also must be prepared to deal with wind, heat, hills, and your competitors. Chapter 28 details race day strategy for competitive runners.

Running Form

Inefficient running form slows you down and contributes to injury. See chapters 29–31 for guidelines.

Injury and Illness

If you don't make it to the starting line healthy, you can't perform at your best. Perhaps the single greatest cause of improvement among runners is remaining injury-free long enough to attain consistent training. Chapters 32–33 review the causes of injury and illness, and detail how to prevent and manage them. Following a good warm-up and cool-down routine improves flexibility and minimizes injury (chapter 34).

Glycogen Depletion

After 1½ hours of running, you begin to deplete your supplies of glycogen—carbohydrates stored in your muscles that serve as the primary fuel for distance running. For marathon running you can minimize glycogen depletion by carbohydrate loading (see page 531) and by doing regular long runs (see chapter 22).

Heat and Humidity

Running in heat and humidity slows you down and can cause serious health problems. See page 466 for guidelines. Drinking fluids before, during, and after running (see chapter 37) is critical to your performance and your health.

Body Composition

The more weight you carry, the harder you must work while running. You need to have a strong engine and a light chassis. See chapter 38 for guidelines.

Wellness

You can be fit, and not be healthy. Runners need to follow a good nutritional program (chapter 36), and balance the stresses in their lives (chapter 39).

Tension

A tense runner is more prone to injury and, because he or she is not relaxed while running, is also a less efficient runner. Pre-race tension and mid-race tension are also factors that limit race performance. See chapter 27 for guidelines.

Part II
AEROBIC TRAINING

5. TRAINING PACE

"No pain, no gain" is a philosophy that may apply to some sports, but not to running. In fact, the most common mistakes made by advanced competitors as well as novice competitors are trying to run too much mileage and trying to do that mileage at too fast a pace. How fast you run your workouts depends upon your goals. Most of your training should be done aerobically, within your training heart-rate range as explained in the previous chapter. It is the daily easy training runs that give you the base of endurance upon which you can sharpen for races with faster speedwork.

BASE PACE

Your base pace is the comfortable, everyday training pace you naturally settle into when you go out for a typical unstructured run. "I'm going for an easy run," you say and head out the door. But what is easy? Too many runners train at a pace faster than necessary, leaving them prone to fatigue and injury, and unable to properly recover from previous speed sessions, long runs, or races. Some runners slop along at too slow a pace, which results in "junk" mileage that produces little or no training effect. Runners are more likely to run too fast than too slow. The secret is to find the slowest pace that will still provide aerobic benefits.

You can estimate your ideal base pace from the following formulas:

		Brisk	Easy
BASE PACE =	10K race pace	+ 1 min, 30 sec	+ 2 min
	5K race pace	+ 1 min, 40 sec	+ 2 min, 10 sec
	Marathon race pace	+ 45 sec	+ 1 min, 15 sec

Select the base pace formula that comes closest to what you consider your everyday running speed. The results should be about the same if you are equally well trained for all three distances. Since the 10K event is raced most frequently, it is usually the best guide and is the one we shall use in this book. See the chart for your base pace training mileage in the Appendices.

You should have a flexible range for your base pace: from easy to brisk. For example, a runner in 45-minute shape (7:15-minutes-per-mile pace) for 10K according to this formula would train within a range of 8:45 minutes per mile for brisk runs to 9:15 minutes per mile for easy runs. Remember, these are *approximate* pace goals based on your present fitness level. As you become more fit, the pace of your training runs will naturally become a little faster. For example, a 45-minute 10K runner would do his or her base runs at approximately a 9-minute-per-mile pace in order to keep within his or her training heart-rate range. After a few years of improvement, this same runner might be a 42-minute 10K performer and would train at an 8½-minute-per-mile pace to keep within the same training heart-rate range. This runner works at the same effort, but picks up the pace of the training run to keep up with his or her development as a distance runner.

How to Use the Base Pace

The base pace is a flexible guide that can help you determine the appropriate speed for your daily aerobic training runs. You shouldn't run much more slowly than the "Easy" figure. The "Brisk" base pace is the estimated fastest pace you can run at and still stay within your training heart-rate range. You may be able to run a little faster than that pace and still be running comfortably. Advanced competitors and above sometimes train at a faster pace, which borders on the discomfort line (can talk, but not with complete freedom). Even these fast guys need to exercise caution; don't leave your race on the training paths. Faster isn't necessarily better. Most runners will find a base pace that will fluctuate from day to day, and even within each run, between the suggested minimum and maximum pace suggested here. For example, the 45-minute 10K runner who trains between 8:45 and 9:15 minutes per mile may run a 9-minute pace most of the time, 9:15 often, and 8:45 occasionally.

If you are running low mileage or training for a short, fast race, your training pace may be at the brisk end of the range. Experienced runners often prefer a brisker pace, but not too hard, because at that pace they are lighter on their feet and use better running form. Running too slowly too often can lead to bad running form habits. If you are running high mileage, perhaps while marathon training, you should do most of your runs at the easy end of the range. Recovery runs after hard speedwork, races, and long runs as well as tapering runs before races should be run at the easy base pace. All long runs for most runners should be easy; advanced competitors may occasionally toughen themselves by running all or part of their long runs at the brisk pace or slightly faster. *Note: Some novice competitors may run 10Ks at a slower pace than their 2–4 mile daily aerobic runs because of a lack of endurance. They must build up their mileage before utilizing the base pace formula.*

Remember to run your base pace at perceived effort. A 9-minute pace effort on your normal flat course in good weather isn't the same as a 9-minute pace on a hilly course on a hot or windy day. Since your training courses may not be accurately measured, be careful not to be led astray. Occasionally time a run for a mile on the local track or over a measured part of a local race course at your base pace effort to get a proper feel for your pace per mile.

The important concept to remember about your base pace is that you should run within yourself to build a base of endurance; train, don't strain.

Note: If you are running faster than the base pace, it may be for one of two common reasons. (1) You are a victim of the "hurry disease" all day and take it with you on the run—slow down. (2) Your 10K race times are too slow; taper for a race and give it a good effort.

6. TRAINING MILEAGE

Each of our runs is measured in miles. In fact, runners are obsessed with mileage: to record in a diary, track on charts and graphs, count and discuss, brag about and exaggerate. Runners even categorize themselves by mileage and are often driven to log more mileage than their friends and their competitors, as if mileage were the only goal in running. Perhaps a cartoon in a popular (nonrunning) magazine summed up "mileage mania" the best. It showed a group of people at a party with the host introducing two men: "10 miles a day, meet 6 miles a day." Surely Mr. 6 miles a day felt inferior. But one man's meat is another man's poison.

More mileage is the runner's solution to almost any problem: the "More is better" syndrome. High mileage, however, is not the goal of training; performance is. Mileage is the backbone of every runner's program. Too little and you fade before the finish line; too much and you don't make it to the starting line healthy.

According to Dr. David Costill in *Inside Running: Basics of Sports Physiology*:

"In its simplest form, endurance training serves as a constructive type of stress. Regular physical activity causes the body to become more tolerant of the demands of exercise so that it can run farther and faster. During each training run the leg muscles demand that energy be rapidly replenished, often at 200 times the resting rate. Day by day such training stress triggers the muscles and circulation to grow stronger and more capable of generating energy."

Too much stress applied on top of stress, however, will result in poor performances or injury. Costill cautions:

"Over the past 15 to 20 years runners have learned to judge their readiness for competition on the basis of their weekly mileage. Conversations among distance runners inevitably turn to 'How many miles per week have you been running?' While most runners think that the more miles you run, the better your chances of success, it is easy to overtrain and perform poorly. It is important to remember that *the purpose of training is to stress the body, so that when you rest it will grow stronger and more tolerant of the demands of long-distance running.* Unfortunately, most runners forget that you can train too hard, or allow too little rest, which overstresses the body and allows no opportunity for growth."

Your training mileage includes aerobic endurance runs as well as the miles you accumulate while doing speed work and races. The faster-paced mileage tears you down; the slower runs build you up for hard efforts and help you recover from them. Aerobic endurance runs, the daily strolls at your base pace, make up the bulk (90 percent or more) of your training mileage. These runs build your foundation base and are used year-round to help maintain fitness.

Aerobic endurance training produces the following physiological benefits:
- increases the efficiency of your heart
- increases your coronary blood supply
- increases the efficient use of oxygen
- improves your respiratory system
- increases the strength and endurance of your leg muscles
- brings about increased neuromuscular efficiency

TYPES OF AEROBIC ENDURANCE RUNS

The following chart lists the three types of aerobic endurance runs you will use:

ENDURANCE TRAINING RUNS	DISTANCE
1. Medium slow distance	3–10 miles
2. Short slow distance	2–6 miles
3. Long slow distance	10–20 miles

The Medium-Distance Endurance Run

This is your average daily run, which makes up the bulk of your training. Balance it with long runs and short runs. This relaxed run takes about 30 minutes to 1½ hours to complete, depending on your level of fitness and the pace that you run. The distance covered ranges from 3 miles for novice competitors to 10 miles for advanced runners. A single medium-distance run will be about 15 percent of your total weekly mileage. If you average 6 miles a day, your medium-distance run will be in the 5–7 mile range. This run is completed over a variety of terrain—mostly flat or moderately hilly.

The primary goal for running medium-distance runs is to "pack in the miles" without placing great stress on your body and mind.

The Short-Distance Run

This is an easy day; enjoy it. This run lasts from about 20 minutes to 45 minutes—the range for an easy recovery day for novices up to advanced runners. The distance stretches from 2 miles to 6 miles, or about 5 to 10 percent of your weekly mileage. The short-distance run is used once or twice a week over even terrain (preferably grass or dirt) with few hills included. The emphasis is on staying relaxed and comfortable. Run it at your easy base pace. Always run well within your capacity. Use this run to accumulate weekly mileage and for fun; it is a time to run with friends, or run for solitude and exploration. This easy run is used primarily as a recovery run, tapering run, or easy training day. It usually precedes or follows long runs, speed workouts, and races.

There are alternatives to doing a short-distance run that will also serve as recovery or easy days: an off day, a long walk, or swimming or biking for 30–45 minutes.

The Long-Distance Run

The long aerobic endurance run is considered a *hard* workout, even if you're running at your easy base pace: it fatigues the legs and depletes your energy reserves. This run takes from 1½ hours to 3½ hours and ranges from 10 miles to 20 miles (even 4 to 6 miles may be long for some novice competitors). On the average, the long run shouldn't be more than one-third of your weekly mileage, and it shouldn't be done more than once a week; twice a month may be often enough for most runners. The last long run before a key race should be no closer than 2 weeks. The long run strengthens your legs, heart, lungs, and mind.

Suggested Long Run Distances

For less than the marathon event, novice runners should do at least two or three runs of two-thirds the race distance you are training for during the 8 weeks prior to the event, and preferably run the race distance or slightly longer. Minimal long runs suggested:

SUGGESTED MINIMAL LONG RUN MILEAGE FOR NOVICE COMPETITORS

RACE DISTANCE	LONG RUN DISTANCE
5K	2–3 miles
10K	4–6 miles
Half marathon	8–13 miles
Marathon	16–20 miles

Experienced competitors need to run long distances two or three times a month for at least 2–3 months prior to their key race. For less than the marathon, these long runs should be longer than the race distance. Suggested long run distances:

SUGGESTED LONG RUN MILEAGE FOR EXPERIENCED COMPETITORS

RACE DISTANCE	BASIC COMPETITOR	ADVANCED COMPETITOR	CHAMPION COMPETITOR
5K	8–10	8–12	12–16
10K	8–12	10–18	15–20
Half marathon	15–18	15–20	18–20
Marathon	18–20	18–20	20–23

The long run's glamour comes from marathon preparation. Thus, we've devoted a complete chapter to this topic (chapter 22) within the marathon section. Nonmarathoners should review this chapter for general guidelines that apply to nonmarathon training.

HOW MUCH MILEAGE?

According to the founder of the aerobics fitness movement, Dr. Ken Cooper, 15 miles a week of running is all that is necessary for maintaining minimal fitness. Anything beyond that, he believes, and you get little return for the increased risk of injury. But competitive runners aren't interested in just minimal fitness, we strive to improve our race times; increased performances are goals well beyond minimal fitness. Thus we choose to improve our conditioning by adding more than the minimal amount of mileage Cooper recommends while attempting to minimize injury.

How much mileage you need and can handle depends on several factors, including goals, age, sex, athletic background, weight, injuries, time schedule, and disposition. You must determine how much mileage you need to meet your *realistic* goals and how much mileage you can tolerate physically and mentally. Unfortunately, what you need and what you can do are not always the same.

Getting to the finish line in reasonable health is enough of a goal for most novice competitors. Later you may wish to run faster, and you will need to increase your mileage to do so. Here the mileage treadmill begins: you need more mileage to run faster. Too much mileage will defeat you mentally and physically; you may never get to the starting line. With too little mileage, however, you'll have trouble getting to the finish line.

MINIMUM AND MAXIMUM MILEAGE GUIDELINES

For races under the marathon distance, you should run at least two times the race distance you are training for each week for 6–8 weeks prior to the race, preferably three times the race distance. For the marathon, you should run a minimum of 35–40 miles a week for 8 weeks prior to the race. These are minimal guidelines for novice competitors and won't guarantee that you will not slow the pace toward the end, or need to take some walk breaks. If your mileage is less than these minimal standards, you may be able to still compete in your race but should plan on taking several walk breaks. We prefer that you first build up your mileage. Novice competitors attempting much more mileage than indicated here may harm their performance. You may not be ready to handle that much. Start from a sound fitness base, and increase gradually. Here's the recommended mileage for novice competitors:

SUGGESTED WEEKLY MILEAGE TOTALS FOR THE NOVICE COMPETITOR

RACE DISTANCE	MINIMAL WEEKLY MILEAGE	SUGGESTED WEEKLY MILEAGE
5K	6–9	10–20
10K	12–18	15–25
Half marathon	25–40	25–40
Marathon	35–40	40–50

Note: These mileages should be averaged for 6–8 weeks prior to tapering for your race. You should complete at least two or three long runs (see chart on page 70) in this 6–8 week period.

As you work to improve your race time, you will also need to increase the minimal mileage in order to race successfully.

Most competitive runners fit into our recommended minimum mileages as charted below. You do not need to maintain this mileage year-round. Take a break after the big race, and lower your mileage level.

SUGGESTED WEEKLY MILEAGE TOTALS FOR EXPERIENCED COMPETITORS

RACE DISTANCE	BASIC COMPETITOR	ADVANCED COMPETITOR	CHAMPION COMPETITOR
5K	25–35	30–40	40–70
10K	30–40	40–60	50–75
Half marathon	40–50	50–60	60–75
Marathon	40–50	50–70	70–90

Note: These mileages should be averaged for 8–12 weeks prior to tapering for your race. Long runs (see chart on page 71) should be completed two to three times per month, depending on your fitness level and racing schedule.

These recommended mileages are less than those recommended in the first edition of *The Competitive Runner's Handbook.* We have learned through research and through the experiences of thousands of runners that high mileage is risky. According to Dr. Costill: "There is a point of optimal distance that will cause the body to adapt to its full aerobic capacity. Based on laboratory observations, we have concluded that the mileage needed for the maximum training benefits varies between 60 and 90 miles per week. There is a point of diminishing returns, a point at which you can increase weekly mileage but see little or no improvement in performance." For the average runner, Costill believes that the mileage limit should be 50–75 miles a week, since "the amount of physiological improvement beyond that is almost insignificant." For runners below the advanced competitive level, weekly mileage limits below 50 miles per week are needed to minimize injury. Remember, what is high mileage for one may be excessive for another.

High-mileage advocates believe that they are training their body to become more efficient at burning fat for fuel, thus sparing glycogen, and that volume training may result in a neuromuscular training effect. High mileage may give you a psychological advantage: you feel strong when you come down off high mileage for an important race; with rest, your legs feel much fresher, and mentally you just *know* you are strong. High mileage is the answer for some runners, but it is not the answer for most.

The Perfect 30-Mile Week

Amby Burfoot, executive editor of *Runner's World*, recommends a 30-mile week for the average runner. He promotes an efficient training program which "is one that yields the best results from the fewest hours of training. Let's face it, we're all busy. Training isn't our occupation; winning big-time road races isn't the way we put food on the table. We have to fit our running in around everything else that goes on in our lives." If you are unable to train as much as you would like to in order to meet your goals, be realistic. By using an abbreviated, but sound, training program you can be healthy and reasonably fit. Amby notes that his program "is the schedule for dedicated runners who want to be all they can be without mortgaging their lives. It's the training week for those smart enough to recognize that there are no shortcuts, and smart enough to avoid the unproductive excess of some programs." Thirty miles a week is very close to the average for *Runner's World* readers. It is on the low end of the recommended range on page 73 for the basic competitive runner training for the 10K. Although you would be stronger and perhaps faster at 40 miles a week, 30 might be a more reasonable program for you. Here's Burfoot's breakdown of the "perfect 30-mile week":

1. A long run of 10 miles (one-third the weekly mileage and within our recommended 8–12 miles for this level runner.)

2. Two days off. Either don't run or do an easy 30–45 minutes of an aerobic alternative. One of the rest days should follow the long run. Rest days allow your body to recover from hard work. Nonrunning days also allow you more time for the responsibilities in your life.

3. Two days of easy running (4 miles).

4. Two days of harder running. For example: a *fartlek* run on Tuesday and three or four times a mile at race pace on Friday.

Here is how a 30-mile week might look:
Monday—off day
Tuesday—speed work (total of 6 miles)*
Wednesday—easy 4-mile run to recover
Thursday—off day
Friday—race pace repeats (total of 6 miles of running)
Saturday—easy 4-mile run to recover
Sunday—10-mile long run

As Amby sums up his program: "That's all there is to it. A week couldn't be perfect without being simple, and this one is. Five days of running, two days off. A long run of 10 miles, two shorter and faster days and two days for recovery running. It's a schedule that's easy to follow, easy to like and geared to producing results."

You would follow such a schedule for 6–10 weeks going into a key race and then back down for a while, eliminating or minimizing the speed training but keeping the mileage near 30 miles (no lower than 20). This schedule works best for the 45-minute-plus 10K runner and will not work for marathon training. It could be adapted to the marathon by merely extending the 10-mile long run (in gradual increases) to 20-milers, yielding a 40-mile training week.

The Perfect 40-Mile Week

We can adapt the program for the 45-minute-plus runner to work for the advanced competitive runner in the 35–45 minute range for 10K who needs to get by on the minimal mileage we recommend (but would most likely do better at 50–60 miles a week). Just extend the long run in the example above from 10 to 14 miles, the recovery runs from 4 to 6 miles, and add another mile to the warm-up for the faster days, and you have a 40-mile week. The schedule still saves the two midweek off days, often an important feature for the working man and woman. This minimal program can be used for the marathon by stretching the long run to 20 miles. Again, back off the speed training and keep the mileage near the peak level when you take training breaks during the year.

*See chapter 9 for a simplified 10-week speed-training program.

Alternative Aerobic Training

A good way to minimize the pounding of running extra mileage is to substitute alternative aerobic training—such as biking or swimming—for some of your running mileage. This system prevents injury, helps you train when nursing an injury, provides a more balanced fitness routine, and gives you a mental break from running. The following chapter details the "running equivalent" method.

FACTORS THAT AFFECT YOUR MILEAGE

Age and Experience

Teenage and younger runners should not run more than 40 miles a week, for doing so may contribute to injury or "burnout." Runners above the age of 40 may be able to run less, especially if they have faithfully put a large reservoir of miles in the bank. Runners who have accumulated many miles for several years often find that they can race well at a lower mileage level than in previous years. Because older runners don't recover as fast from injuries and previous runs, it is often wise for them to run less mileage than their younger friends do.

Time on Your Feet

Elite male runners average about 6 minutes per mile for a 10-mile training run. Thus, they log about 10 miles per hour on the road. An elite female runner and many elite masters runners may cover the same distance at 6:30 to 7:00 per mile. The average runner may take from 9:00 to 12:00 per mile. That is a time range of from 1 hour for the elite runner to 1½ to 2 hours for some average runners on a 10-mile run. Obviously, it takes a lot longer to cover the same mileage at 9–12 minutes per mile than at 6.

The average 9–12 minute-per-mile runner who attempts to match the high mileage of the 6-minute-per-mile superstar will actually spend 50–100 percent more time on the road than the elite runner. Be careful when comparing mileage figures—no matter what the numbers. The slower you run compared with the average runner, the more you should consider time rather than mileage in setting your daily and weekly goals. In fact, some runners prefer to log their training by minutes run rather than mileage, because for these people it more accurately reflects their training. That makes sense, but since races are held over mileage distances and most training information is expressed in mileage, we'll stick to this system for this book.

Runners, regardless of age or sex, who train and race at approximately the same pace can handle similar weekly mileage work loads. Our fitness category system, adjusted for age and sex, recommends a wide range of racing and training paces within each category. Within each racing distance chapter, we recommend flexible weekly mileage goals to adjust for the differences in the amount of time you spend training and your age and running experience. The slower runner should run fewer miles than a faster competitor within the same fitness category, because a slower runner covering the same distance would spend more time training. This additional effort could create a higher risk of injury or fatigue. These adjustments are most critical when doing high-mileage marathon training.

Here are some other points about mileage:

It is harder to keep your mileage up if
- you are running over very hilly terrain;
- you must combat extremes of heat or cold, or snow and ice;
- you are running in the reduced light of early morning or late evening;
- you are carrying extra pounds;
- you are running on business trips or on vacation;
- you just don't enjoy running long and slow, but prefer to run shorter and faster;
- you have achieved your goal and do not have a goal to aim toward;
- you don't have training partners to help you along, especially on long runs;
- you have an inflexible work schedule, or many career and family responsibilities;
- you don't have a coach and teammates to support you.

You must lower your mileage if
- you increase the pace significantly for training runs;
- you add more hard speed work as you sharpen for a race;
- you are tapering for a race, or recovering from a race;
- you are racing very often;
- you are recovering from an injury;
- warning signs of injury or illness, and thus overtraining, appear;
- you have completed your racing season or big race—take a break!

GUIDELINES FOR INCREASING MILEAGE

We have found that by applying these simple rules you can progress safely with little worry of overtraining:

- How you increase your mileage depends first on how often you are running now. If you are running less than 6 days a week, gradually add more days per week until you are running 6 to 7 days consistently. Don't add too much mileage on the new days at first. Later, you may wish to continue taking a rest day, or you may choose to run 7 days per week.

- Once you get up to your maximum number of training days per week, stay at that level for a few weeks. First increase the distance of your long run, and then of your medium run. Gradually lengthen all your runs while maintaining a balance of effort. Be sure to alternate hard (long or fast) days with easy days as you build up your mileage.

- Avoid any sudden changes. Avoid dramatic increases in mileage from day to day, week to week, month to month, even year to year. Don't increase your weekly mileage or long runs by more than 5 to 10 percent; you will invite injury if you do. Be patient, not *a* patient. A common mistake is to increase mileage quickly when you feel good or are in a hurry to build up for a race. The usual result of increasing your work load too rapidly is either fatigue or injury. It may not seem like much if you jump your mileage from 20 to 40 miles per week when you compare yourself with friends who run 70 to 80 miles a week. But don't be fooled into thinking that you are running only 40 miles a week. You have *doubled* your work load, and your body isn't ready for it. A 10 percent increase can range from 2 miles a week (for the 20-mile-per-week runner) to 6 miles a week (for the 60-mile-per-week runner). This is a safe way to progress. A conservative program for the novice competitor wishing to move from 20 to 40 miles a week would be to add 2 miles a week up to 40, and then level off. This progress would take 14 weeks, and you would be gradually tricking the body into handling more mileage.

A typical 14-week progression, starting with 20 miles per week, may look like this: 20, 22, 24, 26, 26, 28, 30, 30, 32, 34, 36, 36, 38, 40, 40. This program increases your mileage by a total of 20 miles a week, but your body can safely handle this increase, since it is gradual.

• Don't continuously move your mileage upward. Here's a math riddle for you. Add 10 percent each week, week after week, until you're running 24 hours a day. How long will this take you? Get the message?

Every few weeks, "level off" for a week or two before adding more mileage. Then reach a planned level that you can handle—such as 40 or 50 miles a week—and stay there for a few weeks or months. Increase slowly, taking a few breaks along the way. Periodically "plateau" for a while, so you can regenerate physically and mentally for another upward push. These plateaus of mileage may increase only from year to year, and are determined by what you can safely handle as you strive to meet your training goals. Rest breaks along the way, or even periods of decreased mileage—planned or unplanned—will help reduce the pressure of constantly building up mileage. You do not have to increase every week. Your goal is long-term, not short-term.

• Back off occasionally, especially after big races and when warning signs of overtraining appear. Progress regularly, and if you find it difficult, back off and choose a more gradual course of buildup.

• You don't *have* to move up the ladder. You can get off the mileage treadmill any time. More isn't necessarily best for you. If you are happy with the level where you are now and have achieved a comfortable balance between running and the rest of your life, don't let peer pressure or your inner guilt feelings drive you to do more. Maintain your present program and be happy with it. You can always move up later if the urge strikes.

• Determine the upper limits of mileage you have time for and can handle physically and mentally at this stage of your running career. If you are not careful about realistic limits, you are going to reach a point where you can no longer increase your mileage without incurring injury. You may be too tired all the time and not looking forward to running. Each of us must determine his or her own upper limits. Don't compare yourself with a runner with more experience and talent. And your limits can be flexible; you may be able to handle more in the good training months of spring and summer than you can in the dismal winter. After several years of running, you may have built to an upper limit of 40 miles a week which is comfortable for you. The next year, however, you may find that because of accumulated miles in the bank and experience, you can safely handle 50 miles a week—a figure that would previously have wiped you out. The important thing to remember is that you should be aware of your limitations and not force yourself to go beyond these realistic boundaries.

TIPS FOR MANAGING YOUR MILES

• Some runners prefer alternating longer weeks with shorter weeks. For example, 50-60-50-60 is an average of 55 miles for the month. By setting *monthly* goals rather than weekly ones, you can be more flexible with your training week and won't be as obsessed with trying to make up miles lost due to a few days off.

• Don't try to make up mileage. You can make up some mileage gradually over a period of weeks, but generally it is better to forget the lost miles and concern yourself with continuing at the rate of so many miles per day on the average.

• Don't count "junk" miles. Running a mile to the subway and then a mile to the office, for example, may save time and may even be enjoyable, but it isn't part of your training. Training mileage shouldn't be logged unless you run at least 4 miles at a time and are running in your training heart-rate range (except for the novice competitor, for whom 2- or 3-mile runs can represent a workout). Don't look for every excuse to put miles in your diary. It is more important that the miles you claim are of reasonable quality.

• Don't be a slave to your training diary. You should plot your mileage regularly in advance—this gives you the motivation to keep it up. But don't feel you absolutely have to run once more late on Sunday night in order to reach your goal so you can record it. Diaries are great coaches—they can make you keep going. They are also lousy coaches—the obsession to write down mileage sometimes causes the runner to lose sight of the quality of his training. In the end, it is the blend of quantity and quality mileage that will help you improve times, not how many miles you write in your diary.

• Measure training by miles or minutes. If you don't know exactly how long your course is, estimate it—on the conservative side. If you are traveling over unknown terrain, estimate mileage by your pace. For example, if you feel you are running 7:30 a mile, that equals 8 miles in an hour. Run up the road for a half hour and return, and log 8 miles in your diary. That is close enough. You don't have to be exact.

• How do you "count" mileage if you did a hard speed workout that didn't cover much mileage? Cheat! The easiest solution if you are obsessed with mileage totals is to credit yourself with whatever mileage you would have run in the time you took to do your speed workout, including the recovery time between runs. For longer speed sessions such as 1-mile workouts, you'll get in adequate mileage. Also, always run before and after each speed workout and race. It'll help you keep your mileage up.

• Establish a realistic range of mileage. If you want to average 40 miles a week, don't go over 45–50, but try not to go under 30–35. Thus, you can adjust for the weather and other variables.

THE TRAINING DIARY

Keep a diary so you do enough—but not too much—mileage. Record your mileage starting with Monday so you are training into weekend races. Starting your diary on a Sunday often encourages runners to do too much back-to-back on the weekend, since they think of Sunday as starting a new week. Think in terms of mileage goals per month—such as 200 miles—rather than being obsessed with achieving a weekly mileage total no matter what.

The running diary will help you keep a record of every aspect of your running life. Whatever your running level, the diary will help you keep an accurate record of your progress up the training ladder.

Why record your progress? The past is a valuable guide to the future. In the diary, you set goals and plan your training program. You describe in it what you did and how it felt. The diary contains the facts of your training and doesn't leave them to memory.

The diary, when filled, also becomes a guide and a reference. It is a record of your training. You will be able to see and measure your growth as a runner. If you are training for your first race, or your next marathon, the diary will help you train regularly and train well. It will contain an accurate daily account of your workouts. Afterward, you will be able to look back to your training schedule to see what you did right (or wrong) in preparing for a race. You can then repeat this training procedure or avoid past mistakes. The goals you set and your training to reach them become results you can review in the diary in the future.

Be consistent in keeping your diary. Fill it in each day after your workouts. It's easier to motivate yourself to get in the minimal mileage required if you record it each day. Nobody likes to see too many unplanned zeros. But don't become a slave to recording mileage—remember, performance is the goal, not accumulating mileage in your diary. You can keep yourself under control and not suddenly find that you ran too much mileage for the week, or from one week to the next, if you have a written record of the mileage being accumulated.

The diary can become your training partner, providing you with goals, feedback, and a sense of continuity over the long haul. Being well organized, planning and recording your runs, is one of the secrets of success for the competitive runner.

You can use a simple wall calendar or a formal book such as *The Runner's Handbook Training Diary* to record your training information. Here are some of the records you can write in your diary:

- daily, weekly, monthly, and yearly mileage totals
- comments on how you feel during each run, what the weather was like, who you ran with, where you ran, pace of run, time of day
- specifics on speed workouts such as number of intervals, recovery period, and times of each running segment
- racing events and race times as well as splits along the way, overall place, age group pace, who you beat, and who beat you
- resting heart rate in the morning when you woke up, training heart rate during your run if you checked it
- body weight on a weekly basis
- running shoes worn and accumulated miles per pair of shoes
- warning signs of injury and status of current injuries/illness and daily treatment
- personal notes such as your birthday run highlights, meeting a new friend, etc.
- personal records for various race distances and your racing goals for the next year

Following is a sample week-at-a-glance diary for a basic competitor from *The Runner's Handbook Training Diary*:

WEEK _____

DAY _____ Time _____ Weather _____

Pace/Type of Workout _____

Where Run _____ Shoes _____

Comments _____ Companions _____

_____ Distance or Time _____

_____

_____

DAY _____ Time _____ Weather _____

Pace/Type of Workout _____

Where Run _____ Shoes _____

Comments _____ Companions _____

_____ Distance or Time _____

_____

_____

DAY _____ Time _____ Weather _____

Pace/Type of Workout _____

Where Run _____ Shoes _____

Comments _____ Companions _____

_____ Distance or Time _____

_____

_____

DAY _____ Time _____ Weather _____

Pace/Type of Workout _____

Where Run _____ Shoes _____

Comments _____ Companions _____

_____ Distance or Time _____

_____

_____

DAY _____ Time _____ Weather _____

Pace/Type of Workout _____

Where Run _____ Shoes _____

Comments _____ Companions _____

_____ Distance or Time _____

_____

_____

DAY _____ Time _____ Weather _____

Pace/Type of Workout _____

Where Run _____ Shoes _____

Comments _____ Companions _____

_____ Distance or Time _____

_____

_____

DAY _____ Time _____ Weather _____

Pace/Type of Workout _____

Where Run _____ Shoes _____

Comments _____ Companions _____

_____ Distance or Time _____

_____

SUMMARY _____

_____ Total: Distance or Time _____

_____ Weight _____

_____ Resting Heart Rate _____

7. ALTERNATIVE AEROBIC TRAINING: THE RUNNING EQUIVALENT

The key to success as a runner is the ability to get to the starting line both physically fit and healthy. Attempting to increase your mileage beyond a level that your body can handle often results in lost mileage over the long run. Add it up—a conservative, consistent program almost always results in more mileage in the bank over a period of several weeks or months than a program where you greedily attempt to keep pushing the mileage up.

The problem runners must cope with is that the musculo-skeletal system betrays us. The heart and lungs—and the mind—have tremendous capacities for work. Competitive swimmers and bicyclists prove that by training many hours more than possible for a runner. But running, unlike swimming and biking, is a weight-bearing activity, a stressful, pounding form of aerobic exercise. The runner's training limit is reached sooner and enforced more strictly.

The more you run, the greater your chances of aggravating your biomechanical weaknesses. Your odds of developing injuries increase dramatically with each mile you run beyond a weekly total of 30. Some runners can go well beyond that, but even the most durable has a breaking point. Every runner should be aware of the nearness of his or her limit and treat it with respect.

If the goal is to improve aerobic endurance, then the runner most often keeps adding more and more mileage, especially when marathon training, until race day or injury occurs—quite often the latter. But since swimmers and bicyclists train longer and harder than runners, shouldn't runners adjust their training to utilize the advantages of these sports? The popularity of the triathlon event has demonstrated to one-dimensional runners the value of "cross-training." Alternative aerobic exercises—swimming, cycling, cross-country skiing, rowing, race-walking, even brisk walking with hand weights—can be substituted for running mileage and speed work to help us combat injury and improve performance.

THE RUNNING EQUIVALENT

The only thing that most runners understand is mileage. How, then, to speak that language and still stop runners from overtraining? Or to make injured runners appreciate the value of sensible alternatives to running? Bob Glover developed a system that he calls the "running equivalent" (RE), and detailed its value originally in a feature article in the December 1985 issue of *Runner's World*. RE is not running, but it is expressed in miles and goes into the training diary. Runners are comfortable with it. Many of Glover's national class female athletes from his Atalanta team use the RE system to help them increase their aerobic base without the added stress that comes with extra mileage.

In the RE system, any high-quality aerobic activity (exercise within your training heart-rate range) can be expressed in terms of miles. Simply replace running minute for minute with your choice of aerobic alternative exercise. Approximate the mileage you would have gone had you spent your exercise period running. If you normally run 4 miles in a half hour, then 30 minutes of any aerobic alternative activity earns you 4 RE miles. Log them in your diary as such: "RE—4 miles." It works the same with speed work: if injury—or just caution—keeps you from doing repeat miles, for example, swim or ride hard on your bike for as long as it would take you to run your mile interval. Take the appropriate rest interval and go again.

RE training works because the heart doesn't differentiate. The heart benefits almost equally from equal amounts of good aerobic activity, provided the pulse is the same. It doesn't much matter what form of exercise gets you into your training heart-rate range. The goal in RE speed work is to drive the heart rate up beyond the aerobic training range. Again, if you work hard enough it's all the same to the heart.

It's important to realize that you can simulate the aerobic value of running and even the anaerobic value of running fast, but no alternative aerobic activity uses the same specific muscle groups as running. You must still get out there and pack in the miles. Hour for hour, running is the best training for the runner. The ideal use of RE mileage to prevent injury and enhance performance would be to limit it to 25 percent of your total aerobic mileage. If injury dictates that all your aerobic work be RE training for a period, don't expect to race well until you've been back on your feet and running for a while.

FORMULA FOR FIGURING OUT YOUR RUNNING EQUIVALENT MILEAGE

1. Figure out your average training pace per mile of running (example: 8 minutes per mile)
2. Divide this figure into the number of minutes spent exercising with an aerobic alternative (example: 40 minutes on an indoor bike)
3. The result is your running equivalent mileage (example: 5 miles RE to record in your diary)

HOW TO USE THE RUNNING EQUIVALENT

There are four major uses for alternative aerobic training:
1. When you can't run at all because of injury.
2. When you are running through or coming back from an injury.
3. To help recover from hard workouts and races.

4. To minimize injury and increase your performance level by allowing you to train harder and longer than you could with a running-only program.

When You Can't Run Because of Injury

Most serious runners get injured. We must learn to accept this fact and intelligently manage our training during injured spells and then seek to prevent further injury. Chapter 33 includes guidelines for the management of injury, and *The Injured Runner's Training Handbook* contains detailed information on how to train despite injury.

Options for the Injured Runner Who Can't Run

You have four options when you are injured and can't run:

Take Time Off. Taking time off is the simplest option—merely rest. This is the best choice for a few days while a minor injury mends. But if you are like most runners, you will want to do some exercise to keep fit and to chase away the feeling of depression associated with not running. Alternative aerobic exercise is the answer.

Maintain Absolute Minimal Fitness. If you know it will be more than a few days before you'll be able to run again—especially if you have to lay off for 2 weeks or more—you may, if your doctor agrees, choose to do some type of alternative aerobic exercise three to five times a week for 30 consecutive minutes each time. This will maintain minimal cardiovascular and musculoskeletal fitness and prepare you to come back sooner. You may also find the easier schedule a mental relief. You may lose considerable fitness from the competitive level, though, so don't press too hard during your return.

Replace Running with an Alternative Exercise. To maintain near-normal fitness when forced off the running trails, you should try to replace your running minute for minute with alternative aerobic exercise. Build gradually to the same amount of time you had spent running: for example, 1 hour a day. If possible, this training should be done at the same vigorous level of exertion as running to achieve aerobic benefit. Aim for a *running equivalent* mileage base similar to or slightly more than your running mileage base. This option will allow you to replace the running habit psychologically, and although you'll lose some fitness, you'll also be able to return to running in good shape.

Impersonate a Competitive Runner. If you really *have* to be ready for a big race, then only a lack of imagination and discipline need stop you. This is the top level, the serious runner who has to lay off running for a while but can still exercise vigorously. Build up slowly, follow the hard-easy system, and include training specific to your goal. The same principles that apply to competitive training apply here. If you are in a buildup stage, long bike rides or swims will build strength and endurance. Build up to the time you would spend on your long runs, or longer. All types of speed workouts can be done on a bike, in a pool, and so on if you need to sharpen close to a race. Later, as you begin to run again, you may be able to do aerobic running without risking injury but choose to continue doing running equivalent speed work or complete your long runs with a combination of running for a medium distance and doing some RE mileage.

Success Story. Angella Hearn is a very determined runner. Both she and her identical twin sister, Chris, were scheduled to return home to run the 1982 London Marathon—the first marathon they had planned to run together and their first race in their native country. After running the 1981 New York Marathon in 2:53, Angella developed a shin injury. It kept getting worse until she was advised by her doctor to completely stop running for several weeks. It was 3 months before the London Marathon, and she was training 80 miles a week. She was determined to continue training, so her coach, Bob Glover, directed her to the swimming pool, where she developed a rigorous program to fit her needs.

She swam for 1 hour each morning before work and for a half hour each evening after work for 4 full weeks. In her 6-day-a-week program she didn't run a step, yet she included speed work to sharpen her fitness work.

After a month without running, Angella began a 2-week program that included the hour swim each morning but replaced her evening swims with some easy runs. She began with a run around the block, just to get the feel of running again. The goal was to return to running slowly to avoid aggravating the injury. She really had to discipline herself, because her heart and lungs were strong enough to allow her to run much farther and faster than her injury could tolerate. Within 2 weeks after she started running again, she gradually moved from running 2 miles a day to running 5 miles a day. She cut her swimming training back to twice a week just for the speed work because she still couldn't do that safely by running. From there she moved up to running 8-mile runs alternated with days consisting of two 5-mile runs. Six weeks before the marathon she was again running 70 miles a week, but being careful not to stress the injury.

Long runs were then extended weekly to 13, 16, and 18 miles and then to a single 20-miler. No speed work was done outside the pool until one month before the marathon, when Angella ran a few half-mile sessions at marathon pace to get a feel for racing again. She ran one 10K race 2 weeks before London to prove to herself that the leg would hold up to the stress.

During this entire period, Angella did weight training three times a week to keep her upper body, quadriceps, and abdominals fit for racing. She also did special exercises to strengthen the muscles in the shin area, where she was injured.

Angella ran a personal record of 2:50:05 and inspired her sister to a 2:56:55 in her marathon debut. In 1987, Angella, then 41, ran the Grandma's Marathon in 2:39:55—the 8th fastest time ever in the world for a female masters runner. In order to increase her performance and minimize further injury, she now uses running equivalents as part of her marathon training. She runs 80 miles a week and adds 2½ hours on her indoor bike at home for an additional 20 miles of REs. Her aerobic mileage of 100 miles a week would make her very prone to injury if accomplished solely through running. She feels that her evening bike rides loosen her up and, combined with strengthening her quadriceps, help prevent injury as she increases her aerobic conditioning. She runs one or two Atalanta speed workouts each week. The following day she runs an easy

6–8 miles at lunchtime and then recovers with a 45-minute bike ride in the evening. She doesn't run at all on Fridays— the day before her long run of 20–22 miles—but instead will bike for 1 hour to give her body needed rest.

When You Are Running Through or Coming Back from an Injury

Aerobic alternatives can be used effectively to help you maintain fitness as you are coming back from injuries or while running through nagging problems. Lower your running mileage to whatever level you can safely handle and make up the difference with running equivalents. The goal should be to gradually ease back to where you can return to running full-time, although it may be wise to continue to reserve 10–25 percent of your aerobic training for REs in order to prevent further injury. As mentioned previously, REs can also be used to aid you with long runs and speed workouts. Here are some success stories that are examples of how to benefit from running equivalents.

Training to Finish a Marathon. Bret Jorgensen was a pre-race-day dropout for the 1984 New York Marathon. He had progressed too quickly—from no running to 30 miles a week in a period of less than 2 months. Soon thereafter he had to give up on his goal of finishing his first marathon. He had tried to do too much too soon. For the 1985 New York Marathon, he followed this book's 26-week buildup program, which he entered with a base of 15 miles a week. He followed a formula of running 4 days a week, biking on his indoor bike 2 days a week, and taking 1 day off. A typical weekly schedule was to take Monday off, run 5 miles on Tuesday, run 8 on Wednesday, bike on Thursday, run 5–6 miles on Friday, and run long on Saturday (building up to 20-milers), and on Sunday he would make up the balance of mileage needed for the week on his bike. He gradually built up to running 30 miles a week plus 10 miles of running equivalents for a 40-mile week, and then peaked with a few weeks of 35-mile running weeks plus 15 miles of REs for a 50-mile week. In addition to minimizing the pounding on a sensitive knee, the biking helped strengthen the quadricep muscles, which also helped prevent further knee problems. He successfully completed his first marathon.

By using alternative aerobic training and common sense, you can still train for a marathon despite injury. Too often runners will stubbornly keep pounding the pavement despite the warning signs of injury and never make it to the starting line.

Still think you can't do it? Dick Traum completed a few marathons using conventional running training. Because of an arthritic knee, he wasn't able to handle the pounding of the running for further marathon attempts, so he used an indoor bike at home to simulate his running training. He would train 3 days a week: 1 day of running up to 5 miles, 1 day of biking for 2 hours, and 1 day of biking 4–6 hours! He would run a 5-mile race and a 20K a few weeks prior to the marathon to test his leg. Following this program, he completed the 1980 New York Marathon in 8:04 and the next year in 7:21. Dick is an above-the-knee amputee and competes with an artificial leg. Using similar methods, approximately 100 physically disabled members of the Achilles Track Club, which Dick and Bob Glover cofounded, complete the New York Marathon each year.

Running Fast Times Despite Injury. Kass Young was a former member of the Oxford University crew team. She is also a very talented but injury-prone runner. At one point she couldn't run for several months because of a series of injuries. She swam for 30 minutes at a time 5 days a week for several weeks until she got totally bored by it. She bought an indoor rowing machine and for the next 9 months ran an easy 10–20 minutes each morning and then rowed a brisk 30 minutes. She did speed work twice a week on her rowing machine. Gradually she built up to where she could run 20–25 miles a week, including one Atalanta team speed session, and combined this with 30–35 minutes of rowing 6 days a week for a running equivalent of 20–25 miles a week. Her total aerobic mileage was 40–50 miles, including one running speed workout and one rowing speed workout. She ran her first race in over a year and a half and won a women-only 5-mile race with a personal record. She now can handle 50 miles a week of running plus her rowing.

Andy Fisher was prepared for a good first marathon at New York in 1984, but the hot weather foiled his bid and he struggled in with a time of 3:51. His training for the 1985 New York Marathon aimed for a sub-3-hour effort. He lowered his 10K personal record from 39:58 to 37:30 and was comfortably handling 70 miles a week of training. Six weeks prior to the marathon he wrenched his back while running. He took off 2 days to ease the pain and then for 3 days biked indoors for 75 minutes—the running equivalent of his normal 10-mile training runs. As the back got better, he would run every other day for 5–6 miles after a 30-minute bike ride, still biking for 75 minutes on the alternate days. Since he had been doing weekly speed runs of four to six times a mile in 6 minutes, he would simulate that workout once a week on the bike. He would also do a few long workouts of biking for 75 minutes followed by a 10-mile run for a running equivalent of a 20-mile run. As marathon day approached, Andy built up to 50–60 miles a week of running plus another 10–20 miles a week of REs. By following this program instead of panicking and continuing to invite further injury by pushing ahead with his normal running schedule, Andy went into the marathon confident and ran a good race.

To Help Recover from Hard Workouts and Races

The daily strain of running causes the muscles to tighten and makes them more prone to injury. Many runners find that a relaxing bike ride or a swim (which has a massaging effect) a few evenings a week helps them loosen up muscles that have been "beaten up" during the daily grind of road training. Others find that a 30-minute bike ride in the morning or prior to a run helps them recover from a hard or long run the previous day and helps them safely warm up (especially on cold days) for another day of running.

Prevention of injury for those who are vulnerable is another key reason for using aerobic alternative exercise. For example, you can follow a long run or a hard speed workout with a day off from running, but yet get in some running equivalent mileage by biking or swimming while minimizing the risk of injury. Your tired legs welcome the opportunity to exercise without being pounded, and the promotion of blood supply to fatigued legs will help flush out waste products and promote recovery.

The use of aerobic alternatives to assist with recovery is especially valuable after a marathon. If you don't do any exercising in the immediate days after a marathon, your legs will get very stiff. But if you pound the ground on sensitive legs and blistered feet, you are likely to cause injury. I advise runners to bike or swim for 30–45 minutes for 3 straight days after a marathon before running a step.

To Minimize Injury and Increase Your Performance Level

The average runner can use the RE method to minimize injury and to improve performance. But even the elite runners, our role models, benefit from the RE method.

Cindi Girard-Klein is as fragile as she is talented. As a high schooler she placed third in the 2-miler in the New York State track meet. Less than a year later she had quit running. Cindi was tired of fighting injuries. She had tried to do too much too soon and had overtrained. She didn't run a step for 3 years and gained twenty-five pounds.

In 1983, she returned to running with all of her talent but less impatience, and that's why she became a national class road racer and qualified for both the 1984 and 1988 USA Olympic Trials Marathon. In the long-range training program she developed with her coach, Bob Glover, the highest priority was placed on minimizing injury, not on harder workouts or high mileage. Over a period of 2 years she gradually increased her mileage base from 30 to 60 miles a week, and then over the next 2 years to 80 miles a week. Throughout this buildup period she consistently supplemented her running with RE mileage on a bike at home. Going into the 1988 Olympic Trials Marathon, she was still biking three times a week for a total RE mileage of 90–100 miles—a figure which if done by running alone would cause certain breakdown.

In her first few years on the comeback trail, as Cindi became stronger she gradually moved her speed work from once or twice a week on the bike only to the track. First one workout per week on the track and one on the bike, and later two on the track (or one on the track and one on hills). The day after hard speed workouts and all races she doesn't run—a bike ride of 30 to 45 minutes helps her recover and minimizes the chance of injury. The day after long runs she bikes for 30 minutes to loosen her stiff legs and then runs 4 to 5 miles. She makes periodic visits to Atalanta's team physical therapist, Robert Kropf, who monitors her muscle balance, her flexibility, and the fluidity of her stride.

Following this program, Cindi ran a 1:13:15 for the half marathon in 1986, one of the all-time bests for an American. She has proven that even the elite can benefit from keeping their mileage within their physical limits and replacing the stressful extra mileage with RE miles. Besides minimizing injury, the RE program allowed her to strengthen her quadriceps, which had always troubled her. Although she was previously fragile and very injury-prone, the RE method allowed Cindi to run injury-free at the national class level for over 3 years. Consistency and attention to proper recovery and injury prevention are more important to performance than trying for the highest mileage possible and the hardest workouts imaginable.

Perhaps a total fitness approach to training is the ultimate answer to how to achieve maximum performance without developing overtraining injuries.

ADDITIONAL VALUES OF ALTERNATIVE AEROBIC TRAINING

Balancing Musculoskeletal Development

Alternative aerobic training benefits the runner in other ways than building endurance. Many aerobic exercises involve key muscle groups not sufficiently developed with a running program. Biking, for example, helps strengthen the quadriceps and thus assists in preventing knee injuries. Swimming helps strengthen the upper body and stretch and relax the back and legs. The following key muscle areas are developed with alternative aerobic exercises:

- Ankles: Swimming
- Shins   Biking (with toe clips)
- Quadriceps: Biking, race walking, cross-country skiing, rowing, swimming
- Low back: Swimming
- Hip: Biking
- Buttocks: Race walking, cross-country skiing, rowing, swimming
- Abdominals: Race walking, cross-country skiing, rowing

Bad weather

Your running paths buried in snow? Try cross-country skiing. Too hot and muggy outside? Jump in the pool or lake. Too cold for you? Try an indoor bike or treadmill. Don't give up; either toughen up and go out and run slowly or look for an alternative to running.

Travel

Always take your running shoes along when you travel, whether for business or pleasure. For many reasons, however, it may not be possible to run, or you may prefer to enjoy another aerobic activity while traveling. Stuck in a hotel in a strange city at night? Try the hotel pool or exercise bike. Check out the pools and indoor exercise equipment at local YMCAs or health clubs.

On a skiing (downhill) vacation, take time to do some cross-country skiing to keep your aerobic conditioning. Be flexible. Going for a hike up a mountain? That's enough hard work. You might jog a little on the flats now and then just to keep the feel for running. Here's an example of a great way to vacation without running and still keep in shape. Nancy Tighe, Atalanta's team president and a top age 55 and over competitor, spends 2 to 3 weeks each year traveling by bike with her husband, John. Although they make it a "fitness vacation" away from career work, she gives up running entirely during this time. They tour the countryside in such places as Ireland, Austria, England, and Vermont. Upon her return, she looks forward to running again. Besides maintaining aerobic conditioning (and recording RE mileage in her diary), the biking has also strengthened her quads considerably.

Change of Pace

Hard competitive training is not always fun. It can become tiring and boring. Give yourself some time off without guilt. Taking a day off, or even a week or two, for another aerobic exercise is an excellent idea. It will give you a chance to rebuild, regenerate.

TRAINING GUIDELINES FOR ALTERNATIVE AEROBIC EXERCISE

Don't just jump into an alternative exercise. You must plan your nonrunning exercise as carefully as you plan your program of running. Here are some guidelines for adding exercise to your running schedule:

• Ease into the activity. Treat your new exercise just as you did running during your first few months: don't overdo it. Too much will be worse than too little. Because your cardiovascular system is in great shape from running, you will think that you can do more of your new activity than a conservative amount. But because different muscles will be used or the same ones in different ways, your body will be very sore the next day if you don't start your new activity gradually. Don't cause an injury by foolishness. Begin the new exercise slowly, and do it every other day, alternating with running if possible.

• Training principles that apply to running also apply to your alternative activity—especially the principles of alternating hard and easy days and training without overstraining.

• Perform your new exercise at a training heart rate, or perceived exertion, equivalent to that of running.

• If new techniques are required, take lessons (for example, in cross-country skiing).

• Whatever you select as an alternative exercise for a change of pace, continue to run a few times each week to keep your "running legs." This will ease the transition when you return to running full-time.

• If you select an alternative exercise to increase your aerobic fitness base and prevent injury, don't overdo it. You should not exceed approximately 25 percent of your total training equivalency doing alternative exercise. Thus, if you are running 30 miles a week at about a 7:30-per-mile pace (8 miles per hour), don't do more than the equivalent of an additional 10 miles a week (such as 1 hour a week of vigorous swimming in your training heart-rate range) in another activity. Don't think you are running 40-mile weeks—it's not quite the same.

• If you wish to cut back your running to rest, to baby an injury, or just for a change of pace, and wish to maintain approximately the same level of aerobic fitness with supplemental exercise, try to cut back no more than one-third of your running time. The runner doing 30 miles a week should cut back no more than 10 miles of running—to no fewer than 20 miles a week—and replace them with approximately 1 hour a week of alternative activity in his or her training heart-rate range.

Biking, swimming, race walking, and cross-country skiing are the best alternative aerobic choices for the runner. But in these, and all alternative exercises, you must keep your intensity up, not cheat, and work hard. Because running forces you to pick up your body weight and push it, it is the hardest activity to cheat at. Also, to give yourself a broader range of activities and benefits, you may want to combine alternatives: biking and weight training, for example, provide good overall workouts for the upper body, legs, and cardiovascular system.

Specific guidelines for aerobic alternative training and sample speed workouts for biking, swimming, race walking, and cross-country skiing are detailed in *The Injured Runner's Training Handbook.*

Part III
SPEED TRAINING

8. INTRODUCTION TO SPEED TRAINING

We've met few runners who don't want to run faster. And we've met few who aren't intimidated by the prospect of doing speed training.

You shouldn't be. The brutal "no pain, no gain" workouts you hear serious competitors, like the Atalanta women, brag about aren't for you. At least not until you improve more as a runner. To safely improve, you need only run a little faster than your comfortable everyday training pace and learn to handle a modest amount of discomfort. Later you may be ready for more advanced speed workouts.

Most runners train every day at a slow, conversational pace. That's fine, much of the time. But if you expect your body to respond with a faster pace on race day, you have to train it to perform at that pace. Your biomechanics (foot strike, stride, arm drive, body angle) are different when you run faster than when you run at an easy training pace. You need to practice your racing form. Racing also causes you to breathe harder and to run more in "oxygen debt"—the physiological state where you can no longer converse comfortably and you start to feel your muscles tightening, your lungs burning, and your body temperature rising.

Speed training will help you improve your running form and leg strength and leave you better able to cope with the discomfort of oxygen debt. It will also help you learn to pace yourself properly, to hold yourself back at the start of a workout—or a race—so that you'll have something left at the end. It will allow you to have a "kick" at the end of your race.

Even more important, though, are the psychological gains you'll make as you run these workouts. Working through small doses of discomfort in training helps you realize you can push a little harder in races without risking falling in a heap.

We've had many students rejoice about running significantly improved race times after only a couple of our speed sessions. It was physiologically impossible for them to have benefited that much that soon. But after learning to push themselves in workouts, they began to feel tougher and faster. Because they *thought* they could race better, they did. Experienced runners too benefit psychologically from speed training. They build confidence going into key races when they are able to run faster and stronger in speed workouts.

The earliest days of road racing saw runners favoring long, slow distance training. Then, spurred by the success of Emil Zatopek, the great Czech runner who dominated the 1952 Olympic Games and ran large quantities of speed workouts on a track, runners shifted to speed training, the new formula for success. In the 1970s, runners shifted back to long, slow distance running (now called LSD). By the 1980s, however, track-trained stars like Allison Roe of New Zealand, Grete Waitz of Norway, and Craig Virgin and Alberto Salazar of the United States took over the road-running events. Many American runners agreed that "long, slow running only teaches you to run slow," and they took off for the track. Speed training again became the secret formula for success.

We believe that neither long, slow runs nor speed training alone is a successful training formula. The key is blending them together into a balanced training schedule. A base of endurance running should be followed by speed workouts on a track, hills, trails, and roads to sharpen for key races. Although some runners may avoid speed work and still race well, most will benefit if it is done properly.

Generally we recommend that 80 to 90 percent of your training be endurance work, and only 10 to 20 percent be speed. The first-time racer and first-time marathoner should do only endurance training. The competitive marathoner runs 90 percent endurance training and 10 percent speed as he or she sharpens for a race. Experienced racers preparing for a 10K or less may do 25 percent speed work; the average racer will do no more than 10 percent. All runners do fewer speed workouts during their training lulls between races. The shorter the race, the more speed workouts you need. The less experienced you are, the fewer speed workouts you should do.

Safety Note: We do not recommend that you begin to add speed work to your training until you (1) have been running *at least* one year, (2) have completed *at least* two races, (3) run *at least* 20 miles a week, and (4) can race 10K at a faster pace per mile than your daily training pace for 5K–4 miles. Runners who are susceptible to injury when doing speed work must be conservative with their workouts or avoid speed work altogether. It is better to enjoy racing at less than optimal conditioning than to be injured and not able to participate.

Here are some guidelines for the experienced racer for blending endurance runs and speed workouts:

RACE	ENDURANCE	SPEED
1,500 m–1 mile	60%	40%
5K–4 miles	75%	25%
10K–half marathon	85%	15%
Marathon	90%	10%

By increasing mileage, without speed work, the average runner finds that he or she can race faster and faster for the first few years of running. Endurance training gets these runners to the finish line comfortably. Eventually, however, as they try to race at a faster pace, they begin to struggle, especially in the 10K-and-under races. Now, with a solid endurance base, these runners are ready for speed work.

Generally, you can benefit from speed work if:

• It is difficult for you to hold a fast pace during a race, but you finish feeling as though you could have run farther at the same pace: "If only the race had been longer."

• You feel uncomfortable with the pace at the start of or during the race, or cannot generate a "kick" at the end.

• You lack the strength to generate power during a race, especially up hills.

• Your racing form needs improvement.

• You need to improve your race pace judgment.

• You want to "sharpen" for a key race or series of races.

• You want to test your limits in a nonracing situation.

Your goal, at all levels, is to improve your stamina: the ability to run a fast pace over long distances. To increase your stamina, you will need to work on three areas: strength, speed, and endurance.

Strength in running means training that increases your muscular strength and endurance and improves your ability to hold a fast pace. Strength workouts include weight training and continuous speed runs (see chapter 10).

Speed work means training to run faster. We break speed work into three categories: strength-training runs, pace-interval-training runs (to improve pace, racing form, and aerobic conditioning), and fast-interval-training runs (to improve speed, strength, and anaerobic conditioning). Each of these speed workouts overlaps with and complements the others.

Strength speed workouts, except for *fartlek,* are run at a steady, continuous pace. *Fartlek* workouts are a combination of strength-training runs and pace-interval and fast-interval runs. They are run continuously with intermittent bursts of speed at race pace or faster over a set distance, with recovery at a moderate pace.

Interval workouts are run in bursts, with recovery periods between them. Speed workouts may be run on a track, roads, or trails. They are often done up hills, and are called "speed work in disguise," because you work very hard without having to run as fast as you would on a track. The training results of these short, fast runs with brief rests are well established. Intermittent speed workouts, run at a fast, even pace, not only condition you to run faster, but also enable you to improve form and style, since they are often run in contained areas (a track or hill) that allow a coach to monitor your technique. Since they are run over measurable distances, you can control the workout better and measure progress. These workouts get the most out of you in the least amount of time and bring rapid improvements in your fitness level after only a few weeks. You can do much more work at a fast pace than would be possible with continuous running.

THE SPEED WORKOUT: 1-2-3 APPROACH

Speed workouts are tough. They will benefit you—and they can also injure you. Minimize the risk of injury with intelligent use of speed work.

Don't just put on your running shoes and go out for a workout. Plan. Speed training is intense, and poor habits surface quickly and can cause loss of training time from soreness or injury. By following a proper speed-training routine, you should complete a good workout and still feel like running the next day. Analyze your body's training needs, and plan your speed workout program to safely meet those needs.

All workouts—both endurance and speed—should follow this 1-2-3 step approach:

Step One. The warm-up lasts about 15 minutes for endurance runs, 30 minutes to 1 hour for speed work and races.
Step Two. The workout lasts from 30 minutes to 1½ hours.
Step Three. The cool-down lasts from 15 minutes to 30 minutes or more.

Allow enough time to do all three steps carefully. If you skip one step, you may get injured. See chapter 34 for a sample warm-up and cool-down routine to use for speed workouts.

The Workout

The speed workout consists of running a set distance at a certain pace, or at various paces. Three variables must be balanced

when planning a speed workout: quantity, intensity, and recovery.

Quantity refers to how many repeat hard runs—popularly
referred to as intervals—you do. Generally you should start
with enough intervals to give yourself a good workout, but not
so many that you can't finish the last run at nearly the same
pace as your average interval. For most average runners four
to six intervals of anything are adequate, since runners usually
aren't patient enough to run them at a very controlled pace.
Advanced competitors can usually handle six to eight intervals,
more if they are near race pace. Generally, the longer the
distance you run, the fewer intervals you run. Consult the
charts in the Appendices for the recommended quantity of intervals.

Intensity (pace) refers to the speed of your workout. To keep
it simple, we use paces that correspond to your approximate
race pace for 1–2 miles, 5K, and 10K. Consult the "Pace for
Speed Workouts" chart in the Appendices for the approximate
pace per mile for your speed workouts, and page 144 for
guidelines on the various speed paces we use in this book.

Generally, the longer the distance of the intervals, the slower
the pace. You should adjust your pace according to how you
feel, the weather, and how aggressively you like to train. You
should find that the second time you do the same workout you
can run the same pace more comfortably, or you can handle
the workout at a slightly faster pace. This shows that you are
progressing with your fitness. However, don't be dismayed if
you run more slowly as a result of poor weather (wind, heat,
cold) or fatigue from increased mileage. The object is to run
some workouts at race pace and some at faster than race pace.
It is also important to learn the value of pacing yourself. Ideally
each of your runs within the workout will be within a few
seconds in time. Don't start too fast and then poop out at the
end. On the other hand, don't underestimate yourself by starting too slowly and having a lot left at the end. In this way,
speed training mimics the pacing of races and helps you learn
to be aggressive, but sensible, about your starting pace.

Recovery (rest) is the easy part. It refers to how much rest you
take between hard runs. The theory behind intervals is that

you can manage a fair amount of hard work in small amounts if you rest the body in between. If you ran very hard with no rest breaks, you would be racing. Your body can't handle too many races, but it can handle weekly speed sessions if you properly use recovery between the intervals. On *fartlek* runs, recovery is easy running at a conversational pace for 1–3 minutes. For short and long hill workouts, the recovery is a slow run back down the hill. Don't be in a hurry; be aware that the body gets beaten up more by running downhill than by running up. Novice competitors may wish to walk part of the way down as they adjust to the work. For track-type workouts (440s, 880s, and miles), recovery is timed. Basically you want to recover by allowing the heart rate and body temperature to get back down to about the level you would be at for a slow jog. For recovery you can jog, walk, or both. Do not sit down or lie down—that would place an abnormal stress on the cardiorespiratory system. Most college track coaches prefer to keep the athletes running in order to keep them loose and ready to go. The average runner, however, is better off walking because it minimizes the amount of pounding on tired legs and because it allows the body temperature to come down further—especially valuable on hot days. Don't be shy about pouring liquids on and into yourself during recovery periods, but don't drink a lot of very cold fluids or you may cause a cramp. Conservative recovery times for the suggested workouts (usually 1–3 minutes) are suggested in the speed workout charts in the Appendices. They should be adequate. If you are still uncomfortable and your pulse isn't below approximately 120, then take more time before you run again or abort the rest of the training session. The harder you run, and the longer the distance, the more recovery time required.

These three variables can be juggled in various ways to make the workout more difficult. Adding to the number of intervals run, increasing the pace, or shortening the recovery period makes the workouts harder. Many college coaches like to sharpen their athletes by emphasizing cutbacks in recovery. We feel that the average runner is best served by keeping the recovery period constant, and slightly increasing the number or pace of the intervals. That's the kind of improvement your stopwatch can capture, and it should build your confidence as you approach your key races.

The Track Workout Language

All speed workouts are written to include the three variables. For example, an interval workout would be indicated: 6 × 440 at 10K pace, 2-min jog. This shorthand means that your track workout will be 6 repetitions of 440 yards in length (quantity), at your 10K pace (intensity), with a 2-minute jog (recovery) between each repetition.

FACTORS INFLUENCING YOUR SPEED WORKOUTS

The quantity (distance), intensity (pace), and frequency of your speed runs depend upon two essential factors: (1) the purpose or goal of your training and (2) what you can tolerate in terms of your fitness level, experience, and environmental, physical, and psychological limitations.

1. Goals

For all speed levels, you should have speed workout goals.

Your goal for each speed workout relates specifically to your racing goal and your present phase of training. If your goal is to build strength and staying power, you may want to run strength speed workouts. If your goal is to develop a sense of pace, improve your race form, or build for longer races, you may select a pace-interval workout. If you wish to improve your raw speed and strength or your ability to run in oxygen debt, or to sharpen skills for a short race, you may choose a fast-interval workout.

Some runners choose training specific to a course. They prepare for hilly races by running hills. Interval workouts over the finishing stretch of a course are also good to give the runner a feeling of confidence for kicking to the finish line. *Fartlek* runs over parts of the course will give you a sense of the battle at strategic points and prepare you for an upcoming race by giving you a feel of landmarks along the way.

2. Fitness and Experience Levels

Your fitness level, training, and racing experience determine how much speed work you can handle. Here are guidelines for our four categories of runners:

The Novice Competitor. This runner has a base of 20 miles per week and has run several races. Don't attempt any speed work until you reach this minimal level. Then safely learn the fundamentals of competitive speed training: how to run a workout, what proper form is, and so forth. The goal is to learn and to get a feel for your running potential rather than to train hard. This runner does fewer repetitions, runs no faster than present race pace, and takes plenty of rests between hard workouts.

To start, we recommend that you try a few quick—but not all-out—"pickups" of about 50 to 100 yards to get the feel of running fast. Do this once or twice a week during your regular training runs; try it only after at least 2 miles of easy jogging, and follow the speed workout with another slow, cool-down jog.

Do about six pickups, and then, over time, gradually extend the distance. This is a modified *fartlek* workout. Next, you may be able to add conservative, pace-interval workouts to your program. Races, of course, are considered speed training for you.

The key words here are caution and patience. Start carefully and allow your body to adapt to the new stress. If possible, start speed work under the supervision of a coach who understands runners at your level. See the following chapter for a sample 10-week program ideal for novice racers.

Safety Note: We recommend that at this level—20–30 miles per week, new to racing and speed work—you run only one speed session per week and that you limit it to a modified *fartlek*, rolling hills, or pace-interval run. Save the long, continuous strength runs and the faster-interval workouts for later when you have become more fit and more experienced.

The Basic Competitor. This runner can safely handle one—perhaps two—speed workouts per week. If just starting speed work, follow the guidelines for the novice competitor. With experience, this runner can benefit from the full range of speed work by adding tougher strength-training runs and faster-interval runs.

After adjusting to one hard speed workout per week, add a second, light one, perhaps a modified *fartlek,* or conservative interval run, before going into key races. You should keep the speed work within your limitations. Most speed-work-related injuries come in this group: the runner wants to progress quickly but hasn't the experience or the "speed miles in the bank." Slow progression is important in both mileage and speed accumulation.

The Advanced Competitor. This runner is experienced at speed work and racing. He or she benefits from speed work 1 or 2 times a week. This runner's biggest problems are finding the time to do all this running and balancing higher mileage with the quality of the speed work.

The Champion Competitor. This runner may run two to three speed workouts a week, depending on the distance of the upcoming race and whether or not he or she is sharpening for it. This runner, benefiting from experience, knows what is best for a champion effort for each race.

Safety Note: All runners must ease back into speed work after a layoff. Don't fool yourself into thinking that you are still in good shape. "Memory training"—remembering how well you ran in the past and thinking you still can do it now—leads to shattered egos and injury. Return slowly, step by step.

---

3. Environmental Limitations

Speed workouts will be influenced by your environment: the weather, altitude, hills, your equipment, the time of day, and the running surface.

Hot Weather. If you train outdoors, weather may be the most important factor. If you train in hot weather, remember the following guidelines:

• The best temperature for running is 45° to 70°F. As temperature and humidity increase, you work harder. You should adjust your goals and your workout accordingly.

• *Continuous runs* should be shortened in the heat. Slow your pace. Take breaks to drink, and drink plenty of fluids.

• For *intermittent workouts,* take longer recovery breaks. Walk instead of jog, drink fluids, and pour them over yourself while recovering. Stay in the shade until ready to run again. Recovery is a battle to bring your heart rate and temperature down. Power workouts may be preferred for hot days since the workout is shorter, recovery time longer, and your muscles looser.

• Don't compare hot-day run times with those run in cool weather. In fact, we seldom time hot-weather workouts; they are meaningless compared with the effort. Make other adjustments: run more slowly, do fewer intervals, change clothing if the weather changes.

• In group workouts, remember not all runners react the same way to heat.

• Be sure you have access to water, shade, and other comforts. Bring your own water and sponges if necessary, or plan your workouts on tracks that have access to water or along roads or in loops where water is available. Never run a speed workout on a hot day without fluids and shade handy.

• Warm up and run the workout in the shade if possible. Run a course near a lake, stream, or pond, so you can jump in after finishing. To avoid the heat altogether, schedule your workouts for early morning or evening, when it's much cooler.

• Remember, drink plenty of fluids *after* the workout.

Cold Weather. Cool, crisp weather allows you to run fast and recover fast. Below 32°F, however, speed work can become dangerous. If you train in cold weather, observe these guidelines:

• Do not attempt short, fast speed workouts, especially fast intervals, when it is extremely cold. The cold weather will cause your muscles, ligaments, and tendons to remain very tight— you won't be able to loosen up adequately—resulting in a lack of efficiency in your motion and possible injury.

• Do light (race pace) runs or brisk strength-training continuous runs to keep moving—and warm.

• If you try to run very hard, your lungs will feel scorched, your throat sore and raspy.

• Cooling occurs very quickly between sessions. Be prepared

to put on a warm-up suit or more clothing between work loads, and towel off to keep from getting cold and wet.

• Adjust your time goals. You are forced to go more slowly, since your body can't go all out in the cold and the extra clothing slows your pace.

• The key is to keep moving and slow the pace. Don't overdress or you'll overheat, even in the coldest of weather. Attach hat, gloves, and windbreaker to your body so you can keep adjusting to the conditions. Don't underdress, or you will be very uncomfortable.

• Take extra time to warm up. Jog 3 or 4 miles before doing anything hard, and then do your first few work loads conservatively to further ease into hard work.

• As soon as you are finished—just as when finishing a race in the cold—take off your wet shirt and put on a dry one; add extra clothing if needed. Keep jogging to prevent tightening up, and then head for a warm place. Remove all wet clothing and replace it with dry things if you are not going home immediately. As soon as possible, take a warm bath or shower, but not until your body has fully recovered from the workout and your heart rate is back to its normal level.

Wind, Rain, Lightning, Snow, and Ice. If you try to train in inclement weather, remember these guidelines:

• A strong wind can ruin workouts. First it blows you faster, then slower; you fatigue more quickly. You should just run at your intended effort level and forget time goals.

• In cold, steady rain, stick to a steady, brisk strength run at a moderate pace. If the track is slippery or full of water, try finding a dry run on hills or along roadways.

• Don't cancel workouts, just modify them. But don't mess with those speedy bolts from the sky. Lightning kills. Get off the track or road.

• Ice and snow can be fun to run in, but risky. Never attempt to run hard on ice or snow; you may get injured. Adjust your workout by running a slower, steady pace so you can be sure of a strong foot plant. Look for bare spots on the course and pick it up on them. Or look for dry hills and do your workout there. You may want to wait for better weather, or run a modified speed session on an indoor track, indoor bike, or treadmill, or in the pool.

Altitude. There is less oxygen at higher altitudes, and you can go into oxygen debt faster. If you are traveling and run in an altitude much higher than the one you live in, skip your speed work unless you will be there for a week or longer. Slowly adjust; allow for a slower pace and a longer recovery period.

Hills. Running a speed workout on a very steep hill may be counterproductive. The hill must be challenging, but not so steep that good racing form is impossible. It's good to include a few steep hills on strength-training runs, but in all cases watch out for the downhills, where injury is possible.

Safety Note: Running downhill is more dangerous than running uphill when doing several repetitions up and down a hill. Be careful to use good form and relax—not brake—when coming downhill. It is better to walk down a steep hill than risk injury.

Shoes. Training shoes are the only equipment most of you need. If you are above the level of basic competitor, you may want racing flats. If you plan to race in racing flats, use them in most of your speed workouts. Do your warm-up in them; don't just switch for the hard work. Racing flats have a lower heel; therefore, do extra stretching for your Achilles tendon and calves. Stick with your training shoes if you are bothered by injuries or if you are doing speed training on hard surfaces. Extra padding in your training shoes will also help. After your speed workout, put on your training flats for the cool-down run.

Do not experiment with spikes in speed sessions or races unless you are used to them and will really benefit from using them for several races on the track or for cross-country. Few road runners should ever use spikes; the risk of injury caused by their flimsy support and low heels is too great.

Time of Day. You run faster during daytime because you see better. If you must run after dark, either select a well-lighted route or slow down. The New York Road Runners Club classes train in Central Park, and during the winter when the lighting is poor, they modify their workouts by slowing down. In summer, when it is lighter, they run faster.

Running Surfaces. For continuous speed runs, just charge along your normal flat or hilly training courses. For intermittent speed work, the best setting is a good hill or your local track.

Most outdoor tracks are 440-yard ovals; newer ones may be 400 meters. The track is ideal for speed workouts, since times and splits are easily measured. (See the pacing chart on page 590 for even-paced splits for track workouts.) The track surface is important. A hard, smooth surface will produce faster times than a soft cinder or dirt track. The fastest surface is the new bouncy synthetic track. The difference may be as much as 2 seconds for the 440, 8 seconds for the mile. Remember this when you run on various track surfaces and compare times. Tracks in poor shape will yield slower times.

If you can't use a track, make up your own speed-workout structure. You can do speed work over measured distances on roads, dirt or wood-chip trails, grassy fields, a shopping center parking lot, park sidewalk, or your own backyard. Just measure off the distances you need, and be sure the course is free from obstacles such as potholes or protruding roots. The Atalanta running team and the New York Road Runners Club classes seldom work out on a track. They run on what they find in New York City.

If you can't run a measured distance, you can run for time. That is, instead of running a 3-minute 880 on a track, run hard along a road or path for 3 minutes and take a recovery jog before starting again. These speed-work variations allow you to do your hard track workouts wherever you go. Remember, the essential thing is the work done. You can even create hills in your flat town by running up a garage ramp, golf course hill, sloped highway grading, or even a flight of stairs.

Running on indoor tracks can cause injury. Beware of them. The tight turns and banked surface create unusual leg stress. Also, you must do eight to twenty-four laps to run a mile. Do speed work indoors only as a last resort. Don't run as hard, and do fewer repetitions. Run only the 440-880 distances, and use the outside lanes to minimize the sharp turns. Unless you intend to race indoors or have access to a good fieldhouse track, avoid indoor speed workouts. Even in the worst weather, it is still usually worthwhile to bundle up properly and get outdoors. Besides, unless they are keying for a cold-weather race, most runners should use the winter to rebuild strength and save the hard track work for the spring and summer. For this reason, Glover refuses to schedule hard indoor track workouts for his Atalanta group in the winter. You can't do hard speed work year-round.

4. Physical and Psychological Limitations

Illness, such as a cold, requires that you run fewer and less intense repetitions and take more time for recovery. This also holds true if you are nursing a minor injury. Stay away from speed work if the illness or injury becomes more serious.

We also find that performance is affected by the runner's mental state. Anxiety, tension, mental fatigue, can require that you take longer recovery periods. Psychological pressures of career, family, or education may cause occasional poor performances. This can be overcome by running with a sympathetic group, or backing off from speed sessions, although sometimes the speed session itself can give runners confidence enough to lift them. Don't take out your stresses on the track. Run a more controlled workout. Runners, like everyone else, have their ups and downs. They just have to learn to take them in stride.

VARIETY

Don't run the same workout every week, week after week. You will soon get bored and stale. Create a variety of workouts by mixing the three types of speed runs with the six basic distances we use—220, 440, 880, mile, short hill, long hill. Keep the distances and speeds fixed throughout each session to keep them simple. Other workouts can be done at varying distances and speeds:

Cut-Downs. Start at a slower than race pace, and increase the pace with each repetition, making the work tougher and tougher.

Pyramids or Ladders. Start with 220, work up to 440, 660, 880—using equal-distance recovery jogs—and then work back down.

Combinations. Alternate 440s and 220s, for example, rather than running only one distance throughout.

Out-and-Back. Run out 1 minute and back to the starting point, and rest for 2 to 3 minutes, then out 2 minutes and back, out 3 minutes and back, and so on until you reach 5 minutes; rest between each out and back. If you are fit, reverse the run and finish by running out 1 and back 1.

GROUPS

To make group running helpful, everyone must stay together at the same pace and make the same effort. For *fartlek* runs, the fastest runners might jog back toward the slower runners and regroup during recovery. The out-and-back and single-file runs are also fun. In the out-and-back, the slower runners, at the turn-around, are in the lead, with the faster runners trying to catch them; at the 5-minute out-and-back, the slower runners might actually finish ahead of the faster. This teaches runners the feel of passing and holding off runners. A similar situation on a track or hill can occur when the slower runners start first. This involves the slower runners of the group, and challenges the faster ones. Each runner starts at approximately the lead time needed so that all the runners will finish at about the same time. For single-file runs, line yourselves up single file and start running. Then the last runner sprints to the front and settles into a steady pace until the next runner sprints to the front, and so forth.

For our classes, we break down the groups by ability so they will help each other and not run against others who are much faster. We break them down into groups of 5K or 10K ability— since interval runs are done at race paces—and each group runs together.

Form Work (Pickups)

As you are easing into faster speed work, you may wish to run a few "pickups." These are *not* speed workouts, but rather brisk intervals with *complete* recovery. Run for 100–220 yards at race pace or quicker (no faster than 1-mile pace), and then jog for several minutes until completely recovered. Do four to six of these "modified" intervals. You can do them on the road as part of your run or on a track. Cindi Girard-Klein, Atalanta's national class road racer, does this workout two or three times per month untimed in order to concentrate on relaxing with good form at a fast pace. It is also a good workout to do 2–4 days before a key race. It allows you to feel peppy and thus sharpens both your racing form and your mental attitude going into a race. Form work, however, should not be run the day before or after hard speed work or long runs.

FINAL TIPS

* Don't procrastinate about getting into speed work; do it.
* Finish all your interval runs feeling exhilarated and tired, but not exhausted. Strength runs should leave you feeling tired all over, with "a tingle," but not as exhausted as an all-out race.
* Speed work should build up your body, not tear it down. Work hard, but keep control. Ease into the work; follow the principle of adaptation to progressive stress.
* Listen to your body for protests about overstress; obey them, and ease back.
* Drop out immediately if you feel anything unusual happen—a muscle tighten, a sharp pain. You can keep going, but you may regret it.
* Train by "going with your strengths." Train specifically for the race you are entering, and don't try to be what you aren't.
* Don't increase both mileage and speed at the same time. Build your mileage and speed carefully. Build your mileage first, and add speed; then cut mileage as you intensify speed.
* Follow the hard-easy method. Always take it easy the day before and after speed workouts.
* Don't jump back into your speed sessions for several days after a short race and for several weeks after a marathon.
* Make no sudden changes in surface, shoes, type, or intensity of workouts.
* Don't race during training—you'll leave your race on the training runs. Don't compete with others, only yourself.

• Run your sets evenly; don't show off on one and sandbag another.

• In group running, help each other by pushing each other. As the late Jumbo Elliott, track coach of many powerful Villanova University teams, said, "Runners make runners."

• Log every run in your diary, and log your complete workouts: quantity, intensity, rest, weather, shoes, type of track. Then you can more accurately compare workouts and measure progress.

• Generally, the shorter the race, the more speed work you do, the faster this speed work is, and the shorter the distance run.

• Build a positive attitude in your workouts, and carry it into your races and your life. Train to be tougher, wiser, faster.

Safety Note: Don't run hard speed workouts on a regular weekly basis for longer than 2–3 months without taking a break. Sharpen, then rest.

---

9. A SIMPLIFIED 10-WEEK SPEED-TRAINING PROGRAM

The following chapters detail advanced speed-training programs. They are especially helpful to runners who want to know all the intricacies of speed training and would like to personalize their speed-training program. Many runners, especially at the novice competitor and basic competitor level, don't care to know the theories behind speed training. They just want to get faster in order to meet their modest goals. "Just tell me what workouts to do and I'll do them," they state. If you wish, plug the following program into the "perfect 30-mile week" mileage schedule on page 74, and you'll have a model program for the runner who must balance career and family responsibilities with the desire to get a little better as a competitive runner.

Review the previous chapter and the following two chapters of this speed-training section for an important overview of speed training. Then, if you choose, just follow this simple schedule for 10 weeks as you prepare to peak for your chosen race. Afterward, take a break from hard training, and then come back to the schedule again when you are ready to prepare for another good race effort.

The following 10-week speed-training program is modeled on the typical 10-week program used for the New York Road

Runners Club classes. Hundreds of runners, from novice to advanced competitor, have benefited from this type of once-a-week-for-10-weeks routine. Our program offers a variety of workouts that will allow you to progress in a conservative manner. It is easy to follow, consisting of simple variations on just a few basic themes.

This is a conservative program. Our students know from experience that too little training when it comes to speed work is always better than too much. The key is to run a few high-quality workouts within a limited time period that will help you get better without overtraining. This process is like playing the stock market. Choose a conservative growth stock, and you'll gradually improve your assets with minimal risks. Or bet your money on a highly volatile stock; you can make big gains quickly, but you're also more likely to crash.

Most runners aim to do well in one or two races each "season." You may wish to train for a very popular 10K or marathon, or just for the local Turkey Trot. The program assumes that you've developed a reasonable fitness base and are ready to prepare for your key races by "sharpening" with a little speed work. To further "sharpen" for a particular race, you'll benefit from running one or two races during the 10-week buildup program—say a 5K and a 5-miler before a 10K, or a 10K and a half marathon before your marathon. Try to time your 10 weeks so that your last hard speed session (number 10 in the sample schedule) is about 10 days before your big race. You may wish to run one additional speed workout—a light *fartlek* run—4 to 5 days before the race. This peppy little run, perhaps over key parts of the race course, should leave you excited and mentally ready but not physically fatigued. Be sure to taper properly for your key race (see page 163).

The sample 10-week program that follows is just that—a sample. You can use it exactly as explained, or you can adapt it to fit your individual needs and environment. You may wish to follow it for your next race and then use the following chapters to expand on it for future races. This program is designed to allow average runners to progress in a simple, conservative manner that should lead to improved performances at distances from 5K to the marathon.

The program assumes that you are only ready to handle one

speed workout per week—because of inexperience as a competitor, vulnerability to injuries, or lack of time and energy owing to other responsibilities. Keep these workouts separated from your long runs by at least 2 days, and from races by at least 4 days (both before and after).

Ability Levels

The following guidelines are categorized into novice competitors, basic competitors, and advanced competitors.

Types of Speed Workouts

For this sample program we stick to six basic types of workouts: *fartlek,* short hills, long hills, 440-yard runs (¼ mile), 880-yard runs (½ mile), and mile runs. See the following chapters for additional types of workouts. Except for *fartlek* and mile runs, you'll do each type of workout twice during the 10 weeks. This will help you measure your improvement.

Speed-Training Guidelines

Make sure to review chapters 8 and 11 for important guidelines for safely running speed-training sessions, including the three key variables of a speed workout: quantity, intensity, and recovery. The sample schedule (page 127) lists conservative ranges for the number of intervals, pace of the intervals, and suggested recovery time. Consult the Appendices for more detailed speed workout charts.

WEEK-BY-WEEK PROGRAMS: 10 SAMPLE WORKOUTS

Week #1: Fartlek

Fartlek is the best way to make the transition between easy running and speed training. See page 130 for information on "modified" *fartlek* recommended for novice and basic competitors and page 132 for information on advanced *fartlek.*

You might enjoy *fartlek* sessions so much that you'll choose to do a few more sessions during the 10-week program as secondary speed workouts. That's fine, as long as you don't overdo it. If you find yourself dragging when it's time for your next primary speed session, cut back on the extra work.

Week #2: Short Hills

Pick a hill that is 100–220 yards in length and that is steep enough to challenge you, but not so steep that it will interfere with good form. Run at least 2 miles before and after this workout to properly warm up and cool down. See chapter 11 for guidelines for short-hill intervals. This type of workout is used early in the program because it represents "speed work in disguise." On hills, you don't have to run very fast to raise your heart rate, so you can ease into faster-paced running. The hills also strengthen your legs for later workouts and help you concentrate on good form. Novice and basic competitors should ease into this workout by running it at 10K pace. If you are bothered by foot or lower-leg injuries, avoid hill workouts.

Week #3: 440s

Jog 1 to 2 miles to warm up and the same to cool down before and after each of your track-type workouts. Doing "quarters"— one lap of a quarter-mile track—helps you ease into running at a pace faster than race speed and conditions you mentally and physically for running at race pace later. It makes speed seem less intimidating. See the speed-training charts in the Appendices if you wish more precise guidelines for the pace of your 440 intervals.

Week #4: Long Hills

Find a hill that's 440 to 660 yards in length but not quite as steep as the one you used for your short-hill workout. Run 1 to 2 miles before and after for your warm-up and cool-down. This type of workout will further increase your leg strength and bolster your confidence in running hills at or near race pace. See chapter 11 for more information on running long hills.

Week #5: 880s

We now move up to two-lap workouts on a track. "Halves" will help you learn to pace yourself properly over a longer distance. Try to run each half of the 880—one lap, if you're running on a quarter-mile track—at approximately the same pace. By running this workout at 5K pace or faster, you'll make the race pace feel more comfortable. See the speed-training charts in the Appendices if you wish more precise guidelines for the pace of your 880 intervals.

Week #6: Long Hills

The 6th week is a repeat of what you did in the 4th week. You may feel confident enough to add an extra one or two hills this time, or to run them slightly faster. You should, by now, notice that you have more strength on the hills than you had before starting this program.

Week #7: 880s

The 7th week repeats what you did in the 5th week. You may choose to run one or two more intervals this time and/or to run them at a slightly faster pace. Thus, you can monitor progress. You should now feel much more comfortable at holding a strong pace over distance.

Week #8: Short Hills

Run short hills slightly faster than you did in week #2 to help you sharpen for your fast-approaching race. You should feel much more in control, and be aware of improved form. Keep lifting those knees and driving those arms!

Week #9: Miles

This one is for the mind. It's the peak workout of the 10-week program. If you're doing mile intervals on a quarter-mile track, try to run each of the four laps at approximately the same pace. For the first 1- or 2-mile intervals, you'll need to hold yourself back, much as you must at the start of a race. For the last 1 or 2, you'll have to concentrate on maintaining good form in order to hold pace—just as you would in the last few miles of a race. Concentrate on the *feel* of being in a race.

You can use this workout to test your fitness level and help predict your race day potential. If you're able to run these miles considerably faster than your previous race-pace goal—and in reasonable comfort—then perhaps this training program has prepared you for a personal record performance and you can feel confident starting the race a little faster than you'd planned. On the other hand, if you struggle here with your expected 10K pace, you should reevaluate your goal. See the speed-training charts in the Appendices if you wish more precise guidelines for the pace of your mile intervals.

Week #10: 440s

This last workout is a repeat of the 3rd week. You should be able to zip through these quarters at a quick (but not all-out) pace, proving that you are sharp and ready for action! Try to exaggerate your race day running form and breathing so that you'll be much more comfortable and confident at race pace.

Summary

Remember, this is a flexible, *sample* program. Follow the pattern established for this 10-week program and use the workouts that you feel are best for you if you wish. Unless you are guided by an experienced coach, don't try to extend your speed-training routine beyond 10 weeks. Give yourself a break. The following two chapters detail advanced speed-training methods: strength runs and intervals. The chapters on training for 5K, 10K, and the marathon also offer specific workout guidelines.

This simplified 10-week program will help the average runner get as ready as he or she can get, with a modest amount of work, for a quality race effort. Good luck!

10-WEEK SPEED-TRAINING PROGRAM FOR THE AVERAGE RUNNER

To follow this program, first decide whether you're a novice competitor (NC), a basic competitor (BC), or an advanced competitor (AC). Do the prescribed workouts in sequence, and do just one speed session per week. "Pace" here refers to your approximate race paces for four different distances: 1 mile, 2 miles, 5K, and 10K. For recovery during hill workouts, novice competitors should walk and jog slowly down the hill ("WJ" in the chart); if you're basic or advanced, jog down ("J"). When doing repeat 440s, 880s, or miles, walk or jog after each interval for the time specified in the chart.

WEEK	QUANTITY NC	QUANTITY BC	QUANTITY AC	PACE NC	PACE BC	PACE AC	RECOVERY NC	RECOVERY BC	RECOVERY AC
1 Fartlek	(See text)								
2 Short hills	4–5	5–6	6–8	10K	10K	5K–10K	WJ	WJ	J
3 440s	4–5	5–6	6–8	5K–10K	5K	2 MI–5K	2–3 min	2 min	1½–2 min
4 Long hills	3–4	4–5	5–6	10K	10K	5K–10K	WJ	WJ	J
5 880s	4–5	4–5	5–6	5K–10K	5K	2 MI–5K	3 min	3 min	2–3 min
6 Long hills	4–5	5–6	6–8	5K–10K	5K–10K	5K–10K	WJ	WJ	J
7 880s	4–6	5–6	6–8	5K	2 MI–5K	2 MI–5K	3 min	3 min	2–3 min
8 Short hills	4–5	5–6	6–8	5K	5K	2 MI–5K	WJ	WJ	J
9 Miles	3	3–4	4–5	10K	5K–10K	5K	3 min	3 min	2½–3 min
10 440s	4–5	5–6	6–8	5K	2 MI–5K	1 MI–2 MI	2–3 min	2 min	1½–2 min

10. ADVANCED SPEED TRAINING: STRENGTH RUNS

When you analyze why a long-distance runner can run fast for up to several hours, you think of endurance and speed. You should also consider strength a significant factor.

Distance-racing strength is a specific form of muscular strength. It enables distance runners to perform with less effort, yet accomplish the same amount of work. Herbert deVries, an exercise physiologist at the University of Southern California, states that "a maximal level of strength should be developed along with the endurance training program. This allows the muscle group to work at a lower percentage of its all-out capacity, and thus, significantly increase endurance." In other words, as you increase the strength of the muscles used for long-distance running, you will require less effort to run at a particular speed. Your level of endurance increases as a result. The stronger you become, the farther you can run at faster speeds without need for additional oxygen or energy.

Strength-training runs are aerobic-anaerobic runs that either are at the borderline of aerobic and anaerobic work—where breathing becomes labored—or that pass back and forth between the two. Training is intense, and brings improvement in your muscular strength and endurance and pushes you into oxygen debt. These runs combine some of the virtues of continuous aerobic endurance runs and intermittent speed workouts. By improving endurance, speed, and strength, they improve your stamina. The term "strength," therefore, refers here not to muscle development with weights, but to the strength of the heart-lung system and the muscular system improved by these runs.

Strength runs cover 4 to 13 miles, and the pace is between 5K and marathon pace. To minimize injury and fatigue, you run the race distance at slower than race pace, *or* run race pace or faster at distances less than your race distance. The increased strength resulting from these runs will give you these benefits:

• added strength to run faster with less effort;
• the ability to maintain a faster pace for a longer period of time without using additional energy reserves;
• the psychological strength to "hang on" during intense continuous races;
• a stronger ability to overcome hills;
• a resistance to fatigue during races that will help you maintain good running form throughout the race.

Strength training also conditions runners' bodies to transport oxygen more efficiently to their muscle tissues. As you become stronger and more efficient, you rely less on your anaerobic system, and your anaerobic threshold—oxygen debt—will be extended. Your body will also tolerate greater levels of lactic acid, your heart will pump more efficiently, and you will develop a better ability to withstand pain from your running effort (not pain from injury). Your body will recover more quickly from workouts.

Endurance runs done at aerobic levels benefit your heart-lung system. By adding strength-training runs, you increase your muscular strength and endurance. By combining endurance runs with strength runs, you improve your overall fitness, and teach your mind and body to run at or near race pace for long periods.

HOW TO IMPROVE YOUR RACING STRENGTH

You improve your racing strength by systematically overloading your muscles. This is done by using strength-training runs to progressively increase the intensity and resistance of your workouts.

1. You increase the *intensity* of your workouts by increasing the *speed* of your strength-training runs. The increased speeds force your body to activate more muscle fibers to propel you forward.

2. You increase the *resistance* of your workouts by including more hills in your strength-training runs, and then increasing the elevation of the hills you run. These hills force your muscles to work harder, and this strengthens them.

3. You increase your strength by including weight training as part of your regular program.

We believe that the best way to improve your racing strength is by using strength-training runs. These runs work at improving the strength of those muscles *specifically* used for racing. Weight training is an excellent source for *general* strength building used as a supplement to your running. Chapter 35 contains detailed information about using weight training to improve your strength and thus your running.

STRENGTH-TRAINING RUNS

There are several types of strength-training runs that will progressively increase the intensity and resistance of your training workouts. These include modified *fartlek,* hill *fartlek,* advanced *fartlek,* surges, fast continuous runs, anaerobic threshold runs, tempo runs.

The Modified Fartlek Run

This is a strength run for novice and basic competitors just beginning to include more strenuous training runs in their workout schedules. It is an introduction to speed work for these runners. It is also used by advanced runners returning from injury who are easing into more strenuous runs, and by those runners easing back into more intense workouts after a long layoff from competitive training.

The modified *fartlek* run is generally done on a level or gently rolling course so that only one overload factor (speed) will be manipulated by the runner. If you add steep hills, you include a second overload factor (resistance), and that is too difficult a challenge at this stage of your development.

This is a continuous run—ideally over grassy fields or dirt trails—at your normal base-training pace. Use your regular training route of 4 to 8 miles if you can't find a more exciting route for your "speed play."

After warming up with a mile or two at your base pace, do "pickups" of 50 to 440 yards at your 5K or 10K race pace. Do approximately six to eight *fartlek* bursts, following each with 2 to 3 minutes of recovery running at or slightly slower than your base pace. Go again when you feel ready, and follow your final pickup with a couple of easy miles to cool down. Be conservative with pace and recovery; the object of modified *fartlek* is to ease into speed training and have a little fun doing it. The more exploring you do and the more varied the terrain, the better. Play games by picking out landmarks to run briskly to—such as the top of a moderate hill or to the next streetlight. The workout gradually introduces you to strength-training runs and speed work, and allows your body to adapt to new stresses with little chance of injury.

You may vary the distance or time you run hard within the same workout according to how you feel. The purpose of the modified *fartlek* is to incorporate speed work into your endurance training. It is much less stressful than the typical track workout. *Fartlek* training can also help you work on your form while you run those short, fast spurts.

The Hill Fartlek *Run*

This strength run introduces resistance work into your training. It is necessary for developing racing strength, and is used by basic, advanced, and champion runners.

Hill *fartlek* includes a fair number of hills that range from ¼ mile to ¾ mile in length. The entire run should cover a distance of 4 to 10 miles, depending on your fitness level. The basic competitor may limit himself or herself to 4 to 6 miles at first. The run should last at least 30 minutes, but no longer than 75 minutes. Run a few easy miles before and after the workout. Choose a course with a series of hills that aren't spaced too close or too far apart.

The run emphasizes the hills. You should approach them in a very positive manner. By "working" or challenging the hills at race pace, you force your muscles to overcome the resistance of the incline, thus increasing your strength. Running downhill, you should work on "falling" instead of resisting the decline. Maintain good hill-running form on uphills and hold a steady brisk conversational pace while running along the flat sections. When you complete this workout, your whole body and soul should tingle.

Hill *fartlek* should help you improve your form. The increased resistance and elevation should force you to use good running form to work up and down the hills. The oxygen debt encountered when you challenge the hills will force your body to work under stress. Your body will become more efficient in supplying oxygen and energy sources to your muscles, enabling you to run better.

Make sure that you progressively increase the resistance of the hills you run against. As you become stronger, run steeper hills, and increase the mileage and number of hills included in your workout. A frequent diet of hill running will make you a tougher hill runner. You will develop confidence and not be frightened when you run up against one of those killer hills during a race.

The Advanced Fartlek *Run*

This workout may be included in all stages of your training. It can be used as an introduction to workouts, or it can be done as an alternative to these types of runs for those who don't like to work out on a track. This difficult workout is not recommended for novice and basic competitors. Basically, this is a transitional workout that includes some pace-interval running and some fast-interval running done intermittently, alternated with endurance running. The workout is very stressful, since it combines both intensity (speed) and resistance (hills) in one workout. It is used only by the advanced and champion competitor. Control the difficulty of the workout to prevent injury. Most runners make the mistake of not taking enough rest between the "speed plays." They become fatigued too early in the workout and begin to force themselves through the run. They may get injured, perhaps straining a muscle or ligament, as they try to "bull" their way through the session.

The advanced *fartlek* run covers varied terrain with some good hills and flat sections. Most *fartlek* sessions are done on trails or golf courses but could be done even in city streets if need be. The distance ranges from 4 to 8 miles, and the entire workout should take 30 minutes to 1 hour. The runner selects a landmark such as a telephone pole or traffic light and runs hard to it, or chooses to run hard for a set time period such as 1 minute. The workout is broken into segments of "hard stressful" runs followed by "easy recovery" runs. The hard portion of the run is done at 10K pace or faster, depending on the length of the segment, which may range from 100 yards to 1 mile. The recovery portion of the run is done at base pace and covers approximately the same distance as the hard run. The faster the bursts, the slower the recovery pace. The distance of the pickups should vary within the workout; for example, 220-rest-880-rest-440-rest, and so forth. The distance may also vary with the terrain, picking up the pace on each hill. The number of pickups per workout varies from 10 to 20; go as you feel. This workout is open to variation. You may vary the length of the hard stressful run as you wish. The workout is done entirely to your "feel" and not structured in any way. This is not a carefree workout, however. It is stressful, placing a large overload on your cardiorespiratory and musculoskeletal systems. The workout is done best alone or in small groups of similar ability. During recovery, faster runners should turn around and jog toward the slower, to regroup. You should run a few easy miles before and after the workout.

Remember, *fartlek* training means getting tired without feeling tired. It is designed to be intense and different. Allow for variations of speed in an informal but intense run.

Surges

Experienced advanced and champion competitors may benefit from another variation of *fartlek* running. Instead of running hard and then jogging for recovery, they run hard "surges" of

1 to 6 minutes of a strong, brisk base pace. Hold that pace for another 4 to 6 minutes before surging again. Another variation is to run a "ladder" workout: surge for 1 minute, 2 minutes, 3 minutes, 4 minutes, and 5 minutes—for example—at 10K race pace or slightly faster.

Surging simulates racing conditions, where you may have to pick up the pace to pass or move away from another runner. This workout gives you the confidence to pick up your pace in a race even when you are already running hard. Caution: This workout is only for those with a strong mind and body.

Fast Continuous Runs

This run stresses speed over a long distance. You want to get the feeling that you are pushing the pace throughout this run. The length and actual speed of the run are secondary to the feel of the run. The fast pace overloads your muscles and cardiovascular system to improve your racing strength. Only runners with the proper preliminary training that has conditioned their bodies to withstand the stress of this workout should try fast continuous runs. Many runners feel that these are the "bread and butter" of their training schedules, rather than lots of long, slow endurance runs. These runners, however, are very fit and experienced.

The fast continuous run is done over a level or gently rolling course where you can move along undisturbed at a fast clip. The pace is steady (about half-marathon pace for 4 to 8 miles, marathon pace for 8 to 10 miles), and you should be able to cover a distance of 4 to 10 miles, depending on your fitness level. Start with the shorter distance. You should complete the entire workout at the same pace. Run an easy mile before and after the workout.

The key here is the fast, steady pace for the entire distance of the run. If you slow down or lose your concentration, you will diminish the overload (speed) force that you are placing on your muscles.

The fast continuous run improves your cardiorespiratory level of fitness. It makes you mentally a tougher competitor by training you to run faster under pressure and improves your confidence that you can do this. Strength-training runs are progressive: be sure to progressively increase the overloading of your system by increasing the speed of the fast continuous runs as you become stronger. You may also want to lengthen the distance of the run somewhat. You should finish these runs feeling that you have really taxed your body.

A good way to utilize this type of workout if you are marathon training is to run a 15K–half marathon race at your-marathon goal pace. This type of fast continuous run builds strength and endurance, enables you to practice running-form biomechanics at race pace, gives you practice at even pacing going into your marathon, and improves your confidence at being able to run a strong, controlled pace over distance.

Anaerobic Threshold Runs

That fine line between aerobic running and anaerobic running is called the anaerobic threshold. At that pace (approximately 85 percent of your maximum heart rate) you begin to have difficulty breathing, lactic acid builds up, your form tends to get ragged, you feel your muscles tensing and tightening.

Generally, runners with the highest maximum oxygen up-take (largely developed with aerobic running) and the ability to push hard with a finishing kick (anaerobic ability developed with fast intervals) are the first to cross the finish line at races. Olympic marathon champion Frank Shorter, however, has a maximum oxygen uptake value much lower than that of other elite runners. Yet his anaerobic threshold is so high that he could run marathons at 85 percent of his maximum, while other athletes could only maintain levels of 75 to 80 percent. No matter what distance you are racing, the higher your anaerobic threshold, the farther and faster you can run before your muscles give in to oxygen debt.

Basic competitive, advanced competitive, and champion runners can benefit from regular anaerobic threshold workouts, particularly when marathon training. The pace you run for this workout is approximately 30 seconds slower than your 10K pace. (See the Pace for Speed Workouts Chart in the Appendices for specific guidelines.) After warming up with a couple of miles, run at your estimated anaerobic threshold pace for 3 to 4 miles. Or you may choose to break it up by running three intervals at your anaerobic threshold pace for 1½ to 2 miles. Jog for 3 minutes recovery. Finish the workout with 1–2 miles of easy running.

Tempo Runs

Similar to the fast continuous runs, these are more structured, with the distance and time being measured and recorded accurately. Tempo runs are done at a slightly faster pace than the fast continuous runs. This run is used *only* by advanced and champion competitors preparing for major races. (Beware of turning tempo runs into an all-out race effort.)

The Russians first introduced tempo runs, wanting to simulate race conditions without exposing their runners to the high stress and pressure of actual races. They like the run to teach their runners a feeling for pace, thus the term "tempo."

This run covers a distance of 4 to 5 miles at very close to your 10K pace (approximately 10–20 seconds per mile slower than 10K race pace). The course should be level, with good footing. Each time you run this workout, you should run the same course and time yourself. As you become more fit, try to improve your time to maintain the overload. This will help increase your racing strength and build your confidence. Run a few easy miles before and after this workout. Be sure to prepare yourself for it, since it is very stressful, and a poor time can be discouraging. Thus, you would taper for a few days going into it.

Safety Note: Be careful when doing the strength-training runs, since they are unstructured and you can't measure accurately how intensely you are training. Ease into these runs.

SUMMARY OF STRENGTH-TRAINING RUNS

STRENGTH-TRAINING RUN	DISTANCE	INTENSITY	RECOVERY PERIOD	HILLS	CATEGORIES OF RUNNERS WHO USE THIS RUN
1. Modified *fartlek*	3–5 miles	Short bursts at 10K pace or faster	Yes	Few, moderate	Novice, basic
2. Hill *fartlek*	4–10 miles	Uphills at race pace	Yes	Many, challenging	Basic, advanced, champion
3. Advanced *fartlek*	4–8 miles	Faster than 10K race pace	Yes	Several, challenging	Advanced, champion
4. Surges	4–8 miles	1-to-6-minute bursts at 5K–10K pace	Yes	Optional	Advanced, champion
5. Fast continuous runs	4–13 miles	Half-marathon pace for 4–8 miles; Marathon pace for 8–10 miles	No	Few	Basic, advanced, champion
6. Anaerobic threshold runs	6–8 miles	30 seconds faster than 10K pace for 3–4 miles	Optional	Few	Basic, advanced, champion
7. Tempo runs	4–6 miles	10–20 seconds per mile slower than 10K race pace	No	None	Advanced, champion

11. ADVANCED SPEED TRAINING: INTERVALS

Interval workouts are speed workouts with incomplete recovery breaks. Technically, the rest breaks you take between each speed run is the "inverval." Over the years, however, track coaches have come to call the actual speed runs "intervals"—thus we shall in this text.

We use two basic types of interval workouts: pace intervals and fast intervals. *Pace intervals* are primarily aerobic and are run near the top of your training heart-rate range, a controlled pace at which you experience only a modest amount of anaerobic discomfort. These runs are at race pace: we use 5K pace intervals and 10K pace intervals in this book. Anaerobic threshold pace runs (see page 137) can also be used as pace-interval runs and are run slightly slower than 10K race pace.

Fast intervals are run faster than pace intervals and are run anaerobically. A faster version of fast intervals, power intervals, can be used by advanced runners who need to run much faster—especially for 220s and 440s—when training for 5K and under.

PACE-INTERVAL WORKOUTS

Combined with aerobic endurance runs and strength work, pace intervals allow you to run faster over longer distances, thus improving your race times.

Pace-interval workouts:

• *Develop a sense of pace and rhythm.* Since you accurately time your workouts, you can teach your body to run at a desired pace. This is helpful for those runners who tend to start races too fast or too slowly. You learn and then practice the pace that is right for you so you will feel it and run it on race day. The interval workout allows you to run at your own selected pace over and over again to get that "feel."

• *Improve speed.* By training at a pace slightly faster than race pace, you progress toward a goal of faster race times.

• *Improve racing form and style.* By training in race-pace form, you will be more efficient, coordinated, and relaxed on race day.

• *Build confidence.* These runs develop your confidence to hold a brisk, steady pace. Since much of interval work is done a little faster than race pace, the speed of your race in the early going will feel within your limits. You learn that you have "staying power" and can maintain pace at the end of your race, even when you are tired, by maintaining pace when tired over the last few sets of interval runs.

• *Increase endurance.* Improves both your aerobic and muscular endurance.

• *Extend your aerobic-anaerobic borderline.* By training, and racing, at a higher level of aerobic capacity, you are not slowed by oxygen debt and can hold your fast pace longer.

• *Sharpen you for races.*

• *Allow for a flexible workout.* Interval workouts are excellent for the novice competitor who needs to ease into speed work, for other runners returning from injury or layoff, and for all runners compensating for bad weather conditions.

• *Measure progress.* When you do *fartlek* runs or endurance runs, you know you are getting fit, but can't prove it. Interval workout improvements are measurable: your times improve, your recovery periods are shorter, you do more repetitions at the same pace. Do not do the same workout every week, however, and expect to improve. Use variety: go back to some of the same workouts every few weeks and compare your times, repetitions, recoveries.

• *Maintain general conditioning.* Moderate interval workouts can be used once a week year-round to help you maintain a high level of base fitness even when not building toward a key race.

• *Improve hill running.* They improve your hill-running ability and form as you gain confidence in your handling of hills at race pace.

• *Speed recovery from races.* About 2 or 3 days after a race, a full week after a marathon, very conservative slow-paced work— low intensity, low quantity, extra rest—will help stretch out your stiff muscles and flush away accumulated waste products. It also helps you psychologically to do something brisk. In our classes on Tuesday evenings following Sunday races we have our runners move back a group or two in speed, or do fewer repetitions at a slower pace. These workouts must be treated as recovery speed workouts, not training speed workouts.

• *Develop a feel for pack running.* By running in a group, you learn to hang on when you want to drop out, or to hold back and be patient. You learn what it is like to run elbow-to-elbow in a race with a pack of runners who can "draft" off each other and help each other run a faster pace. In our classes we group runners together by race pace and encourage them to hang together in a tight pack. You should also run some rhythm workouts alone to learn how to judge your own pace.

FAST-INTERVAL WORKOUTS

These hard efforts combine strength and speed to achieve stamina. You develop increased power doing fast intervals, allowing you to run faster more comfortably. You run in oxygen debt and thereby make friends with what runners call the Bear.

Fast-interval workouts:

• *Develop leg strength*—especially the quadriceps—upper-body strength, and knee lift, resulting in increased leg speed, stride length, ankle flexibility, and ratio of fast-twitch to slow-twitch muscle fibers.

• *Improve raw speed.* They develop your "sprinting speed" by increasing strength and leg speed and improving movement coordination.

• *Condition you for competition.* These workouts, because of their intensity, closely approximate the stress of racing. Repetition of the intense pace improves your mental and physical toughness for racing. Being forced to run through discomfort brings out the competitor in you, and you realize a potential that you didn't know existed until you were pushed hard.

• *Push back your aerobic-anaerobic borderline and improve your ability to run anaerobically.* Like strength and pace-interval speed work, fast-interval workouts help train you to run faster without accumulating lactic acid and being forced to slow down. The workouts push you much further into oxygen debt than other speed workouts, and thus teach you to run more efficiently and confidently when the Bear (oxygen debt) does attack you. The shorter the race, the faster the pace, and the more demand there will be for anaerobic conditioning.

• *Improve your racing technique.* By running very fast, you learn better coordination of your body. This improves your racing form and style and helps you develop your "power gear" to shift into when running up short, steep hills at a fast pace and using a finishing kick. Fast-interval workouts, by exaggerating proper biomechanical movements, also make you concentrate on driving the arms and lifting the knees. You learn controlled breathing at an intense pace.

• *Provide a psychological boost during training.* Coaches may stimulate runners during "down" periods by "popping" short, fast runs.

HOW TO WRITE AN INTERVAL WORKOUT

Putting together your own interval workout requires planning. You can't merely play with the three variables—quantity, intensity, recovery—and hope to come up with the right combinations. Each workout is influenced by many factors, including your training goals, fitness, and experience levels and environmental, psychological, and physical limitations (see page 353). By examining the three variables individually and considering all these factors, you can construct the right workout for yourself. Before starting:

1. Select the distance of your runs, and the number of intervals you want to do *(quantity)*.

2. Determine the amount of rest you will take between each repetition *(recovery)*.

3. Determine the speed of the intervals *(intensity)*. Speed will depend greatly upon the amount of rest you allow yourself and the distance run. The shorter the recovery period and the greater the distance, the slower the intervals. Consult the speed workout charts in the Appendices for suggested amounts for quantity, intensity, and recovery.

Safety Note: Increase the stress of only one variable at a time.

Selecting Quantity

This covers distance and repetitions. Many intervals improve fitness and form. Total mileage (not counting warm-up, cooldown, or recovery running) may range from 1 to 2 miles for novices up to 4 to 6 miles for more experienced runners. In general, you run more intervals and longer distances to prepare for longer races and as your fitness level increases. The greater the distances of the intervals, the fewer you run.

We use six different distances—from 220 yards to 1 mile—for our basic workouts. This keeps things simple, and the distances are fixed for the entire workout. As you improve, you may want to vary these. Our six distances are:

1. *220-yard runs.* Used primarily for short-distance training (5K and under) to improve speed.

2. *440-yard runs.* "Quarters" are used for improving form, general aerobic conditioning at slower paces, and a final prep for shorter races at faster paces.

3. *880-yard runs.* Used at 10K and under to develop speed and simulate racing conditions. For races longer than 10K,

these runs are used for improving aerobic conditioning, form, and pace.

4. *1-mile runs.* Used mostly for 10K to marathon training. Excellent for pace judgment and improving aerobic conditioning. Teaches the ability to hold on to a strong pace. A basic workout for marathoners as they build toward the race. More advanced runners may do 1½-mile and 2-mile sessions.

5. *Short-hill runs (100–220 yards).* Steep enough to challenge, not so steep as to prohibit good rhythm. Excellent for improving form, speed, and strength.

6. *Long-hill runs (440–660 yards).* Not quite as steep as the short hills. Mainly used for psychological purposes. After running a number of these, you begin to feel very confident about running up hills in races. More advanced runners may go as long as ½ mile or 1 mile for these runs. *Note:* See page 118 for the modified interval "form work."

Determining Recovery

Less rest is used for shorter distances, slower speeds, fewer intervals. When peaking for a race, you may keep the quantity and intensity the same, but cut back the rest. More rest may be required for novice competitors, or runners coming back from an injury or layoff.

Your recovery time from interval runs should be enough to allow your heart to return to about 120 beats per minute, or long enough so that you can do the next run at the same pace. You seek *incomplete recovery:* you bring your heart rate up to about 85 percent of maximum and do not let it fall below about 60 percent of maximum. Thus you train aerobically for the entire workout, including the recovery time.

Experienced runners may jog lightly between intervals to stay loose; some may walk briskly. Novices should walk. Do not jog on your toes as the track runners do; they do that in order to keep a "bounce" to their ball-heel foot strike. Don't sit down or stand around, either. Keep moving.

The recommended length of rest for the interval workout varies from 30 seconds to 3 minutes. If you require more than the recommended time to recover, you are running the distance too quickly. You should modify your speed. If you recover too quickly, increase the speed of the run. The amount of rest you take controls how fast you can run.

If you are doing a large number of intervals at a slow pace, you should take as little rest as possible. (Example: 12 × 440 with 30 seconds between each.) If you are training at fast interval paces or want to do some longer intervals (1 mile), you will have to take a longer recovery period. The increased stress of a faster speed or longer distance requires more time for your body to recover.

On hills, rest is determined by how long it takes you to jog down to the bottom. When you reach the top, don't stop. This is a continuous run at intermittent paces. You run up the hill at or near race pace, and down at or near conversation pace. Don't "brake" coming downhill; relax and flow. Run up briskly and and flow down easily. Novice competitors may choose to walk briskly and jog downhill.

Determining Intensity

Pace-interval runs are done near race pace, fast intervals at faster than race pace. Pace intervals give you the feel for your own race pace, and your first run should be at the same speed as your last. They should all be very close in time, just like your splits during a race. You will, therefore, learn to hold back when fresh and keep pushing when tired. Fast intervals exaggerate the intensity of the race and are uncomfortable, thus making it easier to handle the pace on race day.

The speed of your interval runs will vary from 1 mile to slightly slower than 10K pace. Your speed will increase if you want to do work for shorter races or improve race pace. Your speed will decrease if you run more intervals or longer distances, take less rest, or are troubled by various limiting factors.

We use five speed levels as detailed on speed-training charts in the Appendices. These speed levels are reference points to guide you in establishing your specific training paces. Your actual pace may be slightly faster or slower.

1. *10K pace intervals.* All the other speed levels are based on your average pace per mile at your estimated present fitness

level for the 10K. Gradually increase that pace toward your goal pace as your workouts and race times improve. This pace is the safest for novice competitors easing into interval training. For 10K competitors, it conditions you to hold back and run an evenly paced race.

2. *Anaerobic threshold pace intervals.* This pace is 30 seconds per mile slower than 10K race pace. This pace is run as a continuous strength run for 3–4 miles (see page 137) or as an interval run such as three times 1½ miles. This pace is at your approximate aerobic-anaerobic borderline: the speed at which it begins to be difficult to hold pace over an extended period and still breathe comfortably.

3. *5K pace intervals.* This speed is 10 seconds per mile faster than 10K pace: approximately your 10K starting pace. For 10K runners, this quicker speed conditions them to be comfortable at slightly faster than race pace. For 5K runners, this workout conditions them to run comfortably at an even race pace.

4. *Fast intervals.* The speed for this type of interval is 20 seconds faster per mile than 10K pace, 10 seconds per mile faster than 5K pace. It is the approximate starting pace for a 5K race. They are not all-out sprints, but they are run very fast. This the approximate pace that you could hold for approximately 10–11 minutes before having to slow because of the buildup of lactic acid. Exercise physiologists have determined that this is the best speed at which to train to improve your aerobic capacity.

5. *Power intervals.* This is a variation of fast intervals and is run 10 seconds faster per mile: 30 seconds faster per mile than 10K pace and 20 seconds faster per mile than 5K pace. This isn't a sprint, but is getting close. It is approximately your pace for an all-out run of 1–2 miles. This pace is primarily used by advanced competitors training for shorter races and at intervals of 440 yards and less.

Controlling Your Interval Pace

The most difficult problem faced by runners just learning to do interval workouts is regulating their workout pace. It is one thing to know what pace you should be running and quite another to do several repetitions at that exact pace. Many runners, including experienced racers, begin the workout much faster than the planned pace. You should get into the correct rhythm immediately, so that you don't destroy the purpose of the workout. If you start at too fast a pace, you will have to take too long a recovery or you will run too slowly for the remaining repetitions because of fatigue.

If you run the entire workout at a faster pace than planned, consider:

• Cutting back the amount of rest between intervals.

• Doing more intervals.

• Increasing your weekly mileage. Some runners naturally do very good speed workouts but not enough distance training, and therefore don't run as well in distance races. We have had runners in our classes doing interval workouts meant to break 40 minutes for the 10K, but who cannot run under 44 minutes for that distance. Check your weekly mileage. Perhaps you aren't getting enough distance work in your training program.

If you cannot run the workout as fast as you planned, consider:

• Not doing as many intervals. By reducing the number of intervals, you may be able to run the remaining ones at a faster pace.

• Giving yourself more rest between intervals. Here, 15 to 30 seconds can make a world of difference.

• Adjusting your workouts for the next session. You may have misjudged your fitness level and picked a pace you are not ready for yet. Or you may be trying to progress too fast with your workouts.

• That you may need more experience at speed work. Perhaps your marathon time indicates that you should be able to run faster times on a track for your workouts than you can handle. You have been able to "bull" your way to fast race times for longer distance thanks to your endurance. More speed work will improve your times at all distances.

HOW TO INCREASE THE SPEED OF YOUR INTERVAL WORKOUTS

As a competitive racer you will want to run your interval workouts faster as you become more fit and attempt to improve your race times. Rather than haphazardly trying to increase the speed, we offer a safe two-step method of progressively increasing the speed of your workouts.

1. Increase the number of repetitions of your workout. You do this by progressively increasing the number of intervals for each specific distance that you choose to run. You can use the interval workout charts in the Appendices as a guideline for choosing how many intervals to run, beginning with the minimum number recommended and then progressing toward the maximum. In some cases you may feel that you have to do the suggested maximum number before being ready to move on to a faster pace, while in other cases you may feel that after a few weeks of increasing the number of intervals, you are ready to increase the speed of your workouts without having reached the maximum number suggested.

2. Increase the speed of your runs slightly (usually 1 to 2 seconds per 440 yards of your run), at the same time you decrease the number of intervals you have been doing for each particular distance. Then proceed in the same manner as in step one. For example, if you have completed 10 × 440 in 90 seconds and now feel ready to increase the speed of your run, you might try to run the 440s at 88-second pace. However, don't attempt to run them in this initial workout. That would be too difficult for you, might discourage you, and may possibly cause injury. Begin by doing 8 × 440 in 88, for example. If you have trouble finishing the workout, you are probably not yet ready to increase the speed of your runs, and should go back to a 90-second pace.

This two-step approach allows your body enough time to adjust to a specific rhythm before pushing it to faster speeds. If you constantly push yourself to run at faster speeds with every successive workout, you will find that instead of getting faster you will be putting so much strain and pressure on your body that you will end up going more slowly.

You must increase your speed in steps to allow your body to adapt to the increased work loads. Be patient, for it will take some time to increase your pace. In the early training stages, progress may be fairly brisk and you may improve your pace 4 to 10 seconds per mile in the first month or two. However, as you become better, you will find that it becomes more difficult to increase the speed of your intervals. And it may take 4 to 6 months to increase your per-mile pace 2 to 4 seconds.

Safety Note: Never increase both the number of intervals and the speed of intervals at the same time. Changing both quantity and speed will only result in placing a great stress on your body and cause you to run a very poor workout or to injure yourself. You must be prepared to run slower times if confronted with adverse weather conditions.

GENERAL GUIDELINES FOR RUNNING INTERVAL WORKOUTS

Keep the following points in mind:

1. The workout is controlled, with no racing between running partners allowed; work together.

2. Recovery is important for two reasons: (a) it keeps you from running too quickly, and (b) it is essential to the development of your aerobic and anaerobic systems.

3. Concentrate on maintaining a steady pace and don't worry about the speed of your run.

4. Stop the run as soon as the pace falls off sharply. When this happens, it means that you have misjudged your ability to run at a certain pace and a buildup of lactic acid has occurred. Adjust for your next workout.

5. Finish feeling that you have a little left, and are not exhausted. The first, middle, and last interval should always be at the same pace.

6. Your last hard session should be 10 to 12 days before a key race; if it's much earlier, you lose benefits; if it's later, you don't recover in time.

7. Jog into the start of your runs. Don't start flat out as if you were in a race. This places too much stress on your legs.

8. Develop a rhythm to the run and try to stay with it through your workout, even when it becomes difficult toward the end. Stay relaxed throughout the run. If you begin to press, slow down rather than "bull" your way through. The idea of the workout is to run rhythmically and evenly within your ability.

9. Keep moving during the rest period by walking or jogging.

CHARTING YOUR PERSONAL INTERVAL WORKOUT

Instead of juggling variables by trial and error, consult the interval workout charts in the Appendices. We have developed them based on our work with thousands of runners at all levels. All you have to do is determine your flexible speed workout ranges and head for the track.

Follow these simple steps:

Step One: Determine Your Fitness Category. This is for speed work based on the approximate descriptions in chapter 1. Follow the guidelines on the interval workout charts for your category. These are just guidelines. Some experienced runners blessed with natural speed and doing lower mileage may move up a group. Some experienced high-mileage runners who are inexperienced with speed work or are coming off a layoff may move back a group. Older runners may need to move back a group.

Step Two: Determine the Distance of Your Interval Run. Is it 220, 440, 880, mile, short hill, long hill?

Step Three: Determine Your Interval Pace. Is it pace intervals or fast intervals?

Step Four: Determine the Quantity of Intervals. You have a range to choose from on the charts. Start with the lower range; don't go to the higher ranges until ready. You do not have to attempt the highest range. Generally, you work to the highest range before increasing speed, then you reduce the number of intervals to the lowest range, and then build back up.

Step Five: Determine Your Recovery. We use a fixed rest period, but if you need more, decrease the speed of your run. Determine whether you will walk, jog, or do a combination of both for your recovery.

The interval workout charts in the Appendices are only approximate, like any guidelines. So too are the categories of runners we have described. Be flexible with these charts, and you will find they can help you properly set up a good interval speed workout. Consult the more detailed guidelines within the specific racing chapters: 5K, 10K, marathon.

Here are some sample workouts, one for each category, to show you how to set up your own interval workout:

SAMPLE INTERVAL WORKOUT: NOVICE COMPETITOR

Aiming for a 10K, just starting speed work.
   (Consult the 10K interval charts in the Appendices.)
   The workout—pace-interval workout: 6 × 440, 10K pace (9-minute miles), 2-minute walk.
   Step One. *Fitness category* is novice competitor. You are running at least 20 miles a week and have run a few races. Your best time was 9 minutes per mile for 10K. You train at about 10:00 per mile. After you have done some modified *fartlek*, you are ready for some conservative speed work following the novice competitor's chart.
   Step Two. You will begin with the *shorter distances*, then extend to longer distances in future workouts as you become more experienced with speed work. We select here 440 yards.
   Step Three. You will run at 10K pace to teach you the feel of race pace. This will be 2:15 per 440 at a 9-minute-per-mile pace.
   Step Four. You will do *six intervals*. You find this figure on your chart under 440s for pace intervals and pick the lower range under "quantity," since you are a novice at this type of work. This will be enough to give you a feel for pace work.
   Step Five. You will take a *2-minute recovery or rest period* as recommended on the chart. Since you are a novice, your rest will consist of walking.

SAMPLE INTERVAL WORKOUT: BASIC COMPETITOR

Aiming for a 3:30 marathon.
(Consult the marathon training interval chart in the Appendices.)
The workout—pace-interval workout: 4 × 1 mile, 10K pace (7:30), 3-minute jog.
Step One. *Fitness category* is basic competitor. You are running approximately 50 miles a week and have a month to go before the marathon. Your best 10K is about 30 seconds per mile faster than you think you can run for the marathon (7:30 for 10K, and you hope to average 8:00 for the marathon). You are experienced at speed work and are sharpening for the marathon. Follow the basic competitor's interval workout chart.
Step Two. You select *1-mile runs* to help improve your endurance.
Step Three. You will run them at *10K pace* of 7:30 per mile.
Step Four. You will do *three intervals*. Since you have never done mile speed sessions before, don't try for four.
Step Five. *Recovery* will be three minutes of easy jogging to keep loose, or brisk walking, if you prefer.

SAMPLE INTERVAL WORKOUT: ADVANCED COMPETITOR

Aiming for a 6-minute pace for 10K.
(Consult the 10K training interval charts in the Appendices.)
The workout—fast-interval workout: 8 × 440, faster than 5K pace, 1½-minutes walk/jog.
Step One. *Fitness category* is advanced competitor. You are running about 60–80 miles per week and have 2 weeks to go before a big 10K race. Your best time is 38 minutes. Your goal is to bring that down to a 6-minute pace (37:17).
Step Two. You select *440s* to work on your speed.
Step Three. You decide to do them at *fast-interval pace* (20 seconds per mile faster than 10K pace) to help bring your speed down. For you, this is about 5:40 per mile, 10 seconds faster than the pace you plan to go out at for your 10K, which will be held in cool weather and on a fast course. This is 85 seconds per 440.
Step Four. You choose to do *eight intervals*.
Step Five. *Recovery* will be 1½ minutes, which you will do walking until you cool down somewhat from the fast work, and then you will jog a little.

SAMPLE INTERVAL WORKOUT: CHAMPION COMPETITOR

Aiming for sub-6-minute miles for the marathon.

(Consult the marathon training interval charts in the Appendices.)

The workout—pace-interval workout: 10 × 880, 10K pace (5:25), 1-minute jog.

Step One. *Fitness category* is champion competitor. You are running 80 miles per week and have run 5:35 per mile for 10K and 2:42 for the marathon. Three weeks from now you wish to run under 6 minutes per mile—2:35—for the marathon.

Step Two. You select *880s* to give you a feel for a strong pace and to increase endurance.

Step Three. You decide that you will run at 10K pace for the shape you are in now. Thus you do 880s at a 5:25-per-mile pace (2:42.5 per 880).

Step Four. You choose to do *ten intervals,* since you are in good shape and want a really strong workout.

Step Five. *Recovery* will be a 1-minute jog—an easy 110. You will run two laps hard, jog a one-eighth lap, then go around again in constant motion.

Part IV
THE TRAINING SCHEDULE

12. THE TRAINING SCHEDULE

The competitive runner must plan not only every workout, but also his or her complete training schedule leading to a specific racing goal. Mileage and speed work must be balanced and planned to come at the right time and in the right amount. Selecting the proper training runs in correct sequence is essential. We use a simple, flexible program to guide you toward your racing goal.

You begin your race 2 to 6 months in advance. You follow the principle of foundation training and sharpening to build up to, and then race, a quality performance. Taking shortcuts cheats yourself: you won't be well prepared, and you will probably race poorly and may injure yourself.

First, pick the race or races you want to run, and then train toward this goal. The runner who trains aimlessly or inconsistently won't reach his or her potential. You must gear your training for a specific event or distance.

Your training schedule consists of two important concepts: training *cycles* and training *phases*. The training cycle is the training for and completion of your racing season—the seasonal approach. The key steps you must take along the way to prepare for your race or racing season are called training phases.

This chapter details how to utilize cycles and phases when planning your training schedule. Within each racing chapter (5K, 10K, marathon) we give you simplified sample training schedules to follow. Also, chapter 8 details a simplified 10-week training program (a short-term cycle) that will help you build toward a key race and then peak for it with a once-per-week speed-training workout.

YOUR TRAINING CYCLE

This is your running season, when you may run a few races and must design a plan to do that. There are two opposite approaches to competitive training: the one-race season and the year-round season. We recommend an alternative: the long-term or short-term training cycle.

The one-race season covers a long time period, perhaps a year or more, during which every workout is aimed toward one big race. These runners run low-key during the year, make the sacrifice of less signifcant race results by not racing fully to potential, and reach a very high peak for that one big race. The runner aiming for the Olympic Games, for example, may use this approach. This training philosophy isn't recommended for the average runner, however, because it offers no rewards along the way.

At the other extreme is the runner who trains to race almost every week. Overracing is hard to avoid today, since there is a race within jogging distance of almost every runner each weekend. You must restrain your enthusiasm. Unfortunately, the media and race officials often glamorize runners who do ridiculous things like race 20 miles one day and 10 the next or compete the week after a marathon. This runner isn't tough—just stupid. Runners who enter a race week after week, "using it as a training run," are cheating—themselves. They always have an excuse for getting beaten or not running a good time, since they ran a race last week or are just getting ready for the one next week. Whatever your reason for wanting to race often on a year-round basis, we do not recommend it unless you take off at least one full month from serious racing and hard training twice a year.

It is possible to compromise between the extremes of the one-race season and the year-round season. One solution is to build to a high fitness level and race one to two times a month or more. With this system you race year-round, peaking for certain races. Without built-in rest periods or off-seasons, however, this runner sometimes is forced by injury or burnout to ease back. Many of America's leading road racers follow this system. If you do, use it cautiously and back off occasionally. Remember that runners usually run faster times and have fewer injuries by alternating easy training and racing periods with more intense training and racing periods.

We use two basic types of training cycles for our schedules: short-term (2 to 4 months) and long-term (4 to 6 months). Within that time period, we break down your training cycle into five-part phases. You do four basic things: prepare for battle; battle; lick your wounds and bask in the glory; and prepare again.

The length of your cycle depends on your goals and how long you have before your races. We feel that novice and basic competitors benefit most from following the short-term cycle so that they can enjoy the fun of competing sooner and gain racing experience. Marathon training, however, requires the long-term cycle for all levels of runners. Rushing for this event is risky.

The advanced and champion competitors with more racing experience benefit from both types of schedules. With the short-term cycle, these runners can sharpen and thus race sooner for shorter races: mile, 5K, 10K. With the long-term cycle, these runners can improve racing times and continue racing at a high level for a longer period of time (for a series of races at all distances), or go for a quality marathon effort. The longer cycle enables you to build a stronger, more solid base, which lets you train at higher intensities and faster speeds—which equal faster times.

These cycles can also be alternated. You might use the long-term cycle to prepare for a spring marathon and, after rebuilding, use the short-term cycle for a few shorter races in the fall and winter.

The Short-Term Cycle (2—4 Months)

This cycle is most beneficial if you are preparing for races of 10K or less. The short-term cycle allows you to race well several times a year, since you may use this cycle as many as three or four times in a racing year. Since the buildup period is less demanding, your rest between cycles is shorter, so you can return to racing sooner. It doesn't require as much time to prepare physically and mentally, which makes it more practical for the average runner. Its disadvantages include not enabling you to hold your peak for a long time (3 to 4 weeks, or two to three races) and not giving sufficient preparation for longer races, particularly the marathon.

The Long-Term Cycle (4—6 Months)

This schedule benefits three types of runners. First, this cycle helps those runners who want to run very fast in a single race of 10K to a half marathon. It also benefits runners—usually high school or college teams—facing a long racing season of 4 to 8 weeks, with several races leading into one or two championship races. Third, the cycle helps the long-distance runner, especially the marathoner, prepare adequately for maximum effort in one or two long races. The disadvantages include the long time period for training, having to plan far in advance (which may conflict with other aspects of your life), and the long buildup and long recovery, which may require sacrificing some of your favorite races during the early building period and the rebuilding phase. You can use this system only once or twice a year.

Bob Glover's Atalanta team basically uses this system. It allows them to race well from March through May, back off for the hot months of June, July, and August, and race well again for September and October. They then back off for the cold months of November through February.

Using the long-term schedule, you may choose to race during your off-season but shouldn't expect to, or attempt to, race as fast. During this time you cannot expect to run personal records (PRs), and you can expect to get beaten by runners you easily defeated when you were "sharp." Don't be concerned about this. Because some are usually backing off as others are peaking, the only fair way to judge who is the best runner is to line them all up for the key races when everyone is prepared for maximum effort. This is why we prefer the long-term cycle: we want our athletes to do their best when it counts the most.

YOUR TRAINING PHASES

Both the short-term and long-term training cycles include five phases.

Phase I: Endurance. Builds your aerobic foundation with endurance runs.

Phase II: Strengthening. Prepares for more detailed speed work with strength-training runs.

Phase III: Sharpening. Prepares you for quality races with interval and strength-training workouts. Also uses a few hard workouts and races close to your key race to reach your best "peak" performance.

Phase IV: Tapering. Cuts back on your mileage and speed work so you enter a race well rested.

Phase V: Rebuilding. Regenerates the body for a few weeks after the racing season.

We suggest blending the phases together in a progressive building toward quality racing followed by quality rest. You will also blend together the four types of runs we have discussed: endurance, strength, pace intervals, and fast intervals. Before blending is detailed, we need to examine each phase, and discuss its purpose and how to use it.

Phase I: Endurance (Foundation Training)

This is the longest phase, the most important and the easiest to do. The important thing here is putting in plenty of time on your feet and in your training heart-rate range. This initial phase—essential for *every* runner—conditions your cardiorespiratory system and your muscles to run long distances. Your goal is to put in the miles and build to your planned upper limit of mileage. Safely build your foundation. Your starting fitness level is at least 50 to 75 percent of the mileage you intend to build to during this phase.

Long-, medium-, and short-distance runs will improve your aerobic system and comprise all, or at least the majority, of the running done during this phase. Gradually increase the length of your long runs throughout this phase until you reach your goal distance.

During this phase you don't race (except for low-key fun races) or do hard speed work. Don't rush this phase. Cheating on endurance and jumping into early speed work results in running some fast early-season race times but causes you to falter in your races during the late season. The stronger your endurance base, the higher you can aim when sharpening for big races. You can look at the endurance work as filling up your reservoir. Whenever you do hard speed work or race, you withdraw from the reservoir. When you do endurance training and slow rhythm training, you are filling the reservoir. Take out too much from the reservoir, and you will run dry.

You should begin blending a small variety of easy speed runs (strength and pace-interval runs) into your endurance phase after you feel fit enough to handle this slightly more intense work. The 10K pace intervals, modified *fartlek* runs, and hill *fartlek* runs are the easiest types of training runs to include in your schedule, since they are the least intense and easiest to control. Including these speed runs in your endurance phase will help stimulate your body and mind so that you will stay motivated and excited about your training.

Build your base before adding harder speed work. The short-term training cycle requires 3 to 6 weeks in the endurance phase. The long-term training cycle requires 6 to 12 weeks in the endurance phase. The longer this phase, the greater your base of endurance.

Phase II: Strengthening

After building your endurance base, you expand your training program to include strength training, especially emphasizing running hills. The short-term training cycle will take 2 to 4 weeks in this strengthening phase. The long-term cycle will take 4 to 6 weeks. You maintain your mileage base and make the transition into speed work so that your body is prepared for the faster speed work ahead. You can strengthen your body to handle the added stress of running longer at a faster pace by including the various types of strength runs. You now do endurance runs, plus one or two strength runs per week. Some pace-interval runs are also considered strength runs, particularly those workouts done on uphills. These may be included for strength runs during this phase.

You should run one or two races in this phase, but will train through them rather than go for an all-out effort. If you race too soon or too often, however, you will overtrain and peak too early in the season, or never reach a peak. Instead of building strength, the excess racing will take away strength. You may also include a supplemental weight-training program to develop overall strength.

Phase III: Sharpening

The sharpening phase is designed to put it all together—endurance, strength, and speed—to produce stamina and faster race times. You sharpen for your racing season, perhaps peak for a key race at the end of your cycle. The inclusion of fast interval training runs will help you improve your speed. Pace intervals will teach you racing pace, which enables you to carry your speed for the entire length of the race. The short-term training cycle requires that the sharpening phase last 1 to 3 weeks, while the long-term phase covers 3 to 4 weeks.

This phase combines strength and interval runs 1 to 3 times a week, and high mileage (but less than in previous phases) with high quality speed work and racing. You use this phase either to keep racing fit for a long time, or to "sharpen" for a single race or a series of two or three races. This is the phase that some runners who compete at a high level year-round attempt to stay at. These runners can reach "minipeaks." They just lower the mileage for a week or two and increase the intensity of speed work, and are able to race at near-peak performance. This system, however, should only be used by the very fit, and even they should take periodic breaks to rebuild. We suggest you sharpen for a few races and then rebuild.

The sharpening phase adds faster speed work aimed at specific race distances or courses, a series of races designed to help you race yourself into top shape for one or two races at the end of your cycle. As you get closer to your race and increase the intensity of your workouts, don't increase mileage. You should decrease it by some 10 to 15 percent; quality is more important than quantity now. Also, as you approach your key race, go after some PRs in a series of two or three shorter races to add confidence and fitness. Space these races to allow for recovery. You should taper for these races more than you did in previous phases; don't train through these races, but go hard. After adequate recovery from each race, you resume your sharpening phase, except when you finish the last race of your season, when you break and move into your rebuilding phase.

Sharpening isn't used by the first-time racer and first-time marathoner. They don't need the stress of speed work on top of the new high-mileage levels. They move from the endurance-base phase directly into the tapering phase. Novice competitors would sharpen with mostly pace-interval workouts. Basic competitors add fast-interval workouts. The advanced and champion runners sharpen with all levels of speed work. The intensity of these runs varies with the race you are sharpening for. You would sharpen for the mile with intervals at half-mile pace, for the 10K and marathon with intervals of 5K and 10K pace. Guidelines for sharpening for each racing distance are included in the following chapters. The final sessions of your sharpening period should be very specific—on hills if a critical slope approaches you on the race course, on a track or trail if you're going to race there. Try to do some of your runs, if possible, over key points of the course. That helps you "callous" yourself to handle this section of the race when it hits you.

All experienced competitors should sharpen for key races. To us, the term "peaking" means being very "sharp"—achieving a very high level of fitness—at the end of your sharpening phase.

Phase IV: Tapering

This phase involves backing off your mileage and speed work so you are well rested and ready to race. Tapering always follows your sharpening phase (except for the novice racer and novice marathoner, who taper off the endurance phase). If you race during your buildup stage, you will probably not taper but just back off a little the day before a race: you maintain mileage to get the full benefit, and "train through" the race. To race well, you need to be well rested. You can't have it all: high mileage, two or three speed sessions, and a good race—all in one week.

How long you taper depends on the distance of the race, your fitness level, and what feels best for you. Generally, the longer the race and the less fit or experienced you are, the more you need to taper. If you taper too much, you may lose a little of your racer's edge. If you taper too little, you may not perform well from fatigue. With experience, you will learn what is best for you.

Guidelines and examples of tapering programs are included in the training schedules within each specific racing chapter. Here are some key points:

• Get plenty of sleep the last week, especially the second and third nights before the race, which are more important than the night before.

• Try to keep off your feet as much as possible in the last few days going into your race.

• Follow the guidelines in chapter 36 for eating during the last few days before going into the competition.

• Don't take too many days off. You'll feel sluggish. We prefer a day off two days before racing, not the day before.

Many runners feel uncomfortable about cutting back on their training since they worked so hard to get to this point. They're afraid that if they cut back, they are going to lose it all. Tapering is necessary to allow the body to rest and prepare for the big race ahead. If you don't taper, you usually will not respond well in racing situations. Remember—it takes 2 weeks for the training effect to occur, so any work you do in that time period before a race may help you mentally, but could hurt you physically.

Phase V: Rebuilding

Rebuilding consists of two parts. The rest period required after each race is termed recovery. The longer rest period required after your racing cycle is completed is termed rebuilding.

Recovery. The postrace recovery takes anywhere from a few days to several weeks. The less fit you are and the longer the race, the longer the recovery period. Before the race even starts, you should have begun your recovery program. By racing only when you are fit enough for the distance, pacing yourself wisely, and going into the race with flexible muscles and a proper diet, you will minimize the tearing down process that is part of racing. Fluids taken during the race will also aid your recovery. Older runners and those nursing injuries will require more time to recover. Runners racing in heat and over hills will too.

Here is a postrace recovery procedure:

• Keep moving when you finish the race. Don't lie down or sit down. After leaving the chute, drink fluids, put on warmups, walk. For races shorter than a half marathon, try a little jogging (1–4 miles).

• Apply ice—immediately after the race and over the next few days—to any sore or tender areas of your body.

• As soon as possible, take a long, hot bath. Do some gentle stretching. Drink plenty of fluids and eat carbohydrates after a marathon to replenish lost energy resources.

• Later in the day, go for an easy run, swim, bike ride, or walk to aid recovery. Take another bath and do more gentle stretching. Try dancing—believe it or not, it will make an incredible difference the next day. Ask any of the women who danced into the wee hours after the Avon International Marathon in Ottawa. If you just lie around and don't exercise after a race, your legs will feel like concrete. Force yourself to do the unnatural—exercise when your body doesn't want to.

• Start the next morning with another bath—your third! Do more gentle stretching and take a walk or easy run. You may be better off forgetting about running for a few days after a marathon. Stick to non-weight-bearing exercise such as swimming or biking. The object is to recover by forcing blood into the legs to remove waste products, so why abuse the body by compelling it to run on blistered feet and tired legs? After races shorter than a marathon, do some light jogging the next day.

• Get plenty of sleep for several days after your big race, and do lots of gentle stretching anywhere and anytime you can.

• Beware of a "false high" you may get a few days after a big race. Hold back on your training.

• Gradually increase your mileage back to your normal comfortable level. Recovery is your priority for 2 to 3 days after a 5K, up to a week after a 10K-half marathon, and for 2 weeks or more after the marathon. By the 3rd week after the marathon, you may be able to run your normal mileage. Don't rush it. You can usually return to normal mileage within 3 to 5 days after a 5K, 3 to 7 days after a 10K-half marathon, and 3 to 5 weeks after a marathon. Take it easy.

• Experienced runners find that *easy* speed work (pace intervals) a few days after a race of half-marathon or shorter distance helps them recover faster.

The recovery from races of half marathon or less comes, it seems, almost naturally. You listen to your body and ease back into the running and speed work. But recovery from a marathon or longer takes a long time and deserves as much planning as your premarathon schedule. Besides recovering from muscle soreness, you need time to restore your body chemistry to its normal balance. This takes a longer time than you can feel the need for, so you must force yourself to hold back. See chapter 25, "The Aftermarathon."

Race Spacing. How long should you wait before racing again? Here are flexible guidelines for determining when you can race again at any distance after completing a race:

RACE DISTANCE	MINIMUM WEEKS OF TRAINING BEFORE RACING AGAIN FOR NOVICE AND BASIC COMPETITORS	MINIMUM WEEKS OF TRAINING BEFORE RACING AGAIN FOR ADVANCED AND CHAMPION COMPETITORS
5K	1–2 weeks	1 week
10K	2–3 weeks	1–2 weeks
Half marathon	3–4 weeks	2–3 weeks
Marathon	6–8 weeks	4–6 weeks

All runners should wait at least 3 months, preferably 6–12 months, before running their next marathon.

Rebuilding. After your racing season or peak race, you need a break in your training schedule. This marks the end of your seasonal cycle. You need time off to relax and to allow your mind and body to recover from the intense training and racing season. Sometimes after running your big race, you get "the blues" syndrome, when you don't feel like running any more because of the effort to train and race. Your long-sought-after

THE SHORT-TERM (2–4 MONTH) TRAINING CYCLE— FIVE-PHASE TRAINING SCHEDULE (FOR LESS THAN MARATHON DISTANCE/SHORT SEASON)

PHASE	EXPERIENCED COMPETITOR (WEEKS)	NOVICE RACER (WEEKS)
I. Endurance	3–6	6–12
II. Strengthening	2–4	x
III. Sharpening	1–3	x
IV. Tapering	1–2	1
V. Rebuilding	3–4	3–4

Note: The 2-to-4-month (8–16-week) cycle goes from the beginning of phase I to the completion of your hard race or races. Then you enter the rebuilding phase (V), after which you may wish to start over again with phase I or just maintain a good level of fitness and not race again for a while.

THE LONG-TERM (4–6 MONTH) TRAINING CYCLE— FIVE-PHASE TRAINING SCHEDULE (LONG RACING SEASON OR MARATHON BUILDUP)

PHASE	EXPERIENCED COMPETITOR (WEEKS)	NOVICE MARATHONER (WEEKS)
I. Endurance	6–12	16–24
II. Strengthening	4–6	x
III. Sharpening	3–4	x
IV. Tapering	1–3	2
V. Rebuilding	4–8	4–8

Note: The 4-to-6-month (16–24-week) cycle goes from the beginning of phase I to the completion of your long racing season or marathon. Then you enter the rebuilding phase (V), after which you may wish to start over again with phase I or just maintain a good level of fitness and not race again for a while.

goal has been achieved. The rebuilding phase then becomes a necessary vehicle to get you going again.

Rebuilding from the hard training discipline may include some easy running or one of the aerobic alternatives discussed in chapter 7. This stage should consist of easy runs, and should lead into phase I (endurance) when your training cycle begins again. Your mileage base should be cut back, but not by more than 25 to 50 percent of your maximum mileage base. If you cut by more, you will need to take much longer to build your base for the next cycle.

For the short-term cycle, we suggest that your rebuilding phase take *at least* 3 to 4 weeks. For the long-term cycle, we believe *at least* 4 to 8 weeks are needed. *Our basic rule: All runners should take at least two breaks from hard training and racing each year; each break should last a month or more.*

The following charts summarize how the five phases fit into the short-term and long-term training cycles. First-time racers and marathoners skip phases II and III since they need to concentrate on building their endurance base.

BLENDING THE PHASES OF YOUR TRAINING SCHEDULE

You can choose to incorporate the five phases into your training schedule in two ways: the Single-Phase Buildup Method and the Blending Method.

The Single-Phase Buildup Method

This is the system favored by some elite runners. We do not recommend it for the average runner. With this method you concentrate on finishing one complete phase at a time before "stepping up" to the next phase. For example, you would begin your training cycle by doing as much foundation training—the endurance phase—as suggested in our charts or longer. During this phase you do only endurance runs. Then you proceed with the strengthening phase. Here you would concentrate on doing only strength-training runs—mostly hills—alternated with endurance runs for recovery. After completing this phase, you would move into the sharpening phase, which includes doing several interval workouts. From there, you taper for the race. We do not recommend this method for the average runner, since suddenly changing from one phase to another promotes injury. For the elite runner, however, it does allow for a thorough buildup for a key race and is normally done over a long-term training cycle.

The Blending Method

This is our preferred method. You begin with endurance training, introducing easy speed runs (an occasional strength run or pace interval) to allow your body to adapt gradually to harder workouts. You emphasize the endurance runs as the major part of training during this phase, as you continue to increase your mileage base to a peak level.

When you become more fit, stronger, and slightly faster, you blend in more difficult strength and interval runs as you move into the strengthening phase. During this phase, your weekly mileage base will level off and you begin to concentrate on making improvements in your strength and speed by increasing the intensity and quantity of speed work.

The blending process continues during the strengthening phase as you begin to introduce faster speed workouts. Initially you may increase the speed of your *fartlek* runs so that your "bursts" or "pickups" become faster than race pace, and then include one or two fast interval workouts to further blend in speed before moving on to the sharpening phase.

During the sharpening phase, you blend in all types of speed runs done at high intensity in a final effort to "peak" for your key race. Still, most of your runs are endurance runs, used for recovery and maintaining your aerobic fitness level, although you will want to cut back on the weekly mileage levels slightly.

Blending lets you adapt to progressive stress. It allows your mind and body gradually to grow accustomed to more intense training. Blending allows you to continue building your endurance, strength, and speed throughout your training cycle. This system adds variety to your program, since you aren't running the same type of workout every week. Finally, blending makes you better prepared to "gear up" for races because you can modify your training program faster.

Using these guidelines, plan your short- or long-term schedule, and stick with it. The next chapter will teach you how to write that schedule.

TRAINING TO PEAK

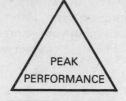

PEAK
PERFORMANCE

TAPERING PHASE
Concentrate on:
 —Lower mileage
 —Rest
 —Final sharpening
  speed work
 —Mental preparation
  for race

SHARPENING PHASE:
 Concentrate on: —Fast speed work
  —Speed work specific
   to key race
  —A few quality races
   before key race

STRENGTHENING PHASE:
 Concentrate on: —Maintaining mileage base
  —Long runs
  —Hill training
  —Faster speed training
  —Controlled racing efforts

ENDURANCE BASE:
 Concentrate on: —Aerobic endurance runs
  —Long runs
  —Introduction of easy speed training

13. HOW TO WRITE YOUR OWN TRAINING SCHEDULE

We can't list a detailed training schedule for each and every runner who reads this book—and we shouldn't. You have to plan and write your own schedule, because only you know which goals you want to pursue, what your training needs are, and how much training you can tolerate. We have included model training programs for each category of runner at the end of each specific racing distance chapter. These models were developed from the guidelines below. Your schedule must remain flexible enough, however, so that when warning signs of fatigue or injury appear, you can back off. That would be the action a personal coach would take. You can't just follow blindly either a training schedule you put together months ago or the model programs we have developed for you.

By now you should have acquired a sound understanding of how to use the various types of runs and why they are used with the five phases that make up your training cycle. Now it is your turn to do the writing. Whether you decide to use a short-term or a long-term training cycle for a 5K race or a marathon, you can begin putting together your own training schedule following a six-step approach.

THE SIX STEPS TO WRITING YOUR OWN TRAINING SCHEDULE

Step One: Determine Your Fitness Category

In order to develop the best training program to fit your needs, you must first decide which of the four fitness categories you will use as your flexible guide for detemining how much mileage you will run and the specific speed work you will do. Refer to chapter 1.

Step Two: Select Your Races and Time Goals

Choose the particular race or set of races for which you wish to train. Your choice should be far enough in the future to fit into your short-term or long-term training cycle. If you decide to train for the marathon, be sure that this race is 4 to 6 months away so that you will have time to follow the long-term cycle. Consider doing one or two early-season races to ease you back into racing and to measure your fitness. Choose two or three races to help you sharpen for the final, key race of your training cycle. These races should be spaced far enough apart to allow time for recovery and to increase the intensity of your speed work. Your selection of the "big race" should be made carefully. Some may choose a national, regional, or local championship. Others may favor a "celebrity race" that attracts big-name runners. Many choose the fastest course around and usually in the cooler months of the year so that they can aim for a very fast time. The race should be important enough to you that you will want to "sharpen" for this particular event.

Mark the date of your selected race or set of races on your training calendar and plan your training schedule so that you gradually build toward these dates. Using our Three-Goal System (chapter 26) set race time goals to help you establish your training goals. *Note:* Although you aim for your best time at the end of the cycle, factors such as bad weather, injury, or hills may interfere. You may run your best race earlier, during your sharpening phase, if conditions are most favorable at this time. The model schedules at the end of each racing distance chapter include examples of race distances and which week to run them. These are only guidelines. Pick the date and distance of your buildup race according to your needs and the racing distances available.

Step Three: Determine Your Training Cycle and Phases

Using the previous chapter as a guide, determine the length of the training cycle—short-term or long-term—that you will follow and how much time you will need to spend with each training phase: endurance, strengthening, sharpening, and tapering.

Step Four: Determine Your Weekly Mileage and Long-Run Goals

Using the guidelines in chapter 6, determine your weekly mileage and long-run goals for your entire cycle. Make sure you can tolerate this level of mileage. If it is a big increase, you may need a longer period of time to build up to this new level. Take that into consideration when selecting the length and date of your races. Gradually increase the weekly mileage over the entire endurance phase until you reach your desired level. This mileage base is maintained throughout the strength phase and then is cut back when more intense sharpening work is included in the training schedule. Cut back your mileage and speed work for a few days going into and after your buildup races. The mileage is cut back further as you taper the last 1 to 2 weeks before your key race. The length of your long runs also gradually increases as you become more fit.

Step Five: Plan Your Individual Workouts

Use the following Guide for Scheduling Your Training Runs to decide when to schedule the various types of training runs. When scheduling far in advance, you must be flexible and realize that it is impossible to run the exact workout and mileage each day of the week as you had planned. But by writing down a plan, you will be motivated to stay reasonably close to your predetermined schedule. Analyze the schedule periodically and make modifications as necessary for such factors as injury, illness, and bad weather. It is important that you have faith in your carefully planned schedule and stick to it as closely as possible. Estimate the specific mileage you wish to run each day, balancing long runs, races, speed work, and easy days. Determine the general type of speed work you need to accomplish each week. Use the interval workout guides within each racing chapter to establish the quantity and intensity of these runs. Determine the exact number of intervals and specific speed of each run a few days before your workout so that you can make adjustments according to how your training has been progressing.

Step Six: Plan Your Rebuilding Phase

Rebuilding is recovering from the entire cycle. Although this 3-to-8-week period following your key race may seem to be anticlimactic, it is essential. Plan this phase in advance, and don't cut it short by rushing back into hard training.

We do not include examples of rebuilding in our model training schedules in the following chapters, since the training should consist entirely of short and medium endurance runs. Following is an example of a 4-week rebuilding phase:

The purpose of the rebuilding phase is to rest and regenerate after a hard training cycle and gradually build up to a conservative level (about 50–75 percent of your peak base) of mileage. The example below shows a runner rebuilding to a level of 30–35 miles a week—about 60–70 percent of his or her peak mileage of 50 miles per week. There should be no long runs, speed workouts, or races included in the schedule during this phase. At the end of this rebuilding phase this runner can continue to maintain basic fitness by running 30–40 miles a week of endurance runs only, or may choose to start a new training cycle by building the mileage back up and adding some easy speed work and long runs during the endurance phase.

GUIDE FOR SCHEDULING YOUR TRAINING RUNS: WORKOUTS TO CHOOSE FROM IN WRITING YOUR INDIVIDUAL TRAINING SCHEDULE

	WHEN USED	WHY USED	CATEGORIES OF RUNNERS
ENDURANCE RUNS:	Year-round, 4–7 times per week	Build aerobic endurance, foundation for speed work and racing	All
1. Short	Year-round, 1–3 times per week	Easy days, recovering, and tapering	All
2. Medium	Year-round, 3–5 times per week	Major source of foundation mileage	All
3. Long	Mainly in endurance and strength phases. Especially important when marathon training. Approximately 1–3 times per month	Build aerobic endurance and mental toughness	All
STRENGTH RUNS:	In preparation for racing season—used in all phases, but emphasized in strengthening phase; 1–2 times per week	Build muscular strength and speed	All
4. Modified *fartlek*	Used in all phases; 1–3 times per month	Introduction to speed work, for a moderate strength run	Novice and basic
5. Hill *fartlek*	Late in endurance phase, throughout strength phase. Used for training for all distances, especially when training for a hilly race; about every other week	Build general strength, confidence over hills	Experienced basic, all advanced and champion
6. Advanced *fartlek*	Used during all phases and for all distances. Particularly important for cross-country training; about once a week	Improve ability to switch gears, running form, confidence on hills	All advanced and champion

GUIDE FOR SCHEDULING YOUR TRAINING RUNS: (Continued)

	WHEN USED	WHY USED	CATEGORIES OF RUNNERS
7. Surges	Used during all phases and for all distances; twice a month or less	Improve ability to switch gears, running form, confidence to break away from opponent	All advanced and champion
8. Fast continuous runs	Strength and sharpening phases; especially for 10K–marathon training, twice a month or less	Build ability to hold a fast pace, used as pace work for marathon training	Basic, advanced, and champion
9. Anaerobic threshold runs	Strength and sharpening phases; especially for marathon, 2–4 times per month	Improve anaerobic threshold, confidence in holding a good pace	Experienced basic, all advanced and champion
10. Tempo runs	Late in strength phase and early in sharpening phase. Mainly used for 1 mile–10K; 1 or 2 times during entire training season	Simulate racing conditions	Experienced advanced and champion
PACE-INTERVAL RUNS:			
11. 440s	Late endurance, strengthening, sharpening and tapering phases; 1–2 times per week	Develop racing pace, build strength and speed	All
12. 880s	Late endurance, strengthening, sharpening, and tapering phases; for all distances, especially 5K–10K; several times per season	Develop sense of race pace, improve racing form	All
	Same as 440s; particularly good as last hard workout 10–12 days prior to a key 5K–4-mile race	Same as 440s	All

GUIDE FOR SCHEDULING YOUR TRAINING RUNS:
(Continued)

	WHEN USED	WHY USED	CATEGORIES OF RUNNERS
13. Miles	Late endurance, strengthening, sharpening, and tapering phases; for all distances, especially 10K–marathon; particularly good as last hard workout 10–12 days prior to a key 10K–marathon race; several times per season	Simulate racing conditions, build confidence, teach ability to hold pace when tired	All
14. Short hills	Strengthening, sharpening phases; for all distances, especially when building for races on hills; several times per season	Improve ability to hold race pace and form on hills, build strength, speed, and confidence	All
15. Long hills	Strengthening, early sharpening phases; used for specific training for hilly courses, especially 10K–marathon	Simulate race conditions over hills, build confidence	All
FAST-INTERVAL RUNS	Late strength, sharpening, and tapering phases; when peaking for key races; several times per season for 10K and under, few times for race training above 10K	Improve speed, race pace, and form; transition into power workouts	Experienced basic, all advanced and champion
16. 220s	Primarily used in sharpening phase; mostly for mile–5K; 1 or 2 times per season	Introduction to fast-interval work	Experienced basic, all advanced and champion

GUIDE FOR SCHEDULING YOUR TRAINING RUNS:
(Continued)

	WHEN USED	WHY USED	CATEGORIES OF RUNNERS
17. 440s	Late strength, sharpening, and tapering phases; all distances, especially mile–10K; few times per season	Make race pace seem more comfortable, improve speed	Experienced basic, all advanced and champion
18. 880s	Same as 440s	Same as 440s	Experienced basic, all advanced and champion
19. Miles	Late strength, sharpening phases; mostly for 10K–marathon; 1 or 2 times per season	Build strength, teach ability to hold pace and form under stress	All advanced and champion
20. Short hills	Sharpening phase; mostly for mile–10K; 1 or 2 times per season	Build strength and speed; improve form for fast paces	Experienced advanced and champion
21. Long hills	Late strength phase; mostly for 10K–marathon; no more than once per season	Build confidence	Experienced advanced and champion
FORM WORK (PICKUPS)			
22. 100s–220s	Strengthening or sharpening phase; 2–4 times per month	Concentrate on racing form; peppy workout prior to a race	Basic, advanced, and champion

WEEK #	MON.	TUES.	WED.	THURS.	FRI.	SAT.	SUN.	TOTAL
1	Short endurance	Off	Short endurance	Short endurance	Short endurance	Off	Short endurance	20 miles
2	Off	Short endurance	Medium endurance	Short endurance	Medium endurance	Short endurance	Medium endurance	30
3	Off	Short endurance	Medium endurance	Short endurance	Medium endurance	Short endurance	Medium endurance	30
4	Off	Short endurance	Medium endurance	Short endurance	Medium endurance	Medium endurance	Medium endurance	35

WRITE YOUR SCHEDULE

Use the blank training schedule on page 181 to write your individual training program. (Step numbers are keyed on the schedule.)

1. *Write in your fitness category* where indicated.

2. *Write in the races* you wish to run building to a key race (in this example, races are indicated for weeks 5, 9, and 12). List race time goals and record actual race times on the Goal Setting/Race Selection Sheet on page 182.

3. *Write in the number of weeks of your training cycle.* This schedule is for 12 weeks—a short-term cycle. For a long-term cycle you may use an 18-week schedule. *Write in how many weeks you will spend in each phase.* In this example: endurance—4 weeks; strengthening—4 weeks; sharpening—3 weeks; tapering—1 week.

4. *Write in your goals for weekly mileage* from the beginning of your cycle through your last race. *Write in your goals for long runs* and when you plan to run them. In this example, we have included four long runs—weeks 2, 4, 6, and 8.

5. *Write in the specific type of run* (consult the Guide for Scheduling Training Runs) *and your daily mileage for the entire cycle.* You have listed your races and your long runs; the next step is to write in your speed workouts. Then balance the hard days—races, long runs, and speed workouts—by writing in the easy days—short and medium endurance runs and off days. In this example, we have demonstrated how to write in each of the three major types of speed runs—strength, pace interval, and fast interval—as well as an endurance run. When recording a speed run, list both the distance of the speed run and the total mileage for the day, which includes your warm-up and cool-down. (Example for week 9: 10 × 440 is 2½ miles of running, and with warm-up and cool-down, the total mileage for the workout is 6 miles.) Fill in all of the speed days first, then the endurance days to complete your schedule.

6. *Write your rebuilding schedule.*

Fitness Category: ①

SAMPLE TRAINING SCHEDULE

PHASE/WEEK	MONDAY	TUESDAY	WEDNESDAY	THURSDAY	FRIDAY	SATURDAY	SUNDAY	TOTAL MILEAGE
③								④ →
1 *Endurance*			⑤ Short Endurance 4					30 ④
2							④ Long Endurance 10	34 ④
3								36 ④
4							④ Long Endurance 10	38 ④
5 *Strengthening*			⑤ Strength Rolling Hills-4 6				② Race	38 ④
6							④ Long Endurance 12	42 ④
7								40 ④
8								40 ④
9 *Sharpening*		⑤ Medium Rhythm 6 10x440					④ Long Endurance 10	40 ④
10							② Race	37 ④
11		⑤ Power 5 4x440						35 ④
12 *Tapering*							② Final Race	30 ④ 20 + Race

Note: For this sample schedule weeks 13–16 would be the rebuilding phase.

GOAL SETTING/RACE SELECTION FOR A RACING SEASON

PREDICTION

DISTANCE	ACCEPTABLE GOAL	CHALLENGING GOAL	ULTIMATE GOAL
5 K	23:00	22:30	22:00
10 K	47:00	46:00	45:00

ACTUAL

RACE DISTANCE	DATE	ACTUAL TIME
5 K	9/18	22:40
10 K	10/16	46:05
10 K	11/16	45:30

Part V
SPECIFIC TRAINING FOR RACING

14. YOUR FIRST RACE _____

Why race?

• It gives your running life a goal, a focus. You circle the race date on your running calendar and train for that day. This helps you get "over the hump" that some runners face who are having trouble moving through dull periods of their training.

• You make friends. Races give you the opportunity to meet other runners. It is often a large social gathering, a party in running shorts. You may meet potential running partners, or even runners who become close friends. You can exchange training tips and experiences. Also, training for a race gives you a great topic of conversation with other runners.

• You can test yourself. Racing gives you a method of measuring your progress toward some specific goal. Finishing a race is a great achievement: you have set a goal and accomplished it; you may also get satisfaction from doing something physical, especially if you have not been successful in athletics in the past. At this early racing level, your competition is entirely against the "old you." Racing lets you discover the new you.

• You aim toward running a marathon. Your first race—which is *not* the marathon—is a stepping-stone along the path toward running the "ultimate challenge." You must start with shorter races.

Some runners don't want to race. They dislike the competition. They run for the pleasure of it. Nina Kuscsik, the first women's division winner of the Boston Marathon, doesn't think of racing as competition but as running with other people "to show off what you can do."

The era of the "fun run" and the "fun racer" is upon us. Now more runners enter races to achieve higher personal goals and to meet friends and see some new countryside. In tougher competitive races, there are a few top-level runners, and a mass of back-of-the-packers to keep even the slowest runner company. The first and foremost goal for all of them is the finish line.

SELECTING YOUR FIRST RACE

Pick a race. The distance should be long enough to challenge you but short enough to be completed without pain. We recommend a distance between 2 miles and 10K (6.2 miles). Choose a local race; traveling to an event adds to your excitement and stress. Pick either a low-key "fun run" or a big mass-participation event filled with fellow runners of every level of training. Keep away from races with killer hills, and don't race on a hot day. In other words, minimize your obstacles. Women may prefer women-only races.

TRAINING FOR YOUR FIRST RACE

If you are now running for 20–30 minutes at a time, 3 to 5 times a week or more, you are ready to train for your first race. Do not concern yourself yet with speed work or the various phases of training used by more experienced runners. You should concentrate on building up your endurance base to the point where you can run and finish a race comfortably, tapering off as you approach that race date.

You need a minimum amount of mileage and long runs to be able to race and reach the finish line with reasonable comfort. Our basic guidelines are the following. Your weekly mileage should be at least two or three times the distance of the race, and you should be running this mileage 6 to 8 weeks prior to the race itself. You should also complete three longer runs, covering at least two-thirds of the race distance, prior to the week before the race. Never try to cram mileage in during the last few weeks before a race. Build gradually. For example, if you plan to run a 4-mile race, you should be running at least 8 to 12 miles a week, with long runs of at least 3 or 4 miles. For a 10K (6.2 miles), you should be running 12 to 18 miles a week, with minimum long runs in the 4-to-6-mile range.

Remember the hard-easy system. Alternate your three types of conversational endurance runs—long, short, medium. Run up and down a few hills if the race route includes them. A few days before your first race, take it easy. No amount of additional training now will help you.

Use the following charts as models for your first race. We prefer that you race 5K–4 miles before your first 10K, but many runners race first at the 10K distance, since it is a more popular and frequently run race.

8-WEEK TRAINING PROGRAM FOR YOUR FIRST RACE (5K–4 MILES)

WEEK	MON.	TUES.	WED.	THURS.	FRI.	SAT.	SUN.	TOTAL MILEAGE
1	Off	2	2	2	Off	2	Off	8
2	Off	2	2	2	Off	2	2	10
3	Off	2	2	2	Off	2	2	10
4	Off	2	3	2	Off	2	3	12
5	Off	2	3	2	Off	2	3	12
6	Off	2	3	2	Off	2	3	12
7	Off	2	3	2	Off	2	3	12
8	Off	2	2	2	Off	2	Race (5K–4 miles)	8 + race

8-WEEK TRAINING PROGRAM FOR YOUR
FIRST RACE (10K)

WEEK	MON.	TUES.	WED.	THURS.	FRI.	SAT.	SUN.	TOTAL MILEAGE
1	Off	2	3	3	Off	2	4	14
2	Off	2	3	3	Off	2	4	14
3	Off	3	3	3	Off	2	5	16
4	Off	3	4	3	Off	3	5	18
5	Off	3	4	4	Off	3	4	18
6	Off	3	4	3	Off	3	5	18
7	Off	3	4	3	Off	2	4	16
8	Off	4	2	2	Off	2	Race (10K)	10 + race

TIPS FOR YOUR FIRST RACE

Goal

Finish. Experience your first race, don't race it. Your first race should be slightly longer or slightly faster than your usual jog. *Run* your first race. Later you can *race*.

Shoes

Wear your faithful, well-cushioned, well-broken-in training shoes. You don't need a fancy new pair just for the race.

Organize Yourself

Get enough sleep the night before your first race. Pack, and check, all your needed "goodies." Arrive early and warm up properly. This may include a little light jogging along the first 100–200 yards of the race course.

Don't Overdress or Underdress

Beginner racers usually wear too much clothing. You should start feeling slightly underdressed. Your body will heat up during the race, and even clothing that was comfortable for training runs may now feel too heavy. If the weather is cool, try dressing in layers. You can remove a hat, gloves, even a sweat-shirt. Tuck them into your shorts or hand them to a friend along the road. Don't discard clothing unless the day is truly warm; a drop in temperature, a sudden wind, rain, or snow, and you'll want it all back. Take layers off progressively until you find the right level. In the heat, cover your body with light, loose, reflective clothing.

Eating

On race day, don't eat or drink anything out of the ordinary. This is not the time to experiment. (Save that for your training days.) Do not eat within several hours of the race. Carbohydrate loading is only for experienced racers and long racing distances.

Put on Your Number

Put your number on long before the race starts, to get the feel of it. Some are on stiff paper that may jab your chest or stomach. Adjust it now, not during the race. Remember, you are only doing a training run with a number on. Relax.

Fear Not

Afraid of finishing last? That's unlikely if you are well prepared and following these guidelines. Some runners will start too fast and struggle in last, or attempt to run the distance without proper mileage "in the bank" beforehand.

Gain confidence by planning your race strategy in advance; break the course into small sections, and know where key landmarks and hills are located. Run from mile marker to mile marker. Be confident in knowing you have prepared well and properly. Everyone is nervous before a race, even elite runners.

Drink

Pour the fluids into yourself and over yourself. In warm weather, drink fluids even for a 2-mile run. You should be used to drinking from your training runs.

Walk

Nowhere on the race application does it say you can't walk. Take walk breaks, especially on those tough hills, but keep moving. Never stop, unless you are hurt, and run the whole way if you can. But if your pulse soars, or you can't "catch" your breath and run at conversation pace, or your legs tire, take brisk walk breaks. Cheat: since you should drink water at the stations and pour it on yourself, walk with your cup of water as you slowly drink it. Everyone will think you are only walking so you can drink! Avoid walking across the finish line; take your walk break earlier, and jog across smiling.

Run with a Partner

Run your first race with a friend, so you can help each other along. Make a promise not to race each other but to finish together, no matter what. If an experienced runner volunteers to run with you, make him or her promise to go at your pace.

Warm-Up and Cool-Down

Stretch thoroughly both before and after your race, just as you do for your workouts. Don't sit down right away after finishing. Walk around and then stretch.

Race Day

Here you are. The morning of your first race may find your heart pounding. Prerace nerves strike the fast and the slow. You may take your leisure in the bathroom, eat toast, drink orange juice (if that's your style), and read the paper. Carefully pack your bag: Vaseline, an extra pair of shoelaces, shoes, shorts, shirt, jock or bra, an extra shirt to wear after the race, tape, liniment, warm-ups, postrace first-aid equipment, toilet paper, a hat in case it's cold, a hat in case it's sunny, gloves in case it's cold, lock, and towel.

Arrive at least an hour before race time so you can check in, warm up, and of course chat with other runners. You should always preregister by mail so you can get right into line and pick up your number and perhaps a free T-shirt. If you don't preregister, you often must stand in line longer, fill out forms at the last minute, pay a higher entry fee, and get yelled at by tired officials. Warning: Not all races accept entries on race day. Better check in advance.

Proceed to the dressing area. Since you arrived early, you get a locker and have ample time to dress and apply your Vaseline, liniment, etc. Pin your number to the lower third of the *front* of your shirt, so the officials can see it as you finish. Fold or cut it so that the extra space at the edges is not in your way. Pin the number on each edge to make sure it is secure. I always bring extra pins in case they don't have enough. Also, memorize your number in case it gets destroyed by rain or splashing water.

Spend the next half hour or more stretching, walking, and talking, and preparing your mind and body for the race. Tense runners arrive at the last minute to find you stretched and relaxed. Periodically jog for a few yards, and then stretch and relax. Half an hour before race time, take one last trip to the john, and be thankful you brought toilet paper. They've probably already run out. Proceed to the drinking fountain, and jog to the starting line.

Ten minutes before the start, peel off your sweats and place them in your easily recognized tagged bag. Carefully place the bag with the others. Very subtly jog behind the bushes for one last visit. Tie your shoes in a double knot. Line up toward the back of the pack to ensure against getting trampled by the speedsters, or getting "pushed" into a fast early pace. Standing there among the crowd of runners, you may suddenly feel all alone, insecure, intimidated.

Lining Up

Stand toward the back so you won't get caught in the opening sprint.

You're Off!

The crack of the gun propels you along with the flowing mass of runners down the road. "Why did I let Bob Glover start me

on this madness?" you scream. But you're off. You fight adrenaline and hold back. Begin slowly, and if you feel good after a
while, pick up your pace toward the end. Another approach is
to start slowly and let as many runners get ahead of you as
possible. (If you start too fast, they'll pass you later anyway.)
Then, as you feel good toward the end of the race, pick up
your pace and pass some of them; you're the tortoise passing
the hares who went out too fast. This gives you confidence and
the excitement of passing runner after runner over the last
mile or two of the race.

Maintain a comfortable, slightly slow pace. Find a group of
runners going at your pace, and join them. All will pull each
other very easily for the first mile. You aren't out there to beat
people. Your goal is to finish. Don't race against anyone who
passes you or whom you pass—you'll lose your sense of an even
pace. Chat with the runners around you, wave to your fans,
laugh, have fun. This is a fun race for you, not a serious race
as it is for those up ahead. Try to run the race as slowly as you
can—that way you'll be sure to set a personal record (PR) in
your next race. Then you hit a tough hill, or just run out of
gas and feel the urge to quit. If you're running with a friend,
encourage each other. Nina Kuscsik says, "You have a choice.
You can quit or keep going. Just the knowledge that you can
always quit sometime is often enough to keep you going to the
finish line."

Don't be a hot dog, finishing the race with a face-twisting,
arm-whirling, mad-hatter sprint. Finish in good form. Be in
control.

Now comes the fun: you can brag to everyone in sight about
how great you felt in your first race. Secretly, you may start
plotting strategy for improving your time in the next race. After
you cool down by walking and stretching, you can cheer the
top runners as they receive their trophies, and know that you
too are a winner.

Analyze the Results

Now that you have won *your* race, think it over. What went
well? What problems did you have, and why? What worked

and what didn't in terms of equipment, starting pace, water, finish, and so forth? Do you need more work on hills? Did you drink enough fluids? Use the experience as background to help you prepare and run your next race. Reevaluate your training program, and select a new racing goal. Make it either farther or faster, but not both—not yet. Don't race too soon or too often.

You may choose to improve your time for that distance race or to increase your race distance. You may want to move from 4 miles to the popular 10K (6.2 miles), and later to 10 miles, the half marathon, and then the marathon. Take these races, as you take your training, step by step. However, you don't have to keep racing longer and longer distances, and if you aren't properly prepared for them, you shouldn't.

Recover

After the race, take it easy the next few days with less and slower running. Even though you will not be racing hard, you will still be under a lot of stress from the excitement and exertion of your first race. Recover carefully.

Don't be in a hurry to make the transition from beginner runner to a more serious racer. The "too much too soon" syndrome will leave you injured or frustrated or both. It can take from 3 to 5 years to progress safely from jogger to veteran marathon runner. The following schedule is a guideline to help you progress from your first race to faster racing times. You are now on the mileage and racing treadmill. It, and you, keep going. You constantly set new goals, and you surprise yourself when you see how far you've come. In this instance, do look back. You'll be pleased. Remember you can level off any time. You can back down a step or more. You can progress at a slower pace. From our experience, we feel that this progression will take you safely to whatever level you seek.

THE RACER'S PROGRESSION—FROM BEGINNER RUNNER TO SERIOUS COMPETITOR

PHASE I: STARTING OUT

1. Beginner runner—build to 30 minutes.   3 mo.
2. Intermediate runner—build to and maintain
   15–20 miles a week.   3–6 mo.
3. Beginner racer—build to *run* first race
   (5K–10K)—an experience.   3 mo.
                                                                  9 mo.–1 yr.

PHASE II: RACING FEVER/MARATHON FEVER

4. Novice competitor—more exposure to races at
   distances up to half marathon—learn to *race* and
   improve times.   6 mo.–1 yr.
5. Novice marathoner—build up to *run* a
   marathon—an experience.   6 mo.
                                                                  1–1½ yr.

PHASE III: GETTING BETTER

6. Basic competitor—train to improve race times
   5K–half marathon.   6 mo.–1 yr.
7. Veteran marathoner—train to *race* a marathon.   6 mo.
                                                                  1–1½ yr.

PHASE IV: GETTING SERIOUS

8. Basic competitor, advanced competitor, and champion competitor—train
   to improve times for 5K–half marathon in order to have the speed to
   improve times for the longer distances. The cycle now repeats itself if
   you choose to race both long and short. Improvements in speed and
   short race times will help improve longer race times. Improvements in
   endurance and stamina from marathon training will also help you to improve your times for shorter races.

15. 10K TRAINING AND RACING _____

The most popular and frequently run distance race in America is not the marathon. The marathon attracts more publicity, but each year more races are held at the 6.2-mile distance, and these events attract more runners—from first-time racers to Olympians—than any other distance.

The 10K is the perfect distance for most runners. The distance serves as a good endurance goal for beginner runners to aim toward, and the weekly mileage level for the average recreational runner/racer—15–30 miles—is sufficient to complete the race distance comfortably. More advanced runners are also challenged by its combined requirement of speed and endurance. Unlike the marathon, it can be raced frequently after short recovery periods, and it doesn't require as much of a time commitment as the marathon.

The 10K also enjoys the status of being the longest standard racing distance on the track for the Olympic Games; thus the average runner can emulate the elite step-for-step for a full 10K distance, and often can line up in road races over that distance with the superstars of the sport. It is also competed at the college track level.

Many runners specialize at this distance. They may lack the raw speed to excel at the mile or 5K, or lack endurance and the ability to handle the high mileage needed for quality marathons. Some runners are psychologically better suited for the 10K than the marathon: they can maintain concentration and confidence for 10K but are too impatient to hold back and run an even marathon pace. This is our recommended upper limit for racing among teenage runners; heavier runners often can't excel (or run safely) beyond this distance.

The 10K is the most common yardstick of performance in our sport. Since it is raced frequently and can be run several times a year, it is a common meeting ground for track runners from one end of the racing spectrum and marathon runners from the other. It is the ideal distance for comparing the ability of runners at all skill levels. If you want to know how good a runner is—whether you are a race director attempting to compare the elite or you are sizing up the ability of some jogging partners—the most common question is: "What is your 10K time?" In fact, we categorize our runners from our New York Road Runners Club speed-training classes according to their 10K race times.

Be careful, however, not to race this distance in excess or you will be burdened with constantly comparing times. You will not be able to improve week after week, since courses vary in difficulty and weather conditions may prove a problem. Additionally, you can't get mentally up for the same distance too often. Take a break from the stress of being measured and run a variety of shorter and longer races, coming back to the 10K again when you feel ready to do it justice. Races of 5K–5 miles help you improve your speed for the 10K; races of 15K–half marathon help you improve your strength for the 10K. The 10K is used by those training for 5K as a strength workout. It is used for "speed workouts" by those sharpening for a fast marathon effort. In fact, we believe that the secret to running faster marathons is to train like a 10K runner and improve times over this distance before concentrating on your next marathon effort. An improvement of 1 minute for 10K increases your potential improvement for the marathon by 5 minutes.

Most runners should train to race the 10K and then add specific training modifications when gearing up for shorter or longer events. The 10K combines speed with endurance; that is, the speed of the 5K with the endurance of the marathon.

The average runner can safely enjoy the full range of road racing if he or she concentrates most of the time on the 10K. For this reason, our 10K training program appears first here, and is the core of our training philosophy. Most road racers have enough mileage to compete well at the 10K distance, but need to concentrate on sharpening with speed training and buildup races in order to achieve ultimate success.

TRAINING FOR 5 MILES, 8K, 15K, 10 MILES, HALF MARATHON

With minor adjustments, the 10K-trained runner can compete successfully from 5 miles to the half marathon. For shorter distances, consult the 5K training chapter for guidelines; for longer distances, consult the marathon training chapter for guidelines. Training and racing for 5 miles–8K is almost exactly the same as for the 10K; you would race at approximately 5 seconds per mile faster. For 15K–half marathon distances, increase your mileage by approximately 10 miles per week (see charts on pages 72–73) and the length of your long runs by approximately 5 miles (see charts on pages 70–71). You would race at approximately 20–30 seconds slower per mile than for 10K.

THE 10K TRAINING SCHEDULE

This 10K program is designed for all four fitness categories and uses the six-step approach outlined in chapter 13.

Step One: Determine Your Fitness Category

Look up your appropriate category in chapter 1 based on your 10K time.

Step Two: Select Your Races and Time Goals

Choose which 10K race you wish to peak for and then start a 12-week training program as described in this chapter (for the simplified 10-week program, see chapter 9). Choose a few buildup races, 2 to 3 weeks apart, to help you get ready for your big effort. You may choose some longer races of 15K–half marathon in the first few weeks of your program to build strength and some shorter races of 5K–5 miles as you get closer to your key race to work on speed. You may choose to run a 10K 2 to 3 weeks prior to your key race in order to become more familiar with the racing distance. Also, you may be blessed with great weather and feel good and run a great race, thus serving as insurance in case the weather is bad for your key race.

Choose time barriers to break for your key 10K efforts. Within this chapter we discuss guidelines for breaking the following popular 10K barriers: 60:00, 56:00 (9:00-minute mile), 50:00 (8:00-minute mile), 43:30 (7:00-minute mile), 40:00 (the most popular goal among fairly serious runners), 37:00 (6:00-minute mile), 34:00 (5:30-minute mile). Use the guidelines in chapter 26 to set challenging, realistic goals.

Step Three: Determine Your Training Cycle and the Length of Your Phases

Most competitors find the 12-week, short-term cycle to be sufficient for the 10K. Determine the length of your training phases by deciding on which areas you need to concentrate the most. If you have a solid endurance and strength background but have done little speed training, you may need to spend more time on the sharpening phase. If you have not spent enough time on endurance and strength, you may need to concentrate on developing a solid base of endurance and strength, and spend less time sharpening with speed work. To be successful at the 10K distance, you will need to develop a well-balanced training program incorporating endurance, strength, and speed.

Here is a guide to selecting your phases for 10K training:

DESCRIPTION	NOVICE	BASIC	ADVANCED	CHAMPION
Length of buildup	12 weeks	12	12	12
Endurance phase	5 weeks	4	4	4
Strengthening phase	4 weeks	4	4	4
Sharpening phase	2 weeks	3	3	3
Tapering phase	1 week	1	1	1
Rebuilding phase	4–6 weeks	3–6	3–4	3–4
Number of races in cycle	3–4	3–4	3–5	3–5

Step Four: Determine Your Weekly Mileage and Long-Run Goals

Since you will be adding speed workouts to your schedule, your body must be strong enough to handle this extra work load. Training for the 10K requires that you have a good mileage base. Long runs, often neglected by the 10K runner, need to be included during the endurance and strength phases. In most cases, don't include long runs during the sharpening and tapering phase of your schedule. They make you feel flat and slow and take away energy that will be needed to handle the more intense speed work.

Follow the *flexible* weekly mileage goals listed in the chart on page xxx to adjust for the amount of *time* spent training and your age and running experience. The mileage ranges reflect an *approximately* equal effort for all levels and all ages of runners. The recommended mileage figures should be averaged for at least 6–8 weeks, preferably 8–10 weeks, prior to tapering for the 10K. See the guidelines for training mileage in chapter 6. The training pace for the daily aerobic endurance runs should be at your base pace: 1½–2 minutes slower than 10K pace (see the guidelines in chapter 5).

Step Five: Plan Your Individual Workouts (See model schedules for each fitness category at the end of this chapter)

Endurance Phase (4–5 weeks): This phase should follow a preendurance phase that will move you up to within 10–15 miles, at least, of your peak mileage goal by the end of the endurance phase. You should do two or three long runs during this phase, gradually easing up near the longest-distance goal you have chosen from the chart on page 200. Your mileage also should have reached the level recommended on this chart by the end of this phase. During the endurance phase you should gradually ease into speed workouts. Novice competitors would start with modified *fartlek* and 10K pace intervals. Basic competitors start with 10K pace intervals and hill *fartlek*. Advanced and champion competitors start with 10K pace intervals and a variety of strength-training runs. Run one low-key race

WEEKLY MILEAGE GOALS FOR 10K TRAINING

	AGE 18–40	AGE 40–50	AGE 50–60	AGE 60+	MILEAGE OF LONG RUNS	LONG RUNS PER MONTH
NOVICE: Men and women	20–30	20–30	20–30	20–30	6–8	1–2
BASIC: Men and women	30–40	30–40	30–40	25–35	8–12	2–3
ADVANCED: Men and women	40–60	40–60	40–50	30–40	10–18	2–4
CHAMPION: Men and women	50–75	50–70	45–60	40–50	15–20	2–4

Train at 1½ to 2 minutes slower than 10K pace (see Base Pace Chart in Appendices).

during this phase to ease into racing. Novice and basic competitors should look for a short race of 5K–5 miles for experience. Advanced and champion competitors should aim for a longer race of 15K–half marathon to work on strength. These races should be run briskly, but not all-out. Save the total effort races for later when you are in peak shape.

The important areas to emphasize during the endurance phase: build a solid base of mileage and long runs, ease into speed training, ease into racing.

Strengthening Phase (4 weeks): Maintain your peak mileage and long-run base during this phase, which is a transition between the endurance buildup phase and the sharpening phase. Run two or three long runs per month. Novice and basic competitors run one speed workout per week, consisting of *fartlek* and 10K pace intervals, and introducing short- and long-hill workouts to build leg strength—especially if you'll be racing on a hilly course. Advanced and champion competitors should run two speed sessions per week, consisting of a variety of advanced strength-training runs, short and long hills, and both 10K and 5K pace intervals—including mile intervals. Run one race during this phase. Novice and basic competitors should run a 10K to get used to racing that distance. Advanced and champion competitors can choose from a variety of options: 5K–5 miles for speed, 15K–half marathon for strength, or 10K to familiarize themselves with racing that distance. Don't expect to run as fast for 10K at this point as you will later after sharpening and tapering.

The important areas to emphasize during the strengthening phase: maintain a solid base of mileage and long runs, gradually intensify speed workouts and emphasize hill workouts, race at a harder effort but not all-out.

Sharpening Phase (2–3 weeks): Novice competitors should maintain their mileage base throughout this phase, but reduce it by 10 percent if it is higher than 35 miles per week. Basic competitors should maintain their mileage base throughout this phase but reduce it by 10 percent if it is higher than 40 miles per week. Advanced and champion competitors will need to reduce mileage by 10 percent or more in order to safely introduce more intense speed training.

At all levels, reduce the length of the long runs to the lower end of the recommended range or less, and only run them every other or every third week. Novice and basic competitors would run one speed workout per week, two for advanced and champion competitors. Novice competitors should concentrate on 5K–10K pace intervals, including a solid 880 or 1-mile workout 8–10 days prior to the final 10K to build confidence in your pacing. Basic competitors will emphasize 5K–10K pace intervals, and can introduce some 440-yard fast intervals to sharpen leg speed. Mile intervals or 880s at 5K–10K race pace 8–10 days prior to the peak race will build confidence.

During this phase, the basic competitor may wish to add a second speed workout per week—most likely a controlled *fartlek* run. Advanced and champion competitors will run two speed workouts per week—one near race pace (5K–10K pace intervals) and one at a faster pace (fast intervals or power intervals). Try to be specific with a few key workouts: run hills if you will race on hills, practice a "finish line drill" to cover the last 440–880 yards of your finishing kick. A final speed session of 880s or mile intervals at a faster but controlled pace about 8–10 days prior to the race will greatly increase confidence for advanced and champion competitors. *Note:* Do not run a hard speed session 8–10 days before your key race if you choose to race 2 weeks before your last key race.

All levels of runners would benefit by running a hard-effort race of 5K–10K distance 2–3 weeks prior to the final key race. Go for a PR: this is your final dress rehearsal for your all-out key race effort. You may very well run your best race on this day, so taper a bit for it. If you have two races that you want to do well in only a few weeks apart, plan your schedule so that they fall at the end of your 12-week training program.

The important areas to emphasize during the sharpening phase: maintain a base of mileage, but lower it to allow for the safer introduction of faster speed training and a final hard tune-up race.

Tapering Phase (1 week): In order to achieve a peak performance, you must go into competition physically rested and psychologically ready. Run no longer than short- and medium-distance endurance runs for 7–10 days before your key race. Novice and basic competitors should cut back on their mileage for 3 to 7 days before the race; advanced and champion competitors, for 2 to 5 days prior. The last hard workout should have been 8–10 days before the race; a final "tune-up" workout of *fartlek* or controlled intervals (220–880) should be run 4–5 days before the race. Cut back on the number of intervals run and make sure to allow for extra rest following each repetition: the goal of this workout is merely to "feel" fresh and fast.

If you race during your buildup stage, you will probably not taper but just back off a little the day before a race; you maintain mileage to get the full benefit, and "train through" the race. To race well, however, you need to taper thoroughly. A full day off 2 days prior to the race is recommended for most runners. Run 2–4 miles at a relaxed pace, perhaps over part of the race course, the day prior to the race to help you control prerace anxiety. Use the final week to sharpen your mental preparation (see chapter 27). Be sure to get plenty of sleep throughout the final week before your key race, stay off your feet as much as you can, and minimize the amount of stress in your life. As you taper your mileage, increase the time spent doing relaxation exercises and perhaps practice race visualization. See the final week in the sample 10K programs at the end of this chapter for a model tapering program for your category.

The important areas to emphasize during the tapering phase: reduce mileage, eliminate long runs, do a final brisk speed session, mentally prepare for a peak effort, rest the body.

Step Six: Plan Your Rebuilding Phase

Take a break! You have trained hard for 3 months and peaked for a big effort. You may be able to run another good race in 2–3 weeks, but don't push your luck. Your body and mind need to regenerate. For approximately 1 month (more if you do not wish to race again for a while), cut your mileage back 10 percent or more (but not more than 25 to 50 percent of your maximum mileage base), and minimize or eliminate long runs. Also eliminate any hard speed training (a light, untimed workout may be used once a week or less) and any racing. See page 340 for guidelines for immediate recovery from a race plus overall rebuilding. See page 343 for a sample rebuilding schedule. You may wish to take a break from running and utilize aerobic alternative training (see chapter 7).

10K RACE STRATEGY

Chapter 28 includes general guidelines for race day strategy. In order to race well at 10K, you need to be much more aggressive from start to finish than at the marathon, but not as aggressive as for the 5K. Novice competitors should line up toward the back of the pack and start at the same pace they wish to average for the entire 10K. Flow with the crowd, using the runners around you to keep you moving toward the finish line. You will be slightly uncomfortable, but not terribly so, since at your level you are still mostly racing on endurance and won't push yourself into oxygen debt. Many basic competitors, and all advanced and champion competitors, should start at 5K pace (10 seconds faster than you hope to average) and attempt to hold that pace for 1–2 miles before settling into a steady pace that will be near your goal pace (faster if you feel good). Think about all the 5K–10K pace work you did as you hold back, and think how easy the pace feels after running fast intervals. Between 2 and 6 miles, maintain concentration (see page 396) and work from race segment to race segment (see page 386). You should be looking for your peers—runners who run near your pace whom you can use to pull you in or to try to beat and thus move up another notch. Unless you start much too fast, or much too slowly, you will not pass or be passed by many runners after the 5K mark.

Thus, it is important to attempt to get into the proper position relative to fellow competitors early in the race. In the first 5K, concentrate on pace, not runners trying to pass you or vice versa. For the second half of the race, try to move up from runner to runner to help you maintain a good pace, or "hitch a ride" when a competitor goes by you. In the late stages, work the hills by reflecting on the hill workouts you accomplished; and think about all the long runs you did to enable you to be strong over the last few miles. Also, reflect on how hard the last few runs of your interval workouts felt—but you made it through them and you will make it to the finish line too by being tough. Those pushing for a fast time, rather than merely aiming to finish in modest discomfort, will need to fight off oxygen debt and leg fatigue by relaxing and really concentrating on good running form. Since you've practiced your finishing kick (see page 449), and have physically and mentally rehearsed running over the last half mile, you should be able to push into the finish line at a strong pace. Run all the way through the finish, but don't forget to stop your watch as you cross the line so you can quickly verify your time.

BREAKING BARRIERS

Breaking barriers can be very rewarding, whether you are aiming to conquer the 1-hour mark or the ½-hour mark. Following are some common barriers and some tips on how to win your race against the clock.

The Sub-34-Minute 10K

Follow the sample schedule for the champion competitor at the end of this chapter. You should run 50–75 miles per week at 7:00–7:30 minutes per mile, and do long runs of 15–20 miles twice a month prior to sharpening. You should run two speed workouts per week, on the average, for 8–10 weeks prior to the key race effort. You should run intervals at these approximate paces: miles—5:15–5:30; 880s—2:30–2:40; 440s—75–80 seconds. At this level of competition, the mind must be willing to push the body through serious discomfort, and confidence in your ability to perform is critical, since the margin or error at this fast pace is slim. Momentary lapses of concentration and confidence can cost you your sub-34:00 performance.

In order to run a sub-34:00, you need to average under 5:29 per mile.

To break 34:00, you should be able to run the following times (or at least be close):

5K	sub-16:40
5 mile–8K	sub-27:00
15K	sub-53:00
10 mile	sub-57:00
Half marathon	sub-1:15

The Sub-6-Minute-Mile 10K (37:11)

Follow the sample schedule for the advanced competitor at the end of this chapter. You should run 50–60 miles per week at 7:30–8:00 minutes per mile, and do long runs of 12–18 miles twice a month prior to sharpening. You should run two speed workouts per week, on the average, for 8–10 weeks prior to the key race effort. You should run intervals at these approximate paces: miles—5:40–6:00; 880s—2:45–2:55; 440s—82–85 seconds. Since you will need to run much faster in the race than you do in your daily runs, it is very important that you practice running faster in speed sessions and in shorter races.

In order to run a sub-6-minute pace, you need to run under 37:11.

To break a 6-minute pace, you should be able to run the following times (or at least be close):

5K	sub-18:15
5 mile–8K	sub-29:30
15K	sub-57:00
10 mile	sub-62:00
Half marathon	sub-1:23

The Sub-40-Minute 10K

Follow the sample schedule for the basic or advanced competitor at the end of this chapter. You should run 40–50 miles per week at 8:00–8:30 minutes per mile, and do long runs of 10–15 miles twice a month prior to sharpening. You should run one or two speed workouts per week for 8–10 weeks prior to the key race effort. You should run intervals at these approximate paces: mile—6:20–6:30; 880s—3:00–3:10; 440s—85–90 seconds. You need enough hard work to enable you to burst through the 40-minute barrier, but must be careful not to overtrain and lose it all. You must hold yourself back in training and over the first few miles of the race, and then run courageously to the finish line. Breaking 40:00, like breaking 3:00 for the marathon, is the most important barrier to smash for the average competitive runner because it symbolizes a high level of achievement. It is thought by many to be the borderline separating the middle of the pack from the top runners.

In order to run a sub-40-minute 10K, you need to average under 6:27 per mile.

To break 40:00, you should be able to run the following times (or at least be close):

5K	sub-19:30
5 mile–8K	sub-32:00
15K	sub-62:00
10 mile	sub-67:00
Half marathon	sub-1:30

The Sub-7-Minute-Mile 10K (43:30)

Follow the sample schedule for the basic competitor at the end of this chapter. You should run 30–40 miles per week at 8:30–9:00 minutes per mile, and do long runs of 10–12 miles twice a month prior to sharpening. You should run one or two speed workouts per week for 8–10 weeks prior to the key race effort. You should run your intervals at these approximate paces: miles—6:50–7:00; 880s—3:15–3:30; 440s—1:30–1:40. You will race at a pace faster than your training pace and thus must be sure to include intervals at race pace to give you experience at pushing at that speed.

In order to run a sub-7-minute pace for 10K, you must run under 43:30.

To break the 7-minute-mile barrier, you should be able to run the following times (or at least be close):

5K	sub-21:30
5 mile–8K	sub-34:30
15K	sub-68:00
10 mile	sub-73:00
Half marathon	sub-1:39

The Sub-45-Minute 10K

Follow the sample schedule for the basic competitor at the end of this chapter. You should run 30–40 miles per week at 8:30–9:30 minutes per mile, and do long runs of 8–12 miles twice a month prior to sharpening. You should run one speed workout per week for 8–10 weeks prior to the key race effort. The sample 10-week speed program in chapter 9 and the "perfect 30-mile week" on page 75 were modeled on the 45-minute 10K runner. You would run your intervals at the following approximate paces: miles—7:00–7:15; 880s—3:25–3:35; 440s—1:35–1:45. You are the average competitor and will improve if you include moderate mileage and moderate speed training. Trying to do too much too soon is the problem most often faced by this runner.

In order to run a sub-45:00, you need to average under 7:15 per mile.

To break 45:00, you should be able to run the following times (or at least be close):

5K	sub-22:00
5 mile—8K	sub-36:00
15K	sub-70:00
10 mile	sub-76:00
Half marathon	sub-1:43

The Sub-50-Minute 10K (Sub-8-Minute Mile)

Follow the sample schedule for the basic competitor at the end of this chapter. You should run 30–40 miles per week at 9:15–10:00 minutes per mile, and do long runs of 8–12 miles twice a month prior to tapering. You should run one speed workout per week at a controlled pace. You should run intervals at the following approximate paces: miles—7:50–8:00; 880s—3:50–4:00; 440s—1:45–2:00. At this level of running, you may not be racing at a much faster pace than your training runs. Endurance is the key to your success, especially long runs of over the 10K distance. You run speed sessions near race pace to help you get used to pushing yourself a little. Start the race holding back and concentrate on good form all the way to the finish.

In order to run a sub-50:00, you need to average under 8:00 per mile.

To break 50:00, you should be able to run the following times (or at least be close):

5K	sub-24:30
5 mile–8K	sub-40:30
15K	sub-78:00
10 mile	sub-84:00
Half marathon	sub-1:55

The Sub-9-Minute-Mile 10K (Sub-56:00)

Follow the sample schedule for the novice competitor at the end of this chapter. You should run 20–40 miles per week at 9:30–11:00 minutes per mile, and do long runs of 6–10 miles two to four times per month. A moderate speed workout once a week for 4–8 weeks will help you improve your form and confidence. They should be run at or near race pace to help you get a good feel for this pace. You should run your intervals at these approximate paces: miles—8:50–9:00; 880s—4:15–4:30; 440s—2:00–2:25. The most important ingredient at this level of running is the long run of 6+ miles. This runner may even be able to run daily runs of 2–3 miles at sub-9-minute pace but can't hold that pace for 10K unless he or she has an adequate base of mileage and long runs. Those with a proper mileage base who train at slower than race pace need to do a few shorter races of 5K–5 miles to learn how to push a little harder.

In order to run a sub-9-minute pace, you need to run under 56:00.

To break the 9:00 barrier you should be able to run the following times (or at least be close):

5K	sub-28:00
5 mile–8K	sub-44:30
15K	sub-1:27
10 mile	sub-1:34
Half marathon	sub-2:07

Note: At this level, you may not be ready to run the times listed beyond the 10K distance.

The Sub-60-Minute 10K (Sub-10:00 Pace)

Follow the sample schedule for the novice competitor at the end of this chapter. You should run 15–30 miles per week at 9:30–12:00 minutes per mile, and do long runs of 5–8 miles two to four times per month. If you are the type of runner who is running slower than 10:00 pace for daily runs, concentrate on once-per-week modified *fartlek* or 5K–10K pace intervals for 880s (4:50–5:00) and miles (9:45–10:00) to help you learn to run a little faster. If you are the type of runner just moving up to 15+ mileage per week and are new to racing, particularly concentrate on getting in long runs of 5–8 miles at a steady pace (taking walk breaks if necessary). For the novice racer, the 1-hour barrier is the first significant achievement as a runner and unofficially separates runners from joggers.

In order to run a sub-60:00, you need to average under 10:00 per mile.

To break 60:00, you should be able to run the following times (or at least be close):

5K	sub-29:30
5 mile	sub-47:00
15K	sub-1:33
10 mile	sub-1:40
Half marathon	sub-2:15

Note: At this level, you may not be ready to run the times listed beyond the 10K distance.

12-WEEK 10K BUILDUP SCHEDULES

The model training schedules on pages 212–215 should be used to help you write your own program. The exact mileage you will run, distance and dates of your buildup races, and the days of your different types of runs will vary with your individual needs, age, sex, and other factors that influence your running. Use these models as a guide to create a specific training program that can help you reach your racing goals. Understand the concepts behind these schedules, don't just follow them blindly. We have not included an example of the rebuilding phase. Follow the model in chapter 13 to write your rebuilding program.

NOVICE COMPETITOR'S 12-WEEK 10K BUILDUP SCHEDULE

PHASE	WEEK	MONDAY	TUESDAY	WEDNESDAY	THURSDAY	FRIDAY	SATURDAY	SUNDAY	TOTAL MILEAGE
ENDURANCE	1	Off (—)	Medium endurance (4)	Medium endurance (4)	Medium endurance (4)	Off (—)	Short endurance (—)	Medium endurance (4)	18
ENDURANCE	2	Off (—)	Medium endurance (4)	Medium endurance (5)	Medium endurance (4)	Off (—)	Short endurance (—)	Medium endurance (5)	20
ENDURANCE	3	Off (—)	Strength Modified *fartlek* (3)	Short endurance (4)	Medium endurance (4)	Off (—)	Short endurance (—)	Long endurance (6)	20
ENDURANCE	4	Off (—)	10K pace intervals 6 × 440 (4)	Short endurance (3)	Medium endurance (5)	Short endurance (2)	Short endurance (2)	Medium endurance (5)	22
ENDURANCE	5	Short endurance (2)	10K pace intervals 4 × 880 (4)	Medium endurance (4)	Medium endurance (4)	Short endurance (3)	Off (—)	Race 5K (5)	22
STRENGTHENING	6	Short endurance (2)	Off (—)	Medium endurance (5)	Strength Modified *fartlek* (5) 3	Short endurance (3)	Short endurance (3)	Long endurance (8)	25
STRENGTHENING	7	Off (—)	Medium endurance (5)	Medium endurance (4)	10K pace intervals 5 × Short hills (4)	Short endurance (2)	Medium endurance (4)	Medium endurance (6)	25
STRENGTHENING	8	Short endurance (3)	10K pace intervals 6 × 880 (4)	Short endurance (4)	Medium endurance (5)	Short endurance (3)	Off (—)	Race 10K (7)	25
STRENGTHENING	9	Short endurance (2)	Off (—)	Medium endurance (4)	Short endurance (3)	Strength Modified *fartlek* (5) 3	Short endurance (5)	Long endurance (8)	25
SHARPENING	10	Off (—)	Strength Modified *fartlek* (3)	Short endurance (3)	Medium endurance (5)	5K pace intervals 5 × Short hills (4)	Short endurance (3)	Medium endurance (5)	25
SHARPENING	11	Off (—)	5K pace intervals 4 × 880 (5)	Short endurance (3)	Medium endurance (4)	Short endurance (3)	Medium endurance (4)	Medium endurance (4)	23
TAPERING	12	Off (—)	Strength Modified *fartlek* (3)	Short endurance (5)	Medium endurance (4)	Short endurance (3)	Off (—)	Race 10K (—)	15 + race

212

BASIC COMPETITOR'S 12-WEEK 10K BUILDUP SCHEDULE

PHASE	WEEK	MONDAY	TUESDAY	WEDNESDAY	THURSDAY	FRIDAY	SATURDAY	SUNDAY	TOTAL MILEAGE
ENDURANCE	1	— Off	5 Medium endurance	4 Short endurance	6 Medium endurance	— Off	4 Short endurance	6 Medium endurance	25
	2	— Off	5 Medium endurance	4 Short endurance	— Off	5 Medium endurance	4 Short endurance	10 Long endurance	28
	3	— Off	6 10K pace intervals 5 × 880	4 Short endurance	8 Medium endurance	6 Medium endurance	4 Short endurance	8 Medium endurance	30
	4	— Off	6 10K pace intervals 3 × mile	5 Short endurance	6 Medium endurance	6 Medium endurance	5 Short endurance	10 Long endurance	32
	5	— Off	6 10K pace intervals 6 × Short hills	6 Medium endurance	8 Medium endurance	6 Medium endurance	— Off	8 Race 5K	34
STRENGTHENING	6	— Off	6 Medium endurance	6 Medium endurance	6 Strength Hill fartlek	— Off	5 Medium endurance	12 Long endurance	35
	7	— Off	8 Medium endurance	5 Short endurance	6 10K pace intervals 6 × 880	5 Short endurance	4 Strength Modified fartlek	8 Medium endurance	35
	8	— Off	6 10K pace intervals 4 × mile	6 Short endurance	8 Medium endurance	6 Strength Modified fartlek	4 Short endurance	10 Long endurance	36
SHARPENING	9	5 Short endurance	5 5K pace intervals 6 × Short hills	4 Short endurance	6 Medium endurance	5 Medium endurance	— Off	8 Race 10K	35
	10	4 Short endurance	— Off	6 Medium endurance	6 Medium endurance	5 Short endurance	6 5K pace intervals 6 × 440	8 Medium endurance	35
	11	— Off	4 Strength Modified fartlek	6 Short endurance	5 5K pace intervals 5 × 880	5 Medium endurance	4 Short endurance	6 Medium endurance	30
TAPERING	12	2 Short endurance	6 Strength Modified fartlek	4 Short endurance	4 Short endurance	4 Short endurance	— Off	— Race 10K	20 + race

ADVANCED COMPETITOR'S 12-WEEK 10K BUILDUP SCHEDULE

PHASE	WEEK	MONDAY	TUESDAY	WEDNESDAY	THURSDAY	FRIDAY	SATURDAY	SUNDAY	TOTAL MILEAGE
ENDURANCE	1	Off —	10K pace intervals 6 × 880 (6)	Medium endurance (6)	Medium endurance (6)	Medium endurance (6)	Short endurance (4)	Long endurance (12)	40
	2	Off —	10K pace intervals 8 × 880 (6)	Medium endurance (6)	Medium endurance (6)	Medium endurance (8)	Short endurance (4)	Medium endurance (10)	42
	3	Off —	10K pace intervals 3 × 1 mile (6)	Medium endurance (6)	Strength Hill *fartlek* (8) [5]	Medium endurance (6)	Medium endurance (6)	Race 15K (12)	44
	4	Off —	Medium endurance (5)	Medium endurance (8)	Medium endurance (8)	Strength Advanced *fartlek* (8) [6]	Short endurance (4)	Long endurance (15)	48
STRENGTHENING	5	Off —	10K pace intervals 8 × Short hills (8)	Medium endurance (8)	Medium endurance (8)	10K pace intervals 10 × 880 (8)	Medium endurance (6)	Long endurance (12)	50
	6	Off —	10K pace intervals 4 × 1 mile (8)	Medium endurance (10)	Strength Hill *fartlek* (10) [6]	Medium endurance (8)	Medium endurance (6)	Race 5K (14)	52
	7	Off —	Medium endurance (8)	5K pace intervals 8 × 440 (8)	Medium endurance (10)	Strength Advanced *fartlek* (8)	Medium endurance (10)	Long endurance (12)	52
	8	Off —	5K pace intervals 6 × 880 (6)	Medium endurance (8)	Medium endurance (8)	5K pace intervals 8 × Short hills (8)	Medium endurance (7)	Long endurance (15)	52
SHARPENING	9	Off —	5K pace intervals 3 × 1 mile (8)	Medium endurance (8)	Medium endurance (8)	Medium endurance (6)	Short endurance (4)	Race 10K (10)	44
	10	Off —	Medium endurance (8)	Medium endurance (8)	Medium endurance (8)	Medium endurance (6)	10K pace intervals 6 × 380 (6)	Medium endurance (10)	46
	11	Off —	Fast intervals 6 × 440 (6)	Short endurance (6)	Medium endurance (6)	10K pace intervals 5 × 1 mile (8)	Short endurance (6)	Medium endurance (10)	46
TAPERING	12	Medium endurance (6)	Fast intervals 6 × 440 (6)	Medium endurance (8)	Short endurance (6)	Short endurance (4)	Off	Race 10K (—)	30 + race

CHAMPION COMPETITOR'S 12-WEEK 10K BUILDUP SCHEDULE

PHASE	WEEK	MONDAY	TUESDAY	WEDNESDAY	THURSDAY	FRIDAY	SATURDAY	SUNDAY	TOTAL MILEAGE
ENDURANCE	1	8 Medium endurance	8 10K pace intervals 8 × 880	6 Short endurance	10 Medium endurance	8 Medium endurance	5 Short endurance	15 Long endurance	60
ENDURANCE	2	8 Medium endurance	8 10K pace intervals 10 × 880	8 Medium endurance	10 Medium endurance	8 Medium endurance	6 Short endurance	18 Long endurance	65
ENDURANCE	3	10 Medium endurance	10 10K pace intervals 4 × 1 mile	10 Medium endurance	10 Strength Hill fartlek	10 Medium endurance	4 Short endurance	16 Race 15K	68
ENDURANCE	4	6 Medium endurance	10 Medium endurance	10 Medium endurance	8 Strength Advanced fartlek	10 Medium endurance	6 Short endurance	20 Long endurance	70
STRENGTHENING	5	10 Medium endurance	10 5K pace intervals	11 Medium endurance	10 Strength Advanced fartlek 8	10 Medium endurance	9 Strength Hill fartlek 7	14 Medium endurance	72
STRENGTHENING	6	10 Medium endurance	10 10K pace intervals 10 × Short hills	14 Medium endurance	10 5K pace intervals 6 × 880	10 Medium endurance	6 Short endurance	12 Race 5K	72
STRENGTHENING	7	10 Medium endurance	10 Medium endurance	10 5K pace intervals 10 × 440	8 Medium endurance	10 10K pace intervals 5 × 1 mile	6 Short endurance	20 Long endurance	72
STRENGTHENING	8	10 Medium endurance	10 Medium endurance	10 5K pace intervals 4 × 1 mile	8 Medium endurance	12 Medium endurance	6 5K pace intervals 10 × Short hills	14 Medium endurance	72
SHARPENING	9	14 Medium endurance	6 Fast intervals 6 × 880	12 Medium endurance	8 Medium endurance	8 Medium endurance	6 Short endurance	10 Race 10K	64
SHARPENING	10	10 Medium endurance	8 Medium endurance	10 Medium endurance	12 Medium endurance	8 Medium endurance	8 Fast intervals 8 × 440	8 Medium endurance	64
SHARPENING	11	12 Medium endurance	6 Fast intervals 8 × Short hills	10 Medium endurance	8 Medium endurance	10 5K pace intervals 4 × 1 mile	8 Medium endurance	10 Medium endurance	64
TAPERING	12	6 Medium endurance	6 Fast intervals 6 × 440	6 Medium endurance	8 Medium endurance	6 Short endurance	4 Short endurance	— Race 10K	36 + race

16. 5K TRAINING AND RACING

The 5K (3.1-mile) distance is becoming increasingly popular. It is just right for the beginner racer and low-mileage recreational runner. The 5K is our preferred distance for your first few races. It is also the ideal distance during the long, hot summer. Take a break from the pressure of trying to run a fast 10K despite the heat, and move down to a distance that is more reasonable on hot days.

If you can run for a half hour, you can easily complete a 5K. But don't think this race distance is a softy. It is raced regularly on the track at high school and college meets, and is a highly contested track distance at the Olympic Games. Milers often race this distance as a transition to road racing; 10K and marathon runners use it as a break from longer races (especially in the summer) and to improve speed. In fact, a 30-second improvement at the 5K distance will result in the ability to improve by a full minute at the 10K distance. Since the 5K requires minimal recovery time, it can be raced frequently: two or three times per month.

Some runners, especially those gifted with lots of speed and those with limited time to train at higher mileage, specialize at the 5K distance. The distance requires a blend of speed and endurance. The racing distance is often taken lightly, and the result is extreme discomfort as oxygen debt causes you to feel as if rigor mortis has set in. A hard 5K will test your ability to hold a fast pace over distance. The event requires good basic speed with a solid background of endurance training.

We feel that all runners, from novice racers to die-hard marathoners, should race this distance more often. It serves as an excellent stepping-stone for novice racers, and the event allows the 10K runner to experience an intensity that will help him or her become a faster, tougher racer at all distances.

To be successful at the 5K, you can't just jump in and do well without specific training. You race at 10 seconds per mile faster than 10K pace and thus must train your body to handle the quicker speed. Almost all runners have enough mileage to run well at this distance, but will need to concentrate on more quality speed training. In fact, you may do better by lowering your mileage while 5K training so that your legs are fresher for speed training.

THE 5K TRAINING SCHEDULE

This 5K program is designed for all four fitness categories and uses the six-step approach outlined in chapter 13.

Step One: Determine Your Fitness Category

Look up your appropriate category in chapter 1 based on your 5K time.

Step Two: Select Your Races and Time Goals

Choose which 5K race you wish to peak for and then start a 12-week training program as described in this chapter. Choose a few buildup races, 2 to 3 weeks apart, to help you get ready for your big effort. You may choose some longer races of 4 miles—10K to build strength and some races of 1–2 miles to work on speed. You should choose to run at least one other 5K a few weeks prior to your big race in order to become more familiar with the racing distance. Also, you may be blessed with great weather and feel good and run a great race, and this will serve as insurance in case of bad weather on the day of your key race.

Choose time barriers to break for your key 5K efforts. Within this chapter we discuss guidelines for breaking the following popular 5K barriers: 30:00 (10:00 mile), 28:00 (9:00 mile), 25:00 (8:00 mile), 22:00 (7:00 mile), 20:00 (6:30 mile), 18:30 (6:00 mile), and 17:00 (5:30 mile).

Step Three: Determine Your Training Cycle and the Length of Your Phases

Most 5K racing goals can be achieved by using a 12-week, short-term training cycle. As long as you have a good foundation of endurance training, you will not need to add too much additional time to get yourself in shape for the 5K. The key is to have the endurance and strength to support the faster speed training of the sharpening phase, which is necessary for success at this distance.

Here is a guide to selecting the length of your training phases:

DESCRIPTION	NOVICE	BASIC	ADVANCED	CHAMPION
Length of buildup	12 weeks	12	12	12
Endurance phase	5	4	3	3
Strengthening phase	4	4	4	4
Sharpening phase	2	3	4	4
Tapering phase	1	1	1	1
Rebuilding phase	3–4	3–4	3–4	3–4
Number of races in cycle	3–4	3–4	3–5	3–5

Step Four: Determine Your Weekly Mileage and Long-Run Goals

The mileage base for the 5K falls somewhere between that for a miler and that for the 10K runner. If you are primarily a 10K runner and are using the 5K for developing more speed and strength, you may want to lower your mileage somewhat (but no more than 10 percent off your weekly 10K rate). If you are a miler using the 5K to develop greater endurance and strength, you may want to increase your mileage slightly (about 10 percent) to broaden your foundation base. For those who consider themselves 5K specialists, follow the guidelines below.

Your needs and goals determine the length of your long runs. If you anticipate running longer races along with the 5K, you will want to include some longer runs in your training. If you wish to concentrate on the 5K, however, you will need to minimize the length of your long runs. Longer runs take away from your ability to handle intense speed work.

Follow these *flexible* weekly mileage goals in training for the 5K. The recommended mileage figures should be averaged for at least 6 weeks prior to tapering for the final race. Runners age 50 + should use the lower end of the recommended mileage range.

FITNESS CATEGORY	WEEKLY MILEAGE	MILEAGE OF LONG RUN	LONG RUNS PER MONTH
Novice competitor	15–25	5–8	1–2
Basic competitor	25–40	8–10	1–2
Advanced competitor	30–50	8–12	1–2
Champion competitor	40–70	12–16	1–2

Endurance Training Pace for the 5K. Most 5K competitors should run medium endurance runs at *approximately* 1½ to 2 minutes per mile *slower* than their *present* 5K race pace. They may run slightly faster for short endurance runs and slightly slower for long endurance runs.

Step Five: Plan Your Individual Workouts (See model schedules at the end of this chapter)

Note that 5K competitors follow the same basic training philosophy as described for 10K competitors with a few specific modifications. In general, the 5K runner runs less mileage, shorter and fewer long runs, and does faster and more frequent speed work than the 10K runner.

Endurance Phase (3–5 weeks): Build your weekly mileage total during this phase to your peak level and hold. Run one or two long runs per month to build strength and confidence. Ease into speed training with one speed sesson per week for novice and basic competitors; and one or two speed sessions per week for advanced and champion competitors. Ease into speed training with *fartlek* runs and 5K pace intervals. You may run a low-key race during this phase to ease into racing. Novice and basic competitors should aim for a 2–4-mile race as they are building up their mileage; advanced and champion competitors will concentrate on easing into speed training and avoid racing, except perhaps for a low-key 2–4-mile effort.

The important areas to emphasize during the endurance phase: build a solid base of mileage and long runs, ease into speed training, ease into racing.

Strengthening Phase (4 weeks): Maintain peak mileage and two long runs per month. Include hill intervals and *fartlek* runs to build strength and 5K pace intervals to learn to feel relaxed at race pace. Ease into fast pace intervals to improve speed. Novice competitors run one speed workout per week, basic and advanced competitors run one or two, champions run two. Novice and basic competitors should run one race during this phase of 5K–5 miles to gain further racing experience. Advanced and champion competitors should run a longer race of 5 miles–10K to build strength.

The important areas to emphasize during the strengthening phase: maintain a solid base of mileage and long runs, gradually intensify speed workouts and emphasize hill workouts, race at a hard but not all-out effort.

Sharpening Phase (2–4 weeks): Novice competitors should maintain their mileage base throughout this phase, but all other competitors who will be doing increasingly intense speed work and racing should lower mileage by at least 10 percent. At all levels, eliminate long runs beyond the lower end on the chart on page 219. Novice and basic competitors run one or two speed workouts per week, advanced and champions run two. Novice and basic competitors intensify interval workouts by adding runs of faster than 5K pace. Advanced and champion competitors run hard speed sessions at both fast and power interval pace. All runners should run one 5K race during this phase. It should be a serious effort, and you should work at being competitive and running relaxed with good form at this fast pace. Go for a PR in this race 2–3 weeks prior to your key race.

The important areas to emphasize during the sharpening phase: maintain a base of mileage, but lower it to allow for faster speed training and a final hard tune-up race.

Tapering Phase (1 week): In order to achieve a peak performance, you must go into competition physically rested and psychologically ready. Run no longer than short- and medium-distance endurance runs for 7–10 days before your key race. Reduce mileage, take a day or two off, rest. A final "tune-up" workout of *fartlek* or controlled intervals (220–880) should be run 4–5 days before the race. Cut back on the number of intervals run, and make sure to allow for extra rest following each repetition: the goal of this workout is merely to "feel" fresh and fast.

As you taper your mileage, increase the time you spend mentally preparing for the race. See the final week in the sample 5K programs at the end of this chapter for a model tapering program for your category.

The important areas to emphasize during the tapering phase: reduce mileage, eliminate long runs, do a final brisk speed session, mentally prepare for a peak effort, rest the body.

Step Six: Plan Your Rebuilding Phase

Take a break! You have trained hard for 3 months and peaked for a big effort. You may be able to run another good race in 1–3 weeks, but don't push your luck. Your body and mind need to regenerate. For approximately 1 month (more if you do not wish to race again for a while), cut your mileage back 10 percent or more (but not more than 25 to 50 percent of your maximum mileage base), and minimize or eliminate long runs. Also eliminate any hard speed training and any racing. See page 340 for guidelines for immediate recovery from a race plus overall rebuilding. See page 344 for a sample rebuilding schedule. You may wish to take a break from running and utilize aerobic alternative training (see chapter 7).

5K RACE STRATEGY

You must remember that you will be running at a faster pace than you may be accustomed to when racing a 5K. It is a very intense race for those attempting to run fast. The mistake most people make is starting out too fast and going into oxygen debt very quickly. Start at the pace you wish to average for novice and basic competitors; advanced and champion competitors start up to 10 seconds per mile faster than goal pace. Keep pushing during the race. Racing a short distance requires constant concentration compared with longer races where you have more time to distribute your energy equally. Make sure you are well warmed up and ready to go at the gun. To be competitive in a short race, you must be physically and mentally alert from start to finish or you will suddenly find yourself off your goal.

Chapter 28 includes general guidelines for race day strategy. Review the strategy for 10K racing on page 204 for tips that relate to the 5K event.

BREAKING BARRIERS

Breaking barriers can be very rewarding, whether you are aiming to conquer the 30-minute mark or the 15-minute mark. Following are some common barriers and some tips on how to win your race against the clock.

The Sub-17-Minute 5K (5:28 per mile)

Follow the sample schedule for the champion competitor at the end of this chapter. You should run 50–70 miles per week at 7:00–7:30 minutes per mile, and do long runs of 10–15 miles twice a month prior to sharpening. You should run two speed workouts per week, on the average, for 8–10 weeks prior to the key race effort. You should run intervals at these approximate paces: miles—5:20–5:30; 880s—2:30–2:40; 440s—75–80 seconds.

The Sub-6-Minute Mile 5K (18:38)

Follow the sample schedule for the advanced competitor at the end of this chapter. You should run 40–50 miles per week at 7:30–8:00 minutes per mile, and do long runs of 10–12 miles twice a month prior to sharpening. You should run one or two speed workouts per week for 8–10 weeks prior to the key race effort. You should run intervals at these approximate paces: miles—5:50–6:00; 880s—2:45–2:55; 440s—82–85 seconds.

The Sub-20-Minute 5K (6:26 per mile)

Follow the sample schedule for the advanced competitor at the end of this chapter. You should run 30–50 miles per week at 7:30–8:30 minutes per mile, and do long runs of 8–12 miles twice a month prior to sharpening. You should run one or two speed workouts per week for 8–10 weeks prior to the key race effort. You should run intervals at these approximate paces: miles—6:20–6:30; 880s—3:00–3:10; 440s—85–90 seconds.

The Sub-7-Minute 5K (21:45)

Follow the sample schedule for the basic competitor at the end of this chapter. You should run 30–40 miles per week at 8:00–9:00 minutes per mile, and do long runs of 8–10 miles twice a month prior to sharpening. You should run one or two speed workouts for 8–10 weeks prior to the key race effort. You should run your intervals at these approximate paces: miles—6:50–7:00; 880s—3:15–3:30; 440s—1:30–1:40.

The Sub-8-Minute 5K (24:50)

Follow the sample schedule for the basic competitor at the end of this chapter. You should run 25–40 miles per week at 9:00–10:00 minutes per mile, and do long runs of 8–10 miles twice a month prior to sharpening. You should run one or two speed workouts per week for 8–10 weeks prior to the key race effort. You should run intervals at these approximate paces: miles—7:50–8:00; 880s—3:50–4:00; 440s—1:45–2:00.

The Sub-9-Minute 5K (27:58)

Follow the sample schedule for the novice competitor at the end of this chapter. You should run 20–30 miles per week at 10:00–11:00 minutes per mile, and do long runs of 5–8 miles two to four times per month. A moderate speed workout once a week for 6–8 weeks will help you prepare for a good race effort. You should run intervals at these approximate paces: miles—8:50–9:00; 880s—4:15–4:30; 440s—2:00–2:15.

The Sub-30-Minute 5K (10:00 per mile)

Follow the sample schedule for the novice competitor at the end of this chapter. You should run 20–30 miles per week at 11:00–12:00 minutes per mile, and do long runs of 4–6 miles two to four times per month. A moderate speed workout once a week for 6–8 weeks will help you prepare for a good race effort. You should run intervals at these approximate paces: miles—9:50–10:00; 880s—4:45–5:00; 440s—2:15–2:30.

12-WEEK 5K BUILDUP SCHEDULES

The model training schedules on pages 249–250 should be used to help you write your own program. The exact mileage you will run, distance and dates of your buildup races, and the days you will do your different types of runs will vary with your individual needs, age, sex, and other factors that influence your running. Use these models as a guide to create a specific training program that can help you reach your racing goals. Understand the concepts behind these schedules, don't just follow them blindly. We have not included an example of the rebuilding phase. Follow the model in chapter 13 to write your rebuilding program.

NOVICE COMPETITOR'S 12-WEEK 5K BUILDUP SCHEDULE

PHASE	WEEK	MONDAY	TUESDAY	WEDNESDAY	THURSDAY	FRIDAY	SATURDAY	SUNDAY	TOTAL MILEAGE
ENDURANCE	1	— Off	3 Medium endurance	3 Medium endurance	3 Medium endurance	— Off	2 Short endurance	4 Medium endurance	15
	2	— Off	3 Medium endurance	3 Medium endurance	3 Medium endurance	— Off	2 Short endurance	4 Medium endurance	15
	3	— Off	4 Strength Modified fartlek 2	2 Short endurance	2 Medium endurance	— Off	3 Short endurance	4 Medium endurance	15
	4	— Off	3 Slow rhythm 8 × 220	3 Medium endurance	3 Medium endurance	— Off	3 Short endurance	6 Long endurance	18
	5	— Off	4 Strength Modified fartlek 3	4 Medium endurance	3 Medium endurance	2 Short endurance	— Off	5 Race 5K	18
STRENGTHENING	6	2 Short endurance	2 Short endurance	4 Medium endurance	5 5K pace intervals 4 × 440	— Off	3 Short endurance	4 Medium endurance	20
	7	— Off	3 5K pace intervals 5 × Short hill	3 Short endurance	— Off	5 Medium endurance	3 Short endurance	6 Long endurance	20
	8	— Off	4 Strength Modified fartlek	3 Short endurance	— Off	5 Medium endurance	3 Short endurance	5 Medium endurance	20
	9	— Off	4 5K pace intervals 5 × 880	4 Medium endurance	4 Medium endurance	3 Short endurance	— Off	5 Race 5K	20
SHARPENING	10	2 Short endurance	3 Short endurance	3 Medium endurance	4 Fast intervals 4 × 440	— Off	3 Short endurance	5 Medium endurance	20
	11	— Off	4 5K pace intervals 5 × 880	3 Short endurance	— Off	4 Fast intervals 5 × 440	3 Short endurance	4 Medium endurance	18
TAPERING	12	— Off	5 Strength Modified fartlek 3	3 Short endurance	2 Short endurance	2 Short endurance	— Off	Race 5K	12 + race

BASIC COMPETITOR'S 12-WEEK 5K BUILDUP SCHEDULE

PHASE	WEEK	MONDAY	TUESDAY	WEDNESDAY	THURSDAY	FRIDAY	SATURDAY	SUNDAY	TOTAL MILEAGE
ENDURANCE	1	Off [—]	Medium endurance [4]	Short endurance [3]	Medium endurance [5]	Medium endurance [5]	Short endurance [3]	Medium endurance [5]	25
	2	Off [—]	Medium endurance [4]	Short endurance [3]	Medium endurance [5]	Medium endurance [5]	Short endurance [3]	Medium endurance [5]	25
	3	Off [—]	Strength Modified *fartlek* [3]	Short endurance [3]	Medium endurance [4]	Medium endurance [4]	Short endurance [3]	Long endurance [8]	25
	4	Off [—]	5K pace intervals 5 × 440 [4]	Short endurance [3]	Medium endurance [4]	Strength Modified *fartlek* 3 [5]	Medium endurance [5]	Medium endurance [6]	27
STRENGTHENING	5	Short endurance [3]	5K pace intervals 5 × Short hills [5]	Medium endurance [5]	Medium endurance [6]	Medium endurance [6]	Off [—]	Race 5K [5]	30
	6	Short endurance [2]	Medium endurance [4]	Medium endurance [4]	Medium endurance [4]	Strength Modified *fartlek* 4 [6]	Off [—]	Long endurance [10]	30
	7	Off [—]	5K pace intervals 6 × Short hills [5]	Medium endurance [5]	Medium endurance [5]	Strength Modified *fartlek* 4 [6]	Short endurance [3]	Medium endurance [6]	30
	8	Off [—]	5K pace intervals 5 × 880 [3]	Medium endurance [5]	Medium endurance [5]	Strength Hill *fartlek* [6]	Short endurance [3]	Long endurance [8]	30
SHARPENING	9	Off [—]	Fast intervals 4 × 880 [5]	Medium endurance [5]	Medium endurance [5]	Short endurance [4]	Off [—]	Race 5K [6]	25
	10	Short endurance [3]	Off [—]	Medium endurance [3]	Medium endurance [5]	Fast intervals 5 × 440 [4]	Short endurance [4]	Medium endurance [6]	25
	11	Off [—]	Fast intervals 4 × 880 [4]	Short endurance [4]	Medium endurance [6]	Strength Modified *fartlek* 4 [6]	Off [—]	Medium endurance [6]	25
TAPERING	12	Off [—]	5K pace intervals 5 × 880 [—]	Short endurance [4]	Medium endurance [4]	Medium endurance [4]	Off [—]	Race 5K [5]	15 + race

226

ADVANCED COMPETITOR'S 12-WEEK 5K BUILDUP SCHEDULE

PHASE	WEEK	MONDAY	TUESDAY	WEDNESDAY	THURSDAY	FRIDAY	SATURDAY	SUNDAY	TOTAL MILEAGE
ENDURANCE	1	— Off	5 Strength Hill *fartlek*	5 Medium endurance	5 Medium endurance	6 Medium endurance	4 Short endurance	10 Long endurance	35
	2	— Off	6 5K pace intervals 8 × 440	5 Medium endurance	6 Medium endurance	6 5K pace intervals 6 × Short hills	5 Medium endurance	7 Medium endurance	35
	3	— Off	6 5K pace intervals 6 × 880	6 Short endurance	4 Strength Advanced *fartlek*	6 Medium endurance	4 Short endurance	12 Long endurance	38
	4	— Off	5 5K pace intervals 8 × 880	6 Short endurance	6 Medium endurance	8 Strength Hill *fartlek*	7 Medium endurance	8 Medium endurance	40
STRENGTHENING	5	— Off	7 5K pace intervals 10 × 440	6 Medium endurance	6 Strength Hill *fartlek*	8 Medium endurance	5 Short endurance	8 Race 10K	40
	6	— Off	6 Medium endurance	8 Medium endurance	8 Strength Advanced *fartlek*	8 Medium endurance	6 5K pace intervals 3 × 1 mile	7 Medium endurance	43
	7	5 Short endurance	5 Strength Advanced *fartlek*	8 Short endurance	6 Fast intervals 6 × 440	7 Medium endurance	7 Medium endurance	7 Medium endurance	45
SHARPENING	8	3 Short endurance	6 Power intervals 6 × 440	5 Short endurance	6 Medium endurance	6 Medium endurance	6 Fast intervals 5 × 880	8 Medium endurance	40
	9	— Off	6 5K pace intervals 3 × 1 mile	6 Medium endurance	6 Medium endurance	6 Fast intervals 6 × 880	8 Medium endurance	8 Medium endurance	40
	10	8 Medium endurance	5 Power intervals 6 × 440	6 Short endurance	6 Medium endurance	8 Medium endurance	— Off	7 Race 5K	40
	11	— Off	6 Medium endurance	6 Medium endurance	6 Medium endurance	5 Fast intervals 5 × 880	4 Short endurance	8 Medium endurance	35
TAPERING	12	6 Medium endurance	4 5K pace intervals 10 × 440	4 Short endurance	5 Medium endurance	5 Medium endurance	— Off	Race 5K	24 + race

CHAMPION COMPETITOR'S 12-WEEK 5K BUILDUP SCHEDULE

PHASE / WEEK	MONDAY	TUESDAY	WEDNESDAY	THURSDAY	FRIDAY	SATURDAY	SUNDAY	TOTAL MILEAGE
ENDURANCE — 1	10 Medium endurance	10 5K pace intervals 6 × 440	8 Medium endurance	8 Medium endurance	8 Strength Advanced *fartlek* 4	8 Medium endurance	12 Long endurance	60
2	10 Medium endurance	10 5K pace intervals 6 × 880	8 Medium endurance	8 Medium endurance	6 5K pace intervals 8 × Short hills	8 Medium endurance	10 Medium endurance	60
3	10 Medium endurance	10 5K pace intervals 3 × 1 mile	8 Medium endurance	8 Strength Hill *fartlek* 6	10 Medium endurance	8 Medium endurance	15 Long endurance	65
4	10 Medium endurance	7 5K pace intervals 8 × 880	8 Medium endurance	10 Medium endurance	8 Strength Advanced *fartlek* 6	10 Medium endurance	12 Medium endurance	65
STRENGTHENING — 5	10 Medium endurance	10 5K pace intervals 10 × Short hills	8 Medium endurance	9 Surges 5	10 Medium endurance	6 Short endurance	12 Race 10K	65
6	6 Short endurance	6 Medium endurance	10 Medium endurance	10 Strength Advanced *fartlek* 6	10 Medium endurance	9 Fast intervals 6 × 440	12 Medium endurance	65
7	10 Medium endurance	10 5K pace intervals 4 × 1 mile	10 Medium endurance	8 Medium endurance	8 Medium endurance	8 Strength Advanced *fartlek* 5	12 Medium endurance	65
SHARPENING — 8	10 Medium endurance	10 Strength Tempo run 4	8 Medium endurance	8 5K pace intervals 10 × 440	10 Medium endurance	6 Short endurance	8 Race 5K	60
9	6 Short endurance	10 Medium endurance	10 Medium endurance	8 Strength Advanced *fartlek* 5	8 Medium endurance	8 Fast intervals 6 × 880	12 Medium endurance	60
10	10 Medium endurance	10 Power intervals 8 × 440	6 Short endurance	6 Strength Advanced *fartlek* 5	6 Medium endurance	6 Short endurance	8 Race 5K	50
11	6 Short endurance	6 Medium endurance	8 Medium endurance	8 Fast intervals 8 × 880	6 Short endurance	6 Power intervals 8 × 220	8 Medium endurance	50
TAPERING — 12	8 Medium endurance	8 Fast intervals 8 × 440	4 Short endurance	6 Medium endurance	6 Medium endurance	— Off	Race 5K	30 + race

17. THE MILE

This event is the focus of most track meets and the basic measure of all runners: you train at an 8:00-per-mile pace and race at a 6:30-per-mile-pace, for example. The Wanamaker Mile in the Millrose Games, in New York's Madison Square Garden, is the classic event of the classic meet of the indoor season, and 19,000 spectators stand to cheer its participants. The excitement of the mile has been with us for decades, even before Roger Bannister broke the elusive 4-minute barrier in 1954. The excitement returned to the headlines in 1981 when Great Britain's Sebastian Coe and Steve Ovett ran world-outdoor-record miles, and the first world-class mile race down a city street saw elite runners sprinting down New York City's Fifth Avenue before thousands of spectators and millions of television viewers.

High school and college runners see the mile as the prestige event for them, and the mile is catching on with adults who run the distance on a track or in the increasingly popular road-mile runs. The mile requires different training and racing methods from those used for the longer road races. Your training schedule should efficiently combine speed, strength, and endurance runs. You will have to keep constantly alert to how your body reacts to the stressful training of the mile. It is very important that you remain flexible in your program and make adjustments when necessary.

Whether you are experimenting with the distance for the first time or have experience in competing at this event, you must keep the following points in mind:

• *Speed Work.* The key to running the mile is power: that means improving both your speed and your strength. Speed work for the mile is much faster than for other distances. Pace intervals are run at 1 mile–5K speed, and fast intervals are done at ½-mile pace. You will run speed work for up to 50 percent of the time when training for the mile, compared with 5 to 15 percent for the 10K-marathon. You will race and train much more anaerobically. You won't hit the Wall (glycogen depletion) in the mile, but you will carry the Bear.

Speed workouts will help your energy system become more efficient and help you handle the oxygen debt incurred when running the mile. Fast-interval runs will force you to become accustomed to running fast while accumulating lactic acid and teach you to run in oxygen debt while maintaining good form and style. Refer to the 1-Mile Speed-Training Chart in the Appendices.

• *Muscular Strength.* Along with increasing your speed, you will need to increase your muscular strength. Your muscles will have to propel you forward in what feels like a sprint. Strength-training runs are included in the miler's regular training routine, as well as weight training for the legs, upper body, and abdominals. You will become stronger overall and, as a result, faster. Fast workouts on the track and hills should be included following a buildup of strength-training runs.

• *Form.* The same running form that you use for your long-distance runs will not help you in the mile. In fact, it may slow you down. You will need to learn the ball-heel foot strike and the power stride.

• *Warm-up.* Because of the intensity of this event from the very start of the race, it is important that you properly warm up and cool down following the guidelines in chapter 34.

• *Flexibility.* Because of changed running form and the increased stress from additional speed training, you will place more strain on your Achilles tendon, lower leg muscles, and major joints. It is very important that you incorporate into your training an extensive program of flexibility exercises for the hamstrings, Achilles tendons, ankles, lower back, knees, and hip flexors.

• *Recovery.* You will need more rest than usual after hard speed work and races. You are using different muscles and a different energy supply system. Use your easy days wisely following the hard days. For the highly experienced miler in the early stages of training, hard workouts 2 days in a row are sometimes used to teach the body to respond to the high intensity of work demanded by the mile. The 3rd day should be easy.

• *Racing Shoes.* Inexperienced milers should wear racing flats, not spikes. Experienced milers should race in spikes only after breaking them in gradually during workouts.

• *Training on the Track.* You should do one or two speed workouts a week on the track to get the feel for its surface and turns, but don't do your endurance runs there. Track running will help you get a feel for racing, and when your laps are timed, you will develop a sense of rhythm and pace for the mile. Speed workouts can also be done on trails, hills, and grass fields for variety.

• *Buildup Races.* Most milers like to race the mile frequently during their training cycle. Some runners even race every weekend. Generally, you should race the mile at least two or three times during your training phase if you are an inexperienced miler, and four to seven times if you are an experienced miler. Racing the mile will teach you a great deal about pace, strategy, and your individual strengths and weaknesses. The more you race, the more you will learn and the faster you will be able to race for the final mile run of your training cycle. If you can't find a track meet to race a mile in, you may need to just do it by yourself as a time trial. If possible, recruit others to run with you and to time you and cheer you on.

CATEGORIES OF MILERS

We have replaced our four fitness categories for road racing with two broad categories for the mile. For the most part, the basic and some advanced competitors would fit into our inexperienced miler category. The novice competitor isn't fit or experienced enough at racing to run the mile all-out. Most champion competitors and many advanced competitors, along with the majority of high school and college track runners, would fit into the experienced miler category.

The Inexperienced Miler

This category includes the following runners:

A. The young runner (age 12–15) who is experimenting with the mile for the first time or is in his or her first few years of running. We recommend that this runner limit his or her mileage to 15–20 miles a week and work on developing leg speed and good racing form. Young runners will have many years ahead of them in which to build endurance with higher mileage. They should also be careful not to overrace.

B. Women who have not run the mile competitively before or have not run faster than a 6:00 mile. Women should be able to run under 50:00 for 10K before attempting to train for the mile.

C. Men who have not run the mile competitively or have not run faster than a 5:00 mile. Men should be able to run under 45:00 for 10K before attempting to train for the mile.

We have included speed restrictions here because training for the mile is very intense work. The inexperienced miler does not have the speed or strength to follow the more difficult training program for the experienced miler. Before racing the mile, you should have run a few shorter races of 5K–4 miles.

The Experienced Miler

This category includes the following runners:

A. The high school runner who has a good training background and, if a boy, can run faster than a 5:00 mile; if a girl, faster than a 6:00 mile. *Note:* Many high school track programs require the runner to race more frequently than we suggest. To adjust, substitute your scheduled races for speed workout days on our schedule and reduce your weekly mileage. Generally, high school milers do not run more than 40–50 miles a week.

B. Women road runners who have competed regularly at 5K–10K and can run faster than a 6:00 mile. This runner should be able to break 42:00 for 10K.

C. Men road runners who have competed regularly at 5K–10K and can run faster than a 5:00 mile. This runner should be able to break 37:00 for 10K.

D. Track-oriented men and women who train to race under 5:00 and 6:00 respectively for the mile.

The following training program is designed for our two categories of milers and uses the six-step approach outlined in chapter 13.

STEP ONE: DETERMINE
YOUR FITNESS CATEGORY

Use either the inexperienced or experienced miler's program. Your decision should be based primarily on how well your body can handle the much more intense work necessary to run the mile competitively.

STEP TWO: SELECT YOUR RACES
AND TIME GOALS

You should run at least two 1-mile competitions during your training cycle. Use the first one to get the feel of the race, familiarize yourself with the speed of the event and the different type of fatigue, strategy, etc. Then use the second mile race to improve your time. You should also pick time barriers to break as you compete. Common barriers to break include (pace per 440-yard lap is noted after each barrier) 7:00 (1:45), 6:30 (1:37), 6:00 (90 seconds), 5:30 (82.5 seconds), 5:00 (75 seconds), 4:40 (70 seconds), 4:30 (67.5 seconds), and 4:20 (65 seconds).

It will take time to reach your goals, perhaps over a number of racing seasons. You may progress rapidly and then stall out for a while. As you become stronger, faster, and more experienced at racing shorter distances, you will eventually reach your realistic goals. Don't rush. Speed must be carefully developed, or you will become an ex-miler.

STEP THREE: DETERMINE YOUR TRAINING CYCLE AND THE LENGTH OF YOUR PHASES

We use a shortened, 8-week schedule for the inexperienced miler. This is the minimal amount of training needed to improve significantly for this event. Much more time spent doing this intense training is liable to cause you either to lose interest or to become injured. The experienced miler should follow a 12-week short-term training cycle to allow for a sufficient buildup of endurance, strength, and speed. All milers should have a good background of mileage before starting the endurance phase.

Here is a guide to selecting your phases for mile training:

DESCRIPTION	INEXPERIENCED MILER	EXPERIENCED MILER
Length of buildup	8 weeks	12
Endurance phase	2	3
Strengthening phase	3	4
Sharpening phase	2	4
Tapering phase	1	1
Rebuilding phase	3–4	3–6
Number of races in cycle	2–3	4–8

STEP FOUR: DETERMINE YOUR WEEKLY MILEAGE AND LONG-RUN GOALS

The mile requires less of a mileage base than do longer-distance events, but training for it requires a balance between easy endurance runs and intense speed work. The miler doesn't need to do long runs for as long a distance as the road racer. In fact, long runs may do more harm than good. During your training for the mile, long runs may make you feel heavy and sluggish, throw off your rhythm for the race, and take time away from specific mile training. Training pace for all endurance runs will be similar to that of the 5K runner (see page 219).

Follow these mileage guidelines when training for the mile:

FITNESS CATEGORY	WEEKLY MILEAGE	MILEAGE OR LONG RUNS
Inexperienced miler	20–40	6–10
Experienced miler	40–60	8–14

STEP FIVE: PLAN YOUR INDIVIDUAL WORKOUTS (See model schedules at the end of this chapter)

Inexperienced Miler

Endurance Phase (2 weeks): Two speed workouts per week; one long run or none; no races. Before starting this phase, it is necessary that you already have put in at least a solid month of endurance training. A short endurance phase is used as a transition to the much faster-paced runs used to train for the mile. Introduce speed work with modified *fartlek* and hill *fartlek*. Interval runs are added, but these are now done at 5K pace. Listen to your body for signs that this harder introductory speed work is too much for you at this point.

Strengthening Phase (3 weeks): Two speed workouts per week; one long run or none; one or two races during phase. During this phase you will begin to work harder at your two speed sessions each week. Do plenty of work on hills to add strength along with a 5K road race. Toward the end of this phase, introduce a race-pace interval run based on your present predicted speed for the mile. Races of 3K–5K are used to improve strength.

Sharpening Phase (2 weeks): Two or three speed workouts per week; no long runs; one or two races per phase. Add fast interval workouts to improve speed. These are done at your predicted speed for the 880, so be very careful not to overstrain and pull a muscle at what will probably feel like an all-out sprint for you. Reduce your weekly mileage. Race a mile during this phase to become familiar with the event.

Tapering Phase (1 week): One or two speed workouts; no long runs; one race—1 mile. Reduce mileage, don't overtrain. One interval workout at the pace at which you feel you can race the mile is used early in the week to give you a final feel for race pace. Use a minimal number of repetitions so as not to take strength away from your final all-out effort for the mile.

Experienced Miler

This runner spends most of his or her time improving strength and speed.

Endurance Phase (3 weeks): Two speed workouts per week; one long run or none; one race or none during phase. Make the transition into faster work by including several strength runs and then interval runs at 5K race pace. Include a 5K or similar-distance race (3K, 2 or 4 mile) to develop strength, endurance, and the ability to maintain a fast pace over longer distances.

Strengthening Phase (4 weeks): Two or three workouts per week; one long run or none; one or two races during phase. Gradually begin to do three hard sessions per week, introducing interval runs at your present 1-mile race pace and finally fast-paced runs at your estimated 880 pace. Include one or two 1-mile races during this phase to gain racing experience and test your fitness level. Don't expect to race fast times in these early races. If you wish to continue working on strength building, run a 5K race instead of a mile.

Sharpening Phase (4 weeks): Two or three speed workouts per week; no long runs; two or three races during phase. You should concentrate on these key areas, increasing your leg speed with short, fast interval runs using proper running form, and improving your ability to run with the Bear on your back. Include at least two 1-mile races in this phase to bring down your time.

Tapering Phase (1 week): Two speed workouts; no long runs; one race—1 mile. It is very important that you not overtrain here after spending so much effort building up for your final mile race. It is better to do too little mileage and speed work in the last week than too much.

STEP SIX: PLAN YOUR REBUILDING PHASE
THE MILE BUILDUP SCHEDULE

The model training schedules on pages 240–241 should be used to help you write your own program. The exact mileage you will run, distance and dates of your buildup races, and the days you will do your different types of runs will vary with your individual needs, age, sex, and other factors that influence your running. Use these models as a guide to create a specific training program that can help you reach your racing goals. Understand the concepts behind these schedules, don't just follow them blindly. We have not included an example of the rebuilding phase. Follow the model in chapter 13 to write your rebuilding program.

Pace Progression

As you begin your training cycle for the mile, your pace- and fast-interval workouts will be slower in each area than at the end of your last mile racing season. Obviously, you were in better shape then. Now, you want to increase the speed of your rhythm runs progressively toward your race goal pace so that your body adjusts to the increased intensity without breaking down. If you find that at the start of your speed program you are having a hard time running workouts at your 5K pace, or that it takes 2 days to recover from the workout, you are not fit enough to handle this intensity. You should either slow down the pace of your runs or increase the number of weeks that you do endurance training.

STRATEGIC TIPS FOR
THE INEXPERIENCED MILER

Starting

Racing the mile may be a new experience for you. First of all, there will probably be only a few other competitors at the starting line. Usually no more than ten can safely compete. Second, everyone runs very fast when the starting gun goes off. There is no shuffling along waiting for a place to open, no time to check your watch or say hello to a friend. You are off and flying, or else. It is important, therefore, that you follow these instructions for the start of the mile:

• Make sure you are ready to run when the starter calls you to the line. You should be finished warming up and ready to go.

• The starter usually gives two commands: he says, "Take your marks," and fires the gun. Be ready to go when the starter tells you to take your mark. Often the starter will fire the gun immediately after the command.

• Make sure that the runners on either side of you give you enough room to run freely. If they squeeze you in, use your elbows to move them away.

Establishing Your Race Pace

Invariably, you will go out faster than your anticipated race pace. Don't panic. Get control of yourself quickly, relax, and settle into your own race pace as soon as possible. This is essential if you are a first-time racer. Try to get your breathing under control and rhythmic. Panic breathing will cause you to stay tight and continue running fast until exhausted. By concentrating on getting your breathing under control, you will also start to settle into your race pace.

Listen for Your Splits

Most mile races are run on a 440-yard or 400-meter track. You will have to go around the track four times to complete the mile. Each time you complete one lap you should hear a time called for that lap. These are your splits (the mile is split into 4×440). Before running your mile race, you should determine your 440 splits. This will enable you to run as even a pace as possible. For example, if you want to run a 6:00 mile, your 440 splits will be 0:90, 3:00, 4:30, and then your final time.

Race Tactics

The inexperienced miler should concentrate only on running an evenly paced race. Leave the tactics of racing against others to the more experienced runners. Get into your pace, stay relaxed, run rhythmically. Don't get caught trying to run with people faster than you. Run *your* race.

STRATEGIC TIPS FOR THE EXPERIENCED MILER

• Start quickly to get into a good position, and then settle into your pace.

• Make no big moves early in the race. These include sprints to discourage opposition or catch another runner.

• Know your natural strengths and use them in the race. If you have good natural speed, wait until the last possible moment to use it. If you are a very strong runner, use your long, extended kick over the final 440 to 660 yards.

• Concentrate on competing rather than on running a certain time. You will run better when battling the competition.

• Don't get "boxed in"—stuck behind slower runners without being able to pass. Run slightly off the right shoulder of the runner in front of you so you can easily pass if this runner slows down.

• Pump your arms when you need to pick up your speed.

• Stay forward on your feet to maintain good rhythm and forward drive, especially when you want to "kick."

Safety Note: Because of the intensity of this event from the very start of the race, it is important that you do the proper warm-up and cool-down routines, following the guidelines in chapter 34.

THE INEXPERIENCED MILER'S 8-WEEK BUILDUP SCHEDULE

MEN: 5-MIN MILE TO 6:30 MILE
WOMEN: 6-MIN MILE TO 7:30 MILE

PHASE	WEEK	MONDAY	TUESDAY	WEDNESDAY	THURSDAY	FRIDAY	SATURDAY	SUNDAY	TOTAL MILEAGE
ENDURANCE	1	— Off	5 / 3 Strength Modified *fartlek*	4 Short endurance	6 Medium endurance	5 / 3 Strength Modified *fartlek*	4 Short endurance	6 Medium endurance	30
ENDURANCE	2	— Off	5 / 3 Strength Hill *fartlek*	6 Medium endurance	5 / 3 Strength Modified *fartlek*	4 Short endurance	5 Medium endurance	5 Medium endurance	30
ENDURANCE	3	— Off	4 5K pace intervals 8 × 220	5 Short endurance	5 Medium endurance	6 Strength Hill *fartlek*	4 Short endurance	6 Medium endurance	30
STRENGTHENING	4	5 5K pace intervals 6 × 440	5 Short endurance	4 5K pace intervals 4 × 880	6 5K pace intervals 3 × 1 mile	7 Medium endurance	— Off	— Race 5K	30
STRENGTHENING	5	4 Short endurance	— Off	5 Medium endurance	5 Fast intervals 4 × 440	5 Medium endurance	6 Medium endurance	5 1-mile pace intervals 6 × 440	30
SHARPENING	6	4 Short endurance	4 1-mile pace intervals 3 × 880	4 Short endurance	5 1-mile pace intervals 8 × 440	4 Short endurance	5 / 3 Strength Modified *fartlek*	4 Short endurance	30
SHARPENING	7	6 Medium endurance	6 Fast intervals 8 × 220	5 Short endurance	5 Short endurance	4 Short endurance	— Off	— Race Mile	27
TAPERING	8	4 Short endurance	4 Short endurance	4 1-mile pace intervals 3 × 880	4 Short endurance	4 Short endurance	— Off	— Race Mile	21 + race

THE EXPERIENCED MILER'S 12-WEEK BUILDUP SCHEDULE
MEN: SUB-5-MIN MILE
WOMEN: SUB-6-MIN MILE

PHASE/WEEK		MONDAY	TUESDAY	WEDNESDAY	THURSDAY	FRIDAY	SATURDAY	SUNDAY	TOTAL MILEAGE
ENDURANCE	1	Medium endurance (7)	Strength Advanced fartlek (7)	Short endurance (5)	Medium endurance (5)	Strength Hill fartlek (7)	Short endurance (5)	Medium endurance (7)	45
	2	Medium endurance (8)	Strength Advanced fartlek (7)	Short endurance (5)	Strength Fast 6 continuous run (5)	Medium endurance (9)	Short endurance (4)	Race 5Km (5)	45
	3	Short endurance (5)	Medium endurance (5)	Medium endurance (8)	5K pace intervals 8 × 440 (10)	Short endurance (6)	5K pace intervals 8 × Short hills (6)	Medium endurance (10)	50
STRENGTHENING	4	5K pace intervals 6 × 880 (7)	Medium endurance (7)	Medium endurance (6)	Strength Advanced fartlek (6)	Short endurance (8)	5K pace intervals 10 × 440 (7)	Medium endurance (10)	50
	5	5K pace intervals 10 × Short hills (8)	Medium endurance (8)	Medium endurance (8)	5K pace intervals 3 × 1 mile (8)	Medium endurance (7)	Medium endurance (6)	Race 1 mile (5)	50
	6	Short endurance (5)	1-mile pace intervals 6 × 440 (5)	1-mile pace intervals 5 × 880 (6)	Strength Advanced fartlek (10)	Medium endurance (10)	5K pace intervals 3 × 1 mile (6)	Medium endurance (8)	50
	7	Medium endurance (8)	Medium endurance (8)	1-mile pace intervals 5 × 880 (10)	Medium endurance (6)	1-mile pace intervals 8 × 440 (6)	Medium endurance (6)	Fast intervals 8 × 220 (8)	50
SHARPENING	8	Medium endurance (8)	1-mile pace intervals 10 × 440 (8)	Medium endurance (8)	Fast intervals 10 × 220 (7)	Short endurance (5)	1-mile pace intervals 5 × 880 (6)	Short endurance (5)	45
	9	Medium endurance (8)	1-mile pace intervals 6 × 880 (8)	Short endurance (6)	1-mile pace intervals 10 × 440 (6)	Medium endurance (8)	Short endurance (5)	Race 1 mile (4)	45
	10	Short endurance (6)	Strength Advanced fartlek (6)	Medium endurance (8)	Fast intervals 6 × 440 (6)	Medium endurance (6)	Fast intervals 8 × 220 (4)	Medium endurance (7)	45
	11	Medium endurance (8)	Fast intervals 10 × 220 (6)	Medium endurance (6)	1-mile pace intervals 10 × 440 (6)	Short endurance (6)	Short endurance (5)	Race 1 mile (4)	40
TAPERING	12	Short endurance (5)	1-mile pace intervals 3 × 880 (5)	Short endurance (5)	Strength Advanced fartlek (5)	Short endurance (5)	Off (—)	Race 1 mile	24 + race

241

18. CROSS-COUNTRY

Bounding down a wooded trail, I suddenly careen to the left, then to the right, and climb a short, steep, rocky hill. I mount the crest, burst down the other side, uncontrollably flowing along meandering paths as birds and other animals scurry away. As I pick up the pace and roller-coaster along, I fantasize that I am pulling away from my competition and powering out of the woods to cross the finish line in an open field.

—BOB GLOVER

No other type of running offers such variety of terrain, scenery, and emotional experiences as cross-country. As every experienced "harrier" knows, cross-country racing is a love-hate relationship. It is a scenic, serene, and rewarding experience only *after* the race is over. The race itself is a gut-wrenching ordeal that demands careful preparation and promises no "runner's high." To the untrained, a 10K cross-country race over a tough, hilly course would be as devastating as a marathon on the roads.

Cross-country runners must prepare for this unique test of their stamina and competitive spirit. Most cross-country courses—usually in parks or golf courses—include numerous hills and valleys, sharp turns, narrow paths, and difficult footing that will quickly make you forget the idyllic setting and force you to respond to the challenge ahead.

The tempo is also very different from road races. In cross-country racing, you will have difficulty settling into a steady pace or rhythm. Throughout the entire race you will be changing speeds as you attempt to negotiate turns, uphills, downhills. Thus the advanced *fartlek* becomes an essential training run. Courses in New York City's Van Cortlandt Park and Philadelphia's Fairmount Park contain hills with such appropriate names as Cemetery Hill and Parachute Hill. In Europe, plowed fields, haystacks, and water jumps are added to the courses to make them more challenging. When Pete Schuder and his Columbia team traveled to England to compete against Oxford, the course included a quagmire of mud a foot deep, the usual impossible hills, and a wide brook. The times for the 5.5-mile course were slow, shoes and uniforms a mess, but the runners had a great time competing against each other and Mother Nature.

If you are still eager, don't make the mistake of jumping into any cross-country race. Your road-running training will be of little use here. You must train specifically for the cross-country event to run the course successfully.

CATEGORIES OF CROSS-COUNTRY RUNNERS: INEXPERIENCED AND EXPERIENCED

As with the mile, we have replaced our four fitness categories for road racing with two broad categories for cross-country. For the most part, the basic and some advanced competitors would fit into our inexperienced category. The novice competitor, like many basic competitors, is not fit or experienced enough to race over difficult terrain. Most champion and many advanced competitors, along with the majority of high school and college runners, would fit into the experienced category.

The Inexperienced Cross-Country Runner

This category includes the following runners:

A. Young runners (age 12–15) who are new to the sport of cross-country or who are in their first few years of running.

We recommend that these runners limit their mileage to 20–25 miles per week and race only at distances of 1½ miles or less. These runners will need to modify our model 8-week schedule by lowering the mileage totals.

B. Men and women road racers who are running cross-country for the first time, or who have previously run the event but only wish to dabble with it. Men should be able to run 45:00 or better and women 50:00 or better for a 10K on the roads before attempting to compete at this event. These runners should limit their cross-country races to 5K.

The Experienced Cross-Country Runner

This category includes the following runners:

A. The high school runner who has a solid background of distance training and is able to run 40–50 miles per week, including hard speed work. This runner is able to run the 5K on the road or track under 19:00 if a boy and under 22:00 if a girl. Since most high school cross-country courses are between 2½ miles and 5K, this runner should follow the training schedule we have developed at the end of this chapter for that distance.

Note: Many high school programs require the runner to race more frequently than we suggest. To adjust, substitute your scheduled races for speed workout days on our schedule and reduce your weekly mileage.

B. Women who have experienced racing cross-country and who are able to run 42:00 or faster for 10K on the roads. Most women's cross-country races are contested at distances from 3K to 5K. Use the training schedule as explained above for the high school runner if you're going to train for this distance, and the 10K cross-country schedule if you're going to race 5 miles to 10K.

C. Men who are experienced at running cross-country and who are able to run faster than 37:00 for 10K on the road. Most open and college cross-country races are contested at distances ranging from 5 miles to 10K. Use the 10K cross-country schedule.

The following training program is designed for our two categories of cross-country runners and uses the six-step approach outlined in chapter 13.

STEP ONE: DETERMINE YOUR FITNESS CATEGORY

Use either the inexperienced or experienced program. Your decision should be based primarily on how well your body can handle the much more intense work necessary to manage the hilly terrain and other challenges that cross-country offers.

STEP TWO: SELECT YOUR RACES AND TIME GOALS

Select only a few races to run during your training cycle. These races are very taxing and require time to recover properly. You must really get mentally "up" for this event, and you can't do that every week. Ideally, space your races, running only one every 2 to 3 weeks. It is very difficult to set a time goal for a particular cross-country course, since all courses are different and usually you are more concerned with beating your competitors and the course itself than the clock. A 38:40 10K cross-country time on one course may be excellent because the course is very hilly, while the same time on a flat course may be slow. As an alternative to reaching for certain time barriers, you may choose to better your time over the same course or to defeat other runners of similar experience in your age group.

STEP THREE: DETERMINE YOUR TRAINING CYCLE AND THE LENGTH OF YOUR PHASES

All runners should have a good background of aerobic training before beginning the endurance phase. The inexperienced cross-country runner should limit his or her training to a short-term, 8-week cycle. This minimum period will allow you to improve at this event without overtaxing your body. The experienced cross-country runner must devote a minimum of 12 weeks (short-term cycle) to train properly for top performances. The strength phase for both categories of runners is very important because of the strength required to race up and down hills. At least 3-5 weeks of strength training, including advanced *fartlek*, hill *fartlek,* and specific hill training, are needed. The inexperienced runner doesn't need to spend as much time sharpening for the race, since he or she is more concerned with running a strong race to the finish than running at fast speeds. The experienced runner will spend much more time on sharpening, especially if the course is short (3K–5K) or flat and fast.

Here is a guide to selecting your phases for cross-country training:

DESCRIPTION	INEXPERIENCED COMPETITOR	EXPERIENCED COMPETITOR
Length of buildup	8 weeks	12
Endurance phase	3	4
Strengthening phase	3	5
Sharpening phase	1	2
Tapering phase	1	1
Rebuilding phase	3–4	3–6
Number of races during cycle	2–3	4–5

STEP FOUR: DETERMINE YOUR WEEKLY MILEAGE AND LONG-RUN GOALS

Your weekly mileage goals are determined by several factors:

1. *Your training phase.* When you include difficult strength-training runs in your schedule, your mileage may drop a little since the runs you do for cross-country are harder than the normal strength workouts you would do for a road race. You may have to give your body more time to recover from the stress.

2. *Cross-country races.* For the inexperienced runner, cross-country racing is more difficult than road racing, so you will need longer rest periods with reduced mileage after each race. Also, all runners will need more mileage if training for a 10K than if training for a 5K.

3. *The weather.* Cross-country training begins in the heat of summer and ends in the snows of winter. Weather will be a major factor in your mileage and running. Cross-country is a fall sport. Use the long, hot summer for endurance training to

build a solid foundation before starting your training cycle.

You should decide what level of mileage you can handle best and benefit from the most. Continue including long runs in your training schedule as though preparing for distance races on the road. These runs will toughen you for the terrain of cross-country. Training pace for all endurance runs would be similar to that of 10K and 5K (see chapter 5).

Follow these mileage guidelines when training for cross-country:

FITNESS CATEGORY	WEEKLY MILEAGE	MILEAGE OF LONG RUNS
Inexperienced competitor (5K)	30–50	10–15
Inexperienced competitor (1½ miles)	20–25	4–6
Experienced competitor (10K)	60–100	15–20
Experienced competitor (5K)	40–60	8–12

STEP FIVE: PLAN YOUR INDIVIDUAL WORKOUTS *(See model schedules at the end of this chapter)*

Inexperienced Competitor

Endurance Phase (3 weeks): One or two speed workouts per week; two or three long runs; one race during phase. The 3-week endurance phase is primarily used to maintain a high level of aerobic fitness and to prepare the body for the more intense strength work necessary for cross-country. Include modified *fartlek* and hill *fartlek* to simulate race conditions. Increase mileage to your peak level.

Strengthening Phase (3 weeks): One or two speed workouts per week, one or two long runs; one or two races during phase. Use this phase to improve your ability to handle hills. Hill training will benefit you greatly even if your races are mainly over flat courses. Do several of your strength and interval runs over cross-country trails rather than on the road or track to familiarize yourself with running cross-country. Your first race should be more of an experience than a competitive race. Keep it low-key so that you will want to come back for more.

Sharpening Phase (1 week): Two speed workouts; no long

runs; no races. This 1-week phase consists of reducing your mileage and doing race-pace rhythm workouts or faster, variable speed runs such as hill *fartlek* and advanced *fartlek*.

Tapering Phase (1 week): One speed workout; no long runs; one race—5K cross-country. Your last speed workout should be 5–6 days prior to your key race and be low-key. Be sure to be well rested for your contest against nature. Remember the lessons learned from the previous races.

Experienced Competitor

Endurance Phase (4 weeks): two speed workouts per week; two or three long runs; one race during phase. A successful cross-country racing season is dependent on building a solid base of mileage *prior* to starting the 12-week buildup schedule. Pete Schuder's Columbia University cross-country team that won the Ivy League Championship in 1979 stayed on the roads from early June until the end of August, and gradually increased each runner's base mileage from about 60–65 miles per week to 80–85 miles. Most of the mileage was run at a comfortable conversational pace, and a few road races were used to maintain interest. When the team members returned to campus in late August, they began specific cross-country training following a 12-week buildup schedule. The 4-week endurance phase should be used to maintain your aerobic base and also to blend in slow rhythm workouts and strength runs that allow your body to adapt to the rigors of cross-country training. A race during this phase is used to gain experience in the unique challenges of cross-country racing.

Strengthening Phase (5 weeks): two speed workouts per week; two or three long runs; one or two races during phase. Include several hill workouts and advanced *fartlek* runs in this phase. Interval hill workouts in particular will improve your leg strength, increase your ability to drive up hills, and improve your racing form. *Fartlek* best imitates cross-country racing conditions. If possible, run some of these workouts on the course you plan to race, or a similar course. *Fartlek*, like cross-country racing, demands that you keep changing your speed and form as you go through the course. Other specific workouts can include runs of 1 to 2 miles over the most difficult portion of the course. Repeat this run three to five times during this workout, depending on the shape you are in. Also, you may choose to run a time trial at 80 to 90 percent effort over the entire course, or parts of it, to get a good feel for the course under racing conditions.

You should run at least one cross-country race during this phase to test yourself both physically and mentally. Run the race at less than all-out effort, but be competitive against your opponents and the course. Reduce mileage coming off this race to ensure proper recovery. Cross-country races demand more recovery time.

Sharpening Phase (2 weeks): two speed workouts per week; no long runs; one race. Include faster-than-race-pace workouts to:

1. Improve your racing speed.

2. Make it easier for you to start out faster than race pace in order to get a good position in a crowded field.

3. Make it easier for you to pick up the pace to pass runners quickly on narrow paths.

Include workouts that are very specific to your races:

1. Hilly courses would require some final short drills over hills.

2. Flat, fast courses or shorter race distances than 10K require that you include longer, race-pace interval runs to help you maintain a steady pace.

3. Run the first 880 yards of your race course at the pace at which you will start to give you a feeling of jumping out in good position for the race.

4. Finish some of your workouts by briskly covering the last 880 yards of the course at race pace. This will help you get your mind and body accustomed to finishing strongly.

Include a cross-country race during this phase, which you should run at all-out effort. Concentrate on staying calm, for any tightness will cause you to lose your ability to run efficiently. Don't allow the course to defeat you by trying to overpower it. Use this race as your final learning experience prior to your big meet. Reduce weekly mileage to accommodate intense training.

Tapering Phase (1 week): One speed workout; no long runs; one race. Allow your mind and body to relax. Reduce your mileage and complete your last race-pace workout early in the week at a reduced work load.

STEP SIX: PLAN YOUR REBUILDING PHASE

CROSS-COUNTRY BUILDUP SCHEDULES

The model training schedules for cross-country on pages 254–256 should be used to help you write your own program. The exact mileage you will run, distance and dates of your buildup races, and the days you will do your different types of runs will vary with your individual needs, age, sex, and other factors that influence your running. Use these models as a guide to create a specific training program that can help you reach your racing goals. Understand the concepts behind these schedules, don't just follow them blindly. We have not included an example of the rebuilding phase. Follow the model in chapter 13 to write your rebuilding program.

RACING TIPS FOR THE CROSS-COUNTRY RUNNER

You will have to react quickly during your cross-country races. Here are some points to look out for in the race.

The Course

Arrive early. Walk or jog key sections of the course, even if you think you know it. You may have overlooked or forgotten some obstacles, or new ones may have been put in just for this race. Check landmarks and direction arrows so you will know where you have to go and how far you have to run. Pick out a point in the course where you want to start your finishing drive.

Clothing

Cross-country is often run in cool weather. Be careful: you may be cool at the start and heat up during the race. A turtleneck shirt under your racing jersey, and perhaps a hat and mittens, should get you through all but the worst conditions. Be sure to bring a dry set of clothes, and change into them immediately after finishing. Don't stand around. If you race in early season, you can encounter heat too. Be sure to drink fluids before the race. But there are no water stations along the course, so back off a little if you begin to feel dizzy or nauseated.

Shoes

Do not wear spikes, even if the course is grass or dirt, unless you have had a great deal of experience running in them. Most good shoe companies have racing "flats" for cross-country that hold the ground and won't snag on roots or rocks.

Starting

Courses are narrow, so watch for flying elbows and legs at the start that might knock you off stride. Novice runners should be alert to the fact that cross-country starts are faster than road races. Do not go out too fast!

Your first ¾ mile to 1½ miles will be faster than your anticipated race pace, even if you go out cautiously. Your breathing will be labored, since your effort to get position will be great. Don't panic! Force yourself to relax and control your breathing. If you continue to take short, shallow breaths, you will go into oxygen debt very quickly and will slow down as you continue the race.

Relax

The most difficult, yet important, part of running a cross-country race is to stay relaxed and just flow along the course. Imagine yourself being swept along a fast-moving stream. If it feels as if you are going against the current, you are not running relaxed.

Pacing

The changing terrain will give you problems. Be prepared to shift gears constantly as you run up and down hills. Try to keep the effort of the run constant, even though your actual speed varies greatly.

Be aggressive, but also be smart as you run. Accept the challenge of the hills, and run them as best you can without trying to "blast" up them. Relax and flow downhill.

Passing

Don't be timid about passing people in the race. Sometimes the only way to get by on the narrow path is to put on a burst. Do it! Yell "track," and you'll get a peephole to bang through.

Strategy

As you wind around the wooded trails, keep contact with others so you don't get lost or have to slow down. Run with teammates or friends in the early going. When Pete Schuder's Columbia Lions won the Ivy League Championships, the top seven went out in a pack and gave each other encouragement along the course. Also, don't stay too close behind a runner, or you won't see roots, rocks, ruts, and other obstacles.

Persevere

You will surely believe that your lungs and thighs are burning, that you are dying or lost or sick. The race is short, remember, and everyone else is suffering with you.

Cross-country is a different kind of sport. You don't just chug along, chatting with the pack. You must conquer not only your competition, but also Mother Nature's obstacles and your protesting body. Cross-country, as we said at the beginning, is best appreciated when it's over. Try a run along the woods one day for a break. Watch a high school or college race one fall weekend. More and more running clubs are sponsoring cross-country races for the average competitor like you. For example, the National Road Runners Club age-group championships are held each November in New York City's Van Cortlandt Park, and hundreds of runners of all ability levels from age 2 to age 70 show up to enjoy the run, the scenery, and the experience.

THE INEXPERIENCED CROSS-COUNTRY COMPETITOR'S 8-WEEK BUILDUP (5K)

PHASE	WEEK	MONDAY	TUESDAY	WEDNESDAY	THURSDAY	FRIDAY	SATURDAY	SUNDAY	TOTAL MILEAGE
ENDURANCE	1	— Off	7 Medium endurance	6 Medium endurance	6 Medium endurance	7 Medium endurance	4 Short endurance	10 Long endurance	40
ENDURANCE	2	— Off	6 5K pace intervals 4 × 880	5 Short endurance	8 Medium endurance	8 / 5 Strength Advanced fartlek	6 Medium endurance	7 Medium endurance	40
STRENGTHENING	3	5 Short endurance	7 5K pace intervals 4 × 880	7 Medium endurance	7 Medium endurance	7 / 5 Hill fartlek	— Off	12 Long endurance	45
STRENGTHENING	4	7 Medium endurance	7 Strength Advanced fartlek	8 Medium endurance	8 Medium endurance	8 Medium endurance	— Off	7 Race X-C—5K	45
STRENGTHENING	5	5 Short endurance	— Off	7 Medium endurance	8 Medium endurance	6 5K pace interval 4 × Long hill	7 Medium endurance	12 Long endurance	45
SHARPENING	6	— Off	7 Hill fartlek	8 Medium endurance	7 Medium endurance	8 / 5 Strength Advanced fartlek	5 Short endurance	10 Medium endurance	45
SHARPENING	7	— Off	7 5K pace intervals 3 × 1 mile	6 Medium endurance	6 Medium endurance	8 / 5 Hill fartlek	5 Short endurance	8 Medium endurance	40
TAPERING	8	4 Short endurance	6 5K pace intervals 5 × 880	4 Short endurance	6 Medium endurance	5 Medium endurance	— Off	5 Race X-C—5K	25 + race

Use the 5K speed-training chart in the Appendices.

254

THE EXPERIENCED CROSS-COUNTRY COMPETITOR'S 12-WEEK BUILDUP SCHEDULE FOR 2½ MILES TO 5K

PHASE	WEEK	MONDAY	TUESDAY	WEDNESDAY	THURSDAY	FRIDAY	SATURDAY	SUNDAY	TOTAL MILEAGE
ENDURANCE	1	6 Medium endurance	6 Medium endurance	6 Medium endurance	6 Medium endurance	6 Medium endurance	5 Short endurance	10 Long endurance	45
ENDURANCE	2	6 Medium endurance	6 10K pace interval 6 × 880	5 Short endurance	5 Medium endurance	8 Strength Advanced *fartlek* 4	7 Medium endurance	7 Medium endurance	45
ENDURANCE	3	6 Medium endurance	7 10K pace interval 4 × 1 mile	4 Short endurance	4 Medium endurance	6 Hill *fartlek*	4 Short endurance	12 Long endurance	45
ENDURANCE	4	4 Short endurance	7 5K pace interval 6 × 880	7 Medium endurance	7 Strength Advanced *fartlek* 4	4 Short endurance	6 Race Cross-country 5K	5 Short endurance	40
STRENGTHENING	5	6 Medium endurance	6 Medium endurance	6 Medium endurance	5 5K pace interval 8 × Short hill	6 Medium endurance	4 Short endurance	12 Long endurance	45
STRENGTHENING	6	4 Short endurance	8 5K pace interval 6 × Long hill	6 Medium endurance	7 Medium endurance	7 Strength Advanced *fartlek* 4	5 Short endurance	8 Medium endurance	45
STRENGTHENING	7	7 Medium endurance	6 5K pace interval 4 × 1 mile	6 Short endurance	4 Medium endurance	7 5K pace interval 6 × 880	7 Medium endurance	8 Medium endurance	45
STRENGTHENING	8	6 Hill *fartlek*	7 Strength Advanced *fartlek* 4	7 Strength Advanced *fartlek* 4	8 Medium endurance	8 Short endurance	5 Race Cross-country 5K	4 Short endurance	40
STRENGTHENING	9	7 Medium endurance	7 Medium endurance	8 Medium endurance	8 Strength Advanced *fartlek* 4	6 Medium endurance	4 Fast interval 4 × 880	4 Short endurance	40
SHARPEN-ING	10	6 Medium endurance	8 Fast interval 8 × 440	4 Medium endurance	6 Medium endurance	6 Short endurance	5 Race Cross-country 5K	4 Short endurance	35
SHARPEN-ING	11	6 Medium endurance	6 Medium endurance	6 Short endurance	4 Strength Advanced *fartlek* 4	6 Short endurance	6 5K pace interval 4 × 1 mile	4 Short endurance	35
TAPER-ING	12	6 Medium endurance	5 Strength Advanced *fartlek* 4	6 Medium endurance	4 Short endurance	— Off	— Race Cross-country 5K	4 Short endurance	25 + race

Use the 5K speed-training chart in the Appendices.

Note: This schedule builds to Saturday races when most high schools compete.

255

THE EXPERIENCED CROSS-COUNTRY COMPETITOR'S 12-WEEK BUILDUP SCHEDULE FOR 5 MILES TO 10K

PHASE	WEEK	MONDAY	TUESDAY	WEDNESDAY	THURSDAY	FRIDAY	SATURDAY	SUNDAY	TOTAL MILEAGE
ENDURANCE	1	10 Medium endurance	10 Medium endurance	6 Short endurance	10 Medium endurance	12 Medium endurance	6 Short endurance	16 Long endurance	70
	2	10 Medium endurance	12 10K pace intervals 6 × 880	6 Short endurance	12 Medium endurance	6 Hill *fartlek*	12 Medium endurance	12 Medium endurance	70
	3	10 Medium endurance	12 10K pace intervals 3 × 1 mile	6 Short endurance	12 Medium endurance	6 Strength Advanced *fartlek*	8 Short endurance	16 Long endurance	70
	4	10 Medium endurance	10 10K pace interval 8 × 880	9 Medium endurance	10 Hill *fartlek*	10 Medium endurance	8 Medium endurance	10 Race Cross-country 10K	65
STRENGTHENING	5	5 Short endurance	8 Medium endurance	8 Medium endurance	12 Medium endurance	10 10K pace interval 10 × Short hill	6 Short endurance	16 Long endurance	65
	6	10 Medium endurance	10 Strength Advanced *fartlek*	6 Short endurance	12 Medium endurance	10 10K pace intervals 6 × Long hill	6 Short endurance	16 Long endurance	70
	7	10 Medium endurance	10 10K pace intervals 4 × 1 mile	6 Short endurance	12 Medium endurance	10 Hill *fartlek*	10 Medium endurance	12 Medium endurance	70
	8	10 Medium endurance	10 10K pace interval 8 × 880	6 Short endurance	8 Strength Advanced *fartlek*	10 Medium endurance	6 Short endurance	10 Race Cross-country 10K	60
	9	5 Short endurance	5 Medium endurance	8 Medium endurance	10 Strength Fast continuous run	6 Hill *fartlek*	7 Fast interval 6 × 880	10 Medium endurance	60
SHARPENING	10	10 Medium endurance	7 10K pace interval 12 × Short hill	8 Medium endurance	6 Strength Advanced *fartlek*	10 Short endurance	4 Short endurance	10 Race Cross-country 10K	55
	11	5 Short endurance	8 Medium endurance	8 Medium endurance	8 10K pace interval 8 × 880	6 Short endurance	8 Fast interval 6 × 880	10 Medium endurance	55
TAPERING	12	8 Medium endurance	6 Strength Advanced *fartlek*	8 Medium endurance	8 Medium endurance	8 Short endurance	— Off	— Race Cross-country 10K	36 + race

Use the 10K speed-training chart in the Appendices.

19. BEYOND THE MARATHON— THE ULTRA

For some runners, the 10K or half marathon is the upper limit. For most, the marathon offers the ultimate challenge. A chosen few, however, enter the world of the ultramarathon.

Ultras are any distance beyond 26.2 miles, most commonly 50K (31.1 miles), 100K (62.2 miles), and 50 and 100 miles. The 50K is considered a long marathon and the transition run between the marathon and an ultramarathon.

Ultras may be run on a road or a track. They may include challenges like seeing how many miles the runners can cover in 24 or 48 hours, or even 6 days. Ultras may be raced or run alone across country.

Who runs ultras? Anyone who can run a marathon comfortably can run an ultramarathon uncomfortably. You only need psychological strength and patience; this race requires discipline over long periods of time. There are two types of ultramarathon runners. One finishes the marathon feeling that he or she could have run longer. They are curious: Can I meet the challenge of the ultra? They want to test themselves, to see if they can complete an ultramarathon run, and then return, hopefully satisfied, to the shorter distances. Other runners run the ultramarathon and get hooked. They run it again and again, by choice, varying their distances and improving their times. Ultra runners drop back to run with the rest of us on occasion, but the ultra is their race, their challenge.

TIPS FOR YOUR FIRST ULTRAMARATHON

Don't consider running an ultramarathon until you have run two 26.2-mile marathons and can complete the marathon in reasonable comfort. In fact, Ted Corbitt, the wily veteran ultramarathoner, advises that a "baby 50"—the 50K—be run before a 50-miler is attempted.

Pick a Distance of 50 Miles or Less

Train like a marathoner. If you are adequately trained—60–70 miles a week with long runs of 20 miles—you don't need any other special conditioning to survive an ultra of 50K or 50 miles. You don't need more mileage or longer runs now. You'll wear yourself out or get injured. Later, when you are ready to race an ultra, you will want to increase your mileage with longer runs.

Run the Ultra Slowly, but Not Too Slowly

This means more slowly than your marathon pace and even more slowly than your training pace. But running too slowly may be unnatural and cause you to tire or become injured.

Take Breaks

Your only goal now is to finish the ultramarathon so you can brag about it. In Bob Glover's first 50K, he ran all the way; it is just 5 miles beyond the marathon. But for his first 50-miler—400 laps around an unshaded track on a hot day—he had to resort to all sorts of tricks to survive. One of them was the planned break. Take walk breaks early to conserve energy for later, rather than running as fast as you can, praying that you can stagger to the finish line. Glover walked ¼ mile after running each 5 miles. Those who didn't passed him early, but he breezed by them later in the run when they were walking—not by choice. The tortoise always beats the hare in the ultra. Glover even changed his clothes during the breaks, including his shoes, and went to the bathroom, drank fluids, and ate a small container of baby food. Break your own ultra into small segments of about 5 miles each. Take short breaks after each one; it's great relief. Most ultramarathons are run around loops, which makes taking breaks easy.

Don't Stop Moving During Your Breaks

If you sit down for a long time, you'll tighten up. Keep progressing toward the finish line. Waste as little energy as possible going in any other direction.

Bring Your Own Support System

Friends can help you with food and drink, counting laps (you won't be accurate at this after a while), handling your equipment, and encouraging you to keep going. They should also recognize when you should stop, and drag you off the course if need be.

Drop Out

If you get injured and start favoring your injury, stop running. You'll make the injury far worse. But if you are merely tired and want to quit, don't. You probably feel better than many of the other runners.

Keep One Goal Firmly in Mind: Finish

Just as with your first race and your first marathon, the goal of your first ultra is to finish the run. You experience your first ultra, you don't race it.

Concentrate on Each 5-Mile Segment

Run the ultra in 5-mile segments at first, and later in 1-mile sections. Thinking too far ahead may destroy you mentally.

Start with the attitude that you are going for a fun run. When you pass the marathon distance, you are an ultramarathoner and should think only about keeping moving; you can walk if you want. Be calm, don't panic. You will run in and out of "bad patches." Take the race after 26.2 miles 1 mile at a time. Remember: The ultra requires extreme patience and mental toughness. In its late stages, the ultra is simply mind over body.

Drink Plenty of Fluids

Pour into yourself water and drinks with sugar and electrolytes. You'll need to replace lost energy sources and minerals.

Eat Little and Conservatively

While eating isn't necessary, if you do eat, be sure it's something that agrees with you. French fries are out. So is pizza. Glover found that baby food digested easily. But it sure tasted bad after baking in a 90° sun.

TIPS FOR RUNNING FASTER ULTRAS

Many of the tips useful to first-time marathoners are also of benefit to first-time ultramarathoners.

Mileage

Start training with a base of 50 to 60 miles a week, and gradually increase to 70 or 100. You won't improve your fitness level much beyond 100 miles a week. Many veteran ultramarathoners, in fact, get by with only 50 to 70 miles a week; they've already got plenty of "miles in the bank," plus a few ultra runs. Most top ultramarathon runners, however, put in high mileage. The key is the accumulation of mileage over a long period of time, combined with long training runs and the experience of surviving ultramarathons.

The Ultra Long Run

As you build mileage for your ultramarathon, also increase the length of your long runs. This conditions you mentally as well as physically. You learn to keep going when you think you can't, and your legs learn to carry your body for long distances. Your body also learns to use fat rather than glycogen as a primary fuel.

Do an exceptionally long run once every 3 weeks, or twice every 4 weeks, as you approach your race. This might be 30 to 50 miles; or run only for time, say 4 to 10 hours. Take many fluid and walk breaks; just complete the distance to get a feel for it. Don't exhaust yourself. You should be able to return to your normal training runs within a few days. Any run beyond 26 miles is specific training for your ultramarathon.

Two suggestions. First, run these long runs point-to-point. (For instance, from one town to another.) That will give you a strong desire to finish. Bring along someone in a car with all your training "goodies" and to get you home. Second, run loops of about 5 miles, and stop after each loop to drink and walk.

Train Progressively

Most of your training runs should be at a slow, conversational pace, but some speed work, such as 1-mile interval runs and short races, will help to build strength. Even the marathon may be speed work for the true ultra runner. Faster running serves as a change of pace, but build slowly on a base of endurance and confidence with consistent mileage and ultra runs. While ultramarathoners will benefit somewhat from speed work and shorter races, 90 to 95 percent of their training should be done just to accumulate time on their feet.

Taper and Rebuild

Follow the marathon tapering program. Rebuild carefully according to your experience and fitness level.

Prepare Mentally

You will experience discomfort—no doubt about it. Restrain your emotions during the early part of the race; don't allow yourself to get too "psyched up." Look at the ultra start as a fun-filled training run with friends. In shorter races you get all charged up and run out with the leaders. But in the ultra, the early leaders seldom even finish. Hold yourself back physically and emotionally. Use your mental energy later, when your physical energy has run dry. Run the race at your pace.

Select a Good Handler

Behind every good ultramarathoner is a great handler. He or she is essential. Make sure that your handler is dependable and knows you well enough to judge when to push you and when to get you to stop.

Run Straight Lines

By running all the way to the inside of a loop course, or by cutting tangents on curves (if allowed), you will save many minutes over the course of an ultramarathon. At the end, the minutes will feel like hours.

Change Your Pace

Periodically change your foot strike, stride, and pace. You will run heel-ball with mostly short, economical strides. Put in a few bursts at a quicker pace, especially if the course is flat and without hills for variety. Use different muscles, and let some of those that are getting tired take a break. For the most part, run an even pace, starting a few seconds a mile faster than your goal pace. Some top ultra runners prefer to start slowly for the first 5 to 10 miles and then pick it up. A few top runners start fast and hold on.

How Does It Feel?

The first 20 miles are like any other training run. You should hit the marathon mark in comfort. If you've trained properly, you'll burn stored fuel (glycogen) for the first 30 to 35 miles. Then, no matter how fit you are, you'll be running on mental strength. You will have exhausted your glycogen reserves; you may be dehydrated and suffering from mineral imbalances. Your legs will be tired, your back stiff, your stomach upset, your feet hurting and probably full of blisters. You may wish that the Bear and the Wall were around—old friends, those—instead of what Glover calls "the death grip."

From 30 to 40 miles during his 50-mile race, Glover thought he was going to die. It was awful. He mentally wrote his will and obituary. By 40 miles, however, he felt somewhat better, perhaps because his body was supplying energy with slow-burning fat. At 45 miles, he suddenly felt "high" as he realized he was going to finish the race. He couldn't slow down, and ran his fastest 5-mile split of the day. In the ultra, you too may run through various moods or even experience hallucinations.

YOUR TRAINING PROGRAM

Here is a typical 7-day training schedule for the serious ultra-marathoner. Aside from the ultra long run, it is very similar in mileage distribution to a marathon training schedule.

MONDAY	TUESDAY	WEDNESDAY	THURSDAY
easy 4–6	easy 5, A.M. easy 5–8, P.M.	15–20	10–15*

FRIDAY	SATURDAY	SUNDAY	TOTAL WEEKLY MILEAGE
10–15	easy 5–10	20–50	90–100

*(Include 4–6 × 1 mile at 30 seconds per mile faster than marathon pace, 3-minute rest.)

The ultramarathoner has extended the previous limits of our physical boundaries. The marathon has become a commonplace run—the challenge now lies beyond. Thousands of runners are exploring their limits by running longer ultra-marathons, or entering the increasingly popular offshoot of the ultra, the triathlon. This is an endurance event consisting of long runs, swimming, and biking in sequence during one tough day.

Like the marathon, when you complete the ultramarathon you will come to know more about your special inner self—a part of our humanness we are just coming to know.

Part VI
THE MARATHON

20. YOUR FIRST MARATHON

"Marathon mania" has swept not only the USA but the world as the symbol and the glamour event of the road-racing boom. The standard marathon event of 26.2 miles (42.195 kilometers) is run through the streets of almost every major city in the United States and the world. It has become a vacation attraction offered by travel agents in such exciting spots as San Francisco, Honolulu, New York, London, Rome, Berlin, Paris, Montreal, Madrid, Stockholm, Rio de Janeiro, Athens, and even Peking and Moscow. What a way to see a city—by running a marathon through its streets!

The marathon is the longest and most difficult race for most runners. It symbolizes the peak of physical and mental performance. Once you finish a marathon, you are a real runner. According to Richard Traum, "Anyone who honestly takes the time to train can finish a marathon. You don't have to be much of an athlete, just patient and disciplined. You have to put in the time." Traum has completed more than eight marathons with an artificial leg, and over 100 physically disabled athletes with the Achilles Track Club compete each year in the New York Marathon. And you're never too old to run your first marathon. Eighty-year-old Ruth Rothfarb made her marathon debut at the 1981 Avon International Marathon in Ottawa, becoming the oldest female (so far) to complete the distance. The youthful octogenarian then danced into the wee hours of the morning to celebrate.

PICKING YOUR FIRST MARATHON

Don't choose a hot one, a hilly one, or a race that won't include a lot of novices like you. If possible, choose one near your home. Your only goal in this first race is to finish.

TRAINING FOR YOUR FIRST MARATHON

Before training for your first marathon, you must have 1 or, preferably, 2 years of running logged in your diary and must have run several races of varying lengths. If you have been running 20 miles a week for the last several months, you may be ready to begin your buildup to the marathon.

You need a minimum amount of mileage and long runs to reach the marathon finish line in comfort. The key here is balance. You don't need speed work or the training phases mentioned earlier. Your only phases will be to build up your endurance base so you can finish the race and to taper your training before the race. Balance the right amount of weekly mileage, the right amount and frequency of long runs. You must be willing to put in the time and not take shortcuts. Also, you must avoid the temptation to overtrain. If you train too little, you won't make it to the finish line. If you train too much, you won't make it to the starting line. The percentage of marathon starters who cross the finish line is much higher than the percentage of runners who start marathon training and make it to the starting line. Follow our minimum and maximum training guidelines for surviving both marathon training and the marathon itself.

Weekly Mileage

As the following charts indicate, you should slowly build to 40–50 miles a week of training. Never increase by more than 2–

3 miles from one week to the next. Plateau at 30 miles for a few weeks and again at 40 miles to allow your body a chance to adjust to the training load. You will benefit little from additional mileage during your 3-week tapering period prior to the race. In fact, you will benefit most by doing less mileage, since that minimizes the chance of an injury and allows your body and mind to restore needed energy to tackle the 26.2-mile challenge. Cramming in last-minute mileage will do more harm than good. By starting to build your mileage 6 months in advance, you will have a huge reservoir of endurance to draw from and thus can lose time along the way to baby a few aches and pains.

Long Runs

Too many runners make the mistake of concentrating on weekly mileage, but not getting in a sufficient number of long runs. The accompanying sample schedules list recommended long runs on Sunday—do them on whatever day fits your schedule. You may find, for example, that a long run on Saturday will leave you fresher for a speed session on Tuesday. The distance of the long run should be gradually increased as you increase your weekly mileage. As you get up to runs of 12 miles and more, alternate running long every other week to minimize the physical and mental fatigue associated with the long run. Take an easy day before the long run and take off the following day (although a short bike ride or swim will minimize stiffness and aid recovery). Twenty miles is the limit on long runs for novice marathoners—anything longer will cause more tearing down than building. Don't worry, on race day your mileage base and the excitement of the crowd will carry you over the last 6.2 miles to the finish line. Your last long run should be at least 2 weeks prior to the marathon.

Races

Novice marathoners should run some races of 10K–25K to learn how to handle pacing, fluid replacement, etc. Do not run these races all-out, but rather as long training runs. Race at least once a month as you are building for the marathon, but not more than twice a month. Your last race should be 2–3 weeks prior to the marathon.

Running Equivalents

You can minimize the wear and tear on your body by replacing up to 20 percent of your mileage with biking or swimming. Do these activities at a pace that will get your heart rate in your training range, and count how many miles you would have run during the alternative training as "running equivalent" mileage.

Injury

Do not attempt to train if you are favoring an injury. Seek advice from a sports medicine expert who is familiar with runners and all their complaints and aches. Replace running with biking or swimming if possible while you recover. If an injury is threatening your health as you approach the marathon, be wise and take advantage of the fact that you can turn in your spot and train for next year's marathon.

The First-Time Marathon 4-Month Training Schedule (from a 25-mile-a-week base)

Thousands of runners have completed their first marathons following the three basic schedules we use. The following 4-month training program is our minimum schedule for those runners training for their first marathon.

THE FIRST-TIME MARATHON 4-MONTH TRAINING SCHEDULE (from a 25-mile-a-week base)

WEEK	MON.	TUES.	WED.	THURS.	FRI.	SAT.	SUN.	TOTAL MILEAGE
1	Off	4	4	4	4	3	6	25
2	Off	4	5	4	4	3	8	28
3	Off	4	5	4	5	2	10	30
4	Off	4	6	4	5	4	10	33
5	Off	4	6	5	6	4	12	37

6	Off	4	6	4	5	4	14	37
7	Off	4	6	4	6	4	16	40
8	Off	6	6	4	6	6	12	40
9	Off	4	6	4	4	4	18	40
10	Off	6	6	4	6	6	14	42
11	Off	4	6	4	6	5	20	45
12	Off	6	6	5	8	6	14	45
13	Off	5	6	4	6	6	18	45
14	Off	4	6	6	6	4	14	40
15	Off	6	6	5	4	10	4	35
16 Race week	Off	4	6	4	Off	2	Race day marathon	16 + Race

Note: When you race, you may need to adjust your daily and weekly mileage downward. Do not attempt to combine long runs and races on the same day or weekend.

The First-Time Marathon 6-Month Training Schedule (*from a 20-mile-a-week base*)

Ideally, you should plan 6 months ahead of your marathon. This obviously allows you more time to prepare for the race, and also gives you a deeper endurance base as well as flexibility in case of lost training time because of illness, injury, or travel. A busy schedule mandates a long-term plan.

The program on page 272 takes exactly half a year—26 weeks of preparation: 1 week for every mile of the marathon. It is basically the same as the 4-month plan, but is our preferred training schedule and builds to a base of 45 miles per week.

The First-Time Marathon 3-Month Training Schedule (*from a 40-mile-a-week base*)

This will work—and not be a disaster—*only* if you have a solid base of endurance: *at least* 1 or 2 months at 35 to 40 miles a week. This foundation will allow you to build for the marathon within 3 months. *This is not a shortcut for the novice competitor.* It is often used for your second marathon after following our longer schedule for your first marathon.

From our base of 40 miles a week, start with Week 15* of

the 26-week schedule on the following page and count down toward the marathon.

THE FIRST-TIME MARATHON 6-MONTH TRAINING SCHEDULE (from a 20-mile-a-week base)

WEEK	MON.	TUES.	WED.	THURS.	FRI.	SAT.	SUN.	TOTAL MILEAGE
1	Off	3	3	3	3	2	6	20
2	Off	3	4	3	3	3	6	22
3	Off	3	4	3	4	3	7	24
4	Off	4	4	4	4	3	7	26
5	Off	4	5	4	4	3	8	28
6	Off	4	5	4	5	4	8	30
7	Off	4	5	4	4	3	10	30
8	Off	4	5	4	4	3	10	30
9	Off	4	5	4	4	3	10	30
10	Off	4	5	4	4	3	12	32
11	Off	5	6	4	5	4	10	34
12	Off	5	6	4	5	4	12	36
13	Off	5	8	5	5	5	10	38
14	Off	5	6	5	5	4	15	40
15*	Off	6	8	5	6	5	10	40
16	Off	5	6	5	5	4	15	40
17	Off	6	8	5	6	5	10	40
18	Off	4	6	5	5	4	18	42
19	Off	6	8	6	6	6	10	42
20	Off	6	6	6	5	4	18	45
21	Off	6	8	6	7	6	12	45
22	Off	6	6	5	4	4	20	45
23	Off	6	8	6	7	6	12	45
24	Off	5	5	5	5	Off	20	40
25	Off	4	6	4	4	4	8	30
26	Off	4	6	4	Off	2	Marathon	16 + Race

TIPS FOR YOUR FIRST MARATHON

Training

• Check with your *physician* before beginning the stressful training for a marathon.

• Find a *partner* or two who is training for the same marathon; run together, and if possible, run the marathon together.

• Train for 2 to 4 weeks in the same trusty *shoes* you'll run the marathon in. *Not* racing flats. If you travel to the race by plane, do not check your shoes, but carry them on board with you. Shoes that are well broken in are the marathoner's most cherished possession.

• Determine your *schedule,* and plan each day to marathon day.

• *Progress gradually* in both mileage and long runs. Long runs build confidence; don't neglect them. Also, one run a day is plenty; no two-a-days yet.

• Take *1 day off* a week, sometimes 2. If you feel tired or get injured, take another day off, or more.

• *Adjust your training* for lost days. You can gradually make up lost time. Be sure to return slowly, however. "Listen to your body," and avoid injury. If your schedule fatigues you or you become injured, back off. You must push through to a small degree, but if you continue to run through fatigue or injury you will do more harm than good. *Return slowly* and gradually take shortcuts to get back into your schedule. You might repeat the week you were out or take 2 to 4 weeks to catch up. Don't panic. A long-term schedule will allow you to miss even a few weeks and still make it to the finish line. You may decide to just stay two weeks behind the schedule—this will be adequate. If you miss a month or more, however, seriously consider skipping this marathon.

• *Stretch* before and after each workout.

• *Respect the heat.* Slow down in hot weather. Cut back your mileage or long run if the heat becomes a burden. Drink lots of fluids, try to run in the morning or evening.

• *Respect the cold.* Wear layers and vent excess heat while you run. Don't toss away gloves or hat too soon. A change in wind direction will make you regret it. Tuck them in your shorts, tie your windbreaker around your waist.

• *Respect the changes in your life,* such as family, work, diet, a new companion or baby, falling in or out of love. Be flexible in your training—but also be consistent.

• *Respect the long run.* It is very important, but requires several days from which to recover.

• Practice *drinking fluids* on your long runs, to find the fluid best for you (we recommend water), and see how your stomach likes it.

• *Practice walking* during your long runs to get the feel of starting again. You don't need to run the whole 26.2 miles on race day.

• *"Train, don't strain."*

• *Keep a detailed diary,* recording every aspect of your training, including diet, shoes, clothing, weather and time of day, unusual stresses, and so forth.

• *Race occasionally.* This is a good way to prevent yourself from starting too fast on race day and blowing all your training. A few races—increasing the distance from 10K to the half marathon or 30K—will give you confidence and a long run. Race at least once a month in the last 3 months prior to your marathon.

• Get more *sleep* as your mileage increases, and *eat moderately, reducing excess weight* without following any crash diet that will be an added stress.

• *Tapering is very important.* Last-minute training will do harm, not good. We actually know of a runner who, 3 days before his first marathon, ran 26.2 miles indoors on a track to see if he could cover the distance. He could—3 days early; but not on race day.

Prerace

• *Eat* carbohydrates during the last 3 to 4 days before, but *don't deplete. Don't stuff yourself* with unfamiliar foods before long runs and races.

• Get to the race early with your *equipment and number* (if you've already picked it up).

• *Don't overdress or underdress.* Peel during the race. Hint: It is better to start out a little cool than just right or too hot.

• Apply Vaseline or foot powder to your feet to *prevent blisters.* You should try this for your training runs. Apply Vaseline around your *crotch and inner thighs* to minimize chafing. Cover your *nipples* with Vaseline or a Band-Aid to prevent rubbing. In cold wind, Vaseline on your *face* will protect your skin.

• *Avoid the premarathon hoopla.* Don't spend hours on your feet walking around to prerace clinics, exhibits, and so forth. Don't get caught up in all the excitement and drain away energy.

• Two days or the day before, *go for a short, easy jog.* Take the other day off.

• Don't avoid *sex* the day or night before the marathon. You'll be more relaxed and sleep better. Do avoid staying up all night looking for it.

• *Wake up* at least 3 hours before starting time if the marathon starts in the morning. If you insist on eating, eat light and at least 3 hours before the race.

• *Stay off your feet* as much as possible before the race.

• *Warm up,* stretch, walk, jog across the starting line and out a few hundred yards to get the "feel" of the course. Use the *toilet* one last time.

• *Drink* fluids 10–15 minutes prior to the start.

• Your *goal:* finishing in comfort. A 12-minute-a-mile jog is a 5-hour marathon. The first-time marathoner often runs between 4 and 5 hours; many finish more slowly than that. But remember—the slower you finish, the easier it will be to improve your time.

• *Fear not.* You won't finish last, and someone will still be at the finish line when you get there. The Honolulu Marathon prides itself on the fact that the last-place finisher comes in over 8 hours.

The Race

• *Drink* plenty of fluids. On a hot day, drink *water* and pour it over yourself.

• Slow down your starting *pace* on a *hot day* by as much as 1 minute a mile.

• *Start* at the back of the pack. Run very *slowly,* well within your ability and training (30 seconds to a minute slower than your normal 10-mile training pace).

• Concentrate on maintaining *good form.* Use a short, economical stride, bringing the knees up just enough so you can keep your legs moving. Use the heel-ball foot strike and shuffle stride.

• If you are *injured* (limping, in pain) or feeling *ill*—perhaps from the heat—walk. If the symptoms remain or increase, go to an aid station. *Leave the race.* You are not a hero for continuing, but a fool. People have pulled muscles, broken bones, and died during marathons. Be sensible.

• *Walk* during the race if you feel tired or if you cramp. In the heat, your legs may feel like cement pillars after 15 miles. Just keep moving briskly; alternate running and walking if need be, but don't sit down no matter how strong the urge.

• No one ever said it was going to be easy. You have to have *fortitude.* If you have trained properly and do not feel ill or are not hampered by an injury, then you should finish as long as you can handle it mentally. Dig down deep for extra strength and keep going. Friends and spectators offer encouragement. This is why you can go those extra 6 miles beyond your 20-mile training run—you have the support of all the runners around you and all the spectators along the course. If you can, find a group to run with during the race to help each other along through periods of weakness. Everyone feels like quitting many times. You are not alone. Keep moving, take it one step at a time, one mile marker at a time, and *smile* when you cross the finish line. You're a marathoner!

Postrace

• *Stretch and walk* after you finish. *Do not sit down.* Drink fluids continuously. Follow our guidelines for eating and drinking after racing.

• Take a *hot bath* as soon as you can, or take a whirlpool or easy swim. *Walk. Stretch* gently. Repeat the following morning.

• Treat all *blisters* and other *ailments* promptly and properly.

• *Return* gradually to *running.* Don't train or race hard for *at least* 4 to 8 weeks. *Recover, rebuild.*

• *Analyze your results.* Your first comment will be "Never again!" Within a few hours you will probably be saying to your non-marathon friends, "If I had only . . ." You will now understand that with a few longer runs, a month or two more of endurance training, some speed work here and there, and an extra helping of spaghetti, you might have lowered your time by 15 minutes. (Okay, so you lie a little.)

• During this recovery period, create *a new marathon training schedule* following our guidelines in chapter 21.

• *Plan well, train intelligently, race wisely.*

SOME CONCLUDING WORDS

You don't ever have to run a marathon. Don't ever let anyone push you into something you don't want to do. The lure of this popular event creates a lot of peer pressure. Desire is the only emotion that will get you through your training and to the finish line. Some runners never race; some love the 10K races or the half marathons. Find your desire and follow it.

Also, if you've entered the marathon but your training is not up to the minimum, don't go. Instead, start training for the next marathon. Treat the marathon with respect. Better to postpone than to fail.

Finally, don't take racing, or marathon running, too seriously. Rumor has it that there is life after running. There is even life after—or without—marathoning. But there is also nothing like that feeling when you cross the finish line of your first marathon. Head up, legs tired but still churning, arms pumping, you hug the runner in front of you in the chute. You congratulate each other. You smile, you laugh, you cry. And—damn!—you know you are *good!*

21. MARATHON TRAINING AND RACING

Participating in a marathon and racing a marathon are not the same. The previous chapter outlines a program that will allow the average recreational runner to become a marathon participant, and a finisher. But to race a marathon, you need the physical preparation and mental toughness to push your body at a pace faster than your 30–60-minute daily aerobic runs for several hours. Your first marathon is a test of survival. Then, as you strive to run faster and faster it becomes more a matter of self-torture. You strive to run near your anaerobic threshold, within your discomfort zone, for mile after mile after mile.

A marathon, says the dictionary, is any test of endurance. But almost every marathon runner knows the legend of a fierce battle on the plains near the small Greek town of Marathon in 490 B.C. The invading Persian army was caught by surprise by the outmanned Athenians, who charged into their ranks and saved the Greek empire. Pheidippides, a Greek soldier, was ordered to run to Athens with the news of victory. His run of about 22 miles from the battlefield is considered the first "marathon," but poor Pheidippides wasn't as fit as the modern marathoner. He entered Athens, exclaimed "Rejoice, we conquer!" and collapsed and died.

The marathon was added to the first modern Olympic Games held in Athens in 1896, and was won by a Greek, Spiridon Loues. Spiridon Clubs (Road Runners Clubs) have been established throughout Europe, and annual marathon runs are held over Pheidippides' route. In the United States, the first marathon was run 35 miles, from Stamford, Connecticut, to New York City. But the event was discontinued until 1970. Boston, with a marathon every year since 1896, remains the city with the oldest continuous marathon in the world.

The distance of the marathon has varied until recent history. Pheidippides ran 38 kilometers as compared with the present standardized 42.195 kilometers (think metric!). From 1896 to 1908, the Olympic marathon distance was unset, but in 1908 the Olympics were held in London, and the races began at Windsor Castle and ended at the new White City Stadium. An English princess, so the story goes, wanted to watch the start of the race from her castle window and then view the finish from her seat at the stadium. The distance, set to please Her Highness, was 26 miles, 385 yards. That was about 2 miles longer than previous marathons, but it became the standardized distance. As you puff along those last few miles, all obscenities should be uttered to "Her Royal Highness," whose vanity created the distance.

In the Munich Olympics of 1972, Frank Shorter, Kenny Moore, and Jack Bachelor finished 1–4–9 for the greatest American Olympic marathon performance to date. Millions of excited Americans watched on television. This American triumph in an event previously dominated by other nations signaled the start of the marathon boom in this country. Within an hour of Shorter's greatest moment, Bob Glover was on the roads training seriously for the first time in 8 years. And so were a lot of other American runners.

Why would anyone want to run a marathon? The glamour and tradition of "the classic distance" captures the imagination. It's also "there," like the highest mountain or the tallest building. As the longest, most grueling, and most unpredictable running event, it is a symbol of superiority in physical and mental performance.

Most beginner marathon runners enter the first race to prove that their minds and bodies can meet the challenge, and their only goal is to finish. Then they may set time goals of breaking 3 or 3½ hours, and training toward those goals. They search to find their limits and then reach beyond them. They also begin comparing themselves with other runners.

As veterans of many marathons, we've learned many "secrets" of survival, although we never guarantee that any one of us will ever experience that beautiful, pain-free, fast marathon of runners' dreams. The marathon event is a true test of the runner. Proper training, diet, race experience, pacing, and so forth are important, but among the elusive elements that make the marathon special are the combination of Mother Nature and Lady Luck, and your mental ability to overcome physical torture for 26 miles, 385 yards. The marathoner learns to discover the peace inside of pain.

The key to marathon running is planning and completing a training program that will prepare both your body and your mind for the 26-mile 385-yard distance. To attempt a marathon without proper training is to risk failure or serious injury. Yet we all hear of marathon runners who just "jump into a marathon" on the spur of the moment. Both of us have done this—with painful and lingering consequences. That's why we both can say with determination that running a marathon on a whim—or considering 6 to 8 weeks of training adequate preparation—can be very risky. Don't get caught up in the popularity of this exciting distance event. Train. Prepare. And then enjoy.

Take the time to plan a long-term training program of about 4 to 6 months, and then follow that schedule as closely as possible before running your marathon. This is necessary for all levels of competitors. Every runner must give this race the respect and training it deserves. You can't expect to train properly for and race more than one or two marathons per year; and only one for novice competitors.

THE MARATHON TRAINING SCHEDULE

This marathon training schedule is for all four fitness categories and uses the six-step approach outlined in chapter 13.

STEP ONE: DETERMINE YOUR FITNESS CATEGORY

Look up your appropriate category in chapter 1 based on your marathon time.

STEP TWO: SELECT YOUR RACES AND TIME GOALS

Choose the marathon you wish to peak for and then start an 18-week training program as described in this chapter.

The 4-to-6-month buildup is a long time to hold your interest. Intermediate goals, shorter races along the way, will help keep you motivated and help you evaluate your progress. By establishing and meeting these secondary goals, you will also salvage your racing season and your training if injury, bad weather, or other factors beyond your control spoil your marathon or cause you to miss it completely. Be careful not to overrace—it will interfere with your ability to maintain the necessary high mileage. Many marathoners, especially inexperienced ones, don't race often enough going into a marathon and thus are out of touch with what a race feels like. Compete at least once a month, but no more than twice a month in your last 3 months of training.

Use races early in your program for fun and to build strength. "Train through" these events without complete tapering. Select a few races in your last month or two (10K–30K), and go for a good time, perhaps even a PR. You will be in very good shape, and recording good performances will give you the incentive to continue training for the marathon. You can determine your fitness level and predict your marathon time from these efforts and thus go into your marathon with increased confidence. See chapter 26 for guidelines for establishing goals and how to use shorter racing distances to predict your marathon potential. If you run times much more slowly than the result that predicts the marathon goal you were aiming for, and don't have a good excuse (hot, hilly course, coming off the flu, etc.), then you need to scale down your marathon goal and your starting pace— or perhaps even cancel your marathon plans until you can prove in shorter races that you are near the fitness level required for a solid marathon effort. If your tune-up race times predict that you are capable of running much faster for the marathon than you had originally hoped, and you have a good base of mileage and long runs, then you should consider starting a little faster and adjusting your goals.

Choose time barriers to break for your marathon effort. Within this chapter we discuss guidelines for breaking the following popular marathon barriers: 4:00, 3:45, 3:30, 3:15, 3:00, 2:50, 2:40. The sub-4:00 barrier is considered the dividing line between marathon survivors and marathon runners; the sub-3:00 barrier is considered the dividing line between marathon runners and very good marathon racers.

STEP THREE: DETERMINE YOUR TRAINING CYCLE AND THE LENGTH OF YOUR PHASES

We recommend a long-term training cycle: a 4-month buildup with the endurance, strengthening, and sharpening phases followed by a 2-week taper, and then at least 4 weeks of rebuilding after the marathon. The entire cycle should last at least 5½ months. If you already have a solid base of endurance and are already near your peak mileage goal, you may be able to use a 3-month buildup. Start by gradually easing into the strengthening phase.

Novice and basic competitors are concerned mostly with the endurance and strengthening phases. They will spend little time (1 to 2 weeks) in the sharpening phase, which primarily consists of reducing mileage and a final short race. If these runners haven't done much base training, more time should be spent on the endurance phase. If you have been running for several years and have a fairly solid foundation of endurance training, you may want to move to the strengthening phase sooner.

Advanced competitors will spend more time in the strengthening phase and less in the endurance phase. The stronger you are, the better you will be at pushing your body through the depletion stages late in the marathon. The sharpening phase is fairly short (3 weeks) and includes a final hard race of 10K-half marathon.

The champion competitor's training program should emphasize the individual talents of the runner. This means that you may choose a long strengthening phase at high mileage if you are a naturally strong runner, or a long sharpening phase at less mileage if you are gifted with good speed. You should work to improve your weaknesses, but concentrate on your attributes. For most champion marathoners, a 3-to-4-week sharpening phase will be used to improve basic speed.

For all runners, to be successful at the marathon distance, you must first build the endurance and strength to go the distance at your normal training pace or slightly faster. Then you must work on speed to enable you to race at a pace which may be more than 1–2 minutes per mile faster than your training pace. If your weakness is not being able to go the distance comfortably, work more on your long runs and the endurance and strengthening phases. If you can easily go the distance but have trouble pushing a fast pace, you need to emphasize the strengthening and sharpening phases to build speed over distance and train more like a 10K runner. By using an 18-week buildup, you should have plenty of time to work on each of the key training phases.

Here is a guide to selecting your phases for marathon training:

DESCRIPTION	NOVICE	BASIC	ADVANCED	CHAMPION
Length of buildup	18 weeks	18	18	18
Endurance phase	10	8	6	6
Strengthening phase	4	6	7	6
Sharpening phase	2	2	3	4
Tapering phase	2	2	2	2
Rebuilding phase	4–8	4–8	4–6	3–6
Number of races in cycle	4–5	4–5	5–6	5–7

STEP FOUR: DETERMINE YOUR WEEKLY MILEAGE AND LONG-RUN GOALS

All runners need to be careful not to increase mileage too fast. Follow the general guidelines for increasing and managing mileage and long runs in chapter 6. See chapter 7 for guidelines for using alternative aerobic training in the management of mileage. Be sure to "plateau" occasionally as you build. Level off at a consistent mileage base at the end of the endurance phase and maintain it throughout the strengthening phase. As you increase the intensity of your speed work, cut back your mileage and cut back more in the tapering phase—over a 2-to-3-week period.

The novice and basic competitors need enough mileage to allow them to run through the Wall, but not so much that they will become overly fatigued or injured. Too much can be as bad as too little.

The advanced and champion runners will have to be very careful about balancing hard days and easy days when doing high mileage. These runners need enough mileage to allow them not to be worried about reaching a "collapse point." They should not fear the Wall itself, but rather the inability to push a fast pace. They must have both high mileage and quality speed work. This is a very demanding schedule, but trying to run as fast as you can for 26.2 miles is a very demanding task.

This is probably the only event you will race for which you haven't completed training runs longer than the race distance. Consistently high weekly mileage and regular long runs are necessary to train your body and mind to rise to this severe challenge. No matter how fast you are or what your experience level, without a solid base of mileage prior to your buildup and throughout your training cycle, you are a potential victim of the Wall. See chapter 22 for guidelines for the critical long training runs.

Follow the *flexible* weekly mileage goals on page 285 to adjust for the amount of *time* spent training and your age and running experience. The mileage ranges reflect an *approximately* equal effort for all levels and all ages of runners. The recommended mileage figures should be averaged for at least 8 weeks prior to tapering for the marathon.

Training pace should be at your base pace: $1\frac{1}{2}$–2 minutes slower than 10K pace (see guidelines in chapter 5).

WEEKLY MILEAGE GOALS FOR MARATHON TRAINING

	AGE 18–40	AGE 40–50	AGE 50–60	AGE 60+	MILEAGE OF LONG RUNS	LONG RUNS PER MONTH
NOVICE:						
Men	35–50	35–50	35–40	35–40	16–20	1–2
Women	35–50	35–50	35–40	35–40	16–20	1–2
BASIC:						
Men	40–50	40–50	40–50	40–50	18–20	2
Women	40–50	40–50	40–50	40–50	18–20	2
ADVANCED:						
Men	50–70	50–70	40–60	40–60	18–20	2–3
Women	50–70	50–70	40–60	40–60	18–20	2–3
CHAMPION:						
Men	70–90	70–90	60–80	50–60	20–23	3
Women	60–80	60–80	50–70	45–55	20–23	3

STEP FIVE: PLAN YOUR INDIVIDUAL WORKOUTS (See model schedules at the end of this chapter)

General Guidelines for Developing the Marathon Training Schedule

Preendurance Phase. Before beginning your marathon buildup, it is essential that you have already been running for several weeks at a mileage base that is within 15–20 miles per week of your peak mileage goal. This running can be done entirely at an easy conversational pace. Additionally, you should do a few long runs of 8–10 miles if you're a novice or basic competitor, and 10–12 miles if you're an advanced or champion competitor, before starting the endurance phase. Without this preendurance-phase work, you will not be able to handle the buildup of mileage and long runs safely.

Endurance Phase. During this phase, all marathoners gradually build up to their target weekly mileage and long runs. Run a few fun races at 5K–10K to maintain enthusiasm for racing. Don't be concerned with your time. Gradually blend in speed workouts: late in this phase for novice competitors, in the middle of the phase for more advanced marathoners. Highly experienced marathoners who already have a good base of fitness may be able to cut the endurance phase short by 4–6 weeks—thus they will only need a 12–14-week buildup because they have already done much of the work for the endurance phase. Be careful, however, not to take shortcuts here. Most runners are not experienced enough to carry their conditioning over from one cycle to another, and should spend more time between cycles rebuilding and then use a longer buildup going into the marathon.

Strengthening Phase. Maintain your peak level of mileage and long runs. Gradually add more speed work to your schedule, especially short and long hills, fast continuous runs, anaerobic threshold runs, advanced *fartlek,* and 1-mile pace-interval runs (at 30 seconds per mile faster than your present marathon pace—or approximately your present 10K race pace). As you get stronger, increase the quantity and intensity of those runs without lowering your mileage. The marathoner does more repetitions and longer distances for speed work than the 10K runner. Run two or three races during this phase of 10–20 miles to improve your ability to hold a strong pace over long distances. Ten-kilometer races are too short to teach this. Use anaerobic threshold runs, marathon-pace fast continuous runs, and your early races to run near your marathon goal pace. This teaches you to run relaxed and with good form at marathon pace. Don't run these races all-out. After several more weeks of high mileage, speed work, and racing, you may be surprised to find that you can run a marathon at the same pace that you ran for an earlier race of 10–20 miles, and possibly faster. Races here should be progressive—gradually improve your relative times. Train through the races, but taper near the end of this phase and run a hard race, going for a good performance. Race about once every 3 weeks during this phase and the following sharpening phase.

Sharpening Phase. Reduce mileage by at least 5–10 miles as you increase the intensity of your speed work. This runner sharpens by increasing the quantity and intensity of long pace-interval runs, anaerobic threshold runs, and fast continuous runs, and by adding fast intervals. One or two hard races of 10K to half marathon are used to help you sharpen and predict your marathon time, and thus your starting pace. Good performances at this point after months of hard work greatly increase your confidence. Taper for the races and go for a good time. Don't try to fit everything—a long run, race, and speed work—into your weekly schedule during this phase or the previous one. It is better during the sharpening phase to skip a long run than to cut back too much on your speed work and racing.

Tapering Phase. Reduce your mileage for the 2-week phase. The last long run for novice and basic competitors is approximately 3 weeks before the marathon, 2 weeks for advanced and champion competitors. The last hard workout (long pace-interval runs) should be 10–12 days before the marathon. Any speed work after that should be brisk, not hard, and with plenty of recovery. (See chapter 23 for more detailed marathon countdown guidelines.)

Novice Competitor

(This runner has experienced at least one marathon, and now wishes to train seriously and improve his or her time.)

Endurance Phase (10 weeks): One speed workout per week after 4–6 weeks of endurance runs; four or five long runs during phase; one or two low-key races. Speed work, which we don't use for the first-time marathoners, is introduced here late in the phase with controlled modified *fartlek* and pace-interval runs. Short races are used for fun and experience; a half marathon is used late in the phase to develop knowledge of pacing over a long distance in preparation for the marathon.

Strengthening Phase (4 weeks): One speed workout per week; two long runs during phase; one race at end of phase. The longer interval runs and continued use of modified *fartlek* are used to build strength and confidence for the marathon. Fast continuous runs of 6–10 miles at marathon pace should be used occasionally to teach you the feel for marathon race pace. Run a serious race at the end of this phase to give yourself a positive lift.

Sharpening Phase (2 weeks): One speed workout per week; one long run 3 weeks prior to the marathon; no racing prior to marathon. Since this runner is more concerned with building endurance and strength, extend the training program used in the strength phase, but cut back the mileage and do pace-interval workouts to improve speed and put a little zip into training.

Tapering Phase (2 weeks): One speed workout per week; no long runs; one race—marathon. A final easy speed workout is used 5–6 days before the race to give you a "peppy" feeling.

Basic Competitor

Endurance Phase (8 weeks): One speed workout per week after 3–4 weeks of endurance runs; four or five long runs per phase; one or two low-key races. Introduce strength workouts and pace-interval runs during this phase to add some zip to your endurance training. Modified *fartlek* and 6–10 mile fast continuous runs at *anticipated* marathon pace are most suitable at this time, since they are fairly easy workouts and will not disrupt your efforts to build your mileage base.

Strengthening Phase (6 weeks): One speed workout per week; two or three long runs; two or three races during phase. Gradually increase the quantity and intensity of your speed runs (including 10K pace intervals) during this phase as your mileage levels off. This will ensure that you continue to improve your strength, speed, and confidence. A race near the end of this phase should be a serious attempt to record a good time.

Sharpening Phase (3 weeks): One speed workout per week; one long run 3–4 weeks prior to marathon; one race at all-out effort during phase. Include some hard, fast workouts to improve your speed and build confidence in your ability to run fast.

Tapering Phase (2 weeks): One speed workout per week; no long runs; final race. A speed workout at marathon race pace is used 8–10 days before the race to give you the feeling of your starting marathon race pace. Your last speed workout (modified *fartlek*) done 5–6 days prior to the race is done at medium effort, on roads similar to marathon surface to familiarize yourself with marathon conditions.

Advanced Competitor

Endurance Phase (6 weeks): One or two speed workouts per week; three or four long runs; one low-key race during phase. Most advanced competitors already have a good mileage base and can therefore spend more time on strength and speed training. Include some strength and marathon-pace fast continuous runs early in the endurance phase to develop your rhythmic flow and feel for marathon pace. Any races run during this phase are trained through, with no special preparation necessary, since they are used to build confidence.

Strengthening Phase (7 weeks): Two speed workouts per week; three or four long runs; two or three races during phase. Include two speed workouts per week whenever you are not coming off a race. Carefully increase speed of interval runs to 10K pace during the phase to improve your speed. Blend in strength-training runs (including advanced *fartlek*, anaerobic threshold runs, and fast continuous runs) of 6–10 miles to build strength and confidence throughout the phase. Increase the quantity and intensity of workouts at a rate where you are able to maintain your present mileage levels. Include a number of hill workouts in both strength runs and interval runs. Do not do more than one track workout per week. The longer distance race run near the end of the phase should be run seriously, so decrease your work load that week to be properly rested for this big effort.

Sharpening Phase (3 weeks): Two speed workouts per week; one or two long runs, the last two weeks prior to marathon; one race. One or two fast interval workouts (5K pace) at the longer distances may be included to help you increase speed and build confidence. Continue using strength runs that include hills, since this type of workout helps improve your form and leg speed and builds confidence for the big races approaching. The 10K race (or a race of similar length) is taken seriously, and you must decrease your work load to get enough rest to make a good run of it.

Tapering Phase (2 weeks): Two speed workouts per week; no long runs; one race—marathon. Reduce both mileage and the intensity of speed work. The last hard workout is a 1-mile, pace-interval workout done 10–12 days before the marathon. The pace you average per mile for this workout is approximately 30 seconds per mile faster than your marathon race pace. Use both this workout and your recent all-out half marathon and 10K race times to help determine your marathon goal time and your starting pace. (See chapter 26 for guidelines for predicting race times.) Use the advanced *fartlek* workout as your final speed workout in a controlled manner as a preparation for your big race.

Champion Competitor

Endurance Phase (6 weeks): One or two speed workouts per week; four or five long runs; one or two races during the phase.

Begin strength speed runs by third week to regain rhythmic flow and racing form. The fast continuous runs of 6–10 miles late in this phase are usually done at *anticipated* marathon race pace. Include some low-key hill training late in the phase to blend in strength work. Any races run during this phase will be low-key with no time taken off from training.

Strengthening Phase (6 weeks): Two speed workouts per week; three or four long runs; two or three races at 10K or longer during phase. Long interval workouts (880-mile) at 10K pace and hard strength runs are emphasized during this phase. "Load up" on the number of repetitions as you gain strength to become mentally tougher for the long haul of the marathon distance. A race at the end of the strength phase (10 miles and up) should be an honest-effort race with a go for a PR.

Sharpening Phase (4 weeks): Two speed workouts per week; two long runs during phase; one race at half marathon or under. Reduce your mileage and the number of repetitions while increasing the intensity of the workouts to emphasize a final speed buildup for fast races at the end of your training cycle. Race for a PR during this phase.

Tapering Phase (2 weeks): Two speed workouts per week; no long runs; one race—marathon. Further reduce mileage and decrease the intensity of workouts while slightly increasing the number of repetitions as a final confidence builder for the marathon. The last hard workout is a 1-mile, pace-interval workout done 10–12 days before the marathon. The pace you average per mile for this workout is approximately 30 seconds per mile faster than your marathon starting race pace. Use both this workout and your recent all-out half marathon and 10K race times to help determine your marathon goal time and your starting pace. (See chapter 26 for guidelines for predicting race times.) Use the advanced *fartlek* workout 5 days prior to the race in a controlled manner as a final preparation for your big race.

STEP SIX: PLAN YOUR REBUILDING PHASE (See Chapter 25, "The Aftermarathon," for Guidelines)

BREAKING BARRIERS

Breaking barriers can be very rewarding, whether you are aiming to conquer the 3-hour mark or the 4-hour mark. Following are some common barriers and some tips on how to win your race against the clock.

The Sub-2:40 Marathon

In order to run a sub-2:40, you need to average 6:06 per mile. To break 2:40, you should be able to run the following times (or at least be close):

10K	men—sub-34:30
	women—sub-35:00
15K	men—sub-53:00
	women—sub-54:00
10 mile	men—sub-57:30
	women—sub-58:30
20K	men—sub-1:12
	women—sub-1:13
Half marathon	men—sub-1:15:30
	women—sub-1:16:30
25K	men—sub-1:31
	women—sub-1:32
30K	men—sub-1:50
	women—sub-1:51

Follow the sample schedule for the champion competitor at the end of this chapter. You should run 70–80 miles per week at 7:30–8:00 minutes per mile. Do long runs of 20–23 miles two or three times per month. You should run speed workouts two times per week, on the average, for 10–12 weeks prior to the marathon. You should run intervals at these approximate paces: miles—5:15–6:00; 880s—2:30–2:40; 440s—75–80 seconds. Basically, you should train like a runner aiming to break the 34-minute barrier for 10K, except that you will do more mileage and longer long runs. The key at this level of training is to

• hold consistent high mileage (for 3–4 months) while warding off serious injury;

• do regular long runs of 20–23 miles (eight or more);

• do quality speed training to enable you to have the speed to race well at 10K and the strength to race well at the 15K–30K range;

• be able to run smoothly for 6–10 miles at 6-minute pace for fast continuous runs.

The Sub-2:50 Marathon

In order to run a sub-2:50, you need to average under 6:30 per mile. To break 2:50, you should be able to run the following times (or at least be close):

10K	men—sub-36:30
	women—sub-37:00
15K	men—sub-56:00
	women—sub-57:00
10 mile	men—sub-60:30
	women—sub-61:30
20K	men—sub-1:16:30
	women—sub-1:17:30
Half marathon	men—sub-1:21
	women—sub-1:22
25K	men—sub-1:37
	women—sub-1:38
30K	men—sub-1:58
	women—sub-1:59

Follow the sample schedule for the advanced competitor or champion competitor at the end of this chapter. You should run 60–80 miles per week at 7:30–8:30 minutes per mile. Do long runs of 20–22 miles two or three times per month. You should run speed workouts two times per week, on the average, for 10 weeks prior to the marathon. You should run intervals

at these approximate paces: miles—5:45–6:00; 880s—2:45–3:00; 440s—82–85 seconds. Basically, you should train like the 36:00–37:00 10K runner, except that you will do more mileage and longer long runs. The key at this level of training is to
- hold consistent high mileage for 3 months while warding off injury;
- do regular long runs (eight or more) of 20–22 miles;
- do quality speed training to enable you to have the speed to race well at 10K and the strength to race well at the 15K–30K range;
- be able to run 6 to 10 miles smoothly at 6:30 pace for fast continuous runs.

The Sub-3:00 Marathon

In order to run a sub-3:00, you need to average 6:51 per mile. To break 3:00, you should be able to run the following times (or at least be close):

10K	men—sub-38:30
	women—sub-39:00
15K	men—sub-59:00
	women—sub-60:00
10 mile	men—sub-64:00
	women—sub-65:00
20K	men—sub-1:21
	women—sub-1:22
Half marathon	men—sub-1:26
	women—sub-1:27
25K	men—sub-1:43
	women—sub-1:44
30K	men—sub-2:05
	women—sub-2:06

Like the sub-40-minute 10K, this is a very popular barrier promoting runners into a highly accomplished group of athletes. Follow the sample schedule for the advanced competitor at the end of this chapter. You should run 50–70 miles per week at 8:00–9:00 minutes per mile. Do long runs of 20–22 miles every other week, on the average. You should run speed workouts one or two times per week for 10 weeks prior to the marathon. You should run intervals at these approximate paces: miles—6:00–6:20; 880s—2:50–3:10; 440s—82–90 seconds. Basically, you should train like the 38:00–39:00 10K runner, except that you will do more mileage and longer long runs. The key at this level of training is to

• hold consistent high mileage for 2–3 months while warding off injury;

• do regular long runs (eight or more) of 20–22 miles;

• do quality speed training to enable you to have the speed to race well at 10K and the strength to race well at the 15K–30K range;

• be able to run smoothly at 6:50 per mile for fast continuous runs of 6–10 miles.

The Sub-3:15 Marathon

In order to run a sub-3:15, you need to average 7:26 per mile. To break 3:15, you should be able to run the following times (or at least be close):

10K	men—sub-41:30
	women—sub-42:00
15K	men—sub-64:00
	women—sub-65:00
10 mile	men—sub-69:00
	women—sub-70:00
20K	men—sub-1:28
	women—sub-1:29
Half marathon	men—sub-1:33
	women—sub-1:34
25K	men—sub-1:51
	women—sub-1:52
30K	men—sub-2:16
	women—sub-2:17

Follow the sample schedule for the advanced competitor at the end of this chapter. You should run 50–60 miles per week at 8:30–9:30 minutes per mile. Do long runs of 18–20 miles every other week, on the average. You should run speed workouts one or two times per week for 10 weeks prior to the marathon. You should run intervals at these approximate paces: miles— 6:20–6:50; 880s—3:00–6:50; 440s—85–95 seconds. Basically, you should train like the 41:00–42:00 10K runner, except that you will do more mileage and longer long runs. The key at this level of training is to

• hold consistent high mileage for 2–3 months while warding off injury;

• do regular long runs (six or more) of 18–20 miles;

• do quality speed training to enable you to have the speed to race well at 10K and the strength to do well at the 15K–30K range;

• be able to run smoothly at 7:20 per mile for fast continuous runs of 6–10 miles.

The Sub-3:30 Marathon

In order to run a sub-3:30, you need to average 8:00 per mile. To break 3:30, you should be able to run the following times (or at least be close):

10K	men—sub-44:30
	women—sub-45:00
15K	men—sub-1:09
	women—sub-1:10
10 mile	men—sub-74:00
	women—sub-75:00
20K	men—sub-1:34
	women—sub-1:35
Half marathon	men—sub-1:41
	women—sub-1:42
25K	men—sub-2:00
	women—sub-2:01
30K	men—sub-2:25
	women—sub-2:26

This barrier separates the marathon runner from the marathon racer. Follow the sample schedule for the basic competitor at the end of this chapter. You should run 40–50 miles per week at 9:00–10:00 minutes per mile. Do long runs of 18–20 miles every other week, on the average. You should run speed work-outs once per week for 8–10 weeks prior to the marathon. You should run intervals at these approximate paces: miles—6:50–7:00; 880s—3:15–3:30; 440s—1:30–1:40. Basically, you should train like the 44:00–45:00 10K runner, except that you will do more mileage and longer long runs. The key at this level of training is to

• hold consistent high mileage for 2–3 months while warding off injury;

•. do regular long runs (six or more) of 18–20 miles;

• do quality speed training to enable you to have the speed to race well at 10K and the strength to do well at the 15K–30K range;

• be able to run smoothly at 8:00 per mile for fast continuous runs of 6–10 miles.

The Sub-3:45 Marathon

In order to run a sub-3:45, you need to average 8:34 per mile. To break 3:45, you should be able to run the following times (or at least be close):

10K	men—sub-47:30
	women—sub-48:00
15K	men—sub-1:14
	women—sub-1:15
10 mile	men—sub-79:00
	women—sub-80:00
20K	men—sub-1:40
	women—sub-1:41
Half marathon	men—sub-1:48
	women—sub-1:49
25K	men—sub-2:08
	women—sub-2:09
30K	men—sub-2:35
	women—sub-2:36

Follow the sample schedule for the basic competitor at the end of this chapter. You should run 40–50 miles per week at 9:00–10:30 minutes per mile. Do long runs of 18–20 miles every other week, on the average. You should run speed workouts once per week for 8–10 weeks prior to the marathon. You should run intervals at these approximate paces: miles—7:20–7:30; 880s—3:35–3:45; 440s—1:40–1:50. Basically, you should train like a 47:00–48:00 10K runner, except that you will do more mileage and longer long runs. Those who run much faster for 10K simply need much more experience at running longer races and should concentrate more on mileage and long runs than on speed training. The key at this level of training is to

• hold consistent high mileage for 2–3 months while warding off injury;

• do regular long runs (six or more) of 18–20 miles;

• develop the endurance, strength, and speed to do well at the 10K–30K range;

• be able to run smoothly at 8:30 per mile for fast continuous runs of 6–10 miles.

The Sub-4:00 Marathon

In order to run a sub-4:00, you need to average 9:10 per mile. To break 4:00, you should be able to run the following times (or at least be close):

10K	men—sub-50:30
	women—sub-51:00
15K	men—sub-1:18
	women—sub-1:19
10 mile	men—sub-1:24
	women—sub-1:25
20K	men—sub-1:47
	women—sub-1:48
Half marathon	men—sub-1:56
	women—sub-1:57
25K	men—sub-2:16
	women—sub-2:17
30K	men—sub-2:45
	women—sub-2:46

This barrier separates the survivor from the marathon runner. Most first-time marathon runners will run over 4 hours and then aim to break the 4-hour barrier. If you are not a first-time marathoner and you are not ready to break the 4-hour barrier, follow the novice competitor schedule in this chapter or the first-time marathoner schedule in chapter 20. The sub-4-hour marathoner will follow the novice competitor sample schedule at the end of this chapter. You should run 35–45 miles per week at 9:00–11:00 minutes per mile. Do long runs of 16–20 miles every other week, on the average. You should run controlled speed workouts once per week for 8–10 weeks prior to the marathon. You should run intervals at these approximate paces: miles—7:50–8:00; 880s—3:50–4:00; 440s—1:45–2:00. Basically, you should train like a 50:00–51:00 10K runner, except that you will do more mileage and longer long runs. Those who run much faster for 10K simply need much more experience at running longer races and should concentrate more on mileage and long runs than speed training. The key at this level of training is to

• hold consistent high mileage for 2–3 months while warding off injury;

• do regular long runs (six or more) of 16–20 miles;

• develop the endurance, strength, and speed to do well at the 10K–30K range;

• be able to run smoothly at 9:00 per mile for fast continuous runs of 6–10 miles.

18-WEEK MARATHON BUILDUP SCHEDULES

The model training schedules on pages 300–307 should be used to help you write your own program. The exact mileage you will run, distance and dates of your buildup races, and the days you will do your different types of runs will vary with your individual needs, age, sex, and other factors that influence your running. Use these models as a guide to create a specific training program that can help you reach your racing goals. Understand the concepts behind these schedules, don't just follow them blindly. We have not included an example of the rebuilding phase. Follow the model in chapter 13 to write your rebuilding program.

THE NOVICE COMPETITOR'S 18-WEEK MARATHON BUILDUP SCHEDULE

PHASE/WEEK		MONDAY	TUESDAY		WEDNESDAY		THURSDAY		FRIDAY		SATURDAY		SUNDAY		TOTAL MILEAGE
ENDURANCE	1	Off	Short endurance	3	Medium endurance	5	Medium endurance	5	Short endurance	4	Medium endurance	5	Medium endurance	8	30
	2	Off	Medium endurance	5	Medium endurance	5	Medium endurance	5	Medium endurance	5	Short endurance	3	Long endurance	12	35
	3	Off	Short endurance	4	Medium endurance	5	Medium endurance	5	Medium endurance	5	Short endurance	2	Long endurance	14	35
	4	Off	Medium endurance	5	Medium endurance	6	Medium endurance	5	Medium endurance	6	Short endurance	4	Race 5K	8	35
	5	Off	Short endurance	4	Medium endurance	6	Medium endurance	6	Medium endurance	6	Medium endurance	8	Medium endurance	10	40
	6	Off	Medium endurance	5	Medium endurance	5	Strength Modified *fartlek*	6 / 4	Medium endurance	5	Short endurance	3	Long endurance	16	40
	7	Off	Medium endurance	6	Medium endurance	8	Medium endurance	8	Medium endurance	6	Short endurance	4	Race 10K	10	42
	8	Off	Short endurance	4	Medium endurance	6	Strength Modified *fartlek*	8 / 4	Medium endurance	6	Short endurance	3	Long endurance	18	45
	9	Off	Medium endurance	6	10K pace intervals 5 × 880	7	Medium endurance	6	Medium endurance	8	Short endurance	4	Race Half marathon	14	45
STRENGTH-ENING	10	Off	Short endurance	4	Medium endurance	8	Medium endurance	8	Strength Modified *fartlek*	7 / 5	Medium endurance	8	Medium endurance	10	45
	11	Off	Medium endurance	8	Medium endurance	6	10K pace intervals 5 × Short hills	6	Medium endurance	6	Short endurance	4	Long endurance	20	50
	12	Off	Medium endurance	8	10K pace intervals 3 × 1 mile	8	Medium endurance	7	Medium endurance	6	Short endurance	4	Race 10 miles	12	45

THE NOVICE COMPETITOR'S 18-WEEK MARATHON BUILDUP SCHEDULE (Cont'd.)

PHASE/WEEK	MONDAY	TUESDAY	WEDNESDAY	THURSDAY	FRIDAY	SATURDAY	SUNDAY	TOTAL MILEAGE
STRENGTHENING — 13	— Off	4 Short endurance	7 Medium endurance	5 Medium endurance	8 Fast continuous run 5	8 Medium endurance	20 Long endurance	50
STRENGTHENING — 14	4 Short endurance	5 10K pace intervals 3 × 1 mile	8 Medium endurance	8 Medium endurance	6 Medium endurance	— Off	10 Race 10K	42
SHARPENING — 15	— Off	4 Short endurance	4 Medium endurance	5 10K pace intervals 5 × Long hills	8 Medium endurance	— Off	20 Long endurance	45
SHARPENING — 16	— Off	6 Medium endurance	6 Medium endurance	8 Medium endurance	8 10K pace intervals 3 × 1 mile	5 Medium endurance	12 Medium endurance	45
TAPERING — 17	— Off	6 Medium endurance	6 Medium endurance	6 10K pace interval 6 × 880	4 Short endurance	4 Short endurance	10 Medium endurance	36
TAPERING — 18	— Off	6 Strength Modified *fartlek*	4 Short endurance	4 Short endurance	— Off	2 Short endurance	26.2 Race Marathon	16 + race

THE BASIC COMPETITOR'S 18-WEEK MARATHON BUILDUP SCHEDULE

PHASE	WEEK	MONDAY	TUESDAY	WEDNESDAY	THURSDAY	FRIDAY	SATURDAY	SUNDAY	TOTAL MILEAGE
ENDURANCE	1	Off —	Medium endurance 6	Medium endurance 6	Medium endurance 7	Medium endurance 5	Medium endurance 6	Medium endurance 10	40
ENDURANCE	2	Off —	Medium endurance 5	Medium endurance 5	Medium endurance 6	Medium endurance 5	Short endurance 4	Long endurance 15	40
ENDURANCE	3	Off —	Medium endurance 6	Medium endurance 8	Medium endurance 5	Medium endurance 5	Medium endurance 8	Medium endurance 10	42
ENDURANCE	4	Off —	Medium endurance 8	Medium endurance 6	Strength Modified fartlek 6 / 4	Medium endurance 5	Short endurance 4	Long endurance 18	45
ENDURANCE	5	Off —	Strength Modified fartlek 8 / 4	Medium endurance 10	Medium endurance 8	Medium endurance 5	Short endurance 4	Race 10K 10	45
ENDURANCE	6	Off —	Short endurance 4	Medium endurance 8	Strength Hill fartlek 8 / 4	Medium endurance 6	Short endurance 4	Long endurance 20	50
ENDURANCE	7	Off —	Medium endurance 10	10K pace intervals 6 × 880 8	10K pace intervals 6 × 880 6	Medium endurance 8	Medium endurance 8	Medium endurance 10	50
ENDURANCE	8	Off —	Medium endurance 6	Medium endurance 6	Strength Hill fartlek 8 / 5	Medium endurance 6	Short endurance 6	Long endurance 20	50
STRENGTHENING	9	Off —	Medium endurance 7	Medium endurance 8	Medium endurance 8	Medium endurance 8	Medium endurance 5	Race Half marathon 14	50
STRENGTHENING	10	Off —	Medium endurance 5	Medium endurance 8	Medium endurance 8	Strength Fast continuous run 8 / 6	Medium endurance 6	Long endurance 15	50
STRENGTHENING	11	Off —	10K pace intervals 5 × Long hills 5	Medium endurance 6	Medium endurance 8	Medium endurance 6	Short endurance 4	Long endurance 20	50
STRENGTHENING	12	Off —	Medium endurance 8	10K pace intervals 4 × 1 mile 6	Medium endurance 10	Medium endurance 6	Short endurance 4	Race 10 miles 12	46

THE BASIC COMPETITOR'S 18-WEEK MARATHON BUILDUP SCHEDULE (Cont'd.)

PHASE/WEEK	MONDAY	TUESDAY	WEDNESDAY	THURSDAY	FRIDAY	SATURDAY	SUNDAY	TOTAL MILEAGE
STRENGTHENING — 13	— Off	5 Medium endurance	6 Medium endurance	8 Strength Hill *fartlek* 5	7 Medium endurance	4 Short endurance	20 Long endurance	50
STRENGTHENING — 14	— Off	8 Medium endurance	8 10K pace intervals 8 × Short hills	8 Medium endurance	6 Medium endurance	5 Medium endurance	10 Race 10K	45
SHARPENING — 15	— Off	6 Medium endurance	8 Medium endurance	6 5K pace intervals 6 × 880	6 Short endurance	4 Short endurance	20 Long endurance	50
SHARPENING — 16	— Off	6 Medium endurance	6 Medium endurance	6 10K pace intervals 6 × Long hills	6 Medium endurance	6 Medium endurance	15 Long endurance	45
TAPERING — 17	— Off	6 Medium endurance	5 Medium endurance	8 10K pace intervals 4 × 1 mile	5 Medium endurance	4 Short endurance	10 Medium endurance	38
TAPERING — 18	— Off	5 Strength Modified *fartlek* 3	4 Short endurance	4 Short endurance	— Off	3 Short endurance	26.2 Race Marathon	16 + race

THE ADVANCED COMPETITOR'S 18-WEEK MARATHON BUILDUP SCHEDULE

PHASE	WEEK	MONDAY	TUESDAY	WEDNESDAY	THURSDAY	FRIDAY	SATURDAY	SUNDAY	TOTAL MILEAGE
ENDURANCE	1	— Off	6 Medium endurance	10 Medium endurance	6 Medium endurance	8 Medium endurance	5 Short endurance	15 Long endurance	50
ENDURANCE	2	— Off	8 Medium endurance	10 Medium endurance	6 Medium endurance	8 Medium endurance	8 Medium endurance	10 Medium endurance	50
ENDURANCE	3	— Off	8 Strength Advanced *fartlek*	6 Medium endurance	10 Medium endurance	8 Medium endurance	5 Short endurance	18 Long endurance	55
ENDURANCE	4	— Off	8 Medium endurance	10 Fast continuous run	8 Medium endurance	10 Medium endurance	8 Medium endurance	11 Race 10K	55
ENDURANCE	5	— Off	8 Medium endurance	8 Medium endurance	8 10K pace intervals 8 × 880	10 Medium endurance	6 Medium endurance	20 Long endurance	60
ENDURANCE	6	— Off	10 Strength Advanced *fartlek*	10 Medium endurance	9 Medium endurance	8 Anaerobic threshold run	8 Medium endurance	15 Long endurance	60
STRENGTHENING	7	— Off	8 10K pace intervals 8 × Short hills	10 Medium endurance	10 Fast continuous run	12 Medium endurance	6 Medium endurance	14 Race 10 miles	60
STRENGTHENING	8	— Off	10 Medium endurance	10 Medium endurance	8 10K pace intervals 4 × 1 mile	10 Medium endurance	6 Medium endurance	21 Long endurance	65
STRENGTHENING	9	— Off	8 10K pace intervals 10 × 880	10 Medium endurance	10 Medium endurance	10 Medium endurance	6 Medium endurance	16 Race 20K	60
STRENGTHENING	10	— Off	8 Medium endurance	10 Medium endurance	10 Medium endurance	10 Strength Hill *fartlek*	5 Short endurance	22 Long endurance	65
STRENGTHENING	11	— Off	8 Medium endurance	8 10K pace intervals 4 × 1 mile	10 Medium endurance	10 Fast continuous run	6 Medium endurance	20 Long endurance	62
STRENGTHENING	12	— Off	10 Medium endurance	10 5K pace intervals 8 × 880	10 Medium endurance	8 Medium endurance	6 Medium endurance	15 Race Half marathon	60

THE ADVANCED COMPETITOR'S 18-WEEK MARATHON BUILDUP SCHEDULE (Cont'd.)

PHASE	WEEK	MONDAY	TUESDAY	WEDNESDAY	THURSDAY	FRIDAY	SATURDAY	SUNDAY	TOTAL MILEAGE
SHARPENING	13	— Off	8 Medium endurance	10 Medium endurance	6 Anaerobic threshold run	12 Medium endurance	9 Medium endurance	15 Long endurance	60
SHARPENING	14	— Off	8 10K pace intervals 5 × 1 mile	6 Medium endurance	8 Medium endurance	8 10K pace intervals 8 × Long hills	5 Short endurance	22 Long endurance	57
SHARPENING	15	— Off	8 Medium endurance	8 5K pace intervals 8 × 880	8 Medium endurance	6 Medium endurance	4 Short endurance	10 Race 10K	42
SHARPENING	16	— Off	7 Medium endurance	6 Medium endurance	6 Medium endurance	12 Fast continuous run	4 Short endurance	20 Long endurance	60
TAPERING	17	— Off	8 Medium endurance	7 Medium endurance	8 Medium endurance	10 Strength Advanced *fartlek*	5 Short endurance	12 Medium endurance	50
TAPERING	18	— Off	5 Strength Advanced *fartlek*	3 Medium endurance	4 Short endurance	— Off	3 Short endurance	26.2 Race Marathon	23 + race

THE CHAMPION COMPETITOR'S 18-WEEK MARATHON BUILDUP SCHEDULE

PHASE/WEEK		MONDAY	TUESDAY	WEDNESDAY	THURSDAY	FRIDAY	SATURDAY	SUNDAY	TOTAL MILEAGE
ENDURANCE	1	8 Medium endurance	8 Medium endurance	10 Medium endurance	10 Medium endurance	8 Medium endurance	8 Medium endurance	18 Long endurance	70
	2	10 Medium endurance	8 Medium endurance	12 Medium endurance	12 Medium endurance	8 Medium endurance	8 Medium endurance	12 Medium endurance	70
	3	10 Medium endurance	10 Strength Hill *fartlek*	8 Medium endurance	10 Medium endurance	12 Medium endurance	5 Short endurance	20 Long endurance	75
	4	5 Short endurance	14 Medium endurance	14 Fast continuous run	12 Medium endurance	10 Medium endurance	10 Medium endurance	10 Race 10K	75
	5	8 Medium endurance	8 Medium endurance	12 Medium endurance	12 Medium endurance	12 Strength Advanced *fartlek*	8 Medium endurance	20 Long endurance	80
	6	5 Short endurance	10 10K pace intervals 10 × Short hills	12 Medium endurance	12 10K pace intervals	14 Fast continuous run	7 Medium endurance	20 Long endurance	80
STRENGTHENING	7	6 Short endurance	10 10K pace intervals 8 × Long hills	10 Medium endurance	12 Medium endurance	12 Medium endurance	14 Medium endurance	16 Race 10 miles	80
	8	6 Short endurance	8 Medium endurance	12 Medium endurance	14 Strength Advanced *fartlek*	12 Fast continuous run	6 Short endurance	22 Long endurance	80
	9	5 Short endurance	12 10K pace intervals 4 × 1 mile	12 Medium endurance	12 Medium endurance	12 Medium endurance	10 Medium endurance	17 Race 20K	80
	10	4 Short endurance	12 Medium endurance	12 Medium endurance	12 Fast continuous run	12 Strength Hill *fartlek*	8 Medium endurance	20 Long endurance	80
	11	5 Short endurance	10 10K pace intervals 5 × 1 mile	12 Medium endurance	12 Medium endurance	12 Medium endurance	7 Medium endurance	22 Long endurance	80
	12	8 Medium endurance	8 Medium endurance	12 5K pace intervals 8 × 880	10 Medium endurance	10 Medium endurance	4 Short endurance	18 Race Half marathon	70

306

THE ADVANCED COMPETITOR'S 18-WEEK MARATHON BUILDUP SCHEDULE (Cont'd.)

PHASE/WEEK	MONDAY	TUESDAY	WEDNESDAY	THURSDAY	FRIDAY	SATURDAY	SUNDAY	TOTAL MILEAGE
SHARPENING 13	Short endurance 4	Medium endurance 10	Medium endurance 14	Medium endurance 10	Strength Advanced fartlek 10 / 6	Medium endurance 12	Long endurance 15	75
SHARPENING 14	Medium endurance 8	10K pace intervals 6 × 1 mile 10	Medium endurance 8	Medium endurance 10	5K pace intervals 10 × Short hills 12 / 6	Short endurance 5	Long endurance 22	75
SHARPENING 15	Short endurance 6	Medium endurance 12	5K pace intervals 8 × 880 12	Medium endurance 12	Medium endurance 8	Short endurance 4	Race 10K 12	64
SHARPENING 16	Short endurance 6	Medium endurance 12	Medium endurance 12	Medium endurance 10	Fast continuous run 10 / 8	Short endurance 5	Long endurance 20	75
TAPERING 17	Off —	10K pace intervals 6 × 1 mile 10	Medium endurance 10	Medium endurance 8	Strength Hill fartlek 8 / 6	Medium endurance 10	Medium endurance 14	60
TAPERING 18	Short endurance 5	Strength Advanced fartlek 8 / 6	Short endurance 6	Short endurance 4	Off —	Short endurance 4	Race Marathon 26.2	27 + Marathon

22. THE LONG RUN ___

The single most important ingredient to marathon success is the long run. For this reason we devote a complete chapter to that hallowed weekend tradition which is despised and loved, feared and looked forward to, bragged about and complained about. Whether you like long runs or not, one thing remains clear: you have to run them if you want to maximize your potential on marathon day. The long run can make you physically and psychologically stronger or it can destroy you, turning running into a painful task. The long run mirrors the marathon itself: it demands attention and respect.

WHY LONG RUNS?

The long run provides the marathoner with several critical benefits:

• It improves the capacity of your muscles to utilize fat as fuel, sparing glycogen. Long runs teach your body to utilize both fats and glycogen in producing muscular energy. If you only burned glycogen you would run low on fuel and "hit the Wall." By utilizing fat, and not depleting your glycogen storage, you have sufficient energy reserves to keep up a good pace in the late stages of a marathon. The long run combined with carbohydrate loading and intelligent marathon pacing allows you to push back the wall.

• It improves your nervous system's ability to recruit muscle fibers. According to Dr. David Costill, during the first 15–20 miles of the marathon you primarily use slow-twitch (endurance-oriented) muscle fibers. They become exhausted late in a marathon, contributing to leg fatigue. Long runs train your body to search for help from fast-twitch (speed-oriented) muscle fibers, which can be trained to assist slow-twitch fibers for a marathon effort.

• It strengthens the heart muscle and oxygen delivery system because you spend 2–3 hours or more running aerobically within your training heart-rate range.

• It strengthens your leg muscles, feet, and ankles, enabling them to keep you moving at a good pace for several hours.

• It teaches you to stay relaxed and run with efficient form for long periods despite fatigue.

• It allows you the opportunity to test your body's reaction to water, athletic drinks, potential racing shoes and clothing, prerun eating habits, etc., under marathon-like conditions.

The Mind

Above all, the long run is for the mind. Forcing yourself to get out the door and run for approximately 3 hours on a regular basis in all kinds of weather involves discipline. Your reward for your effort is increased confidence and mental toughness. As you see your long runs build from 10 to 20+ miles, you have measurable proof that your training is making you stronger. This motivates you to keep up your rigorous training schedule. By experiencing what it feels like to keep running when tired, you're not afraid of having to run the last few miles of the marathon while tiring. You learn the difference between fatigue and exhaustion by forcing your body to finish long runs. The long run teaches you to finish despite the objections of the mind and the body. Once you can handle 20 miles, you know you can handle the whole distance.

The long run also trains you to be patient—a very important

virtue when racing long distances. Most marathoners succeed in direct proportion to how well they can hold back and run slowly. Many runners are always pushing the pace, day after day. The long run forces them to slow down and pace themselves wisely—just as they must do in the marathon.

HOW LONG?

For the 10K and other popular racing distances, we recommend long runs a few miles beyond the length of the race. For the marathon, however, that would require runs of 26–30 miles. Although some experienced marathoners will run a few runs of that length, the average runner would suffer more than he or she would benefit from such a practice. More than one runner has run 26+ miles in practice to prove he or she could do it before the marathon and then was unable to toe the line for the real race because of injury or illness.

Long runs cause wear and tear on the musculoskeletal system. With every stride you take, you pound the pavement with three times the force of your body weight. When you get much past 20 miles, your body is fatiguing rapidly and additional pounding greatly increases your chance of injury. As you tire, your running form deteriorates, further increasing your vulnerability to injury. Runs beyond 20 miles seriously deplete your energy reserves and the minerals in your body.

First-time marathoners and novice competitors can complete a marathon with a series of long runs in the 16–18 mile range. If you wish to race a marathon, however, you will increase your chances of doing well by running longer.

We recommend long runs of up to 20 miles for novice and basic competitors. Runs beyond this level for these runners will put them on their feet for well over 3 hours. A few radical coaches have even novice marathoners run 26–30 mile runs, which would put them on their feet for 4–6 hours. The potential gain beyond 3½ hours of running (our suggested time limit for all runners) isn't worth the risk. Save the destructive effects of such lengthy runs for the marathon itself or you may not make it to the starting line. Additionally, runners attempting such long runs are more vulnerable to failing to finish their practice attempt, dealing them a severe psychological blow.

Advanced and champion competitors who are experienced at long runs may benefit from runs up to 23 miles. These slightly longer runs will put the highly competitive marathoner on his or her feet for approximately the same time they will be running on marathon day.

HOW FAST?

This is where most runners err. The long run should be done entirely at conversational pace, within the base pace range detailed in chapter 5. This pace will be 1½ to 2 minutes per mile slower than your 10K race pace. Elite runners who run 4:30 minutes per mile for 10K will run long at 6:00–6:30 pace. That is the same as a 7:30-minutes-per-mile 10K runner doing long runs at 9:00–9:30 pace. The purpose of the run is to build you up, not tear you down. If you want to tear yourself down as much as possible for a long run, do it on marathon day—and then follow it with a long rebuilding phase. You should set a goal of being completely recovered from your long run in 2 days. In order to accomplish this, you must train and not strain during your long run.

To prevent yourself from running too fast, you may wish to run without wearing a watch. Thus, you won't be tempted to try to "beat" your previous time over your 20-mile loop and wear yourself out. Another good tactic: run out for 1½ hours, then turn around and come back for a 3-hour run over an unmeasured course—preferably one you made up while exploring on the run. Approximate the distance you ran and log it in your diary.

Highly experienced marathoners may wish to pick up the pace over the last few miles of the long run to simulate battle conditions. They must be cautious not to turn it into a race, however. The best way to practice marathon race pace is with fast continuous runs of up to 13 miles, not during long runs.

HOW OFTEN?

Veteran marathoners developed the tradition of running long every weekend in order to toughen themselves. Unless you have a fun group to run with each week, you may soon grow to hate this routine. Besides, it may result in chronic fatigue as you never completely recover from the previous long runs.

On the other hand, the mistake most often made by aspiring marathoners is to suddenly get to a few weeks prior to the big race lacking enough long runs. The runner may be running adequate weekly mileage—40+ per week—but no single runs beyond 8–10 miles. You are training to run 26.2 miles in a single run, not to run 40-mile training weeks. Several months in advance of the marathon, ease into long runs with once- or twice-per-month runs of 10–12 miles. Then ease into running 10–12-milers weekly. From that base, you can gradually increase the length of the long run by no more than 2 miles per week. Just as you increase weekly mileage slowly to prevent injury, so too be cautious in the long run buildup. Then alternate running a medium-length run (10–15 miles) or a race with gradually increasing long runs of 18–22 miles rather than running long each week. If you plan well in advance, you can get in an adequate number of long runs by running two per month rather than forcing yourself to squeeze in weekly long runs as the marathon looms ahead.

We recommend that novice and basic competitors run at least six long runs of 18–20 miles, averaging two per month over the 3 months leading into the marathon. Advanced competitors should run at least eight long runs of 20–22 miles, averaging two per month over the 4 months leading into the marathon. Champion competitors should run at least eight long runs of 20–23 miles, averaging two or three per month over the 4 months leading into the marathon.

The last long run should be 2–3 weeks prior to your marathon. The week before the marathon, run no longer than 10–12 miles. Taper your long runs as you taper your weekly mileage.

MAKING IT EASIER

The long run can be something to look forward to, or it can be drudgery. Here are some tips to make them more enjoyable and thus more productive:

- Make a date with a friend to run long. Running long week

after week alone gets boring. Make sure your friend is willing to run within your base pace range. If your friend can't run the whole distance with you, it is preferred to have your partner hook up with you for the last miles of your run in order to give you a welcomed boost of energy. If you can't get a runner to go along, seek out your spouse, child, or friend to ride along on a bike. It is helpful to run some of your long runs alone, but the distraction of social chattering will make your runs more manageable, even fun.

• Join or start a regular group run. Bob Glover used to run the 20-mile loop around Lake Delta in Rome, New York, with the same group of dedicated runners. They developed quite a bond of friendship during hot summer runs and freezing cold winter runs. Afterward, they had breakfast together. Another group Glover trained with ran from mid-Manhattan to New York City's George Washington Bridge and back every Wednesday night for several years. Their runs were followed by several beers at a local pub. One of the runners who used to enjoy this routine was comedian Robin Williams—before he made it big. Many groups meet year-round and run 10–15-milers most of the time and then increase the runs when marathon training. For such runners, the weekly long run isn't training, it is a social outing: an opportunity to gab and gossip on the run.

• Avoid heat, hills, and head winds. Start your runs early in the morning to avoid the heat of the day, and seek courses that offer shade. You should incorporate some hills in your long run course to toughen you, but avoid too many killer hills. Long runs are taxing enough as it is! In the winter, plan your runs to avoid freezing head winds, or at least run into the wind on the way out rather than facing it (and potential frostbite) when you are tired and sweat-soaked.

• If the weather is very bad, consider postponing your long run until the next day or even the next weekend. Be flexible; you don't have to force yourself to be uncomfortable.

• Run long on Saturday if possible so that you can rest on Sunday. That will make it easier on you when you have to go back to work on Monday morning.

• Use long races as long runs occasionally. The New York

Road Runners Club has a 25K "tune-up" race a few weeks before the New York City Marathon each year. Many runners will run a few miles before the race and then run through it at long run training pace. This way they have plenty of company, get to practice drinking at aid stations, and can socialize with hundreds of runners after the race. You can use this system even for shorter races. Or you can run the opposite direction of the race (if you can't trust yourself to hold back), and enjoy watching it while getting in your mileage. Beware of using marathons as "long runs." It is a good training practice if you run at your normal long run pace and stop no later than the 20-mile mark. Unfortunately, few runners have the discipline either to hold back their pace or to stop before the finish line.

• Run over a variety of courses. New terrain to explore is invigorating, and you can see a lot of scenery on a 20-mile run. Ask other runners to recommend good long run courses for an occasional change of pace. In general, however, you are wise to stick to a few trusty courses where you know the distance and where to get fluids.

Many runners look forward to their long runs. It is a time to relax and just run slow and easy. You can do plenty of deep thinking on solitary runs or enjoy the company of a group of runners. If you look at the long run as something to savor rather than a dreaded task that you must get out of the way, you will learn to look forward to it.

CAUTIONS

• Beware of running long on slanted surfaces. Seek well-paved surfaces if you can't run on dirt trails (which are much kinder to the body over the long run). Try to avoid congested areas: dodging cars, bikes, dogs, kids, etc., when fatigued is not easy.

• Pour plenty of fluids on and into yourself on hot days. *Stop* every 20 minutes to get your fluids and cool off prior to starting off again. Slow the pace if it is hot, and stop the workout if you start to feel warning signs of heat problems.

• Do not attempt to run long if you are not fully recovered

from illness or injury. Bail out of long runs if you feel an injury coming on, or if you turn an ankle, fall and bang a knee, etc. Stubbornly pushing ahead may cause you to lose several days of training—or worse. When returning from injury, you may be able to ease back into long runs by combining a run with a bike ride or swim for a long workout.

• Wear well-cushioned, well-broken-in (but not broken-down) shoes. The effect of inadequate shoes is greatly exaggerated over the course of a long run.

• Treat the long run as a hard day, even though you run at an easy pace. Come into it well rested by running easy the day before. Follow it with at least 1, if not 2, easy days. You may wish to minimize injury and maximize recovery by biking or swimming rather than running the day after a long run.

• Recover properly immediately after a long run. Replenish your body with fluids and carbohydrates. Cool down and stretch properly. A relaxed walk, bike ride, or swim later in the day will aid recovery.

• Do not attempt to race one day and run long the next. This is often the case for runners trying to squeeze everything into a weekend. If you plan well in advance, you can skip a few weekend long runs and enjoy a race.

• Be flexible. If you have properly built up your mileage and long runs well in advance, you can skip a long run here and there and not lose out. Don't panic if you miss a long run owing to unforeseen circumstances. One run won't make a difference if you will have several long runs under your belt prior to marathon day. With proper depth of training, you can take a few days off and miss a few long runs without guilt or loss of fitness.

• A poor long run when too tired or too hot, or trying to run too fast, can lead to a negative feeling rather than building fitness and confidence. The secret to success for the long run: rest, run long under control, recover.

23. MARATHON COUNTDOWN

The marathon countdown begins with 2 weeks to go to marathon day. You must taper your training and focus your mind from this point on in order to be prepared for a peak performance. Tapering and mental preparation are important for all distance races, but it becomes much more critical for the marathon, since you invest so much more time and energy into your race buildup. If you make mistakes here, you may waste 4 months of carefully planned training. Unlike a 10K, you can't do it again in a few weeks, so you must be sure to count down for your marathon wisely.

The last 2 weeks before a marathon are very difficult for many runners. This period poses a dilemma for the nervous marathoner hoping for a good race: how can you maintain a high level of fitness and yet rest up for a good marathon effort? You can continue training at a high level if you are obsessed with cramming in as much training as possible in an effort to get more fit. You can completely stop running in order to give your body total rest. The answer, of course, lies about halfway in between.

There is very little physiological value in any mileage, long runs, or speed work you do within 2 weeks of a marathon.

Cutting back here will affect your fitness level in the weeks after the marathon, but that is of no concern to you, since you will be recovering from a hard effort then anyway. You will be as fit as you are going to get 2 weeks prior to the race. Hard training from that point will only make you risk being over-trained or injured. You will benefit from some training, however, since you will wish to burn calories to prevent an unwanted weight gain, and you can continue to train the mind. Easy, paced short and medium aerobic endurance runs will allow you to burn calories and make you feel better about yourself—runners suffer from depression when they are forced to totally withdraw from running.

Tapering Mileage

Many runners fear that they'll lose the fitness base they worked so hard to build if they cut back too much before a marathon. But actually they are far more likely to do too much than too little. Dr. David Costill's research team studied highly competitive swimmers during their prerace tapering routine. Those swimmers who reduced their training by two-thirds for 2 weeks prior to a big meet increased their muscle power, produced less lactic acid during the race, and raced faster than when they didn't taper. Costill's advice for runners who want to achieve a maximum performance on marathon day: cut back to one-third your normal training mileage for 2 weeks before the marathon. Certainly this is comforting news to the runner who is favoring an injury or illness: he or she can back off and heal while not losing fitness.

We feel that Costill's tapering program is too radical for the average runner. He may very well be right, but the ideal tapering program may require a little more running because of the psychological stress of cutting back mileage substantially. We recommend that you cut back your mileage by 25–50 percent from your peak level for the week preceding the final countdown week and then cut further the following week to 15–25 miles in the 6 days prior to the marathon. Sample mileage tapering programs are included in the marathon training schedules for each category of runners at the end of chapter 21.

We prefer that you take 1 or 2 days off on marathon week, including 2 days before the race. We do not recommend taking off the day before the marathon, since tension is usually high then and a *short* run will relax you. If possible, jog over the last 2–3 miles of the course to the finish line and visualize yourself recording a good time.

Your last long run should be 2–3 weeks prior to the marathon, and your last race should also be 2–3 weeks prior (but not the same weekend as the long run). Run a good speed workout, but not all-out, 10–12 days prior to the marathon. Your final speed workout should be about 5 days before and should be brisk, not fast, and include extra recovery time and a reduced number of intervals. It is merely a psychological tune-up, not a real speed session, so control your body, which is rested and raring to go.

None of your training mileage in the last 2 weeks will significantly improve your marathon performance, and it could hinder it. Taper! If you are nursing an injury, back off—perhaps even take several days off, or swim and bike for a half hour. Many runners develop all kinds of aches and pains as they taper, and anxiety increases as the race approaches. You may also feel sluggish and irritable. These are common symptoms of runner's withdrawal: your body and mind are rebelling because of reduced training at the same time your emotions are heightened as the marathon approaches. These psychological problems will disappear when the race begins if you concentrate on keeping as relaxed as possible.

Summary: If you are not in shape for a good marathon effort with 2 weeks to go, you should devote your energy to prayer, not last-minute hard training.

Prerace Planning

Review the prerace anxiety, prerace checklist, and race-day rituals guidelines in chapter 28. Become familiar with the course by running parts of it in advance and reviewing it by car; segment the course in your head.

The Mental Race

Review chapter 27 for guidelines on self-image, motivation, relaxation, and visualization; and chapter 28 for guidelines on maintaining concentration while racing and running through pain and fatigue.

Marathon Morning

Wake up at least 3 hours before the race. Eat lightly, if at all, and take a warm shower to loosen up and calm you down. Put your marathon shoes and your number on before you leave for the race; otherwise you risk getting nervous and forgetting them. Keep warm right up until the start. If you want to wear fancy warm-ups to make you feel better, that's fine. But you'll have to check them in or hand them to a friend well before the start, so if it's cool, have some throwaway clothes on hand that you can discard just prior to the start, or even a few miles into the race.

Keep off your feet. Every 15 minutes get up and walk around and then sit down again. Stretch lightly, but don't nervously overstretch. You do not need to go for a warm-up run, as you would for a 10K. Save your energy for the long run ahead. Make sure you have extra toilet paper on you in case they run out at the official toilets or you need to use an "unofficial" location prior to or during the race. Avoid tense runners, and hang out with confident runners before the race. Remain calm, feel the energy within you relaxing and waiting to be unleashed.

Eating and Drinking

See the important guidelines for carbohydrate loading, the prerace meal, and prerace and race day fluid intake in chapters 36 and 37. As you cut back your mileage during the 2-week countdown, slightly cut back your caloric intake. Extra weight means extra work on race day. Don't nervously eat like a pig as you get close to the big day. You can expect to gain a few extra pounds, however, while carbohydrate loading, because of the added water you are storing. This weight will quickly disappear during the early stages of the race.

MARATHON COUNTDOWN TIPS

Stretching

As you taper your mileage, increase the amount of time you spend doing relaxation and stretching exercises so that you will be as flexible and loose as possible going into the race. Do not, however, overdo it and nervously overstretch: this could cause an injury.

Racing Shoes

Lightweight, experienced marathoners may choose to use racing flats. They make the runners "feel" lighter and allow them to flow more easily at a fast pace. A few ounces of weight saved here may be helpful to the runner trying to race at a very fast pace. However, this runner isn't out on the course as long as the average marathoner and thus doesn't absorb as much pounding. For this reason, training shoes should be used by novice and basic marathoners and by all heavy runners. These runners do not benefit by sacrificing shock absorption for a few less ounces of shoe weight. Hilly marathon courses are safer to race in training shoes; foot or leg injuries may require that you use the shoe that gives you the most protection. Much of the difference between training and racing shoes is psychological.

When Bob Glover ran a 2:37 marathon effort in the 1978 Carolina Marathon, a PR at the time by several minutes, he raced in training shoes. Somehow he had misplaced one of his racing shoes and didn't discover the error until race morning; so he was forced to race in his trusty training shoes. His worries about being slowed down by a heavier shoe disappeared when the gun went off and he had to concentrate on his race. He didn't remember until the next day that he had run a strong race without benefit of racing shoes. In fact, his legs and back ached less in the final stages because of the extra cushioning.

We recommend lightweight racing shoes for a fast feather-weight; lightweight training shoes for the average marathoner; and regular training shoes with excellent cushioning for novice and basic competitors and heavy runners. Use the shoes you will race in for several speed workouts and a few races as you sharpen for the marathon. Also, make sure that the shoes are not too tight, especially in the toe box. Unlike in shorter races, your feet will swell significantly during the marathon, and you will need room in the shoes for them to expand. You can test this by doing a long run in these shoes. Be careful not to get your feet, shoes, and socks soaked during a race—your shoes get heavy and your feet will slip around in them. Direct people to spray water over your head, not on your feet.

Menstruation

It is not unusual for a woman to start her period right before the big race. Since you are tapering off your running and reducing the stress to the body, your body may relax or fatten up just enough to think it is period time. Remain calm. World records have been set by women during their periods. It may or may not affect your race; it certainly will if you dwell on the negative.

Sleep

Get extra sleep during the last week before the marathon, especially 48 hours prior to the race. The sleep you get the night before isn't as critical, so there is no use staying up all night worrying about not being able to get to sleep. In the last few weeks, do not attend any late-night parties, work until the wee hours, or do anything else that will throw off your sleep pattern. You've worked too hard to blow it all now. There will be plenty of time for all-night partying during the postmarathon recovery period.

Sex

As Casey Stengel, the zany but wise baseball manager, once said: "It ain't the sex that kills ya', it's the staying up all night looking for it." You don't need to abstain during the marathon countdown; in fact a healthy amount of sex will help keep you relaxed. But don't let it interfere with your regular sleeping pattern.

Extra Energy

As you taper, you'll have lots of extra time and energy. Too many runners use it to clean out the garage, wash the floors, or chop wood. Any physical activity that you are not used to could cause injury. Stick to less physical ways to spend your time—like reading a book or going to the movies—and save your energy for the marathon.

Calm, Calm

Throughout the marathon countdown, think calm. Focus your life as much as possible on staying relaxed for the marathon. You can expect to feel edgy as the big day gets closer. This is normal. Your body has energy to spare, and it misses the hard training you are denying it. You will have to deal with withdrawal symptoms at the same time you are coping with prerace anxiety. Don't start thinking you are losing your fitness and panic. You are not. Remember this: there is nothing you can do now to help you improve your fitness, but you can make mental errors that will ruin your race. Concentrate on how confident you are. Keep emphasizing the slogan discussed in chapter 27: calm, calm, calm.

Prerace Hoopla

Minimize all the prerace clinics and other events. Attend a few of them for a few minutes to enjoy the atmosphere, but don't spend a lot of time on your feet. If you hang around large crowds of runners at prerace events, it tends to make you more nervous and drain you of energy. Go out to dinner with a few calm, confident friends and relax. Sight-seeing is a problem for runners who travel to an exciting place, such as New York. Tell your spouse to go ahead and sightsee and you stay behind, except perhaps for a bus tour where you can sit down. Don't get caught up going shopping, or you will spend not only a lot of money, but a lot of time on your feet. Ideally, plan your trip so that you can stay for a few days after the race. Use your walking tours as part of your postrace recovery. You can better enjoy your minivacation once the stress of the marathon is out of the way.

24. MARATHON STRATEGY___

Chapters 26–28 include general guidelines for goal setting, mental preparation, prerace planning, and race strategy. Review this information before reading the following specific guidelines for marathon strategy.

The marathon is unforgiving. If you start too fast, surge too hard during the race, or don't take proper fluids, for example, you blow your race. Not only do you suffer physically and mentally in order to make it to the finish line (or before dropping out), you can't "make up" for your errors in a week or two as you can in a 5K or 10K race. Nor can you try again in a few days if you finish feeling you could have pushed harder and run a faster time. For most marathoners, the body can only handle one serious effort per 6–12 months. Here are some tips to help you maximize your chances of success on marathon day:

Choose the Right Race

If you need a fast time to qualify for the Boston Marathon, break the 3-hour barrier, or meet another important time goal, choose a race that is certified and well organized, has a history of being relatively fast, and has a good chance of being run in good weather. A hilly course with a lot of turns held in the middle of the summer with few mile markers and time splits is obviously not an ideal choice. You will want to be able to get a good, clean start and have enough, but not too many, runners around you to push and pull you to a good time. Ideally, you would also like to have a large, enthusiastic crowd along the course to help cheer you on.

If you aren't obsessed with a fast time, but would like to do well on a traditional local course, or in an exciting big-city event like the New York Marathon, then you must adjust your time goal expectations.

Race Planning

Plan for your marathon, train for it, and then go for it with confidence. Don't chicken out at the last minute because you think you need one more long run or some other extra training, and decide to wait a few weeks for another marathon. Don't start the race with the attitude that you will drop out early if you don't feel good. You must go into it believing that you will finish, and finish well. However, it is sometimes wise to pick a backup race a week or two later in case a sudden snowstorm or heat wave makes running a strong marathon impossible. Don't waste a marathon on an extremely bad day. A marathon effort will tear you down physically and mentally. You can't just go out the next week or two after completing a poor marathon—or even if you dropped out en route—and jump into another one for a second chance.

Start Healthy

If you lost a lot of training because of injury or illness, you aren't going to pull off a miracle on race day. If you lost a slight amount of training, and perhaps kept in shape with alternative aerobic training while coming back from injury, you may have an honest chance of running well. If you are favoring an injury before you even start a marathon, you are taking a chance of not only running poorly, but of developing a long-term injury. Don't be a fool!

Establish Challenging but Realistic Goals

Bob Glover works very closely with his Atalanta athletes in goal setting. He feels that a good athlete should not attempt a marathon until his or her race times for 10K–30K "predict" a quality marathon performance. For example, you should be able to run 1:25 or better for a half marathon before you are ready to make an honest shot at a sub-3-hour marathon. If you run a 1:27 2 months prior to your marathon on a warm day or over a hilly course and your training is going well, then you still have a reasonable chance of meeting your marathon goal. However, if you run a 1:29 and struggle to the finish, you should quit dreaming and either adjust your goal or move your marathon plans back until you are fit enough to have a reasonable chance of meeting your challenging goal. Consult the charts that show the times you should be able to run for shorter races in order to break certain marathon goal barriers in chapter 21 and the race-time prediction system in chapter 26.

Marathons take too much time and effort to prepare for to waste. If you aren't ready, don't toe the line. Running a marathon because it is there on the schedule and your friends are running it is common for the less than serious recreational runner. But if you want to get the most out of yourself as an athlete, set a realistic goal that will challenge you and train toward it faithfully. Then "predict" with buildup races that can be used to establish your goal time and race pace. This step is essential to developing your marathon race strategy.

Countdown to the Marathon

The previous chapter details the important steps to take right up until the starting gun in order to peak mentally and physically on marathon day. Without this preparation, your race day strategy will not be effective.

Segment the Course and Visualize the Entire Race

Follow the guidelines on page 386 for breaking the race down into bite-sized pieces and then attacking them one at a time. A sample visualization program for a marathon is included on page 373.

Fluids on You and in You

Starting 10 minutes before the race, drink plenty of fluids and keep your body wet to fight off dehydration and heat exhaustion. Review chapter 37 before your marathon. Fluids are much more essential for the marathon than for shorter races.

Start Your Watch and Watch It

You can't depend on the timed splits along the course being accurate. Many marathons will have each mile marked, but only give splits every 5 miles. Thus you can tell by checking your watch at each mile marker if you are running an even pace and quickly detect errors in timing. Additionally, mile markers are sometimes inaccurate and you should quickly detect major errors, since you will know approximately what time you should arrive at each mile mark. Be prepared, keep an eye on your watch, and don't panic if mile markers or splits seem to be off occasionally. By regularly consulting your watch, you help yourself concentrate on the race; you keep in tune with your goal and your desire to hold pace. Play a little game: see how close you can come to running mile after mile at the same pace per mile.

Don't forget to stop your watch when you cross the finish line (but try to do it while looking up or you'll ruin any photo taken of you finishing): it may be a long time before you get the official results. Believe it or not, fatigued runners are prone to look at the digital clock at the finish and—because of fatigue-induced disorientation—not remember it a few minutes later.

Lining Up, Starting Out

It is more crucial in a 5K or 10K race for an advanced or champion competitor to get up front and off to a fast start. In the marathon, you need to be near the front and in a position to get out and into a flow in a reasonable time period. If you get started a little slowly, you can easily make it up over the first mile or two. Don't frantically weave in and out of people in an effort to move up: you'll waste energy and risk injury. It is more important to avoid getting started too quickly and then get nervous about being in trouble already. Be prepared to follow out those competitors who are experienced runners and are known for sensible pacing. You may pick some teammates or friends, or make a friend at the start, and make a pact to help each other over the first few miles and to keep each other from starting too slowly or too fast. Be calm at the start, not aggressive as you may be for a short race. Hold back the energy for later.

Novice and basic competitors should line up according to their predicted pace per mile. Starting too far up front not only will be unfair to those behind them whom they'll slow, but will seduce them into starting too fast. This runner will especially benefit from having a group of two to five runners who will attempt to start together at a mutually beneficial pace. There is usually safety in numbers: surely one of you is wise enough to control the urge to start too fast. Be careful when running with a pack of runners, however, that someone doesn't start pushing the pace too much or that the pack doesn't slow down and get behind your goal pace.

The First Few Miles: Test the Water

Ease into the race both in terms of your starting pace and your emotional involvement. If you start more than 10 seconds per mile faster than what you plan to average, you are asking for trouble. Slow down gradually and remain calm if you find that your first mile or two are too quick. You can't get away with "putting money in the bank" for too many miles, or your body will rebel in the later stages of the race. A modest 10-second-per-mile "cushion" per mile would result in running 260 seconds—4 minutes and 20 seconds—faster than an even splits at goal pace. This is plenty fast enough.

Most novice and basic competitors are better off starting at exactly the pace they wish to average until they are well warmed up (3–6 miles) and then slightly pick it up (5–10 seconds per mile) in order to have a little margin for error. Most advanced and champion competitors will start 5–10 seconds per mile faster than their realistic goal pace and then run equal *effort* to the finish line. As you get more tired, you may slow the pace slightly but still have a good "lead" on your goal pace. Having this lead will inspire you to keep working and pump up your confidence level. If you are running right on pace or slightly slower, you may get nervous about slipping behind. The key here is to get a little ahead of pace early in the race when you can go a little faster with little effort—resulting in a lot of confidence boosting. Most runners are more willing to tough it out during the inevitable bad patches that they will experience in a race if they are ahead of schedule and running a very good time than if they are slipping slightly behind pace.

Emotionally, stay as calm as possible. Treat the first 10 miles like what they are: a controlled run quite similar to your daily training runs in effort. Try to get in with a pack of runners who are flowing comfortably and help each other. Make note of the runners in the first few miles who sprint past you. Most likely you'll see them a few miles later as you pass them. The 10K pace and faster speed training you have accomplished will allow you to run comfortably at a good pace over the first few miles. Your 1-mile interval workouts and practice races taught you how to start at a controlled pace.

Obstacles: Heat, Hills, Wind, Turns

These factors can seriously affect 5K and 10K races, but they play havoc with your race plans much more dramatically for a marathon. See chapter 28 for guidelines. Hills in marathons need to be climbed much less aggressively than in shorter races. The chart on page 392 demonstrates how heat can slow the runner. It would be wise to adjust your running pace according to the chart from the beginning of the race rather than be forced to painfully slow to those average paces in the late stages.

Exercise physiologist Jack Daniels emphasizes the dramatic effect of a steady wind with the following chart from *Runner's World's Guide to Running the 1986 New York Marathon.*

EFFECT OF WIND ON YOUR RUNNING TIME
(IN SECONDS PER MILE)

PROJECTED FINISH TIME	5 MPH HEAD WIND	10 MPH HEAD WIND	5 MPH TAIL WIND	10 MPH TAIL WIND
2:30	+ 9	+22	− 7	−16
3:00	+11	+25	− 8	−18
3:40	+13	+30	− 9	−22
4:00	+15	+32	−10	−24
4:40	+17	+37	−11	−28
5:00	+19	+39	−12	−30

A runner aiming for a 3-hour marathon, for example, and facing a steady 5-mile-per-hour head wind, would lose 11 seconds per mile from a 6:51-per-mile effort, resulting in a finishing time of approximately 3:04:46. The same 5-mile-per-hour wind from behind would mean a gain of 8 seconds per mile, resulting in an approximate time of 2:56:32. Head winds slow you down more than tail winds assist you. Because of increased time exposed to heat or head winds, the slower runner will be more affected in terms of time loss than faster runners. Unfair, but true.

Halfway Analysis

This is a critical point psychologically for most runners. If your goal is 3 hours and you hit the halfway marker in exactly 1½ hours and feel pretty good, you know that if you continue to concentrate and work on good form you can reach your goal. If you are slightly behind schedule, you can still pick it up and have an honest chance to reach your goal. If you are more than 2 minutes, 10 seconds (representing 10 seconds per mile for 13 miles) behind an even paced half-marathon time, you will have to average better than 10 seconds per mile faster for the second half than the first half: an unlikely task. You should accept the time—realizing that you may have to adjust for a tough course, poor weather, or just a bad day for you—and make the best of it. If your halfway time is 30 seconds to a minute faster than the pace necessary to make your target finishing time, you are in good shape: keep working. If you are up to 2 minutes faster, you may be all right if you feel good but should consider slowing a little to conserve energy for the last few miles. If you are more than 2 minutes faster than an even split half-marathon time, you probably blew the race and will suffer for it over the last few miles. Reaching the halfway mark on or slightly ahead of schedule is an important psychological point in the race. You have put yourself in position to weather the hardest part of the race.

Many marathons are run on out-and-back courses where you turn around at the half-marathon mark (or at other points in the course) and return over the same route. If possible, count the number of runners you see heading back to you so you can estimate your place. Set a goal for moving up in the field over the last half of the race. For example, you may be in 200th place at the halfway point and finish 150th.

The Second Half: Concentration, Form, Relaxation, Mental Toughness

This is where the race begins. In a 5K or 10K race, you battle oxygen debt and discomfort for a few minutes. In a marathon, fatigue tries to capture you for at least 1–2 hours of time and 10–15 miles of distance. The marathon runner must maintain concentration (see page 396), keep relaxed, and remain confident and goal directed. Reflect back on the exaggerated running form used in key workouts to help you maintain proper form. Occasionally change your form a little to provide relief: drop your arms to your sides for a few seconds, shorten or lengthen the stride for a few yards, thus using muscles differently. When you hit bad patches where you are physically fatigued or hurting (see tips for winning this battle on page 397) or psychologically low, hang in there.

Think about all that training time and all those hard workouts that would be wasted if you let up just because you were uncomfortable. Many runners miss their goal time because they are unable to keep pushing through short lapses of self-doubt. They lose confidence, slow down, and fall behind their pace schedule. Relax, and believe in yourself. Have faith in your training program. Work hard to get the most out of your body so that after the race is over you won't feel that you have cheated yourself by giving in to temporary discomfort.

Use runners around you by working to catch them one by one as they tire more than you (making you feel good), or "hitch a ride" for a while if a runner passes you at a reasonable pace that you should be capable of running. Release the aggression that you held back in the first half of the race. Feel pride as you are running ahead of pace and passing runner after runner and use it to build energy toward a personal record finish. Feel anger if you are fighting off a bad patch. Use it to talk tough to yourself: "I'm not going to let that runner ahead of me get away from me." Or, "I'm a well-trained marathoner, I'm going to conquer fatigue . . . let's go!" Don't tense up as you release excitement or anger, control it and use it to your advantage. Internalize the cheers from the crowd and the fellowship of the runners around you to make you stronger. Accept discomfort. It is real. But use all your mental resources and your background of solid training to keep it from slowing you down.

The Wall

The Wall is a myth if you are properly prepared. If you have laid a solid base of endurance mileage, frequently logged long training runs, carbohydrate loaded, and started at a reasonable pace, you will not suddenly fall apart at the Wall. Runners who are not properly prepared and start too fast will most likely experience a dramatic drop-off of pace, suddenly slowing by a minute or more per mile somewhere near the 20-mile mark, when the body runs low on glycogen supplies.

Bail Out

If you are running favoring an injury, are feeling weak and dizzy because of heat—don't be a hero. Bail out at any point during the race. If you are way behind schedule and aren't enjoying yourself, balance the trauma of giving in and dropping out with the value of eliminating further wear and tear on the body, and make an intelligent decision that you can live with. Don't feel that you are a failure if you make an intelligent decision to drop out for reasons of personal safety. Prove yourself in the next marathon on your schedule.

10K to Go

You will hit two key mile markers in the marathon: the half-way mark and the 20-mile mark. Not only does the 20-mile barrier represent the popular conception of where you will hit the Wall, it also represents the start of a new race. From here to the finish you run a 10K race. Of course, it isn't anywhere near the same effort as starting a 6.2-mile run without already logging a hard 20-miler, but at least you can convince your mind that you are familiar with the distance. You can also play a quick mental game. If, for example, you are aiming for a sub-3-hour marathon and hit 20 miles in 2:15, you can break 3 hours by running a sub-45-minute 10K. Since your 10K PR is probably around 38 minutes, this task will not be overly intimidating even though you are starting to feel the effects of fatigue. Think at this point what you need to run for 10K to reach your goal and start a new race. Don't look at the 20-mile mark negatively, but rather positively.

Even though a well-trained runner won't be clobbered by the Wall, all runners will experience various degrees of discomfort over the last few miles. Over the last 3 miles in particular, the mind must take over from the body. You've come this far and your body certainly will feel tired. The willpower that forced you to train through heat, cold, rain, and snow for hour after hour must now be unleashed. Keep the arms pumping and keep picking up the knees. Somehow you will keep going forward at a good pace if you can keep the arms and knees in motion.

Break up the course mile marker by mile marker, landmark by landmark, even block by block—but keep knocking them off. Work on the runners around you—use them to push or pull you as often and as far as you can. Start thinking in terms of time left until the finish. First get under the 30-minute-to-go barrier, then 20, then 15, and finally 10: you know you can suffer for these amounts of time which seem less threatening than mileage to go. You have two major mileage markers to go: the 25-mile mark and the 26-mile mark. If possible, gather your energy and start a final push to the finish by slightly picking up the pace. You can do it! Dig down deep into your energy reserves, lift your knees, drive your arms, and go for it. As you cross the 26-mile mark you have only 385 yards— less than a quarter mile—to go. Look at your watch and know what you will need to run to break your barrier (even split goal pace for 26 miles subtracted from finish goal time), and use the noise of the crowd and the runners ahead to challenge you, and *guts* to push toward the finish line. As you sight the digital clock over the finish, use it to pull you in under your goal time.

The Finish

Run hard to a point 10 yards beyond the finish line; if you ease up as you approach the finish, you'll lose a few seconds that could cost you a barrier-breaking time. Also, there are often a few seconds of error as the masses crowd into chutes and are tabulated. As you move into the chutes, keep moving. *Do not, under any circumstances, fall or sit down and give in to fatigue and exhaustion.* See the following chapter, "The Aftermarathon," for guidelines on what to do for the next few minutes, hours, days, and weeks. If you ran a great race, exhault in the glory! If not, analyze what went wrong and plan new goals and new strategies.

25. THE AFTERMARATHON___

Thousands of runners each year put in hundreds of hours of physical and mental preparation to run the marathon. Very little time or planning, however, is devoted to what happens after the marathon. The scene at the finish line of a major marathon resembles a disaster area. The marathon tears down the body, which has been built up for months in anticipation of a strong effort. Injury and illness are frequent not only during and immediately after the marathon, but also in the days and weeks following. The body is weak, and the mind is undisciplined because the immediate goal has been achieved. A post-marathon runner is very vulnerable. How well you recover from a marathon effort and prevent injury from developing depends on how effectively you deal with the three key phases of marathon recovery:

1. your prerace preparation
2. *race day* strategy and execution, and environmental influences
3. *postrace* recovery procedures and training for several weeks following the marathon

Many runners come down with injuries resulting from carelessness in the "after-marathon" period. Because we feel that most runners seriously neglect the not-so-glamorous days following the excitement of a marathon, we want to call attention to that period here by devoting a full chapter to it.

PRERACE PREPARATION

Training

The better trained you are for the marathon, the better your chances of a healthy, quick recovery. The first-time marathon runner who builds to a minimum of 40–50 miles per week will take longer to recover fully and will be more vulnerable to injury than the veteran marathoner who logs 60–70 miles per week. Another factor is the frequency of long runs in the 3 to 4 months before a marathon. At least two runs a month of 18–20 miles will train the body to race better—and recover from—the marathon event. A proper tapering program will not only help you run a faster race, but also help you recover faster and minimize injury. A rested, fresh body is less prone to injury when subjected to the rigors of a marathon race.

Remember this key point: most injuries during the buildup stage are a result of overtraining; many injuries during the marathon and the postmarathon period are caused by undertraining. If you feel that you may not be properly trained for a good marathon effort, then wait for next year's event, when you will be more likely to run faster and emerge from the marathon uninjured.

Prerace Injury

Stubbornly starting a marathon with an injury could make the injury far worse or create another even more serious than the first one. The officials of New York Marathon, aware that runners would do anything to compete in their event, started a policy that allows runners to cancel because of injury or undertraining and be guaranteed entry into the race the following year. Each year over 2,500 of 20,000 accepted applicants take advantage of this offer. Over one-half of those surveyed said that if it had not been for this policy they would have tried to compete, even though they were injured, rather than pass up the opportunity to participate in this highly publicized event. If you take a chance and start a marathon with an injury, the odds are high that you'll be a double loser. You'll run poorly, if not be forced to drop out; and you'll be laid up with the injury for several weeks or more, thus losing out on future racing goals.

Racing Weight

The more you weigh, the more force you hit the ground with at each foot strike. The more you weigh above your ideal racing weight, the greater your chances of becoming injured during or after the marathon.

Flexibility and Muscle Balance

Poor flexibility and muscle imbalance will affect your recovery rate. The marathon severely taxes relatively weak muscles, such as the quadriceps, and tightens the muscles primarily used in running, the antigravity muscles in the back and legs. If you experience tightness in your hamstrings before the marathon begins, you will be prone to injury after the event.

Age and Experience

Marathon runners peak out physically somewhere between the ages of 25 and 35. You might still be able to improve your times after that, but most people start slowing down after age 35. Another major consideration for older marathoners is recovery. The older you are the longer your body takes to recover adequately and thus the greater your danger in trying to come back to hard training and racing after a marathon effort.

For the most part, the more marathons you have run the easier it is to recover and the less prone you are to injury. This is not only because you are in better shape, but because you have learned valuable lessons about how to listen to your body's warning signs during the critical rebuilding periods after your previous marathons.

Pre-race-Day Food

A marathoner can increase glycogen storage and minimize the tearing-down effect of glycogen depletion by carbohydrate loading.

Pre-race-Day Fluid Intake

For 2 weeks before the race, drink plenty of water, especially the last few days as you load with carbohydrates. Water is needed in correct balance to keep the body healthy; an even greater quantity of water is needed when you are carbohydrate loading because extra fluid is required to store the added glycogen properly.

RACE DAY PREPARATION

Correct Pacing

If you start too fast, you'll suffer much more at the end of the marathon than if you run an evenly paced race. Start no more than 10 seconds per mile faster than the pace you realistically expect to average for the race. A properly paced race will significantly minimize damage to your body and speed up the recovery process.

Proper Form

Errors in running form cause many injuries. The impact of these form faults is greatly magnified when repeated over and over during 3–5 hours of hard running. Even someone with good running form can lose control of it in the late stages of a race when fatigue, glycogen depletion, and—if the race isn't going well—depression can combine to produce running form errors that could make the runner more vulnerable to injuries following the marathon by overtaxing key parts of the musculoskeletal system. Attempt to concentrate on proper form even when you are fatigued so you can improve your race time, increase recovery time, and minimize injury. If—because of extreme fatigue—your form in the late stages of the marathon and your race pace are very poor, seriously consider dropping out to protect yourself from losing a lot of training time as a result of injury.

Injury

As with extreme fatigue, if you are losing good form because of injury, you are liable to cause further injury. Drop out! Swallow your pride and use common sense. Consider this: one runner in the New York Marathon continued running through pain until she was forced to stop when her leg broke less than a half mile from the finish line. Respect pain, don't be afraid to drop out to prevent serious injury and/or an extended loss of training time. Be especially careful of continuing to run while favoring painful blisters.

Shoes

Well-cushioned training shoes protect you better from pounding than racing shoes—especially on downhills. They also have higher heels, which minimize strain on the Achilles tendons, shins, and calves. If you insist on wearing racing shoes in an attempt to race a fast marathon, be aware that it may take you longer to recover. The average marathoner is better off opting for protection from injury rather than lightness of the shoe.

Heat

The lingering effects of dehydration during a hot marathon will make you vulnerable to injury. You can minimize this danger by starting more slowly and adjusting your race goal. If you start fast and unrealistically challenge the heat, you'll pay for it for several weeks.

Wind

Strong head winds wear you down and slow not only your time, but your recovery as well. They also make you lean forward, taxing the lower legs even more. Bob Glover fought strong head winds for over 20 miles in the 1983 Long Island Marathon—his first in 5 years—and his recovery time was slowed by a full 2 weeks. Beware once again of coming back too strong when coming off a marathon that presented you with special weather hazards on top of the challenge of racing 26.2 miles.

Hills

Hilly courses, particularly those with several steep downhills, cause extra damage to your muscles. You have to be especially careful when recovering from races such as the Boston Marathon, noted for its downhills. Cold, wet weather combined with downhills causes the muscles to become even more stiff and prone to injury.

Fluids

It is very important—in order to minimize the dangers of dehydration and improve recovery time—to be adequately hydrated before and during the marathon. Fluids consumed during the last 2 or 3 miles may not help you in your race, but they will aid in your recovery.

POSTRACE RECOVERY

Immediately after finishing the marathon you must fight the urge to lie down and give up the hope that your pain and fatigue will go away. Force yourself to begin the very important but largely neglected postrace recovery process. If you fail to take care of your aching body properly after the marathon, your legs will soon become very tight and you will be extremely prone to injury over the next few days and weeks of running.

This is the postrace recovery procedure that is most effective in helping runners to recover safely and quickly.

The First Hours

Keep moving when you finish the race. Don't lie or sit down for long periods of time. If you do sit down, try to keep your feet elevated. After leaving the chute, drink plenty of fluids, put on warm-ups, walk. Then get off your feet for a few minutes and drink some more fluids. Have any blisters treated immediately by medical personnel at the finish area. Apply ice to any painful areas in the major leg muscle groups, and repeat the process along with taking aspirin for the next few days to combat inflammation. It is the swelling around the traumatized muscles that causes soreness and tightness. Do some very light stretching, but don't overstretch fatigued muscles.

We recommend that you avoid heat treatment of the painful areas for 48 hours. However, some people find that a hot bath or whirlpool bath will relax them. If you do take a hot bath, treat the injured area with ice first. After the bath, take a short nap or at least lie down and rest. After you have gained some strength, go for a 10–15-minute walk and eat some food.

Later in the day, go for another walk (15–30 minutes), swim, ride a bike, or go dancing. The purpose of this activity is to pump blood into the legs in order to help flush away the waste products that have accumulated. Force yourself to do the unnatural—exercise when your body doesn't want to. Apply more ice and stretch some more before going to bed.

Fluids

Start replacing fluids as soon as you cross the finish line. Sip fluids if you cannot gulp them. When your stomach settles, pour them in. In hot weather, consume cold drinks to bring down your body temperature as well as replace the fluid loss. In cold weather, also drink some cold water to replace lost fluids, but then add something warm to prevent chill.

You should drink plenty of fluids throughout the day in proportion to the amount of weight you lost. An average runner might lose as much as 8 pounds of water weight running a marathon. Keep drinking until you have clear urine; dark urine is a symptom of dehydration. Force yourself to drink extra fluids. Watch your body weight for the next 24 hours. Generally this is enough time to get your fluids—and your weight—back to normal.

Beware of chronic dehydration, which can be caused by going several days without properly replenishing lost fluids. This is a dangerous condition that is frequently overlooked. It lowers a runner's tolerance to fatigue, reduces the ability to sweat, elevates the rectal temperature, and increases stress on the circulatory system. According to Dr. David Costill, "Probably the best way to guard against chronic dehydration is to check your weight every morning before breakfast. If you note a two or three pound decrease in body weight from morning to morning, efforts should be made to increase your fluid intake. You need not worry about drinking too much fluid, because your kidneys will unload the excess water in a matter of hours."

Food

Runners who are obsessed with proper diet before a race often ignore it afterward. But what you eat and drink for several days after a marathon will affect your recovery. A balanced diet, with an emphasis on carbohydrates, will replenish all your energy stores of fat and glycogen and allow you to return sooner to a normal training and racing routine.

A marathon will especially deplete your glycogen stores. To recover, and to replace lost glycogen, you should eat plenty of carbohydrates. In effect, this is a carbohydrate reloading to get glycogen back into your muscles and liver. Dr. Costill says, "Probably the first meal after the marathon should be like the last big meal before. You want to recover as much of that used-up glycogen as possible. It often takes three to five days to recover the glycogen. That's part of the problem of recovering from a marathon. A lot of people don't go after the carbohydrates hard enough, and that is part of the cause for the fatigue and difficulties in getting back into running form again."

THE DAYS FOLLOWING THE MARATHON

Joe Henderson commented in his book *Run Farther, Run Faster*, "Recovery seems to go backward at first. You feel worse the morning after the race than you did right after, and worse yet the second day. It takes that long for the 'drunk' to wear off, and the soreness and fatigue to settle in completely. You typically hit bottom about forty-eight hours after racing. You aren't tempted to do much running in this state, and you aren't thinking much about racing again. After another twenty-four or forty-eight hours pass, the worst of the hurts disappear. You think you're ready to start training for another race, but that's where you're wrong—perhaps dangerously wrong. Recovery isn't finished when your legs loosen up; it has only begun.

"Racing tears you down in more ways than one. I see at least three stages of recovery. They are: (1) muscular, (2) chemical, and (3) psychological. Recovery from muscle soreness and fatigue comes quickest. Even marathoners get over it within a few days. But it takes longer to restore body chemistry to its normal balance, and still longer to forget how bad this race felt so you can start looking forward to the next one."

Here are general guidelines and a sample program to follow for the first week following a marathon.

• The morning after the marathon take another bath to relax, but remember to treat injured areas with ice first. Do more gentle stretching, and take a walk or easy run. You may be better off forgetting about running for a few days. Stick to non-weight-bearing exercise, such as swimming or biking. The object is to recover by forcing blood into the legs to remove waste products, so why abuse the body by compelling it to run on blistered feet and tired legs?

• Treat injured areas with ice for the first 48 hours. You may later use heat treatments such as whirlpool baths or ultrasound and massage to promote circulation. Do gentle stretching exercises in the first 48 hours, and be cautious— remember, your muscles will be tight.

SAMPLE PROGRAM FOR ONE WEEK
FOLLOWING A MARATHON

Monday	Walk for 30 minutes in the morning; swim or bike for 30 minutes in the evening.
Tuesday	Walk for 30 minutes in the morning; swim or bike for 30 minutes in the evening.
Wednesday	Walk for 15 minutes and then run for 15–30 minutes in the morning; swim or bike for 30 minutes in the evening.
Thursday	Run 4–6 miles easy.*
Friday	Run 4–6 miles easy.
Saturday	Run 4–8 miles with a few brisk pickups of 100 yards at 10K pace.
Sunday	Run your average medium-distance day—approximately 6–10 miles

*If you find it difficult to run with good form because of injury or tight muscles, continue to use aerobic alternatives until you can comfortably run again.

• Get plenty of sleep for several days after your big race. Go to bed early, and take naps if possible. It is extremely important to get much more than the normal amount of sleep.

• Beware of a false high you may experience a few days after a strong marathon effort. Hold back. Even though you feel as if you are very strong, you are not. Also be careful following a disappointing race not to punish yourself by running hard in an effort to improve immediately for your next race.

REBUILDING—THE NEXT FEW WEEKS

Recovery is your priority for 2 weeks or more after the marathon. By the 3rd week you may be able to run your normal mileage. Don't rush it. Recovery can take 4 to 8 weeks, and it deserves as much planning as your premarathon schedule. Besides recovering from muscle soreness, you need time to restore your body chemistry to its normal balance and time for you again to desire to train properly for your next race. First-time marathoners and those who run behind the middle of the pack shouldn't race any distance for 5 to 8 weeks after the marathon; advanced marathoners shouldn't race for 4 to 6 weeks.

Postmarathon Depression

You put in a lot of time and effort, making many sacrifices along the way, to attempt to race a good marathon. But the marathon is a risky event. If you have a bad day, catch a stitch, develop bad blisters, have problems with your shoes, have an old injury act up, or trip and bang your knee, all your preparation can go down the drain. This is why we encourage you to go for good times for a few shorter races in the last weeks prior to the race. You will have something to show for all your training if the marathon race ends up being a disappointment.

Even if you ran a good race, you may feel depressed for the next few weeks. Just as in postpartum depression, your "baby" has reached the finish line and your long-sought-after goal, around which your life revolved for months, has been achieved, leaving you feeling empty. Take some time off from serious running and enjoy activities that you had to give up because you were spending most of your nonworking time running. Maintain minimal mileage levels, however, by doing a few easy runs per week. Then when you feel the urge to train again, set new racing goals and write a new training schedule. We recommend that you now train for shorter races.

Part VII
RACING

26. GOAL SETTING AND RACE-TIME PREDICTION

Competitive runners have three goals: finishing, running a good time (perhaps a PR), and placing high among their peers, or even winning. For the first-time racer and marathoner, the goal is finishing. Perhaps later you'll set a goal to finish in the top 50 percent of the field, and still later, as you improve, to finish among the top 25 percent. Eventually, you may set a goal to place in your age division, or even win a race.

Goals are fundamental to improvement. They establish the direction of our training. As Kay Porter and Judy Foster note in *The Mental Athlete:* "The effects of a goal-setting system are cumulative. As you achieve your first goals, you will become more certain of what you want from yourself and your sport and just how to accomplish it. Learning to set short-term, intermediate, and long-term goals is one of the most powerful tools any athlete can use to increase measurably the level of his or her performance. Your goals become the framework that guides your training and your competitions. Your goals, whatever they may be, and the desire to achieve them, are the motivation that pushes you through the rain and snow, through pain and injuries, and through the times when you may feel stuck at a certain competitive level or plateau."

For most competitive runners, the goal isn't finishing or winning, but improving their times. In effect, they race against themselves every time. This is a wonderful contest that can go on for years and lead you, year after year, to better racing times. Goals challenge you one step at a time: for example, finishing a marathon, breaking 4 hours, then a few years later, breaking 3½ hours.

Your progress will come quickly at first and then slowly, in amounts that will still be satisfying. You may reach plateaus, or even regress slightly, before moving ahead again. Goals must be challenging but realistic. Base them, for example, on how much training you can accomplish with a full-time job and a family rather than if you were single or only worked part-time. There is a difference between realistic goals and ideal goals. Few of us train under ideal conditions. You also must be committed to reaching your goals. You can't just dream about running certain times, you have to put in the hard work to prepare for a better performance. Dr. Jerry Lynch notes in *The Total Runner:* "My work with elite marathoners at the U.S. Olympic Training Center and experience as a competitive distance runner has helped me to realize that the difference between those who reach their goals and those who fall short can be attributed to their level of commitment. The stronger the commitment, the better their chances for obtaining objectives. I see this trend with recreational-competitive runners as well. They complain about not reaching their goals; either they are unrealistic in their desires or simply not committed to the goal. Perhaps other aspects of their life are more important yet they don't realize it. If the job, family or other worthwhile endeavors are more important, then running goals should and will take a back seat—for now. Admitting this to yourself will help relieve the frustration and disappointment with an activity like running that you thought was most important. The *key* in this situation is to choose your priorities carefully and create your goals accordingly."

You need to set both short-term goals—steps up the ladder—and long-term goals. Long-term goals may be for a year from now, or 4 years from now. They give you general direction—like moving up from novice to basic competitor. We believe the most important goal you set is the one for a year from now. This goal should change as you improve. It should always be a year away—a tantalizing objective, out of reach, guiding you in the direction of improvement. By keeping your goal a year away, you won't be in a rush to try too much too soon.

Short-term goals are both the goals of your racing season and the immediate goal of your next race. We suggest three levels of short-term goals to guide our runners, and we call it the Three-Goal System:

Goal 1: The Acceptable Goal. This is a preselected minimum race time. It takes into account factors of weather, training, personal health, and so forth—as should each of our goals. It represents reasonable progress. Usually this goal time would be to improve the previous PR by a few seconds.

Goal 2: The Challenging Goal. This goal represents a significant improvement in your race time. It is a challenging, realistic goal that requires you to put out a strong effort; it is also a goal you can reach. It would be a solid new PR.

Goal 3: The Ultimate Goal. This is your dream time. If everything goes right, maybe you can hit this very demanding goal. Usually you take 6 months to a year to reach this goal. But "popping" one of these fast times helps you enter a much higher level of competition.

Going into the 1981 Boston Marathon, Marilyn Hulak Cofnuk's greatest dream was to break the 3-hour barrier. This was a realistic goal, since her previous best, 6 months prior, was 3:11. But her training was going very well, and she kept racing faster and faster times. She amazed everyone by running a 1:20 half marathon 6 weeks prior to Boston, which her coach, Bob Glover, figured predicted a sub-2:50 marathon time. After the race, he confided to her: "Marilyn, you are way ahead of schedule; you can be a national class runner a year from now if you want it badly enough." He was being conservative; she was already almost there, but even so she was shocked by his statement. She trained very hard for the next few weeks to sharpen for the big race.

They set three goals for her for the Boston Marathon. Her acceptable goal had to be adjusted, because of her progress, from just improving her time to breaking 3 hours. That was her biggest barrier—anything else would be gravy. The challenging goal would be low 2:50s, a possible time after her half-marathon result. The ideal, ultimate goal would be to improve upon her half-marathon quality effort and break the national class standard of 2:50. She was advised not to tell anyone of her secret goals—others might think she was crazy, and it would put too much pressure on her. She stated that her goal was just to try to break 3 hours. She approached the race with enthusiasm and confidence. Without the benefit of a goal-setting plan and race-time prediction she would only have aimed for a 3-hour marathon and probably finished with a lot left over. Instead, she started at a pace that would allow her to break 2:50 and held on to become the first New York finisher with a national class time of 2:45:57. "Where did Marilyn come from?" New Yorkers asked. They didn't know that she had carefully followed a secret plan. She went on to run 2:39:55 at the 1984 Olympic trials.

Use the race-time prediction system detailed on the following pages to help you establish challenging goals. Don't be satisfied with setting a "soft" PR if your training and other race times indicate that you are capable of more if you give a good effort. Take a look at what times others are running for the marathon, for example, who are racing similar times as you for the 10K. When your other race times and the race times of your peers are pointing out that it is possible to make a significant improvement, go for it. The saying "What you can conceive you can achieve" fits here. If you believe a lofty, but realistic, goal can be achieved, it can. Go for it!

Your Purpose

If you are just rounding into shape, you may not be able, or want, to race well. You may prefer to use the race as a hard strength run without tapering. You adjust your goals and are not concerned about time. Or you may decide to use the race for pace work for a longer race later. A half marathon, for example, may be run strongly at comfortable marathon pace rather than all-out. In this case, your goal will be to hold an even marathon pace throughout the race.

Your Fitness Level

Maybe you are tired, overtrained, and need to take it easy during the race. Or you haven't put in the training you planned and need to adjust your goals downward.

You're Coming Back

After an injury, illness, or layoff from competition, you will need to adjust your goal times.

Your Age

Slowly we grow older, and the times come harder. You may have to set new goals. Eventually, all of us have to give in and adjust our time goals downward with age. But we get new goals as we enter new age divisions, and thus can start all over again by setting new PRs for our new age group.

Your Weight

If you've added a few pounds since your last race, you may have to subtract some time for the extra baggage.

Your Environment

Heat and cold, snow, rain, ice, wind—all of Mother Nature—may slow you down. You should adjust your race goals. On the other hand, consider a tailing wind when you analyze race results. Heat slows every runner at one time or another: if you expect to run a 40-minute 10K and the temperature is 80°F, chances are you will run at least a minute or two slower. Start with a pace appropriate to your revised goal, and consider in your postrace analysis the factors you encountered—especially the weather.

The Course

Hills, poor footing, or turns may make you adjust your race goals. You may run faster on a flat course than on your normal hilly one and should adjust your goal pace accordingly. If you race over the same course again, you can more accurately set racing goals.

Your Head

If you are "psyched up" for a race and know you are really fit, you may "go for it" and start off at a pace aimed for your ultimate goal time. On the other hand, stress, poor training, or fatigue may undermine your confidence, and you probably should take the pressure off and aim for a conservative goal.

The Crowd

If the start of the race is packed and you cannot start as fast as you wish, take this into consideration. Time how long it takes to get going at your intended pace after reaching the starting line, and give yourself two goal times—from where the gun went off and from where you got rolling. Crowded races also make it difficult to pass, or get fluids at water stations. Some runners also run slower times in small races where they run alone without benefit of other racers pushing them.

Look around you at the start. You know who usually finishes just ahead of or just behind you. Start off pacing yourself off the runners you want to catch up to and beat. Don't be intimidated and assume they're bound to beat you just because they always have in the past. After the race, if your time was off, see what your competitors did. If everyone ran, say, 3 minutes slower than normal because of heat and hills, you can better gauge how to evaluate your performance relative to your goals. Spectators also make a difference. If you need a crowd to pick you up, a marathon in the country with only the cows watching may result in slower times. In summary, consider the impact of crowds on your performance and goals, both in the race and along its course.

PREDICTING RACE TIMES

Consider all of the above factors. Be fair to yourself. To set your goals, disregard super race times, which are questionable measures of performance owing to special circumstances: strong tail wind, downhill course, or the possibility of a short course.

Knowing in advance what your finishing time *should* be—approximately—and therefore what your starting pace should be, is a great advantage. Without such a goal, you won't know how and when to push yourself or even what pace to start with. We have developed a system that helps predict what times our runners are capable of racing over given distances. We determine what they should run or a specific distance based on their times for other races and in workouts, and then adjust the goal times upward or downward based upon the influencing factors above. With experience at measuring the factors that influence your race times, and a feel for what you are capable of doing, you can use this system to predict accurately your racing times. While neither this or any other system is foolproof, most of the time we are correct within a few seconds of our predictions.

Different runners and coaches have different systems. German track expert Toni Nett based his time-prediction rules on statistical data. His formula, developed over two decades ago, for predicting the results of 10K time from the 5K time was 10K time equals 2 times your 5K time plus 1 minute. Going the other way, Nett said 5K time equals your 10K time minus 1 minute and divided by 2. (For example, if you run 16 minutes for the 5K, your 10K time would be 33 minutes.)

Manfred Steffny, former German Olympic marathon runner and coach of Christa Vahlensieck when she was the women's world record holder for the marathon, devised a theory for predicting marathon times based on 10K times he had collected. Steffny's theory was originally published in the March 1975 issue of *Spiridon* magazine and later in his book *Marathoning*. His theory goes like this: *A ratio of approximately 1:5 exists between 10K times and marathon times. Starting with a 10K time of 30:00 equaling a marathon of 2:20:00, add or subtract 5 minutes for every change of 1 minute in the 10K time.* For example, 31:00 for the 10K would be 2:25:00 for the marathon. This formula compares well with computerized time comparisons detailed in *Computerized Running Training Programs* by James B. Gardner and J. Gerry Purdy. Consult this excellent text for more detailed race-time comparisons from 100 meters to 50 kilometers.

After analyzing many race times for 10-mile and half-marathon distances, we predict that approximately every 30-second difference in the 10K time is a difference of 50 seconds for 10 miles and 1 minute 15 seconds for the half marathon. These predictions are listed in the Race-Time Comparison and Predictor Chart in the Appendices. They teach a basic lesson. There is a relationship between your pace per mile for all distances. These relationships are consistent for all levels of runners; we all slow down at about the same rate over longer distances. Here's another interesting relationship: an increase or decrease in performance for the following times is equal:

5K—15 seconds
10K—30 seconds
10 miles—50 seconds
half marathon—1 minute 15 seconds
marathon—2 minutes 30 seconds

Theoretically, if you improve your time by 30 seconds for the 10K, for example, you should be able to race the other distances faster as well, and by the times noted. Thus, if the marathon runner does speed work aimed at improving his or her 5K and 10K times, with added speed and specific marathon training, he or she can also improve marathon times.

HOW TO USE THE RACE PREDICTION SYSTEM

Using the chart to predict your times, you can do the following:
• Set your three goals more efficiently.
• Establish a starting pace based on your time prediction for every race you enter.
• Analyze your race results and compare them with race times at various distances to determine your best performances, and perhaps your best events.

Goals

Assume you have run a 10K in 42:00, and that in 2 weeks you will run a half marathon and 4 weeks later an important marathon. You should set goals for both races based on your 10K time. Consult the Race-Time Comparison and Predictor Chart in the Appendices and note that 42:00 for the 10K is equivalent to 1:35:00 for the half marathon and to 3:20:00 for the marathon. You can use these times, assuming conditions are similar for all three races, to set realistic goals. For example:

1. Acceptable Goal: a present PR for these distances
   half marathon: 1:40:00
   marathon: 3:35:00

---

2. Challenging Goal: as predicted from the chart
   half marathon: 1:35:00
   marathon: 3:20:00

---

3. Ultimate Goal: faster than predicted
   half marathon: 1:32:00
   marathon: 3:15:00

By hitting your challenging goals for your sharpening races, you may have conditioned yourself physically and mentally to take a good shot at your ultimate race-goal time for your final peak race.

Establishing Pace

Before you run, you must know the pace you will start out with. Dare yourself with your ultimate goal pace; test yourself with your challenging goal pace; or be conservative and start at your acceptable goal pace. Consult the Pacing Charts in the Appendices to find the pace per mile that you must average for the race distance. For example, to run 1:35:00 for the half marathon, the goal pace from the chart would be 7:15 per mile. To achieve 1:35:00 for the half marathon—a challenging goal— start no faster than a 7:05 pace and no slower than a 7:10 pace. The key is to start a few seconds per mile faster than your goal pace based on your race-time prediction.

Analyzing Your Results

After you have finished the race, analyze your time and compare it with your best performance at other distances. Perhaps you ran a 1:35:00 half marathon and then ran a strong 3:15:00 marathon. Comparing race times, you can see that your marathon time is much better than the 10K and half-marathon times. You have moved up a notch in your competitive running. Now use this time as a gauge by which to seek improvement at other distances. Record in your diary your race time, pace per mile (from the Pacing Charts in the Appendices), and perhaps your equivalent times for other distances, and use this information to set your goals for the next racing cycle. If you see a trend emerging—better relative times for either the shorter, longer, or middle distances—you may determine that these are your best events, or that you need more specific training for the events that you are behind on.

All time comparisons and predictions, here and anywhere else, are obviously estimated. Use them to set *flexible* goals; adjust those goals for the various influencing factors. The accuracy of your predictions increases when the race distance you are predicting from is close to the race distance you are setting a goal for—for example, predicting a half-marathon time from a 10-mile time. Predicting marathon times from 5K or even 10K times, or vice versa, is more difficult. The comparisons assume that you will do the required specific training for each distance (more mileage for the marathon, more speed work for the 5K, and so forth). Some runners lack speed but have plenty of endurance, while others can run fast but not over long distances. Women, who have less muscle power than men, often find they run faster for the marathon than for the 5K or 10K. Time comparisons are most accurate when based on your performance in a series of races peaking for a big race. This system will guide you to faster times as you confidently measure progress.

Setting Your Goals

As stated, goals need to be both challenging and realistic. To be effective, they also need to be specific and measurable. Write your goals down in advance and adjust them as you record your actual race times. Use your training diary for this purpose or make a simple chart like the one below to establish tangible racing goals.

NAME John Smith	RACE DISTANCE 10K	
DATE January 1, 1988	PERSONAL RECORD 51 min	
	ACCEPTABLE GOAL	**CHALLENGING GOAL**	**ULTIMATE GOAL**
Short-term (within 30 days)	50	49	45
Intermediate (within 3 months)	49	48	45
Long-term (in 1 year)	47	45	42

Establish a separate chart for each of your key racing distances. Adjust your goals as your race times improve or as dictated by changes in your training or environment. Compare race times at different distances using the chart in the Appendices to help establish new goals at all distances after a good race effort.

In the above example, John Smith has established a challenging, but realistic, goal system that is quite flexible. The "perfect" scenario for this runner would be to run a sub-50-minute 10K within a month, a sub-49-minute within 3 months, and a 45-minute 10K in a year. He may progress faster or slower than this goal system. By establishing written goals, he is more likely to succeed. So are you.

27. MENTAL PREPARATION FOR RACING

Mental preparation is perhaps the most neglected factor in racing. Many runners set racing goals and prepare themselves physically to meet them. They reach the starting line in superb condition, but something happens before they finish. These runners don't reach their athletic potential because they only train themselves physically and don't prepare mentally. At the U.S. Olympic Training Center in Colorado, sports psychologist Dr. Jerry Lynch asked a dozen elite marathon runners what percentage of a runner's success is due to each of the following: (a) natural ability; (b) diligent training; (c) positive mental attitude; (d) good coaching. The answer: "An overwhelming majority of the athletes said that the greatest percentage of a runner's success is due to *positive mental attitude*." Obviously, in addition to developing a carefully planned training schedule, you must also have a positive mental attitude about yourself and your running.

If you enter a competition in the same physical shape as another racer, most often the one who finishes first will be the one who was stronger mentally. In fact, over 80 percent of elite runners believe that the difference between the top runners on race day is who had the best race mentally.

Average runners are concerned less with defeating others than with defeating the clock, but nevertheless they too can gain from good mental preparation. We've often found that runners improve their race times by large margins after only one or two of our classes. Can our workouts be that great? No. But our pep talks are. In class we tell people to search for the athlete within and work hard. In speed sessions you find that you can push harder than you thought possible. Transferring this knowledge and confidence to a race often results in improved performances. These runners didn't get better, rather they didn't underperform from lack of confidence. With a belief in your value as an athlete, even a 60-minute 10K runner can run faster.

Bob Glover received a long-distance phone call from 40-year-old Roberta Brill within a few minutes after she crossed the finish line of the 1987 Boston Marathon. "It worked! You were right! I can't believe it," she exclaimed. Glover had noticed that Roberta always smiled during our speed workouts and during races, and yet was disappointed with her race times. "Save the smiling for after the race," was his stern command. She read and reread the sections of this book on goal setting and mental preparation and then went for it. Despite a head wind, she improved her PR from 3:22 to 3:10. Two months later she lowered her time to 3:06. "I owe it all to mental preparation," she concluded. Before, she didn't believe in herself and didn't set her goals high enough. You too can get more out of your body if you train your mind to succeed.

The following key ingredients are essential to yor mental fitness.

GOALS AND COMMITMENTS

As detailed in the previous chapter, goals need to be challenging, realistic, and specific. Mental fitness starts with goal setting. However, to be effective you have to be committed to reaching your goals. You need to examine why you want to reach certain goals and whether you are willing and able to put in the time and effort to achieve your goals as a runner.

Bob Glover, for example, *wants* to run a sub-2:30 marathon.

It is unlikely that he ever will, although he is most likely capable of doing it and would really be happy to reach that goal. However, running his own business (and writing this book) takes a lot of energy, and he values the time he has to play baseball and other sports with his son. This doesn't leave him with enough time or energy to train *ideally*. He has made a choice not to be highly committed to running. You don't have to be either 100 percent committed to running or become a jogger. You can choose how much of a commitment you can make: from 0 percent (those who totally give up) to 100 percent (those who are totally addicted). Neither extreme is recommended. Chapter 39 offers advice on balancing running, career, and family. Most of us can find the time and energy to set and reach *realistic* but not *ideal* running goals. You need to schedule your time well, follow a vigorous, progressive training program, and be mentally tough.

SELF-IMAGE AND CONFIDENCE

You are an athlete. Yes, you! Whether you run a 5-minute mile or a 10-minute mile; are 15 years old or 65; are a corporate president or a housekeeper; run with two legs or on crutches. You strive to do your best—just like the elite runners up front who wouldn't seem so important if it weren't for people like you behind them. Your goals are just as important as those of anyone else in a race. That's the reason for the great popularity of mass running events: everyone can be a winner.

Feel proud of yourself as a runner. Even if you are a novice, you are a big shot. How many people at the office can even run around the block, and you can complete a 10K! Don't compare yourself with the skinny, fast guys and feel substandard. The runners in front of you don't beat you, they are running in a different race. You will win your race. Compare yourself with the millions of people you are superior to in terms of aerobic fitness, the old out-of-shape you, or the slower-paced runner you once were. When you are running and racing, "feel" like an athlete. Think about how smoothly or powerfully you can move your body. Envision yourself running like a deer or like your running hero.

To win—whatever "winning" means to you (finishing a race, a modest PR)—it is essential to develop a winning attitude and a positive self-image. As you reach your personalized running goals, success will build upon success and you will increase your self-confidence.

You must learn to want to be successful. As Flip Darr, former U.S. World Games swim coach, said: "It takes a hungry person to be a champion. Although the true champions don't let it show, they are on ego trips. The ego satisfaction they get from winning makes the necessary hours of effort worthwhile." All of us are champions to various degrees, and all of us have egos that demand satisfaction. Learn how to satisfy your ego and accept achievement. Don't put yourself down. Build yourself up, physically and mentally. When another runner says, "Nice race," reply, "Thanks. I worked hard for it." You did; don't reject a compliment with "I was just lucky" or "I should have done better." Be quietly confident before the race, show reserved pride after the race.

Long training runs and consistent mileage build confidence. Increasingly faster times during speed workouts and buildup races also contribute to your physical and mental confidence. On race day, concentrate on your own positive feelings, rather than on how good some of the other runners look. Pump yourself up with a spirited pep talk. You've trained well: you're ready. Go get 'em!

If by some chance you have a bad race, don't panic. We are entitled to a few disappointments. Figure out the likely causes: too hot, started too fast, too hilly, coming off the flu. Write it off. Forget about it. Concentrate on the previous good race and how you will do well in the next race.

Sports psychologists recommend increasing your level of confidence and enhancing self-image by developing a list of positive self-affirmations. Write them down and look at them regularly; think about them while running and racing. Change them periodically. Here are some examples:

—I am getting stronger each week of consistent mileage (or long runs).
—I feel faster with every speed session.
—I am going to break 3 hours for the marathon.

—I am going to beat my boss in the 10K.
—I am strong going uphill.
—If I keep pushing in the race, Sally will not be able to catch me.

Affirmations can be particularly useful to help change negative thinking to positive thinking. If you get very nervous during a race and tighten up, for example, your positive statement could be "I become calmer as the race gets longer." Make up sayings that rhyme and are easier to remember. Memorize famous quotes, or even fortune cookie statements, to help you enhance your self-image.

MOTIVATION

You can have a strong commitment to your running and still fail if you lack strong motivation. Clear, reachable goals—winning an award, achieving a time, finishing a distance, beating a competitor—give you the focus to train. But along the way you often get discouraged, impatient, or bored. You will need to keep motivating yourself. Don't race the same distance all the time. Some runners do one 10K race after another and are too obsessed with improving with each race. Others only train for the marathon and miss out on the fun of achieving goals at shorter distances. Seek variety. Set goals to improve first at 10K, for example, and then move down to 5K, 4 miles, or 5 miles. Then perhaps aim for a PR at 15K, 10 miles, or the half marathon. The greater variety of distances you race, the more opportunity you have to be motivated to aim for a PR.

When you reach a point where you can't get motivated to run another 10K, search for another distance and get "psyched up" for a good race. The 10K distance is the most frequently raced and is a common measure for progress. But it can also be an annoying stress. Who wants the pressure of comparing 10K times week after week? Get away from some of the racing distances that are the most common and come back to them when you are hungry to be measured again. You can even be out of shape and run a PR if you haven't raced an odd distance in a while. Look for a 12K or a 7.3-mile race. You'll be relaxed and enjoy it, since it will be a new distance and a certain PR.

Adjust your goals as you get older. A 40-year-old, for example, should start all over recording PRs when he or she reaches 45 and then again at age 50. Or record separately your best times after an operation or perhaps after having a baby. Use your imagination. Look for new goals to motivate you to keep training.

Don't run the same races year after year. After a while you won't be able to improve your times over the course, and you'll lose your enthusiasm. Search out a few new races. Or schedule a trip to an exciting new place: try for the London Marathon, or a winter 15K in Florida or 10K in the Bahamas.

Here are some more motivational tips:

Support System

Let your family and friends share in your excitement. Encourage them to travel with you to some races. Make it an exciting adventure for all—it doesn't matter if they don't know anything about running. Having people cheering for you along the course—and waiting for you at the finish line—and knowing they will be out there, will inspire you to work harder in training and on race day. Have your family time you for some of your training sessions, or ride along on a bike. It will give you a boost, and respite from the often lonely training days.

Training partners are sometimes hard to find but are great motivators. Make a date with others for a run, and you will make sure not to miss it, and will be unlikely to cut the run short. It is especially helpful to have a group to meet on a regular basis for long runs. Lots of small running clubs across the country meet every Saturday or Sunday morning for a sociable run. Bob Glover once ran a 20-miler every Sunday for 3 straight months despite a tough upstate New York winter because he was motivated by a dedicated group of veterans who forced each other out the door. On their own, few of them would have been motivated to keep consistent with their training. Come spring and the Boston Marathon, they all ran confident and strong.

Join, or form, a running team. Most local teams welcome runners of all ability levels. Teammates pick each other up and help motivate each other. The feeling of "belonging" makes you feel like a better, more dedicated runner. If you feel that way, then you are. In races, when you see teammates doing well, let that push you to dig down a little more. "If John and Sally up ahead can keep going up that hill, then I can," you say. Bob Glover's elite women's racing team Atalanta thrives on the excitement created when some of the athletes do well. This in turn motivates the others to train and race harder. In races, they enjoy the *blue wave* approach. Most of the women line up for the same race, and a steady stream of blue uniforms up front inspires each of them to push harder, dig a little deeper. Pride in wearing your team uniform and not wanting to let your teammates down can certainly contribute to your performance.

Even your competitors can be a key part of your support system. If you hear that a runner you've been beating ran a real fast 10K, then you are motivated to beat that time. During a race you push extra hard if you see a peer up ahead, or fear that he or she is gaining on you from behind.

A coach, or at least an adviser, is very helpful. He or she can give you positive feedback about your training, help establish goals, give you pep talks, and brag about your achievements. If you don't have a coach, use this book to help pep you up, and brag about your achievement to anyone who will listen (even the dog).

Variety

If your mileage is getting up there and you are getting tired of the same old training routes, look for a few new ones. Get in your car if need be and drive to a new venue. It will pick you up. If you are tired of weekly 440s on the track, run some 660s or try a ladder workout (220–440–660–440–220, for example). Forget the track and head out for a *fartlek* run over dirt trails. Use your imagination. As mentioned, race over a variety of distances. Maybe even try something new like running a mile on a track or entering a cross-country race. Try some fun events like a relay race or even a triathlon for a change of pace.

Read/Watch

Read an inspiring book about running, or pick up a copy of *Runner's World* and read articles about great achievements accomplished by elite or just average runners like yourself. Such stories are often an inspiration. Watch an inspirational movie about sports. Go to a road race and, instead of running, view the excitement of the up-front racing. Or go to a track meet, such as the thrilling Millrose Games in New York City's Madison Square Garden. Reread some especially inspirational articles or books going into a key race. Tape the highlights of an exciting race on TV and replay them before a race while you "feel" yourself in the middle of the action.

Take a Break

Take periodic time-outs from competitive training. Cut back the mileage, cut out racing and speed training for a while. Give your body and your mind a break. When you start feeling hungry again, it will be easier to get and stay motivated for quality training and racing.

RELAXATION

One of the most important, and often overlooked, aspects of running is relaxation. Running itself is a form of relaxation for many people. But running, particularly hard racing, also causes tension to build. Runners need to learn how to relax before and during competition in order to race well. Bud Winter, author of *Relax and Win: Championship Performance in Whatever You Do,* believes that the key to a good performance is the ability to stay relaxed.

Tense muscles aren't as flexible and are more prone to injury. Relaxation exercises (see page 508) should precede the prerun stretching routine. Tightness in your running form contributes to inefficiency. See chapter 30 for guidelines for a relaxed running style. A tense mind makes mental errors—such as starting too fast—and contributes to sudden losses of confidence before and during a race. Winter adds: "Fatigue is largely mental and, like the first pangs of hunger, is only a preliminary warning of things to come and should be treated as such by those who would learn to relax, refresh and restore themselves." He emphasizes: "Relaxation helps distance runners by keeping their antagonistic, or unused muscles relaxed. They run with as few muscles as possible." To avoid tensing up, Winter says, you must learn to work at 90 percent effort rather than at 100 percent. You learn to let the muscles not directly involved with running—such as the muscles in the face, neck, and shoulders—relax. Winter states it this way: "Let the meat hang on the bones." Of particular importance to runners is the ability to "turn off" the hamstring muscles when the opposing quadricep muscles are contracted, and vice versa. Tension here causes the leg muscles to tighten.

Relaxation techniques help you control the stress in your life and improve your total well-being. Learning to relax before and during training runs and races helps you maintain proper form, improves your level of confidence, and results in faster race times.

Methods of relaxation include transcendental meditation, yoga, zen, hypnosis, biofeedback, flotation tank therapy, deep breathing, and progressive relaxation. Good sources of relaxation programs helpful to runners include *The Relaxation Response* by Herbert Benson, *The Total Runner* by Dr. Jerry Lynch, and Winter's *Relax and Win*. Relaxation exercises can be done any time of the day—perhaps on your lunch break—when you can get a free and quiet 15–30 minutes of time.

The process of learning to control tension in specific muscles by tensing and then releasing tension from one muscle group at a time was pioneered in 1920 by Dr. Edmund Jacobson, author of *Progressive Relaxation*. Here's a sample progressive relaxation routine that Bob Glover has found effective:

- Lie on your back, knees flexed.
- Shut your eyes, take several deep breaths.
- Lower your right leg, then raise it a few inches off the ground; tighten all the muscles in the leg, concentrating on the tension for 15 seconds. "Feel" the tension escape as you let go, lower the leg, return to flexed position, and take several deep breaths. Repeat with the left leg.

- Tighten all the muscle in your butt and hold for 15 seconds, concentrate on the tension. Slowly let go, then breathe deeply.
- Raise your right arm a few inches off the floor, tighten your fist and all the muscles in your arm, concentrating on the tension for 15 seconds. Slowly let go and then lower the arm. Take several deep breaths. Repeat with the left arm.
- Hunch your shoulders up and tighten all the muscles in your neck and shoulders, concentrating on the tension for 15 seconds. Slowly release. Take several deep breaths.
- Tighten all the muscles in your face and hold for 15 seconds, concentrating on the tension. Release and take several deep breaths.
- Flex your knees, shut your eyes, breathe slowly, and "feel" your body floating in warm water in the Bahamas. Let yourself go. Often, this results in a brief but deep and relaxing nap.
- Slowly stretch the body, like a cat, roll over, and slowly stand up.
- You should feel very calm and relaxed.

Relaxation exercises should always be done before stretching and running. The relaxation routine we recommend on page 508 can be used before and after each workout and race. You must enter each competition mentally "psyched up" for a strong effort, yet relaxed.

Winter notes: "The best attitude going into an athletic contest is one of cool confidence. So maybe before these situations, we should set your minds to be cool and confident. To set your mind, you make up a short slogan that expresses the attitude in which you want your mind during a pressure situation. Then you get into as total a relaxation state as you can. When totally relaxed, repeat the slogan over and over, at least three or four times." The word Winter favors to trigger a relaxation response is "calm." Try it. Say and think calm before races and even during a race when you start to feel tense. Be calm, be cool, be relaxed.

Relaxation exercises are also essential to get rid of mental tensions so that you can free up the mind for positive visualization of your racing. We suggest belly-breathing exercises combined with shoulder shrugs for 5 to 10 minutes, once or twice a day, during the days leading into a big race, to help you prepare for visualization. Then five or six deep breaths, or sighs, should leave you feeling relaxed enough to visualize clearly your upcoming race. You may want to sit quietly while doing this, and you may want to continue the deep breathing for several minutes. The idea here is to get into a deeply relaxed state. Too many runners experience stress before hard workouts or races (this routine can also help you with your training runs). They become anxious about their opponents, or the distance, or the Wall. "Such anxiety," says Dr. Lynch, "interferes with the fluidity of the muscle function. When the muscles begin to tighten and become less fluid, the mind begins to send messages to quit. The thought of stopping in a race increases anxiety, creating a vicious cycle. Relaxation and visualization techniques can decrease anxiety, allow you to burn less energy because you're not in a state of stress, and thus improve your coordination and increase your endurance. Relaxation also has the effect of clearing the mind and enhancing your concentration, perhaps the most important ingredient in athletic excellence."

VISUALIZATION

Visualization is a mental game used by leading athletes in every sport to enhance performance. But you don't have to be an elite runner to benefit. As long as you have a solid goal and a strong desire to reach it, all you need is a good imagination. Basically, visualization is rehearsing for success. You imagine what you would like to have happen (such as breaking 4 hours for a marathon) and thus convince yourself that you can do it. You see and feel success so that when it is actually happening you are not afraid to succeed, but rather embrace it as an old friend. You have to dream that the difficult is not only possible, but that it *will* happen.

Whether your realize it or not, you practice visualization daily. You envision an upcoming event in your life—such as a presentation to your boss or an explanation to your spouse that you must cancel a social engagement to get in a long run—and then play out the scenario in your head.

Visualization trains the athlete to experience mentally the event as if he or she were living it. Dr. Thomas Tutko, author of *Sports Psyching: Playing Your Best Game All of the Time,* tells athletes to "relive" their best performances over and over until they actually can achieve them almost automatically. "It's like putting a tape into your brain, as you would with a computer." Rerun some of your best races and workouts to give you a feel for visualization. Then imagine running an upcoming race. You control the imagery; you should actually imagine your muscles in action as you rehearse your race. Neurons will fire just as they do in a race, and muscles contract in minute but detectable amounts.

Kay Porter and Judy Foster, authors of *The Mental Athlete: Inner Training for Peak Performance,* note: "Each time you 'see' yourself performing exactly the same way you want with perfect form, you physically create neural patterns in your brain. These patterns are like small tracks permanently engraved on the brain cell. It is the brain that gives the signal to the muscle to move. It tells each muscle how to move, when to move, and with how much power. . . . Our performance will be tremendously more powerful if we have also trained our minds and created the neural patterns to help our muscles do exactly what we want them to do perfectly."

The technique works because it follows the psychological principle that the closer one comes to simulating an actual situation, the greater one's chances of developing the skill to perform it. By imagining yourself successfully running, you will actually improve your form and racing speed. By training the subconscious mind to perform in the way we want, it will "tell" our conscious mind to perform in that manner. Obviously you can't just dream about a fast time and then do it, but a realistic, challenging goal can be achieved more readily when it has first been "practiced" in your mind.

Visualization is a three-step process: (1) set a goal and create a positive self-image; (2) achieve a state of deep relaxation; (3) imagine yourself succeeding.

Visualization begins with goal setting and a positive self-image. Write your goal on a piece of paper and tape it to your wall, or take a digital clock and set it for your race time—2:59

for a sub-3-hour marathon, for example—then unplug it and place it in a prominent place so you can see it often. Seeing it often, your mind accepts it as a realistic goal. You then begin to imagine yourself crossing the finish line in that time, making the time seem even more possible. Think about it often, including during your training runs and in the race itself. If your goal is directed toward beating others rather than achieving a time, "see" yourself making key strategic moves during the race and outrunning your competitors. To help you improve your self-image, place pictures of top runners running with good form on their way to their victory where you can see them often. Or place photos of yourself running well in past races in prominent locations to remind you of past successes. Set your goals, believe in them, desire them, expect them, and practice reaching them.

The next step is to achieve a state of deep relaxation as described on page 369. Then focus on your goal. Mentally rehearse the entire race, being as specific and positive as possible. Use all of your senses: "see" the crowd, "hear" the noise, "smell" the air, "feel" your body relax. Visualize the warm-up area, the starting line scene, the course, the spectators, the runners, etc. See, feel, hear, and smell the entire experience. Visualize yourself starting your race full of energy, conquering the hills, running with good form, outracing your competitors, reaching mileage markers at your goal times, and finishing ahead of your competitors within your time goal. Repeat the whole mental process several times before your key race. You become a movie director and run the movie of your race through your mind.

Visualization can be practiced at quiet times during the days leading into your race, and before your training runs. Some runners continue "visualizing" in brief flashes into their runs and races by "seeing" themselves running up an approaching hill, or finishing the workout or race strongly. It may take a few sessions to get the hang of the technique of visualization. Be patient, be consistent. Practice it for 5–10 minutes several times a week over the last 2–4 weeks going into a key race. Don't go all out in your visualization process for every race; save the mental power for the most important events.

Avoid too much mental rehearsing the night before the race. It may leave you emotionally drained. Instead, you may wish to do the relaxation exercise to help you get to sleep. On race day, you may benefit from going through your race one more time in your head as a final tune-up. Others find that it leaves them either too hyped up or too relaxed.

When visualizing, you should practice the "perfect" race. But on occasion you should also incorporate some unforeseen problems and see yourself reacting to them calmly. For example: your shoelace comes untied, you lose time because of a crowded start. When visualizing, develop a low-key "feeling" for your goals. Concentrate on the actual race itself, one step at a time.

With positive visualization you can be in charge of mental factors, rather than allowing them to be in charge of you. Whether you follow these visualization techniques conscientiously, or merely occasionally daydream about your race, you can see yourself as a confident, successful runner. But remember that you must have a solid training program to back up your visualization. It is not enough just to dream about running fast without putting in the hard training.

Sample Visualization

Here is a visualization program that Bob Glover uses with his New York Marathon training class. Modify it for your race at any distance. Remember to first achieve a state of deep relaxation.

You wake up the morning of the New York Marathon feeling relaxed and refreshed. Feel yourself yawning and stretching like a cat. Taste the cup of orange juice and muffin with jelly that you choose for breakfast. It hits the spot. See yourself putting on your racing uniform and pinning on your official number. You look in the mirror and see yourself as being trim and fit. Feel yourself putting on your socks and shoes—which feel very comfortable. See yourself double-checking the bag of race goodies—extra clothing, toilet paper, etc.—that you packed last night. Feel yourself walking toward the buses, your legs stretching out.

You have casual conversation with other runners waiting for

the bus. You hear some talking negatively, some positively. Some look very fit and intimidating, others look like they'll never make it. You are prepared for these distractions and calmly take them in. You sit on the crowded bus and smell the various ointments that runners have covered their bodies with. You hear lots of chatter that you can't understand since the bus is full of foreign runners. People ask you what you are aiming for, how you will do. Hear yourself say with both modesty and confidence: "I'm ready to do my best." Hear the bus start up for your journey to the start and feel the nervousness in your stomach. Repeat your slogan: *calm, calm.*

See the bridge you will cross at the start, knowing that you are near the starting area. Hear the voices in the bus become more nervous as you approach the staging area. See yourself calmly getting off the bus and finding a quiet area in which to relax. Every 15 minutes you get up and walk around, then sit and relax. Feel yourself holding the excitement back, saving energy for the race. You see others wasting energy by getting too involved with prerace nervous talk. You analyze the weather prediction and adjust your race accordingly. If it will be hot or windy, you will start a little more slowly. If it looks like great weather, you will be prepared to go for it.

Hear the announcement to go to the starting line. Feel your heart beating faster and your stomach growling. Feel your positive thoughts emerging. You are not afraid to get started, you welcome the opportunity to unravel your successful race. Feel the runners elbowing each other and hear them chattering as you make your way to the start. See yourself lining up and feel yourself breathing deeply, relaxing as the final minutes are counted down to the start. Repeat your slogan: *calm, calm.* Feel the wind whipped by the loud helicopters overhead, and then hear the cannon explode. Feel your hands touching the runners on each side to protect you from falling, feel your feet making short little strides at the start and then longer ones as you gain room to run. See the time on your watch as you hit the starting line and say to yourself that your race begins now, don't try to make it up all at once.

Feel the powerful vacuum sucking you up the hill and over the bridge. You feel like a powerful horse being reigned in.

Repeat your slogan: *calm, calm*. See yourself flowing down the other side of the bridge with proper form. See yourself winding around and then straightening out as you flow in next to the other starting group on Fourth Avenue. You hear the crowds now for the first time, and they are loud and enthusiastic. Feel yourself holding back your energy, not allowing the crowd, the slight downhills, or the overeager runners around you to let yourself go out too fast. See your split at each early mile mark and adjust your pace accordingly—slightly picking it up or slowing down. Hear yourself say that you must subtract the time it took you to reach the starting line from your time to determine how fast you really are moving. Think of how smart you are not to try to make up the time.

See yourself passing runners who started too fast and being passed by others who are full of energy. Feel how your legs are moving smoothly, your breathing is relaxed, you feel in control. Feel the wind. Is it against you, behind you? If it is against you, see yourself tucking in behind others who become shields. See yourself taking water from an aid station; taste the water in your mouth, and feel the second cup you grab as you pour it over your head and down your chest. Repeat this throughout your visualization.

Concentrate on reaching your next goal—the 5-mile split. You see it up ahead and you reach it feeling real good near your expected goal split. Feel yourself smiling. Hear other runners talking, but you remain quiet, saving energy. You feel patches of weakness and then hear the crowd and use their energy to feel stronger. See yourself reaching the point where the men and women merge near 7 miles. You welcome the added "scenery." Your next goal is the big clock tower looming ahead at 8 miles. Feel the energy from it pulling you like a magnet. You now aim for the 10-mile mark. Feel your form getting a little ragged and feel yourself picking up the knees, using the arms, breathing comfortably and regaining control of your form. Repeat your slogan: *calm, calm*. See the 10-mile split near your goal time. You feel confidence surging. See a friend jumping out of the crowd and yelling at you.

Your next goal is a big one—the half-mile mark at the Pulaski Bridge. See yourself approaching it up a short, but what feels like a steep, hill at this point in the race. Record your split in your mind, multiply it by 2. You will run a great race by keeping the same pace now for the second half of the race. Even if you slow a little, you will do well. Hear yourself giving yourself a pep talk. You can do it. You feel happy to have the first half under your belt. You feel full of confidence. Repeat your slogan: *calm, calm.*

The next goal is to get up and over the 59th Street Bridge. You reflect on your hill-training sessions and see yourself changing your form to get up the hill. You see your split at 15 miles near the start of the bridge—again near your goal time. You feel your quads working, your arms pumping, your knees coming up to get over the hill. You see yourself running stronger than those around you who let the hill attack them. You attack the hill with cool confidence. You feel the wind whipping at the top of the bridge, and feel your feet caressing the carpet. You see the majestic New York City skyline and let the power from it pull you like a magnet to the top of the bridge. Repeat your slogan: *calm, calm.*

You feel yourself flowing down the hill now, like a free-falling roller coaster. See yourself holding back slightly, running with good form. Feel the strain on your legs. Hear the loud noise up ahead, and anticipate the surge you will feel as you hit First Avenue. Hear and feel the crowd as you zoom around the corner onto Fifth Avenue. Feel the slight uphill, but feel your form powering you along. Feel the fatigue in your legs, but the confidence in your head allows you to relax and keep moving. See all the struggling runners who are now walking, and you increase in confidence as you power by them—knowing that you paced yourself more wisely, trained yourself better, and have a stronger mind. See friends stationed at this point jump out and encourage you, giving you a rush of new energy. Repeat your slogan: *calm, calm.*

Your next goal is to reach 18 miles—the halfway point between the bridge and the Wall at 20 miles. See yourself hitting it and talking to yourself—saying, "Okay, Wall, you aren't going to get me." See yourself at the end of your long training runs and eating all those carbohydrates. See yourself laughing at the Wall. Yes, it slows you slightly. But as you hit the 20-mile mark you picture yourself smashing through a brick wall and raising your fist in victory. You feel tired, but full of purpose and confidence. A 10K to go. Only a 10K race now. Envision what your finishing time will be by adding a 10K at your goal pace. Sounds good! See yourself patting yourself on the back and saying, "Let's go for it." Repeat your slogan: *calm, calm.*

See yourself shortly after 20 miles, making the turn and heading south toward Central Park. You are on your way home now! Just calm down, concentrate on working the arms and picking up the knees, breathing in a relaxed manner, keeping the neck and shoulders loose. Now you run from mile marker to mile marker, even block to block as you see the street numbers get smaller as you aim for 110th Street—the start of Central Park. Hear the crowds cheering you on, saying, "You're looking good!" Believe them, keep moving. Keep pushing. Don't let up or you will lose time. Hear yourself talking to yourself. Extolling your body to keep moving. You feel bad off and on but keep moving down the long blue line. See that line. Trust that it will pull you to the finish line. Repeat your slogan: *calm, calm.*

See the trees up ahead—it is Central Park. You hit 110th Street and get a surge of mental toughness. You know you can do it now! Keep the legs moving. Feel the uphill stretch on Fifth Avenue to 102nd Street, and then the short steep hill as you enter the park. Think about how you practiced this hill and just become a robot, running it by memory with good hill-running form. See the 23-mile banner across the road near the top of the hill. Only 3.2 miles to go. Think about how you ran this comfortably 2 days ago and remember how it felt to run up and down the rolling hills. Remember the joke Glover made: "You only have to run 23 miles on race day, since we're practicing the last 3.2 miles now; you can just become a robot the rest of the way on race day." A friend jumps out of the crowd and yells in your ear. You hear him: "You can do it, go for it." You feel heavy in the legs, but strong in the mind and heart. Think of how tough you are, think about all those long runs you made, all the mileage, all the sacrifice. This is your moment now. This is not the time to give in to fatigue. You concentrate on good form, on feeling relaxed, on being in control. Your body is tired, but it is moving! "I'm going to do it!" Repeat it over and over. Repeat your slogan: *calm, calm.*

The crowd is very excited. They know you will do it. See the 90th Street and Fifth Avenue entrance to the park. A large crowd there gives you a fresh blast of energy. See yourself reaching the 24-mile mark ½ mile later. Your next goal is a long, steep downhill at 80th Street. See yourself flowing down the hill. Then look up. You see the New York skyline. Feel the power from the skyscrapers pulling you like a magnet toward them. Repeat your slogan: *calm, calm.* See yourself turning left to leave Central Park as you go under the 25-mile marker. How fast can you run 1.2 miles? Even if you jog it you will have a good time. See what your time will look like at the finish if you finish at goal pace. You are flowing downhill, full of determination. A friend screams at you, you see yourself looking proud in front of him.

Hear the crowd roar as you leave the park and turn onto Central Park South at 59th Street. They become part of you. Their screaming, your willpower, are becoming one powerful machine now. You are too tired to feel graceful. But you do feel powerful. See the quarter-mile-long slight uphill grade ahead, and see the struggling runners you are passing. Feel a few runners who pass you with a finishing rush and see yourself holding on to some of them and going for a ride. See yourself cresting the gradual incline and feel yourself going down now. You are so close! You can hear the announcer at the finish line. Feel the tears welling in your eyes. Feel the anticipation in your heart.

See yourself turning at Columbus Circle, feel your feet crossing the wooden planks over a short grassy stretch and then returning to pavement. This is it. You are on the last stretch on Central Park Drive. See the crowd up ahead, the balloons, hear the deafening roar of the crowd. You hear them all yelling for you, as you are winning your race. See yourself moving to the right (men's finish) or to the left (women's finish). See yourself running under the 26-mile banner. Feel yourself going up the final hill to the finish line. Feel the excitement, feel the pain and the joy of the others around you. You help each other now, push each other toward the moving numbers on the digital

clock. See the numbers coming into focus now. See the time—
your goal time—and see yourself finishing with great form.
See yourself throwing your hands up, your chest out as you
cross the finish line. See yourself hugging the runner next to
you. You are trembling in fatigue and joy. You did it! See
yourself smiling at last. See your family and friends congrat-
ulating you. Hear yourself saying to others: "I set a challenging
goal, I trained hard, I worked hard during the race, I felt real
strong except for a few times, I was determined to do it, I did
it! I am so happy and so proud of myself!"

YOU'VE GOTTA BELIEVE

Remember the "amazin' Mets"? They won the World Series of
baseball after they had been laughed at for being a bunch of
losers ever since starting as an expansion team in New York.
Their battle cry during their improbable year was: "You've
gotta believe." Positive thinking is essential to success. No one
believed that the 4-minute barrier for the mile could be broken.
Medical experts said it was impossible. But Roger Bannister
didn't believe it was impossible, and broke the barrier. In the
next 1½ years fifty others followed. It was now easier since the
mental barrier had been broken.

Set imposing, perhaps impossible, ultimate goals for down
the road. Your in-between goals will then no longer be intimidating. If your eventual goal is to break 40 minutes for 10K,
your present goal of breaking 45 minutes is less threatening.

Think positive. Don't say before a race in an effort to diffuse
anxiety: "I'm just running through the race," or "I didn't taper,
I'm just doing the race easy." If you speak and think negatively,
you will most likely act that way. Lynch warns runners about
this psychological problem, which he refers to as the "self-
fulfilling prophecy." On the other hand, if you say and think
you can do something, chances are you will.

Bob Glover remembers his best race—an even 5:30 pace for
30K. He trained very hard for it with a cocky, confident, sometimes bizarre runner—Jim Ferris. They exchanged insults and
challenges daily to push each other through very difficult workouts. Ferris told Glover that he (Ferris) was "going beyond,

entering a new dimension." He invited Glover to follow. The pair of Vietnam vets reminded each other that this war would be "a piece of cake." Glover followed him out at the start, inspired by his aggressive, confident charge. He hit a PR at 5 miles and was frightened. Then he saw Ferris up ahead, "hammering." He thought "going beyond" and kept going. He hit PRs every step of the way from 5 miles to a 1:43 finish. Late in the race, Glover saw runners within striking distance whom he had never been close to before. Up ahead, he saw Ferris pass them and responded to the challenge and passed them too. Glover's finishing time was the equivalent of a 2:28 marathon. Only 5 years before, his ultimate goal had been to break 3½ hours in order to qualify for the Boston Marathon. His mind had indeed entered a "new dimension" and dragged his body along for the ride. You too can "go beyond" your perceived limits.

28. PRERACE PLANNING AND RACE DAY STRATEGY___

During the prerace hours you need to take care of certain prerace details as described in this chapter. See chapters 36–37 for prerace guidelines for eating and drinking and chapter 34 for prerace warm-up routines. You also need to plan—and execute—race day strategies. Your mental race begins a few weeks in advance and continues to the postrace analysis.

DEALING WITH PRERACE ANXIETY

Your prerace planning should include learning how to deal with prerace anxiety. According to sports psychologist Dr. Robert N. Singer in *The Physician and Sportsmedicine* magazine: "Any meaningful event is bound to produce heightened arousal (perhaps too much), anxiety, and tension within athletes. Emotions that get out of control are a problem for many athletes, regardless of their sport.

"Obviously, thought processes and elevated emotions need to be quieted. Many coaches make the mistake of trying to stimulate athletes just before competition. Although some may need to be stimulated, many others may need to be more relaxed to attain an optimal arousal state. An optimal arousal state exists for each person for each event. Athletes must train themselves to be in this state, just as they train to develop the mechanical skills necessary to succeed in an event."

You need to learn to reach the emotional state that will give you the best results. Getting "psyched up" for a shorter race may help you get off to a good, confident start, but such a tactic could backfire in the marathon, where you need to start off more slowly and reserve your emotional energy for late in the race when your physical resources run low.

The competitive runner on race day must be prepared to manage thoughts of the physical and mental stress he or she will face during the actual race. Self-imposed stress is necessary in practice to help the athlete cope with this pressure. According to Singer, "Athletes must take practice seriously and believe that a practice run . . . is the real thing. They should develop the necessary attitudes and emotions to be psychologically prepared to compete. It is difficult to be a good contest competitor without being a good practice competitor." Relaxation exercises and visualization of your race on race morning will also help you conquer prerace nerves.

Athletes who run superior workouts and race well in low-key races but then perform poorly in big races must analyze the reason for "choking." They may be victims of the fear of failing—letting down their coach, family, or friends—or the fear of success. The runners should discuss their fears with others, if possible with a well-trained sports psychologist. For these athletes, Dr. Singer recommends that they develop a positive attitude on race day and over the days leading into the race by mentally visualizing and reliving their successes in practice and in other races.

As mentioned in the last chapter, be aware of the value of positive thinking and the "self-fulfilling prophecy" theory. Besides thinking positively yourself, try to surround yourself with positive-thinking people. Avoid running friends who are emotional wrecks before the race, full of negative statements. This is especially true the night before and the morning of a big race. Hearing others talk negatively and nervously will take energy away from you. Seek calm, strong-minded runners to socialize with in the final hours before a big race. Or seek out nonrunning friends who are very confident people and are very supportive of your race efforts.

THE PRERACE CHECKLIST

To free yourself to focus on your positive mental attitude and imagery, be sure to eliminate prerace details from your concern. Make a checklist of what must be done before the race, and do it. Here are a dozen tips:

• Enter the race early. Don't train for it and then find that you missed the entry deadline.

• Plan your prerace tapering and eating routine day by day. Also plan your race day fluid intake. Remember to drink fluids 10 to 15 minutes before the start.

• Pack your running shoes first. Then work your way from your feet up your body to your head. Pack one item at a time the night before leaving for the race. Include extras of everything, especially shoes, and pack for the weather. Remember toilet paper, Vaseline, Band-Aids, extra pins, soap, towel, lock, and a dry set of postrace clothes. Never check your bag of racing gear with an airline or other service.

• Arrive at the race 2 hours before the start. Plan all travel arrangements with this in mind. If possible, arrive 1 or 2 days before the race. Stick with your regular time schedule if the race is in another time zone, unless you can arrive much earlier than a day or two before the race. A good rule of thumb is to allow one day of acclimatization for every hour time change; therefore, if you live in New York and run the London Marathon, you should arrive in London 5 to 6 days before the race to adjust to the change. If you are traveling from New York to California, for example, and will arrive only 2 days before a race, plan to eat, sleep, and run according to your New York time zone. Use the most comfortable means of travel you can arrange and afford. Driving for several hours should be avoided if possible. If not, break it up with walking, stretching, and running breaks. Don't travel more than 1 to 2 hours in the morning on a race day—it's too hectic. It is better to arrive the night before and stay over, starting the day relaxed.

• If possible, check in and pick up your number a few days

before the race. If not, get your number at least an hour before race time. Pin it on your running shirt right away so you don't lose it. Also, double-check the time and location of the start.

• A good night's sleep is most important *two* nights before the race. Follow your normal routine, and go to bed early. Also, follow your normal training diet.

• On race day, get up 3 hours before the start. Have someone awaken you as a backup to your alarm. Remember—if you insist on eating, do it at least 3 hours before the race, and eat light.

• Get the weather report, and adjust your clothing to it.

• At the starting point, turn in your sweats early. If it's cool, wear an old throwaway outfit or a clean plastic bag to keep warm.

• Make a final bowel movement and empty your bladder well before the start of the race. Don't be modest. Your comfort is at stake, and the bushes may be your only choice.

• Take all safety precautions and apply all skin protection— Vaseline, suntan lotion, etc.—well before the start.

Race Day Rituals

One way many runners deal with prerace tension is to follow race day rituals. These rituals really are meaningless, but help boost confidence by making you feel more prepared. A basketball player may shoot exactly five foul shots before each game, or not take off his warm-up jacket until the moment the horn blows signaling the teams to line up. Runners may benefit from making a list of prerace details—as listed above—and checking them off the morning of a race. Your race day ritual may be to have exactly one glass of juice and one piece of toast exactly 3 hours before the race, to wait until exactly 15 minutes before the start of the race to put on your racing shoes, to start your warm-up jog 30 minutes before the race and run exactly 1 mile up the course and 1 mile back. Some runners always wear the same racing singlet because they are most comfortable wearing "an old friend." Some read a novel the night before every race. Don't feel stupid if you have silly rituals. Many elite athletes in all sports possess idosyncratic behavior patterns that they use to help them cope with the emotional pressures of athletic competition. Be consistent with your race day rituals and you will be rewarded with the support of familiar stimuli.

Know the Course

If you want to perform well in a race, make sure that you know the course. You'll have periodic mental letdowns during the race, and by knowing what challenges are coming up you can set short-term goals: "Make it to the top of that next hill and then I get to go downhill for a while." By knowing what the course actually looks and feels like, your visualized "rehearsals" will be more effective.

If you live near the course on which you'll be racing, practice key sections in advance of race day. They'll become familiar and less threatening. Here are some sample tricks Bob Glover uses to prepare runners for the popular L'Eggs Mini Marathon held in New York City's Central Park:

• Since the race is run clockwise and most runners in Central Park tend to run counterclockwise for their training runs, do a few runs in the same direction as the race. It's surprising how different that makes the hills and turns look. Glover's Atalanta team runs the entire race course as a group, doing *fartlek* surges at key points.

• Since the Central Park course has two tough hills at the midway point, runners should cover them often in training at race pace, or slightly faster, while picturing themselves as being in the race.

• If you can't practice on the course, find some similar hills. Run up and jog down once a week several times going into the race. When you hit the previously dreaded section on race day, you'll look forward to it, because you'll have an advantage over most of the runners around you. Attack the hills (gently please!) before they attack you. A course conquered in practice is one you'll beat again on race day.

• Practice the finish. At L'Eggs, it's a 440-yard gradual uphill stretch. Run anywhere from 440 to 880 yards into the finish line at race pace or slightly faster and repeat 4–6 times. This will give you a "feel" for the finish, and on race day you'll automatically shift into your well-practiced finishing gear. Feel proud each time as you cross the finish line, just as you will on race day. On race day jog into the finish one more time, just to reinforce the feeling of finishing.

• If you're visiting an out-of-town course, practice the last mile the day before the race or even on race day. It's important to get a feel for the finish. If you're a woman, find out in advance if women will finish in a certain area (usually women to the left, men to the right). This way you can start moving toward that side of the road as you approach the finish and save precious seconds. Know what the last mile will feel like, know exactly where the finish line will be. You'll be more confident early in the race if you know what to expect at the end.

• If you can't run the entire course, you might wish to review it by bike or car. Memorize landmarks, and visualize yourself running strong and passing them. Some less confident runners will get "psyched out" by touring a marathon course, since it seems so long. But the confident runner has the advantage of knowing where the hills, turns, etc., will hit him or her on race day and will not be surprised by them.

Segment the Course in Your Head

Break the race distance up in your head and set short-term goals to reach. For example:

—Reach the 1-mile mark within 10 seconds of goal pace, perhaps right behind a friend who is aiming for a similar time.
—Hit the top of the hill at $2\frac{1}{2}$ miles with good form.
—Flow down the hill at 3 miles.
—Look good at 4 miles because your spouse and kids will be waiting for you.
—Survive to 5 miles by hanging on to the runners around you.
—Concentrate on relaxation and good form from the turn at 5 miles to 6 miles.
—Kick in to the 10K finish just like you've practiced.

You can segment the course by landmarks or by mile markers, or both. By breaking up the course into bite-sized pieces, you can keep yourself pushing to a goal that is possible to reach. When you begin thinking only of a finish line miles away, it's too easy to get mentally fatigued.

RACE STRATEGY

Lining Up and Starting Out

Where you stand at the start of the race is a good measure of your level of confidence and common sense. Don't just line up next to your friend—he or she may be too fast or too slow for you. Don't line up in the front of the pack with the 5-minute milers if you're a 9-minute-per-mile runner. Not only will you get in the way of others, but you will most likely start too fast and ruin your race. On the other hand, don't line up in the back of the pack unless you are a beginner only interested in finishing. Line up with confidence with or slightly ahead of other runners of your ability level. Look for runners you know and position yourself accordingly. If you see a runner who is slightly better than you and who runs a good steady pace, line up behind him or her and use that runner as a guide in the early going. Later try to keep him or her in sight if you can't keep up, but don't be afraid to pass if you feel strong.

Top women and masters runners who want to be competitive with their peers usually line up close to the front even if they aren't as fast as the men around them. But they need to get a good start for their "race within a race." So don't lose contact if you wish to be competitive with others. They'll usually settle into an appropriate pace soon after the start. Many races post signs according to your expected pace per mile. Since most people cheat at this, line up slightly ahead of the pace signs appropriate for you and look for runners who are your pace.

Be prepared when the starting time gets close. Don't rush off to the toilet or to change a shirt and miss the start. Also, sometimes races suddenly start with little or no warning, so while standing at the start remain alert so you don't get tripped up by an unexpected start. Flow with the crowd until you can establish your own pace. Keep your hands up to maintain balance, keep your feet low to avoid tripping. Ease into a faster pace until you can get more running room.

Don't start off in a sprint in an effort to get a good start unless you are an up-front runner trying to establish a position over the first 100–200 yards before settling into a fast race pace. The average runner will pay for it later if he or she starts fast. But be alert and get out as quickly as possible or you'll suddenly find yourself trapped behind slower runners. Beware of the vacuum effect. A wave of runners up front starts off fast and pulls everyone out very fast. Next thing you know, you and everyone around you are running too fast. If you are stuck in a slow start, don't panic and swerve in and out of people, passing others like a madman. Not only will you risk injury to yourself and others, you will waste a lot of physical and mental energy.

In mass races like the L'Eggs Mini Marathon, Bay to Breakers in San Francisco, or Atlanta's Peachtree Race with thousands of entrants, you have no choice but to start slowly—most likely writing it off as a fun run. If you wish—especially in a large marathon with a crowded start like Boston or New York—start your watch when you get to the starting line and time your personal effort. In these events, don't attempt to run fast the first mile or two in an effort to make up for lost time. It is better just to adjust to the situation and run the same effort you would have run starting from the point where you could establish your desired pace.

Race Pacing

There are three ways you can run a race: against yourself (for a PR), against the course (for time), and against your competitors (for place). Your race strategy and pace will reflect that choice, as will the course, weather, and the fitness level of you and your competitors.

Here are six basic variations for pacing when running against yourself or time:

• Start slowly, gradually pick it up, finish fast. This is best for novices and those runners returning to racing after a layoff.

It challenges you only minimally, however. This may also be the only pacing strategy available in a crowded mass start.

• Start slowly, pick it up to a strong pace, and hold that pace to the end. You open at slower than goal pace, then after a few miles increase your pace to 10 to 15 seconds per mile faster than goal pace, and continue to the finish—although you may slow the pace somewhat as you tire. Many runners run better when they can get warmed up first with an easier pace, plus they feel less tense in the early going. You pick up confidence as you start to pass runners when you pick up the pace after a few miles.

• Start fast and hold on. This method often brings failure, especially to the inexperienced racer. Those who start this way often find themselves running the second half of the race, and particularly the last few miles, at a much slower pace. If you start too fast, you could very well blow the race and finish in a much slower time, and much more uncomfortably, than if you had paced yourself more wisely. Sometimes by "building a cushion," you can dare yourself to hang tough and finish with a good time. Usually, however, the result is that your pace slips away as does your confidence, particularly if many runners pass you. Then you begin to fall apart mentally as well as physically, resulting in an even worse time, often in dropping out.

• Start fast, relax in the middle but keep pushing, and pick it up at the end. This is a good method for many top runners.

• Pace yourself evenly for time or effort. This is the most efficient system. In fact, Bob Glover ran his best marathon time by running each mile within 5 seconds of the others, including the 1st and the 26th. If you are aiming for an even 9-minute pace, for example, the first few miles will seem easy and thus can serve to warm you up. You will have to really concentrate and push from the middle of the race on in, however, because with this system you do not build up a cushion of time ahead of your finishing time goal. Lack of concentration here can quickly put you behind your goal pace.

Recommended Pacing Schedule

First, establish your challenging goal time by utilizing the race-time prediction system (chapter 26). Then, figure out what pace per mile you would need to run with even pacing to hit that time (for example, 7:14 minute-per-mile pace for a sub-45-minute 10K). Start 5–15 seconds per mile faster than that pace— no faster. Then attempt to run an even pace at that effort for the entire race. This may mean that you will slow slightly toward the end. But by starting out slightly faster than your goal pace, you leave a little room for error in case you are slowed later by a big hill, head wind, or misplaced mile marker. Another advantage of starting slightly faster: you pick up confidence mile after mile as you add a few more seconds to your cushion, and you may be able to keep it up and really "pop" a good time. Here are some valuable pacing tips:

• Learn the patience of holding yourself back in the early going so that you will be stronger at the end in your race-paced speed workouts and practice races. Temper the excitement of the start with common sense; your mind should say "whoa" because your body will say "go!"

• Run from mile marker to mile marker and play a little game—see how close you can come to keeping an even pace.

• Adjust your pace according to the time "splits" along the course and according to your body signs. Keep in mind that uphills and head winds may contribute to slower splits, and downhills and tail winds to faster ones.

• Memorize or write down and carry your split-goal times, so you can easily adjust. Write them on paper and wrap the paper in plastic for protection, or write them on your hand or arm.

• Don't panic if you find yourself ahead or behind schedule. Gradually adjust your pace. If you are well off pace and feeling real bad, you might just need to relax and enjoy the rest of the race as a fun run, or drop out to minimize risk of injury or fatigue. Persevere if possible, but don't try to be a hero if you're fighting injury, extreme fatigue, overheating, or mental burnout.

• If you are past the halfway point and feeling good, don't be afraid to pick up the pace slightly and go for a really good time. Take advantage of days when everything feels great, we don't have a lot of them.

• When you begin to tire, the effort necessary just to hold

pace will increase. Then you begin to think of the last few interval workouts where you strived to maintain pace by increasing effort slightly and concentrating on relaxing and holding good form.

• Split times and mile markers are occasionally inaccurate. Wear your own watch to check splits. Don't panic. Racing experience and pace work on a track will help protect you against inaccurate mile markers.

Usually you will start slightly ahead of goal pace, begin to run at goal pace or slightly slower as effort increases later in the race (but still ahead of goal time), and hold on to the end where you can put together a final drive to the finish. Even pacing means being close to the ideal, steady effort all the way rather than actually running the same pace per mile every step of the way. You should be flexible, but consistent with your pace.

Eventually you will automatically flow into the proper pace for you, but you must concentrate on keeping it going or you will unconsciously slow down and lose valuable time. With experience you will learn to "red line," to run at the edge of your physical and mental limits. With experience at racing and with race-pace workouts, you will learn to feel what pace is right for you by monitoring your breathing. You will know that you can pick it up or should slow it down, despite what the watch says. Don't let the watch cause you undue pressure and make you run too fast or too slowly. Don't become dependent on a watch. It is used as an aid, not a crutch. Many elite runners purposely don't wear watches in races—they feel that they run better when they "listen to their body" and pace themselves according to their internal pacer.

A Note on Unfair Pacing Assistance: Novice racers and novice marathoners will benefit greatly if a faster, experienced runner runs with them to help pace them and provide psychological comfort. Runners in the pack may choose to use such a "pacer" to help them along to a PR. However, once a runner gets to a point where he or she is competing for awards in races—overall or age-group categories—then such a practice is unfair to those who are competing without this advantage. Racing is a sport where one should have to deal with the psychological factors on one's own, without the assistance of a coach, boyfriend, or husband. Pacing of women by men, in particular, is both un-sportsmanlike and against the rules of the sport. Practice good sportsmanship, whether you are racing in the local 2-miler where the only awards are cheap medals, or the New York Marathon where first prize is several thousand dollars.

Fighting the Elements: Heat, Hills, Wind, and Turns

Your race pace, and your finishing times, need to be adjusted to account for heat, hills, wind, and turns.

Heat

See page 466 for guidelines for racing in the heat. If you properly adjust your starting pace and goal time, think "cool" while keeping relaxed, and pour plenty of fluids into and on yourself, you will outsmart and thus defeat competitors who stubbornly kept to their ideal weather race strategy. You can run relatively well in the heat if you run smart and think positively.

Be prepared, however, to run slower times. Here's how much heat is likely to slow you over a 10K (it could be worse in humidity or over a marathon):

TEMPERATURE	RACE PACE SLOWED BY THIS AMOUNT
50 degrees	Ideal, go for it
60 degrees	5 + seconds per mile
65 degrees	10 + seconds per mile
70 degrees	15 + seconds per mile
75 degrees	20 + seconds per mile
80 degrees	25 + seconds per mile
85 plus degrees	Run for fun in the sun

Note: These estimates are most accurate for runners in the 6–8-minute-per-mile range; runners slower than that are often affected even more by the heat.

When finishing, compare your times with those of your peers. You can usually figure out what you would have to run *if* the weather were cooler by seeing how you rank among those who run a little faster and more slowly than you. If it is hot, start the race more slowly by the paces noted above for the warm temperature noted. Remember too—this is only an estimate of the effect of the heat on you.

Hills

The best way to "attack" hills is just that. Don't let hills beat you psychologically. Attack them gently with confidence gained from training on hills and knowing where the hills will come on the course. The best way to handle a hilly course is to try to maintain an even *effort,* not necessarily pace per mile, going up and down hills. Don't be intimidated by a big hill. Shift into your uphill racing gear (see chapter 31), concentrate on keeping in contact with your competitors, and stay relaxed. Don't try to blast away from a competitor; you'll most likely pay for that move later. If competitors quicken the pace dramatically on you, let them go but try to maintain a reasonable distance behind them. Unless they are super fit, they'll come back to you.

If you race over a hilly course at an equal effort on the flats, uphills, and downhills, you will end up with a slower time than if you raced at that same equal effort over a flat course. According to exercise physiologists at the Nike research laboratory, your cost of energy increases 12 percent when you go up a one-degree slope, but you only gain back 7 percent if you come back down that same slope: on a hilly out-and-back course you would lose 5 percent in terms of cost of energy for every hill you encountered. Unfortunately, you can't totally make up the loss of energy and time on uphills when you come back down the other side. But you can minimize the loss with proper pacing and good hill-running form.

Run uphill at an effort similar to the one you use on the flat. This may cause you to lose a little time, but you will reach the top of the hill relatively fresh and can make up some of the time on the flats and on later downhills. Trying to keep the same speed, or increase the speed, going uphill will drive your heart rate above your training range and quickly put you in oxygen debt, resulting in early fatigue that will be hard to shake off.

If you are a good hill runner, you will increase your lead over the distance. Try to stay close to the others so they will "pull" you over the hills. When running uphills, pick landmarks along the way as short-term goals to make it easier. Make your moves at the crests, where many runners let up momentarily, or on the downhills, where many runners coast.

Also maintain even effort on downhills. Don't jog up a hill and then sprint down. Bob Glover tries to stay close to his competitors who are pulling away on uphills, and then he relaxes and gradually catches and pulls away from them on downhills, since he runs very efficiently downhill and can run quite fast with very little effort. See chapter 31 for downhill racing form guidelines. Beware of downhills early in the race, like the one in the Boston marathon, which lure you into starting too fast.

If you are a novice racer, or perhaps not well trained on hills, be prepared to walk on tough hills. If you begin having trouble breathing or if your legs start wobbling, don't hesitate to take a brisk walking break. Hills aren't the place for heroics, particularly if you're overheating on a hot day. By alternately running and walking as necessary, you can regain control of your body temperature, breathing, and leg muscles. Besides, you'd be surprised how fast some people can walk hills. Glover found that out when he ran the Mt. Washington Road Race in New Hampshire. It is an 8-mile race with only one hill. Trouble is, the one hill is 8 miles up to the top of the highest peak in the Northeast. Glover blasted out with the leaders, and by the time he reached the timber line he was in big trouble. Not only was he overheating, his legs were aching, stomach was heaving, and lungs and head were screaming—and his right foot fell asleep. On top of that, a bunch of old-timers started passing him. Even worse, before long, old-timers who had been walking while he was still running passed him. He watched them: they would run, then walk briskly, run, then walk briskly. More efficient when you get tired on tough hills, they said. He tried it, and the technique helped him get to the top of the hill, right after all the 60-year-old billy goats.

Wind

When running into the wind, try to tuck in behind others to reduce the wind resistance. Look for a big runner and keep as close as you can to properly "draft." According to Chester Kyle, a professor of mechanics at California State University at Long Beach, you can cut your wind resistance by 31 percent if you stay 10 feet behind another runner; by 51 percent if you're within 5 feet. It isn't sportsmanlike to steal the advantage from others for a lengthy period. If you're with a pack of runners of equal ability on a windy day, take turns shielding each other from the wind. Try to hang with the group as long as you can. The effort will be far easier than if you have to battle head winds alone. When you have a tail wind, try to take full advantage of it by moving away or to the side of a pack of runners who are behind you.

If you have a tail wind for much of the race, you will not have to work as hard to run your desired pace. You may find you are hitting your goal splits ahead of schedule without added effort. Take advantage of this situation and go for a good time. For example: a 10-mile-an-hour tail wind would allow a runner on 6-minute pace for a marathon (2:37) to run nearly 8 minutes (5 percent) faster. On the other hand, a 10-mile-an-hour head wind will cause the 2:37 marathoner to run over 12 minutes slower (8 percent). That is a range of from 2:29 to 2:49 for an even-effort 6-minute paced marathon! Obviously you must take the effect of the wind into consideration when comparing race times. Don't be too disappointed if you run several minutes slower if you battled head winds. On the other hand, don't think that because you ran a super fast time with a strong tail wind (or a downhill course) you've entered a new dimension as a runner.

If you are running an out-and-back course, don't think that the tail wind section will even out the head wind section. It won't. A head wind will slow you down more than a tail wind will assist you. According to exercise physiologist Dr. Jack Daniels, to hold a given pace in a 13½-mile-per-hour head wind, you'd have to work more than 15 percent harder than if there were no wind, but you'd save only 8 percent of your energy with that same wind behind you. Nonetheless, your best strategy on windy days is the same as when confronting uphills and downhills: maintain equal *effort.*

One advantage of a head wind: it helps to keep you cool on a hot day. But a tail wind will interfere with your cooling process and can cause you to overheat even on a cool day. When running into a head wind, try to keep as relaxed as possible. Fighting the wind will cause tension, poor form, and further loss of efficiency and thus time.

Turns

The fastest course available would be downhill, with a tail wind and in a straight line. Rounding turns forces you to slow down and interrupts even pacing. Be sure to run "shortcuts" at each turn by running it in a tangent. The shortest route you can possibly take when rounding a turn will save you precious seconds. It will give you an advantage over your competitors if they are running the full turn and thus going a farther distance. If you are leading competitors, throw in a burst right after you go around a turn. When they come around and see you again you'll have gained distance on them and given yourself a psychological advantage.

Concentration

"The ability to concentrate," says sports psychologist William Morgan, "is the single element that separates the merely good athletes from the great ones. Concentration is the hallmark of the elite runner."

During the race, concentrate on pace, your opponents, and flowing rhythmically with good style and form. Some mind-wandering is inevitable, but the key is to recover quickly and get back into your concentrated effort, or you will lose precious seconds. Look straight ahead. You are not sight-seeing if you are going for a good time. You don't have the energy to waste waving and smiling at your fans. Thank them for their support after the race. Think of yourself as strong but relaxed.

Some runners "disassociate"—they enter a trance state by repeating a mantra over and over, relive part of their lives, or stare at another runner's back or ear—in order to avoid the pains of racing. Although a few top runners have success with this method, most attempt to "associate" with the pain and discomfort of the race, which tell them how hard they can push themselves. Morgan conducted a study that showed that top marathon runners constantly monitor body signals of respiration, temperature, heaviness of the legs, etc. They keep thinking, "Stay loose," "Keep the pace up," "Form together." The average runner may find that by disassociating while running up a troublesome hill, for example, he can conquer it, but he should return to monitoring his body's signals. The runner who associates can better preserve fuel and avoid injury. Interestingly, Morgan found that top runners don't "hit the Wall." They feel only minor discomfort, since they read their bodies, adjust pace, and avoid trouble.

Concentration must begin before the race. You zero your thinking in on the race at hand for the last few days. You must focus on it. Distractions like attending too many running clinics and parties will interfere with your mental preparation. So too will stressful business and family responsibilities. Try to arrange for a "time-out" from other responsibilities for the last few days and hours going into a really important race.

You can learn to concentrate in your workouts. Running a few long runs alone improves concentration late in a race. So too do long repeats such as 1-mile intervals. *Fartlek* runs also teach you to pay attention to your running. Workouts on a treadmill or an indoor bike, without the distraction of music or TV, will also give you practice at concentrating. Running mindlessly with headphones will do the opposite: teach you to lose concentration. This is why runners with headphones have been known to run into the sides of moving cars and stationary street signs.

All runners have momentary lapses in concentration while racing. You might think about quitting because it is too hot or hilly, or worry that you're not fit enough, that you're not prepared properly, etc. Make sure these are passing thoughts that you don't dwell on. You must pay attention to your form, your pace, your competitors, or you will daydream away the success of your race and waste all your solid physical and mental preparation.

Running Through Pain and Fatigue

If you just run races for the fun of it, you experience very little discomfort. But to get the most out of your body, you will need to experience agony in order to earn the ecstasy of a great performance. Speed workouts and practice races will help you physiologically and mentally adjust to the discomfort of oxygen debt. Long training runs condition the mind to handle mental fatigue. Carbohydrate loading and long runs prepare the body to better handle the fatigue that sets in when you run low on glycogen supplies. You must learn the difference between discomfort and pain. The warning sign of injury is pain. Trying to "gut it out" when in pain is foolish. You are likely to injure yourself seriously and be forced off the running paths for a long time.

But how much discomfort can you take? Some runners are "mentally tough," and others are softies. You must work to improve your psychological strength during races. If you give in when the going gets tough, you'll never be a complete athlete. Glover tells his elite Atalanta athletes that if you run a truly great race, you'll feel like you're on the verge of death every step of the way. You'll walk the tightrope of agony and maintain—somehow—physical and psychological balance. The great runners can handle a lot of discomfort. The average recreational competitor who wants modest race results can handle a reasonable amount of agony. Those unwilling to pay the price at all will always be underachievers. Overachieving runners thrive on discomfort during a race. They "go beyond pain."

Fatigue limits your performance. It is a physical reality, but much of it is psychological and thus can be dealt with. When you lose confidence during a race, you start to let go and fatigue rushes in for the kill. Here are a few tips to help you fight off fatigue and maintain your race pace:

• Acknowledge fatigue and pain if they try to attack you, says New York City physical therapist Robert Kropf, who uses mental techniques to help many top runners recover from injury and race more efficiently. Instead of thinking "Oh no, my hamstring is tightening up," think, "Hello, hamstring, are you reminding me to loosen up and relax again?" This technique reduces anxiety, although it sure sounds silly. Carry on a conversation with pain or fatigue (but not out loud or they'll lock you up!). By recognizing the problem, you will not let it take control. According to Kropf: "The central theme is to avoid panic or anxiety. It is important that the runner learn how to turn a possibly disastrous turn of events into a win situation by taking charge of the pain or tight area, not allowing that area to take charge of him. Sooner or later this will happen to all runners in a race. Once they use some of these techniques successfully, they will have another ace up their sleeve for the next race."

• Kropf suggests that at the first sign of pain or fatigue— or even before it appears in anticipation—heighten your awareness in the area. If you often feel tightness and fatigue in your quads late in a race, for example, tighten those muscles momentarily and then let go. This will reduce anxiety, and help you fight off fatigue with relaxation.

• Repeat your relaxation slogan (see page 369). For example, chant "calm, calm, calm" if you feel fatigue setting in. Kropf recommends specific visualization. Become familiar with anatomical drawings of the various muscles of the body, particularly ones that often cause you trouble in a race. "See" those muscles widening and lengthening as they are being relaxed. This will ward off the tension that will cause the fatigued muscles to tighten and shorten.

• Kropf believes that attention to posture is important. When fatigue sets in, the chest moves forward, the low back arches, the spine shortens, and the head lowers. A series of compensations take place that in effect shorten the runner, placing key muscle groups in biomechanical disadvantage. This leads to poor form and the inability to maintain pace. Kropf recommends that at first you give in to the tension and fatigue— momentarily. Let your body go in the direction it wants. Exaggerate the poor form that fatigue creates only momentarily rather than fight it. Then, after breaking the pattern of fighting fatigue, you can concentrate on relaxed, good form. Feel your jaw loosen, your neck and shoulders relax, the torso widen and lengthen, and imagine the head floating into a hat 1 inch above your head. Feel yourself getting taller, feeling relaxed and more efficient.

• Talk to yourself. Think about how much you—and your family and friends—have sacrificed to prepare for this race. Think about how badly you want to beat your competitor. Or about how you don't want to let down your teammates. Tough pep talks will help you through bad patches of fatigue.

• Pick up the pace. That's right. Believe it or not, by slightly picking up the pace you may be able to fight off fatigue. A quicker pace uses different muscles, allowing some of the tired ones to rest momentarily. After 100 yards, return to your goal pace. A course with gently rolling hills offers a natural way to utilize different muscle groups.

• Concentrate on how close you are to the finish. If you are 2 miles to the finish, for example, reflect on how easy it is to run that 2-mile loop around your local park. It might be easier to think in terms of time to go rather than distance: 20 minutes to go or 5 minutes to go seem less threatening when you are battling fatigue.

• Get mad. When a runner passes you, get angry—but remain reasonably relaxed. Or get mad at a comment made by a spectator or competitor. The sudden rush of adrenaline will give you a psychological boost and break the hold of fatigue.

Racing Tactics

Most runners race against themselves, for time. Some, however, strive to place high in the field, or perhaps high in their age group. Perhaps your goal is to beat your friends (or enemies). To win "your race," pick one of the following tactics.

• Pace yourself to run your best time and hope that will be good enough to outdistance your rivals.

• Burst out and lead from the start. This can be dangerous. Your opponents know where you are and can pick you off. You can also burn out. It is a tremendous psychological burden to know you are being followed. This strategy works only if you are fit enough to hold the lead to the end. You may be able to get enough of a lead to discourage your opponents and steal a victory. Unless you are sure you can break away, however, don't lead.

• Run with or follow and work off the energy of your opponents, and move away from them in mid-race. You can gradually increase the pace until your opponent "breaks," or use a series of surges—short, quick accelerations—to push into the lead and hold it. If someone bursts on you, slowly move back to him or her; don't respond immediately. Decide in advance—while studying the race course—where you will make a strategic move; at the crest of a hill runners are vulnerable, or you can use your downhill skills to open a lead. Most races are won or lost with such tactics, but they are very dangerous for the non-elite runners, since they require suberb conditioning.

• Outkick your opponent at the end. If you have superior speed, hang back in contact with your opponents and then outsprint them at the end. This takes careful timing. You can sprint out too soon, run out of gas, and be passed again. Respond to kickers by moving with them and then, if possible, outkicking them from behind. These methods may result in a win, but could also cause you to run more slowly. Sometimes you must choose to go for either time or place.

Strategy and confidence building start long before you reach the starting line. But a good strategy, planned ahead of time, will give you an extra mental edge. The following strategy tips may help you defeat your competitors, whether you are fighting for the win or to beat a "friendly" rival back in the pack.

• Don't worry about other runners before the race. Concentrate on your image and your goals. Don't look at flashy uniforms or fancy shoes, or listen to bragging or complaining. Beware of competitors trying to "psyche you out." Focus on yourself.

• Your strategy will differ with each race distance. In a 5K race, if you don't hold close contact with your opponents from the start, you cannot make up the distance. You must go out and run with them from the opening gun. In marathons, you can follow far enough behind to see them, relax, set your pace, and have plenty of time to catch up.

• Look around at the start and during the race. Pick some runners who are better than you to pace off, and then try to reel them in as the race progresses. Early in the race, don't be as concerned with your place as with staying within striking distance of your opponents. During the race, get aggressive, and set small goals of passing each runner as you go along.

• Analyze the course and the weather. Make sure you know where all the hills come and *exactly* where the finish line is. With a downhill course and a tail wind, you can start faster and will get some help over the last few miles. Conversely, you'll need to save energy if the course is hilly near the end and the wind against you. Many of the runners on the course tour bus for the 1982 Avon International Marathon in San Francisco got "psyched out" because the bus took several hours to cover the route (making the course seem very long), and the hills began to look even worse than they were as the moans on the bus increased. By riding the course himslf along with some of his Atalantans, Bob Glover was able to determine that a change of strategy was needed: throw away the time goals and race against the other runners instead. Starting paces were adjusted by 10 seconds, and the runners were advised to aim to place in the top 30 in order to win a medal and help the team score, and completely forget about running a fast time. Knowing this decision, team members no longer feared the course, and they had a big advantage over other runners who didn't rise to the challenge of the hills and didn't go over the course first and stubbornly went ahead with their previous race-time goals.

• Work together. On the hilly Avon course the Atalantans worked together, sharing the pace through the hills for most of the race. The result was that they placed in the top 31 runners in a world-class field and led the team to its fourth straight Avon International Championship and the 1982 National Athletics Congress Championship. They won despite the fact that on paper several teams were stronger. But over the hills of San Francisco, they were mentally superior and thus physically superior to twenty other clubs.

• Use the runners around you. You can use them to hold or push your pace, break the wind, or help you up hills. Take turns sharing the pace so everyone gets a fair ride. If the group's pace slows, make a move toward the next group. If it's too fast, back off and look for runners coming up.

• Never panic. If your opponent passes you, watch him or her closely for signs of fatigue. Switch gears easily and glide back into contention gradually. Stay relaxed.

• Run the first half of the race, especially the marathon, controlled. Hold back your emotions until the last stages of the race, when the going gets tough. Become more aggressive gradually. When you feel bad, remember that runners around you feel worse.

• Be alert at all times. If an opponent tries to surge, be mentally prepared to go with him or her. If you think he or she is going too fast, ease back and later slowly reel him or her in. Make a big move only toward the end, unless you know you are fit enough to pull it off earlier.

• Listen to and watch your opponents. If they are breathing hard, or their form is getting sloppy, take advantage of this "bad patch" and move ahead.

• A good time to pass an opponent is when he or she is taking water. But remember: you've got to drink too. You should practice getting your fluids in quickly so you can take advantage of an opponent's temporary pause.

• Pass runners decisively so they know you are feeling strong and let you go. A few yards down the road you can settle back into your pace. Only throw in these bursts to break away from a serious competitor. For most of the race, especially back in the pack, you should pass people only at your even race pace. Usually passing really means going past runners who are slowing down because they started too fast. See chapter 31 for guidelines for switching into your passing gear when you really want to break away from a competitor. Even if you don't feel good when passing, fake it. A quick "You're looking good, see you later, I'm feeling great" as you pass may "psych them out." Don't pay any attention to what your competitor says to you. He or she is most likely trying to "psych you out."

• Get aggressive when the going gets tough. Flash back to previous races where you ran tough, or to the hard training runs leading into this race. This will boost your commitment to keep pushing. Sometimes directing anger at your competitor or picking up the pace will overcome fatigue. Change your form for a few strides when you feel tired. Slowing down is the easiest thing to do, but it will defeat you psychologically.

• Use strategy that best fits your mental and physical strengths, and consider those of your opponent. Atalanta's Marilyn Hulak won a 25K race in Central Park and a trip to the Rome Marathon with some daring strategy. She started out very fast and opened a large lead over her rival, who had greater speed and usually beat her. With the physical strength of 100-mile training weeks and the mental goal of going to Rome, Marilyn caught her opponent by surprise and held on for victory. She then placed second in Rome.

• Don't let your opponents get such a big lead that you can't make it up. On the other hand, don't go out very fast with them and risk blowing up. It is better to go out faster than normal to keep within striking distance but still be reasonably comfortable. Don't wait until it is too late to track down an opponent from behind. Make a move to get near him or her with at least 2 miles to go, and then concentrate on closing ground.

The Finishing Kick

Develop a strong finishing kick. This might be a strong move to defeat others or to shave precious seconds off the clock. Most road races are won by staying with or slightly behind the leaders and then making a strong move toward the end. (Where that "end" point is differs, of course, from a 5K to a marathon.) If you have a strong finishing kick, try to keep the pace slow and wait until the last minute to make your move. Otherwise, gamble early. If you can't break a faster opponent early with surges or a hard early race, start your final kick at least ¼ mile or ½ mile from the finish and try to wear him or her down.

Let's detail some techniques about your finishing kick. This is as much a mental as a physical weapon. Your kick demands more than pure speed or strength at the end of the race. It also requires positive thinking, concentration, and the conviction that you can "turn it on" and win. Your ability to finish fast gives you the psychological edge of knowing that you have another "gear" you can use.

The kick demands leg strength at the end of a race. You will improve that strength by aerobic endurance runs, with weight training and speed work, and by running an evenly paced race. Most competitive runners have enough strength at the end of a race but cannot find the gear to sprint because they lack leg speed.

You can develop a finishing kick by spending some time on

it during your training. There are six parts to making a finishing kick: speed, strength, racing form, concentration, positive thinking, and practice. Concentration and positive thinking, as we've said, give you the confidence that you have the strength and speed to win with a finishing kick. If you believe you have it, you do.

Practice pulls all these elements together. There are several ways that your training runs can be adjusted to help develop your finishing kick. First, incorporate fast "pickups" into some of your distance runs to simulate the finishing kick. Do some fast 220s or 440s as you visualize the race finish. If possible, practice your kick over the finish line of the course. Also, you may run the final repetition at a faster pace than the rest of your workout to simulate kicking late in a race. When doing this, be sure that you are prepared for the added stress. Ease into this training. Do this type of training late in the season, after your strength and speed have developed.

During a race, start your kick early (880 yards to 1 mile out) if you're not blessed with natural speed. Otherwise, start your kick later (220–440 yards). It isn't the fastest runner who wins, but the runner who with brain and brawn reaches the finish line first. Don't ever give up. You can pick up precious seconds or places by concentrating on your finishing drive all the way *through* the finish line. *Please:* Don't be a runner who sprints only the last few yards to the cheers of the undiscriminating crowd. By now, every serious runner knows the difference between the hot stuff and the hot dog. If you've got that much left, you should have run faster sooner.

Burnout

A runner approached Bob Glover with a problem as he was writing this chapter. She had improved by leaps and bounds since starting his classes, in fact dropping her 10K time from 46 minutes to 40 minutes in a few months. But then she ran a series of poor races. Her times didn't improve. Worse, she hated the experience. She wanted to quit. Analysis of the problem quickly found the source of her troubles. She was physically and mentally burned out. She was racing too often, which left her body tired. She was racing so often that she could no longer get mentally up for each race. Racing had lost its excitement.

As a runner you will improve by leaps and bounds at first, then level off before improving again. When you make huge improvements in race times, often these are followed by difficulty in shaving off seconds when previously you were improving by minutes.

Runners need to take several "time-outs" a year. Rebuild, refresh, rest. You can't train hard year-round and expect to keep improving. You can't race hard several times a month and keep improving indefinitely. Either your body or your mind will break down.

Glover's advice for the "burned out" runner is to back the mileage down for a few weeks, stop hard speed training for a few weeks, don't race again until you are very hungry for competition. Don't toe the line until you really want to do well. Set a goal for several months away, and then gradually build toward it. Don't just jump into the next race on the schedule. Build excitement toward a new PR, for moving up to a marathon, down to a 5K, a trip to a new and exciting, perhaps faraway, race.

Your mind must be prepared to race or the body won't respond the way it did when you were "psyched up." Don't force yourself to keep challenging goal after goal, race after race, under pressure to keep running faster and faster. Work in streaks of energy and mental buildup. In between, take a break before racing breaks you.

The "DNF"

Almost every runner has a few "DNFs" in his or her diary: a Did Not Finish. When the going gets tough in a race, all of us think about dropping out. The pain and pressure get difficult and we momentarily lose confidence. But mentally tough, well-trained runners hang in there and quickly get back their confidence and finish well. If you are overwhelmed with the strong desire to quit because you feel very unhappy, then quit. Walk off the course without feeling like a failure. Analyze your problem—perhaps overtraining, too much pressure at home or work, etc.—and deal with it. Ease back into your training and start racing again with a low-key effort before taking another shot at a competitive effort.

If you find yourself favoring an injury or are very uncomfortable because of overheating, the effects of a cold or flu, or other ailment, don't be a hero—drop out. Dropping out for intelligent safety reasons will save your body and mind a lot of abuse. You will recover from the effort much faster than if you forced yourself to finish. But will you recover from the disappointment and embarrassment of being a DNF? If you are a confident runner, you know that the runner who was struggling out there wasn't the real you and that you will return next time and do well.

If at all possible, avoid DNFs. Finishing despite having a tough day makes you that much tougher and faster when things are going good for you. Learn to differentiate between troubles that are fleeting and not a threat to your health—physical and mental—and those that justify a DNF.

The "Bad" Race

Perhaps you were able to finish the race, but wish you hadn't when you see your time. We can't have a good race each time out. Professional baseball teams don't win every game each season. The best teams have lots of good games and only a few bad ones. Aim for the same for yourself: seek consistency. Often runners pop a new PR for 10 miles, and the next time out run a relatively poor time for a 5K, for example. The great race raised your expectations. But everything went right that day, and perhaps on the day of the poorer performance the weather was warmer, you were stressed out from your job, etc. Write off "bad" races as learning experiences. Take a couple of easy training days, set a new goal, and get back to work. Of course if you still feel lousy several days after a race, you are headed for injury or burnout and should take an extended physical and psychological break from competitive racing and training.

ANALYSIS

Analyze the entire race the day after you run it, and make notes in your diary about your performance. Learn from your successes and mistakes.

- Was my prerace mental preparation adequate?
- Did I execute my race strategy properly?
- Was my pacing effective?
- Were my start and finish good?
- Did I concentrate during the race on pace, form, breathing, etc.?
- Was I in control?
- Did I run the time I had planned? Why or why not?
- How can I improve next time?

The best runners are not always the ones who will win. You can defeat runners who are physiologically superior if you are mentally superior. At the top level of competition, it is mental preparation and mental toughness that separate the winners from the losers. For all levels of runners, the ability of the mind to get the most out of the body is the difference between a good performance and a great one. The mind, not the body, is therefore the most important single factor in racing success.

Part VIII
TECHNIQUE

29. RUNNING FORM

The most ignored ingredient in successful racing is *technique*. This is the art of blending form and style to produce a more efficient, faster runner. *Running form* refers to the biomechanics of running. (Biomechanics is the biology of motion, the study of the mechanisms of movement.) Running form, according to Dr. Peter Cavanagh, professor of biomechanics at Pennsylvania State University, "involves the most economical use of physiological resources with the least risk of injury." *Running style* is how you look and feel when you run.

Various studies have demonstrated that some runners are much more efficient than others. This means that in most cases, improving a runner's form will improve his or her running results. Some runners have form quirks that apparently offset musculoskeletal asymmetrics naturally and shouldn't be changed. Bill Rodgers, for example, flails his right arm to compensate for a short left leg; still, no one is going to change his form for better results.

You should run naturally, as long as that is biomechanically sound. Former University of Oregon and U.S. Olympic coach Bill Bowerman wrote in *Runner's World:* "Every human being is built on the same basic set of biomechanical functions: muscles working in concert with each other, muscles moving and augmenting bone structures, joints connecting rigid bones to allow them to support the body in differing planes. Every runner, therefore, starts with the same machine. No two bodies, however, have the same interaction of parts. Some are more efficient than others. Working with a runner's basic running form as dictated by the biomechanical structure, certain modifications can be made that merely make what nature gave the runner function more efficiently."

The four basic biomechanical principles of running are:
1. foot strike
2. forward stride
3. body angle
4. arm drive

These general principles apply to everyone, but no one form works for every runner. The main thing is to have the best biomechanical form and still run with a relaxed, flowing, rhythmic style.

Long, slow distance training can cause the competitive runner to lose touch with proper racing form. When the runner needs to go faster in races, he or she finds it difficult to master that skill. To be comfortable with a racing form, you must practice it regularly. It is a skill that you will learn, and then sharpen consistently—or lose. Practice your running form both at race pace and faster.

In a race, poor form leads to fatigue. And fatigue will lead to poor form. Thus you must keep working on your form. By concentrating on its main aspects—without trying to run perfectly—and running in a relaxed style, you will be more efficient, and thus a more productive racer.

If you are new at racing and speed workouts, a concerted effort at making improvements in your running form may result in dramatic improvements in your racing performances. We have seen novice competitors improve their 10K times by 2 to 5 minutes after spending up to 10 weeks working on form in our classes with the New York Road Runners Club. As you become a more experienced competitor, continued emphasis on proper running mechanics will enable you to move up in the pack.

FOOTSTRIKE

One of the greatest controversies in running concerns how your feet should hit the ground: foot strike. Coaches, elite runners, sports doctors, exercise physiologists, and even the authors of this book disagree on what method is best. Most track coaches promote ball-heel foot strike in order to achieve maximum speed. Generally, doctors and fitness experts prefer the heel-ball method, which minimizes injury. Pete Schuder spent most of his life running ball-heel; he had to use this method as a national class quarter-miler. As a track coach, he mostly trained runners in distances under 10K—events that require more speed. Bob Glover, on the other hand, spent most of his life running heel-ball as a marathoner. As a fitness teacher, he promotes heel-ball for safety reasons. But as Glover got much faster as a runner, he started naturally running more ball-heel in races and then in training runs. He still uses heel-ball when he isn't in top shape, but learned from Pete how to perfect ball-heel form to help improve his race times. In turn, Pete learned from Bob that the average runner cannot handle the stress of the ball-heel foot strike. Our combined experiences form the position taken in this chapter.

Clearly, there is a lot of confusion about footstrike, including the terms. We use these five in this book:

1. Heel Strike

Not recommended. Avoid this extreme of the heel-ball method. You should not make initial contact with the ground by jamming your heel into it and then slapping your forefoot down hard. It puts a tremendous stress on your body and may cause injury.

When we tell you to land on your heels, we mean that you gently land on the heel and then allow the forefoot to come down quietly as the body rolls over the foot and pushes off the ball. The difference is in impact: proper heel impact must be gentle, heel-ball.

2. Toe Strike

Not recommended. Avoid this extreme of the ball-heel method. Landing high on your toes should be restricted to the ballet dancer and the sprinter. With this method, you may quickly develop injuries of the shin, calf, or forefoot. Some elite runners may appear to run on their toes. But they are actually landing ball-heel-ball: hitting just behind the ball of their foot, touching down gently on the heel, and pushing off the ball.

3. Flat-Foot Strike

In the flat-foot strike, the entire sole meets the ground at one time, but as lightly as possible. Knee lift is quick and the entire action similar to riding a bike. Some runners are more comfortable landing flat-footed or on the outside of the entire foot instead of on the heel. This is all right as long as you are comfortable. However, we find it hard to believe that anyone can run fast using the flat-foot strike. Runners who think they are may be using a subtle variation of ball-heel or heel-ball: hitting almost flat-footed, landing near the heel and easing to the ball, or hitting low on the ball and easing lightly to the heel. Since this is a minor modification of the heel-ball or ball-heel foot strike, we don't use the flat-foot strike as an option.

4. Heel-Ball Strike

Recommended for beginners, for injury prevention, for heavier runners, for a slower pace. This method is used with the shuffle stride.

This technique involves touching gently on the outside of the heel, rolling inward lightly to the ball of the foot with your knee slightly bent to absorb shock, and lifting off from the big toe. Done properly, this is more of a shock-absorbing light flick than a bone-jarring crash. The slight rocking motion between heel contact and push-off ensures proper cushioning and effective forward propulsion. The result is a hitting and springing motion that is less jarring and increases acceleration. Your toes should be pointing as straight forward as possible.

5. Ball-Heel Strike

Recommended for highly conditioned light runners who want speed and can safely coordinate the method to help them train for and maximize their running speeds. This method is used with the power stride.

According to Pete Schuder, the heel-ball foot strike does not allow you to increase the length of your stride and thus gain speed. In fact, he says, because of the position of your body as your heel hits the ground, you must keep your stride very short in order to keep your balance. As your heel first hits the ground, your center of gravity is located behind the support leg, forcing you to pull your body forward. If you attempt to increase your stride by reaching out with your lead leg, you will find it hard to pull your body forward without losing your balance. Your hamstrings are not strong enough to do this. To propel yourself forward with the heel-ball method, Pete says, you must use a short shuffling action in which your legs only slightly reach out in front of you. The pulling action of the legs forces you into a "squat" from which you cannot lengthen your stride. To run faster with the heel-ball method, you would have to increase the number of steps you take per second: your stride frequency.

The ball-heel method, Pete argues, allows you to increase both your stride length and your stride frequency. This advanced method of foot strike enables you to place your center of gravity over your support leg. Your foot is now in perfect position to drive your body forward with a strong pushing action. The length of your stride is now dependent on how hard you push forward and not how far you reach ahead of your body.

Your foot strike with the ball-heel method touches the ground behind the ball of the foot, on the outside edge, and as the foot rolls inward, the knee bends slightly to absorb shock. The heel gently touches the ground so that the entire sole of the shoe makes contact. Then you roll up to the ball of the foot for lift-off, pushing off the big toe. You should concentrate on "popping" off the ground with a light flick rather than pounding into the ground. If you use this foot strike method correctly, you may wear out your running shoes on the balls of the feet as quickly as on the heels.

Should you change your running foot strike? There are more than a dozen points to consider:

Fitness and Experience. Beginning runners, racers, and marathoners should run heel-ball. With experience and improved fitness, you may want to change to the ball-heel method. Novices do not have the strength in the lower leg and ankle to safely master the ball-heel technique. Many experienced competitive runners will train most of the time using heel-ball foot strike and use ball-heel strike in races, although perhaps not for the marathon distance, and in speed workouts.

Injury. Even an experienced ball-heel runner may be forced to train heel-ball when suffering from such injuries as Achilles tendonitis, shin splints, or back injury. This would lessen stress on impact and the pull on the Achilles and calf. Runners prone to stress fractures or injury in the Achilles tendon, ankle, or calf will want to run heel-ball, which is the safest running foot strike. (Injuries from heel-ball strike usually come from hitting too hard on the heel or overstriding.)

Speed of Runs. Don't use ball-heel until you are able to run at a quick pace (about a 6:00–7:00 mile). At that pace you can run with a lighter foot strike. It is difficult to run a 6:00-per-mile pace on your heels. Generally, the faster you run in training or racing, the more likely you are to use the ball-heel method. Jogging ball-heel at a slow pace places a stress on the lower leg.

Mileage. If you are running 50 miles a week using the ball-heel method and gradually increase to 70 miles, you may find that the additional pounding on your legs is fatiguing and is making you vulnerable to injury. You may want to train heel-ball. This often occurs naturally. Conversely, if you cut back your mileage and mostly run heel-ball except in races, you may feel bouncier and quicker and switch to ball-heel more often in training. Most runners, except the very top competitors, run more heel-ball in training to give them more cushioning.

Distance of the Race. You are likely to run ball-heel during shorter races when you'll be going faster. A middle-of-the-pack and up runner in a 10K will do better with ball-heel if comfortable. You must be very fit to stay up on the balls of your feet for long races.

Coach, Doctor, Running Idol. Coaches tend to treat all runners the same. Beware of the coach who wants you to change your foot strike. Make sure it is right for you. If you get injured and your doctor tells you to run heel-ball for safety, you may be concerned about returning to ball-heel. You should do so only after your injury mends, and return gradually. The elite runner often weighs very little and is very light on his or her feet. Don't try to copy your running idol—what works for him or her may not work for you.

Weight. You increase the force of impact on your body by three pounds for every pound you are overweight. The heavy runner, therefore, must emphasize shock absorption. Run heel-ball.

Foot Type. A runner with a high arch and dropped forefoot may be more comfortable running ball-heel.

Surface. Running on ice or snow may require a flat foot or heel-ball strike to achieve a firmer grip.

Terrain. Run uphill ball-heel and run downhill as you do on the flats. You may lessen shock by running ball-heel downhills.

Age. It may be too late, after years of running, to change styles without injury. It is safer to use heel-ball. The best time to learn ball-heel is when you are young and being taught the proper mechanics of distance running and sprinting.

Habit. Most men learn to play pivot sports on the balls of their feet: soccer, football, basketball. When they start running, they often start that way too. It is safer to start heel-ball, however, and then return to ball-heel when ready.

Comfort. Three major factors to consider are the safest way, the fastest way, the easiest way. Experiment, but don't change unless it feels right for you. We don't have all the answers to what is best for the runner. Your body will give you clues.

Switching to the Ball-Heel Method

Most runners start with the heel-ball method. Then, as they reach a faster level, they may want to switch to ball-heel. How should you do this?

First, allow your body to adjust to the new method. Give your legs time to get used to the new position of your feet. Remember: Changing foot strike is almost like starting to run all over

SUMMARY OF WHO LANDS WHERE

	HEEL-BALL	BALL-HEEL
Novice runners and racers, most marathoners	X	
Heavy runners	X	
Runners with lower-leg injuries	X	
Training and/or racing at 6–7 min per mile or faster	X	X
Training and/or racing at 7-min pace or slower	X	
Most middle-of-pack and back runners	X	
Most elite runners		X
Most runners between middle and elite	X	X
Most track racers		X
Finishing kick		X
Uphill		X
Downhill	X	X

again. If you start too quickly, and try to do too much too soon, you may become very sore or injured. Be sure to stretch and strengthen your muscles, especially your Achilles tendon and calf.

Start by jogging a little with your foot hitting behind the ball of the foot. Do this before and after your usual workouts. Just get the feel of landing behind the ball. Pete Schuder helps runners by having them imagine they are jumping rope. When you do this, you should land right behind the ball of the foot. Slowly introduce the ball-heel foot strike into a light training session, preferably a 220-yard slow interval speed session or an uphill workout. Periodically during your training runs and races, concentrate on using the new method. Finally, after many workouts, use the foot strike throughout a short race. Be patient. You are learning a new skill that may take several months to master.

FORWARD STRIDE

The second biomechanical principle of running is forward stride.

Stride length is the distance between successive ground contacts of the right and left feet, heel to toe as measured in distance covered on the ground. *Stride frequency* is the total number of right- and left-foot ground contacts per minute. *Running speed* can be defined as the product of the length and frequency of stride. Therefore, there are only three ways to increase your speed:

1. Increase the length of your stride.
2. Increase the frequency of your stride.
3. Increase the length and frequency of your stride.

Stride Length

At the 1984 Women's Olympic Trials Marathon, Dan Buckalew filmed elite women marathoners at various points in the race and then analyzed the results on a digitizer. The results of his computerized study were published in the *International Journal of Sport Biomechanics*. The runners' strides deteriorated over the course of the race, and two major points emerged from the film: the biggest declines in stride efficiency occurred between 20 and 24 miles; the faster marathoners consistently maintained a higher stride length throughout the race. Stride length, not stride rate, is the most important factor separating the elite from the average marathoner. Studies have proven that two runners of comparable aerobic capacity will most likely be separated at the finish line by running economy.

Buckalew's research points out that the top runners have less vertical displacement of center of gravity (bounce), less overstride (distance the foot reaches forward of the center of gravity as the lead foot hits the ground), and less time that the driving foot is in contact with the ground (causing braking). Trials winner Joan Benoit-Samuelson scored significantly better than the average runner she faced on race day in all of the above categories that reflect a runner's economy of stride.

Increasing stride length will help you increase your speed. But "reaching out" in an attempt to increase stride will not be effective. "Trying to stretch the lead leg out in front of the body will have a negative effect," Buckalew says. "You have to have the propulsion from your rear leg." Hill training, speed work, and weight training will increase rear leg propulsion. Increased flexibility will also help lengthen your stride and improve running economy. Overstriding is not only inefficient, it causes extra impact shock, resulting in an increased vulnerability to injury. It is better to understride than overstride. Studies show that the average runner overstrides, while Dr. Peter Cavanagh and others at Pennsylvania State University have discovered that elite runners have shorter strides than slower runners.

Stride length will shorten on uphills and lengthen on downhills, but must remain under control. At any given pace, everyone has a stride length that is best for him or her; usually it is the most comfortable. Stride length must not be copied from any other runner nor imposed by coaches. There is no one optimal stride length for all runners.

Stride Frequency

Running faster also involves increasing the frequency of your stride. Dr. Cavanagh's studies also showed that the stride frequency of elite runners was 9 steps per minute faster than that of the average runner. Buckalew's study showed that the top elite women in the trials had a slightly faster stride rate than those a few minutes behind them at the finish. Quicker strides, therefore, are better, but not as important as longer, but controlled, strides.

There are two basic types of runners: the shuffler and the power runner. Don't try to change your stride if it is best for you. You can improve by learning to "switch gears" when you need to. For some, this will be the finishing kick, for others, shorter races; and for the gifted few, the full marathon.

The Shuffler

This runner runs very low to the ground with little vertical lift. He or she skims the surface with short, rapid strides, little knee lift or back kick. As a heel-ball runner, this runner moves along in a very efficient manner with few extraneous motions. The heel-ball action allows the runner to increase his or her frequency of stride and thus increase speed with little difficulty. But this runner's center of gravity is slightly behind the support leg, pulling the body forward and making it difficult to increase stride length. If this runner reaches out too far in front to increase stride length, he or she will overstride. This may cause imbalance, inefficiency, or even injury. This runner can generate more speed only by increasing the frequency of his or her stride, not its length.

Distance runners who spend many hours on the roads learn to run with as little effort as possible. Their bodies take short, shuffling steps to conserve energy. Derek Clayton wrote in *Runner's World:* "When I started training for the marathon, my form changed naturally. Running 20 miles a day shortened my stride length. It also eliminated the tendency to lift my knees. Gradually, my power stride evolved into one of economy . . . I developed a very natural leg action I call 'the Clayton shuffle.' Through miles and miles of training, I honed my leg action to such a degree that I barely lifted my legs off the ground. It was economical and easy on the body. But it 'happened.' It grew slowly through many hours of training." Alberto Salazar, who broke Clayton's world record with a 2:08:13 in the 1981 New York Marathon, also changed his stride over the years into his own "shuffle stride." Amby Burfoot, the 1968 winner of the Boston Marathon, is another notorious shuffler.

Obviously the shuffle stride is widely used, and over the long distance its efficiency may be preferred over the speed of the power stride.

The Power Runner

This runner uses the ball-heel foot strike, runs with a slight forward lean, "pops" off the ground, and has more knee lift and a longer stride.

To run fast using this method, you must lift your knees and open your stride. Proper knee lift requires that you bring your knees forward ("lead with the knees") and high enough so that your legs can follow through and extend themselves to the longest possible length without strain, and then drop naturally in front of you. If you keep your knees low, or throw your forefoot out in front of you, you will prevent yourself from getting that full, natural stride. Instead, you will take short, choppy steps. If you raise your knees too high, your body will lean too far back, and you will bounce up and down as you run and lose your forward drive.

A marathon runner, of course, will not run that distance with high knee action. It is important to maintain knee lift relative to the speed being run. To hold form, strong quadriceps are needed; they may be strengthened by running hills and by weight training.

For the ball-heel runner, Newton's Third Law of Motion—for every action there is an equal and opposite reaction—becomes the key ingredient in attempting to make improvements in speed. Your ability to run faster is dependent not only on stride frequency, as is the case for the shuffler, but also on how well you are able to push off with the support leg. By keeping your center of gravity (hips) in front of your support leg, you are able to push hard into the ground with the support leg. This force into the ground is countered with an equal and opposite force that propels your body forward. The greater the drive into the ground, the greater the thrust forward.

The power stride increases the ground distance covered with each stride without forcing you to reach out to do so. This happens not because the foot hits farther out by reaching, but because you are covering more ground in the air as a result of increased power at push-off. You increase force, thus ground distance. Many runners are confused by this, and reach out and thus overstride. In baseball, for example, base runners are taught to run through first base, not jump toward it, since running through is faster.

If you are going at a relatively slow pace, the drive into the ground is minimal, resulting in a fairly small stride length. However, if you wanted to increase your speed quickly, you would begin to push your body forward by powerfully driving off your support leg. Your stride opens, resulting in your being able to cover a greater distance in a similar period of time.

The most important point to remember in increasing your stride length using the ball-heel foot strike is to keep your hips in the proper position. If you allow yourself to sit back too far, so that your center of gravity is behind the support leg, you will be forced to *pull* your body forward, thus cutting down your stride.

After you make initial contact with the ground just behind the ball of your foot, it is important to allow your entire foot to then touch the ground. *Do not* try to stay up on the ball of your foot. Total contact with the ground gives you a larger surface area with which to generate a counter force in pushing you forward. Allowing all of your foot to make contact with the ground also allows your hips to move ahead of the support leg prior to push-off. You should also have your support leg bent slightly at the knee so that your hips can come directly over the lead leg.

The ball-heel runner increases speed by increasing the frequency of the stride and the length of the stride. The heel-ball runner, as we've described, increases his or her speed by increasing the frequency of the stride. But this runner can only minimally increase stride length without overstriding.

The power stride is used by most track runners, elite runners, and runners powering uphill or finishing with a kick. Only the very fit use this stride for marathons. The power stride may produce more speed, but it is less efficient over long distances than the shuffle stride. Many runners train with a slight shuffle stride and race marathons with that stride; they usually race shorter distances with the power stride.

BODY ANGLE

Too many runners worry about how they should run: erect, bent over, or whatever. The best advice is to relax. Allow your body to move as freely and with as little rigidity as possible.

Bill Bowerman emphasizes that an erect, but not stiff, posture is the most essential element in a smooth and efficient running form. He notes: "The best postural position for a distance runner is an upright one. You should be able to drop a plumbline from ear level and it would fall straight down through the line of the shoulder, the line of the hip and then onto the ground." This suggests that the runner runs perfectly erect. Leaning too far forward from the waist forces the muscles to work to maintain balance, causing potential injury to the lower leg muscles and back. Leaning backward has a braking effect and places a severe burden on the back and legs. The heel-ball runner using the shuffle stride runs nearly erect, but relaxed.

Body angle is important for the ball-heel runner. According to Brooks Johnson, the 1984 Women's Olympic track coach and Pete Schuder's coach when Pete was an AAU All-American, "We must place the body in a position of jeopardy; we must lean forward, or otherwise upset our equilibrium. Simply stated, running is a series of falls and recoveries." The important point to emphasize is that the runner normally runs relatively upright. While running quickly with the ball-heel foot strike, you should employ a very slight forward lean, which allows for a more fluid stride.

Three areas are important to your running posture:

Hips

Keep your hips relaxed, forward, and up; pull in your "caboose" and bring the pelvis forward slightly. This allows your legs to push your body forward, since your center of gravity is in front of you, and it also enables your legs to rotate unrestricted through their entire range of motion. If you allow your hips to drop down and back, however, you will become a "squat" runner, which is a very inefficient way to move quickly.

Upper Torso

Keep your upper body up and out in front of you in an unrestricted and relaxed manner. The back should be as straight as is comfortable. The shoulders should "hang" in a relaxed manner. Don't pull your shoulders so far back that you pinch your shoulder blades together and build up tension. Just keep the shoulders relaxed, and even allow them to curve a little. Your chest should feel flat, never thrust out at military "attention." If your upper torso leans too far forward, bending at the waist, you will force your hips too far back and drastically cut down on the length of your stride.

Head

Your head will help keep you erect. If you bring your head too far forward, you will start to lean forward, bending at the waist. Don't look at your feet; keep your eyes straight ahead. Bring your head too far back, and you will force your body to be too erect, or worse, you'll lean backwards. Tilting your head to one side or the other will also throw off the efficiency of your movement. The head weighs about ten pounds (more for our thick-headed friends), so keep it centered on your shoulders in a natural, relaxed position.

A few more points about your running posture. Good posture is essential to good body mechanics. It results from good muscle tone, which gives you the ability to keep your body at a proper running posture, especially late in a race when you're tired.

ARM ACTION

In running, your arms are in some ways as important as your legs. They are not just along for the ride. If you use your arms properly, they will make your legs go faster by propelling your body forward. You will also maintain good rhythm and balance and conserve energy.

Position

Your arms should hang loosely from the shoulders. If you carry them too high, the result will be a shortened stride, shoulder twisting, muscle fatigue, and tension in your shoulders and upper back. Arms carried too low contribute to forward lean or a side-to-side and bouncing motion. Too little forward or backward arm swing will result in a lack of proper forward drive, lift, and balance. Either flopping your arms or rigidly holding them in position contributes to inefficiency of motion.

Carry your arms between your waistline and chest. On the upswing, your hand should come close to your body at about your pectoral muscles. On the downswing, your hand should lightly graze the side seam of your running shorts. The arms naturally swing in front of your torso, but your hands should never cross the midline of your chest. Arms moving across the body cause side-to-side motion and a shortened stride. Keeping your elbows unlocked and slightly away from your body will help maintain proper arm motion. Every runner will vary slightly in arm position. The main objective is to carry your arms in a relaxed and efficient manner.

Motion

Arms balance the runner. Their motion helps propel you forward. Your arms should move in a vertical plane from front to rear, and should synchronize with the opposite leg. The arms act as a lever and balance for the leg drive and should move in the same plane as the leg. As the left leg pushes into the ground, your right arm is driven down at the same instant, adding to the driving force. When the right leg drives into the ground, your left arm propels downward. The faster the beat, the quicker the arms move.

You might want to practice arm and leg synchronization before a mirror, perhaps to the beat of music. First try your arm swing, and then synchronize it with an easy lifting of your legs, moving from heel to toe and back while standing in place. Get the feel of arms and legs in rhythm with each other.

Forearm and Elbow

When you swing your arms, concentrate on moving them from the elbow down, driving from the forearm. *This is the most important ingredient in proper arm drive.* Many runners swing from the shoulder, locking their arms at the elbow. This is a slow and inefficient method that requires a great deal of energy to move the large muscles of the shoulder and the length of the entire arm. When driving your arms hard in a race or workout, you should end up feeling a little stiff the next day in the forearms, not in the shoulders.

Imagine that you are cross-country skiing, and pushing yourself along the trail with your poles. The motion is very similar to running, and the movement is from the forearm down, which makes your elbow open and close with each swing. Do not lead with the elbow, but with the hands, wrists, and then forearms. Keep your elbows unlocked, and swing your arms from them as though on hinges.

Try swinging your arms first from the shoulders—the wrong way—and then from the elbow. Grab your upper right arm just above the elbow with your left hand. Do not allow the elbow to move backward as you raise the arm up and then drive it down, using the elbow as a hinge. See how much easier it is to swing the arms from the elbow? This is because the radius of your swing is very short, compared with swinging from your shoulders, and also you get more driving action downward, which propels you forward. Don't lock your elbow; this common error makes the shoulders sway and dip and will not allow you to drive downward with the arm. The elbows should be "open" and should bend and straighten a little with each arm swing. They should neither point away from the body nor be tucked in close to it.

The Hands

Proper hand position is essential to correct arm drive. Percy Cerutty, the famous Australian coach, emphasized that "all natural running begins in the person's fingers and is transferred to the legs and feet." Your hands should be held loosely, so that your thumb and forefinger or middle finger just touch, "cupping." The thumbnail faces up. Fists clenched or fingers held stiffly create tension; hands hanging loosely cause the arms to flail. Both create an inefficient running motion.

The Wrist

The wrists should be relaxed and loose. At the top of the swing, cock your wrist slightly upward. At the bottom, flick your wrist as if lightly snapping a whip, turning your palm somewhat down and in. The snapping allows you to stay loose and rhythmic.

Arm Drive

For slower running, hold your arms in a comfortable, relaxed position and keep their action to a minimum. When you want to go faster, your arms should swing from the chest just past your hips. There should be a pulling action, as in swimming, or a snapping motion, as in snapping a whip, on the downward swing. Dr. Cavanagh's research indicates that proper arm motion "increases running speed by providing small amounts of 'lift' and 'drive.' " Arm action reduces the amount of force needed to lift the body from the ground, and also aids in propelling the body forward. Without using their arms at all, Dr. Cavanagh found, runners needed 4 percent more oxygen to run at the same speed than when using their arms. You can test the theory by running uphill first with your arms at your side, then using your arms properly.

Keep your arms and shoulders relaxed and strong. The success of your arm drive will be enhanced by improving your upper body strength. The use of weight training, and hand weights, will help.

TOTAL FORM

By driving the arms, maintaining proper body angle and utilizing the proper foot strike and forward-stride techniques—all together—you will have arrived at near-perfect form, for you. Form must be practiced as a unit, not just piece by piece. The proper form for running along at training pace is best practiced by training regularly with comfortable form and periodically checking out your form body part by body part. Proper form for racing needs to be practiced in speed workouts. Race-paced training runs help you adjust to the biomechanics of race pace. Fast training runs exaggerate your form and thus force you to concentrate on it more, making it easier to learn and remember. Form runs or "pickups" (see page 118) should be used often to help you improve and maintain good racing form.

We have found with our classes and teams that the best way to teach proper form is to do runs up a short, steep hill. The hill should be approximately 100 yards long and steep enough to challenge you, but not ridiculously steep. After proper warm-up, and followed by proper cool-down, you should run repetitions up the hill at 10K race pace, concentrating on the following:

1. *Foot strike.* Keep up on the ball of the foot and "pop" off the road.

2. *Forward Drive.* Push off the back foot, lift the knee (lead with the knees), and drive up and forward.

3. *Body Angle.* Lean slightly into the hill, push the hips forward and up. Keep the head up.

4. *Arm Action.* Drive the arms downward in a vertical plane from the elbow in short, quick strokes, keep the shoulders down and relaxed, don't lock the elbows.

The steepness of the hill forces you to use better form in order to get up it. If you were to practice your form on the flat at first, you would tend to stay down on your heels, stay erect, and not drive forward with your arms. Later, after a few hill sessions, you should practice your total form by doing pick-ups of 100 yards on the road or track.

For your first attempt at hill training, 4 to 6 hills (4 for novice competitors, up to 6 for veterans who have never done speed work) at a medium effort, with a jog back to the start, will be enough. Since it helps to run with others, get a group together if possible to help each other along. As you go up the hill, try to keep an even-paced rhythmic flow to your run. If you really run hard up the hill, you may never get through the workout. Remember, the major purpose of this workout is to emphasize proper running form. The secondary benefit is that you will get a good workout from this exercise, but don't let that take precedence. Work on form, even if it means having to slow down to do it.

After you have concluded this drill, do an easy recovery jog on the flat, every once in a while concentrating on push-off, knee lift, and arm swing. By doing this type of workout about once every 2 or 3 weeks for a few months, you will find that you have made dramatic improvements in your form. But you can't quit then—form doesn't come to you automatically, but it leaves you quickly. Periodically return to doing workouts on the track and hills that emphasize keeping your good form together.

To go faster using proper form, remember the four "drives":

1. *Drive off* the back foot.
2. *Drive up* with the knee.
3. *Drive forward* with the hips.
4. *Drive down* with the arms.

30. *RUNNING WITH STYLE*

You can spot your running friends way off in the distance. Some shuffle, some flow, some rock, and some roll. Runners have individual styles: their running "signatures." Many experts in the field say that little should be done to change your style of running (how you look and feel when you run). We shouldn't fool with Mother Nature. Others feel that improvements can be made.

Some runners have tried to attain the perfect style and failed—but not necessarily as racers. Australian Derek Clayton wrote in *Runner's World:* "I don't think I have a particularly pretty style. If I had my choice, I would rather look Like Frank Shorter. Frank's movements are so effortless that he makes it look like running doesn't hurt. He is light on his feet, has fluid arm movements, and seems effortless in his breathing. To me, Frank Shorter looks the way a runner should.

"I made an unsuccessful effort to alter my style. I would consciously try to keep my head from rocking and run so that my shoulders didn't sway. I felt like a tin soldier, and probably looked like one as well.

"By running the 'right' way, I had suddenly lost interest in running. It became extremely painful for me to have to think of what I was doing every step. My aim in life was to become a world-record holder. If it meant looking bad to get it, then so be it. I realized that you can't copy someone else's style. With imitation, you risk injury and, more important, you can kill the joy of running."

For the most part, you are born with a certain style that changes as you do. As youngsters we seemed to have a natural tendency to run with a very rhythmic and fluid style. As we grow older, many of us lose strength and flexibility as we cut back in physical activity. When the adult returns to exercise, he or she often lacks knowledge of proper running form and style.

The best we can do for you is to help you clean up bad habits. Running doesn't have to look right, but it should feel right. What is right for Frank Shorter or Derek Clayton may not be right for you.

When done properly, your style will flow as a complete, unconscious action. We believe that you can make improvements in your style and form. But we encourage you to work at correcting the most common errors rather than trying to emulate "the perfect style." At first, trying to make improvements in your running style may seem very difficult. But if you are patient, you may very well find that you will begin to look and feel more relaxed and efficient as a runner.

Ideally, to improve your style you should have a coach or knowledgeable runner watch you run. If no one is available to help you, check your style by catching your reflection in mirrors or store windows. Analyze the following four points of running style in detail.

1. RHYTHMIC FLOW

Running should be a graceful and elegant form of locomotion. Developing a rhythmic flow to your running style means learning to run to an "inner beat." If you ever learned to type or took piano lessons, you may remember how difficult it was to establish a cadence or rhythm. Typing and music teachers use metronomes to help their students learn the rhythm of finger movement. Runners need to learn a rhythmic style of running.

Most of us find it occasionally, but too often it is a one-run, momentary thing and hard to recapture. Since you cannot take a metronome with you when you run, here are some skills that will help you understand running rhythm and make it part of every run:

• During your training runs, try visualizing yourself as a very well-coordinated athlete. Concentrate for a few moments on emulating that gifted runner. This may also be done during a quiet moment *before* you run.

• Do short repetitive runs of 100–220 yards, and concentrate on running smoothly and being relaxed. Work at keeping everything in step. This is best done with a group of runners who run at your level and stride: attempt to keep in step with one another for the entire distance, like marching in a band. Or do the same on a slight downhill course of similar distance. A downhill slope of a few degrees will help you learn to flow.

• Play a fast song on your stereo, and run in place. Keep step to the beat. Count as you run—1-2-3-4/1-2-3-4—keeping the count steady and in step with the leg stride. Breathe out every time you count 4 to help keep a cadence.

2. LIGHT FEET

Heavy-footed running may indicate problems in your running form. If you hear yourself making hard, slapping noises with your feet as you run, think seriously about making some changes. "Grinders," as these heavy-footed runners are affectionately known, usually do not survive the rigors of distance running. They suffer painful foot, leg, and hip injuries and are frustrated because they can't increase their speed.

Running "light," on the other hand, is the style of the runner who floats along the roads making scarcely any sound. This is easier to visualize than attain. But many of the drills used to develop running rhythm can also be employed here, since light, gentle running is rhythmic too. Some other drills that will help you run light:

• Jump rope at double beat. Make yourself jump twice per rotation. Jumping quickly forces you to be light on your feet. When you first try this, jump only a short time. You will be using muscles in your legs and ligaments in your joints that you haven't used before. About 2 to 5 minutes of rope jumping per day is sufficient; you aren't a springtime schoolgirl in the play yard. One runner we know started jumping rope when at the Laundromat waiting for his weekly wash. After 30 minutes of rope jumping, his clothes were clean, but he could hardly walk. He had to take two days off from running to recover. Moral: Don't do things in extremes, especially new things. Begin slowly, build slowly. Another hint: Try rope jumping without the rope. You won't trip as often. (If you're tripping over imaginary ropes, see your doctor immediately!)

• Run noiselessly. While out on a run, concentrate on not making any noise. See how close you can get to your friends before they hear you coming. Just focusing on this will help you run more gently and easily.

3. RELAXATION

Many runners find that their running style is restricted by tightness and the inability to relax. You hear coaches yell this all the time: "Relax! Relax!" But it's easier said than done. In fact, when someone is told to relax, the opposite usually occurs: he or she tenses up. A more positive phrase might be "hang loose," and that's what we really mean.

Here are some points to remember to help you run more relaxed:

• Let your chin hang loosely. Too often we see runners who grit their teeth from the start of the race to the finish. Keep your mouth slightly open and loosen your jaw. This will keep the muscles in your neck and shoulders relaxed. Occasionally let the head roll from side to side and then return, shrug the shoulders and let them drop, or drop your arms loosely at your side to promote relaxation.

• Check yourself every once in a while as you run. Make sure your shoulders haven't risen to your ears, causing your arms to rise and become ineffective. Check your hands and make sure the fingers are still cupped and not held tightly together. Squeezed hands cause your arms to tighten and restrict your free-flowing movement.

• Check your wrists to be sure they are loose. Do they flick at the bottom of the swing as they should, thus helping you keep a steady beat to your rhythm?

• Check your breathing.

4. BREATHING

If listened to carefully, this one sound will tell you a great deal about yourself. Quick, shallow breaths may indicate nervousness; we've known runners who actually hyperventilated at races. "Panic breathing" can cause your entire body to tense up. Other runners start too fast, and never "catch" their breath during the run. Make a determined effort to slow down your breathing by taking deeper breaths that are regular and rhythmic. Breathing, then, is part of your running rhythm and style.

Pete Schuder suggests that to establish a cadence, a runner should breathe out every second right step for part of the run. Force the breath out and then slowly breathe it in. Other runners count their breaths, which is also a form of distraction during a particularly difficult long run.

Regular rhythmic breathing is no different on the run from while you are at rest. The rate remains about the same, while breathing volume uniformly rises. Make your breathing your metronome; use it to measure the pace of your runs.

Some runners enjoy breathing in time to their foot strike, while others feel this is a nuisance. There are two basic suggestions here. Breathing should be relaxed, and should follow the principles of "belly breathing." Most of us breathe backward: we suck in the stomach as we take a breath. With proper abdominal breathing, the belly expands as you breathe in, flattens as you breathe out. The expansion of your abdomen means that your diaphragm is fully lowered and your lungs are inflated to the maximum, allowing more efficient intake of oxygen. Improper breathing can also cause the dreaded side stitch.

As Bob Glover said in *The Runner's Handbook,* there are three R's to running: run tall, run relaxed, run naturally. These will contribute to your running style.

31. RACING TECHNIQUE

Form and style during a training run differ greatly from form and style during a race. In racing, you must concentrate on your technique to maximize your potential. Efficient racing technique will shave seconds, even minutes, off your time and give you an edge over your competitors who are breathing out of control, carrying their arms too high, or barely lifting their feet.

Race technique involves the ability to maintain good form and style throughout an evenly paced race and to be able to shift gears, making necessary alterations in form. The competitive runner must be prepared for six variations in his or her race:

1. Starting
2. In the Race
3. Passing
4. Uphills
5. Downhills
6. The Finish

1. STARTING

In crowded races, you may just be shuffling along at the start. Run cautiously with your hands up in front of you to ward off other runners and help maintain balance. Flow into a steady running rhythm as soon as possible. The serious competitor may wish to get out front quickly and establish his or her position in the field. This start requires some adjustments:

• Swing your arms as soon as you begin to run. This will help you generate some speed for the first 50 to 100 yards. Bring your knees up and run briskly with "quick feet," but do not sprint. Do not overstride. Keep in control. Often, runners panic-breathe because they start too quickly. If your breathing is too fast, slow it down and get it in rhythm with your running.

• Stay loose and relaxed. Don't run tight. As soon as you can, get into your race pace and establish a good rhythm. Make that rhythm as comfortable as possible, yet push your physical limits.

The secret of a good start is to move quickly into your flow—the pace your body is trained for—as soon as you stake your position in the crowd.

2. IN THE RACE

After you have settled into your race pace, concentrate on your style and form. This should now be your greatest concern—even more than the runners around you. Don't leave your technique lessons on the training road—use your knowledge to fight off bad habits and the fatigue that tries to ruin your form. Check yourself periodically throughout the race. Better yet, have your coach or a friend meet you at various spots along the way to check your form and yell any corrections at you. Hearing the words called out to you will help you keep a good racing technique. Here is what your coach or friend should look for, and yell:

• "Don't overstride!" Don't grind or squat. Keep your hips forward.

• "Lead with the knees! Get your knees up!"

• "Run tall and easy!" Think relaxed.

• "Stay up on your feet!" If you are trying to maximize your speed by using the ball-heel foot strike, concentrate on staying "forward and up" throughout the race. It is easy to lose concentration and fall back on your heels to a heel-ball foot strike.

• "Push off your back foot!"

• "Use your arms!" Swing from your forearms. Don't lock your elbows. Drive down, not across your body.

• "Keep your hands and wrists loose!"

• "Rhythm breathe!"

• "Flow!" Keep a nice rhythm.

3. PASSING

You will have to change your running form in order to pass a competitor in a race. You will have to increase the speed of your run and use as little energy doing so as possible. Hard, forceful surges may be costly and bring on fatigue and slower times. Proper passing technique will get you by your opposition with enough left for a strong finish. Passing requires that you concentrate on the following:

• Increase your arm swing. Pump your arms faster and your legs will go faster.

• Increase the power drive with your support leg.

• Lift your knees. This will help you run faster.

• Return to race pace. Having passed your opponent, settle back into your race pace by slowing down your arm swing, decreasing the power drive, and decreasing your knee lift. Allow yourself to relax and develop your racing rhythm by concentrating on doing rhythmic breathing.

Passing a runner requires that you stay relaxed and use little extra energy. This is particularly important early in a race, where an all-out effort to pass someone will spell disaster for you later. Do not floor your accelerator and blast past your competition. Use your fuel cautiously; accelerate gradually and smoothly.

4. UPHILL

When you round the bend and see the Big Hill, don't wince. Prepare! Learn to shift gears—both mental and physical—and use proper technique to propel yourself up that hill. Attack the hill before it attacks you, by changing your form; too many runners go uphill out of control without using their arms and foot drive. Hill-running techniques can improve your racing times dramatically.

Runners combat hills three ways: in daily training runs, in hill-training speed sessions, and in races. Each is approached slightly differently. In hill speed training, you run uphill to improve overall form, strength, and speed. You might practice an exaggerated knee and arm drive and drive up the hill ball-heel. You wouldn't use this exaggerated motion in a race unless you were sprinting up a final hill or trying to power away from a competitor on a hill as a surge strategy.

For most hills, you should try to maintain, as nearly as possible, the rhythm and form you use on the flats. A few changes are necessary, however, to compensate for the incline and increased resistance.

Running hills in daily running and at normal race pace involves trying to get up the hill with a fluid, economical technique. In your daily training, run up hills fairly quickly and practice proper technique (see below). Surprisingly, it is easier to run uphill quickly with good form than slowly in poor form. Technique differs slightly for different hills and in different racing conditions. Basically there are three methods, or "gears," for running uphill:

Gear 1: Training Pace and Evenly Paced Racing

Keep a steady stride throughout the climb. First, increase your knee lift. If you don't, the angle of the hill will cut down the length of your stride and you won't be able to get your feet up and out in front of you. It's like climbing stairs: you want to pick up your feet more.

• Increase your cadence slightly, but don't overstride. Tighten your stride for economy. By maintaining a normal or slightly shorter stride, you will keep your center of gravity over or slightly in front of the drive leg. Consequently, your force is directed up and forward, which is the precise direction you want to go. In a race, you will be maintaining normal stride length owing to the added push-off and knee lift but will feel as if you are shortening your stride.

• Increase your arm swing slightly. By driving the arms a little bit more, you will overcome the pull of gravity. But don't exaggerate the arm drive. Uncontrolled, jerky motion will slow you. The arms should move as described previously, bending at the elbows with a smooth rhythm that matches the frequency of your stride. Don't reach out in front of you; keep your elbows slightly away from your body, hands relaxed.

• Push harder off your back foot. The faster you wish to run, the harder you push. Do not try to bounce up the hill; drive up the hill.

• Lean into the hill slightly. This increased lean will help you keep your center of gravity forward; you lean forward slightly just to maintain an upright position relative to the pull of gravity. The steeper the hill, the greater your lean. Keep your hips slightly forward, chest forward, back straight, chin up, and eyes ahead. If you look down near your feet, your hips will fall back, destroying your erect, efficient posture.

One other trick here: focus your eyes on an object 10 to 15 yards and watch it pass, and then focus on another object. Psychologically, you can also pull yourself uphill with your eyes.

• Don't tense up. Don't bring up your arms to fight the hill, and don't tighten your neck, hands, forearms, shoulders. This tension diverts energy from the real struggle of racing uphill and may cause fatigue and a slower time. Run relaxed.

• Maintain an even, steady rhythm. Races are won by runners who get up the hills with the minimum loss of energy. Attack the hills with finesse, not muscle, by steadily moving uphill with good form and reasonably controlled breathing.

Gear 2: Steep- or Long-Hill "Downshift"

If you face a steep or long hill, the first thing to do is cut back your stride. Just as you downshift your car when going up steep or long hills, so too you downshift in running. To do this you must:

• Cut down the length of your stride and increase your stride frequency.

UPHILL TECHNIQUE

	ARMS	BODY ANGLE	KNEES	FOOTSTRIKE	STRIDE
Gear 1 Medium speed	Slight increase in swing	Slight forward lean; hips forward	Increase lift	Ball-heel, push off back foot	Maintain stride and slightly increase frequency, maintain actual stride length
Gear 2 Steep-hill downshift	Quicken drive, short strokes	Forward lean, hips forward	Increase lift	Ball-heel, reduce drive off back foot	Shorten stride, greatly increase stride frequency
Gear 3 Power up	Drive hard, with intense, short swing	Forward lean, hips forward	Greatly increase lift	Ball-heel, push hard off back foot	Shorten stride length, increase frequency, don't overstride

• Swing your arms faster and keep the swing short and controlled.

• Reduce the amount of drive off your back foot; since you are going slower, you will not need to drive forward as hard.

• Lift your knees slightly so that your stride isn't too short and choppy.

• Continue to lean into the hill with your hips.

• Don't panic! Stay relaxed.

Gear 3: "Power Shifting"—for Hill Training and for Your Win

You only use this gear in a race when you know you have the power to use it and still finish. Most runners don't want to challenge a hill, and so they hold back, waiting to make their moves on the downhill and flats. You may be able to move away from your competitors if you can power uphill.

As you power uphill, keep the following in mind:

• Drive your arms faster. Make your arm stroke short, deliberate, and quick, with the movements beginning at your chest and ending at the top of your hip. Keep your arms close to your body. Don't allow them to swing out in front of you or way behind you. Don't raise your arms and try to "box" your way to the top.

• Lean your body forward. Lean from your hips, not from your waist.

• Lift your knees. Make the effort to get your knees up so you can maintain good stride. If you try to run up a hill keeping your knees low, you will lose power.

• Power hard off your back foot. Your efforts will be unrewarded unless you push off your back foot with power.

• Don't overstride; it will cause you to lose power and thus run slower.

• Keep relaxed. Impossible to relax while hammering up a steep hill? Not so: belly breathe; keep your shoulders, neck, and jaw from tensing up. Let your legs do the power work assisted by your arms. You'll recover your breath at the top.

5. DOWNHILL

Downhill technique is ignored by most coaches—and most books. Uphill technique is more glamorous. But once you've passed 'em going up, don't let 'em pass you going down. Most runners think downhill running is easy: take off the brakes, and roll. It is essential to let gravity do much of the work, but you must master the technique of letting yourself go while running in a controlled manner. This takes practice.

In an attempt to get down a hill as quickly as possible, some runners flail their arms and legs all over the place; they may get injured or lose their rhythm and speed. Others fight the downhill and lean back, shorten their stride, dig in their heels, and raise their arms to "brake" them.

You should develop a feel for downhill running. Some runners compare it to "throwing" themselves downhill; others feel like a mountain stream flowing smoothly with the hill. You can actually improve your race times more by perfecting your downhill technique than by perfecting your uphill technique. The speed with which you run downhill is regulated by the lean of your body and the length of your stride. With these two regulators, you can use three gears to run downhill:

Gear 1: Maintaining a Steady Race or Training Pace

As you start downhill, try to keep your form as close as possible to that used on the flats. Allow gravity to do most of the work for you.

Forward Lean. Keep your body perpendicular to the ground, back straight (don't bend at the waist), and your hips pushed forward over your lead leg. Your forward momentum will keep you from falling on your face. The angle of your lean helps determine how fast you go downhill. To maintain a steady pace, hold the angle of your body so that the center of gravity is over your lead leg. If you lean too far forward, you will pick up speed; leaning back will cause you to slow.

Stride. Maintain your stride length by bringing your knees up. As you lean forward going downhill, you will have to lift your knees higher to maintain your stride length. You can help control the speed of your run by where you place your lead leg. On a steep descent, you will want to shorten the length of your stride slightly to hold back your speed. On a gradual decline, you may have to push off your back foot to keep a steady forward speed.

Arm Swing. Keep your arm swing under control. Unlike running uphill, downhill running uses the arms mostly to maintain balance and rhythm. There is no need to swing the arms hard; gravity is powering you downhill. Don't swing your arms wildly, windmilling all over the place as you go downhill; this causes you to lose balance and rhythm. Keep your elbows slightly away from the side of your body. Get your arms in rhythm with your legs.

Foot Strike. Use the same foot strike that you use on the flats. However, Dr. Steve Subotnik suggests: "Concentrate on landing on the ball of the foot. If you're landing on your heels, you've overstriding. This is important because the foot and leg absorb shock much better when you land on the ball of the foot under a bent knee, than when you land on the heel in an almost straight-knee position." The ball-heel form absorbs shock and helps you hold forward motion as you run. But it may be uncomfortable. If you strike behind the ball of the foot, concentrate on lifting your feet quickly, hitting lightly, and pushing off against the slant of the running surface. If you are more comfortable running heel-ball, concentrate on hitting the heel very gently and quickly rolling your foot forward so you don't jam your heel into the ground. Most important, do not bounce on your toes or overstride by landing hard on your heels.

Relax. Keep your arms, shoulders, neck, and chin relaxed. Practice will help alleviate tension. But as Dr. Subotnik warns: "I tell runners to master this downhill technique, then to avoid it whenever possible. That is, even if you are a great downhill runner, you should do as little of it as you can. No one can tolerate a lot of hard downhill running and no one should try."

Gear 2: Downshifting for Very Steep or Long Hills

Sometimes you may want to slow down as you run downhill. Some races feature "super hills" down which it would be dangerous for you to "fly like an eagle." To help you slow down without losing form or putting on your brakes, here are some suggestions for downshifting:

The Forward Lean. Although this is difficult to do, try to lean forward slightly, allowing your hips to ride directly over your support leg. The natural tendency, especially on steep hills, will be to lean backward.

Reduce the Length of Your Stride. A shorter stride will slow down your speed. As you decrease the length of your stride, you will increase its frequency. Be sure to bend your knee slightly as you land to allow for greater shock absorption and to keep your center of gravity over the lead leg. Don't jam your heel into the ground.

Use Your Arms for Balance and Rhythm. To keep your balance, bring your elbows farther away from the sides of your body. This will help you stabilize yourself.

Relax. Allow your body to move freely but keep it under control. Tension will create fatigue and soreness, so relax.

Gear 3: Power Shifting and Increasing Your Speed

Good downhill runners gain a huge advantage when they can increase the speed of their descent without using much energy. Running fast downhill without losing balance or rhythm requires concentration on keeping a controlled yet free-flowing movement. You can significantly increase your downhill speed by using the following techniques:

Increase Your Forward Lean. As noted above, the more you lean forward as you run downhill, the faster you will have to run to maintain your balance. The result is that your stride frequency increases. Initiate your forward lean with your hips, not your upper body. If you bend forward at the waist, you will force your center of gravity behind your support leg, which will cause you to slam your heel into the ground as you plant your lead leg.

Increase the Length of Your Stride. Do not attempt to lengthen your stride by reaching farther out in front of you. Reaching out will cause you to overstride, which makes you land hard on your heels and actually brakes your forward progress. In-

DOWNHILL TECHNIQUE

	ARMS	BODY ANGLE	KNEES	FOOT STRIKE	STRIDE
Gear 1 Medium speed	Normal-to slightly faster swing, elbows slightly away from body	Forward, keep perpendicular to surface	Increase lift	Ball-heel or heel-ball	Normal stride length, maintain stride frequency
Gear 2 Steep-hill downshift	Same	Same	Increase lift	Same	Shorten stride length, increase frequency
Gear 3 Faster speed power shift	Same, faster swing	Same, increase lean	Increase lift	Ball-heel	Increase stride length and frequency

crease your stride length by increasing push-off and knee lift.

Swing Your Arms Vigorously and Keep Your Balance. As you increase your leg speed, increase your arm swing to keep a smooth and flowing rhythm. Control your arm swing by moving the arms up and down rather than flailing them side to side or way out in front of you. Keep your elbows away from the side of your body.

Rhythm Breathe. Since you are running downhill at a fast pace, your breathing rate may increase or even become labored. Concentrate on maintaining rhythmic breathing; continue breathing deeply and avoid shallow panic breathing.

Relax. Learn to "let go" and allow your body to "fall" downhill. Just as in skiing, you are less likely to fall and get injured and will have more control if you learn to push fear out of your mind, relax, and let yourself go.

6. THE FINISH

In the ideal race, you will have run at an even pace and left a little strength for a strong finish. More likely, you will be just holding on or tailing off. Although this may seem to be an inappropriate time to be concerned with running form, proper technique will help you finish strong and cut seconds from your time.

For years, Pete Schuder thought he was helping his long-distance runners by yelling at them near the end of their races, "C'mon, move faster! Gut it out to the finish!" It wasn't until Pete tried a hard marathon himself that he realized that the most annoying thing that can happen to runners is to have someone yell at them to run faster near the finish line. Trying to gut it out may make runners tense up. Instead, someone should yell, "Stay loose, keep your arms moving, knees up." The emphasis should be on a relaxed rhythm and efficient technique; otherwise, you may finish with head rolling, arms and shoulders high, shortened stride, or "survival shuffle." Finish with finesse, not brute force.

Holding On—Maintenance Finish

When you've extended yourself beyond your limits, worked hard to run fast, you don't want to lose it all. How do you hold on until the end?

• Maintain your form as well as possible. Keep your arm swings in a vertical plane from the elbow forward. Don't lean backward. Keep leading with the knee, and concentrate on proper stride.

• Keep your breathing rhythmic. This will help you maintain your rhythmic flow.

• Don't panic. Stay relaxed, keep your confidence up. Believe you'll finish, and you will.

Tailing Off—Survival Technique

There are times when you miscalculate your pace or are undertrained. You find yourself coming up short near the finish. You may have met the Bear, or in a longer race, you have hit the Wall.

Finishing with the Bear on Your Back (Oxygen Debt). You may feel stiff and heavy and unable to make your muscles move. You should follow the same techniques as mentioned above in Holding On, but shorten your arm drive, cut down your stride, and thus use less energy to move yourself forward. Stay rhythmic, don't panic, shuffle on in.

Finishing Through the Wall (Glycogen Depletion). Inadequate energy supplies may cause you to develop leg cramps. Your body will want to quit. You don't feel winded; you just cannot make your legs go. You feel like going to sleep. You have hit the Wall. This usually happens—if it does—at around 20 miles. Jack Shepherd, however, used the survival technique for the last 11 miles of the 1978 New York Marathon. If you hit the Wall, follow the guidelines for Finishing with the Bear on Your Back and run as easily as possible. Take the course in small segments. One woman we know ran the New York Marathon from water station to water station. Shepherd ran from one block to the next. Walk when you want to, and stretch your leg muscles to get rid of cramps. If you walk, pick the spot ahead of you where you'll start running again, and do it. Run slowly and keep going. Even well-conditioned runners sometimes find themselves struggling to the finish line. National class marathoner Marty Cooksey crawled across the line on her hands and knees after her legs gave out at the 1978 New York Marathon. We won't teach you the techniques of a finishing crawl. But if you feel that bad, consider walking in or dropping out. We know of another woman who pushed herself too hard in New York and collapsed ¼ mile from the finish with a broken leg. The desire to finish, obviously, must be tempered with common sense.

Finishing Kick

This may be a gradual shifting of gears and buildup of speed over the final mile, or a sudden acceleration during the last 50–100 yards following a buildup of speed over the final ¼ mile.

The trick is to move into a new pace, switch gears, and put new form and reinvigorated muscles to work. You will usually have a finishing kick, even when you feel exhausted. The key is to find and push that special button, shift gears, and finish strong. Here's how you should see yourself:

• Vigorously increase your arm drive to initiate the kick and carry it through to the finish. Remember: The faster you swing your arms, the faster you move your legs.

• Increase your power drive off the support leg to lengthen your stride. The stride will become snappier and longer. In the kick, you want to increase both stride length and frequency.

• Greatly increase knee lift to allow proper follow-through of your lead leg.

• Move farther up on the ball in your ball-heel strike. Push off over the big toe. Your heel should come off the ground more quickly in the recovery stage. Hit the ground less with a push and more with a "pop." Feel that you are "popping" your feet and knees up from the road or track.

• Run tall; look 20–30 yards ahead and then at the finish line through to the end. Lift from the hips.

Stay relaxed, and maintain a rhythmic cadence to your breathing so you can continue your finishing kick all the way to the finish line. Think of the form you have used in speed workouts. Continue the drive through the line; don't let up just as you approach it.

Part IX
INJURY AND ILLNESS

32. TWENTY-FOUR CAUSES OF INJURY AND ILLNESS

Competitive running contributes little to health and fitness. In truth, it tears you down more than it builds you up. But competitive runners are running for sport, not fitness. Like other athletes, they must learn to accept the inevitability of injury and illness; they must also try to minimize their effect on ability to perform.

It is safe to say that every year of competitive running will find you injured or ill at least a few times. Your best and safest response is to be conservative—hold back, and return to running cautiously. For the competitive runner, there is a fine line between overtraining and undertraining. Too much training may lead to injury or illness, too little may lead to underachievement. You will determine these outer limits for yourself and strive for the injury-free competitive area between. Often this is what makes the difference between winning and losing at all levels of competition. Many runners get into great shape only to become injured or ill and never make it to the starting line. The runner who loses training time again and again will be in worse shape than the conservative and consistent runner. An important part of competitive training is learning to prevent injuries and illness and knowing how and when to return to running.

QUESTIONS TO ASK WHEN INJURED OR ILL

These are some of the questions we ask runners who become sick or injured. The goal is to discover the reason or reasons you developed your problem. Often more than one factor is involved. The basic question is, What have you done differently in your running or your daily routine that may have caused the injury or illness? Use the following checklist to help you determine the cause of your problem or, better yet, to help prevent a problem from occurring:

1. Are your feet or legs structurally weak? (Your doctor may have to answer this for you.)
2. Do you have good flexibility?
3. Do you warm up and cool down properly for all runs?
4. Do you overstretch?
5. Are your opposing muscles weak? (Abdominals, quadriceps, etc.)
6. Do you have any previous injuries that might make you vulnerable?
7. Did you return from an injury or illness too quickly?
8. Is your running form proper?
9. Have you made any sudden changes in the quantity or quality of your runs: mileage, speed, hills, surface?
10. Has running on snow or ice changed your running pattern or form?
11. Are you undertrained for the races you are running?
12. Are you racing too frequently?
13. Are you taking time to recover from races and hard workouts?
14. Have you changed running shoes, or are thy worn down, or have you started wearing racing shoes?
15. Has your weight changed? Are you overweight or underweight?
16. Is your diet adequate for your training level?
17. Are you taking proper care of your feet?
18. Have you changed any daily habits, such as driving or sitting more?
19. Are you under additional stress?
20. Are you getting enough sleep?
21. Have you been doing other sports that might affect your running?
22. Have you changed running surfaces, or are you running on uneven or slanted terrain?

"Diseases of exellence," as Dr. George Sheehan calls running injuries, are a part of the sport. The runner must accept this fact. You must be constantly aware of the warning signs and prepare to analyze the causes of these problems. They are seldom a result of accident, although most often they seem to "just happen" for no reason at all.

The causes of injury and illness seem to fall into one of three areas: training errors, inherited physical weaknesses, and environmental influences. Rather than dealing in detail with the treatment of specific injuries, which many running books have already covered, we will explain the causes of injury and illness and how training may be affected. (For detailed treatment of injuries and illnesses, consult *The Runner's Handbook* or *The Injured Runner's Training Handbook.*)

Here are twenty-four causes of injury and illness:

1. BIOMECHANICAL: WEAK FEET AND UNEQUAL LEG LENGTH

Many runners have biomechanically weak feet. This means that the foot has some basic physical flaw that, aggravated by running, leads to foot, leg, or knee injuries. A distance runner's foot strikes the ground over 1,000 times during every mile of running. The force of impact on each foot is approximately three to four times the runner's weight. With weak feet, the force exerted upon foot strike causes an abnormal strain on the supporting tendons, muscles, and fasciae of the foot and leg. Arch supports (orthotics), either commercially made or custom fitted by a podiatrist, may help runners with biomechanically weak feet.

If your legs are of different lengths, you may experience pain in your back, knee, or hips. In many cases, unequal leg length causes no injury. When it does, the injury often occurs first on the long leg. Structural shortages may occur anywhere in the leg: the upper leg, the lower leg, and below the ankle. Heel lifts or orthotics to balance leg length may help; placed inside the shoe, they should never exceed half an inch. Exercises to stretch and strengthen the affected area are also beneficial.

If you experience back, hip, or knee problems, have a sports-medicine expert check for leg-length discrepancy before you spend a lot of money for other treatment. This is one of the most neglected causes of running injuries and one of the easiest to repair.

2. OLD INJURIES

Running may create a new problem from an old, forgotten injury. A person who suffered a severe ankle injury or had a childhood disease may have latent weaknesses that existed prior to running and that may be reactivated with the extra stress of running. The site of a previous injury may also prove to be a vulnerable area for a stress fracture. Scar tissue also develops from muscle tears caused by running or other sports, and you may experience recurring problems after you think the injury is healed. Bob Glover's old ankle sprains from his youthful basketball-playing days, and the big toe he once dropped a steel plate on, make periodic "comebacks" to trouble his running—even though the original injuries occurred 20 years ago!

3. POOR FLEXIBILITY AND OVERSTRETCHING

The vast majority of runners do not allow enough time for stretching. Ask any runner how much he or she stretches and the most common reply is, "Not as much as I should." From laziness or lack of discipline, we set ourselves up for injuries resulting from a lack of flexibility. Tight or shortened muscles are more easily injured than stretched muscles, and cause a variety of biomechanical problems.

In a few cases, runners can be too flexible. You may be naturally too flexible in the ankles, for example, which would make them more liable to pronate too much. Flexibility in the calf muscles can also lead to injury. In these cases, you may not benefit from stretching.

Overzealous or careless stretching can do more harm than good, and it has been blamed for many injuries. The fact is that stretching isn't to blame, but rather straining. Do not stretch injured muscles. Stretching an injured muscle will only aggravate it and delay healing. Leave it alone until tenderness and swelling disappear, then work gradually to improve its flexibility. If you have a recurring problem such as back pain, don't do any exercise that aggravates it.

4. MUSCLE IMBALANCE

It is important that muscles be strong and that opposing muscles have a proper balance of strength. The prime contracting or agonist muscles (buttocks, hamstrings, and calf muscles) become overdeveloped and tight with running. Stretching exercises for these muscles coupled with strengthening exercises for the opposing antagonist muscles are essential to restore muscle groups to proper balance. Otherwise, imbalances lead to injury. Strengthening exercises to prevent injuries include those for the abdominal muscles (easing back pain), shin area muscles (shin splints), and quadriceps in the thigh (hamstring and knee pain).

The competitive runner who regularly includes speed work, especially hill training, in his or her routine has less need for supplemental exercises for the quadriceps, buttocks, and other muscle groups because these types of runs build strength. But the competitive runner who runs aerobically, mostly on the flat, using the same muscle groups repetitively, is often prone to injury from muscle imbalance.

5. IMPROPER INJURY AND ILLNESS REHABILITATION

Take your time! Allow an injury to heal before running hard or long again, and don't resume training too soon after illness. Relapses are common, resulting in even more training time lost. Many serious injuries result from ignoring or favoring a minor injury. It is always wise to back off. Take your time off; you've earned it.

6. ERRORS IN RUNNING FORM

Technique is important for both fast running and healthy running. A pronounced forward lean will result in extra pressure on the lower leg. Leaning backward, "braking," will cause pressure on the back and hamstring muscles. Swaying side to side and running too "tight" may also cause injury. Overstriding—when your foot hits in front of your center of gravity—causes the surface to push your body back, and this stress often causes shin splints and stress fractures.

Heel-ball foot strike allows for increased shock absorption, but excessive hitting on the heel causes jarring and sometimes leg and back injury. Videotapes of leading runners in long-distance races reveal that most of these elite runners land ball-heel instead of heel-ball. Most of the back-of-the-packers, however, land heel-ball. Videotapes of injured average runners at the George Washington University Clinic and Sports Medicine Center reveal that they often cannot tolerate this ball-heel foot strike and tend to develop overuse injuries such as shin splints, calf tightness, and stress fractures.

When concerned about preventing injury, run heel-ball. When concerned about improving speed, run ball-heel; but be alert to warning signs of injury.

7. OVERTRAINING—TOO MUCH MILEAGE, SPEED, OR HILL WORK

Too much mileage too soon may be the leading cause of injury to all runners. In his studies, Dr. David Brody, medical director of the Marine Corps Marathon and an orthopedic surgeon, has found that injuries are most frequent among beginner runners and among all other runners who are trying to increase their mileage. Even if you build up your mileage gradually, beyond a certain point you may be unable to handle more. Dr. Lyle Micheli, director of the Division of Sport Medicine at Children's Hospital in Boston, adds that he sees "a real increase in injuries when people get beyond 50 miles a week in running. It's like a medical barrier. All kinds of problems develop, from tendonitis of the heels to irritation of the soles of the feet, to knee problems." The solution may be orthotics, or holding the mileage at a level below that which causes problems until the body is ready to accept more mileage. Most mileage-related injuries are minor and treatable. Risks can be minimized by using common sense and moderation—in getting started, in increasing distances, and in judging how much running is enough for you.

Pete Schuder is a frequent victim of what he calls "memory running." Good weather often finds him thinking about the good old days when he was a national class quarter-miler, and he finds himself training at higher mileage than his rusty chassis can handle. The "too much too soon" dilemma applies to both the runner on the way up and the runner coming back—or in Pete's case, over the hill.

Speed work helps you race faster. Unfortunately, it also increases your chance of injury. There is a very fine line between speed work that produces physiological benefits and that which causes injury. With experience, you will develop a feel for what is safe for you and still provides training benefits.

Be careful not to increase the speed of your training pace too rapidly. Sudden changes in the speed of your daily runs may result in fatigue and injury. Also, be careful when your pattern of training changes as, for example, where you find yourself regularly running with a group or individual much faster than you. Run the pace that is best for you.

Hill work is a specialized type of speed training. Sprints uphill place a severe stress on the lower leg and can cause low-back and hamstring injury. Keep away from hill workouts when your Achilles tendons, shins, or calves are troubling you or you are recovering from hard races or long runs.

Ease into this type of speed training, whether you are new at it or returning to it as preparation for a key race. Also, beware that sudden changes in the difficulty—hilliness—of your daily runs may cause injury. Be especially careful if you're ordinarily a flatlander and find yourself in a hilly section of the world while traveling.

Safety Note: Beware of the urge to train harder and harder after a few successful races. Restraint and common sense are as important as desire and hard work.

8. DOWNHILLS

Running downhill puts a severe strain on the body. According to Dr. David Costill, it "forces the leg muscles to do eccentric work. They stretch out much farther than normal. This causes a lot of minute tears in all the connective tissues." Much more shock is absorbed by your body at impact when running downhill. If you "brake" going downhill, you may cause the muscles along the backs of your legs and in your back to fight against gravity, creating additional stress. Downhill running, therefore, is especially hard on runners with knee or back problems. You should be relaxed and roll downhill with good form. Run ball-heel to minimize shock.

Racing downhills makes strain and stress that much more pronounced. In addition, the racer is prone to blisters and jammed toes caused by the foot sliding forward in the shoe. Stitches are another problem. After a race such as the Boston Marathon, known for its many downhills, you will find that your quads will be very sore from the straining they take racing downhills. If you're racing or training on downhills, wear well-cushioned shoes. Avoid practicing downhill racing technique unless you really need it to improve your position in races.

9. UNDERTRAINING

You must have the mileage base and speed training to be prepared for races. If you put in only 20 miles a week and then run a marathon, you are asking for injury. If you do all your running at 9-minute miles and then race at 6-minute miles, you're asking for injury. You may get away with it and reach the finish line, but the toll on your body could be serious. The collapse-point theory refers not only to falling apart in the race in terms of ability to keep pace, but also to risking musculoskeletal collapse by pushing the body beyond endurance levels for which it was prepared. Overtraining often causes you to break down before you reach the starting line. Undertraining often causes you to break down before you reach the finish line.

10. GREED: OVERRACING

You can stress yourself physically and mentally with too much racing. "Going to the well" once too often will cause injury or illness. Select your races wisely, space them wisely, and allow yourself to recover before applying the race stress again.

11. INADEQUATE RECOVERY

The training effect won't take place if you don't allow your body to recover from stress. Follow the hard-easy system of training. You may need additional easy days or even days off following stressful workouts and races. Allow much more time to recover from marathons.

12. SURFACES AND TERRAIN

Ideally, your runs should take place on slightly rolling courses, without too many steep uphills or downhills. The rolling terrain gives more muscle groups a workout while not taxing them.

It is generally good to change surfaces frequently; however, this may cause problems for some runners. In your daily routine, don't make sudden changes in surface. A medium-hard synthetic path, a dirt trail, or even level grass fields are the best training surfaces. But if you intend to run in road races, you're going to have to run the roads for training. Force yourself to train on pavement two or three times a week. (Conversely, if you run on roads a lot, try to take a break on a softer surface occasionally.)

Cement or concrete are harder than asphalt; you'll get less shock on the road than on the sidewalk. Switching from a very hard to a very soft surface late in a run, or the reverse, may cause injury. If possible, do your speed workout on soft trails with good footing or on a track where you'll get more shock absorption.

Also, beware of obstacles—ruts, rocks, loose or uneven turf, or holes—that may cause injury. They are just as dangerous as potholed streets. On paved surfaces, you face at least three dangers. First, running along sidewalks requires you to leap off the curbs, which increases the shock on the body. A fatigued runner may injure himself or herself; stress fractures occur this way. Second, most roads and sidewalks are banked or crowned for drainage. When you run on them, you are running along an incline; your upper foot is twisting inward with every step, and you're giving yourself a short leg. If possible, run in the middle of the road where it is more level, or cross over the road every mile or so. Strangely, some runners find that they can run on roadbeds slanted one way but not the other. If you go for a postrace run, don't go in the same direction as you raced. Your muscles will be tired and you'll be prone to injury running on the same slant. Third, watch out for vehicles. Common sense tells you to run facing traffic. But to alter your impact on a slanted road, you'll have to change that idea. Look for extra-wide aprons where you can safely do some running with the traffic.

Always run defensively. Watch every car, and be alert for zooming bikers, roller skaters, skateboarders, even other runners. Watch out for dogs—on and off leashes. Your best bet to avoid bumping into one of these dangers is to run only in the early morning in crowded parks or meridians popular with other activists.

Beach running may look tempting. Avoid it. In soft sand, your heels sink in and pull your Achilles tendons. On the firm, damp sand you run on a slant. Then there are seashells, broken glass, and driftwood to avoid.

Indoor running can be a blessing in the winter months, but it can also cause more trouble than it is worth. Since you are running around sharp turns, often on a slanted, hard surface, you are severely stressing the inside leg. Ideally, you would minimize injury by changing direction every five minutes, but this is usually impossible, since most tracks are crowded. Therefore, you should limit your indoor runs to 30 to 45 minutes.

Speed work can be helpful indoors if you really must sharpen for a race and all the roads are full of ice and snow. When confined indoors for your speed training, cut back on the intensity and number of repetitions to minimize stress on your legs. One of the leading causes of injury to top college athletes is intense training on indoor tracks with tight turns. Competitive road runners, unaccustomed to such tracks, are even more prone to injury. Save your hard track work for spring, when you can run more safely outdoors as you sharpen for key races.

Some injuries require that you run on certain surfaces. Achilles tendon problems, for example, require even, hard surfaces that don't create a pull on the damaged tendon. Knee injuries, on the other hand, are aggravated by hard surfaces. Running on trails or grass may lessen the shock to your body and strengthen muscles not used on hard surfaces. This may alleviate fatigue and injury. However, don't run on soft, uneven surfaces when injured, or you may aggravate a leg injury: the soft surface puts the leg through a greater range of motion than a hard surface.

For most of us, it is impossible to avoid the roads, and thus we must learn to adjust to them, especially since that is where we race. Using an efficient stride and well-cushioned shoes, the runner with good flexibility who follows a sensible training program should not worry about the hardness of the road ahead. Just pack in the injury-free miles.

13. WEATHER

Cold

The cold-weather runner is less flexible and thus more vulnerable to injury. The main weather-related cause of injuries is poor footing during winter months. According to Dr. Paul Taylor, winter running injuries most often come from being tight when trying to guard against slipping. Tense muscles, whether consciously or unconsciously tightened, are more prone to strains and other overuse injuries. The runner usually alters his or her running form to increase traction, which leads to further problems. Lateral foot slippage also occurs on icy spots, and if the foot slips, a pulled muscle or tendon may result. Running in a few inches of snow forces you to work muscles normally not taxed. If your quadriceps become fatigued, knee injury could result. Beware of the obvious—if you slip and fall, try to land lightly and then immediately stop your run and put ice on the injured area.

The most common winter running injuries are groin and hamstring pulls caused by slipping and sliding through the snow. These nagging injuries require rest, or they will still be with you when the snow has melted.

Training must go on, with or without dry surfaces. The best prevention is to make sure you warm up well, maintain good flexibility, and run relaxed, not allowing yourself to tense up out of fear of falling. When running on slippery surfaces, shorten your stride slightly and shuffle along, maintaining good balance. Be especially careful on downhills and turns and when running in the dark, when you can't see where your feet are landing. Don't attempt fast running under slippery conditions. Studded shoes that aren't overly worn are the best in snow—just like the snow tires you put on your car for better traction. In the fall, be wary of wet leaves, which can be just as slippery as ice.

Cold weather brings the danger of frostbite and hypothermia. To prevent frostbite, keep covered, keep dry, keep moving. Frostbite can result in the loss of fingers or toes and has even caused death. Frostbitten skin is cold, pale and firm to hard to the touch. The first step in treatment is to warm rapidly without excessive heat. Use water at about body temperature. Do not massage or, in the case of toes, walk on the injured area. Do not run with snow. Take the frostbitten runner immediately to where he or she can get medical aid.

The danger of cold includes the wind, which when combined with air temperature produces the "windchill factor." Running into the wind lowers the windchill factor, while running with the wind may speed you along to produce a sweat. Therefore, begin your runs into the wind on out-and-back courses. Otherwise you'll build up a good sweat with the wind at your back and then turn into the biting wind for the return, which may cause frostbite or at least extreme discomfort.

Hypothermia is the lowering below normal of the central or core temperature of the body. As the temperature falls, the body responds with shivering, which is the muscles' attempt to produce heat. If not attended to, the runner could next become incoherent and then lapse into a coma, even die. Hypothermia usually strikes when you are wearing wet clothing. If your clothes are soaked from getting splashed with slush or if you sweat too much from overdressing, you should change right away rather than keep going. Take off wet clothing immediately after running, or hypothermia may strike you.

Follow these guidelines for training and racing in the cold:

• It's never too cold to train, but exceptionally cold weather makes racing times slower and is very uncomfortable.

• Let someone know where you are going and when you expect to return.

• Dress in layers that can be easily adjusted. You can always remove a layer if you get too warm and tie it around your waist. The key is to trap the heat naturally produced by the body. Wear up to three layers, four if it is extremely cold. Two layers are enough for most racing conditions. The innermost layer should be absorbent and nonirritating, such as a cotton T-shirt. Polypropylene undergarments are very lightweight and transmit moisture away from the body, allowing your inside layer, and you, to remain dry and warm. The second insulating layer is usually a long-sleeved turtleneck or a hooded wool sweatshirt, or long underwear. The outer shell is usually designed to break the wind. A nylon windbreaker or the newer Gore-Tex fabrics, which "breathe" better than nylon and repel water as well as wind, are most often used. Most of the time, the inner layer plus a turtleneck are enough for racing.

The legs usually stay warm with one layer of clothing. If two layers are needed, try tights, long wool underwear, or polypropylene bottoms under sweatpants or nylon windbreakers. For racing, tights or long underwear covered by shorts to help protect the privates are preferred.

• Keep the extremities covered. Mittens are warmer than gloves. An old pair of wool socks will do just fine. Make sure the wrists are covered. Ears should be protected by a ski cap or wool headband. The most important area to keep warm is the head. As much as 50 percent of body heat is lost through the head, as through a chimney. In extremes of cold, a ski mask may be used to keep the face and nose warm. Coating your face with petroleum jelly will also help.

• Feet endure best. Wool running socks are excellent and all you need. If you keep moving and don't get wet, your feet won't get cold.

• If you get hot when training or racing, remove your hat

first (tuck it in your shorts), then your mittens, then unzip your outer layer, and then remove it and tie it around your waist. As you cool, replace this clothing in opposite order.

• Be prepared—dress properly. Be flexible. On a single run the conditions may change several times. Don't toss away your gloves and hat when you are racing unless you are positive you won't need them again.

• There is great danger not only in underdressing, but also in overdressing. You should open your clothing as soon as sweat starts to build up. You will get cold much more quickly in sweat-soaked clothing.

Heat

Running in hot weather can be trouble; racing in it can be dangerous. The effects of heat on long-distance running mustn't be taken lightly. Problems you face may include muscle cramps, blisters, and fatigue. The symptoms of heat exhaustion include profuse sweating, dizziness, weakness, and dehydration. With a further increase in body temperature, often exceeding 105°F, heat exhaustion may be followed by heat stroke, which can be fatal. Listen to the warning signs of heat: headache, dizziness; disorientation; nausea; decrease in sweat rate; pale, cold skin. Don't try to run through these symptoms. Stop, walk, or rest. Find shade and pour water on yourself immediately, and seek medical help. If these symptoms develop after the race, lie down, raise your legs, and ask for help.

Air temperature is one factor to consider when running. Humidity is another. The key to regulating body temperature in hot weather is sweat evaporation, which accounts for as much as 90 percent of heat removal. Under very humid conditions, little sweat can vaporize; it is difficult for the body to lose heat. An air temperature of 60°F with 95 percent humidity could be more dangerous than a temperaure of 90°F in a dry climate. A head wind facilitates evaporation, but a tail wind eliminates most of the air flow over the skin and therefore reduces sweat evaporation and heat loss. The position of sun and clouds is also a factor. Direct sunlight at high noon results in a rapid rise of body heat; cloud cover, of course, shields the runner.

The runner must understand that he or she can only partially adjust to heat. You cannot run faster in heat, so the next choice is to prepare yourself to be more competitive in the heat then the other runners. Heat affects some runners more than others and even affects the same runner differently on different days. Since serious runners must train in the heat and often are forced to race in it, they should make adjustments in their training and racing in order to achieve their goals. The following guidelines to running in the heat apply to all runners, regardless of level of ability:

Be in Shape. An unconditioned runner places an extra burden on his or her body by running in the heat.

Avoid the Heat. If you don't plan to race in it, don't train in it. Run during the cool of the early morning or late evening. Look for running paths that are shaded, and run on the shady side of the road.

Run in the Heat. Acclimate yourself to the heat. Allow 10 to 14 days of slowly progressive training to get used to new heat conditions. Run at least a few times a week in the heat of the day if you intend to race in the heat. If you live in a cool area and must race in a warmer area, you can "heat train" by running three or four times a week for several weeks in double sweats to create an artificial heat stress. Don't run in a rubber suit, however, since it is not properly ventilated.

Adjust Your Pace. Start out more slowly and run a steady pace in both training runs and races. You may need to adjust your starting pace for races by as much as a minute and make further reductions in pace along the way. Run within yourself and try to outsmart your opponents rather than trying to outrace them *and* the heat. The result is likely to be disastrous if you challenge the heat.

Adjust Your Distance. On a hot, muggy day, forget your planned long run—cut it short and reschedule it for a cooler day. In the summer months, choose shorter races, preferably 10K and less.

Keep Your Body Wet. During runs and races, pour water over your head. Use sponges to douse your body with water. During workouts, dunk your shirt in water and drape it over your head and shoulders. Ice is great on hot days. Put it under your hat, and just let it melt. Or rub it across the base of your neck and under the arms.

Drink Plenty of Liquids. Do this before, during, and after your workouts and races.

Run on Cool Surfaces. Hot pavement burns your feet, and the heat from the road pushes your temperature up. Try running on the dirt shoulders. Search for dirt or grass surfaces. Pavement sprinkled with water is cooler.

Keep Cool Before and After Your Race. Warm up and cool down in the shade. Try to keep your body temperature as low as possible before racing, and bring it down as quickly as possible after.

Dress Carefully. In direct sunlight, provide the body with shade. Wear white or other bright colors that reflect the sun. A hat should protect your head and shoulders. It should be white, lightweight, and well ventilated.

On exceptionally sunny days, wear a full, loose-fitting T-shirt, not a tank top, to protect your shoulders. Cotton is better than nylon because it absorbs water and "breathes" more readily.

14. SHOES AND ORTHOTICS

Running shoes designed to prevent injury often contribute to it. While the competitive runner owes his or her existence to the remarkable advances made by shoe manufacturers, and the massive running boom has been made possible by well-cushioned, flexible, and comfortable running shoes, it's also true that runners of all types are made to serve as guinea pigs for the shoe business.

According to Dr. Richard Schuster, running injuries vary year to year in response to the latest advances in running shoes. Changes in the flexibility of the shoe and the rigidity of the heel counter, for example, may help some runners but cause problems for others. As shoes get lighter with the use of new materials, the most common breakdown is a result of weak heel counters. The wide-flared heel, designed to prevent injury, caused widespread knee problems. The air shoe was a great improvement in increasing shock absorption, but it also aggravated knee problems because it allowed runners to pronate or supinate more than usual. The softer-soled running shoes created a similar problem and wore out faster doing it. Also, the heel sinks further down in the shoe, causing potential cases of Achilles tendonitis and shin splints.

To minimize injury, running shoes must offer flexibility, cushioning, support—and they must fit your feet. Monitor the wear of your shoes daily. Uneven wear of the soles will cause injury, as this affects the angle of your foot strike, causing your foot to roll abnormally. Also check for loss of support in the upper shoe.

When buying shoes, always purchase from a dealer who specializes in running shoes and can help you make the right selection. Always have two pairs of training shoes going at all times to minimize injuries. This way you won't get hurt trying to get a few extra miles out of an aging shoe as you break in a new one, or get blisters from having to rush a new shoe into service if your trusty shoes are lost or destroyed. If you try to resole your shoes or use shoe-saving devices, be careful that you don't overcompensate and cause injuries.

Should you own a pair of racing flats? A common mistake among runners is to wear racing flats when they are not necessary. The average competitor should use the same shoe for both racing and training. This is especially true for the heavy runner. A racing shoe gives less shock absorption and is designed for running on the ball of the foot. It also has less heel lift, and can lead to Achilles tendon injuries. Racing shoes should be worn only for shorter races at first, and then for races beyond 10 kilometers when you will be running at a pace much faster than your training pace. Use your racing shoes for occasional short runs and speed workouts to minimize the risk of injury when you switch to them for races. Many training shoes are now made light enough to be used for both racing and training.

Sudden switches to spikes can also cause injury, since they have very low heels and little cushioning, and force you to run on the balls of your feet. Many college cross-country coaches, including Pete Schuder, prefer studded flats for cross-country events. Pete also recommends them for 10K races on tartan tracks because he feels they are safer. Since most road racers would wear spikes only once or twice a year in competition, they're seldom worth the expense and injury risk.

The type of shoe you purchase may be determined by the kind of injury you are susceptible to. You may need a firm heel counter if you pronate and have a knee problem, or a flexible shoe if you have shin splints, or a very well-cushioned shoe if you have heel spurs, and so forth. Your sports-medicine specialist will guide you in a selection of shoes that will minimize your particular problem.

Faults in shoes may also cause injury. Look for good quality and check for bad: stitching that isn't properly secured, parts in the wrong position, heels that lean to one side, improper placement of the studs or waffles on the sole. In the shoe industry, unfortunately, a good thing isn't left alone. You can be certain that as soon as you've found your perfect running shoe, the manufacturer will stop making it. Or a good model will be "upgraded" next year and at a higher price. Old, trusty models don't stick around long.

Orthotics have become a status symbol. Glover was a running cripple when he was saved by a series of orthotic devices developed by Dr. Schuster. However, he has also seen runners with mild problems that became much worse after wearing orthotics. Before submitting to the expense of custom-made orthotics and the agony of adjustments—you must follow your doctor's advice for easing into them or you'll cause additional injury—first try exercise and commercial arch supports. Our friend in Vermont, Jack Shepherd, suffered from excruciating back and leg pain for a while. He bought a pair of ready-made orthotics, tried one, tried 'em both, the pain disappeared, and he wore the things until they wore out. Then he threw them away, and the pain never returned. You figure it out.

Dr. George Sheehan claims there are several reasons why orthotics fail to work: they are difficult to fit and mold; they impair the runner's flexibility; rear-foot correction is sometimes excessive; they need adjusting and runners don't bother following up with the adjustments. Badly fitted orthotics, Dr. Sheehan says, "can make you worse as well as better."

Pay attention as well to the shoes you wear when not running. Wearing training shoes all day, or even another pair of the same model, may make you susceptible to injury because of the lack of variety of stress. Wearing street shoes that have a hard surface may hurt your feet if you are used to wearing well-cushioned shoes. Dr. Hans Kraus, author of *The Causes, Prevention, and Treatment of Sports Injuries,* solves this problem by painting his running shoes black so he can wear them at the office. High-heeled shoes, for both men and women, are very bad for runners. Constantly wearing these shoes will shorten your Achilles tendon or create ankle problems. The competitive runner who wants to dress up and go dancing in high heels takes chances with his or her Achilles tendons and ankles. Wear lower heels—or dance barefoot. (Just be careful not to get stomped on by a nonrunner wearing spike heels.)

15. BODY WEIGHT

Many competitive runners, when in superb shape, weigh as much as 20 percent less than the average person of the same height. A very fit runner often looks very gaunt, but there is a fine line between looking underweight and feeling underweight. Your bone structure, metabolism, and personal preference will dictate what is too little or too much weight for you. Losing weight too rapidly may make you weak and ill; being underweight may have the same effect. However, says Dr. Edward Colt, an endocrinologist at New York City's St. Luke's Hospital, "The lighter you are, within certain limits, the less likely you are to become injured. The limits are set by your own constitution—each individual has an optimum weight below which he or she feels tired and becomes susceptible to infections." Dr. Colt considers excessive weight loss "a running injury" similar to the overtraining syndrome.

Being overweight is a well-known and well-documented problem. If you are 20 percent or more over your "ideal" weight, you must get your weight down before racing, to prevent injury. The overweight runner stresses the cardiovascular and musculoskeletal systems and isn't able to handle heat as well as slimmer running friends. The runner who is 30 pounds overweight slams the ground with 20 percent more force than normal. The heavier runner, whether overweight or just big boned, needs well-cushioned training shoes.

Bulimia and anorexia nervosa are psychiatric disorders that are becoming increasingly serious health problems in our stress-filled society. Bulimia is a fear of getting fat, for which the solution is to eat large amount of food and then induce vomiting. Anorexia is a refusal to eat almost anything at all, even though the individual is hungry and obsessed with food. The anorexic desires to achieve extreme thinness. Bulimia often leads to anorexia, or follows it once the anorexic has returned to eating.

These disorders mainly strike adolescent women from middle- to upper-class homes, but older women and men of all ages are also susceptible. According to Dr. David Herzog of the Eating Disorders Clinic at Massachusetts General Hospital in Boston, as many as one in five college students are believed to have bulimia. Sherrye Henry, Jr., a top cross-country runner at Yale University, conducted a survey at the Women's Ivy League Track and Field Championships. She found that women who ran 45 miles a week or more showed anorexic-type behavior, according to an Eating Attitudes Test (EAT) developed at the University of Toronto. Since sprinters and field-event athletes scored very low on the test, the survey suggests that long-distance runners are more prone to this illness than the average person and most other athletes.

As Sherrye Henry, who dropped from 120 to 90 pounds, concludes in an article in *The Runner:* "While there is no conclusive evidence that links anorexia nervosa to long distance running, as runners, we ought to remember that while thin is good, thinner is not always better. And in the case of a runner with anorexia, perfection can kill."

Most runners will find a good racing weight, however, and will have little trouble staying at that level.

16. INADEQUATE DIET

The well-balanced diet of fresh fruits, raw vegetables, and protein (but not too much meat) is recommended for runners. Some top runners, however, are notorious junk food addicts, but they pack that stuff in on top of a reasonably balanced diet.

Poor diet will cause immediate problems. The runner who doesn't eat enough carbohydrates and essential vitamins and minerals may find himself or herself feeling weak. Women runners are prone to anemia (for known medical reasons) and should take iron supplements as a precaution. A one-a-day general vitamin and mineral supplement may also be of value to all runners, even if they follow a good diet.

Avoid—and beware of—"special diets." Nothing that you ingest will make you faster. A lot of things you eat, or don't eat, may make you slower, however. Frances Sheridan Goulart noted in *The Jogger* that a low-calorie diet reduces your overall nutrient intake as well as your weight. Fewer calories mean less A, D, E, C, and B complex vitamins as well as sports-specific minerals like iron. A low-carbohydrate diet, by contrast, may produce fatigue, calcium depletion, dehydration, and/or hypoglycemia (low blood sugar).

If you eat and compete on a low-fat diet, you run the risk of depleting key fatty acids and may suffer impaired cellular function because of low levels of vitamins A, D, and E. On the other hand, if you reduce protein and emphasize carbohydrates, your body may go into negative nitrogen balance. The result is fatigue, from depletion of B vitamins. High-protein diets, however, may cause excessive losses of sodium and water and of whole-body energy reserves.

Dr. Edward Colt warned runners at a New York Road Runners clinic: "The healthy diet does not cause obesity, heart attack, colon cancer, diabetes, spastic colitis or appendicitis. The unhealthy diet does cause these disorders—at least there is much evidence to implicate it." Eat a balanced diet, and don't fool around with fads.

17. IMPROPER FOOT CARE

Treat your feet like good friends. Wash them daily in warm water, dry them thoroughly, and sprinkle them with anti-fungus powder. Fungus also feeds on dead skin tissue, so clean your feet with a nail brush, emery board, or pumice stone. It is also important to wear dry, clean socks. Corns, warts, infections, slivers, ingrown toenails, and the like should be taken care of immediately by your podiatrist.

Take care of blisters, and catch 'em when they're small. Blisters are caused by something rubbing—shoes that are too big or too small, abrasive socks, faults in shoe or sock stitching, downhill running, etc. Friction can be minimized by using a petroleum jelly (but don't destroy your leather orthotics with it), friction-reducing insoles, or talcum powder. If the blister is small and not painful, leave it alone. If it is large and painful and interferes with your running, stop running until you no longer favor it. Favoring a blister has been known to cause many knee and other injuries. Dr. Murray Weisenfeld knows his way around blisters and in his book *The Runner's Repair Manual* suggests the following operation (for those with a surgeon's hands):

Sterilize a razor blade, nail clippers, or scissors with antiseptic (usually alcohol). Make a small slit in the blister and press out the fluid. Clean the opening with antiseptic. With cotton, soak up the fluid. Cover the blister. Dr. Weisenfeld doesn't like Band-Aids because they are usully plastic and keep air out. He prefers a square of gauze with tape at the edges; at night, remove the gauze and let the blister air. Don't peel the cap off the blister. Let it wear off.

For basic foot care, Dr. Weisenfeld suggests talcum powder between the toes to absorb moisture and reduce friction (protecting against blisters). He suggests cream on your heels in fall and winter to prevent cracking, which can be very painful. Keep your toenails short; long nails jam into the front of your shoes, causing black toenail or ingrown toenails. Dr. Weisenfeld suggests cutting the nails straight across, not in a curve, to prevent ingrown toenail. Rub calluses with an emery board to reduce them. Very thick calluses should be removed by your podiatrist.

All of this will benefit your two friends down there. Treat your feet well and listen to 'em hum while you run.

18. POOR DAILY HABITS

A sudden change in daily habits can cause the runner problems, especially back pain or sciatica. You should be careful lifting heavy objects; always use your powerful legs to do the work and not your back. Sleeping on your back or stomach may also cause problems, and a pillow under your knees or hips respectively may help. Comfort is the key to sleeping correctly, but the preferred position is on your side, knees flexed—the fetal position. The bed should be very firm and a bed board should be placed under the mattress. Lifting and carrying around a baby may cause back pain in both men and women. There are also occupational hazards: standing or sitting too much, reaching, or lifting. A change in posture at home or office may be the cause of pain. If you spend a lot of time sitting, make sure you have good back support. If possible, elevate your feet regularly too.

Driving can cause tightened muscles, strains in the back, and tension. Pushing the gas pedal or clutch for long periods can cause leg, knee, and back pain for some runners. You may want to put a small pillow behind the small of your back for support, or move the driver's seat forward or back to find the most comfortable position. Not all runners find driving troublesome, but some do, and others don't realize that this can be the source of leg or back pain. Remember not to drive (or ride) for too long a period just before a race. If you have pain, always look for a change in personal habits as a possible cause.

19. STRESS

Stress is essential to life, but a cause of death. It is everywhere in our daily lives. It may be pleasant, damaging, or helpful. Its negative effect on our bodies may be long lasting, even occurring after the stressful event itself has ceased. What causes it? Work pressures, social readjustment, geographical change, a sudden surprising event. "Stress," says Dr. Hans Selye, author of *Stress Without Distress* and *The Stress of Life,* "is essentially the wear and tear in the body caused by life at any one moment."

There are various kinds of stress: emotional (from a family argument, the death of a loved one), environmental (from excessive cold or heat), and physiological (from an outpouring of the steroid hormones from the adrenal glands, which are extremely sensitive indicators of stress). Stress changes us physically and may cause a variety of medical ills, some imagined and some very real, painful, even lethal. Each period of stress, Dr. Selye says, especially from frustrating, unsuccessful struggles, leaves some irreversible chemical scars. When we are burdened beyond our stress tolerance, we become ill, or develop emotional problems, or suffer the physical breakdowns of athletes. Stress takes its physiological toll. Our emotions affect our muscles, and our muscles reflect our emotional problems. Dr. Selye and other medical authorities believe that most ailments, especially back pain, are the result of too much stress.

Some runners run with stress, carrying their tensions visibly during a workout. They run with tight muscles, tense and high shoulders, and short, choppy strides. They are too busy to relax, warm up, stretch, and begin running slowly before beating their bodies into the hard-paved roads. They think cooling down is for other runners and risk serious injury by forgoing that series of exercises too. They often pay the penalty of tight calves and hamstrings, as well as back pain.

In the beginning, as you take up the sport of running, the exercise helps you cope with stress. But after you get into competitive racing, it can become an additional stress that may overwhelm you. Stress, whether caused by the drive to become a better runner or by external factors, makes you vulnerable to illness and injury.

Dr. Hans Kraus, author of *Backache, Stress, and Tension,* notes that "tension is the root of all evil." When faced with such stresses as marriage, a baby, lack of sleep, final exams, pressures at work, etc., the runner must adjust his training—back off the mileage and speed work and maybe skip the big race. Take a "time out," and just run for relaxation and stress management rather than for competitive training. Otherwise you risk not only poor performances but serious injury or illness.

20. INADEQUATE SLEEP

Beginning runners often find that they sleep better; perhaps they even need less sleep than the average of about 7½ hours. But as you start training competitively, you may find just the opposite: that you require more sleep than average, perhaps up to 10 hours a day. Many elite runners take regular naps between daily workouts.

The average runners can't do this because running isn't their job. They often find themselves saving time for other duties by stealing sleep time with late-night runs—which may leave them too tired to get to sleep—or they may awaken very early in order to pack in miles before work. If you lose sleep, remember: you can't burn the candle at both ends. You will destroy yourself if you don't back off for a few days until your body recovers.

Sleep patterns are important. You develop a regular rhythm of sleeping and waking. If this rhythm is disrupted, stress results and you will be more susceptible to injury and illness.

. Some runners require more sleep than others. Some require much more when training hard. When a runner overtrains, he or she frequently develops insomnia. He or she gets to sleep easily, but wakes up often during the night and frequently has trouble getting back to sleep. When the warning signs of overtraining hit you, take a break and get some rest. Fatigue tends to accumulate quickly if you don't sleep enough, leaving you susceptible to illness and injury and feeling stale. If you can't get enough sleep, back off your training. Sleepless nights, for whatever reason, must be followed by easy days and lots of sleep. Otherwise you'll end up having plenty of time to sleep, because you won't be running at all.

If you keep accumulating a sleep deficit night after night, warns Dr. Julius Segal of the National Institute of Mental Health, you are in for serious physical and psychological consequences. Adequate sleep is essential. "We sacrifice it," notes Segal, "at considerable peril to our bodies and minds."

21. OTHER SPORTS

Runners sometimes injure themselves playing other sports. For example, a member of a New York Road Runners class once complained of a pain in his chest. Remembering a similar problem he had faced in the past, Bob Glover asked if he had been playing other sports recently. Sure enough, the cause was identified. He had caught a few elbows playing basketball, which had never bothered him in his prerunning days, but running and breathing hard aggravated the otherwise undetectable injury. The beating you take in other sports is magnified by the pounding of running.

When you reach the competitive level of running, you have to decide which other sports you want to do and what the benefits and risks might be. Downhill skiing, basketball, soccer, tennis, handball, and other activities, while fun, carry the risk of sprains and breaks that may take months to heal. And besides such obvious risks of injury, these activities may contribute to injuries in a way you may not readily identify.

When combining running with other sports, follow the basic principles discussed in chapter 3. Don't forget your warm-up and cool-down routine. Many runners who faithfully stretch before running neglect this important principle before playing sports such as tennis, and end up straining muscles. Never do hard workout days in other sports and then race or do speed workouts the next day. Also, don't play other sports in running shoes—they are not made for lateral movement, and you can easily turn your ankles and put strain on your knees. If you want to participate in other sports as well as maximize your potential as a runner, be very moderate in your activity. You should do much *less* of another sport than you can handle in terms of heart and lung conditioning because your muscles will not tell you that you have overdone it until it is too late—a day or two later.

22. AGE AND SEX

As we age, our bodies betray us. We recover more slowly from long or hard runs, and we require more easy days. If the aging runner—even in his or her 30s or 40s—doesn't adjust, injury results. As we age, we become more brittle, more inflexible, and gradually lose muscle strength—thus, we are more injury prone. The gradual loss of bone mass—especially in women— increases the risk of fractures and retards the healing of bone injuries. Our ability to regulate body temperature also decreases, which makes us more susceptible to heat stroke and frostbite. Dr. Murray Weisenfeld finds that his older patients are more prone to heel-spur formation but generally have fewer injuries than younger runners. Maybe they are wiser. Older newcomers are usually more cautious, and wily veterans of the roads have experienced every possible injury and know how to hold them off.

Young runners are susceptible to disease where tendons attach to bones at the heel and the knee. These soft plates—called apophyses—are involved with growing. The plates gradually close with adolescence, but serious damage to them can stunt growth. Some medical people are concerned that very young runners who try long-distance running can be seriously injured; others find little scientific justification for that concern. Dr. Weisenfeld has found that 10–12-year-olds often develop a separation at the heel bone, usually because they hit too hard on their heels, or their shoes lack proper cushioning in the heels. Girls age 11 to 14, and slightly older boys, are prone to Osgood-Schlatters disease, which is a separation of the epiphyseal line where the head of the tibia meets the shaft of the tibia.

The incidence of injuries to women is no greater than to men. As Dr. Leslie S. Matthews of Baltimore's Union Memorial Hospital Sports Medicine Center joked, "Women are equally entitled to athletic injury." Most injuries women suffer are sports related, not gender related, he said. Common female-related injuries are pelvic fractures—because of the fact that women have a broader pelvis—and groin injuries. Dr. Weisenfeld also sees a lot of injuries from wearing high-heeled shoes. Besides the Achilles tendon and calf injuries that one would expect, these women often develop calluses and pain under the ball of the foot. When you wear high heels, your weight is placed on the ball instead of the padded heel, which results in the wearing down of the padding under the ball of the foot. Running hard, especially when you have to get up on the balls of the feet, can then cause injury.

23. POOR ADVICE

Everyone gives medical advice to runners. You can go to an orthopedist, podiatrist, chiropractor, physical therapist, osteopath, running coach, trainer, or running buddy. You can be Rolfed, have your foot held and massaged, join a group standing on its head. Your running friends and enemies, even your sedentary grandmother, will freely offer advice.

Beware. There are no quick cures. Sports-medicine experts pop up everywhere. Instant coaches are a national nuisance. Remember: If you ask people for advice, they will give it. A coach's job is to keep you healthy, not to help you run faster at all costs. A running friend may mean well but know nothing. Every runner and every coach has his or her own system. You need to develop your own system, gradually, through your own experiences. In the meantime, follow the commonsense guidelines of highly recognized experts.

A competent medical person will refer you to another source if he or she has been unable to help you or feels that your specific problem should be handled by a specialist. Beware of doctors who don't run, or who have all the answers, or who set up running programs for you. Doctors shouldn't coach, and coaches shouldn't doctor. In the long run, follow any advice only after thinking about it carefully.

24. MARATHONITIS

> WARNING; THE SURGEON GENERAL HAS DETERMINED THAT MARATHON RUNNING IS DANGEROUS TO YOUR HEALTH!

This statement, like those on cigarette packages, should be stamped across the toes of every running shoe. Too many people are training for and running in marathons before they are prepared. Hundreds of men, women, and children each year take up running after watching or hearing about a marathon. They take it up specifically to run a marathon. Incredible, but true! For most, there is no in-between. It is all or nothing— 26.2 miles or bust. For many of them it's bust. Very few who take up running and racing can escape the lure. It's like a magnet. You are driven to meet the ultimate challenge—as hyped by the media and all those veterans of the marathon wars.

We constantly urge beginner runners to wait several years before running a marathon. But too many runners attempt the distance during their first year of training. Patience! We prefer a much longer period of buildup and adjustment.

Actually, marathons themselves cause few injuries. But overmileage or improper preparation wipes out thousands of runners. At the New York Marathon, more than 2,000 runners out of the 20,000 accepted for the prestigious race never get to the starting line even though their racing numbers are worth their weight in gold. They were injured. Any sports-medicine person in a city with a big marathon will acknowledge the increase in patients for several weeks before and after a marathon. Those who get injured during the marathon are mostly undertrained runners or those who ran with injuries against their doctors' advice and aggravated them. An additional problem is that injuries developed or aggravated en route are most often ignored during the marathon. In a shorter race the runner would probably drop out, but the marathoner feels obligated to suffer, since it is part of the glory.

The majority of veteran marathoners would be best off limiting their marathons to two or three a year—two or less for less experienced racers. This event is not a joke. It hurts. Proper training and preparation are essential. For some, their body type precludes running a marathon. But for too many, the pressure from their friends proves too much to resist. They should heed the above warning. Or take the advice of a running friend who was undertrained for his first New York Marathon and finished in pain. "All I looked foward to those last torturous miles was having a warm bath and a cold beer," he notes. His solution the following year: "I watched it on TV and then had a warm bath and a cold beer."

By the way, why didn't Pheidippides "listen to his body" and stop at 10 kilometers?

DONATING BLOOD

Physiologists have found that physical performance decreases by approximately 30 percent and maximal oxygen uptake by about 13 percent when 800 cubic centimeters of blood are removed. You feel the biggest effect the second day. It takes

2 weeks for maximum oxygen capacity to return to normal. The effect of withdrawing a pint (500 cubic centimeters) would be less, but still significant. If you choose to donate blood, which we encourage, make sure you do so during a period of your training when you are taking it easy and won't be racing or doing hard workouts or heavy mileage.

33. PREVENTION AND MANAGEMENT OF INJURY AND ILLNESS

Prevention of injury and illness means eliminating their causes and reacting to their warning signs. Most injuries and illnesses can be prevented, but once they occur you must treat the cause, treat the injury, and rehabilitate your body in order to return to competitive fitness.

WARNING SIGNS

Many running-related injuries and illnesses can be prevented, either by minimizing the causes or by adjusting to the warning signals our bodies send us. The physical and mental symptoms of overstress and impending injury or illness warn us to take heed. As Dr. George Sheehan preaches, "Listen to your body, it will tell you when you are doing too much, when you are close to injury."

Here are some of the warning signs your body may give you:

1. Mild tenderness or stiffness that doesn't go away after a day of rest or after the first few miles of your daily run. Any indications that your musculoskeletal system has been over-taxed.

2. A desire to quit or an unexplained poor performance

in workouts and races. Also, an uncharacteristic lack of interest in training, racing, and life in general.

3. A tired feeling after a full night's sleep or a sluggish feeling that continues for several days. You may also have difficulty falling asleep, or may wake up often in the night and find it difficult to go back to sleep.

4. An increase in your morning pulse rate. Record your pulse in your diary each morning—take it when you first wake up. Note significant increases as a sign that you haven't recovered from the previous day or days of stress. A pulse ten or more beats higher for the average runner and five or more beats higher for the highly trained runner is an indication of trouble.

5. A continued thirst despite replacement of fluids lost after your run. Check your urine. Normal urine is almost clear and odorless. A runner who is dehydrated will pass a darker urine.

6. A significant loss of body weight as measured each morning. A temporary loss of a few pounds from sweating is normal. Check your weight daily and record it in your diary. A sudden loss of two or more pounds is not normal—fluid weight loss should be replaced by morning.

7. The feeling of a sore throat, fever, or a runny nose coming on, which may indicate your susceptibility to a cold or flu. Any signs that your body is fighting infection. Also, skin blemishes and cold sores.

8. Muscle cramping (resulting from mineral depletion).

9. Upset stomach, diarrhea, constipation, or loss of appetite.

10. Increased irritability, feelings of tension, depression, and apathy—a sure sign of the overtraining syndrome.

Respond to any of these warning signs by cutting back your mileage, minimizing or eliminating your speed work, getting more sleep, and taking off a day or two. If the symptoms persist, seek medical attention as a precaution. Don't be cheap here: you'll save on medical bills in the long run by seeking help early.

The most obvious warning sign is *pain*. Pain is a sure warning of something wrong. Pain should be heeded. Your body yells at you for a reason—without pain signals you would continue to train and more serious injury would result. Runners can push through *discomfort.* There's a difference. Injury and illness cause pain. Oxygen debt and muscle fatigue are discomfort barriers that runners can push through. But pain is the early warning of injury and must not be ignored. Try to push through the discomfort of hard training and racing, but not through the pain signals of injury and illness. While training and racing, runners should listen to their bodies, not try to prove toughness by running through an injury or attempting to ignore it. To prevent injuries, therefore: (1) eliminate the causes; (2) back off your training and racing when warning signs appear.

Most early warning signs will be mild. Don't ignore them. Too many runners—especially men—feel that cutting back, resting, taking time off, makes them seem weak. Don't stop running at every muscle twitch, but balance your observation. Watch for what troubles you or gives you pain. Act wisely. Sometimes you can run through the stresses of competitive training and racing. But if you err, err on the side of caution. When in doubt—back off.

One helpful device is the running diary. Enter into it all of your discomforts and pains, your warning signs, plus the training and racing information. This record will not only help you train in a consistent and injury-free pattern, but it will also help you note when pain or discomfort lasts a long time. Our memories on these matters are unreliable. A detailed diary will often reveal the cause of injury and illness. Rereading your past experiences will help prevent future problems.

Perhaps the wisest way to prevent injury is occasionally to take a few days or even weeks off from serious training before major warning signs appear. By choosing to take time off, rather than being forced to by injury, you are giving your body a well-deserved rest without having to suffer physical and mental pain. You will have made an investment in your health by heading off an injury "at the pass."

FOUR SPECIAL ILLNESSES

1. Colds

Running won't protect you from the common cold, which is transmitted by hand contact with an infected person or object.

You are more likely to catch a cold by shaking hands than by kissing. The cold is also one of the early warning signs of over-training and emotional stress: during the Olympic Games, most of the visits to physicians by the athletes are for treatment of the common cold. Stress, poor nutrition, and contact with an infected person all lead to colds. At the Olympic Games, colds easily spread through the village filled with fatigued, highly stressed runners. Moral: Olympians should kiss more, shake hands less.

Easy running at a slow pace may break up the symptoms of a minor cold. Vigorous exercise during infection or fever, how-ever, is not a good idea. If your temperature is more than 100°F, you are better off not exercising at all. After the fever breaks, wait for the sore throat phase to pass before resuming your running. It usually takes 5 to 7 days for the cold to run its course. Remember, when you have a cold, cut back your mile-age, slow down your pace, and run within the limitations of your energy.

When you resume, if you don't notice any daily improvement in your health and running, stop and rest more. Do not train hard until you have completely recovered. However, coughing after you run is normal, doctors tell us, a reaction to deep breathing that can help clear your lungs.

You'll be surprised how quickly you can lose your endurance. After a cold or flu, the results may be even more discouraging than after a layoff resulting from injury. A University of Upp-sala (Sweden) study shows that colds with muscle pain often keep competitors from regaining full strength for more than 4 months. Remember: If you don't take time off and care for that cold, your layoff period will be much longer, or you may injure yourself in other ways. Sometimes you should look upon a cold as a blessing: since you probably caught it from over-training, it will force you off your feet and into bed, where you cannot injure yourself—at least not from running.

A cold may be a symptom that your body is drained physi-cally, mentally, or emotionally. Frequent colds for a runner may indicate overtraining. If you decide to go out and run when you have a cold, it could become worse and even develop into something more complicated, like bronchitis. The rapid onset of fatigue could also lead to a variety of injuries.

A cold is a virus. Antibiotics will not help: they kill bacteria, not viruses. Medications—sprays, "tiny time capsules," cold remedies—may do more harm than good. They may provide temporary relief, but may also delay return to full health. There are lots of healthful and well-meaning remedies that many runners swear by and that may offer various benefits: chicken soup, peppermint and elder flower tea, wheat germ oil, vitamin C, Mexican food, bee pollen, even acupuncture. We suggest rest, little or no running, lots of natural fruit juices or water, aspirin, a humidifier to increase moisture in the room (if your nose is feeling stuffed up), and even a nice steam bath. Remember the three R's here: rest, relax, recover.

2. The Flu

Fever and flu are more dangerous than the common cold. The body is weak and cannot tolerate the stress of running. When the flu bug hits, your only interest is, and should be, survival. You won't want to run. Running with fever and flu, says Dr. Sheehan, can be dangerous. "Sudden death can occur if the virus is also affecting the heart muscle, which it frequently does."

The rule of thumb is to expect to feel terrible as long as your fever lasts, and then take twice that time to overcome the flu symptoms. Take your time getting out to run. In fact, a walk-run program for a week or so might be wise until your strength returns. Then start your runs slowly and return gradually. When you come back, it is often difficult to determine if you feel tired from physical reasons or mental, because you still *think* you are sick. Dr. Sheehan advises testing yourself to see if you are ready to run yet: "Start your runs very slowly until you reach the point where you start to sweat. This usually takes about six minutes. At this point, you should feel like running no matter how you felt in the beginning. If you don't and five more minutes confirms it, pack it in." Relapses from the flu are common, and weakness caused by the flu can also lead to other injuries.

The body weakened by heavy training may be more vulnerable to the flu virus. Despite your high level of fitness, it can still knock you off your feet. Flu viruses spread rapidly, and many strains are highly contagious. Treatment is similar to that of a cold; antibiotics may be necessary to fight off related infections.

3. The Stitch

There may be no other pain that strikes the runner with the suddenness and devastation of the stitch—a.k.a. the dreaded side stitch. Sometimes it feels like a knife jabbed into the edge of your rib cage, hips, or shoulders; almost always it occurs when you're running hard and ceases when you slow down or stop. The stitch can be both prevented and treated on the run.

The actual cause of the stitch remains unknown. Dr. Gabe Mirkin theorizes that the stitch occurs "when the diaphragm is deprived of oxygen supply due to an obstruction of blood flow caused by pressure from the lungs above and the abdomen below." The result is a spasm in the diaphragm. Another theory is that the diaphragm is forced downward as the lungs and heart work hard, distending the ligaments that connect the diaphragm to the skeleton.

The cause, however, may be traced to one of the following possibilities:

Faulty Breathing. "Belly breathing" is the proper way of breathing on the run. Improper breathing often results in a strain on the diaphragm. You should practice "belly breathing" in your workouts.

Sometimes stitches occur in races when you start "panic breathing"—pushing hard to catch another runner, or to hold one off. Even when you strain harder, you must learn to breathe relaxed, belly out.

Weak and Tense Abdominal Muscles. Diaphragm cramps can be prevented with strengthening and stretching exercises. These should be done daily, not just when the stitch strikes. There are three exercises that will help:

A. Bent-knee sit-ups. Or for advanced sit-ups, put your feet against a wall, cross your arms, and grasp opposite elbows. Exhale, pull your chin to your chest so your head lifts off the floor, contract the stomach to lift your upper chest; release by laying one vertebra at a time back down on the floor.

B. Wall push-ups. Stand several feet from the wall; lean forward, put hands on the wall, and do ten or more push-ups against it.

C. Backward bend. Cup hands behind head; raise elbows as high as possible; bend slowly backward to the point of maximum extension of torso. Repeat thirty times.

Exercises should be repeated daily. It will take several weeks to condition the diaphragm and stomach properly.

Running Too Soon After Eating. Food in your stomach requires blood to be pumped to the intestinal tract to aid digestion. When running, your muscles need more oxygen, and blood supply to the intestines may be diminished, resulting in intestinal cramps. Each person's system dictates how long before running he or she can eat and avoid stitches. The range is from 2 to 6 hours.

Gas. According to Dr. Mirkin, the lower intestine forms gas during the breakdown of food. Exercise speeds up intestinal contractions and pushes the gas toward the rectum. If the gas cannot be passed because hard stools are in the way, the colon stretches like a balloon and a stitch occurs.

Diet and Constipation. Improper diet can lead to constipation and belly pains. Too much sugar and starches may contribute to a stitch; some people have an intolerance for milk or wheat products. Greasy foods, such as bacon or french fries, can also burden you.

Fluid Intake. Drinking very cold water during strenuous exercise has been known to cause a stitch. Also, commercial drinks may cause stitches in some runners. During the Avon International Women's Marathon in Ottawa, Atalanta's Marilyn Hulak charged from 30th place to a few yards out of 10th place late in the race, and then got a side stitch. It may have been caused by the tension of pushing toward the top, but Coach Glover theorized that it was something other than Marilyn's race that did her in. Race officials had put out water cups with plastic lids and straws, and while this made drinking more efficient, pulling water through a straw draws in more air—and thus produces gas. This, together with pushing on downhills, Glover feels, caused the problem.

Downhills. Stitches often appear when you pick up the pace or after a hard downhill stretch that jars the tight muscles in your abdomen. Some runners are very prone to stitches when they drink cold water and then race downhill. Running downhill, you should not let your arms come up, or lean back, or land too hard on your heels. All of these movements put more pressure on, and cause jarring of, fatigued abdominal muscles. Relax running downhill and remember to belly breathe.

Improper Warm-up. Before your hard runs, stretch your abdominal muscles and jog easily. Then do some pickups to prepare your body for the sudden heavy breathing.

Starting Too Fast. This may put you into oxygen debt and place an added burden on your diaphragm muscles. Start within your fitness level and gradually build to your race pace.

Fitness Level. Stitches are more common among beginner runners and racers than among veterans, owing to the vets' stronger cardiorespiratory systems and abdominal muscles. The competitive runner, however, often finds himself or herself undertrained—trying to run longer or faster than he or she has trained for. The result is often a stitch. These runners should run at race pace or faster once or twice a week to minimize stitches caused by the stress of competitive racing on their bodies. You are most prone when race day tension and excitement is combined with hard running.

Dr. Mirkin adds that if you develop a stitch, you should decrease the pressure on the lungs and abdomen enough to let blood flow back into your diaphragm. To do this, he suggests that you stop running and empty your lungs by pursing your lips and blowing hard. This should release air trapped in your lungs. To relieve abdominal pressure, bend over and raise your knee on the stitch side while pressing yor fingers deep into the painful area. The pain will usually disappear, and you can continue running.

If you get a stitch during a race, however, you may not want to stop. You might try several options:

• As you run, bend over as much as you can and press the stitch with the fingers of your hand. This sometimes relieves the pain.

• Try the George Sheehan-Ted Corbitt method. They suggest breathing out against a slight resistance—belly breathing—

even if you groan a little. Listening to Sheehan and Corbitt, a former Olympic marathoner, during a race is unpleasant, but they claim it works, and they pass other runners as they moan and groan, grasping at their sides. Try breathing in very deeply and noisily. Exhale deeply with a groan. Don't be shy. Your PR may be at stake.

Some runners find that doubling their rate of breathing rids them of the dreaded stitch. Others raise their arms overhead, breathe deeply, expand their stomachs, and, as they lower their arms, exhale loudly and contract their stomachs. (This is no time to worry about appearances!) Still other runners slow their pace until the pain subsides or stop running and lie on their backs, raising arms overhead.

• A few runners get away with not thinking about the pain, and continuing. Try thinking about something else or talking to the runner next to you. A magical minority do something bizarre: Jim Ferris, a former training mate of Bob Glover and ex–University of Oregon runner, used to cure his side stitches by doing a quick somersault in the middle of a race. It worked—and really "psyched out" the opposition.

Toughing it out may be the option of last resort. Just remember that no one has ever died from a side stitch, although you may feel you are going to be the first. If you have tried all the treatments and eliminated all the causes and are still troubled by the stitch—check with a doctor. You may have internal problems that should be handled medically.

1. The Overtraining Syndrome, and the Blahs

Competitive running involves stress, and stress involves a three-step process. Step one is the stress of training. Step two is the buildup of resistance (training effect) as a response to the stress. This will not take place unless stress is balanced with recovery. Step three must be avoided: overstress and exhaustion.

The overtraining syndrome may be the biggest medical problem doctors see from competitive runners. The basic symptom is a breakdown of some kind: cold, flu, nagging injury, running performance. Overtraining lowers resistance to disease; the runner may lose interest in training, have trouble eating or sleeping, find it difficult to work or study, become irritable. Fatigue or sluggishness may envelop him or her, sometimes accompanied by constipation, diarrhea, or loss of weight. With overly enthusiastic competitive runners, the coach's biggest task is not making them run harder but convincing them to cut back when they should.

The best solution is to cut both mileage and pace sharply, eat carbohydrates and sweets to replace lost glycogen, get plenty of rest (including afternoon naps), and relax. Do something else for a while. Veteran racers, who call this problem "breaking down," are usually much more adept at recognizing the warning signs and remedying the situation.

The blahs are a bad case of apathy. We often find runners with this problem. They are usually victims of overtraining and often appear before us one or two months before a big marathon when the training is getting routine, tough, and boring. Sometimes they are victims of overracing. There are two other types of "blah" runners. One is the depressed runner who has just finished the big race, usually a marathon, and is suffering from postrace blues: the big event is over. What's next? The other is the runner without goals, whose training has no purpose. This runner needs to focus on something, even a simple race, or else take a break and do something different.

The overtraining syndrome and the blahs can usually be cured by the above methods. If they persist, however, do not overlook them. See your doctor to make sure the symptoms don't become too severe. Competitive runners, especially young ones, who attempt to train through these states often experience burnout and never return to their previous level of racing. Serious cases of mononucleosis are also common among overtrained athletes.

RUNNING THROUGH AN INJURY

The competitive runner cannot lay off every time he or she gets a minor blister, ache, pain, or sniffle. Yet by forcing yourself to continue at a high level of training, or any training at all, you may make things worse. Often a day or two off to allow a bad blister to heal, for example, will let you return sooner to quality training than if you had continued, and aggravated the injury. However, total rest beyond 2 or 3 days will not help many injuries. You may as well continue to run, but within certain limits. Gentle exercise will help you heal and will also help you maintain a base of fitness. The trick is to train enough to provide these benefits while allowing the injured area to rest by doing relatively less work that does not aggravate the injury. More serious injuries or illness will require good judgment by you and your doctor about whether or not you should continue training or rest. Absolute rest from the stress of running for a few weeks (but not necessarily from other forms of exercise) may be required to allow some injuries to heal properly.

We use the following dozen rules to guide those who decide to run through their injuries:

1. Be aware of pain and other warning signals. Pain should protect you from overdoing.

2. Unless you can walk briskly with little or no pain for a mile, don't run.

3. Don't run if your pain makes you limp or otherwise alters your form. You may cause another injury, and it may be far worse than the one you already have. Bravely limping through a run is stupid!

4. You can run with discomfort, but not with pain. If the pain worsens as you run, stop. Beware! Your body produces its own pain-killing drugs, which may allow you to run or race and forget your pain. But after the run, you will be in agony and may have further aggravated your injury. There is danger in pushing hard through workouts and races when you started in pain that disappeared after a few miles.

5. Never use pain-killing drugs to allow you to run. You must feel the pain to adjust to it—either to continue or stop.

6. Avoid hills, speed work, races, long runs, and slanted or soft surfaces that aggravate your injury and intensify your pain.

7. Analyze and treat the cause of your injury. Pain is a signal. If your pain lessens when you change shoes, for example, or when you switch to the other side (and slope) of the road, you have learned its cause and can treat it.

8. After running, treat your injury by applying ice, and take aspirin.

9. Warm up thoroughly and cool down thoroughly with each run.

10. Do specific exercises to strengthen or improve flexibility, if it helps heal your injury. Do not overstretch or stretch injured parts until they have recovered.

11. Adjust your training if need be. You may try running twice a day for less time or distance in order to get in the miles with less continuous pounding; this will minimize aggravation of the injury. Injury-prone runners may need to run for 3 or 4 days and then take a day off to allow the body to rebuild and keep ahead of the breakdown. Alternate forms of training may be used on these off days. In more extreme cases, alternate days of running with days off, or alternate running with walking for each exercise session. You may find that you can't run more than a mile without having to stop. This is too frustrating. Try alternately running up to the edge of your capacity and then, before you feel pain, walking briskly. With this form of training you can cover 4 or 5 miles, which is psychologically satisfying and can help maintain minimal fitness. These same rules can apply when coming back from a layoff resulting from injury.

12. Be patient, and persevere.

The key to running through your injury is to develop a feel for your limits. If during a training run you aggravate an injury or develop one which causes you to change your form and/or is painful, stop and take a cab home or call for a ride. Don't force yourself to get a few more miles in so you can keep on schedule. During a race or speed workout, if you feel an injury or tightness coming on, stop. Don't be foolish and feel you have to finish—you'll be a hero today and a painful fool tomorrow.

Distance runners sometimes develop high levels of tolerance for pain. This probably means that they are good at putting up with the discomfort of low-level pain, but are aware of it and adjust or train accordingly. All runners must develop a sense of their limits. This may mean, for example, running up to 5 miles before the knee acts up and later increasing to 7 miles, as the knee strengthens. Since you are the one experiencing the pain, only you can determine the limits of training you can handle. You must balance the need to continue in order to build or maintain fitness with the need to prevent the destruction of your health—and thus your training. Better to play the limits wisely than to challenge those limits and risk long-term setback.

TREATMENT

When you are injured, you can respond in one of four ways: ignore the injury and run through it, often making it worse; quit running and pray that it will go away; attempt self-treatment; seek medical help. Most runners deal with an injury in that order: ignoring it, quitting for a few days, attempting self-treatment, and finally seeing a doctor. Runners usually injure tissue, bone, tendon, or muscles. As Dr. Joan Ullyot says in *Women's Running*, "The immediate response of the body to the damage is the same: a local outpouring of fluids and cells release substances that cause an inflammatory response, with more leakage of blood cells and lymph—and the results are the classic five signals: heat, redness, pain, swelling, and loss of function."

As most runners already know, disability can be minimized by keeping the swelling down. This is done with ICE (ice, compression, elevation), which are used immediately after the injury occurs and continued for a day or two. After 48 hours or so, you should start promoting circulation, because increased blood flow to the injured area will help remove waste products and fluid, which speeds healing. Heat, massage, gentle exercise, and even ultrasound will hasten this healing process. Relaxation of the injured area is itself beneficial because most of the pain around the injury is caused by muscle spasms.

Dr. Murray Weisenfeld prepared the following table to aid runners in the treatment of common minor injuries. Extended treatment of all ailments, and early treatment of serious injury, should be administered by a medical doctor.

DR. WEISENFELD'S SUGGESTED TREATMENT FOR COMMON INJURIES TO THE COMPETITIVE RUNNER

INJURY	TREATMENT
Runner's knee	—Ice after running (10 minutes). —Check training paths for banked surfaces. —Try commercial arch supports. —Strengthen quadricep muscles. —Try pointing toes slightly inward while running. —Improve flexibility of calf and hamstring muscles.
Achilles tendonitis	—Ice after running (10 minutes). —No stretching until pain is gone, then stretch calves, hamstrings, and Achilles tendons. —No hill work or speed work. —Run more erect, heel-ball. —Elevate heels.
Shin splints	—Ice after running (10 minutes). —Elevate heels. —Run more erect, heel-ball. —No hills or speed work. —Make sure shoes are flexible at ball. —Do strengthening exercises for muscles in shin area; stretching exercises for the Achilles tendons, calves, and hamstrings. For tenderness at inner side of the leg also: —Try commercial arch supports. —Try changing shoes; soft-soled shoes may cause trouble. —Check for leg-length discrepancy. —Avoid banked surfaces.
Stress fracture	—Rest. No running for 6 weeks. —Use alternate exercises.
Back pain/sciatica	—Avoid hills. —Check for leg-length discrepancy. —Check for banked surfaces. —Shorten stride. —Strengthen abdominals; stretch hamstrings, calves, and back muscles. —Do relaxation exercises. —Take frequent warm baths, massage.

Black toenail	—If out to end of toe, slit with sterile blade, soak, and use antiseptic. —Have podiatrist drill a hole to relieve pressure and drain the blood. —Use longer shoes, tighter laces; pad the tongue. —Put a slit in shoe over injured area.
Heel spurs or bruise	—Ice for 10 minutes after run. —Use soft sponge or Sorbothane heel lifts in both shoes. —Do wall push-ups.
Ankle sprains	—Immediately pack in ice, 15 minutes on, 15 minutes off, and repeat; in between gently rotate ankle. —Elevate. —If pain and swelling persist, seek medical attention.
Arch pain	—Try commercial arch supports. —Raise heels. —Do wall push-ups. —Ice for 10 minutes after run.
Hamstring pain	—Shorten stride. —Don't stretch until pain subsides. —Apply ice for 10 minutes after run. —Raise heels; check for leg-length discrepancy. —No hills; check for soft-soled shoes.
Calf pain	—If there is sharp, sudden pain—indicating torn muscle—elevate the heel and rest. —If pain comes on gradually, raise heels. —Don't stretch muscle. —Ice after running. —No hills; run erect and heel-ball. —Make sure shoes are flexible across the ball of the foot.
Pain in ball of foot	Usually a bruise of metatarsal head or heads: —Ice after running. —Pad behind bruise. —No speed or hills. —Run heel-ball.

Groin pain	—Check for leg-length discrepancy.
	—Run with sore groin as the long leg (closer to curb).
	—Rest.

DETRAINING

According to Dr. David Costill in *Inside Running:* "Unfortunately, the fitness gained from miles and miles of running is quickly lost when the runner stops all training. With the cessation of training, improvements in maximum oxygen uptake, maximal cardiac output, skeletal muscle capillarization, and the aerobic capacity of the leg muscles vanish at varied rates."

How quickly will performance be affected after the runner stops training? Costill answers: "In general, there is no loss for five to seven days. As a matter of fact, running performance may even be improved after two to five days of inactivity. Such rest periods allow the muscles and nervous system to recover and rebuild from the stress of training and provide the runner with improved energy reserves and tolerance of endurance exercise." Beyond that period we decondition quickly. Costill notes that beyond 1 week of inactivity the runner's muscles lose 10–50 percent of their aerobic capacity; the number of capillaries that surround each muscle fiber decreases by 10 to 20 percent within 5 to 12 days after the last training session, which results in the impaired ability to deliver and produce energy; within the first 5 to 12 days of inactivity, the combination of a lower maximal cardiac output and a smaller blood flow around the muscle fibers lessens the transport of oxygen to the runner's muscle fibers and slows the removal of waste materials from the working muscles. Costill adds: "By the fourth week of inactivity, muscle glycogen levels in an idle athlete may be no better than those in an untrained individual."

Costill sums up the detraining dilemma: "The physiological gains from training are short-lived with the cessation of regular activity. Though moderate amounts of running can maintain performance levels for many weeks, total inactivity can mean a loss of all training benefits within a few months. Our laboratory tests have shown that even the most gifted distance runners are indistinguishable from the sedentary population after six to twelve months of inactivity."

Whether injured or ill, you will need 2 or 3 days of rehabilitation training for every day lost. Even if you were in racing shape when you stopped, it generally takes 2 weeks of aerobic endurance training plus a week of sharpening for every week lost before you can return to combat-level fitness. If you're out a month, you may need 9 to 12 weeks to return to your level of conditioning. If you are concerned about keeping the racing edge, you will shorten the time required to return to reinjury condition if you replace your running time minute for minute with an aerobic equivalent and by some anaerobic work.

See chapter 7 for guidelines for using aerobic alternatives to help you keep in shape when you can't run. Biking, swimming, and other activities will help you keep in shape while injured, but they still do not use the leg muscles the same way running does; thus some loss of training will occur. Running in water is the best form of exercise to minimize detraining. You can run in thigh-deep water, which minimizes the stress of impact. Try deeper water if this puts pressure on the injury. An alternative is to use a flotation device (or the commercially made "Water Vest") in deep water and run in place. Simulate the running motion and the time period you would normally run as much as possible. *The Injured Runner's Training Handbook* contains more detailed information on how to manage running injuries while maintaining fitness.

When you lay off, you will feel a sense of loss. You may be cranky. A layoff may be a blessing in disguise: you will appreciate the joys of being able to run, and it will stimulate you to set new goals and go out and attain them. In fact, establish two goals for yourself: a return to your old PR level, and improving your time.

COMING BACK

Coming back depends on how long you were off, what alternative workouts you have done, and what put you out in the first place. Each injury or illness has its own special road to recovery. A minor cold, for example, may go away soon and allow you light running at a slow pace within a day or so. A more serious flu, or injury, will obviously take longer. When you are better, put together a recovery plan (see below), and start without any pain or changes in form. Losing a week or two may only require a week or two of gradually progressive training starting at one-half to one-third the preinjury distance. Longer layoffs for more serious injuries require a more conservative comeback. Return after long layoffs by following a program of alternating running and walking, just like a beginner's program except that you can progress more quickly since you can return in less time than you needed to build up the first time. Also take days off between running days. Start slowly: you'll feel side stitches, wobbly knees, muscle soreness, weakness. Beware: Veteran runners often find that their heart and lungs can return much faster than their musculoskeletal systems; you may be more vulnerable to muscle strain and injury than you realize.

After a long layoff, you might start with a 3 to 5 mile distance covered either with 3 minutes of walking, 3 minutes of normally paced running, or ½ mile of walking, and ½ mile of running. Jogging very slowly may aggravate your injury or cause another. Thus, it may be better to run a fairly normal pace and take walk breaks to prevent continuous pounding. Slowly increase the running period and decrease the walking until you can run nonstop comfortably. Then slowly build back up to your normal training base; never increase your distance by more than 10 percent a week. Don't attempt hills and speed work until you've run at least 2 weeks at your previous distance level.

Here are some further guidelines:

• Reach the base your body can tolerate, and stay there until you feel strong. That might be 40 miles a week instead of the 60 miles that caused the breakdown. Learn your limits and gradually increase your base.

• If you lost a day or two to minor injury or a cold, don't try to make them up. So what if you don't get in your 60-mile week? Proceed "at the rate of," and pick up where you can on your normal schedule as soon as it is safe. Making up may only set you back instead of getting you back on schedule.

• Since so many runners feel better going uphill, it can be part of rehabilitation. It is therapeutic because the body absorbs only about two-thirds the stress of running on the flat and only half the stress of downhill running. It is safer than doing speed work on a track and gives a similar training effect. But avoid hills if you suffer from lower-leg injury.

• You should also set goals well below your threshold of further injury. Avoid frustration. Give yourself the sensation—and the fact—of making slow and steady progress.

• Approach your racing goals differently. Run the first few races after your layoff only for "reexperience." Just get the feel again. Next, aim to approach your prelayoff times, and then match and exceed them. But don't be in a hurry.

• Reanalyze again and again the *cause* of your injury or illness. The Chinese say: "Fool me once, shame on you; fool me twice, shame on me." Learn from your mistakes and don't repeat them.

Most runners stop running when they are injured, and those who don't often become ex-runners. When you can't run, you need an alternative way to stay fit. It is your choice how active you want to be. If you are patient and disciplined during your alternative training period, you will return to running with a toughened mental attitude about your ability to cope with training obstacles.

Injury, in fact, may be helpful. It can force you to back off and rest. It may also encourage you to condition neglected parts of your body, which in turn will help you to perform at a higher level later. The enforced rest may make you mentally hungry for competition and serve as a means of avoiding the blahs that often accompany overracing and overtraining.

Part X
SUPPLEMENTAL EXERCISES

34. THE WARM-UP AND COOL-DOWN ROUTINES

Every workout should follow the 1-2-3 approach: warm-up, run, cool-down. A proper warm-up and cool-down of relaxation, stretching, and easy running is essential for most runners. The key is to follow the routines properly. Since running strengthens muscles at the back of the legs and back and makes them stronger and less flexible than the opposing, or antigravity, muscles in front, a balanced program of stretching tight muscles and strengthening opposing muscles should be followed to minimize injury. The warm-up and cool-down routines help you prepare for and recover from each run in three ways:

1. Relaxation exercises calm you down so that you don't carry tension with you on your run. The cool-down relaxation leaves the run behind and makes you feel surprisingly fresher. These routines are transitions allowing body and mind to move safely from your hectic life into running and calmly back again.

2. Walking and easy running at the start help your breathing and heart rate respond to exercise gradually. This permits a safe transition into running. For speed work and racing, "pickups" put your cardiorespiratory systems in tune with the de-

mand of the workout. Following your runs, you need to slow your heart rate down and allow that extra blood needed to bring fuel to your legs to return to your heart and other vital organs.

3. Stretching increases your athletic ability and efficiency. Runners lengthen their strides and increase their fluidity with less muscle tightness and leg cramping.

The first requirement for increasing your flexibility is to learn how to relax. A few minutes of relaxing and limbering exercise releases tension so that muscles can be stretched properly. Stretching exercises should condition the muscle and connecting tissues. A muscle works best when at its maximum length. Static stretching should be done, which involves slow and rhythmic movements, stopping and holding at the point of first discomfort.

It is important to perform about 10 to 15 minutes of static stretching exercises before vigorous activity. The time you spend here will save time that would be lost to injury. At least 10 minutes of stretching and relaxation should be done after your workouts to prevent muscle tightness. The exercises are also of value performed during the day whenever you can, perhaps while you're on the phone. It all adds up to increased flexibility and a more fit body.

GUIDELINES FOR STRETCHING

• Easy does it. Don't force it!
• Don't bounce or swing your body freely against a fixed joint—such as forcing a toe-touch with knees locked.
• Avoid overstretching. Too much is worse than too little. You can be injured by overstretching.
• Don't stretch injured muscles. Stick to easy limbering movements until the muscle is healed and ready to be stretched.
• Don't overdo stretching after a hard workout or race.
• Avoid exercises that aggravate a preexisting condition— especially knee or back pain.
• Don't try advanced exercises too soon. Ease into each stretching routine just as you do with your running.
• Breathe properly. Do belly breathing while stretching, just

as you do when running. Take a deep abdominal breath and let it out slowly as you reach forward with your stretch.

• Warm the muscles. A muscle can be stretched safely only when it is relaxed and warm. Do relaxation exercises before starting. Some experts suggest that you run a few minutes first to warm up the muscles before stretching. We advise this before speed workouts and races, but not before your daily runs. Runners aren't likely to start their daily run and then after a mile stop to stretch. Start your daily run with easy relaxation and limbering exercises, and then some gentle stretches. Then stretch more thoroughly after you run.

• Include all major joint movements in your stretching.

• Include stretching for specific areas: hamstrings, calves, Achilles tendons. This is especially good when doing speed work.

• Older runners should work especially hard to remain flexible.

• Stretching in the morning, when you are stiff, can be a problem, especially the day after a hard race or workout. Try easy limbering and walking, followed by an easy run. A hot bath or shower first may help. Stretch more thoroughly upon returning.

• In cold weather, warm up thoroughly indoors, especially for speed work and races. Perhaps a bath or shower would help, on an indoor stationary bike ride before your run.

• In warm weather don't let feeling warm fool you into thinking you are warmed up and stretched. Be sure to stretch thoroughly.

• Don't be in a hurry. Take your time, and do the stretching step by step and thoroughly. Use the same basic routine every day so you feel comfortable with it; know it, and stay with it. You should never cut short your stretching just to get in an extra mile.

• Add to your stretching routine exercises for other parts of your body: sit-ups for your abdominals, push-ups for your arms and upper body. You may even add a few special exercises to your routine for specific strengthening or stretching: leg extensions for your quadriceps, for example, or additional stretches for your groin area.

Remember: When a muscle is jerked into extension, it tends to "fight back" and shorten. When the muscle is slowly stretched and held, it relaxes and lengthens. Reach easily and hold; do not tug and pull. The relaxed, lengthened muscle is more efficient, less prone to injury, and recovers sooner from stress. Reach to the point of first discomfort, and hold for a count of 10. Then relax for a count of 10 before repeating.

THE ROUTINES

Use the same basic exercises for your warm-up and cool-down, and the same exercises before each type of run that you do. Here is a basic sample program for you to follow for all your runs. If you want variety or need to add a few specialized stretching exercises for specific problems to your program, refer to the book *Stretching* by Bob Anderson and *The Runner's Handbook* by Glover and Shepherd.

The basic exercises are the same for your three types of workouts—daily endurance runs, speed workouts, races—although your total warm-up and cool-down routine will change to prepare you for faster running. Here is the sample warm-up and cool-down routine used for daily training endurance runs, plus guidelines for adapting that routine to speed work and races.

The warm-up consists of three steps: relaxation exercises, stretching and strengthening exercises, and the cardiorespiratory buildup. You begin with relaxation to "break" muscle tension that frequently causes muscular strain, especially back pain. These exercises also warm up muscles that are tense and difficult to stretch.

Here is a sample 15-minute warm-up routine. Lie on the floor with your knees bent. (You should always have your knees flexed when lying on your back, to relieve pressure on the lower back.) Do the following exercises in order:

Relaxation Exercises

1. *Belly Breathing.* Close your eyes. Take a deep breath and concentrate on letting your stomach rise as you breathe in. Let

go slowly and breathe out. Repeat two more times. To be certain you are breathing properly, place your hands on your stomach. They should rise as you inhale.

2. *Head Roll.* Same position. Roll head slowly to one side and let it relax there and go limp. Roll head slowly back to the center, and then roll to the other side. Let go. Repeat three full rolls, right to left and left to right being one roll.

3. *Shoulder Shrug.* Same position. Relax, and as you take a deep breath, slide your shoulders up toward your ears and hold for a few seconds. Exhale, letting your shoulders drop limply to a relaxed position. Repeat two more times.

4. *Arm Limbering.* Same position. Raise your right arm 10 inches off the floor, clench the fist tightly for 10 seconds, then let the arm drop limply to the floor. Repeat with your left arm.

5. *Leg Limbering.* Same position. Slowly slide one leg forward until it is stretched flat on the floor, and let it go limp. Raise the leg 10 inches off the floor, and flex all the leg muscles for 10 seconds. Let the leg drop and relax, and slowly return it to the flexed position. Repeat with the opposite leg.

Lying-Down Stretches

1. *Double Knee Flex.* Same position. Pull both knees to your chest as far as you can without raising your hips. Then hug your knees with your arms, and bring your head to your knees. Let go, bring your arms back down to your sides. Lower your legs slowly to the flexed position with feet on floor. Repeat at least three times, up to twenty.

2. *Double Knee Roll.* Same position—arms outstretched, palms down. Roll both knees together to one side until the outside knee touches the floor. At the same time, turn your head to the opposite direction, and hold. Remain in this position for a few seconds. Then roll to the opposite side. Do one complete set three times.

3. *Lying Hamstring/Calf Stretch.* Same position. Bring one knee to your chest and slowly straighten the leg toward the ceiling, pointing the toe (hamstring stretch). Slowly lower the leg to the floor and relax. Return to the flexed position. Alternate legs, and repeat for a total of two full sets. Then repeat the process,

pointing the heel toward the ceiling (calf stretch), for a total of two full sets.

4. *Back Arch.* Same position, but with feet as close to buttocks as possible with heels on floor. Grasp you heels with your hands, and as you take a deep breath, arch your back, lifting your bottom off the floor but keeping your heels flat and shoulders level. Hold; exhale as you return. Repeat twice.

5. *Cobra.* Lie on your stomach, arms at your side. Arch your back and look toward the ceiling. Hold, relax, and repeat.

Sitting Stretches

1. *Ankle Rolls.* Sit cross-legged. Grasp right foot with both hands and rotate ankle. Reverse direction. Repeat with left ankle.

2. *Groin Stretch.* Same position. Place the soles of your feet together. Push down on your knees. Gently bend your head toward your feet. Hold the position with head down for a few seconds. Sit up; repeat two more times.

3. *Sitting Hamstring, Calf, and Back Stretch.* Sit with legs straight and spread, both hands overhead. Inhale, and then exhale slowly, and slide your arms along your left leg toward your left toe (keep the back of your knee flat against the floor). Reach as far as you can comfortably, and hold for a 10-count. Inhaling, bring arms back overhead; sit up straight. Exhale as your arms reach toward your right toe, and hold at the point of first discomfort. Don't worry if you can't reach your toes. Repeat twice for each leg.

4. *Sitting Quadriceps Stretch.* Tuck your legs under you, sit on them, and lean back on your hands. Push your hips gently forward. Hold to a count of 10. Repeat two more times.

5. *Hip Stretcher.* Sit with your legs straight out. Bend your left leg across the right and hug it with your arms, knee to chest. Hold; count to 10; repeat with your other leg. Repeat twice with each leg.

Standing Stretches

1. *Total Body Stretch.* Stand with legs apart, arms extended toward the ceiling. Grab air with your right hand, then your

left, alternating as you rise on your toes. Do this for 10 seconds, then let your upper body slowly bend forward at the hips, breathing out, and hang loosely as you slightly flex your knees. Slowly rise to a standing position as you inhale.

2. *The Wall Push-up.* Stand about 3 feet from a wall, tree, or lamppost. Place your hands on the wall, keeping your hips and back straight, heels firmly on the ground. Now slowly allow your straight body to lean close to the wall. Drop your forearms toward the wall so that you touch it with your hands and elbows. Keeping your back straight and heels flat, now tuck your hips in toward the wall. Then straighten your arms and push your body back to the starting position. Repeat twice. Hold to a 10-count.

Next, stand close to the wall, feet together, hands on the wall. Bend at the knees, keeping your feet flat on the ground. (This is good for your Achilles tendon.) Hold for a 10-count. Repeat two more times.

3. *Standing Quadriceps Stretch.* Lean against the wall with your right hand. Reach behind you with your left hand and grasp the top of your right foot. Gently pull your heel toward your buttocks. Hold for a count of 10. Do twice with each leg.

4. *Upper Back, Arm, and Hamstring Stretch.* Stand with legs apart, hands clasped behind your back. Bend forward, bringing your arms overhead, tucking your chin into your chest. Hold for 10 seconds. Slowly rise back to a standing position.

5. *Side Stretches.* Stand with legs apart, right hand on the side of your right leg, left hand overhead. Bend to the right at the waist, also stretching overhead arm to the right. Look up to outstretched hand. Hold for 10 seconds, and alternate stretch to the other side. Repeat each side one more time.

Strengthening Exercises

1. *Push-ups.* Lie on the floor on your stomach. Then rise off the floor, back straight, so only your hands and toes touch. Form is important. Do five and work up to fifteen or so with good form. Back straight, fanny high, touch only your chest to the floor.

2. *Sit-ups.* Lie on your back, knees bent. Have someone hold your feet, or anchor them under a chair, bed, or bleacher. Put

your hands behind your head and roll up smoothly to a sitting position with your head close to your knees. Exhale slowly as you roll up and inhale while rolling down. Start with a few and work up to more. Do as many as you comfortably can with good form.

> *Safety Note:* If you do not have the time to do the whole series of exercises properly select as many of them as you can do without rushing. It is better to do a few well than to do none at all or do all of them haphazardly.

The Cardiorespiratory Warm-up

After stretching, begin a 5-minute brisk walk. Pick up your pace as you near the starting point of your run. Or start jogging slowly for 5 minutes, and then ease into your training pace. Don't go full throttle as soon as you start your run. Allow your pulse to move up gradually and settle into your training range.

SAMPLE 15-MINUTE WARM-UP AND COOL-DOWN ROUTINES

RELAXATION EXERCISES
1. Belly Breathing
2. Head Roll
3. Shoulder Shrug
4. Arm Limbering
5. Leg Limbering

LYING-DOWN STRETCHES
1. Double Knee Flex
2. Double Knee Roll
3. Lying Hamstring/Calf Stretch
4. Back Arch
5. Cobra

SITTING STRETCHES
1. Ankle Rolls
2. Groin Stretch
3. Sitting Hamstring, Calf, and Back Stretch
4. Sitting Quadriceps Stretch
4. Hip Stretcher

STANDING STRETCHES
1. Total Body Stretch
2. The Wall Push-up
3. Standing Quadriceps Stretch
4. Upper-Back, Arm, and Hamstring Stretch
5. Side Stretches

STRENGTHENING
1. Push-ups
2. Sit-ups

Note: For cool-down, do the exercises in reverse order, from standing stretches to relaxation, ending with belly breathing. Then close your eyes and rest for 2 minutes.

The Cool-Down

This is the warm-up in reverse: cardiorespiratory cool-down, stretching, relaxation exercises. It is also the easiest step to skip. But runners who miss their cool-down get injured because they haven't stretched and relaxed their muscles after a run.

After your workout, slowly walk for about 5 minutes. Follow this walk with the same stretching exercise routine as above, in reverse order, perhaps skipping a few stretches to make it a 10-minute routine. Don't do any push-ups or sit-ups. The purpose of the cool-down is to return the body to its preexercise level, ensuring the return of normal blood flow from the extremities to the heart and preventing muscle tightness. It is also important to slow your heart rate; your recovery pulse should be under 100 beats per minute at the conclusion of your cool-down. Take your pulse after your cool-down walk and stretch.

SPEED WORKOUTS AND RACES

The Warm-up Routine

Before any fast runs, prepare your body for the stress. Bring your heart rate and breathing up to your aerobic exercise level, and prepare your muscles and joints for hard work. Your warm-up includes the following:

1. *Relaxation and Easy Stretching.* Loosen up. Follow relaxation and lying-down stretches in the sample on page 512.

2. *Warm-up Run.* Continue your prespeed workout routine wih a low 10-to-30-minute jog before stretching further. For long races like the marathon jog only about 5 minutes. This is a slow, leisurely, warming-up jog. The purpose is to loosen the body and warm it so that you can stretch more thoroughly. Some runners also find that easy runs of 2 to 4 miles in the morning before an early-afternoon speed workout, or a run at noon before an evening workout, helps loosen them.

3. *Stretch.* Continue with the sitting and standing stretches in the sample on page 512.

4. *Pickups.* Run a set of six to twelve "pickups" or "strides" of about 60 yards on grass (if smooth) or on the road or track, at increasing speeds. These should be brisk but not all-out. Do the first two or three slowly, concentrating on warming up your body and moving easily. Pick up the speed as you become loose; concentrate on good running form. This routine is specific dynamic stretching for the muscles and joints used in speed work and racing, and brings your heart and breathing up to the rates used during the hard work ahead.

5. *Relax and Limber Up.* Now do a 2 or 3 minute period of light exercises, including head rolls, leg shakes, Achilles tendon, and groin stretches, and any other relaxed stretching you may need. Do specific stretching for any area you feel is tight. Do not, however, perform these stretches in a nervous, haphazard manner. You are now ready for your speed workout or race.

6. *Ease into It.* If you are doing a continuous strength-training run, start at an easy pace to get your heart rate up into your training range and your muscles warmed before stepping on the gas. For intermittent track work or hills, run your first repetition conservatively, as a continuation of the warm-up. Jog into each start—never use a standing start.

For races, if the start is delayed after your carefully planned warm-up (begun 30 minutes before race time), keep moving, jogging easily, and walking briskly. Avoid last-minute nervous stretching, which can be dangerous. Try to do a few more pickups right before the start, to bring your heart rate closer to race level. For the marathon, however, keep calm and try to conserve energy.

The Cool-Down Routine

This is perhaps the most important—and often most neglected—part of your routine. It helps you recover from your workout and be ready for the next day.

1. *Walk or Jog.* After your workout or race, walk around or jog easily to cool down. An easy jog of 1 to 4 miles will help you recover from the stress of the run. Next, walk around slowly for a few minutes until your heart rate returns close to normal. Novices, or those running marathons, probably will be

too tired to do any more running. They should walk; do not sit or lie down. If you do, you'll tighten up.

2. *Stretch*. Follow your daily run routine. If your muscles are very tired and tight, do fewer stretches and don't force them. You may not be able to work your muscles as thoroughly, since they are fatigued. Be careful. Overstretching here can lead to injury.

3. *Relax*. End your routine with easy relaxation exercises. An easy swim, walk, or bike ride may help you recover from your workout—now, later in the evening, or the next morning. Afterward, of course, there is the runner's reward: the post-workout beer!

35. WEIGHT TRAINING

A supplemental program of weight training will improve both your strength and your running times. Runners who compete in distance races need upper-body strength and muscular endurance. Just holding up your arms during the long races or finding that extra leg power through those last few miles requires added muscular strength.

Strength-training runs such as *fartlek,* rolling hills, fast continuous runs, and brisk workouts over hills will develop specific muscle groups such as the hamstrings, calves, quadriceps, and buttocks. Weight training generally strengthens all the muscle groups of your body when properly selected lifts are included in a weight-training program.

Proper weight training can also help prevent injury resulting from imbalanced muscle groups and strengthen your body for better performance. Increased overall strength will help a runner drive up hills and continue running fast even during the latter stages of a long-distance run.

A strength-training program will also benefit the runner who needs to increase the drive in his or her arms to help propel the body forward to the finish line. Some runners train with weighted gloves two to three time a week to improve strength and arm drive. In the late stages of the marathon, when attacking hills or the finishing line, the runner with a stronger arm drive will do better. And that arm drive comes from weight training; running itself does little to strengthen your upper body.

Weight training is especially valuable to women runners, who usually have less well-developed muscles than men. Their arms and shoulders may be underdeveloped. Dramatic improvements in running performance are possible for women who develop some upper-body strength, usually through a weight program.

You should design a specific weight-training program and routine, similar to the one you follow for your running workouts. The three-step approach for weight training is as follows: (1) the warm-up; (2) the workout; (3) the cool-down.

THE WARM-UP AND THE COOL-DOWN

The warm-up for lifting weights is basically the same as that for preparing to run. You should do about 15 minutes of stretching exercises using the four groups of stretching exercises outlined in chapter 34. These exercises will loosen up the muscles connecting tissues and joints, and allow you to work all areas with little danger of damaging yourself because of tightness.

You should do some warm-up lifting, 10 to 12 relaxed repetitions using very light weights. This will allow your muscles to warm up and loosen.

The cool-down, as with running, is the warm-up in reverse. Walk or swim 5 to 10 minutes, and then do your stretching and relaxation exercises.

THE WORKOUT

Several books give detailed theories on weight training. There are a few general rules everyone adheres to:
- Heavy weights with few repetitions build strength and bulk.
- Light weights and many repetitions increase muscular endurance.

• Medium weights lifted about ten to fifteen times build both muscular strength and endurance while increasing bulk very little if at all.

Weight-training equipment such as Universal and Nautilus machines are the easiest and safest weight-lifting apparatus to use. The weights are connected to the main housing, which prevents you from dropping them on the floor or on your running toes. Weights can be changed quickly and easily by moving small levers or rods. Working out with a basic set of barbells or dumbbells, however, is also worthwhile, and they may be more easily accessible. Be careful if you have not lifted weights before. If possible, start weight training under the supervision of a professional instructor.

The following routine is one we have used successfully with our athletes. It can be done with any equipment, is simple to follow, and requires only abut 15 to 20 minutes twice a week. We select a medium-weight workout to build stamina. Each weight-training routine consists of the following steps:

1. Select the exercise and the weight to be lifted.

2. Do the specified number of repetitions, exhaling as you lift the weight, inhaling as you release the weight.

3. Rest 1 minute at the completion of the first set to recover, and do some flexibility exercises to keep your muscles and joints loose.

4. Do the second set the same way as the first set.

5. Rest 1 minute at the completion of the second set, doing flexibility exercises to maintain looseness and complete range of motion.

6. Do the third set (if possible) the same way as the first two sets.

7. Rest 1 minute at the completion of the third set, do flexibility exercises, and set up your next exercise.

8. Continue with the next exercise following the above seven steps.

SELECTING WEIGHTS AND MAKING PROGRESS

The difficult part of weight training is knowing how much weight to lift and when to increase the weight for each particular exercise.

Rule One: Start Light

You should always start off working with a very light weight. Allow your body to adapt to the increased resistance. Do only a small number of repetitions. We recommend one set of ten to fifteen repetitions.

Rule Two: Increase the Weight Gradually

You should increase the amount of weight you lift for a particular exercise after you can do three sets of the recommended repetitions easily. Then increase the weight, but only by 5 to 10 pounds. Reduce the number of sets to two, and gradually work your way back up to three sets at the recommended number of repetitions.

THE EXERCISES

The Bench Press

Lying flat on your back, face up, press the weight straight up from your body. This exercise strengthens your arms, chest, and upper torso.

   Do three sets of fifteen repetitions.

Sit-ups with Weights

Lying on the floor, with knees bent and feet hooked under an immovable object, put your hands behind your head and bring your upper body, bent at the waist, to your knees. Lift a light weight behind your head as you become stronger. This exercise strengthens your abdominal muscles.

   Do three sets of twenty repetitions without weights.

   Do three sets of ten repetitions with weights.

Step-ups

Standing, holding the weight with both hands behind your neck, put one foot on a stationary box about 18 inches high, and step up with the other. A set is complete when the recommended number of repetitions is done with each leg. This exercise strengthens the Achilles tendons, calves, and quadriceps.

Do three sets of ten repetitions with each leg.

Toe Raises

Standing, holding the weight behind your neck (as with step-ups), raise yourself up onto your toes. This exercise strengthens your calf muscles, Achilles tendons, and ankle joints.

Do three sets of fifteen repetitions.

Reverse Curls

Standing, hold the bar with the weights palms-down in front of you, resting the bar on your quadriceps. Keep your back straight, thus not allowing your body to swing, and bring the bar up to your chest. This exercise develops the forearm for better arm swing.

Do three sets of fifteen repetitions.

GENERAL RULES FOR WEIGHT TRAINING

• Weight training is progressive, just like running. You begin with low weights and gradually increase the weights as you become stronger.

• You lift twice a week, allowing 2 to 3 days between each lifting session to let your muscles rebuild themselves. Weight workouts should be separate from your runs; or lift first and run second, taking it easy.

• Limit the number of repetitions to ten to fifteen and the number of sets to two or three in order to build muscle strength without building bulk.

• Begin each weight-training session by exercising the large muscle groups first and then the smaller muscles. Alternate upper-body lifting with lower-body lifting.

• Do flexibility exercises before, during, and after each repetition lift.

• All lifts should be done through a full range of motion to work the muscles completely.

• Lifting is done to a 4-count pace: count to 4 as you lift the weight, and count to 4 as you release the weight.

SUPPLEMENTARY EXERCISES WITHOUT WEIGHTS

Important muscles can also be strengthened without the aid of weights. Here are some special exercises that you might add to your running program for specific purposes—to prevent injury and to make your running stronger:

Abdominals

Weak abdominals contribute to poor form and to back pain. Do bent-knee sit-ups.

Upper Body

Weak arms and chest muscles can be strengthened to improve arm drive. Do push-ups.

Quadriceps

Weak quads, especially in relation to strong hamstrings, can cause imbalance, which affects the pull on your kneecaps. These muscles also help pick up your legs and are important in the late stages of long runs and for running uphill. Some supplementary exercises:

• Sit in a chair, straighten the leg, and tighten it, holding the kneecap parallel to the floor. Hold for 20 to 30 seconds in isometric contraction. Repeat ten to twenty times.

• Sit on a table and lift any type of weight suspended from the legs, with legs straight. (One leg at a time.)

• Walk up several flights of stairs regularly.

• Walk in water, emphasizing knee lift.

• Hike or run on hills.

• Tuck your toes under a desk or couch and try to lift it with your toes. Your knees can be either bent or straight. Hold for 10 seconds. Relax. Repeat ten times.

• Stand with your back to the wall. Lift one leg as high as you can, keeping the knee straight. Hold for a 5-count. Now bend the knee to relax for the count of 5. Straighten the knee again. Do each leg five times, increasing to ten.

Adductor Muscles

These muscles contribute to inner leg pain and groin pull. For strengthening the adductors, try the following:

Lie on your right side with your right hand supporting your head. Your left hand is placed on the floor in front of you for support. Your left foot is flat on the floor in front of your right leg. Your right leg should be slightly ahead of your body. Now, flex your right foot so that the toe points up toward the knee. Keep the knee firm and straight throughout the exercise. Then lift the right leg as high as you can, and then lower it. Start with five to ten repetitions and work up to twenty. When you lower the leg each time, do not touch the floor with your foot and do not relax your leg. Keep it firm throughout this exercise. This can also be done with a one-pound weight on your ankle. Turn on your left side, and repeat with your left leg.

Hamstrings

Here is a strengthening exercise to prevent pulls.

Attach a one-pound weight to each ankle. Lie on your back on the floor, arms at your sides. Your knees are bent, feet flat on the floor. Stretch your right leg up as straight as you can. Then put your foot back on the floor. Repeat ten times. Now repeat with the other leg. Your aim is to straighten the leg so that it is almost at a 90-degree angle to the floor. Start with three sets of ten extensions for each leg. At first, do this without the weights.

Arch

The following exercises may relieve arch pain.

• Pick up marbles with your toes.

• Roll a bottle under your foot.
• Stand on a towel with your toes over its edge and pick up the towel with your toes.

Postural Muscles

These muscles are important for good running form. The following exercises should strengthen the abdominals, the gluteal muscles (fanny), and the erector spines (back muscles along your spine).

• Lying on your back, tilt your pelvis toward the floor, tighten your buttocks and stomach, and push the lower back into the floor. Hold. Count to 10. Relax. Repeat two more times.
• Stand with your back against a wall, push your lower back toward the wall as you tighten the buttocks and stomach. Count to 10. Relax. Repeat two more times.

Shins

These exercises will strengthen the anterior leg muscles to minimize shin splints.

• Lying down or sitting in a chair, put your right foot on top of your left foot. Now try to pull your lower foot toward your body as your upper foot pushes it away. Hold for 10 seconds. Switch feet and push-pull for 10 seconds. This is one set. Do five sets.
• Sit on a table with your legs hanging freely over the sides. Flex one foot to lift a weight, perhaps a bucket of pebbles or a sandbag or other weight supended over the foot. Do not try to lift too much. Do ten lifts with each foot. Repeat once.
• Attach a rubber bicycle inner tube to a board. Standing, slip your toes under the tube and lift them against it. Hold for a 10-count and switch legs. Do two or three sets.
• Turn your feet inward while standing and make a rolling motion. Do for a few seconds with each leg. Repeat.
• Stand on the edge of a towel and curl your toes to pull the towel under your feet.

Part XI
FOOD, DRINK, AND WEIGHT

36. EATING AND RUNNING

Food is a fuel and a source of nutrients. Proper nutrition means that essential nutrients—carbohydrates, fats, proteins, vitamins, minerals, and water—are both consumed and absorbed for optimal health. A runner's basic needs aren't very different from those of other healthy people, although the high-mileage runner will need to consume more calories and carbohydrates. The runner training in hot weather will need to make some important adjustments to preserve the body's fluid and mineral balance. Some alterations are also advisable during the final days before a marathon and in the days following the event.

According to Dr. David Costill: "Proper nutrition can play an important role in distance running performance. The key to success is the availability of carbohydrates for muscle energy, though fat serves as an alternative fuel source and contributes to the energy pool during the long, slower events. Muscle glycogen stores depend on a rich carbohydrate diet, though a complement of all the basic food groups, vitamins, and minerals are essential for peak performance. Repeated days of intense training can result in a slow recovery of muscle glycogen, leading to a chronic state of fatigue. Periods of reduced training and diets supplemented with carbohydrate foods promote good training and the adaptations needed for improvement."

A well-balanced diet is important for the runner going into competition. A few weeks before the race, some runners neglect their diets. This is a mistake. As you begin to taper your mileage, *do not* taper your food intake as well: you'll cut out needed nutrients. But don't increase it either: you'll gain weight.

What we eat depends on many factors—most of them related to our habits and culture, along with taste. Generally, the runner should keep away from saturated fats and foods high in cholesterol, as well as excess protein, sugar, and highly processed foods. Concentrate more on complex carbohydrates: fruits, vegetables, pasta, and grains (simple carbohydrates include "nasty junk food").

Too many runners with poor diets have died of heart attacks precipitated by high cholesterol. Running itself doesn't protect you from heart disease: it must be combined with a healthy diet. It is advisable for runners to have periodic cholesterol checkups. Mary Rodriguez, for 5 years in a row the New York Road Runners Club's top 60+ racer and an ultramarathoner, decided to have a blood cholesterol test after reading an article by Dr. George Sheehan warning that you can be fit and not be healthy. She was shocked to find out that years of eating fatty foods had clogged her arteries: she had serious heart disease despite being a national-class runner.

DIET DEFICIENCIES IN RUNNERS

Nancy Clark, the Boston-based running nutritionist and author of *The Athlete's Kitchen: A Nutrition Guide and Cookbook,* points out four major dietary deficiencies that interfere with a runner's health and performance: iron, calcium, carbohydrates, and breakfast.

Iron. Even former world-record holder at the marathon distance Alberto Salazar suffered through subpar race efforts because of an iron deficiency. Iron assists in the oxygen-carrying capacity of the blood. Excessive fatigue in both men and women runners may be due to running-related anemia. Also, a study at Canada's Simon Fraser University concluded that "the presence of latent iron deficiency without anemia may reduce work capacity and impair race performance."

Women, because of blood loss during menstruation, are very prone to iron deficiencies. Men are also prone to this problem since they tend to lose iron through heavy sweating and internal bleeding during periods of intense training (especially in the hot summer when marathon training). Runners interested in lowering their cholesterol level tend to eliminate red meat, a good source of iron, from their diet.

Clark notes: "If you're running regularly yet not improving, feeling needlessly tired and eating little beef, pork or lamb, you might want to have your blood tested for anemia. Be aware that the standard tests (hemoglobin and hematocrit) may not detect the problem. The blood tests that measure serum ferritin and total iron binding capacity better reflect your iron stores."

Iron supplements may be helpful to prevent anemia, but should be taken with the recommendation of a doctor. Eating lean meat will contribute iron to your diet, as will leafy green vegetables and dried fruits. Cooking food regularly in a cast-iron skillet will contribute iron as will iron-enriched cereals, bread, etc. By drinking juice or taking some other source of vitamin C (such as vitamins) with your iron source, you will double the body's ability to absorb this mineral.

Calcium. Bones are active and require 800 to 1,200 milligrams of calcium per day to maintain their strength. Bones reach their peak density at 30–35 years of age, and the amount of bone mass you have at that age is critical to your susceptibility to fractures as you get older. Studies have shown that running contributes to stronger bones, so a runner who consumes a sufficient amount of low-fat milk and yogurt and other calcium-rich dairy products has a reduced risk of fractures and osteoporosis.

Carbohydrates. The typical American diet—30 percent carbohydrates, 45 percent fat, and 25 percent protein—is not only inadequate for performance, it is unhealthy. According to Costill, the ideal diet for the average person who runs 20–30 miles a week should contain 50 percent carbohydrates, 30 percent fat, and 20 percent protein. The runner who logs high mileage—more than 70 miles a week—needs more than 1,000 additional calories a day, consisting of 70 percent carbohydrates, 20 percent fat, and 10 percent protein. Runners in the 30–70-

mile-a-week range should aim for at least 60 percent of calories coming from carbohydrates.

Here are some recommended meal patterns that are high in carbohydrates. For breakfast, pass on bacon and eggs, which are full of fats and cholesterol, and go for toast, bagels, muffins, or pancakes—go easy on butter and syrup (or eliminate them and use some jam). Or orange juice with carbohydrate- and iron-rich cereal topped with a banana. For lunch, pass on the hamburger and french fries, and select a salad, broth-based soup, muffin, and yogurt. For dinner, pass on the juicy steak (except when you need some iron in your diet and then go with a lean cut), and go for steamed vegetables, pasta with tomato sauce, potato (without sour cream), and some fruit.

Breakfast. Clark notes: "Breakfast skippers not only lag in energy, but also tend to binge on grease and goo at nine P.M." Breakfast is the most important meal in the day; start the day off right nutritionally. Key ingredients for the runner's breakfast: carbohydrates, bran, vitamin C, calcium, iron, potassium. A good breakfast choice for the runner in a hurry: cereal that includes plenty of bran, iron, and carbohydrates, topped with a banana, with low-fat milk, plus orange juice, and perhaps a muffin with jam.

VITAMINS AND MINERALS

Runners who eat a well-balanced diet often take vitamin and mineral supplements in the belief that they will help them perform better. In truth, they may only be passing expensive urine and getting no additional benefits. A good diet supplies all the essential vitamins and minerals; however, a competitive runner who is not following the best diet may indeed benefit from a moderate amount of supplements. We recommend a standard multivitamin and mineral supplement, with extra vitamin C (which helps you recover from the stress of training), and perhaps iron, taken in moderation. Clark stresses: "You need sufficient amounts of vitamins to function optimally, but an excess of vitamins offers no competitive edge. No scientific evidence exists to prove that extra vitamins enhance performance."

Minerals aid in warding off fatigue and cramps, and they

maintain the body's delicate water balance. Potassium and magnesium are especially important to minimize cramping—they are lost in body sweat and can be depleted while training in hot weather. If you are prone to cramping, you may wish to take potassium and magnesium supplements. Potassium is available naturally in fruits (especially cantaloupes, strawberries, oranges, apricots, dates, and tomatoes), and magnesium is found in various nuts and grains. As previously mentioned, iron is a very important mineral for the runner.

Contrary to popular belief, you should not take salt tablets or add salt to your diet to replace that lost in sweat. You have plenty of salt in your diet already, although most of it is hidden.

CARBOHYDRATE LOADING

Glycogen is a stored carbohydrate made from simple sugar. It is stored in the muscles and liver. Glycogen serves as the body's basic fuel and converts into sugar for the bloodstream when you need more energy. Carbohydrates create glycogen, which aids endurance. The average runner can store enough glycogen to last about 20 miles—the point at which you "hit the Wall" by literally running out of energy.

In the late 1960s, Swedish exercise physiologist Eric Hultman developed the idea of "carbohydrate loading," a means of manipulating the diet in order to increase glycogen stores. The classic 7-day diet based on his studies worked this way:

1. Seven days before the race, go for a long run of 2 to 3 hours in order to help deplete glycogen stores in your muscles.

2. For the next 3 days, eat a diet high in protein and fats and low in carbohydrates in order to deplete your glycogen stores further. Regular running is maintained during this phase to burn off still more glycogen.

3. For the last 3 days before the race, the diet is reversed. The runner "loads" on carbohydrates and minimizes running in order to store up glycogen levels.

This diet was based on tests that showed that athletes who followed this regimen would be able to improve their performances because the depleted muscles would soak up more glycogen during the loading period than nondepleted muscles.

The athlete would increase glycogen storage by as much as 100–300 percent.

We do not, however, recommend the classic regimen that was used effectively for several years by many runners, including Bob Glover. He can attest that the depletion phase is very taxing physically and psychologically. Fortunately, more recent research has proven that you can carbohydrate load just as effectively without having to go through the depletion phase. The long run and deprivation of carbohydrates are replaced with tapering of training mileage.

Exercise physiologist William Sherman studied runners at the University of Texas and had them taper down by running 90 minutes, 40 minutes, 40 minutes, 20 minutes, and 20 minutes on 5 consecutive days. On the 6th day, the day before their race, they rested completely. For the first 3 days of the study, the runners consumed a normal 3,000 calories a day of which 50 percent was carbohydrates. For the final 3 days, they ate the same total number of calories but increased the carbohydrate percentage to 70. Sherman then performed muscle biopsies on the runners. The result was that the runners had stored as much extra glycogen as in the classic regimen with the depletion stage.

Thus our recommended carbohydrate-loading procedure for anyone wishing to improve his or her performance in endurance events lasting longer than 90 minutes (you don't taper for 10Ks) is as follows:

1. Start cutting back on your training for 2 weeks going into a marathon event. Especially minimize your running for the last 3 days going into the event while you are increasing your carbohydrate intake. Dr. Costill suggests cutting back mileage to as much as one-third your normal training mileage for 2 weeks going into your event. Remember, when you run high mileage you are using stored glycogen as a fuel. As you are attempting to increase your glycogen stores to better assist you on marathon day, you need to minimize your running. See chapter 23 for guidelines for marathon tapering.

2. Stick to your normal diet until 3 days before the marathon, then concentrate on foods high in carbohydrates. Do not overeat; maintain the same caloric intake. Approximately 70

percent of your calories should be carbohydrates. Don't totally cut out proteins. Look at it this way: substitute pancakes for eggs for breakfast, spaghetti for a hamburger for lunch, and lasagna for steak for dinner. Don't pig out on ice cream and other "goodies." They have carbohydrates, but also plenty of unwanted fat. Try to emphasize complex carbohydrates: pasta, vegetables, fruits, beans, bread, rice, carbohydrate-rich cereal. Pizza with extra thick crust is a popular choice. Italian restaurants are popular with runners who are loading, but Chinese restaurants also offer plenty of carbo-loading fare. Some runners develop digestive problems when they increase their carbohydrate percentage. Liquid carbohydrate supplements may be helpful.

3. Drink plenty of water as you are loading. Water is stored in muscle tissue along with glycogen, and your muscles will take it from other organs if enough isn't supplied from the outside, which could lead to dehydration. Going into the race you may feel bloated and heavy from extra water in the body. This is normal and will go away a few miles into the race after you've started sweating.

By tapering and loading, you will most likely feel very "antsy" and raring to go on race day. Be careful! Hold back on your pace in the early stages of the race when you are so full of energy. This routine won't help you run faster; it is designed to help you maintain your pace longer. Start at an even pace and let your carbohydrate-loading program contribute to your performance over the last 6–10 miles of the race.

THE LAST SUPPER

The fuel that you use on race day for the most part comes from food eaten a few days earlier: carbohydrates stored as glycogen in your muscles and liver. You can skip your evening meal and your morning meal before races of half marathon or less if you have digestive problems that interfere with your racing. You will feel hungry and your blood sugar may be a little low, but your performance may not be affected. It is generally recommended, however, that the evening before a shorter race you eat at least a light meal. You need not be obsessed with eating carbohydrates, since you are not going to need to pack in more glycogen for such a short racing distance. Make sure what you do eat, however, is something that agrees with you. Don't go out for Mexican food or try out a new, spicy menu the night before a race, or the combination of prerace nerves and hard-to-digest food may ruin your race.

The evening meal before a marathon is very imporant. Use it to pack in more carbohydrates. The typical "last supper" for marathoners is spaghetti with bread and plenty of fluids—ideally water. If you choose to load with Chinese food rather than Italian, be sure to eliminate MSG, which may contribute to the inability to sleep well. Drinking too much cola or coffee the night before combined with prerace nerves will contribute to both an upset stomach and the inability to get to sleep. Don't drink too much alcohol (one beer is enough) close to the race, or it will contribute to dehydration.

For any racing distance, don't eat a big meal too late at night: you need more time to digest. Eat at approximately 5:00–6:00 P.M. and don't stuff yourself. It is easy to keep shoving food in your mouth, especially at prerace parties, when you are nervous. A light snack around 9:00 or 10:00 P.M. will pack in a few more carbohydrates, but don't overdo it. This is especially helpful if you plan to skip eating the morning of the marathon. If you are traveling to a race, make sure you make reservations if you plan on going out to eat. Don't upset your stomach by being unable to get into a restaurant late at night. If you are dining at the official prerace spaghetti feast, get there early— sometimes they run out of food and you'll have to wait for more. Avoid standing in line for too long the night before just to eat. Be flexible. If the prerace feast is too crowded, find a local restaurant. A meal in your hotel room may be the most relaxing alternative of all. Follow it with a relaxing walk.

THE PRERACE MEAL

The race day meal may do more harm than good. At this last moment, you cannot eat your way to a better time; you can, however, eat your way out of the race. Follow two important rules: don't eat anything you haven't eaten in the past before a previous race (or at least a few long runs or hard workouts), or you may be unpleasantly surprised; and don't eat too close to the starting time.

When to Eat. Eat 3–5 hours before your race if at all on race morning. You may be able to shorten this time for your training runs. Also, use your training runs for just that: to find out what foods you can eat before running that will be beneficial, and that you won't end up either fighting or flinging out on the road. By eating too close to race time, you are asking your stomach to aid in the digestive process. But when you run, extra blood is required by the working muscles to provide fuel. Combining these two demands weakens both processes. You have less energy for running, and you are also likely to have gastrointestinal problems such as diarrhea, nausea, and perhaps vomiting and stitches. The actual time it takes to digest food depends on when you eat, what you eat, and your emotional state. You should enter competition with an empty colon and stomach. Stay away from high-roughage foods like bran, salads, etc., for 2 to 3 days before going into the race. Stress may prolong digestion, and a large, exciting race, or an important one, may create special digestive problems. Do yourself a favor: eat less when under stress, and eat only foods that you have previously eaten when under stress and digested without difficulty.

For shorter events, time your last meal (or don't eat) to make sure you can digest properly. According to Liz Applegate, in *Runner's World:* "The purpose of eating prior to exercise is largely to ease feelings of hunger and to maintain constant blood-sugar levels. During events lasting longer than two hours, a prerace meal also provides the carbohydrates needed to delay the draining of valuable muscle-glycogen stores."

Timing the last meal before a marathon is a bit complicated. Exercise physiologists David Costill and William Sherman reported research in the *American Journal of Sports Medicine* that demonstrates that fasting will cause reduced stores of liver glycogen, the body's major source of glucose, and carbohydrates eaten too near race time will result in early and unnecessary fatigue. They suggest that marathoners eat a light meal about 3 to 5 hours before the race.

What to Eat. Costill and Sherman recommend that the marathoner's prerace meal should consist of easily digestible carbohydrates such as cereal, pancakes, waffles, and breads. They also advise runners to stay away from fat and protein at this time if possible, because these digest slowly. Applegate notes that complex carbohydrates and starches gradually release sugar to the bloodstream when they are digested, but simple carbohydrates or sugars cause a rapid rise in blood sugar, which can lead to low blood sugar or hypoglycemia. For runners bothered by prerace stomach jitters, liquid meals may be best. They empty from the stomach faster than solids, and thus cause fewer problems. Because of this, they may be ingested up to 2 hours before a race without interfering with performance.

How Much to Eat. For shorter races, eat enough to curb your hunger a bit, but not so much that you feel bloated at the starting line. For many runners this will consist of a cup of coffee or a glass of juice and a piece of toast. For the marathon, Costill and Sherman recommend a light meal of 500 to 1,000 calories.

When you find the right combination of when to eat, what to eat, and how much to eat, write it down. Stick to it. Don't try to become a prerace gourmet. Some runners have goats' stomachs and can train and race after eating. Others can eat before training, but never before a race. When in doubt, drink but don't eat.

EATING AFTER THE RACE

Runners obsessed with proper diet before a race often ignore it afterward. But what you eat and drink for several days after your race, especially a marathon, will affect your recovery; a proper diet will help minimize injury and illness and allow you to return to a normal training and racing routine sooner.

You may be tired of pasta and long for steak and eggs. But besides eating what you want—and your body will often tell you what it needs—you should follow your prerace diet for several days after a long race. A marathon will especially deplete your glycogen stores. To recover, and replace lost glycogen, you should eat plenty of carbohydrates afterward as well as before. In effect, this is a carbohydrate reloading to get glycogen back into your muscles and liver. Dr. Costill says, "Probably the first meal after the marathon should be like the last big meal before. If the night before you have spaghetti or some other heavy carbohydrate, the meal after competition should be very much the same. You want to recover as much of that used up glycogen as possible. It often takes three to five days to recover the glycogen. That's part of the problem of recovering from a marathon. A lot of people don't go after the carbohydrates hard enough and that is part of the cause for the fatigue and difficulties in getting back to running form again."

Exercised muscles are twice as receptive to glycogen replacement if you eat within the first 2 hours following competition than they are after 2 hours, according to research conducted by exercise physiologist John Ivy at the University of Texas at Austin. This is true not only right after a race, particularly a marathon, but also after hard or long training runs. By eating carbohydrates soon after running, you will quickly replenish lost energy reserves, resulting in increased recovery time and the ability to better prepare for your next run.

Here's a chance to expand your intake and knowledge of carbohydrates. Go beyond mere pasta. Nancy Clark, author of *The Athlete's Kitchen,* suggests rice pilaf, stuffing, sweet potato, winter squash, corn, split pea soup, banana bread, corn muffins, biscuits with jam, apple crisp, date squares, fruit cup/sherbert.

The extra amount of protein you need to replace after a long race is not significant. Your normal American diet—which usually includes two to three times the amount of protein needed—will be more than adequate. Two containers of yogurt after the race will take care of your protein needs. Eating fatty foods isn't recommended either, despite the fact that you have burned fat as a fuel during the race. Fat supplies are plentiful in your body. Sodium, a component of salt, is an electrolyte lost when you sweat. But the average American diet contains ten to sixty times the required amount; you don't need to replace it. If your body craves it, try pretzels, popcorn, or cheese as a snack to satisfy your urge. Salt losses are best replaced by foods rather than fluids. The clear conclusion of all this is that a balanced diet, perhaps with an emphasis on carbohydrates, will replenish all the energy stores of fat and glycogen plus other essential vitamins and minerals. Fluid intake is important and should be maintained and watched carefully. Remember, the balanced, healthful diet is all any runner needs.

37. DRINKING AND RUNNING

Drinking enough fluids is essential for the competitive runner. On race day, in fact, fluids are more important than food. Runners don't die of hunger pangs, but dehydrated runners can, and have, died from lack of fluids.

1. WHAT TO DRINK IN YOUR DAILY DIET

Your body is mostly water; thus, it needs a good fresh supply of water every day to maintain its balance and function normally. There is little danger of consuming too much water; any excess is flushed away by your kidneys. Chronic dehydration causes an increase in appetite, and thus could cause weight gain.

Your body requires at least six glasses of fluid every day; some fluid replacement will come from the foods you eat. When you exercise, you need much more fluid, at least two to three quarts daily, and half of this should be water. Drink water before and during your meals. Also remember that fluids are important during carbohydrate loading to prevent dehydration.

Water is the main component of our cells, urine, sweat, and

blood. When you are dehydrated, your cells become dehydrated and chemical reactions are impaired. The cells can't build tissues or utilize energy efficiently. You don't produce urine, and consequently toxic products build up in your bloodstream. You don't sweat, so your temperature rises. Your blood volume decreases, and you have less blood to transport oxygen and nutrients through your body. The result is that your muscles become weak, and you are soon in danger of collapse.

Runners, of course, drink other beverages besides water. Two popular but controversial ones are coffee and beer.

Coffee

Coffee contains caffeine, which is a drug. Excessive intake of caffeine causes irregular heartbeats, and in some people may aggravate conditions such as ulcers, gout, or high blood pressure. It is a stimulant and can cause hyperactivity and even stomach spasms. It should be cut back on or eliminated from our diets.

Americans consume a lot of caffeine unintentionally. It is commonly added to foods, beverages (coffee and the colas), and over-the-counter drugs. Adverse effects—including headaches, sleeplessness, and anxiety—may result from drinking four or five cups of brewed coffee daily, ten to twelve cups of instant coffee, or fifteen 12-ounce servings of caffeinated soft drinks. This may seem like a lot, but it's not exceptional; according to the American Council on Science and Health, some 11 million Americans consume this much caffeine daily. Too much coffee or cola late in the evening after a workout when your body may already be jittery can result in troubled sleep.

Beer

Nectar of the gods, ambrosia of those who seek fast times—beer may be the runner's fuel. It doesn't take a scientific study to know that a majority of competitive runners, including those of world class, drink a lot of beer and argue (sometimes loudly) that it helps them. Dr. Peter Wood, of the Stanford University Disease Prevention Program, discovered that runners outdrank nonrunners by two to one. We're still trying to find out if that's cans or pitchers.

A quart of beer supplies about 450 calories, which will quickly replenish depleted energy reserves. That quart contains about the same amount of carbohydrates as a quarter pound of bread, but goes down much faster and is metabolized quickly. Beer also contains B complex vitamins and other nutrients. Studies indicate, however, that one beer lowers heat tolerance for as long as 3 days. Alcohol promotes urination, and can thus help cause dehydration. If you have a slow metabolic rate or if you don't keep your mileage up, beer consumption will add weight; many runners prefer the low-calorie beers.

We recommend as part of your daily diet, if you wish, two or three glasses of beer. But that's it! If you're knocking down a six-pack a day, you not only have a weight problem but also a drinking problem. We do not recommend beer to excess. A beer or two in the evening may help you relax and promote sleep, especially the night before a big race. Before one Boston Marathon, a top-level marathoner couldn't get to sleep because he was so nervous. Bob Glover suggested he have a couple of beers. He drank two—and became quite dizzy. He woke up on the floor with a hangover, and ran a terrible race. He didn't tell Glover that he had never had a drink before in his life. However, the postrace, postworkout beer will replace lost fluids and minerals and help you relax. Whoever heard of a runner's party without beer?

Whatever you drink—water or juice—drink more of it the day before a race in hot weather. If you drink too much, you will urinate more, but you want to have a full tank of fluids prior to race day.

2. DRINKING BEFORE RUNNING AND RACING

Some runners argue that caffeine ingested before a race improves their times. The evidence on this is still inconclusive. About an hour before the race, these runners drink a cup of unsweetened tea or coffee or swallow two caffeine pills. The theory is that the caffeine releases fatty acids into the bloodstream as fuel, thus sparing and slowing the use of muscle glycogen and the onset of fatigue until much later in the race than normally.

Dr. Costill's work shows that caffeine intake may increase the ability to perform work by as much as 16 percent in some people. He warns, however, that caffeine is a drug, and that some people do not benefit from it; in fact, about 20 percent of the population have a negative reaction. Some runners have found that caffeine before a race produces jitters and diarrhea. Studies have also shown that caffeine can increase heat production, which is bad on a hot race day.

If you want to see what caffeine might do for, or to, you, practice drinking one to three cups of tea or coffee before a long training run and see how your body reacts. Don't experiment on race day. We would prefer to see you improve your race times by following the training guidelines in this book, however, rather than by experimenting with a drug that may harm you as much as help you.

Avoid sugared drinks for 1 to 3 hours before a race. You may have an insulin reaction that will temporarily lower your blood sugar, leaving you with less fuel for energy. Dr. Costill has determined that runners who drink sugared beverages a few hours before exercising become prematurely exhausted.

You should drink very little fluid in the 2 hours before you race. It takes 1 to $1\frac{1}{2}$ hours for your body to eliminate excess fluids through urination. So if you drink fluids between $\frac{1}{2}$ and $1\frac{1}{2}$ hours before the race, you may have to urinate at the starting line or shortly after the race begins. The world's largest urinal, *over 200 feet long*, near the start of the New York Marathon, draws plenty of business because nervous runners drink too much in the hours immediately before the start.

The American College of Sports Medicine recommends that runners drink 13–17 ounces of fluids 10–15 minutes prior to racing (or for that matter prior to long runs). Normally the kidneys shut down as you start running so that your last-minute fluid intake that doesn't reach the kidneys will remain in your body. Thus, you are actually "fluid loading." This extra fluid will be immediately available for sweat, which helps cool the body on a hot day. The extra fluids will help prevent or delay dehydration and overheating.

Look for water stations at the starting area. Water is your safest bet before the race. Avoid fruit juices, sweetened athletic drinks, alcoholic beverages, and anything you aren't used to.

3. DRINKING ON THE RUN

In warm or hot weather, especially during long runs, it is important to drink on the run. There are at least three basic reasons:

1. As you run, your body temperature rises as body fluids are depleted. This loss dehydrates you and can cause serious damage to your circulatory system. Fluid intake on hot days especially is essential to your health because it minimizes dehydration and helps cool the body. See page 550 for warning signs of dehydration.

2. Important minerals and chemicals known as electrolytes (sodium, potassium, magnesium) are lost through the pores in perspiration. Fluids containing these minerals can be ingested before and during the race to replace those lost. Electrolyte depletion could result in fatigue or leg cramping, or upset the body's water balance.

3. Sugar solutions supply glucose (used for energy) to the body, offsetting that lost during exercise, especially late in a long run.

The body loses fluids more rapidly than they can be absorbed through the stomach. On hot days, you should drink more than you think is necessary. Don't rely upon your thirst: you could be down one to two quarts of sweat before your mouth even feels thirsty. Drink as much as you can without upsetting your stomach—a further reason for drinking mainly water. Dr. Costill says: "During the marathon, you can't even come close to replacing the fluids you lose. Drinking at aid stations may replace only one tenth of the fluids you lose. But this 10 percent is important."

In general, a weight loss of 2 percent or more of one's body weight by sweating affects performance. A loss of 5 to 6 percent affects health. A weight loss of 5 to 7 pounds is not uncommon during long runs. A runner may lose about 3 or 4 pounds per hour during a marathon, but he or she can only absorb about

1.8 pounds of water from the stomach in the same period. Obviously, regardless of how much a runner drinks, he or she cannot keep up with the weight loss from sweating. Thus, a runner will dehydrate twice as fast as he or she can replace fluids during a race and will finish dehydrated.

You can lose a pound of sweat in as little as 2 miles. Dehydration also affects your body's ability to control body temperature. The combination of dehydration, heat buildup generated by work, and warm air temperatures can dramatically increase your body temperature. Your normal body temperature is 98.6°F. Commonly, it can rise as high as 106°F on hot days, which is extremely dangerous if prolonged. Temperatures as high as 108°F might be fatal, so it is critical to keep the body temperature down by replacing lost fluids. In studies by Costill, it was shown that rectal temperatures in runners were 2 degrees (F) cooler when the runners drank fluids during a 2-hour run than when they did not.

So start drinking about 10 to 15 minutes before the start of the race, and then drink about every 15 minutes during the race on hot days (somewhat less often on cool days). Fluid stations should be located about every 2 miles. Your body can absorb about 6 ounces of fluid every 15 to 20 minutes. Therefore you should take a full cup of fluid every 2 to 3 miles. More than two cups at one time may distend your stomach and cause problems with proper breathing. Remember: It takes up to 20 minutes for the fluid to be absorbed and take effect, so don't wait until you feel hot and thirsty to begin drinking. By then it will be too late. Fluids taken during the last 2 or 3 miles may not help in your race but will aid in your recovery.

You don't have to wait to reach fluid stations before you drink. Some runners carry their drinks with them and don't stop at the water stops at all. In most major marathons, spectators line the course and supply you with fluids. Just be careful of what you take. Water is the safest to accept from a stranger. By supplementing the official fluid stations, you don't need to down as much fluid each time—downing a full cup at once without spilling it isn't easy. Some races don't supply fluids often enough to meet your demands. Also, in some big races it is very hard to get fluids without literally standing in line and fighting for them. So it is helpful to have a backup system of fluid supply.

A good choice, then, is to have friends stationed along the course with plastic squeeze bottles of your favorite road-tested beverage. This will involve forming a team—friends, kids, relatives—and making them part of your racing success. This way you know what you are getting, and you're getting it from encouraging supporters.

Fluid replacement is critical in short races too. Even in 5K races, the slower runner will benefit from drinking fluids. The faster runners will only waste time because they will finish before the fluids are absorbed. Prerace fluid intake, however, is still essential in short races. As a rule of thumb, if you are racing longer than 30 minutes, it is important to drink fluids during the race as well as before. And don't neglect fluids on a cold day. Running will raise your body temperature and deplete fluids even when the spectators are wearing fur coats.

Drinking in a race can be tricky. Most runners try to grab a cup of liquid and throw it down quickly as they run. This is difficult to accomplish and hard on your stomach; it may spoil your rhythm more than stopping altogether. Some runners will try to carry the drink and finish it off in a few mouthfuls. The easiest way to drink on the run is to use a plastic squeeze bottle with a nozzle. You can control your intake, and you don't have to worry about spilling a drop. Of course, you need someone to hand the bottle to you and take it back.

The surest way to make sure you get that needed full cup is to stop and drink it or drink it while walking. For some, this is a good excuse to take a break. You may find that you will lose less time overall if you pause for a drink rather than trying clumsily to drink on the run.

Race directors should tell you before the race starts where the water stations are located—at which mile marks and on which side of the road—and they should post warning signs (or have someone call out) when stations are coming up. Slower runners should take their time, drink a cup of fluid, and then move along. Faster runners, however, may limit their stops to avoid losing ground to competitors. Sometimes, in an effort to break away, a runner will skip a fluid station if he or she sees an opponent take a drink. Some races have been won this way. But others have been lost by competitors who suddenly fell apart from failing to replace lost fluids.

When in doubt, be cautious. Drink. Research shows that time lost drinking is more than made up for in performance by the average long-distance runner. He or she doesn't slow down from dehydration and overheating.

Fluids are also essential for your long training runs, whatever the temperature. On hot days, drink often. In New York City's Central Park, for example, runners break up their 6-mile loop by stopping at a water fountain every 3 miles. On longer runs on humid days, they stop more often. If there are no handy drinking fountains along your route, try running an out-and-back course and stashing a plastic squeeze bottle in the grass along the way. Or scout out a friendly gas station, school, or home along your route. Never think that not drinking during training runs will toughen you for hot weather racing.

4. WHAT DRINKS ARE BEST ON THE RUN

Should you drink water, juice, soda, or commercial athletic drinks? Some prefer to make up their own concoction. For the most part, however, plain water is best. Here are some of the other options available to runners:

Special Electrolyte Drinks

These fluids—such as ERG, Gatorade, Body Punch—make a lot of claims and have avid supporters, who argue that when we sweat, we lose more than water. We lose electrolytes—minerals such as sodium, potassium, magnesium, calcium, and phosphate. These losses may cause cramping and impair your body's normal functioning. Despite advertising claims for these special drinks—and their use in marathon events and by athletic teams—they may not be all that is claimed for them. Dr. Costill's research indicates that we may not need to replace electrolytes lost through sweat during competition because the loss is very small. These drinks also contain sugar.

Sugared Drinks

Some runners and competitive cyclists drink sugared fluids—
in athletic drinks, soda, and other beverages. The cyclists claim
that these drinks eliminate "bonking"—running out of liver
glycogen—which causes dizziness, hypoglycemia, and confusion. You can recover from bonking by consuming sugar immediately. But runners are mostly concerned with muscle—
not liver—glycogen losses. Some studies indicate that sugar
taken during competition goes into the bloodstream and is used
by our muscles to delay the burning of stored glycogen, thus
prolonging endurance. Others indicate that the glycogen stored
previously in the muscles is the determining factor in "hitting
the Wall"—not the circulating glucose (sugar) in the bloodstream.

Researchers at Miami University in Ohio studied the effect
of "glucose polymer," which unlike regular glucose leaves the
stomach as fast as water does, on ultra-endurance cyclists. They
found that drinks such as Exceed, Max, and Carboplex II with
weak concentrations of glucose, in the 5–7 percent range, improved performance. The fluids were absorbed by the body
quickly, contributed some fuel to help push back fatigue, helped
maintain a normal blood sugar level, and enhanced the ability
to concentrate in the late stages of a race.

Sugar may or may not help you beat the Wall, but it may
help you feel less fatigued, especially if you aren't a highly
trained marathoner. According to Dr. Joan Ullyot, author of
Women's Running: "The blood sugar level is kept up mainly by
metabolism of liver glycogen and to some extent by what you
digest. That's why I think things like ERG are so important
during a race. They keep your blood sugar up which makes
you feel better. Blood sugar doesn't do anything for the muscles, though. The brain needs sugar. The brain is the only organ
in the body that needs sugar all the time. If the mind perceives
that the blood sugar is low, you are going to feel fatigue whether
or not you have plenty of fuel. But the trained marathon runners who have been tested during the marathon all had very
high blood sugar levels. The ability to maintain blood sugar
level is developed through training." Thus, the average runner

and the novice need sugar during the race more than the well-trained runner does. Sugar intake, however, delays the absorption of fluids. On a cool marathon day, sugar solutions may be helpful, but on a hot day, play it safe and stick to cool water.

The American College of Sports Medicine advises race sponsors to mix fluids and small amounts of sugar—less than 2.5 grams glucose per 100 ml water—to help absorption. Some runners down cola during races. Cola should be defizzed and diluted with water. Frank Shorter used defizzed cola en route to his 1972 Olympic Marathon victory. Others take both water and the race fluid and drink half of each to dilute the drink further, aid absorption, and lessen the chances of getting an upset stomach. Some runners take sugared iced tea, which packs the water, sugar, and the supposed "boost" of caffeine.

Your choice of drinks depends on:

Your Preference and Needs. Sugared drinks or drinks high in citric acid may upset your stomach, but you may benefit from them. Whatever you drink, practice drinking it on your long training runs and in low-key races—noting both its effect on you and how easily it can be consumed while you run. Your best bet is to choose a drink based on your own experience with it. For some runners, dehydration is more of a problem than for others. Some of us run well in the heat, others need all the fluids we can get just to survive.

Heat. Studies show that water is absorbed 50 percent faster than a sugar solution, which means it works faster to prevent dehydration or overheating. Anything mixed with water delays its absorption. Your preferred drink on a hot day should be water: it is more important to get fluids quickly into your system than to worry about replacing lost energy substances. Cold water absorbs faster than warm fluids. Cold drinks—contrary to the old myth—will not cause cramps. The ideal fluid temperature for absorption is 40°F. In cooler weather, water isn't as necessary, but some fluid intake is always advisable. You may wish to drink more sugared drinks, but switch to water if the weather warms up during the race.

Distance. Under 10 miles, water is all you need. For the marathon, sugared drinks *may* help you through the last miles—

through the Wall—but if you dehydrate, you are in worse trouble. The Wall doesn't kill—dehydration does. Alberto Salazar had to be given emergency fluids intravenously when his body temperature dropped to 88°F after winning the 1982 Boston Marathon on a hot, sunny day. He had lost an enormous amount of body fluids and was dangerously dehydrated.

5. WHAT TO DRINK AFTER YOU RUN

After your workout or race, you should replace lost fluids, electrolytes, and energy reserves. Studies show that sweat loss may result in an 8 percent loss of body weight and a 13 to 14 percent reduction of body water. Marathoners often lose 6 to 12 pounds, or the equivalent of as much as 1 to 1.5 gallons of fluids. This is not a weight loss, but a fluid loss, and is not permanent. You'll actually burn off only enough calories to lose less than a pound of body fat.

To rehydrate adequately takes between 24 and 48 hours. Weigh yourself before and after every workout and race to see how much fluid weight you are losing. You should replace lost body weight by drinking plenty of fluids after long, hot runs—twice as much as you feel is necessary. One gallon of water equals about 8.5 pounds. That works out to more than a pint of fluids to replace each pound of weight loss.

Start replacing fluids as soon as you finish your run. Sip, if you cannot gulp fluids. When your stomach settles, pour them in. In hot weather, consume cold drinks to bring down your body temperature as well as replace the fluid loss. Studies show that runners who drink two cups of ice water absorb half of it in 20 minutes—twice the amount of those who drink warm water. In cold weather, also drink some cold water to replace lost fluids, but then add something warm to prevent chill—hot chocolate, tea, coffee, or soup.

You should drink plenty of fluids throughout the day in proportion to the amount of weight you lost. Dr. Jack Scaff, former director of the always hot Honolulu Marathon, advises runners to keep drinking until they have clear urine. Dark urine is a symptom of dehydration. Dr. Costill warns: "The human thirst mechanism is quite slow. As a result, you may be eight pounds dehydrated and have a couple of glasses of fluid and feel satisfied. But an hour later you will be thirsty again. You have to just force yourself to drink some extra. Watch your body weight for the next 24 hours. Generally this is enough time to get your fluids back."

Beware of chronic dehydration caused by going several days without properly replenishing lost fluids. This is a dangerous condition that is frequently overlooked. It lowers a runner's tolerance to fatigue, reduces his ability to sweat, elevates his rectal temperature, and increases the stress on his circulatory system. "Probably the best way to guard against chronic dehydration," says Dr. Costill, "is to check your weight every morning before breakfast. If you note a two or three pound decrease in body weight from morning to morning, efforts should be made to increase your fluid intake. You need not worry about drinking too much fluid, because your kidneys will unload the excess water in a matter of hours." Better too much fluid for the kidneys than not enough. According to Dr. Edward Colt, "There is a lot of evidence that runners are suffering from chronic dehydration which becomes even more severe during long runs or marathons. The evidence for this is the sixfold increase in kidney stones among marathon runners which Paul Milvy, John Thorton and I reported in the *Journal of Sports Medicine and Physical Fitness*. Kidney stones occur much more frequently in people who are dehydrated. Susceptibility to urine infections also results."

But what should you drink after your long run or race? You need to replace what you lost—sweat. The fastest, simplest, and safest way to do that is by drinking cold water. But you have also sweated out electrolytes that help your body function properly. Shortages in these minerals will affect your recovery. However, the mineral loss isn't high. A few normal, well-balanced meals and a few glasses of orange, pineapple, or tomato juice should easily replace most lost minerals. Soda pop has very little potassium, and the special athletic drinks have even less. The athletic drinks are more valuable during your race than after, since they are diluted to enable your body to absorb them better while exercising. Soda pop will help you replace lost fluids, supply sugar to help replace depleted glycogen reserves, perhaps satisfy your taste. We do not recommend coffee, milk, wines, or liquor as fluids after running. Alcohol makes you urinate more frequently and thus causes you to lose fluids when you are trying to replenish your supply. Before celebrating with a postrace beer, drink several glasses of water, and then eat something nutritious with the beer.

38. RUNNING AND YOUR BODY WEIGHT

Elite runners are lean and mean, but most runners need to work at reducing body fat and weight. We need only essential fat (about 4 percent for men and 10 percent for women) and enough weight for muscle strength to power us through training and races. We should strive for stronger engines, lighter chassis, and good health.

To determine your best weight, consider the following list and then consult the chart estimating the best racing weight for you. Remember: Estimates are generalizations; you alone (perhaps together with your doctor) can determine your best weight.

WHAT DID YOU WEIGH AT 18–25?

During these years most of us were light: we were too active to get fat. Theoretically, we stop growing in our early twenties. According to Dr. Irwin Maxwell Stillman, author of *The Inches-Off Diet,* no one should weigh more than he or she did at age 25. Life-insurance weight charts—which show that people weigh more as they age—merely reflect what is happening, not what should be happening. As we age, our metabolism slows. To counteract this slowdown, we should eat less and exercise more, and level off our weight instead of continuing to gain. Your weight at age 25, therefore, should be a first goal.

HOW DO YOU LOOK AND FEEL?

Dr. Ken Cooper, the author of *Aerobics,* suggests that you stand nude in front of a full-length mirror and look at yourself critically. If you *look* fat, you are. Now the unfair test: try running in place and look for jiggles, especially the thighs and stomach. Very fit runners are often gaunt in the face because their body fat percentage is so low.

A runner may lose inches from the waist but weigh the same, because muscle weighs more than fat, although it takes up less space. With proper weight training, you may actually gain weight, but lose body fat. If you are running to control your weight, you need to run and diet at the same time to reach the level you wish. If your goal is to run faster, you need to weigh as little as you can and still feel strong.

HOW DO YOU PERFORM?

Generally, you will pick your ideal weight by the process of self-selection. As your mileage approaches a high, consistent level, you will find a comfortable and efficient weight for you. Veteran runners can tell what they weigh by how their training is going. Bob Glover is 6'1" and weighs 160 pounds when running very little. He weighs 157 at 50 miles a week, 155 at 70 a week, and 152 at 100 a week. He can guess his weight within a pound by feeling how his body reacts to training.

Check your diary to see what you weighed when you ran your best workouts and races. Weigh yourself daily (but not after runs, when you have temporarily lost body fluids), and record your weight.

Some runners perform poorly when just a few pounds over their ideal body weight; others, when a few pounds under. Being too much overweight can dramatically slow your race time. But you can also perform poorly and be prone to injury and illness if you are underweight. You can actually burn away essential muscle and thus lose strength in key muscle groups, which can make you more vulnerable to injury.

WHAT ARE YOUR GOALS?

You may wish to race lighter for marathons than for other races. Often marathoners will train at a comfortable weight and then, as the marathon approaches, bring the weight down a little. Some choose to improve upper body strength, and will thus gain some weight to help them perform better at shorter distances.

BODY FAT PERCENTAGE

Your body consists of two types of tissues: fat and lean body tissue—bone, organ, and muscle. The amount of fat you carry is called your body fat percentage. It is determined by dividing your total body weight by the weight of your fat. Body fat percentage is commonly estimated by using calipers to measure the fat under the skin (skinfolds) or by an underwater weighing technique. The latter is more accurate, but both are estimates. You can have a skinfold estimate taken at your local YMCA.

Body weight and body fat percentage are closely linked. According to Dr. David Costill, each pound of fat added or lost can result in an increase or decrease in body fat percentage of as much as half a point, which will affect performance. Some runners may weigh within the standard limits, while having a high percentage of body fat. They are underweight and overfat. Big-bodied runners and some other athletes, such as professional football players, may be heavier than the weight charts suggest, but low in body fat percentage. They are overweight, but "underfat." For some of them, losing weight is equated with losing strength—an undesirable result. Consequently, when predicting your best weight, you need to consider several things. The most important is how lean you are. Here are normal body fat values.

	MEN	WOMEN
Elite marathoner	8%	15%
Advanced and champion competitive runners	10	18
Novice and basic competitive runners	15	22
Overweight	20+	25+

DETERMINING RACING WEIGHTS FOR MEN

The Elite Runner

The most widely used rule of thumb for determining racing weight for men is the 2:1 ration—2 pounds of body weight for every inch of height. We have tested this theory on hundreds of runners, and it is very accurate for runners around the average height for male marathon runners, 5'10" (70 inches), where the average weight is around 140 pounds. (To determine your best running weight, multiply height in inches by 2.) Elite runners at the 1980 U.S. Olympic Trials averaged 70 inches and 139 pounds. The chart on page 556 for elite marathoners follows the 2:1 ration for heights from 5'7" to 6'2" in men. Adjustments are made below 5'7" (or the runner has it too easy) and above 6'2" (or the runner has it too hard).

You should not aim for this 2:1 ratio unless you can do it without sacrificing strength. Weighing what an elite runner weighs will not by itself make you fast; and it could, by weakening you, make you slow. Most elite runners weigh what they do because their high training mileage (100–140 miles per week) burns up enormous amounts of calories (more than 5,000 a day); they have small frames on average heights, and a very low body fat percentage (4 to 8 percent).

If your times and mileage are approaching those of the elite runner, you might benefit from being within 2 pounds either way of the weights shown on the chart above. For the lighter-weight elite, the loss of only 2 pounds going into a race might

RACING WEIGHTS FOR MALE ELITE RUNNERS

HEIGHT	WEIGHT IN POUNDS
5′4″ (64″)	119
5′5″ (65″)	125
5′6″ (66″)	129
5′7″ (67″)	134
5′8″ (68″)	136
5′9″ (69″)	138
5′10″ (70″)	140
5′11″ (71″)	142
6′0″ (72″)	144
6′1″ (73″)	146
6′2″ (74″)	148
6′3″ (75″)	153
6′4″ (76″)	158

Note: As with all charts, consider each of the charts in this chapter as estimated guidelines only. The charts have been proven to be quite accurate for most runners; they are most likely to be inaccurate at the extremes. Shorter people or those with very small frames perhaps weigh a little less. Taller people or those with very big frames may weigh a little more. The bottom line is your body fat percentage, not your total weight.

result in improved performance, although others may find even that much loss weakening. The elite runner, through experience, can tell what weight is best for him or her, and generally it will be close to what is listed on this chart.

Advanced and Champion Competitors

These runners are serious about their training and wish to be as efficient as possible by running as light as they can and still maintain enough strength for both their running and their workday (most elite runners have to worry only about their running). They should weigh within 10 percent of the elite runner's weight at the same height. (See chart below.) By bringing their weight closer to 5 percent of the elite runner—perhaps for important races—they may get into even better shape. Reaching the elite weight may be impossible; it may require both taking the time to run 100 or more miles a week and not getting injured doing it.

These runners usually compete at about 10 percent body fat on a small-to-medium frame. It is essential to watch the diet; extra weight will affect performance.

RACING WEIGHTS FOR MALE ADVANCED AND CHAMPION COMPETITORS

HEIGHT	WEIGHT IN POUNDS
5'4" (64")	131
5'5" (65")	137
5'6" (66")	142
5'7" (67")	147
5'8" (68")	149
5'9" (69")	152
5'10" (70")	154
5'11" (71")	156
6'0" (72")	158
6'1" (73")	160
6'2" (74")	163
6'3" (75")	168
6'4" (76")	174

By way of comparison with yourself, the average height for serious male competitors in the 1981 Boston Marathon (who had to qualify with times of 2:50 or better, 3:10 for masters) was 69 inches. Using the height-in-inches-times-2 formula and adding 10 percent, we predict a weight of 152 pounds. Their average weight was 148 pounds.

Novice and Basic Competitors

These runners' weight range is listed on the chart below, for men over age 25. Note that the ranges are listed by body frame type. Since all such charts are merely guidelines, you may be better off using the lower figure in your range; when in doubt, select the lighter frame. These are minimal fitness standards. The closer you come toward the weight of the competitive runner, the better you will look, feel, and run. The runners have a body fat percentage of about 15 percent.

RACING WEIGHTS FOR MALE NOVICE AND BASIC COMPETITORS*

HEIGHT	SMALL FRAME	MEDIUM FRAME	LARGE FRAME
5'4"	118–126 pounds	124–136	132–148
5'5"	121–129	127–139	135–152
5'6"	124–133	130–143	138–156
5'7"	128–137	134–147	142–161
5'8"	132–141	138–152	147–166
5'9"	136–145	142–156	151–170
5'10"	140–150	146–160	155–174
5'11"	144–154	150–165	159–179
6'0"	148–158	154–170	164–184
6'1"	152–162	158–175	168–189
6'2"	156–167	162–180	172–194
6'3"	160–171	167–185	178–199
6'4"	164–175	172–190	182–204

*Developed by the Metropolitan Life Insurance Company.

DETERMINING RACING WEIGHTS FOR WOMEN

Unfortunately, the formula that works so well for men doesn't work for women. They have a different body fat/body muscle makeup. And since women are new to competitive racing, large numbers of highly trained women have yet to be studied. We have, however, arrived at a formula that has so far proven accurate for most women runners. Note, however, that women's weights may increase slightly during menstruation. Also, women should be careful not to place too much value on thinness and loss of weight at a sacrifice to health and strength. Each runner type has similar characteristics to men, and should follow the same guidelines listed for her male counterpart in this chapter.

The Elite Runner

The elite female runner, who runs about 70 to 100 miles a week, has a body fat percentage of 10 to 15 percent. The average elite female runner is 5'6" tall and weights 108 pounds. To determine the weight of the elite runner, subtract 10 percent from weight listed for your height for the advanced and champion competitive runner on page 559.

RACING WEIGHTS FOR FEMALE ELITE RUNNERS

HEIGHT	WEIGHT IN POUNDS
5'0"	81
5'1"	86
5'2"	90
5'3"	95
5'4"	99
5'5"	104
5'6"	108
5'7"	113
5'8"	117
5'9"	122
5'10"	126

The elite female runner may weigh a little more, on the average, than the chart above indicates.

Advanced and Champion Competitors

The average runner in this category is 5'6" and weighs 120 pounds. She has a body fat percentage of 15 to 20 percent. Dr. Joan Ullyot's theory for the proper weight for women runners is used as the formula here: start with 5 feet in height and 90 pounds in weight; add 5 pounds for each additional inch. A 5 percent reduction in weight from this will improve times for many women runners.

RACING WEIGHTS FOR FEMALE ADVANCED AND CHAMPION COMPETITORS

HEIGHT	WEIGHT IN POUNDS
5'0"	90
5'1"	95
5'2"	100
5'3"	105
5'4"	110
5'5"	115
5'6"	120
5'7"	125
5'8"	130
5'9"	135
5'10"	140

All of the dozen or so sub-3-hour marathoners that Bob Glover coaches with his Atalanta team fall at or just below this figure.

Novice and Basic Competitors

These runners run 20 miles a week or more and have a body fat percentage of 20 to 25 percent. The weights, listed on the chart below, are for women over age 25. Note that the range is listed by body frame type, and use the chart only as a guideline. The closer you come to the weight of the advanced and champion competitive runners, the better you are likely to run.

RACING WEIGHTS FOR FEMALE NOVICE AND BASIC COMPETITORS*

HEIGHT	SMALL FRAME	MEDIUM FRAME	LARGE FRAME
5'0"	96–104	101–113	109–125
5'1"	99–107	104–116	112–128
5'2"	102–110	107–119	115–131
5'3"	105–113	110–122	118–134
5'4"	108–116	113–126	121–138
5'5"	111–119	116–130	125–142
5'6"	114–123	120–135	129–146
5'7"	118–127	124–139	133–150
5'8"	122–131	128–143	137–154
5'9"	126–135	132–147	141–158
5'10"	130–140	136–151	145–163

*Developed by the Metropolitan Life Insurance Company.

THE BIG-BODIED RUNNER

This runner isn't fat, just overweight. His or her body wasn't designed for running. It is usually large-framed, with large muscle mass and average or higher body fat percentage. He or she is a victim of heredity. A 7-foot basketball player will never be a great marathoner no matter how fit; he is too tall. But then, Bill Rodgers will never do a whirling, in-your-face, slam-dunk in the Boston Garden either.

RUNNING, CALORIES, AND WEIGHT

The runner burns off one calorie per kilogram (2.2 pounds) of body weight for every kilometer (.62 miles) run. This is approximately 100 calories per mile—3,500 calories equal 1 pound. Thus, you have to run 35 miles to run off 1 pound of permanent fat; how fast you run that mile means little. Running twice as fast will only increase your caloric expenditure by 10 percent. A heavier person will burn a few more calories per mile than a lighter person. Fortunately, you don't have to run 35 miles to burn 1 pound of fat. According to Dr. Gabe Mirkin, "There are three mechanisms activated by regular exercise that control weight gain. First of all, with regular running exercise, you will find that you eat less. This is because the 'appestat'— the mechanism that is in your brain—tells you when and how much to eat. As a beginner, you will eat less. Later, as a competitor, you may eat more, but the appestat helps prevent you from overeating. However, for some runners it doesn't do a good job. Second, you burn extra calories after you stop exercise. For four to six hours after exercising, your pulse rate and temperature continue to increase. During the course of a year, the extra calories that are burned from increased metabolism after exercising can amount to a weight loss of five to ten pounds. Third, you absorb less food.

"It is quite easy for a runner who eats too much and doesn't watch the scales to balloon up quickly. Some runners have a slower metabolic rate than others, or their appestat may be set too high. Those with a low metabolic rate can eat like a sparrow and still have a weight problem. For these runners, the solution is often higher mileage when the body can handle it."

When Bob Glover was the physical director at the Rome, New York, YMCA, he used to run with Pat Merola, a big-boned Italian with a high appestat, slow metabolism, and a weakness for his wife's Italian cooking. If Pat cut his mileage back even slightly, he would gain as much as 20 pounds in 2 weeks. According to Dr. William Haskell, professor of medicine at Stanford University, although active, slim people take in about 600 calories a day more than their inactive, overweight friends, their appestat prevents them from consuming more than they will run off. This is why some people can eat twice as much and not gain weight.

Runners eat much more than the average person, who consumes and burns 1,500 calories a day on an inactive schedule. Studies show that marathon runners consume and burn as much as 5,000–6,000 calories a day. This is why many of them munch on junk food all day long—they need more energy to keep their weight up, and their appestat tells them to eat.

Losing Weight

Improper or fad dieting can result in too low a level of calories, fat, carbohydrates, or protein, resulting in health impairment. Just a few calories added or not burned per day will, in time, allow fat to creep up on you. Here are some tips for the runner trying to lose weight:

• The key is to run more, eat less; burn more calories, consume less.

• Watch what you eat. Try to switch to lower-calorie alternatives—water instead of soda, an apple instead of a candy bar.

• Eat smaller amounts, more often. Research shows that you can gain more on one big meal than on six smaller ones. Or eat the same food in smaller proportions. Cut out desserts.

• Be disciplined. Keep a weight diary to force yourself to stick with your goal. Set a reasonable goal, such as 5 to 10 pounds off before your next big race. Then more for your next race, and so on.

• Don't reduce liquid intake—you must replace lost fluids from sweat.

• Forget spot-reducing gimmicks! Running combined with some weight training should take care of specific contours. Spot reducing is a myth.

• Run long and slow. Runners who run at a comfortable aerobic pace burn more fat than those who train at a higher heart-rate level.

You can't follow both a strict diet and a strict training program. One runner we know was determined to lose weight. He lost over 50 pounds and completed the New York Marathon. Then he tried to shave off a few more pounds by combining a diet of only 1,000 calories a day with an 80-mile training week. Both were extremes that should have been avoided. The result was that he became extremely weak in the middle of one of his runs to work (because of glycogen depletion) and was forced to call a taxi. After that experience, he upped his caloric intake slightly and reduced his mileage slightly, along with the extra pounds.

Problems Caused by Being Overweight

Weight works against the runner. Every excess pound is an extra burden. Try running with 10 pounds of weight strapped in your backpack. Here's how weight affects running:

• The runner hits the ground at a force of impact three times his or her body weight; the more you weigh, the harder you hit. Thus, you are more prone to injury.

• Heavier runners do not handle heat well. Body fat works as an insulator, trapping in heat built up while running. Heavier runners lose more fluids and risk dehydration. Drink extra fluids.

• Extra weight makes the heart work harder, possibly overtaxing it.

• Excess weight affects performance by lowering your aerobic capacity.

Aerobic Capacity and Weight

As mentioned previously, aerobic capacity is the ability to take in and use oxygen to do the work: running. Since your aerobic capacity (maximum oxygen uptake or consumption) is measured by dividing the amount of oxygen you can consume per minute by your body weight, each pound or kilogram of extra weight reduces your aerobic capacity and thus your race times. There are three ways to improve this capacity:

1. Increase your ability to consume oxygen by improving your aerobic fitness level.

2. Decrease your body weight, making you more efficient at your present ability to consume oxygen.

3. Or both—increase aerobic fitness as you lose weight. As you increase your mileage, you gain by increasing cardiovascular fitness and by losing weight.

According to exercise physiologist K. J. Cureton at the University of Georgia, tests on runners showed that their aerobic capacity declines by 1 milliliter of oxygen per kilogram of weight per minute for every 1 percent of added weight. Studies of marathoners show that a 5 percent drop in body weight results in a 5 percent improvement in performance.

The bigger and stronger your engine and the lighter your chassis, the faster you can race—up to the point where loss of weight would make you weaker.

WEIGHT AND RACE TIMES

We have developed the following formula, which has proved to be fairly accurate at estimating how much faster you could run if you lost weight and kept your level of fitness and lean body weight (muscle and bone) the same.

Men

Consult the racing weight charts on pages 556–558 and find the weight recommended for your height. To calculate your race times, add or subtract minutes according to this formula:

• For the 10K, add approximately 2½ minutes per 10 pounds of extra weight above the figure listed.
• For the marathon, add approximately 10 minutes per 10 pounds.

MEN—WEIGHT AND RACE TIMES

WEIGHT	10K TIME (+2:30 PER 10 LBS)	MARATHON TIME (+10 MIN PER 10 LBS)
150	39:30	3:10
160	**42**	**3:20**
170	44:30	3:30
180	47	3:40
190	49:30	3:50

For example, take a 6′1″, 160-pound competitive runner who runs about 42 minutes for the 10K and a 3:20 marathon. If he were to weigh 20 pound more, he would run approximately 47 minutes for 10K and 3:40 for the marathon.

At the top of the opposite page is a chart showing comparisons for this particular size male runner—6'1" and about 160 pounds. You can see how excess weight may limit his potential.

Women

Consult the racing weight charts on pages 559–560 and find the weight recommended for your height. Calculate your race times by adding or subtracting minutes according to this formula:

- For the 10K race, add approximately 4 minutes per 10 pounds of extra weight above the figure listed.
- For the marathon, add approximately 20 minutes per 10 pounds.

For example, take a 5'4", 110-pound woman competitor who runs the 10K in 40 minutes and the marathon in 3:05. If she were to weigh 20 pounds more, her times would be 48 minutes and 3:45. Here's a chart on her potential:

WOMEN—WEIGHT AND RACE TIMES

WEIGHT	10K TIME (+4 MIN PER 10 LBS)	MARATHON TIME (+20 MIN PER 10 LBS)
100	36	2:45
110	**40**	**3:05**
120	44	3:25
130	48	3:45
140	52	4:05

Note: For both men's and women's formulas, improvements by weight loss cannot be expected beyond 10 pounds less than the starting weight: the weight of the competitive runner of your height. Weight loss below the starting figure may not result in faster times without increased training and a certain amount of inherited talent. The charts are only guidelines to show you how excess weight slows you down. With time and training, you will find the best weight for your height and competitive level.

Part XII

BALANCING THE STRESSES IN YOUR LIFE

39. THE RUNNER'S TRIANGLE

When the running boom first spread across America, one of the popular clichés of the time was that running itself created a positive addiction. It was an excellent way of overcoming the stress in our lives and of adding purpose and direction. Many of us found running to be, indeed, a positive force in our lives. But when we cross over into competitive running, for some of us, that can change. Competitive running can become too all-encompassing; it can become our primary reason for living. Competitive racers at the top make running their way of life and accept the commitment, pain, and failure with the success and, often, financial rewards. For them, the addiction to running has tangible benefits. But for most of us who run races and train hard but also have lives away from running, becoming too dedicated, too committed to running can create a very real problem: negative addiction.

Bob Glover, seeing the wreckage of bodies and dreams after the hot 1978 New York Marathon, coined the phrase "the runner's triangle of life." He was distressed that so many competitive runners had invested too much of their emotional, as well as their physical, being into that race, only to lose it all against the heat and the sun. The runner must balance the triangle of life: body, mind, and soul. He or she must balance the physical side of running, the intellectual and career side of life, and the spiritual and emotional side.

Running can be the central focus in our lives and can give us a positive reward, something we succeed at. But we need to balance it with other parts of our lives or running will become negative, draining the good in us. The runner who puts virtually his or her entire reason for living into running a race, or a series of races, is probably psychologically wounded. He or she is missing the point. Running must be fun; it must balance your life (making you more fit, less sedentary); it should bring you new friends, goals, a fresh sense of who you are and where you are going. It should not damage your career, family, love life; it should not make you into something you are not meant to be.

If you are under pressure at work, back off the running. Exercise for stress management, and cut the distance, speed, and structure of your runs until the stress eases. Open yourself up and talk to other runners about stress. Don't take out the stresses of your life on your running. You will make yourself more tense and injury prone. Pounding out your tension on hard pavement is a one-sided battle.

One middle-aged woman we know went through an emotional divorce, precipitated in part by her new independence as a runner, which her husband didn't understand. She turned all her frustrations loose on her running, and improved her times and filled her trophy case. But she was obsessed. She was showing him—she was having an affair with running. When she finally crashed—a cold led to pneumonia and bed rest— she realized that she had lost perspective; she had neglected her children and herself. She put running into perspective, reassembled her family and modified her career goals. She rebuilt her triangle, but not without pain and hard-learned lessons.

Dr. Edward Colt believes that many running-related injuries are caused by overuse as a result of blind addiction to running. "Running addiction cannot be gauged by mileage. Some runners who run 140 miles per week know exacly when they should ease back or stop their training. Some runners who run as little as twenty miles per week may be strongly addicted. Running addiction is predictable. The addictive personality is a lifelong disorder and an afflicted individual will have shown unmistakable signs before he ever starts to run. Overindulgence in one or more of the following: food, alcohol, drugs, sex, gambling, cigarettes, and so forth is usually evident in the past history of the running addict. Often running is used as therapy for these more harmful addictions. If you are a running addict, face it and be careful. If you are not a running addict, you are a most unusual person."

Runners think that because they are running they are automatically mentally healthy. The sport does indeed help us improve our self-image, and that carries over into other activities. It is false, however, to believe that running by itself will make us happy, healthy, or emotionally balanced.

One of the better New York City runners jumped out of a window to his death. His running didn't save him from other stresses. A 45-year-old British executive died from an overdose of aspirin. In his suicide note, he said that life was not worth living: he couldn't run because of a knee injury. That man had lost his perspective; running had become an obsession, a distortion of reality.

Putting running ahead of living soon distorts our runner's triangle. Noel Carroll, a former Irish Olympic runner, wrote in *The Runner's Book:* "The reality of the runner's life is that somebody else is always affected by his running. It may be a spouse, or a girlfriend, or a boyfriend, or a mother and father, or the children. To ignore the fallout is to court disaster. It can create an atmosphere that does nobody any good—and certainly not the runner."

What runners need is balance. Sacrifices do need to be made, but these should be balanced with the whole of one's life. With good scheduling, you can balance your triangle: keep running (body), job or school (mind), and family or friends (soul) in perspective.

WORK

According to William P. Morgan, director of the Sports Psychology Laboratory at the University of Wisconsin: "As the individual becomes more aware of self, he starts losing interest not only in his relationships, but also in such matters as vocational achievement. Promotions are, in fact, often a bother. They can mean increased responsibility, additional stress, the possibility of relocation, and less time and attention for self. . . . Needless to say, such a point of view not only can limit 'professional growth,' but it can jeopardize one's actual employment."

Some serious runners hold running-related jobs that carry limited responsibility and flexible hours, but also limited income. Bill Rodgers and Frank Shorter sacrificed for years to become the best in their sport and became financially independent only after achieving a certain status. Sacrifices must be balanced with the possible payoff. If you have only limited ability, but work in a running-shoe store to have time out to train, perhaps you should reevaluate your situation.

If both partners work and there are no children, the couple may have some flexibility. One may be able to work less in order to be able to train more. Sacrifices are balanced with realistic payoffs. To throw away a potential in sport is a waste. But to throw away your life to chase a futile dream is a greater waste.

Success in a running program, as in business, often depends on developing a routine. It is much easier to plan your running time if your work hours are consistent and regular than if your hours are constantly changing. You may find your lunch hour to be a convenient time to run as long as there is a place to sponge and change when you are done. If you are within distance, running to and from work, using a small backpack to carry your clothes, will let you make good use of your commuting time and interfere less with family and work.

FAMILY AND FRIENDS

When you start a running program or build for a big race, you should make your family circle or friends into allies, a support group. It takes skill to handle family members. The best way to win at the game is to be flexible, sharing your running interest with your family and friends and accommodating household duties and baby-sitting in your schedule.

The Glovers learned all about planning when baby Christopher arrived in 1981. Bob, like so many new fathers, suddenly found himself in many roles: husband, father, breadwinner, coach, author, and sometime runner. He started jogging with his wife to help her get back into shape, pushing Christopher in his carriage as they jogged. They became quite an attraction in Central Park: "Awwww, look at that *family!*"

But are running and marriage compatible? A *Parade* magazine article titled "Running Out of Marriage" stated: "The more runners run, the more conflicts they experience with spouses or close relatives. A poll taken in the Boston area indicated that runners who averaged more than 70 miles a week were far more likely to have marital problems than occasional or moderate runners.

"Nearly half the full-time runners admitted that their partners felt neglected. In 40 percent of the cases, the friction from running was serious enough to lead to divorce."

Forty percent of married runners putting in more than 70 miles a week got divorced! Is it difficult to train seriously and keep others happy? You must work at keeping others happy as much as you do at running. Running can become an affair—it can become a demanding lover that breaks you apart from your friends, family, or loved ones. The divorce rate, for example, among New York Marathon runners is 3.5 times the national average.

Let's talk about partners. A "partner" here is the other person in your life who means a lot to you. There are two types of running partnerships: both partners run together; one runs but the other doesn't. When both run, they have a shared interest; running together adds time together. Many romances begin as runners meet—both of us got "caught" this way.

The biggest problem, we have found, occurs when the woman (especially if she is the wife) runs and the man doesn't. Or where both run, and the woman runs better (faster, more competitively). Held back by our society both as an athlete and in her career, she now finds more self-confidence and becomes more independent. She may rebel against some of the traditions of marriage imposed by her husband (who does the shopping, who cooks, who tends the kids?) or lose respect for him if he is overweight and underexercised. He, in turn, may become jealous of her new independence and her new running friends.

Small issues lead to larger ones: dinner is late while she runs; she postpones having a baby as her running increases in importance.

She might try making him into a cheerleader; he could supply her with liquids at spots along the way during races. But she should never try to make him into a coach, and he must never try to coach her (particularly if he doesn't run himself). Coaching and marriage make a volatile mixture.

The woman runner carries more pressures than a man. She oftentimes balances a career, running, and marriage, and then must decide whether to accept the physical limitations of pregnancy and the time limitations of motherhood. Some women runners postpone all of these choices except running.

Most runners view their running as well integrated with other aspects of their lives and even making a positive contribution to their nonrunning side. But the line beween positive and negative addiction is thin. Some ten out of twelve runners interviewed by Michael Sachs and David Pargman of Florida State University said that they had a psychological or physiological dependence on running; they were placing running first in their lives. Some runners lose perspective altogether. Running becomes an end, not a means. The final stages of this negative addiction occur when running becomes your job and your job is viewed avocationally, when loved ones and friends are placed second, when the exercise addict (like the alcoholic or heroin addict) will not stop running even when faced with serious injury.

When most runners move over the line from dedication to obsession, Dr. Brent Waters, a clinician and researcher in exercise psychology at Royal Ottawa Hospital, says, it is a transient overindulgence. "Nevertheless, obsession with running appears to be becoming a more serious problem. Avoidable overuse syndromes are becoming all too frequent, and the families of some runners are becoming more vocal in their justified complaints that they are being relegated to a secondary role in the runner's life."

Scary? Look around you. Look inside yourself. Don't let the runner's triangle collapse on you and your loved ones in exchange for more mileage and faster times.

APPENDICES

Basic Physiology Terms
Base Pace for Training Mileage
Speed-Training Charts
Race-Time Comparison and Predictor Chart
Pacing Charts
Pace Chart for Track Races and Workouts
Mile-Kilometer Time Comparisons
Racing-Distance Conversions
Selected Reading List
Running Publications
Running Organizations

BASIC PHYSIOLOGY TERMS

1. *Aerobic:* Running "with oxygen" at a conversational pace well within your training heart-rate range. All easy endurance runs are done aerobically.

2. *Aerobic capacity (maximum oxygen uptake):* The ability to supply oxygen to the muscle tissues. Highly conditioned runners have higher aerobic capacities and can race at a faster pace more comfortably than less-conditioned runners. A runner with a higher aerobic capacity may fail to beat another runner, however, since performance is affected by such things as form, style, mental toughness, ability to run with lactic acid, proper pacing, natural speed, muscle strength, endurance, and so forth.

3. *Cardiorespiratory systems:* Endurance running improves the efficiency of both your ability to transport blood and oxygen by the heart and blood vessels (cardiovascular system) and your ability to breathe in air and exchange oxygen and carbon dioxide through the lungs and pulmonary arteries (circulorespiratory system). We combine these systems in the term "cardiorespiratory systems."

4. *Anaerobic:* This means "running without oxygen." When this happens, oxygen debt occurs, lactic acid accumulates, breathing becomes heavy, and the Bear may jump on your

back. Anaerobic running is running above your training heart-rate range. All racing includes some anaerobic and some aerobic running. The shorter and faster the race, the more you will run (and thus need to train) anaerobically. Fast speed-training runs will condition you to this.

5. *Aerobic-anaerobic borderline:* This is running at the edge of being out of breath, near 85 percent of your maximum heart rate, the top of your training heart-rate range. As you become better conditioned, you will be able to run at a faster pace before reaching this point; thus, you can extend your aerobic-anaerobic borderline and race faster. Some training runs are done at this borderline in order to push it back—condition you—so you can run at this intense pace. It is also called the "anaerobic threshold."

6. *Lactic acid:* A chemical substance released in the bloodstream when you run very fast—anaerobically, or in oxygen debt—that leads to muscle fatigue.

7. *Oxygen debt:* When you can't supply enough oxygen by normal aerobic means, you borrow energy, chemically causing a buildup of lactic acid in your muscles. When you slow down or stop running, you repay the debt—recover—and continue to function aerobically.

8. *Glycogen:* A starchlike substance stored in muscle tissues that is created from carbohydrates and used as the principal fuel for long-distance runners.

9. *The Bear:* The feeling of extreme fatigue and tightness caused by a buildup of lactic acid. The Bear will "jump on your back" when you try to sprint very hard or during short, fast races, because you cannot supply the needed oxygen to meet the demand. You go into oxygen debt.

10. *The Wall:* The point during a long run or race at which your body is running out of glycogen and shifts more to fat as an energy source. This happens at about 20 miles. You feel weary, heavy-legged, because you can't supply your muscles with energy fast enough to keep working efficiently. The result is often a dramatic slowdown in pace as you "hit the Wall." You may be able to push back the Wall by carbohydrate loading—which supplies extra glycogen storage—and taking long training runs, which condition the body to burn fat more efficiently.

11. *Fast-twitch muscle fibers:* One of two types of fibers. These contract rapidly and exhaust glycogen quickly during fast sprinting. Track sprinters have a predominance of these fibers. If you lack leg speed, it is largely because you weren't born with enough of these fibers in proportion to slow-twitch fibers.

12. *Slow-twitch muscle fibers:* These fibers burn glycogen slowly and efficiently during long-distance runs. Runners with approximately 70 percent slow-twitch fibers and 30 percent fast-twitch are usually better at the 5K–10K distances. Most marathon runners have a higher proportion of slow-twitch fibers, 80 to 90 percent.

13. *Training effect:* The pace you must train at to benefit from your exercise (at least 60 to 70 percent of maximum heart rate). The upper limit of your training heart-rate range for aerobic endurance running is 85 percent of maximum heart rate.

BASE PACE FOR TRAINING MILEAGE

10K RACE TIME (MINUTES: SECONDS)	10K RACE PACE	BRISK BASE PACE (10K + 1½ MIN)	EASY BASE PACE (10K + 2 MIN)
32:00	5:09	6:39	7:09
32:30	5:14	6:44	7:14
33:00	5:19	6:49	7:19
33:30	5:24	6:54	7:24
34:00	5:29	6:59	7:29
34:30	5:33	7:03	7:33
35:00	5:38	7:08	7:38
35:30	5:43	7:13	7:43
36:00	5:48	7:18	7:48
36:30	5:53	7:23	7:53
37:00	5:58	7:28	7:58
37:30	6:02	7:32	8:02
38:00	6:07	7:37	8:07
38:30	6:12	7:42	8:12
39:00	6:17	7:47	8:17
39:30	6:22	7:52	8:22
40:00	6:27	7:57	8:27
40:30	6:31	8:01	8:31
41:00	6:36	8:06	8:36
41:30	6:41	8:11	8:41
42:00	6:46	8:16	8:46
42:30	6:51	8:21	8:51
43:00	6:56	8:26	8:56
43:30	7:00	8:30	9:00
44:00	7:05	8:35	9:05
44:30	7:10	8:40	9:10
45:00	7:15	8:45	9:15
45:30	7:20	8:50	9:20
46:00	7:25	8:55	9:25
46:30	7:29	8:59	9:29
47:00	7:34	9:04	9:34
47:30	7:39	9:09	9:39
48:00	7:44	9:14	9:44
48:30	7:49	9:19	9:49
49:00	7:54	9:24	9:54
49:30	7:58	9:28	9:58
50:00	8:03	9:33	10:03

50:30	8:08	9:38	10:08
51:00	8:13	9:43	10:13
51:30	8:18	9:48	10:18
52:00	8:23	9:53	10:23
52:30	8:27	9:57	10:27
53:00	8:32	10:02	10:32
53:30	8:37	10:07	10:37
53:30	8:37	10:07	10:37
54:00	8:42	10:12	10:42
54:30	8:46	10:16	10:46
55:00	8:51	10:21	10:51
55:30	8:56	10:26	10:56
56:00	9:01	10:31	11:01
56:30	9:06	10:36	11:06
57:00	9:10	10:40	11:10
57:30	9:15	10:45	11:15
58:00	9:20	10:50	11:20
58:30	9:25	10:55	11:25
59:00	9:30	11:00	11:30
59:30	9:35	11:05	11:35
60:00	9:40	11:10	11:40

Note: See guidelines for base training pace in Chapter 5.

SPEED-TRAINING CHARTS

Use the following speed training charts to help you develop your workouts. These are conservative suggested guidelines. Consult the specific racing chapters (1 mile, cross-country, 5K, 10K, marathon) for more precise guidelines.

The following abbreviations are used:

Q—quantity of intervals to be run

I—intensity or pace of the intervals

R—recovery period between intervals (in minutes)

1m—pace-interval speed for 1-mile training

880—fast-interval speed (880-race speed) for 1-mile training

5K—5K pace intervals

10K—10K pace intervals

F—fast-interval pace (20 seconds faster per mile than 10K)

P—power-interval pace (30 seconds faster per mile than 10K)

WJ—alternate walking and jogging to recover coming back down a hill workout

J—jog back down at training pace to recover on hill workout

1-MILE SPEED-TRAINING CHARTS

DISTANCE	PACE INTERVALS			FAST INTERVALS		
	Q	I	R	Q	I	R
INEXPERIENCED MILER						
220	6–8	1m–5K	1	6–8	880	2
440	6–8	1m–5K	2	4–6	880	3
880	3–4	1m–5K	3			
Mile	2–3	5K	3			
EXPERIENCED MILER						
220	8–10	1m–5K	1	8–10	880	1
440	6–10	1m–5K	2	6–8	880	3
880	3–6	1m–5K	3			
Mile	2–3	5K	3			

5K SPEED-TRAINING CHARTS

DISTANCE	PACE INTERVALS			FAST INTERVALS		
	Q	I	R	Q	I	R
NOVICE COMPETITOR						
440	4–6	5K	2–3	4–5	F	3
880	4–6	5K	3	3–4	F	3
Mile	3	5K	3			
Short hills	4–5	5K	WJ			
Long hills	3–4	5K	WJ			
BASIC COMPETITOR						
440	5–8	5K	2	4–6	F	3
880	5–6	5K	2–3	4	F	3
Mile	3–4	5K	3			
Short hills	5–6	5K	J			
Long hills	4–5	5K	J			
ADVANCED COMPETITOR						
220	10–12	5K	1–2	6–10	F-P	1–2
440	8–12	5K	1–2	6–8	F-P	2
880	6–8	5K	2	4–6	F-P	3
Mile	4	5K	3			
Short hills	6–10	5K	J	5–6	F-P	J
Long hills	6–8	5K	J	4–5	F-P	J
CHAMPION COMPETITOR						
220	10–16	5K	1–2	6–10	F-P	1–2
440	8–12	5K	1–2	6–8	F-P	2
880	6–10	5K	2–3	6–8	F-P	2–3
Mile	4–5	5K	2–3			
Short hills	8–12	5K	J	6–10	F-P	J
Long hills	6–10	5K	J	5–6	F	J

10K AND MARATHON SPEED-TRAINING CHARTS

DISTANCE	PACE INTERVALS Q	I	R	FAST INTERVALS Q	I	R
NOVICE COMPETITOR						
440	4–6	5K–10K	2–3	3–4	F	3
880	4–6	5K–10K	3			
Mile	3	5K–10K	3			
Short hills	4–6	5K–10K	WJ			
Long hills	3–5	5K–10K	WJ			
BASIC COMPETITOR						
440	5–8	5K	2	4–5	F	2–3
880	5–8	5K–10K	2–3	4	F	3
Mile	3–4	5K–10K	3			
Short hills	5–8	5K–10K	J			
Long hills	4–6	5K–10K	J			
ADVANCED COMPETITOR						
220	10–12	5K	1–2	6–10	F-P	1–2
440	8–12	5K	1–2	6–8	F-P	2
880	6–10	5K–10K	2–3	4–6	F-P	3
Mile	4–5	5K–10K	3			
Short hills	6–10	5K–10K	J	5–6	F-P	J
Long hills	6–8	5K–10K	J	4–5	F	J
CHAMPION COMPETITOR						
220	10–16	5K	1–2	6–10	F-P	1–2
440	8–12	5K	1–2	6–8	F-P	2
880	6–12	5K–10K	2–3	6–8	F-P	2–3
Mile	4–6	5K	2–3			
Short hills	8–12	5K–10K	J	6–10	F-P	J
Long hills	6–10	5K–10K	J	5–6	F	J

PACE FOR SPEED WORKOUTS

10K TIME (MIN:SEC)	ANAEROBIC THRESHOLD PACE (10K + 30 SEC)	10K PACE INTERVALS	5K PACE INTERVALS (10K−10 SEC)	FAST INTERVALS (10K−20 SEC)	POWER INTERVALS (10K−30 SEC)
32:00	5:39	5:09	4:59	4:49	4:39
33:00	5:49	5:19	5:09	4:59	4:49
34:00	5:59	5:29	5:19	5:09	4:59
35:00	6:08	5:38	5:28	5:18	5:08
36:00	6:18	5:48	5:38	5:28	5:18
37:00	6:28	5:58	5:48	5:38	5:28
38:00	6:37	6:07	5:57	5:47	5:37
39:00	6:47	6:17	6:07	5:57	5:47
40:00	6:57	6:27	6:17	6:07	5:57
41:00	7:06	6:36	6:26	6:16	6:06
42:00	7:16	6:46	6:36	6:26	6:16
43:00	7:26	6:56	6:46	6:36	6:26
44:00	7:35	7:05	6:55	6:45	6:35
45:00	7:45	7:15	7:05	6:55	6:45
46:00	7:55	7:25	7:15	7:05	6:55
47:00	8:04	7:34	7:24	7:14	7:04
48:00	8:14	7:44	7:34	7:24	7:14
49:00	8:24	7:54	7:44	7:34	7:24
50:00	8:33	8:03	7:53	7:43	7:33
51:00	8:43	8:13	8:03	7:53	7:43
52:00	8:53	8:23	8:13	8:03	7:53
53:00	9:02	8:32	8:22	8:12	8:02

54:00	9:12	8:42	8:32	8:22	8:12
55:00	9:21	8:51	8:41	8:31	8:21
56:00	9:31	9:01	8:51	8:41	8:31
57:00	9:40	9:10	9:00	8:50	8:40
58:00	9:50	9:20	9:10	9:00	8:50
59:00	10:00	9:30	9:20	9:10	9:00
60:00	10:10	9:40	9:30	9:20	9:10

Notes:

1. Chart is based on pace per mile (for example, 8:00 minutes per mile). To figure out your pace per quarter mile for 440s, divide by 4 (for example, 2:00). To figure out your pace per half mile for 880s, divide by 2 (for example, 4:00).

2. *10K race time* is estimated from your present fitness level.

3. *Anaerobic threshold runs* are 30 seconds per mile slower than 10K pace; they are run near your aerobic-anaerobic borderline.

4. *10K pace intervals* are based on the average pace per mile for the 10K race time.

5. *5K pace intervals* are based on the average pace per mile for the 5K race time as predicted from your 10K time. This is 10 seconds per mile faster than 10K pace, and approximately your starting pace for a 10K race.

6. *Fast intervals* are 20 seconds faster per mile than 10K pace; this is approximately your starting pace for a 5K race.

7. *Power intervals* are 30 seconds faster per mile than 10K pace; this is approximately between your 1-mile and 2-mile race pace.

8. For *1-mile training*, pace intervals are at 1-mile–5K speed and power intervals at 880-yard (½-mile) speed.

RACE-TIME COMPARISON AND PREDICTOR CHART

5K	10K	10 MI	HALF MARATHON	MARATHON
14:00	29:00	48:20	1:02:30	2:15:00
14:15	29:30	49:10	1:03:45	2:17:30
14:30	30:00	50:00	1:05:00	2:20:00
14:45	30:30	50:50	1:06:15	2:22:30
15:00	31:00	51:40	1:07:30	2:25:00
15:15	31:30	52:30	1:08:45	2:27:30
15:30	32:00	53:20	1:10:00	2:30:00
15:45	32:30	54:10	1:11:15	2:32:30
16:00	33:00	55:00	1:12:30	2:35:00
16:15	33:30	55:50	1:13:45	2:37:30
16:30	34:00	56:40	1:15:00	2:40:00
16:45	34:30	57:30	1:16:15	2:42:30
17:00	35:00	58:20	1:17:30	2:45:00
17:15	35:30	59:10	1:18:45	2:47:30
17:30	36:00	60:00	1:20:00	2:50:00
17:45	36:30	60:50	1:21:15	2:52:30
18:00	37:00	61:40	1:22:30	2:55:00
18:15	37:30	62:30	1:23:45	2:57:30
18:30	38:00	63:20	1:25:00	3:00:00
18:45	38:30	64:10	1:26:15	3:02:30
19:00	39:00	65:00	1:27:30	3:05:00
19:15	39:30	65:50	1:28:45	3:07:30
19:30	40:00	66:40	1:30:00	3:10:00
19:45	40:30	67:30	1:31:15	3:12:30
20:00	41:00	68:20	1:32:30	3:15:00
20:15	41:30	69:10	1:33:45	3:17:30
20:30	42:00	70:00	1:35:00	3:20:00
20:45	42:30	70:50	1:36:15	3:22:30
21:00	43:00	71:40	1:37:30	3:25:00
21:15	43:30	72:30	1:38:45	3:27:30
21:30	44:00	73:20	1:40:00	3:30:00
21:45	44:30	74:10	1:41:15	3:32:30
22:00	45:00	75:00	1:42:30	3:35:00
22:15	45:30	75:50	1:43:45	3:37:30
22:30	46:00	76:40	1:45:00	3:40:00
22:45	46:30	77:30	1:46:15	3:42:30
23:00	47:00	78:20	1:47:30	3:45:00

23:15	47:30	79:10	1:48:45	3:47:30
23:30	48:00	80:00	1:50:00	3:50:00
23:45	48:30	80:50	1:51:15	3:52:30
24:00	49:00	81:40	1:52:30	3:55:00
24:15	49:30	82:30	1:53:45	3:57:30
24:30	50:00	83:20	1:55:00	4:00:00
24:45	50:30	84:10	1:56:15	4:02:30
25:00	51:00	85:00	1:57:30	4:05:00
25:15	51:30	85:50	1:58:45	4:07:30
25:30	52:00	86:40	2:00:00	4:10:00
25:45	52:30	87:30	2:01:15	4:12:30
26:00	53:00	88:20	2:02:30	4:15:00
26:15	53:30	89:10	2:03:45	4:17:30
26:30	54:00	90:00	2:05:00	4:20:00

Note: The two basic formulas: to predict your 10K time from your 5K time, multiply by 2 and add 1 minute; to predict your marathon time from your half-marathon time, multiply it by 2 and add 10 minutes. This chart is based on statistics and is only an approximate comparison. The predicted marathon times for women may be inaccurate (slow) by up to 5 minutes. Generally women can run 1–2 minutes faster than listed on the chart for the marathon.

PACING CHARTS

How to Use

This chart explains what pace you race per mile for the most common racing distances—both in miles and kilometers. It can be used these ways:

1. *As a guide to even pacing.* For example, if you wish to run an even pace at 7 minutes per mile for a marathon race, your "splits" should be: 5 miles—35:00; 10 miles—70:00; half marathon—1:31:42; 15 miles—1:45:00; 20 miles—2:20:00; and at the marathon finish—3:03:32. If your course is marked in kilometers, your splits should be: 5K—21:45; 10K—43:30; 15K—1:05:15; 20K—1:27:00; 25K—1:48:45; 30K—2:10:30; and marathon—3:03:32.

2. *To help you select a starting pace.* If you wish to break 3½ hours for the marathon, for example, you can refer to the chart and find that this means you must average 8 minutes per mile. Thus you may choose to go out right at 8:00 pace, or perhaps at 7:50 per mile.

3. *To determine your average pace per mile for the race after you have finished.* If you ran 45:21 for 10K, for example, the chart indicates that you averaged 7:18 per mile.

(Times on this chart are in minutes:seconds or hours:minutes:seconds. Example—49:43, 3:29:45.)

MILE PACE	5K	5 MI	10K	15 K	10 MI	20K	13.1 MI	15 MI	25K	30K	20 MI	MARATHON 26.219
4:30	13:59	22:30	27:58	41:57	45:00	55:55	58:57	1:07:30	1:09:55	1:23:54	1:30:00	1:57:59
4:31	14:02	22:35	28:04	42:06	45:10	56:08	59:10	1:07:45	1:10:10	1:24:12	1:30:20	1:58:25
4:32	14:05	22:40	28:10	42:15	45:20	56:20	59:23	1:08:00	1:10:25	1:24:30	1:30:40	1:58:52
4:33	14:08	22:45	28:16	42:25	45:30	56:33	59:36	1:08:15	1:10:41	1:24:50	1:31:00	1:59:18
4:34	14:11	22:50	28:23	42:34	45:40	56:45	59:49	1:08:30	1:10:56	1:25:08	1:31:20	1:59:44
4:35	14:14	22:55	28:29	42:43	45:50	56:58	1:00:03	1:08:45	1:11:12	1:25:26	1:31:40	2:00:10
4:36	14:17	23:00	28:35	45:52	46:00	57:10	1:00:16	1:09:00	1:11:27	1:25:46	1:32:00	2:00:36
4:37	14:21	23:05	28:41	43:02	46:10	57:22	1:00:29	1:09:15	1:11:43	1:26:04	1:32:20	2:01:03
4:38	14:24	23:10	28:47	43:11	46:20	57:35	1:00:42	1:09:30	1:11:59	1:26:22	1:32:40	2:01:29
4:39	14:27	23:15	28:54	43:20	46:30	57:47	1:00:55	1:09:45	1:12:14	1:26:42	1:33:00	2:01:55
4:40	14:30	23:20	29:00	43:30	46:40	58:00	1:01:08	1:10:00	1:12:30	1:27:00	1:33:20	2:02:21
4:41	14:33	23:25	29:06	43:39	46:50	58:12	1:01:21	1:10:15	1:12:45	1:27:18	1:33:40	2:02:48
4:42	14:36	23:30	29:12	43:48	47:00	58:25	1:01:34	1:10:30	1:13:00	1:27:36	1:34:00	2:03:14
4:43	14:39	23:35	29:18	43:58	47:10	58:37	1:01:47	1:10:45	1:13:16	1:27:56	1:34:20	2:03:40
4:44	14:42	23:40	29:25	44:07	47:20	58:49	1:02:00	1:11:00	1:13:31	1:28:14	1:34:40	2:04:06
4:45	14:45	23:45	29:31	44:16	47:30	59:02	1:02:13	1:11:15	1:13:47	1:28:32	1:35:00	2:04:32
4:46	14:49	23:50	29:37	44:26	47:40	59:14	1:02:27	1:11:30	1:14:03	1:28:52	1:35:20	2:04:59
4:47	14:52	23:55	29:43	44:35	47:50	59:27	1:02:40	1:11:45	1:14:19	1:29:10	1:35:40	2:05:25
4:48	14:55	24:00	29:50	44:44	48:00	59:39	1:02:53	1:12:00	1:14:34	1:29:28	1:36:00	2:05:51
4:49	14:58	24:05	29:56	44:54	48:10	59:52	1:03:06	1:12:15	1:14:50	1:29:48	1:36:20	2:06:17
4:50	15:01	24:10	30:02	45:03	48:20	1:00:04	1:03:19	1:12:30	1:15:05	1:30:06	1:36:40	2:06:44
4:51	15:04	24:15	30:08	45:12	48:30	1:00:16	1:03:32	1:12:45	1:15:20	1:30:24	1:37:00	2:07:10
4:52	15:07	24:20	30:14	45:22	48:40	1:00:29	1:03:45	1:13:00	1:15:36	1:30:44	1:37:20	2:07:36
4:53	15:10	24:25	30:21	45:31	48:50	1:00:41	1:03:58	1:13:15	1:15:51	1:31:02	1:37:40	2:08:02
4:54	15:13	24:30	30:27	45:40	49:00	1:00:54	1:04:11	1:13:20	1:16:07	1:31:20	1:38:00	1:08:28
4:55	15:17	24:35	30:33	45:50	49:10	1:01:06	1:04:24	1:13:45	1:16:23	1:31:40	1:38:20	2:08:55

MILE PACE	5K	5 MI	10K	15 K	10 MI	20K	13.1 MI	15 MI	25K	30K	20 MI	MARATHON 26.219
4:56	15:20	24:40	30:39	45:59	49:20	1:01:19	1:04:38	1:14:00	1:16:39	1:31:58	1:38:40	2:09:21
4:57	15:23	24:45	30:45	46:08	49:30	1:01:31	1:04:51	1:14:15	1:16:54	1:32:16	1:39:00	2:09:47
4:58	15:26	24:50	30:52	46:18	49:40	1:01:43	1:05:04	1:14:30	1:17:10	1:32:36	1:39:20	2:10:13
4:59	15:29	24:55	30:58	46:27	49:50	1:01:56	1:05:17	1:14:45	1:17:25	1:32:54	1:39:40	2:10:39
5:00	15:32	25:00	31:04	46:36	50:00	1:02:08	1:05:30	1:15:00	1:17:40	1:33:12	1:40:00	2:11:06
5:01	15:35	25:05	31:10	46:45	50:10	1:02:21	1:05:43	1:15:15	1:17:56	1:33:30	1:40:20	2:11:32
5:02	15:38	25:10	31:17	46:55	50:20	1:02:33	1:05:56	1:15:30	1:18:11	1:33:50	1:40:40	2:11:58
5:03	15:41	25:15	31:23	47:04	50:30	1:02:46	1:06:09	1:15:45	1:18:27	1:34:08	1:41:00	2:12:24
5:04	15:44	25:20	31:29	47:13	50:40	1:02:58	1:06:22	1:16:00	1:18:42	1:34:26	1:41:20	2:12:51
5:05	15:48	25:25	31:35	47:23	50:50	1:03:10	1:06:36	1:16:15	1:18:58	1:34:46	1:41:40	2:13:17
5:06	15:51	25:30	31:41	47:32	51:00	1:03:23	1:06:49	1:16:30	1:19:14	1:35:04	1:42:00	2:13:43
5:07	15:54	25:35	31:48	47:41	51:10	1:03:35	1:07:02	1:16:45	1:19:29	1:35:22	1:42:20	2:14:09
5:08	15:57	25:40	31:54	47:51	51:20	1:03:48	1:07:15	1:17:00	1:19:45	1:35:42	1:42:40	2:14:35
5:09	16:00	25:45	32:00	48:00	51:30	1:04:00	1:07:28	1:17:15	1:20:00	1:36:00	1:43:00	2:15:02
5:10	16:03	25:50	32:06	48:09	51:40	1:04:13	1:07:41	1:17:30	1:20:16	1:36:18	1:43:20	2:15:48
5:11	16:06	25:55	32:12	48:19	51:50	1:04:25	1:07:54	1:17:45	1:20:31	1:36:38	1:43:40	2:15:54
5:12	16:09	26:00	32:19	48:28	52:00	1:04:37	1:08:07	1:18:00	1:20:46	1:36:56	1:44:00	2:16:20
5:13	16:12	26:05	32:25	48:37	52:10	1:04:50	1:08:20	1:18:15	1:21:02	1:37:14	1:44:20	2:16:47
5:14	16:16	26:10	32:31	48:47	52:20	1:05:02	1:08:33	1:18:30	1:21:18	1:37:34	1:44:40	2:17:13
5:15	16:19	26:15	32:37	48:56	52:30	1:05:15	1:08:47	1:18:45	1:21:34	1:37:52	1:45:00	2:17:39
5:16	16:22	26:20	32:44	49:05	52:40	1:05:27	1:09:00	1:19:00	1:21:49	1:38:10	1:45:20	2:18:05
5:17	16:25	26:25	32:50	49:15	52:50	1:05:39	1:09:13	1:19:15	1:22:04	1:38:30	1:45:40	2:18:31
5:18	16:28	26:30	32:56	49:24	53:00	1:05:52	1:09:26	1:19:30	1:22:20	1:38:48	1:46:00	2:18:58
5:19	16:31	26:35	33:02	49:33	53:10	1:06:04	1:09:39	1:19:45	1:22:35	1:39:06	1:46:20	2:19:24

MILE PACE	5K	5 MI	10K	15 K	10 MI	20K	13.1 MI	15 MI	25K	30K	20 MI	MARATHON 26.219
5:20	16:34	26:40	33:08	49:43	53:20	1:06:17	1:09:52	1:20:00	1:22:51	1:39:26	1:46:40	2:19:50
5:21	16:37	26:45	33:15	49:52	53:30	1:06:29	1:10:05	1:20:15	1:23:06	1:39:44	1:47:00	2:20:16
5:22	16:40	26:50	33:21	50:01	53:40	1:06:42	1:10:18	1:20:30	1:23:22	1:40:02	1:47:20	2:20:43
5:23	16:44	26:55	33:27	50:11	53:50	1:06:54	1:10:31	1:20:45	1:23:38	1:40:22	1:47:40	2:21:09
5:24	16:47	27:00	33:33	50:20	54:00	1:07:06	1:10:44	1:21:00	1:23:53	1:40:40	1:48:00	2:21:35
5:25	16:50	27:05	33:39	50:29	54:10	1:07:19	1:10:58	1:21:15	1:24:09	1:40:58	1:48:20	2:22:01
5:26	16:53	27:10	33:46	50:39	54:20	1:07:31	1:11:11	1:21:30	1:24:24	1:41:18	1:48:40	2:22:27
5:27	16:56	27:15	33:52	50:48	54:30	1:07:44	1:11:24	1:21:45	1:24:40	1:41:36	1:49:00	2:22:54
5:28	16:59	27:20	33:58	50:57	54:40	1:07:56	1:11:37	1:22:00	1:24:55	1:41:54	1:49:20	2:23:20
5:29	17:02	27:25	34:04	51:06	54:50	1:08:09	1:11:50	1:22:15	1:25:11	1:42:12	1:49:40	2:23:46
5:30	17:05	27:30	34:11	51:16	55:00	1:08:21	1:12:03	1:22:30	1:25:26	1:42:32	1:50:00	2:24:12
5:31	17:08	27:35	34:17	51:25	55:10	1:08:33	1:12:16	1:22:45	1:25:41	1:42:50	1:50:20	2:24:38
5:32	17:11	27:40	34:23	51:34	55:20	1:08:46	1:12:29	1:23:00	1:25:57	1:43:08	1:50:40	2:25:05
5:33	17:15	27:45	34:29	51:44	55:30	1:08:58	1:12:42	1:23:15	1:26:13	1:43:28	1:51:00	2:25:31
5:34	17:18	27:50	34:35	51:53	55:40	1:09:11	1:12:55	1:23:30	1:26:29	1:43:46	1:51:20	2:25:57
5:35	17:21	27:55	34:42	52:02	55:50	1:09:23	1:13:08	1:23:45	1:26:44	1:44:04	1:51:40	2:26:23
5:36	17:24	28:00	34:48	52:12	56:00	1:09:36	1:13:22	1:24:00	1:27:00	1:44:24	1:52:00	2:26:50
5:37	17:27	28:05	34:54	52:21	56:10	1:09:48	1:13:35	1:24:15	1:27:15	1:44:42	1:52:20	2:27:16
5:38	17:30	28:10	35:00	52:30	56:20	1:10:00	1:13:48	1:24:30	1:27:30	1:45:00	1:52:40	2:27:42
5:39	17:33	28:15	35:06	52:40	56:30	1:10:13	1:14:01	1:24:45	1:27:46	1:45:20	1:53:00	2:28:08
5:40	17:36	28:20	35:13	52:49	56:40	1:10:25	1:14:14	1:25:00	1:28:01	1:45:38	1:53:20	2:28:34
5:41	17:39	28:25	35:19	52:58	56:50	1:10:38	1:14:27	1:25:15	1:28:17	1:45:56	1:53:40	2:29:01
5:42	17:43	28:30	35:25	53:08	57:00	1:10:50	1:14:40	1:25:30	1:28:33	1:46:16	1:54:00	2:29:27
5:43	17:46	28:35	35:31	53:17	57:10	1:11:03	1:14:53	1:25:45	1:28:49	1:46:34	1:54:20	2:29:53

MILE PACE	5K	5 MI	10K	15 K	10 MI	20K	13.1 MI	15 MI	25K	30K	20 MI	MARATHON 26.219
5:44	17:49	28:40	35:38	53:26	57:20	1:11:15	1:15:06	1:26:00	1:29:04	1:46:52	1:54:40	2:30:19
5:45	17:52	28:45	35:44	53:36	57:30	1:11:27	1:15:19	1:26:15	1:29:19	1:47:12	1:55:00	2:30:46
5:46	17:55	28:50	35:50	53:45	57:40	1:11:40	1:15:33	1:26:30	1:29:35	1:47:30	1:55:20	2:31:12
5:47	17:58	28:55	35:56	53:54	57:50	1:11:52	1:15:46	1:26:45	1:29:50	1:47:48	1:55:40	2:31:38
5:48	18:01	29:00	36:02	54:04	58:00	1:12:05	1:15:59	1:27:00	1:30:06	1:48:08	1:56:00	2:32:04
5:49	18:04	29:05	36:09	54:13	58:10	1:12:17	1:16:12	1:27:15	1:30:21	1:48:26	1:56:20	2:32:30
5:50	18:07	29:10	36:15	54:22	58:20	1:12:30	1:16:25	1:27:30	1:30:37	1:48:44	1:56:40	2:32:57
5:51	18:11	29:15	36:21	54:32	58:30	1:12:42	1:16:38	1:27:45	1:30:53	1:49:04	1:57:00	2:33:23
5:52	18:14	29:20	36:27	54:41	58:40	1:12:54	1:16:51	1:28:00	1:31:08	1:49:22	1:57:20	2:33:49
5:53	18:17	29:25	36:33	54:50	58:50	1:13:07	1:17:04	1:28:15	1:31:24	1:49:40	1:57:40	2:34:15
5:54	18:20	29:30	36:40	54:59	59:00	1:13:19	1:17:17	1:28:30	1:31:39	1:49:58	1:58:00	2:34:42
5:55	18:23	29:35	36:46	55:09	59:10	1:13:32	1:17:30	1:28:45	1:31:55	1:50:18	1:58:20	2:35:08
5:56	18:26	29:40	36:52	55:18	59:20	1:13:44	1:17:44	1:29:00	1:32:10	1:50:36	1:58:40	2:35:34
5:57	18:29	29:45	36:58	55:27	59:30	1:13:57	1:17:57	1:29:15	1:32:25	1:50:54	1:59:00	2:36:00
5:58	18:32	29:50	37:05	55:37	59:40	1:14:09	1:18:10	1:29:30	1:32:40	1:51:14	1:59:20	2:36:26
5:59	18:35	29:55	37:11	55:46	59:50	1:14:21	1:18:23	1:29:45	1:32:56	1:51:32	1:59:40	2:36:53
6:00	18:38	30:00	37:17	55:55	1:00:00	1:14:34	1:18:36	1:30:00	1:33:12	1:51:50	2:00:00	2:37:19
6:01	18:42	30:05	37:23	56:05	1:00:10	1:14:46	1:18:49	1:30:15	1:33:28	1:52:10	2:00:20	2:37:45
6:02	18:45	30:10	37:29	56:14	1:00:20	1:14:59	1:19:02	1:30:30	1:33:44	1:52:28	2:00:40	2:38:11
6:03	18:48	30:15	37:36	56:23	1:00:30	1:15:11	1:19:15	1:30:45	1:33:59	1:52:46	2:01:00	2:38:37
6:04	18:51	30:20	37:42	56:33	1:00:40	1:15:24	1:19:28	1:31:00	1:34:15	1:53:06	2:01:20	2:39:04
6:05	18:54	30:25	37:48	56:42	1:00:50	1:15:36	1:19:41	1:31:15	1:34:30	1:53:24	2:01:40	2:39:30
6:06	18:57	30:30	37:54	56:51	1:01:00	1:15:48	1:19:55	1:31:30	1:34:45	1:53:42	2:02:00	2:39:56
6:07	19:00	30:35	38:00	57:01	1:01:10	1:16:01	1:20:08	1:31:45	1:35:01	1:54:02	2:02:20	2:40:22
6:08	19:03	30:40	38:07	57:10	1:01:20	1:16:13	1:20:21	1:32:00	1:35:16	1:54:20	2:02:40	2:40:49
6:09	19:06	30:45	38:13	57:19	1:01:30	1:16:26	1:20:34	1:32:15	1:35:32	1:54:38	2:03:00	2:41:15

MILE PACE	5K	5 MI	10K	15 K	10 MI	20K	13.1 MI	15 MI	25K	30K	20 MI	MARATHON 26.219
6:10	19:10	30:50	38:19	57:29	1:01:40	1:16:38	1:20:47	1:32:30	1:35:48	1:54:58	2:03:20	2:41:41
6:11	19:13	30:55	38:25	57:38	1:01:50	1:16:51	1:21:00	1:32:45	1:36:04	1:55:16	2:03:40	2:42:07
6:12	19:16	31:00	38:32	57:47	1:02:00	1:17:03	1:21:13	1:33:00	1:36:19	1:55:34	2:04:00	2:42:33
6:13	19:19	31:05	38:38	57:57	1:02:10	1:17:15	1:21:26	1:33:15	1:36:34	1:55:58	2:04:20	2:43:00
6:14	19:22	31:10	38:44	58:06	1:02:20	1:17:28	1:21:39	1:33:30	1:36:50	1:56:12	2:04:40	2:43:26
6:15	19:25	31:15	38:50	58:15	1:02:30	1:17:40	1:21:53	1:33:45	1:37:05	1:56:30	2:05:00	2:43:52
6:16	19:28	31:20	38:56	58:25	1:02:40	1:17:53	1:22:06	1:34:00	1:37:21	1:56:50	2:05:20	2:44:18
6:17	19:31	31:25	39:03	58:34	1:02:50	1:18:05	1:22:19	1:34:15	1:37:36	1:57:08	2:05:40	2:44:45
6:18	19:34	31:30	39:09	58:43	1:03:00	1:18:18	1:22:32	1:34:30	1:37:52	1:57:26	2:06:00	2:45:11
6:19	19:37	31:35	39:15	58:52	1:03:10	1:18:30	1:22:45	1:34:45	1:38:07	1:57:44	2:06:20	2:45:37
6:20	19:41	31:40	39:21	59:02	1:03:20	1:18:42	1:22:58	1:35:00	1:38:23	1:58:04	2:06:40	2:46:03
6:21	19:44	31:45	39:27	59:11	1:03:30	1:18:55	1:23:11	1:35:15	1:38:39	1:58:22	2:07:00	2:46:29
6:22	19:47	31:50	39:34	59:20	1:03:40	1:19:07	1:23:24	1:35:30	1:38:54	1:58:40	2:07:20	2:46:56
6:23	19:50	31:55	39:40	59:30	1:03:50	1:19:20	1:23:37	1:35:45	1:39:10	1:59:00	2:07:40	2:47:22
6:24	19:53	32:00	39:46	59:39	1:04:00	1:19:32	1:23:50	1:36:00	1:39:25	1:59:18	2:08:00	2:47:48
6:25	19:56	32:05	39:52	59:48	1:04:10	1:19:45	1:24:04	1:36:15	1:39:41	1:59:36	2:08:20	2:48:14
6:26	19:59	32:10	39:58	59:58	1:04:20	1:19:57	1:24:17	1:36:30	1:39:56	1:59:56	2:08:40	2:48:41
6:27	20:02	32:15	40:05	1:00:07	1:04:30	1:20:09	1:24:30	1:36:45	1:40:11	2:00:14	2:09:00	2:49:07
6:28	20:05	32:20	40:11	1:00:16	1:04:40	1:20:22	1:24:43	1:37:00	1:40:27	2:00:32	2:09:20	2:49:33
6:29	20:09	32:25	40:17	1:00:26	1:04:50	1:20:34	1:24:56	1:37:15	1:40:43	2:00:52	2:09:40	2:49:59
6:30	20:12	32:30	40:23	1:00:35	1:05:00	1:20:47	1:25:09	1:37:30	1:40:59	2:01:10	2:10:00	2:50:25
6:31	20:15	32:35	40:30	1:00:44	1:05:10	1:20:59	1:25:22	1:37:45	1:41:14	2:01:28	2:10:20	2:50:52
6:32	20:18	32:40	40:36	1:00:54	1:05:20	1:21:12	1:25:35	1:38:00	1:41:30	2:01:48	2:10:40	2:51:18
6:33	20:21	32:45	40:42	1:01:03	1:05:30	1:21:24	1:25:48	1:38:15	1:41:45	2:02:06	2:11:00	2:51:44

MILE PACE	5K	5 MI	10K	15 K	10 MI	20K	13.1 MI	15 MI	25K	30K	20 MI	MARATHON 26.219
6:34	20:24	32:50	40:48	1:01:12	1:05:40	1:21:36	1:26:01	1:38:30	1:42:00	2:02:24	2:11:20	2:52:10
6:35	20:27	32:55	40:54	1:01:22	1:05:50	1:21:49	1:26:15	1:38:45	1:42:16	2:02:44	2:11:40	2:52:37
6:36	20:30	33:00	41:01	1:01:31	1:06:00	1:22:01	1:26:28	1:39:00	1:42:31	2:03:02	2:12:00	2:53:03
6:37	20:33	33:05	41:07	1:01:40	1:06:10	1:22:14	1:26:41	1:39:15	1:42:47	2:03:20	2:12:20	2:53:29
6:38	20:37	33:10	41:13	1:01:50	1:06:20	1:22:26	1:26:54	1:39:30	1:43:03	2:03:40	2:12:40	2:53:55
6:39	20:40	33:15	41:19	1:01:59	1:06:30	1:22:39	1:27:07	1:39:45	1:43:19	2:03:58	2:13:00	2:54:21
6:40	20:43	33:20	41:25	1:02:08	1:06:40	1:22:51	1:27:20	1:40:00	1:43:34	2:04:16	2:13:20	2:54:48
6:41	20:46	33:25	41:32	1:02:18	1:06:50	1:23:03	1:27:33	1:40:15	1:43:49	2:04:36	2:13:40	2:55:14
6:42	20:49	33:30	41:38	1:02:27	1:07:00	1:23:16	1:27:46	1:40:30	1:44:05	2:04:54	2:14:00	2:55:40
6:43	20:52	33:35	41:44	1:02:36	1:07:10	1:23:28	1:27:59	1:40:45	1:44:20	2:05:12	2:14:20	2:56:06
6:44	20:55	33:40	41:50	1:02:46	1:07:20	1:23:41	1:28:12	1:41:00	1:44:36	2:05:32	2:14:40	2:56:32
6:45	20:58	33:45	41:57	1:02:55	1:07:30	1:23:53	1:28:25	1:41:15	1:44:51	2:05:50	2:15:00	2:56:59
6:46	21:01	33:50	42:03	1:03:04	1:07:40	1:24:06	1:28:39	1:41:30	1:45:07	2:06:08	2:15:20	2:57:25
6:47	21:04	33:55	42:09	1:03:13	1:07:50	1:24:18	1:28:52	1:41:45	1:45:22	2:06:26	2:15:40	2:57:51
6:48	21:08	34:00	42:15	1:03:23	1:08:00	1:24:30	1:29:05	1:42:00	1:45:38	2:06:46	2:16:00	2:58:17
6:49	21:11	34:05	42:21	1:03:32	1:08:10	1:24:43	1:29:18	1:42:15	1:45:54	2:07:04	2:16:20	2:58:44
6:50	21:14	34:10	42:28	1:03:41	1:08:20	1:24:55	1:29:31	1:42:30	1:46:09	2:07:22	2:16:40	2:59:10
6:51	21:17	34:15	42:34	1:03:51	1:08:30	1:25:08	1:29:44	1:42:45	1:46:25	2:07:42	2:17:00	2:59:36
6:52	21:20	34:20	42:40	1:04:00	1:08:40	1:25:20	1:29:57	1:43:00	1:46:40	2:08:00	2:17:20	3:00:02
6:53	21:23	34:25	42:46	1:04:09	1:08:50	1:25:33	1:30:10	1:43:15	1:46:56	2:08:18	2:17:40	3:00:28
6:54	21:26	34:30	45:52	1:04:19	1:09:00	1:25:45	1:30:23	1:43:30	1:47:11	2:08:38	2:18:00	3:00:55
6:55	21:29	34:35	42:59	1:04:28	1:09:10	1:25:57	1:30:36	1:43:45	1:47:26	2:08:56	2:18:20	3:01:21
6:56	21:32	34:40	43:05	1:04:37	1:09:20	1:26:10	1:30:50	1:44:00	1:47:42	2:09:14	2:18:40	3:01:47
6:57	21:36	34:45	43:11	1:04:47	1:09:30	1:26:22	1:31:03	1:44:15	1:47:58	2:09:34	2:19:00	3:02:13
6:58	21:39	34:50	43:17	1:04:56	1:09:40	1:26:35	1:31:16	1:44:30	1:48:14	2:09:52	2:19:20	3:02:40
6:59	21:42	34:55	43:24	1:05:05	1:09:50	1:26:47	1:31:29	1:44:45	1:48:29	2:10:10	2:19:40	3:03:06

MILE PACE	5K	5 MI	10K	15 K	10 MI	20K	13.1 MI	15 MI	25K	30K	20 MI	MARATHON 26.219
7:00	21:45	35:00	43:30	1:05:15	1:10:00	1:27:00	1:31:42	1:45:00	1:48:45	2:10:30	2:20:00	3:03:32
7:01	21:48	35:05	43:36	1:05:24	1:10:10	1:27:12	1:31:55	1:45:15	1:49:00	2:10:48	2:20:20	3:03:58
7:02	21:51	35:10	43:42	1:05:33	1:10:20	1:27:24	1:32:08	1:45:30	1:49:15	2:11:06	2:20:40	3:04:24
7:03	21:54	35:15	43:48	1:05:43	1:10:30	1:27:37	1:32:21	1:45:45	1:49:31	2:11:26	2:21:00	3:04:51
7:04	21:57	35:20	43:55	1:05:52	1:10:40	1:27:49	1:32:34	1:46:00	1:49:46	2:11:44	2:21:20	3:05:17
7:05	22:00	35:25	44:01	1:06:01	1:10:50	1:28:02	1:32:47	1:46:15	1:50:02	2:12:02	2:21:40	3:05:43
7:06	22:04	35:30	44:07	1:06:11	1:11:00	1:28:14	1:33:01	1:46:30	1:50:18	2:12:22	2:22:00	3:06:09
7:07	22:07	35:35	44:13	1:06:20	1:11:10	1:28:27	1:33:14	1:46:45	1:50:34	2:12:40	2:22:20	3:06:36
7:08	22:10	35:40	44:19	1:06:29	1:11:20	1:28:39	1:33:27	1:47:00	1:50:49	2:12:58	2:22:40	3:07:02
7:09	22:13	35:45	44:26	1:06:39	1:11:30	1:28:51	1:33:40	1:47:15	1:51:04	2:13:18	2:23:00	3:07:28
7:10	22:16	35:50	44:32	1:06:48	1:11:40	1:29:04	1:33:53	1:47:30	1:51:20	2:13:36	2:23:20	3:07:54
7:11	22:19	35:55	44:38	1:06:57	1:11:50	1:29:16	1:34:06	1:47:45	1:51:35	2:13:54	2:23:40	3:08:20
7:12	22:22	36:00	44:44	1:07:06	1:12:00	1:29:29	1:34:19	1:48:00	1:51:51	2:14:12	2:24:00	3:08:47
7:13	22:25	36:05	44:51	1:07:16	1:12:10	1:29:41	1:34:32	1:48:15	1:52:06	2:14:32	2:24:20	3:09:13
7:14	22:28	36:10	44:57	1:07:25	1:12:20	1:29:54	1:34:45	1:48:30	1:52:22	2:14:50	2:24:40	3:09:39
7:15	22:31	36:15	45:03	1:07:34	1:12:30	1:30:06	1:34:58	1:48:45	1:52:37	2:15:08	2:25:00	3:10:05
7:16	22:35	36:20	45:09	1:07:44	1:12:40	1:30:18	1:35:12	1:49:00	1:52:53	2:15:28	2:25:20	3:10:31
7:17	22:38	36:25	45:15	1:07:53	1:12:50	1:30:31	1:35:25	1:49:15	1:53:09	2:15:46	2:25:40	3:10:58
7:18	22:41	36:30	45:22	1:08:02	1:13:00	1:30:43	1:35:38	1:49:30	1:53:24	2:16:04	2:26:00	3:11:24
7:19	22:44	36:35	45:28	1:08:12	1:13:10	1:30:56	1:35:51	1:49:45	1:53:40	2:16:24	2:26:20	3:11:50
7:20	22:47	36:40	45:34	1:08:21	1:13:20	1:31:08	1:36:04	1:50:00	1:53:55	2:16:42	2:26:40	3:12:16
7:21	22:50	36:45	45:40	1:08:30	1:13:30	1:31:20	1:36:17	1:50:15	1:54:10	2:17:00	2:27:00	3:12:43
7:22	22:53	36:50	45:46	1:08:40	1:13:40	1:31:33	1:36:30	1:50:30	1:54:26	2:17:18	2:27:20	3:13:09
7:23	22:56	36:55	45:53	1:08:49	1:13:50	1:31:45	1:36:43	1:50:45	1:54:41	2:17:38	2:27:40	3:13:35

MILE PACE	5K	5 MI	10K	15 K	10 MI	20K	13.1 MI	15 MI	25K	30K	20 MI	MARATHON 26.219
7:24	22:59	37:00	45:59	1:08:58	1:14:00	1:31:58	1:36:56	1:51:00	1:54:57	2:17:56	2:28:00	3:14:01
7:25	23:03	37:05	46:05	1:09:08	1:14:10	1:32:10	1:37:09	1:51:15	1:55:13	2:18:16	2:28:20	3:14:27
7:26	23:06	37:10	46:11	1:09:17	1:14:20	1:32:23	1:37:23	1:51:30	1:55:29	2:18:34	2:28:40	3:14:54
7:27	23:09	37:15	46:18	1:09:26	1:14:30	1:32:35	1:37:36	1:51:45	1:55:44	2:18:52	2:29:00	3:15:20
7:28	23:12	37:20	46:24	1:09:36	1:14:40	1:32:47	1:37:49	1:52:00	1:55:59	2:19:12	2:29:20	3:15:46
7:29	23:15	37:25	46:30	1:09:45	1:14:50	1:33:00	1:38:02	1:52:15	1:56:15	2:19:30	2:29:40	3:16:12
7:30	23:18	37:30	46:36	1:09:54	1:15:00	1:33:12	1:38:15	1:52:30	1:56:30	2:19:48	2:30:00	3:16:39
7:31	23:21	37:35	46:42	1:10:04	1:15:10	1:33:25	1:38:28	1:52:45	1:56:46	2:20:08	2:30:20	3:17:05
7:32	23:24	37:40	46:49	1:10:13	1:15:20	1:33:37	1:38:41	1:53:00	1:57:01	2:20:26	2:30:40	3:17:31
7:33	23:27	37:45	46:55	1:10:22	1:15:30	1:33:50	1:38:54	1:53:15	1:57:17	2:20:44	2:31:00	3:17:57
7:34	23:31	37:50	47:01	1:10:32	1:15:40	1:34:02	1:39:07	1:53:30	1:57:33	2:21:04	2:31:20	3:18:23
7:35	23:34	37:55	47:07	1:10:41	1:15:50	1:34:12	1:39:21	1:53:45	1:57:48	2:21:22	2:31:40	3:18:50
7:36	23:37	38:00	47:13	1:10:50	1:16:00	1:34:27	1:39:34	1:54:00	1:58:04	2:21:40	2:32:00	3:19:16
7:37	23:40	38:05	47:20	1:10:59	1:16:10	1:34:39	1:39:47	1:54:15	1:58:19	2:21:58	2:32:20	3:19:42
7:38	23:43	38:10	47:26	1:11:09	1:16:20	1:34:52	1:40:00	1:54:30	1:58:35	2:22:18	2:32:40	3:20:09
7:39	23:46	38:15	47:32	1:11:18	1:16:30	1:35:04	1:40:13	1:54:45	1:58:50	2:22:36	2:33:00	3:20:35
7:40	23:49	38:20	47:38	1:11:27	1:16:40	1:35:17	1:40:26	1:55:00	1:59:06	2:22:54	2:33:20	3:21:01
7:41	23:52	38:25	47:45	1:11:37	1:16:50	1:35:29	1:40:39	1:55:15	1:59:21	2:23:14	2:33:40	3:21:27
7:42	23:55	38:30	47:51	1:11:46	1:17:00	1:35:41	1:40:52	1:55:30	1:59:36	2:23:32	2:34:00	3:21:53
7:43	23:58	38:35	47:57	1:11:55	1:17:10	1:35:54	1:41:05	1:55:45	1:59:52	2:23:50	2:34:20	3:22:19
7:44	24:02	38:40	48:03	1:12:05	1:17:20	1:36:06	1:41:18	1:56:00	2:00:08	2:24:10	2:34:40	3:22:46
7:45	24:05	38:45	48:09	1:12:14	1:17:30	1:36:19	1:41:32	1:56:15	2:00:24	2:24:28	2:35:00	3:23:12
7:46	24:08	38:50	48:16	1:12:23	1:17:40	1:36:31	1:41:45	1:56:30	2:00:39	2:24:46	2:35:20	3:23:38
7:47	24:11	38:55	48:22	1:12:33	1:17:50	1:36:44	1:41:58	1:56:45	2:00:55	2:25:06	2:35:40	3:24:04
7:48	24:14	39:00	48:28	1:12:42	1:18:00	1:36:56	1:42:11	1:57:00	2:01:10	2:25:24	2:36:00	3:24:30
7:49	24:17	39:05	48:34	1:12:51	1:18:10	1:37:08	1:42:24	1:57:15	2:01:25	2:25:42	2:36:20	3:24:57

MILE PACE	5K	5 MI	10K	15 K	10 MI	20K	13.1 MI	15 MI	25K	30K	20 MI	MARATHON 26.219
7:50	24:20	39:10	48:40	1:13:01	1:18:20	1:37:21	1:42:37	1:57:30	2:01:41	2:26:02	2:36:40	3:25:23
7:51	24:23	39:15	48:47	1:13:10	1:18:30	1:37:33	1:42:50	1:57:45	2:01:56	2:26:20	2:37:00	3:25:49
7:52	24:26	39:20	48:53	1:13:19	1:18:40	1:37:46	1:43:03	1:58:00	2:02:12	2:26:38	2:37:20	3:26:15
7:53	24:30	39:25	48:59	1:13:29	1:18:50	1:37:58	1:43:16	1:58:15	2:02:28	2:26:58	2:37:40	3:26:42
7:54	24:33	39:30	49:05	1:13:38	1:19:00	1:38:11	1:43:29	1:58:30	2:02:44	2:27:16	2:38:00	3:27:08
7:55	24:36	39:35	49:12	1:13:47	1:19:10	1:38:23	1:43:43	1:58:45	2:02:59	2:27:34	2:38:20	3:27:34
7:56	24:39	39:40	49:18	1:13:57	1:19:20	1:38:35	1:43:56	1:59:00	2:03:14	2:27:54	2:38:40	3:28:00
7:57	24:42	39:45	49:24	1:14:06	1:19:30	1:38:48	1:44:09	1:59:15	2:03:30	2:28:12	2:39:00	3:28:26
7:58	24:45	39:50	49:30	1:14:15	1:19:40	1:39:00	1:44:22	1:59:30	2:03:45	2:28:30	2:39:20	3:28:53
7:59	24:48	39:55	49:36	1:14:25	1:19:50	1:39:13	1:44:35	1:59:45	2:04:01	2:28:50	2:39:40	3:29:19
8:00	24:51	40:00	49:43	1:14:34	1:20:00	1:39:25	1:44:48	2:00:00	2:04:16	2:29:06	2:40:00	3:29:45
8:01	24:54	40:05	49:49	1:14:43	1:20:10	1:39:38	1:45:01	2:00:15	2:04:32	2:29:26	2:40:20	3:30:11
8:02	24:58	40:10	49:55	1:14:53	1:20:20	1:39:50	1:45:14	2:00:30	2:04:48	2:29:46	2:40:40	3:30:38
8:03	25:01	40:15	50:01	1:15:02	1:20:30	1:40:02	1:45:27	2:00:45	2:05:03	2:30:04	2:41:00	3:31:04
8:04	25:04	40:20	50:07	1:15:11	1:20:40	1:40:15	1:45:40	2:01:00	2:05:19	2:30:22	2:41:20	3:31:30
8:05	25:07	40:25	50:14	1:15:20	1:20:50	1:40:27	1:45:53	2:01:15	2:05:34	2:30:40	2:41:40	3:31:56
8:06	25:10	40:30	50:20	1:15:30	1:21:00	1:40:40	1:46:07	2:01:30	2:05:50	2:31:00	2:42:00	3:32:22
8:07	25:13	40:35	50:26	1:15:39	1:21:10	1:40:52	1:46:20	2:01:45	2:06:06	2:31:18	2:42:20	3:32:49
8:08	25:16	40:40	50:32	1:15:48	1:21:20	1:41:05	1:46:33	2:02:00	2:06:21	2:31:36	2:42:40	3:33:15
8:09	25:19	40:45	50:39	1:15:58	1:21:30	1:41:17	1:46:46	2:02:15	2:06:36	2:31:56	2:43:00	3:33:41
8:10	25:22	40:50	50:45	1:16:07	1:21:40	1:41:29	1:46:59	2:02:30	2:06:51	2:32:14	2:43:20	3:34:07
8:11	25:25	40:55	50:51	1:16:16	1:21:50	1:41:42	1:47:12	2:02:45	2:07:07	2:32:32	2:43:40	3:34:34
8:12	25:29	41:00	50:57	1:16:26	1:22:00	1:41:54	1:47:25	2:03:00	2:07:23	2:32:52	2:44:00	3:35:00
8:13	25:32	41:05	51:03	1:16:35	1:22:10	1:42:07	1:47:38	2:03:15	2:07:39	2:33:10	2:44:20	3:35:26
8:14	25:35	41:10	51:10	1:16:44	1:22:20	1:42:19	1:47:51	2:03:30	2:07:54	2:33:28	2:44:40	3:35:52

MILE PACE	5K	5 MI	10K	15 K	10 MI	20K	13.1 MI	15 MI	25K	30K	20 MI	MARATHON 26.219
8:15	25:38	41:15	51:16	1:16:54	1:22:30	1:42:32	1:48:04	2:03:45	2:08:10	2:33:48	2:45:00	3:36:18
8:16	25:41	41:20	51:22	1:17:03	1:22:40	1:42:44	1:48:18	2:04:00	2:08:25	2:34:06	2:45:20	3:36:45
8:17	25:44	41:25	51:28	1:17:12	1:22:50	1:42:56	1:48:31	2:04:15	2:08:40	2:34:24	2:45:40	3:37:11
8:18	25:47	41:30	51:34	1:17:22	1:23:00	1:43:09	1:48:44	2:04:30	2:08:56	2:34:44	2:46:00	3:37:37
8:19	25:50	41:35	51:41	1:17:31	1:23:10	1:43:21	1:48:57	2:04:45	2:09:11	2:35:02	2:46:20	3:38:03
8:20	25:53	41:40	51:47	1:17:40	1:23:20	1:43:34	1:49:10	2:05:00	2:09:27	2:35:20	2:46:40	3:38:29
8:21	25:57	41:45	51:53	1:17:50	1:23:30	1:43:46	1:49:23	2:05:15	2:09:43	2:35:40	2:47:00	3:38:56
8:22	26:00	41:50	51:59	1:17:59	1:23:40	1:43:59	1:49:36	2:05:30	2:09:59	2:35:58	2:47:20	3:39:22
8:23	26:03	41:55	52:05	1:18:08	1:23:50	1:44:11	1:49:49	2:05:45	2:10:14	2:36:16	2:47:40	3:39:48
8:24	26:06	42:00	52:12	1:18:18	1:24:00	1:44:23	1:50:02	2:06:00	2:10:29	2:36:36	2:48:00	3:40:14
8:25	26:09	42:05	52:18	1:18:27	1:24:10	1:44:36	1:50:15	2:06:15	2:10:45	2:36:54	2:48:20	3:40:41
8:26	26:12	42:10	52:24	1:18:36	1:24:20	1:44:48	1:50:29	2:06:30	2:11:00	2:37:12	2:48:40	3:41:07
8:27	26:15	42:15	52:30	1:18:46	1:24:30	1:45:01	1:50:42	2:06:45	2:11:16	2:37:32	2:49:00	3:41:33
8:28	26:18	42:20	52:37	1:18:55	1:24:40	1:45:13	1:50:55	2:07:00	2:11:31	2:37:50	2:49:20	3:41:59
8:29	26:21	42:25	52:43	1:19:04	1:24:50	1:45:26	1:51:08	2:07:15	2:11:47	2:38:08	2:49:40	3:42:25
8:30	26:24	42:30	52:49	1:19:13	1:25:00	1:45:38	1:51:21	2:07:30	2:12:02	2:38:26	2:50:00	3:42:52
8:31	26:28	42:35	52:55	1:19:23	1:25:10	1:45:50	1:51:34	2:07:45	2:12:18	2:38:46	2:50:20	3:43:18
8:32	26:31	42:40	53:01	1:19:32	1:25:20	1:46:03	1:51:47	2:08:00	2:12:34	2:39:04	2:50:40	3:43:44
8:33	26:34	42:45	53:08	1:19:41	1:25:30	1:46:15	1:52:00	2:08:15	2:12:49	2:39:22	2:51:00	3:44:10
8:34	26:37	42:50	53:14	1:19:51	1:25:40	1:46:28	1:52:13	2:08:30	2:13:05	2:39:42	2:51:20	3:44:37
8:35	26:40	42:55	53:20	1:20:00	1:25:50	1:46:40	1:52:26	2:08:45	2:13:20	2:40:00	2:51:40	3:45:03
8:36	26:43	43:00	53:26	1:20:09	1:26:00	1:46:53	1:52:40	2:09:00	2:13:36	2:40:18	2:52:00	3:45:29
8:37	26:46	43:05	53:32	1:20:19	1:26:10	1:47:05	1:52:53	2:09:15	2:13:51	2:40:38	2:52:20	3:45:55
8:38	26:49	43:10	53:39	1:20:28	1:26:20	1:47:17	1:53:06	2:09:30	2:14:06	2:40:56	2:52:40	3:46:21
8:39	26:52	43:15	53:45	1:20:37	1:26:30	1:47:30	1:53:19	2:09:45	2:14:22	2:41:14	2:53:00	3:46:48

MILE PACE	5K	5 MI	10K	15 K	10 MI	20K	13.1 MI	15 MI	25K	30K	20 MI	MARATHON 26.219
8:40	26:56	43:20	53:51	1:20:47	1:26:40	1:47:42	1:53:32	2:10:00	2:14:38	2:41:34	2:53:20	3:47:14
8:41	26:59	43:25	53:57	1:20:56	1:26:50	1:47:55	1:53:45	2:10:15	2:14:54	2:41:52	2:53:40	3:47:40
8:42	27:02	43:30	54:04	1:21:05	1:27:00	1:48:07	1:53:58	2:10:30	2:15:09	2:42:10	2:54:00	3:48:06
8:43	27:05	43:35	54:10	1:21:15	1:27:10	1:48:20	1:54:11	2:10:45	2:15:25	2:42:30	2:54:20	3:48:33
8:44	27:08	43:40	54:16	1:21:24	1:27:20	1:48:32	1:54:24	2:11:00	2:15:40	2:42:48	2:54:40	3:48:59
8:45	27:11	43:45	54:22	1:21:33	1:27:30	1:48:44	1:54:38	2:11:15	2:15:55	2:43:06	2:55:00	3:49:25
8:46	27:14	43:50	54:28	1:21:43	1:27:40	1:48:57	1:54:51	2:11:30	2:16:11	2:43:26	2:55:20	3:49:51
8:47	27:17	43:55	54:35	1:21:52	1:27:50	1:49:09	1:55:04	2:11:45	2:16:26	2:43:44	2:55:40	3:50:17
8:48	27:20	44:00	54:41	1:22:01	1:28:00	1:49:22	1:55:17	2:12:00	2:16:42	2:44:02	2:56:00	3:50:44
8:49	27:24	44:05	54:47	1:22:11	1:28:10	1:49:34	1:55:30	2:12:15	2:16:58	2:44:22	2:56:20	3:51:10
8:50	27:27	44:10	54:53	1:22:20	1:28:20	1:49:47	1:55:43	2:12:30	2:17:14	2:44:40	2:56:40	3:51:36
8:51	27:30	44:15	54:59	1:22:29	1:28:30	1:49:59	1:55:56	2:12:45	2:17:29	2:44:48	2:57:00	3:52:02
8:52	27:33	44:20	55:06	1:22:39	1:28:40	1:50:11	1:56:09	2:13:00	2:17:44	2:45:18	2:57:20	3:52:29
8:53	27:36	44:25	55:12	1:22:48	1:28:50	1:50:24	1:56:22	2:13:15	2:18:00	2:45:36	2:57:40	3:52:55
8:54	27:39	44:30	55:18	1:22:57	1:29:00	1:50:36	1:56:35	2:13:30	2:18:15	2:45:54	2:58:00	3:53:21
8:55	27:42	44:35	55:24	1:23:07	1:29:10	1:50:49	1:56:49	2:13:45	2:18:31	2:46:14	2:58:20	3:53:47
8:56	27:45	44:40	55:31	1:23:16	1:29:20	1:51:01	1:57:02	2:14:00	2:18:46	2:46:32	2:58:40	3:54:13
8:57	27:48	44:45	55:37	1:23:25	1:29:30	1:51:14	1:57:15	2:14:15	2:19:02	2:46:50	2:59:00	3:54:40
8:58	27:51	44:50	55:43	1:23:34	1:29:40	1:51:26	1:57:28	2:14:30	2:19:17	2:47:08	2:59:20	3:55:06
8:59	27:55	44:55	55:49	1:23:44	1:29:50	1:51:38	1:57:41	2:14:45	2:19:36	2:47:28	2:59:40	3:55:32
9:00	27:58	45:00	55:55	1:23:53	1:30:00	1:51:51	1:57:54	2:15:00	2:19:58	2:47:46	3:00:00	3:55:58
9:10	28:29	45:50	56:58	1:25:27	1:31:40	1:53:56	2:00:11	2:17:30	2:22:25	2:50:54	3:03:20	4:00:22
9:20	29:00	46:40	58:00	1:27:00	1:33:20	1:56:00	2:02:22	2:20:00	2:25:00	2:54:00	3:06:40	4:04:44
9:30	29:31	47:30	59:02	1:28:33	1:35:00	1:58:04	2:04:33	2:22:30	2:27:35	2:57:06	3:10:00	4:09:06
9:40	30:02	48:20	60:05	1:30:07	1:36:40	2:00:10	2:06:44	2:25:00	2:30:12	3:00:15	3:13:20	4:13:28
9:50	30:33	49:10	61:07	1:31:40	1:38:20	2:02:14	2:08:55	2:27:30	2:32:47	3:03:21	3:16:40	4:17:50
10:00	31:05	50:00	62:09	1:33:14	1:40:00	2:04:18	2:11:07	2:30:00	2:35:23	3:06:27	3:20:00	4:22:13

PACE CHART FOR TRACK RACES AND WORKOUTS

How to Use

This chart can be used to select even-paced splits for races or speed workouts on a quarter-mile (440-yard) track:

1. If you wish to run a 6-minute mile, for example, you can determine that your splits should be: 45 seconds at 220 yards, 1:30 after one lap (440 yards or ¼ mile), 2:15 at 660 yards, and 3 minutes after two laps (880 yards or ½ mile). To find your splits at 220-yard or 440-yard intervals beyond 880 yards, add the time under those columns to the 880-yard time. Example: the split for ¾ mile for a 6-minute mile is 4:30 (3:00 + 1:30).

2. If you did a speed workout on the track and wish to determine your pace-per-mile average, locate your average time for that distance and refer to the left-hand column for your average pace per mile. Example: 8 × 440 yards averaging 1:40 each is a pace of 6:10 per mile.

Note: Since 400 meters is very close to 440 yards, this chart also can be used for approximate pacing for 200 meters, 400 meters, 600 meters, 800 meters, and 1,600 meters.

(Times on this chart are in minutes:seconds.tenths of seconds. Example—1:07.5.)

1 MILE	220 YDS (⅛)	440 YDS (¼)	660 YDS (⅜)	880 YDS (½)
4:30	33.75	1:07.5	1:41.25	2:15
4:40	35.0	1:10.0	1:45.0	2:20
4:50	36.25	1:12.5	1:48.75	2:25
5:00	37.5	1:15.0	1:52.5	2:30
5:10	38.75	1:17.5	1:56.25	2:35
5:20	40.0	1:20.0	2:00.0	2:40
5:30	41.25	1:22.5	2:03.75	2:45
5:40	42.5	1:25.0	2:07.5	2:50
5:50	43.75	1:27.5	2:11.25	2:55

6:00	45.0	**1:30.0**	2:15.0	**3:00**
6:10	46.25	**1:32.5**	2:18.75	**3:05**
6:20	47.5	**1:35.0**	2:22.5	**3:10**
6:30	48.75	**1:37.5**	2:26.25	**3:15**
6:40	50.0	**1:40.0**	2:30.0	**3:20**
6:50	51.25	**1:42.5**	2:33.75	**3:25**
7:00	52.5	**1:45.0**	2:37.5	**3:30**
7:10	53.75	**1:47.5**	2:41.25	**3:35**
7:20	55.0	**1:50.0**	2:45.0	**3:40**
7:30	56.25	**1:52.5**	2:48.75	**3:45**
7:40	57.5	**1:55.0**	2:52.5	**3:50**
7:50	58.75	**1:57.5**	2:56.25	**3:55**
8:00	**1:00.0**	**2:00.0**	3:00.0	**4:00**
8:10	**1:01.25**	**2:02.5**	3:03.75	**4:05**
8:20	**1:02.5**	**2:05.0**	3:07.5	**4:10**
8:30	**1:03.75**	**2:07.5**	3:11.25	**4:15**
8:40	**1:05.0**	**2:10.0**	3:15.0	**4:20**
8:50	**1:06.25**	**2:12.5**	3:18.75	**4:25**
9:00	**1:07.5**	**2:15.0**	3:22.5	**4:30**
9:10	**1:08.75**	**2:17.5**	3:26.25	**4:35**
9:20	**1:10.0**	**2:20.0**	3:30.0	**4:40**
9:30	**1:11.25**	**2:22.5**	3:33.75	**4:45**
9:40	**1:12.5**	**2:25.0**	3:37.5	**4:50**
9:50	**1:13.75**	**2:27.5**	3:41.25	**4:55**
10:00	**1:15.0**	**2:30.0**	3:45.0	**5:00**

MILE-KILOMETER TIME COMPARISONS

How to Use

It is easy to figure out what your pace per mile is for an odd racing distance in miles, such as 7 miles. Just divide your time by your mileage—in this example, 7. But for odd racing distances in kilometers, it isn't as easy. This chart shows you what a pace per mile is equivalent to per kilometer. If you race an 8-kilometer race, for example, in 48 minutes, divide this time by 8 to determine the pace per mile for 1 kilometer. Then look to the left-hand column to see what your pace per mile was for 8 kilometers. Forty-eight divided by 8 equals a pace of 6 minutes per kilometer, which is a pace of 9:40 per mile. You can also figure it the other way. If your goal is a 9:40-per-mile pace, you should hit each kilometer split in slightly over 6 minutes—for example, you would hit 2 kilometers in 12 minutes.

(Times on this chart are in minutes:seconds.tenths of seconds. Example—2:47.80.)

MILE	KILOMETER	MIN/ MILE	MIN/ KILOMETER
4:30	2:47.80	7:20	4:33.46
4:40	2:54.02	7:30	4:39.67
4:50	3:00.23	7:40	4:45.89
5:00	3:06.45	7:50	4:52.10
5:10	3:12.66	8:00	4:58.32
5:20	3:18.88	8:10	5:04.53
5:30	3:25.09	8:20	5:10.75
5:40	3:31.31	8:30	5:16.96
5:50	3:37.52	8:40	5:23.18
6:00	3:43.74	8:50	5:29.39
6:10	3:49.95	9:00	5:35.61
6:20	3:56.17	9:10	5:41.82
6:30	4:02.38	9:20	5:48.04
6:40	4:08.60	9:30	5:54.25

6:50	**4:14.81**	9:40	**6:00.47**
7:00	**4:21.03**	9:50	**6:06.68**
7:10	**4:27.24**	10:00	**6:12.90**

RACING-DISTANCE CONVERSIONS

ENGLISH TO METRIC	
ENGLISH	METRIC
220 yards	201.168
440 yards	402.336
880 yards	804.672

METRIC TO ENGLISH	
METRIC	ENGLISH
200	218y, 2'2" (0.124 mi)
400	437y, 1'4" (0.249 mi)
800	874y, 2'8" (0.497 mi)

RACE	CONVERSION	RACE	CONVERSION
1 mile	1,609 meters	1,500 meters	0.93 miles
2 miles	3,219 meters	3,000 meters	1.86 miles
3 miles	4,828 meters	5,000 meters	3.11 miles
5 miles	8,047 meters	8,000 meters	4.97 miles
6 miles	9,656 meters	10,000 meters	6.21 miles
10 miles	16,193 meters	15,000 meters	9.32 miles
Half marathon	21,098 meters	20,000 meters	12.43 miles
15 miles	24,140 meters	25,000 meters	15.53 miles
20 miles	32,187 meters	30,000 meters	18.64 miles
Marathon	42,195 meters	Marathon	26.22 miles
30 miles	48,280 meters	50,000 meters	31.07 miles
50 miles	80,467 meters	100,000 meters	62.14 miles

Note: The English measurements and the metric ones beside them are the standard races and are approximately the same distance.

SELECTED READING LIST

THE RUNNER'S HANDBOOK SERIES

The Runner's Handbook: The Classic Fitness Guide for Beginning and Intermediate Runners by Bob Glover and Jack Shepherd. The original Penguin best-seller published in 1978 and revised in 1985. A 370-page encyclopedia of running information essential to the novice runner.

The Runner's Handbook Training Diary by Bob Glover and Jack Shepherd (Penguin, 1978).

The Injured Runner's Training Handbook by Bob Glover and Dr. Murray Weisenfeld (Penguin, 1985). The running coach and the runner's podiatrist team up to give the injured runner detailed guidelines for preventing, running through, and coming back from injury.

SPECIAL TOPICS

Physiology

Inside Running: Basics of Sports Physiology
by David L. Costill
Benchmark Press, Indianapolis
1986

A very comprehensive book by the acknowledged leader of exercise physiology research on runners in the USA, director of the Human Performance Laboratory at Ball State University, and contributing editor for *Runner's World* magazine.

Sports Medicine

The Runner's Repair Manual
by Murray Weisenfeld, D.P.M.
St. Martin's Press, New York
1980

A guide in down-to-earth language to help the runner treat common injuries.

Nutrition

The Athlete's Kitchen: A Nutrition Guide and Cookbook
by Nancy Clark
CBI Publishing, Boston
1981

A commonsense guide by the popular sports nutritionist.

Wellness

The Aerobics Program for a Total Well-Being
by Kenneth Cooper, M.D.
M. Evans, New York
1982

Details the interrelationship between exercise, diet, and emotional balance and emphasizes the difference between being fit and being healthy.

Running Without Fear
by Kenneth Cooper, M.D.
M. Evans, New York
1985

Examines the death of running guru James Fixx and establishes guidelines to reduce the risk of heart attack and sudden death during aerobic exercise.

Stretching

Stretching
by Bob Anderson
Shelter Publications, Bolinas, Calif.
1980
  A complete illustrated guide to hundreds of stretches.

Computerized Training

Computerized Running Training Programs
by James B. Gardner and J. Gerry Purdy
Track and Field News Press, Los Altos, Calif.
1970
  A computerized guide to setting your own workouts and comparing race results. Used by track coaches across the country.

Psychology

The Total Runner: A Complete Mind-Body Guide to Optimal Performance
by Dr. Jerry Lynch
Prentice-Hall, Englewood Cliffs, N.J.
1987
  How to use mental training to improve performance.

The Mental Athelete: Inner Training for Peak Performance
by Kay Porter, Ph.D., and Judy Foster
Wm C. Brown, Dubuque, Iowa
1986
  How to use mental training to improve performance.

Women's Running

The Woman Runner: Free to Be the Complete Athlete
by Gloria Averbuch
Cornerstone Library/Simon and Schuster, New York
1984
  Special tips particular to women and motivation for the beginner runner/racer.

Women's Running
by Joan Ullyot, M.D.

Stephen Greene Press, Brattleboro, Vt.
1984

Training tips and general guidelines for women from the women's editor of *Runner's World* magazine and a world-ranked masters runner.

Motivation

Running and Being: The Total Experience
by Dr. George Sheehan
Simon and Schuster, New York
1978

The national best-seller by the popular columnist for *Runner's World* magazine. Sheehan examines more than the "how to" or "why" of running. He looks at who we are—the runners.

Relaxation

Relax and Win: Championship Performance in Whatever You Do
by Bud Winter
A. S. Barnes, La Jolla, Calif.
1981

The classic on the subject by former San Jose State coach and the coach of several Olympians.

RUNNING PUBLICATIONS

Runner's World

The best source if you want to keep up-to-date with the latest in training, equipment, nutrition, etc. Also features well-written articles of general interest to runners of all levels. Executive editor Amby Burfoot is the a former winner of the Boston Marathon, and consulting editors include such big names in the sport as Joan Benoit-Samuelson, Frank Shorter, Bill Rodgers, Don Kardong and Hal Higdon. Regular columnists include Dr. George Sheehan, Joe Henderson, Dr. Joan Ullyot (women), Mike Tymm (masters), Liz Applegate (nutrition), Tom Brunick (shoes). The latest research in health and exercise physiology is contributed by Dr. Peter Wood, Dr. David Costill, and Dr. Jack Daniels. Bob Glover writes a column on the basics of training. A sleek monthly that in 1987 merged with *The Runner* magazine to boost circulation to over 400,000.

Runner's World
Rodale Press
33 East Minor Street
Emmaus, PA 18098

Running Times

"The National Calendar Magazine for Runners" features race results from across the country and a very comprehensive listing of upcoming races—big and small—from across the USA and beyond. A monthly magazine with a low-key approach to running.

Running Times
2029 Century Park East
Suite 3800
Century City, CA 90067

"Running Commentary"

A "newsy" newsletter written twice a month by longtime *Run-*

ner's World editor and running book author Joe Henderson, one of the early leaders of the "running revolution." Joe keeps you up-to-date on the latest running gossip as well as the most recent research findings.

"Running Commentary"
2645 Alder Street
Eugene, OR 97405–4117

"Running Stats"
  A weekly newsletter that rushes out the top weekend race results from around the world within a few days.

"Running Stats"
1085 14th Street
Suite 1260
Boulder, CO 80302

National Masters News
  The bible of masters track and field and road racing. Contains race results, dates of upcoming masters races, stories of interest for the age 40+ runner. A must if you are a masters runner who wants to keep abreast of what's happening in your sport.

National Masters News
PO Box 2372
Van Nuys, CA 91404

Track and Field News
  "The bible of the sport." Interviews with top athletes from track and field plus comprehensive track-meet results from around the world. Includes high school and college results and rankings.

Track and Field News
Box 296
Los Altos, CA 94022

"FitNews"

A monthly newsletter published by the American Running and Fitness Association. Includes several brief nuggets of information on a variety of topics including fitness, health, sports medicine, diet.

"FitNews"
American Running and Fitness Association
2001 S Street, NW
Suite 540
Washington, DC 20009

RUNNING ORGANIZATIONS

Achilles Track Club (physically disabled)

A New York City—based organization under the auspices of the New York Road Runners Club cofounded by Bob Glover and amputee-runner Richard Traum. The club has chapters around the world and encourages disabled runners to write for information on running for the disabled. Also active in running for physically disabled youth.

Richard Traum
Personnelmetrics
356 West 34th Street
New York, NY 10001
212—967—9300

American Running and Fitness Association (ARFA)

A membership organization for those interested in running and fitness. Membership includes the newsletter "FitNews."

American Running and Fitness Association
2001 S Street, NW
Suite 540
Washington, DC 20009

The Athletics Congress (TAC)

The national governing body for track and road racing. All competitors racing internationally or in national events sanctioned by TAC are expected to be members. For information on your regional TAC office, contact:

The Athletics Congress
PO Box 120
Indianapolis, IN 46206

The Fifty-Plus Runners

An organization for age 50 + runners that provides research

information and motivational materials to its members through newsletters and annual meetings.

Fifty-Plus Runners
PO Box D
Stanford, CA 94305

The Melpomene Institute
   An organization devoted to research and education in the area of women's athletics. Holds frequent seminars and publishes research in a newsletter.

The Melpomene Institute
2125 East Hennepin
Minneapolis, MN 55413

The New York Road Runners Club (NYRRC)
   Conducts hundreds of races, classes, and clinics for all levels of runners. Membership (over 25,000) includes subscription to *New York Running News* magazine and "What's Happening" newsletter. International Running Center is home of a very complete running library.

The New York Road Runners Club
9 East 89th Street
New York, NY 10128
212–860–4455/2280

Road Runners Club of America (RRCA)
   Over 200 member clubs across the country promote the sport of running. For the address of your local RRC organization or for information on starting a chapter in your area, contact:

Henry Gibble, President
Road Runners Club of America
629 South Washington Street
Alexandria, VA 22314
703–836–0558

Tacstats
   Under the Athletics Congress, this organization is respon-

sible for keeping records for age groups at all major racing distances.

Tacstats
7745 Southwest 138th Terrace
Miami, FL 33158

Robert H. Glover and Associates, Inc.
   Corporate and club fitness consultants; available for lectures; running classes for all levels from beginner runner to advanced competitor.

Robert H. Glover and Associates, Inc.
236 East 78th Street, Box #6
New York, NY 10021
212–737–7480

INDEX